iddicombe
Hammonds
yl Fox
ny Schmidt
arilyn Williams
erry Rasberry
Judi McClellan
Leoni McVey
G & S Typesetters, Inc.
10/12 Sabon

ge Provincetown Abstraction by Marsden Hartley;
Oil on paperboard, 1916 1983.169
Amon Carter Museum, Fort Worth

Address for Editorial Correspondence
The Dryden Press, 301 Commerce Street, Suite 3700, Fort Worth, TX 76102

Address for Orders
The Dryden Press, 6277 Sea Harbor Drive, Orlando, FL 32887
1-800-782-4479, or 1-800-433-0001 (in Florida)

ISBN: 0–03–074809–7

Library of Congress Catalogue Number: 93–70170

Printed in the United States of America

3 4 5 6 7 8 9 0 1 2 039 9 8 7 6 5 4 3 2 1

The Dryden Press
Harcourt Brace College Publishers

INTERME
MICROECON
and its applicati

Sixth Edition

Walter Nicholson
Amherst College

The Dryden Press
Harcourt Brace College Publishers

Fort Worth · Philadelphia · San Diego · New York · Orlando · Austin · San Antonio
Toronto · Montreal · London · Sydney · Tokyo

Publisher   Liz W
Acquisitions Editor   Rick
Developmental Editor   Da
Project Editor   A
Production Manager   N
Art Director
Copy Editor
Indexer
Compositor
Text Typ

Cover Im

To Susan

The Dryden Press
Series in Economics

Asch and Seneca
Government and the Marketplace
Second Edition

Baker
An Introduction to International Economics

Baumol and Blinder
Economics: Principles and Policy
Sixth Edition (also available in micro and
macro paperbacks)

Baumol, Panzar, and Willig
*Contestable Markets and the Theory of
Industry Structure*
Revised Edition

Berch
*The Endless Day: The Political Economy of
Women and Work*

Breit and Elzinga
*The Antitrust Casebook: Milestones in
Economic Regulation*
Second Edition

Brue
The Evolution of Economic Thought
Fifth Edition

Campbell, Campbell, and Dolan
Money, Banking, and Monetary Policy

Claudon and Olsen
Eco Talk

Demmert
Economics: Understanding the Market Process

Dolan and Lindsey
Economics
Seventh Edition (also available in micro and
macro paperbacks)

Eckert and Leftwich
The Price System and Resource Allocation
Tenth Edition

Edgmand, Moomaw, and Olson
Economics and Contemporary Issues
Second Edition

Estey
*The Unions: Structure, Development, and
Management*
Third Edition

Friedman
Milton Friedman Speaks (Video)

Gardner
Comparative Economic Systems

Glahe
Microeconomics: Theory and Application
Second Edition

Green
Intermediate Macroeconomics

Gwartney and Stroup
Economics: Private and Public Choice
Sixth Edition (also available in micro and
macro paperbacks)

Gwartney and Stroup
*Introduction to Economics: The Wealth and
Poverty of Nations*

Heilbroner and Singer
*The Economic Transformation of America:
1600 to the Present*
Second Edition

Hirsch and Rufolo
*Public Finance and Expenditure in a Federal
System*

Hirschey and Pappas
Fundamentals of Managerial Economics
Fourth Edition

Hirschey and Pappas
Managerial Economics
Seventh Edition

Hoerneman, Howard, Wilson, and Cole
*CAPER: Computer Assisted Program for
Economic Review*

Hyman
*Public Finance: A Contemporary Application
of Theory to Policy*
Fourth Edition

Johnson and Roberts
*Money and Banking: A Market-Oriented
Approach*
Third Edition

Kaufman
The Economics of Labor Markets
Fourth Edition

Keating and Wilson
Fundamentals of Managerial Economics

Keating and Wilson
Managerial Economics
Second Edition

Kennett and Lieberman
*The Road to Capitalism: The Economic
Transformation of Eastern Europe and the
Former Soviet Union*

Kidwell and Peterson
Financial Institutions, Markets, and Money
Fifth Edition

Kohn
Money, Banking, and Financial Markets
Second Edition

Kreinin
International Economics: A Policy Approach
Sixth Edition

Landsburg
Price Theory and Applications
Second Edition

Link, Miller, and Bergman
*EconoGraph II: Interactive Software for
Principles of Economics*

Lott and Ray
Applied Econometrics with Data Sets

Nicholson
*Intermediate Microeconomics and Its
Application*
Sixth Edition

Nicholson
*Microeconomic Theory: Basic Principles and
Extensions*
Fifth Edition

Ormiston
Intermediate Microeconomics

Puth
American Economic History
Third Edition

Ragan and Thomas
Principles of Economics
Second Edition (also available in micro and
macro paperbacks)

Ramanathan
Introductory Econometrics with Applications
Second Edition

Rukstad
*Corporate Decision Making in the World
Economy: Company Case Studies*

Rukstad
*Macroeconomic Decision Making in the World
Economy: Text and Cases*
Third Edition

Samuelson and Marks
Managerial Economics

Scarth
*Macroeconomics: An Introduction to
Advanced Methods*
Third Edition

Smith and Spudeck
Interest Rates: Principles and Applications

Thomas
Economics: Principles and Applications
(also available in micro and macro
paperbacks)

Wachtel
Labor and the Economy
Third Edition

Walton and Rockoff
History of the American Economy
Seventh Edition

Welch and Welch
Economics: Theory and Practice
Fourth Edition

Yarbrough and Yarbrough
The World Economy: Trade and Finance
Third Edition

Zimbalist, Sherman, and Brown
*Comparing Economic Systems: A Political-
Economic Approach*
Second Edition

The Harcourt
Brace College
Outline Series

Emery
Principles of Economics: Macroeconomics

Emery
Principles of Economics: Microeconomics

Emery
Intermediate Microeconomics

The goal of *Intermediate Microeconomics and Its Application* is to provide a clear, concise introduction to the ways in which economists analyze the operations of markets. This goal has remained unchanged over the various editions of this book, and I hope the sixth edition moves even closer to its attainment. This most recent updating seeks to provide students with a clear introduction to the tools they will need if they wish to delve deeper into economics, together with a presentation that is interesting enough so that they will want to do so. All of the topics presented here are developed in nontechnical, intuitive ways, and the requirements for using the book are quite modest—a course in introductory economics and a bit of algebra (which is reviewed in Chapter 2) should suffice.

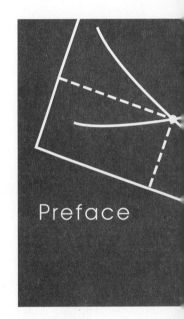

Preface

New to the Sixth Edition

The organization and format of this edition are quite similar to that of the fifth edition. Users seemed to be enthusiastic about the outline adopted previously (which develops the entire competitive model before exploring other cases), so the changes adopted here have been focused primarily on making the presentation work even better. Several new topics have been added to fill in holes that existed in the previous edition, and many new, up-to-date applications have been developed in ways that more clearly illustrate the various concepts in the book.

■ New Topics

The new topics added to this edition are intended primarily to complete the coverage of competitive and noncompetitive analysis in the text and to include a bit more about topics in the rapidly expanding areas of the economics of uncertainty and information. Specific additions include:

- A new chapter on competitive model applications that extensively uses the concepts of consumer and produced surplus in order to analyze the welfare consequences of various market changes (Chapter 13).
- A completely revised chapter on game theory clarifying the relationship between strategic thinking by firms and the more customary topics of pricing and entry decisions (Chapter 18).
- A revised chapter on monopoly, including a simplified treatment of a number of topics related to the theory of price discrimination (Chapter 16).
- Substantial additional material on the economics of information, especially with respect to issues related to adverse selection (Chapters 7 and 15).

Many other changes have been incorporated into the text in every chapter in order to improve readability and to bring the existing material into line with recent theoretical advances.

■ New Applications

The applications in this edition have been thoroughly revised both by the updating of information and by the replacement of many older applications with more recent ones that better illustrate some of the concepts. A few of the new topics included are:

- Shortages in Formerly Communist Countries
- Economic Sanctions against Iraq
- Frequent-Flyer Programs
- Valuing Clean Air
- The Microelectronic Revolution
- The Video Rental Market
- Voluntary Export Restraints on Automobiles
- First-Mover Advantages
- Are Any Resources Scarce?
- Saving the Elephants
- Jokes about Economists

In all, the book now has approximately 120 applications, of which roughly half are new to this edition. All of the applications have been thoroughly revised in an effort to make them more readable, interesting, and thought-provoking.

■ New Learning Pedagogy

Considerable attention has been paid to improving the various learning elements already in the fifth edition. The Review Questions have been thoroughly rewritten to focus more explicitly on fundamental issues, many new problems have been added (the text now has nearly 250 problems), and the end-of-book solutions have been expanded to improve readability and clarity. I hope this edition, therefore, will be even more helpful to students than its predecessors.

Again, Frank Westhoff has produced an excellent workbook and study guide, *Problems and Exercises for Intermediate Microeconomics*, to accompany the text. The computer graphics employed in this edition are remarkable. (See, for example, the very useful exercises associated with consumer and producer surplus in Chapter 13.) Users of the previous edition of this workbook have found Frank's patient approach to pedagogy very useful, and I believe this edition is even better.

To the Instructor

In some ways the sixth edition is little changed from the fifth, so only modest changes in the approach taken are needed. The most important new material is contained in the new Chapter 13 on applications of the supply-demand model, and I believe most instructors will want to use this chapter. To do so will require an explicit introduction to the concept of producer surplus, a topic that was not well covered in the previous edition. Because covering this topic in some detail (especially with regard to the nature of producer surplus in the long run) helps to tie together interactions between goods and input markets, I believe the insights provided more than justify the costs of adding a new topic.

Two other topics new to this edition may be covered more selectively. The "state-preference" approach to decisions under uncertainty is now briefly introduced in the concluding sections of Chapter 7, and I believe this provides a good introduction to the burgeoning research in the economics of information. The material may be skipped without any loss of continuity, however. Similarly, the new chapter on game theory (Chapter 18) provides a simple introduction to a number of new topics in the field of industrial organization, but this material is not essential to the text itself.

Specific suggestions about class scheduling and alternative approaches that might be applied to the material in class are included in the *Instructor's Manual* and *Test Bank* accompanying this edition. The *Instructor's Manual* also includes solutions to all of the problems in the text and an extensive set of multiple-choice and essay-type questions, and is available on computer disk. Over the six editions of this text, I have received many helpful suggestions from users that I have tried to incorporate either into the book directly or into the manual. I'm sure I still have a lot more to learn, however, so any additional comments or suggestions would be most appreciated.

To the Student

This book is primarily intended for you, the student. I hope you find the applications interesting and up-to-date, that the extensive rewriting has made even complex matters clear, and, most of all, that the presentation will encourage you to learn more about this fascinating and ever-changing field. Of course, I'm sure there are still sections of the text that could stand improvement, and I hope you will let me know about them. Just as this edition owes a large debt to previous student users for their helpful suggestions, so, too, would I appreciate any thoughts that you might have about changes that should be incorporated into new, future editions.

Acknowledgments

As for previous editions, most of the good ideas that I have included in this writing came from friends, colleagues, and students who have used the book. Specific, detailed reviews of the fifth edition were provided by:

- Hamid Bastin, Shippensburg University
- George Bittlingmayer, University of California, Davis
- Doug Brown, Georgetown University
- Victor Brajer, California State University, Fullerton
- K. W. Chu, California State University, Fullerton
- Cliff P. Dobitz, North Dakota State University
- Steven M. Goldman, University of California, Berkeley
- Ronald Grieson, University of California, Santa Cruz
- Clifford B. Hawley, West Virginia University
- Edward R. Kittrell, Northern Illinois University
- Richard Schoenberger, University of Wisconsin, La Crosse
- John R. Tedford, Clarkson University
- S. Y. Liu, Virginia State University
- Heather M. O'Neill, Ursinus College
- David C. Rose, University of Missouri, St. Louis
- Hossein Salehi, University of California, Los Angeles

These reviewers offered a variety of good advice, especially about my new chapter on the applications of supply and demand; I have tried to do all that was suggested. I truly appreciate all of the ideas the reviewers and other users gave me for new applications, and I have shamelessly stolen them in order to make it appear that I actually know something about the vast subjects covered. If I have mangled any of the facts, I hope more-knowledgeable people will let me know.

I should once again stress my debt to the generations of Amherst students who have contributed to the development of the problems in the book. Mark Bruni, Stephanie Cogen, Adrian Dillon, David Macoy, Katie Merrell, and Jeff Rodman should be explicitly mentioned, both as designers of some of the best problems and as perpetrators of much of the groan-producing humor. Many other students have made good suggestions on how specific problems might be improved. Indeed, even those students who made egregious errors on problems helped me by showing me some of the pitfalls that lie within what appears to be the most straightforward exercise.

The sixth edition survived Dryden's move from Hinsdale, Ill., to Fort Worth, Texas, with only minor inconveniences. Rick Hammonds was especially helpful in providing strong support for the text and in helping to untangle some difficulties with the art program. Daryl Fox was a great help in developing this edition by offering many thoughtful questions that forced me to focus on what I was doing. The actual production of the text was coordinated by Amy Schmidt, who invariably caught my errors and came up with better ways to do things. How she kept all of the book's pieces together is a mystery to me. To these efforts were added a fine copyediting job by Judi McClellan and (as you will see) some exceptional design work by Terry Rasberry that resulted in a first class product. Once again, I am greatly indebted to these professionals at Dryden, without whom the publication of a book such as this one would be impossible.

The Word-for-Word empire of my secretarial assistant, Happy Cramer, keeps expanding. Nevertheless, once again, she managed to find the time to organize this project and keep things moving. Her ability to get things done shames all of her authors into keeping on schedule.

My children, Kate, David, Tory, and Paul, probably don't care very much any more about seeing their names in print, but tradition is hard to break. All are now fully capable of reading this book, but, so far, they have felt no great urgency about the task. My wife, Susan, is another matter. Not only has she read the book, but she has volunteered her insights into and her disagreements about practically every page. The dedication to her is both intended to recognize her courage for undertaking the job and to express my appreciation for keeping me humble about what economists think they know.

Walter Nicholson
Amherst, Massachusetts
October 1993

Walter Nicholson is the Ward H. Patton Professor of Economics at Amherst College. He received a B.A. degree in mathematics from Williams College and a Ph.D. in economics from the Massachusetts Institute of Technology. Professor Nicholson's primary research interest is in the econometric analysis of labor market policy. He has published papers on such topics as unemployment insurance, welfare policy, and the domestic labor market impact of international trade. He is also the author of *Microeconomic Theory: Basic Principles and Extensions,* 5th ed. (The Dryden Press, 1992). He and his wife, Susan, live in Amherst, Massachusetts, where they are continuing to worry about college and how to pay tuition for their children, Kate, David, Tory, and Paul.

About
the
Author

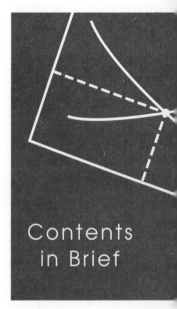

Contents
in Brief

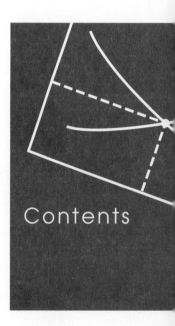

Contents

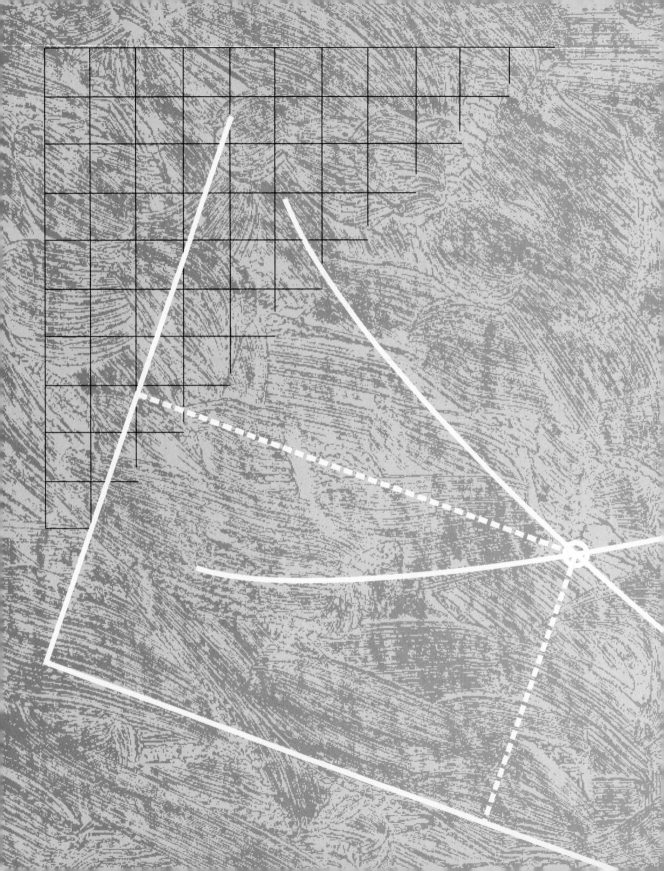

> "Economics is the study of mankind in the ordinary business of life."

> Alfred Marshall

> *Principles of Economics,* 1890

Part 1 provides some background for your study of microeconomics. Chapter 1 examines a few definitions of economics and shows how economic tools help us understand the way real-world economies work. The chapter also briefly reviews some basic principles of supply and demand, which should look familiar from your introductory economics course. This review is especially important because supply and demand models serve as a starting point for much of the deeper theory covered later in this book. Chapter 1 ends with a short outline of the text that shows how several important themes are repeated throughout.

Mathematical tools are now widely used in practically all areas of economics. Although the math used in this book is not especially difficult, Chapter 2 provides a brief summary of what you will need to know. These basic principles are usually covered in an elementary algebra course. Most important for our purposes are the relationships between algebraic functions and the representation of these functions in graphs. Because we will be using graphs heavily throughout the book (and because they are widely used in the field of economics as a whole), it is important to be sure you understand this basic material before proceeding.

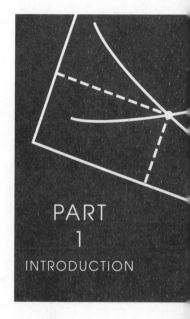

PART
1

INTRODUCTION

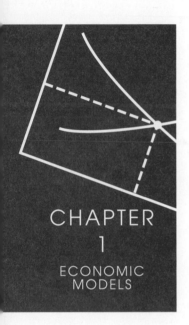

CHAPTER 1

ECONOMIC MODELS

In 1789 the British political philosopher Edmund Burke observed, "The Age of Chivalry is gone: that of sophisters, economists, and calculators has succeeded."[1] What was true in eighteenth-century England is even truer today—chivalry is long gone, and the age of economists (and other unsavory characters) is upon us. Not a day goes by when the economy is not front-page news. Sweeping economic changes in the former Soviet Union, rapid fluctuations in oil or food prices, and complex environmental concerns (such as global warming) increasingly affect our lives. Just because economic issues have become an important part of our lives, however, does not mean they are well understood. There is probably no field in which uninformed opinions can be both so prevalent and so wrong as in economics. Hopefully, after learning how to use the tools presented in this book, you will be better able to tell good economic arguments from bad ones. That should help you make informed judgments about today's pressing economic questions.

This first chapter introduces you to the philosophy behind the study of economics. It first defines the subject and then looks at some simple theoretical models that economists use for making sense out of the economy. The chapter ends with an overview of the remainder of the textbook.

---

[1] Edmund Burke, in *Reflections on the French Revolution,* F. G. Selby, ed. (London: The Macmillan Co., 1902), p. 84.

Defining Economics

Several definitions of **economics** are in use today. The most widely quoted definition describes economics as the "study of the allocation of scarce resources among alternative end uses." This definition introduces two important aspects of society that concern economists: *scarce resources* and *alternative end uses*.

Resources are scarce; there are simply not enough available to satisfy all human wants and desires. The amount of land, labor, and capital that is available and the technology that exists for using them limit what society can produce. These scarce resources can be devoted to many alternative end uses, however. For example, a society may choose to have television sets or automobiles or clean air or beautiful cities. In fact, a society is likely to choose some combination of all of those desirable end uses for its resources. Economists are particularly interested in studying how those choices are made. As Application 1.1: Scarcity in the Natural World shows, the problem of scarcity is a universal one. Economic tools can help us understand the choices that necessarily arise in the face of such scarcity.

A second definition, building on these ideas, describes economics as the "study of the ways in which choices are made." Not only does society as a whole, through governmental decisions, choose how its resources are used, but, more importantly, the people in society also make a wide variety of decisions on their own. They choose what to buy with their incomes, how to spend their leisure time, for whom to vote, how many (if any) children to have, and so on. Beyond these personal decisions, people also make choices with regard to their jobs. A manager of a firm, for example, must decide which techniques to use and which resources to obtain (both labor and raw materials) to make the firm's products. An employee must decide whether working conditions in his or her job are acceptable or whether it is time to look for work elsewhere. As we will see, **microeconomics** studies all of these kinds of individual choices.

A final, not entirely serious, definition of economics describes it as "what economists do." This circular definition shows how difficult it is to describe all the questions that interest economists. Economists ask the *big* questions, such as whether capitalism or socialism is better or what the proper role of government in a free market economy is. They also study *minor* questions, such as why farmers choose to plant hybrid seeds to grow corn or what rates an electric utility company should charge its customers. Even though these questions are very different, all economic studies use similar methods to focus general principles on a particular issue. This book is about those general principles.

Economics
The study of the allocation of scarce resources among alternative end uses.

Microeconomics
The study of the economic choices individuals and firms make and how those choices create markets.

Why Economists Use Theoretical Models

The most striking feature of any developed economy is its overall complexity. Thousands of firms produce millions or even billions of different products and

APPLICATION 1.1

Scarcity in the Natural World

Scarcity is as critical in the nonhuman biological world as it is in the human world. Just as humans choose how to use their resources, animals also must make "choices" about how to use their resources. Of course, even the most social and intelligent animals' choices do not reflect the complexity, sophistication, and free will that characterize human choices. Biological societies usually evolve slowly through time in response to various environmental pressures. But these pressures are in many ways similar to the forces that shape the evolution of human societies. Consequently, it is no accident that Charles Darwin, perhaps the greatest evolutionary biologist, drew extensively from the writings of nineteenth-century economists on scarcity.

Foraging for Food

All animals must expend time and energy in their daily search for food. In many ways, this poses an "economic" problem for them in deciding how to use these resources most effectively. Biologists have developed general theories of animal foraging behavior that draw largely upon economic notions of weighing the benefits and costs associated with various ways of finding food.[1]

Two examples help to illustrate this economic approach to foraging. First, in the study of birds of prey (eagles, hawks, and so forth), biologists have found that the length of time a bird will hunt in a particular area is determined both by the prevalence of food in that area and by the flight time to another location. These hunters recognize a clear trade-off between spending time and energy looking in one area and using those same resources to go elsewhere. Biologists have found that theoretical models based on such factors as the types of food available and the mechanics of the bird's flight explain observed hunting behavior well.

A second, related observation about foraging behavior is the fact that no animal will stay in a given area until all of the food there is exhausted. For example, once a relatively large portion of the prey in a particular area has been consumed, a hawk will go elsewhere.

Similarly, studies of honeybees have shown that they generally do not gather all of the nectar in a particular flower before moving on. To collect the last drop of nectar would not be worth the time and energy the bee would have to expend to get it. Such weighing of benefits and costs is precisely what an economist would predict in the presence of scarcity of time and energy.

Social Organization

The impact of scarcity is also apparent in the behavior of "social" insects such as ants or termites. These insects face scarcity with regard to the availability of food and the amount of work each individual insect is able to do. In order to ensure their survival (which is based on the survival of their queens) an elaborate caste system has evolved. Different members of the species perform different, specialized tasks to promote the overall welfare of the hive. For example, worker insects forage for food or nurse the young, and soldier insects defend the hive.

A number of biological researchers have applied economic logic to the degree of specialization in various species of termites and ants.[2] Social insects in tropical climates tend to have a greater number of castes than do those in temperate climates due to tropical climate problems such as floods and droughts. Similarly, the number of insects in each caste in a given hive is also based on the frequency of regularly recurring problems. There are more insects in castes that must deal with the most frequently recurring problems. Later chapters show how the logic economists develop to study scarcity predicts exactly these results: Specialization and the allocation of resources among members of society with specialized skills is a principal reaction to resource scarcity.

To Think About

1. Does it make sense to argue that animals or insects consciously "choose" an optimal strategy for dealing with the scarcity of resources?
2. Evolution selects those genetic traits that favor long-term survival. How does this explain altruistic behavior where animals take actions that are not directly beneficial to them?

---

[1] See, for example, David W. Stephens and John R. Krebs, *Foraging Theory* (Princeton, N.J.: Princeton University Press, 1986).

[2] See E. O. Wilson, "The Ergonomics of Caste in the Social Insects," *American Economic Review* (December 1978): 25–35.

services. Millions of people work in all kinds of jobs and buy a bewildering variety of products, ranging from plastic yoyos to expensive yachts. These actions must somehow work together. Wheat, for example, must be harvested at the right time; the farmer must ship it to a miller, who grinds it and ships it to a baker, who bakes it into bread. Enough bread must be sent to the grocery store for people to buy. To describe every action of an economy in complete detail would be impossible—lengthy books on every product and job could be written! Instead, economists develop simple **models** to capture the essentials of how the economy works. Just as a road map does not need to show every house to be useful, economic models are useful in understanding the real world even though they do not record every feature of the economy. This book covers the most widely used economic models.

The use of models is widespread both in the sciences (including economics) and in everyday life. In physics, for example, scientists use the abstractions of a "perfect" vacuum to study the force of gravity in a simplified setting. Chemistry uses the atom or the molecule as a very simplified model of the structure of matter. In more everyday life, architects use scale models to plan buildings. Television repairers use wiring diagrams in their work, and dressmakers use patterns and plans.

In much the same way economists use models to understand the infinitely complex real world. These models show how people make decisions, how firms make decisions, and how these two types of decisions are coordinated in the marketplace. As an illustration we will briefly review the development of one such model, a model that you have undoubtedly encountered before.

Models

Simple theoretical descriptions that capture the essentials of how the economy works.

Supply and Demand: The Development of an Economic Model

"Even your parrot can become an economist—just teach it to say 'supply and demand.'" Like many catchy slogans, this one reflects a basic truth—economists use notions of supply and demand practically all the time in order to explain economic events. The **supply-demand model** of price determination is such a familiar staple of introductory economics courses that it is hard to imagine what the subject would be like without it. In fact, however, this model is a relatively recent one developed in the latter part of the nineteenth century. Showing how that model was developed illustrates why the process of economic theorizing is greatly aided by using models and also provides a chance for a brief review.

Supply-demand model

A model describing how a good's price is determined by the behavior of the individuals who buy the good and the firms that sell it.

■ Early Economists

Commodities have had prices throughout human history. Money has been used as a way of making transactions for at least three thousand years, and before the invention of money, early peoples engaged in widespread barter transactions. Even though prices were a familiar feature of virtually all societies, however, few people tried to develop any general explanation for these prices.[2] Instead, most economic theorizing was done by traders who hoped to make a profit by buying goods where they were "cheap" and selling them where they were "dear." A crafty merchant who could become wealthy by buying and selling (say, salt or spices) had little need to delve more deeply into the general determinants of prices. Not until the latter part of the eighteenth century did writers begin to display an interest in developing a general theory of price determination.

■ Adam Smith and the Invisible Hand

The Scottish philosopher Adam Smith (1723–1790) is generally credited with being the first true economist. In *The Wealth of Nations* (published in the year 1776) Smith examined a large number of the pressing economic issues of his day and tried to develop economic tools for understanding them. Smith's most important insight was his recognition that the system of market-determined prices that he observed was not as chaotic and undisciplined as most other writers had assumed. Rather, Smith saw the prices that arose from the market system as providing a powerful "invisible hand" that directed resources into activities where they would be most valuable. Prices play the crucial role of telling both consumers and firms what resources are "worth" and thereby prompt these economic actors to make efficient decisions about how to use them. To Smith it was this ability to use resources efficiently that provided the ultimate explanation for a nation's "wealth." At many points later in this book we will return to this fundamental insight about the role of market prices to see whether recent thinking tends to support or to contradict Smith's conjectures.

Because Adam Smith placed great importance on the role of prices in directing how a nation's resources are used, he needed to develop some theories about how those prices are determined. He offered a very simple and, as we will see, only partly correct explanation—the prices of goods are determined by what it costs to produce them. Since, in Smith's day (and, to some extent, even today), the primary costs of producing goods were costs associated with the labor that went into a good, it was only a short step for him to embrace a labor-based theory of prices. For example, to paraphrase an illustration from *The Wealth of Nations*, if it takes twice as long for a hunter to catch a deer as to catch a beaver, one deer should trade for two beavers. The relative price of a deer is high because of the extra labor costs involved in catching one. Of course, producing many kinds of economic goods is not as simple a process as catching a deer or a beaver, but Smith believed that most

---

[2] Perhaps the most important early writer on economics was Aristotle, who introduced a distinction between the "value in exchange" (price) of a good and its "value in use." Although most economists do not make such a distinction today, the notion that some goods might be "worth" more or less than their market price played an important role in economic decisions of "just prices" in the Middle Ages and continues to influence some modern Marxist economists. See, for example, J. A. Schumpeter, *History of Economic Analysis* (New York: Oxford University Press, 1954), Chapters 1 and 2.

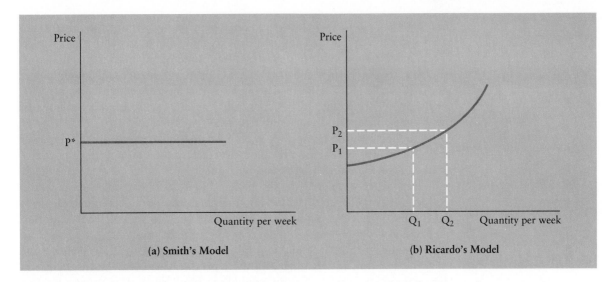

To Adam Smith the relative price of a good was determined by relative labor costs. As shown in the left-hand panel, relative price would be P* unless something altered such costs. Ricardo added the concept of diminishing returns to this explanation. In the right-hand panel, relative price rises as quantity produced rises from Q_1 to Q_2.

Figure 1.1
Early Views of Price Determination

differences in relative prices could ultimately be traced back to differences in underlying labor costs.

Smith's explanation for the price of a good is illustrated in Panel a of Figure 1.1. The horizontal line at P* shows that any number of deer can be produced without affecting the relative cost of doing so. That relative cost sets the price of deer (P*), which might be measured in beavers (a deer costs two beavers), in dollars (a deer costs $200 whereas a beaver costs $100), or in any other units that this society uses to indicate exchange value. This value will change only when the technology for producing deer changes. If, for example, this society developed better running shoes (which would aid in catching deer, but be of little use in capturing beavers), the relative labor costs associated with hunting deer might fall. Now a deer would trade for, say, 1.5 beavers, and the supply curve illustrated in the figure would shift downward. In the absence of such technical changes, however, the relative price of deer would remain constant, reflecting relative costs of production.

■ David Ricardo and Diminishing Returns

The early nineteenth century was a period of considerable controversy in economics, especially in England. The two most pressing issues of the day were the effects that expanding international trade was having on the economy and the effects that industrial growth was having on the availability of good farmland and other natural resources. It is testimony to the timelessness of economic questions that these are some of the same issues that dominate political discussions in the United States (and elsewhere) today. Much of the rhetoric in today's discussions is virtually identical to that which was heard in London streets more than a century and a half ago. One of the most influential contributors to the earlier debates was the British financier and pamphleteer David Ricardo (1772–1823). Throughout this book we will encounter Ricardo's many contributions to economics. Here we will examine only one of them—the concept of diminishing returns.

Although Ricardo generally accepted Adam Smith's views about the power of market prices to influence the allocation of resources and of the importance of labor costs in determining prices, he argued that Smith's view of price determination was incomplete. Ricardo believed that labor and other costs would tend to rise as the level of production of a particular good expanded. He drew this insight primarily from his consideration of the way in which cultivation of farmland was expanding in England at the time. As new and less fertile land was brought into use, it would naturally take more labor (say, to pick out the rocks in addition to planting crops) to produce an extra bushel of grain. Hence, the relative price of grain would rise. Similarly, as deer hunters exhaust the stock of deer in a given area, they must spend more time locating their prey so the relative price of deer would also rise. Ricardo believed that the phenomenon of increasing costs was quite general, and today we refer to his discovery as the **law of diminishing returns.** This generalization of Smith's notion of supply is reflected in Panel b of Figure 1.1 in which the supply curve slopes upward as quantity produced expands.

The problem with Ricardo's explanation was that it really didn't explain how prices are determined. Although the notion of diminishing returns undoubtedly made Smith's model more realistic, it did so by showing that relative price was not determined by production technology alone. Instead, according to Ricardo, the relative price of a good can be practically at any level depending on how much of it is produced and the extent to which diminishing returns are encountered.

To complete his explanation, Ricardo tended to rely on a subsistence argument. If, for example, the current population of a country needs Q_1 units of output to survive, Panel b of Figure 1.1 shows that the relative price would be P_1. With a growing population, these subsistence needs might expand to Q_2, and the relative price of this necessity would rise to P_2. Ricardo's suggestion that the relative prices of goods necessary for survival would rise in response to diminishing returns provided the basis for much of the concern about population growth in England during the 1830s and 1840s. It was largely responsible for the application of the term "dismal science" to the study of economics.

■ Marginalism and Marshall's Model of Supply and Demand

Contrary to the fears of many observers (most notably, Thomas Malthus, whose name has become synonymous with concerns over population growth), relative prices of necessities did not rise significantly during the nineteenth century. Instead, as productive technologies improved, prices tended to fall and levels

---

Law of diminishing returns

Hypothesis that the cost associated with producing one more unit of a good rises as more of that good is produced.

of material well-being improved rather dramatically. As the notion of subsistence became a less plausible explanation of the amounts of particular goods consumed, economists found it necessary to develop a more general theory of demand. In the latter half of the nineteenth century they adapted Ricardo's law of diminishing returns to this task. Just as diminishing returns mean that the cost of producing one more unit of a good rises as more is produced, so too, these economists argued, the willingness of people to pay for that last unit declines. Only if individuals are offered a lower price for a good, will they be willing to consume more of it. By focusing on the last, or *marginal*, unit bought, these economists had at last developed a comprehensive theory of price determination.

The clearest statement of these ideas was presented by the English economist Alfred Marshall (1842–1924) in his *Principles of Economics,* published in 1890. In it Marshall showed how the forces of demand and supply *simultaneously* determine price. Marshall's analysis is illustrated by the familiar cross diagram shown in Figure 1.2.

As before, the amount of a good purchased per period (say, each week) is shown on the horizontal axis, and the price of the good appears on the vertical axis. The curve labeled "Demand" shows the amount of the good demanded at each price. The negative slope of this curve reflects the marginalist principle: because people are willing to pay less and less for the last unit purchased, they will buy more only at a lower price. The curve labeled "Supply" shows the increasing cost of making one more unit of the good as the total amount produced increases. In other words, the upward slope of the supply curve reflects

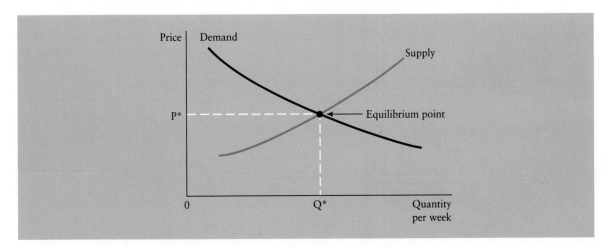

Marshall believed that demand and supply together determine the equilibrium price (P*) and quantity (Q*) of a good. The positive slope of the supply curve reflects diminishing returns (increasing marginal cost) whereas the negative slope of the demand curve reflects diminishing marginal usefulness. P* is an equilibrium price. Any other price results in either a surplus or a shortage.

Figure 1.2
The Marshall Supply-Demand Cross

increasing marginal costs, just as the downward slope of the demand curve reflects *decreasing* marginal usefulness.

■ Market Equilibrium

In Figure 1.2, the demand and supply curves intersect at the point P*, Q*. At that point, P* is the **equilibrium price.** That is, the quantity that people want to purchase (Q*) is precisely equal to the quantity that suppliers are willing to produce. Because both demanders and suppliers are content with this outcome, no one has an incentive to alter his or her behavior. The equilibrium P*, Q* will tend to persist unless something happens to change things. This illustration is the first of many we will encounter in this book about the way in which a balancing of forces results in a sustainable equilibrium outcome. To illustrate the nature of this balancing of forces, Marshall used the analogy of a pair of scissors: just as both blades of the scissors work together to do the cutting, so, too, the forces of demand and supply work together to establish equilibrium prices.

■ Nonequilibrium Outcomes

The smooth functioning of market forces envisioned by Marshall can, however, be thwarted in many ways. For example, a government decree that requires a price to be set in excess of P* (perhaps because P* was regarded as being the result of "unfair, ruinous competition") would prevent the establishment of equilibrium. With a price set above P*, demanders would wish to buy less than Q*, whereas suppliers would produce more than Q*. This would lead to a surplus of production in the market—a situation that (as we shall see) characterizes many agricultural markets. Similarly, a regulation that holds a price below P* would result in a shortage. With such a price, demanders would want to buy more than Q*, whereas suppliers would produce less than Q*. In Application 1.2: Shortages in Formerly Communist Economies, we illustrate how the setting of artificially low prices by governments resulted in shortages on a large scale.

■ Change in Market Equilibrium

The equilibrium pictured in Figure 1.2 can persist as long as nothing happens to alter demand or supply relationships. If one of the curves were to shift, however, the equilibrium would change. In Figure 1.3, people's demand for the good increases. In this case the demand curve moves outward (from curve D to curve D'). At each price people now want to buy more of the good. The equilibrium price increases (from P* to P**). This higher price both tells firms to supply more goods and restrains individuals' demand for the good. At the new equilibrium price of P** supply and demand again balance—at this higher price the amount of goods demanded is exactly equal to the amount supplied. In Chapter 2, we will illustrate how the extent of this price rise might be

---

■

Equilibrium price

The price at which the quantity demanded by buyers of a good is equal to the quantity of the good supplied by sellers.

APPLICATION 1.2

Shortages in Formerly Communist Economies

The governments of communist countries in Eastern Europe and the former Soviet Union made widespread use of price controls to keep prices of basic consumer goods low. Frequently, such price controls resulted in shortages of various goods, illustrated by long lines of consumers waiting to buy what little was available. Some humorous aspects of this situation were captured in the 1984 film, *Moscow on the Hudson,* starring Robin Williams, which detailed the star's ingenious searches for items such as toilet paper and gasoline. The absence of waiting lines in Bloomingdale's department store was one of the factors that motivated Williams' character to attempt to stay in the United States.

Soviet Housing

Housing was one of the goods most subject to price control in the former Soviet Union. The Soviet constitution required that all housing availability would be subject to public control in order to assure that the financial status of demanders did not influence what they received. One result of this provision was the development of a large scale housing bureaucracy that maintained extensive waiting lists of people who wished to move to better accommodations. In some cases Soviet citizens had to wait more than a decade to improve their living conditions.

A 1988 study based on interviews of emigrés from the Soviet Union suggests that the disequilibrium created by this method of housing price control was not sustainable.[1] Because people wanted to purchase more housing at the government set price than was available, they developed a number of ways to make such purchases through the underground economy. A direct method was to bribe the bureaucrats in charge of housing allocations in order to get a better place on the waiting list. An indirect method was to find someone with a better apartment who was willing to swap living quarters for a substantial cash payment. Overall, such manipulations resulted in a rise of the effective price of desirable housing and a reassertion of the influence of a family's purchasing power on the type of housing they received. Widespread cynicism about the ways in which many consumer goods were distributed was undoubtedly one factor that led to sweeping changes in the former Soviet Union during the early 1990s.

The Polish Experience

Price controls and the shortages they bring characterized many of the communist economies in Eastern Europe. In Poland, for example, food prices were controlled at below equilibrium levels for many years. Attempts by the government to raise these prices in the early 1980s resulted in widespread public dissatisfaction that helped give rise to the Solidarity Union movement. Eventual freeing of food price controls in 1989 resulted in rapid inflation rates (averaging over 20 percent a month), posing major problems for the Solidarity government that took control in September of that year.

Some economists believe that most formerly communist nations in Eastern Europe operated with chronic shortages of consumer goods induced by price controls.[2] This situation led to major problems, as in the case of Poland, when these countries tried to make the transition to market economies in the early 1990s. Not only did the repressed inflation in food prices become visible as price controls were relaxed, but many countries discovered that the price controls had distorted production decisions made by their farmers. Although the agricultural sectors of many Eastern European countries have significant advantages in production, it may take some time to put these to good use in the world trading system.

To Think About

1. Should the Soviets have tried to stamp out the underground economy in apartment units? Who are the gainers and losers from such illegal transactions?
2. If consumers from the former communist countries faced shortages in most goods, what did they do with their incomes? How might the transition to market economies be made more difficult by a history of shortages?

---

[1] Michael Alexeev, "Market vs. Rationing: The Case of Soviet Housing," *Review of Economics and Statistics* (August 1988): 414–420.

[2] The case was made most strongly by the Hungarian economist, Janos Kornai. See, for example, *The Economics of Shortage* (Amsterdam: North Holland, 1980).

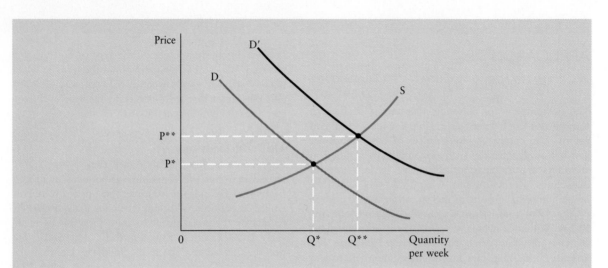

Figure 1.3
An Increase in Demand Alters Equilibrium Price and Quantity

If the demand curve shifts outward to D' because there is more desire for the product, P*, Q* will no longer be an equilibrium. Instead, equilibrium occurs at P**, Q**, where D' and S intersect.

predicted if algebraic expressions for the supply and demand curves were known.

A shift in the supply curve also affects market equilibrium. In Figure 1.4, the effects of an increase in supplier costs (for example, an increase in wages paid to workers) are illustrated. For any level of output, marginal costs associated with the supply curve S' exceed those associated with S. This shift in supply causes the price of this product to rise (from P* to P**) and consumers respond to this price rise by reducing quantity demand (from Q* to Q**) along the demand curve, D. As for the case of a shift in demand, the ultimate result of the shift in supply depicted in Figure 1.4 depends on the shape of both the demand curve and the supply curve.

Marshall's model of supply and demand should be quite familiar to you since it provides the principal focus of most courses in introductory economics. Indeed, the concepts of marginal cost, marginal value, and market equilibrium encountered in this model provide the starting place for most of the economic models you will learn about in this book. Although today we tend to regard Marshall's model as a fairly obvious application of a few simple ideas, our brief sketch of the history of the development of the model shows that was not always the case. Notice how earlier economists constantly refined their models of price determination in the light of real-world observations and experiences. As we shall see in later chapters, this process continues to this day as economists seek to explain a constantly expanding set of economic issues. The simple Marshallian model can be a very good way to start investigating many

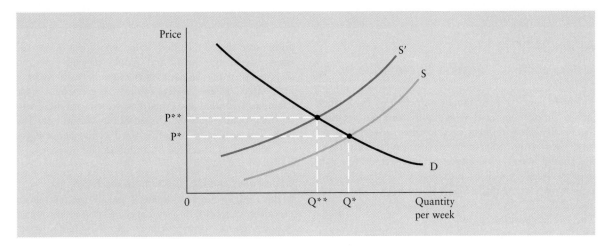

A rise in input costs would shift the supply curve upward to S′. This would cause an increase in equilibrium price from P* to P** and a decline in quantity from Q* to Q**.

Figure 1.4
A Shift in Supply
Alters Equilibrium
Price and Quantity

questions, however, as Application 1.3: History of the U.S.-Russian Wheat Trade clearly illustrates.

Models of Many Markets

Probably the most important shortcoming of Marshall's model of supply and demand is that it does not show how many different markets work together in an economy. The basic model pictured in Figures 1.2 to 1.4 is a **partial equilibrium model** of a single market. It does not show how results in one market affect those in another. For example, Figure 1.3 shows how an increase in demand for a good causes its price to rise, but not how that price increase might affect other markets.

If we were examining the market for imported French wine, say, we know that an increase in demand would result in a rise in its price. But it also seems likely that this price rise would have effects on the market for California wine where demand would increase as people shifted from French to California wine. Indeed, the effects could be far more widespread than this, including repercussions in the market for fine cheeses (to consume with wine), for wine glasses and corkscrews, and possibly even affecting the wages of California grape harvesters. And, to complicate the story, some of these effects may have repercussions on the original market with which we started our discussion (the market for French wine). Suppose, for example, that California grape harvesters just happen to like French wine. Then a rise in their wages might cause

Partial equilibrium model

An economic model of a single market.

APPLICATION 1.3
History of the U.S.-Russian Wheat Trade

The inefficiency of agriculture production by the former Soviet Union combined with highly variable weather has resulted in a frequent need for their government to buy wheat from other countries—most notably from the United States. Not surprisingly, this trade has had wide political as well as economic consequences as a brief history of the trade clearly illustrates.

The 1972 Wheat Purchase
On July 8, 1972, the Soviet Union announced it would purchase 400 million bushels of wheat from the United States—nearly one-fourth of total annual U.S. wheat production. The size of the proposed sale caught both wheat farmers and traders in the wheat market by surprise. As might have been predicted, such a large increase in demand resulted in a rapid escalation in prices. At the end of June, the price of hard winter wheat (which figured predominantly in the sale) was about $1.60 per bushel. By mid-September the price had risen to $2.25 per bushel—more than a 40 percent increase in just over two months.

The 1975 Grain Purchase Agreement
As a result of the sharp run-up in wheat prices in 1972, farmers increased their planting of wheat significantly. Acres harvested rose by nearly 50 percent from 43 million acres in the 1970–1971 growing season to over 65 million acres in the 1974–1975 growing season. The 1972–1973 experience also set the stage for a long-term wheat purchasing agreement between the United States and the Soviet Union signed in 1975. A stated purpose of the agreement was to regularize grain trade between the two countries and thereby lead to "fewer surprises" in the future.[1]

The 1980 Grain Embargo
The next surprise in the U.S.-Soviet wheat trade came when the Soviets invaded Afghanistan in the spring of 1980. In response to this action, President Carter announced that the United States would not honor the wheat trade agreement and would instead embargo shipments to the Soviets. This move seemed to have little effect on the Soviets' ability to get wheat since Canada, Australia, and Argentina were more than willing to provide what the United States would not. The embargo resulted in a shift inward in the demand for U.S. wheat and prices fell by about 15–20 percent.[2]

Grain Policy and U.S. Elections in the 1980s
In the 1980 election candidate Ronald Reagan attacked President Carter's grain embargo, thus making major political gains. Many farmers felt they had lost an important part of their market to foreign competition. Lingering problems in the wheat market reemerged in the 1988 election debates as candidate George Bush attacked Michael Dukakis over the Carter embargo— even though Dukakis disavowed any thought of pursuing such a program in the future (he did, however, make the absurd suggestion that U.S. wheat farmers might consider growing Belgian endive).

Grain Demand and Privatization
With the demise of the former Soviet Union and the increasing importance of market incentives, grain production in the Ukraine and Russia will undergo many changes. Over the long term, these actions are likely to result in increasing grain yields and a consequent reduction in demand for U.S. wheat. The short term effects of privatization on grain yields may, however, be negative. Existing state farms have inadequate equipment and use farming techniques that are inappropriate for the smaller size farms that privatization will bring.[3]

To Think About
1. Suppose the Soviets had decided to buy their wheat from Canada or Australia only. Would U.S prices have been affected as much as they actually were?
2. Would U.S. farmers be better off under such a system of regular grain purchases or under a system in which the same total quantity is bought, but at unexpected intervals?

[1] For a discussion, see C. B. Luttrell, "Grain Export Agreements—No Gains, No Losses," *Federal Reserve Bank of St. Louis Review* (August/September 1981): 23–29.
[2] See U.S. Council of Economic Advisors, *Economic Report of the President, 1984* (Washington, D.C.: U.S. Government Printing Office, 1984), Chapter 4.
[3] For a discussion, see Padma Desai, "Reforming the Soviet Grain Economy," *American Economic Review* (May 1992): 49–54.

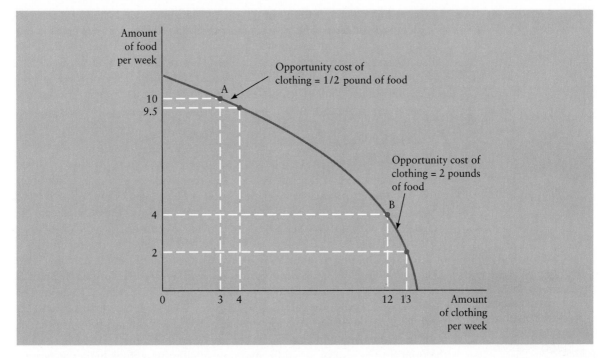

The production possibility frontier shows the different combinations of two goods that can be produced from a certain amount of scarce resources. It also shows the opportunity cost of producing more of one good as how much of the other good then cannot be produced. The opportunity cost at two different levels of production of a good can be seen by comparing points A and B.

Figure 1.5
Production Possibility Frontier

---

them to buy more of this product, and that would disturb the initial equilibrium. To show all the effects of a change in one market on other markets, we need a **general equilibrium model**, which includes workings of all markets together. Later sections of this book look closely at some of these multimarket models.

■ The Production Possibility Frontier

Here these models are introduced using another graph you should remember from introductory economics—the **production possibility frontier.** This graph shows the various amounts of two goods that an economy can produce during some period (again, say, one week). Because the production possibility frontier shows two goods, rather than the single good in Marshall's model, it is used as a basic building block for general equilibrium models.

Figure 1.5 shows the production possibility frontier for two goods, food and clothing. The graph illustrates the supply of these goods by showing the combinations that can be produced with this economy's resources. For example, 10 pounds of food and 3 units of clothing can be made, or 4 pounds of

■
General equilibrium model

An economic model of a complete system of markets.

■
Production possibility frontier

A graph showing all possible combinations of goods that can be produced with a fixed amount of resources.

food and 12 units of clothing. Many other combinations of food and clothing can also be produced. The production possibility frontier shows all of them. Combinations of food and clothing outside the frontier cannot be made because not enough resources are available. The production possibility frontier is a reminder of the basic economic fact that resources are scarce—there are not enough resources available to produce all we might want of every good.

■ Opportunity Cost

■
Opportunity cost
The cost of a good or service as measured by the alternative uses that are forgone by producing the good or service.

This scarcity means that we must choose how much of each good to produce. Figure 1.5 makes clear that each choice has its costs. For example, if this economy produces 10 pounds of food and 3 units of clothing at point A, producing 1 more unit of clothing would "cost" ½ pound of food. In other words, to increase the output of clothing by 1 unit means the production of food would have to decrease by ½ pound. Economists would say that the **opportunity cost** of 1 unit of clothing at point A is ½ pound of food. On the other hand, if the economy initially makes 4 pounds of food and 12 units of clothing at point B, it would cost 2 pounds of food to make 1 more unit of clothing. The opportunity cost of 1 more unit of clothing at point B has increased to 2 pounds of food. Because more units of clothing are produced at point B than at point A, both Ricardo's and Marshall's ideas of increasing marginal costs suggest that the opportunity cost of an additional unit of clothing will be higher at point B than at point A. This effect is just what Figure 1.5 shows.

The production possibility frontier provides two general equilibrium results that are not clear in Marshall's supply and demand model of a single market. The first of these is that producing more of one good means producing less of another good because resources are scarce. Economists often (perhaps too often!) use the expression "there is no such thing as a free lunch" to explain that every economic action involves opportunity costs. An important part of economic analysis is to discover those costs. A second result shown by the production possibility frontier is that the extent of these opportunity costs depends on how much of each good is produced. The frontier is like a supply curve for two goods—it shows the opportunity cost of producing more of one good as the decrease in the amount of a second good. The production possibility frontier is therefore a particularly useful tool for studying the way in which diminishing returns affect several markets at the same time. Application 1.4: Economic Sanctions illustrates how these findings might be applied when examining the results of recent political actions.

How Economists Verify Theoretical Models

Of course, not all models are as useful as Marshall's model of supply and demand. For example, Ptolemy's theory of planetary motion put the earth as the center of the universe; it was finally discarded when it could not explain

APPLICATION 1.4

Economic Sanctions

In recent years economic sanctions have been employed on several occasions in an attempt to discourage a country from pursuing actions thought of as undesirable. For example, the United Nations has adopted long-standing sanctions against South Africa (protesting the *apartheid* system), extensive sanctions against Iraq following its August 1990 invasion of Kuwait, and more limited sanctions against Libya adopted in 1992 in response to evidence of Libya's possible involvement in two aircraft bombings. The purpose of economic sanctions is to increase the costs associated with the undesirable actions the targeted country is undertaking.

Theory of Sanctions

Figure 1 shows the production possibility frontier for a country that is the target of economic sanctions. This country produces two general types of goods: exports (X) and imports (Y). Domestic levels of production of these goods is indicated by point A on the frontier whereas domestic consumption prior to sanctions is indicated by point B. Pre-sanctions trade permits this country to operate beyond its production possibility frontier by trading some export goods ($X_A - X_B$) in exchange for import goods ($Y_B - Y_A$).

Institution of comprehensive economic sanctions can be illustrated in Figure 1 by assuming that the sanctions prevent all international trade. This requires that the country alter its consumption from point B to its no-trade production levels represented by point A. This move is costly to the nation for two reasons: first, it forces it to do without the benefits of international trade—the country can no longer consume a combination of goods beyond its production possibilities; second, at least over the short term, the consumers in this country are forced to consume the combination of goods represented by point A—a combination they may not find very desirable.

Sanctions Against Iraq

This analysis can be used to evaluate the impact of sanctions adopted against Iraq by the United Nations in the

Figure 1
The Effect of Economic Sanctions

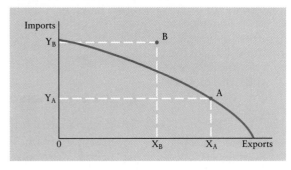

Prior to sanctions $X_A - X_B$ is being exported; $Y_B - Y_A$ is being imported. Comprehensive sanctions cause consumption to move from point B to point A, which may impose a variety of costs.

fall of 1990. Prior to its invasion of Kuwait, practically all Iraqi exports consisted of oil whereas imports included a variety of both military and civilian items. Cessation of international trade therefore meant that Iraq had far more oil than it needed together with shortages of military and civilian items. This result could have imposed significant costs on the people of Iraq but several factors mitigated the effects. The U.N. trade blockade was not fully effective, and imports continued to flow into Iraq. The Iraqi harvest in 1990 proved to be quite good, so food supplies were not severely restricted. Finally, and perhaps most important, the authoritarian rule of Saddam Hussein made it difficult for consumer costs to be translated into political action. Hence, the sanctions seem to have had little effect, and that prompted the U.N.'s decision to take direct military action against Iraq in early 1991.

To Think About

1. What determines the potential costs of economic sanctions? In what situations would these costs be high? When might they be low?
2. Who pays the costs of economic sanctions? How does this correspond with the actual people whose behavior the sanctions seek to change?

the movement of the planets around the sun. An important purpose of scientific investigation is to sort out bad models from good ones. Two methods are used to provide such a test of economic models. The **direct approach** looks at the assumptions upon which a model is based; the **indirect approach,** on the other hand, uses the model to see if it can correctly predict real-world events. This book uses both approaches to try to illustrate the validity of the models that are presented. We now look briefly at the differences between these two approaches.

■ The Direct Approach

The direct approach to testing the assumptions of an economic model might begin with intuition. Do the model's assumptions seem reasonable? Unfortunately, this question is fraught with problems, since what appears reasonable to one person may seem preposterous to someone else (try arguing with a noneconomics student about whether people usually behave rationally, for example).

Assumptions can also be tested with empirical evidence. For example, economists usually assume that firms are in business to maximize profits—in fact, much of our discussion in this book is based on that assumption. Using the direct approach to test this assumption with real-world data, you might send questionnaires to managers asking them how they make decisions and whether they really do try to maximize profits. This approach has been used many times but the results are often difficult to interpret and do not shed much light on the profit-maximization assumption. Like many opinion polls, surveys of business managers do not provide evidence that economists find very convincing.

■ The Indirect Approach

Many economists, such as Milton Friedman, do not believe that a theory can be tested by looking only at its assumptions.[3] They argue that all theories are based on unrealistic assumptions; the very nature of theorizing demands that we make what may appear to be unrealistic assumptions. Such economists believe that in order to decide if a theory is valid, we must see if it is capable of explaining and predicting real-world events. The real test of any economic model is whether it is consistent with events from the economy itself.

Friedman gives a good example of this idea by asking what theory explains the shots an expert pool player will make. He argues that the laws of velocity, momentum, and angles from classical physics make a suitable theoretical model, because the pool player certainly shoots *as if* he or she followed these laws. If we asked the players whether they could state these physical principles, they would undoubtedly answer that they could not. That does not

Direct approach

A method of verifying economic models that examines the validity of the assumptions on which the model is based.

Indirect approach

A method of verifying economic models that asks if the model can accurately predict real-world events.

---

[3] Milton Friedman, *Essays in Positive Economics* (Chicago: University of Chicago Press, 1953), Chapter 1. Another view stressing the importance of realistic assumptions can be found in H. A. Simon, "Rational Decision Making in Business Organizations," *American Economic Review* (September 1979): 493–513.

matter, Friedman argues, because the physical laws give very accurate predictions of the shots made and are therefore useful as theoretical models.

Going back to the question of whether firms try to maximize profits, the indirect approach would try to predict the firms' behavior by assuming that they do act *as if* they were maximizing profits. If we find that we can predict firms' behavior, then we can believe the profit-maximization hypothesis. Even if these firms said on questionnaires that they don't really try to maximize profits, the theory will still be valid, much as the pool player's disclaiming knowledge of the laws of physics does not make these laws untrue. The ultimate test in both cases is the theory's ability to predict real-world events.

■ Using Empirical Examples

This book is about economic theories. Because our real objective is to learn about the real world, we must be able to decide whether those theories are acceptable. This book uses both the direct and indirect methods to test the models presented. Occasionally, we will follow the direct approach by pointing out that a model is based on reasonable assumptions. More often, however, we will look at examples from the real world in which behavior can be predicted using economic theory. These applications are included not only because they are interesting illustrations of economics in their own right, but also because they are used as empirical support for the theories presented here. They are especially important to understanding economic model building. Application 1.5: Poor Models that Forgot about Supply and Demand looks at some inaccurate predictions based on rather poor economic models and shows why we might reject those models.

Positive versus Normative Economics

So far we have been talking about **positive economic analysis,** which uses the real world as an object to be studied—it seeks to explain real economic events. Positive economics tries to determine how resources actually are used in an economy. A somewhat different use of economic theory is **normative analysis.** In this type of economic theory, economists seek to say something about how an economy's resources *should* be used. For example, an economist engaged in positive analysis might explain health care prices in terms of the behavior of doctors, patients, hospitals, insurance companies, and so forth. The economist might also measure the costs and benefits of devoting more resources to health care. But if the economist argues that more resources *should* be allocated to health care, he or she has moved into normative analysis. By suggesting what policies should be undertaken, the economist is making judgments that go beyond basic analytical questions about how prices and quantities of health care are determined and has moved into the role of an advocate for some specific policy.

■

Positive economic analysis

Theories that explain how resources actually are used in an economy.

■

Normative analysis

Theories that make judgments about how the economy's resources should be used.

APPLICATION 1.5
Some Poor Models that Forgot about Supply and Demand

Adam Smith's "Invisible Hand" image was intended to suggest that equilibrium prices brought about by the interaction of supply and demand play a major role in determining the allocation of resources. Consequently, the price mechanism is central to most models of the economy. Sometimes, however, model builders tend to forget Smith's lesson.

The Limits to Growth Models
In the early 1970s many books and reports predicted dire consequences for the future of humanity. *World Dynamics* by Jay W. Forrester and *The Limits to Growth* by Donnella H. Meadows et al. (based largely on the Forrester book) were very influential.[1] Using complex computer models, these books strongly suggested that by the mid-1980s and on into the twenty-first century the world would experience major economic disruptions.

Economists criticized these books because they did not consider how people might change their behavior in response to changing market situations. For example, the models assumed that a certain amount of natural resources was needed for each unit of goods produced by the economy. Increasing demand would therefore put increasing strains on the world's resources. This assumption, however, ignores how the price of resources works to make producers use these resources more efficiently. One of the most dramatic recent examples is the case of energy, particularly oil. During the 1970s the real price of oil to users increased more than sixfold. This huge price increase led to large increases in the prices of all types of energy. The world economy responded to these energy price increases by cutting back on the use of energy in many ways, such as by developing more efficient, smaller cars and more efficient industrial machines. In the United States, for example, real energy prices rose about 60 percent between 1973 and 1980, but energy use per dollar of real gross national product declined by nearly 20 percent. The models used in the *Limits* book did not, however, allow for such possibilities. They therefore vastly exaggerated the problems that economic growth causes.

The Ehrlich-Simon Bet
A related example concerns prices of natural resources during the 1980s. In 1980, the environmentalist Paul Ehrlich bet the economist Julian Simon $1,000 that by the end of the decade natural resources would be much more expensive than they were then. Ehrlich's claim was (implicitly) based on the notion that resources are finite, so increasing demand must lead to an increasing real price. In the end, however, all five of the resources Ehrlich chose (chrome, copper, nickel, tin, and tungsten) declined in price, and Simon won the bet hands down.[2] How could Ehrlich have been so wrong?

Ehrlich's key mistake (as Simon knew) was his focus on the finiteness of resources. Certainly the earth is of finite dimensions, but that matters very little to resource prices since the amounts of resources available throughout the entire earth are vast (see Chapter 21). What matters is how the forces of supply and demand interact. During the 1980s demand for natural resources grew rather slowly while supply, enhanced by new discoveries and better extraction technology, expanded rapidly. The observed price trends only reflected these basic forces. Those who bet against such forces will usually lose.

To Think About
1. What does it mean to be running out of some resources? Hasn't the world been running out of resources since Adam and Eve?
2. Can you think of examples where the failure to consider both supply and demand resulted in wildly erroneous predictions? Did rising gasoline prices in the 1970s, for example, cause problems for automobile companies?

---

[1] J. W. Forrester, *World Dynamics* (Cambridge, Mass.: Wright Allen Press, 1971) and Donnella H. Meadows et al., *The Limits to Growth* (New York: Universe Books, 1972).

[2] See Stephen Moore, "So Much for 'Scarce Resources,'" *The Public Interest* (Winter 1992): 97–107.

Some economists believe that only positive analysis is proper. They argue that economics should be as *scientific* as the physical sciences and should only describe and possibly predict real-world events. According to this view, the choice of a particular health care policy should be left to the political process, not to the economist who should have no more influence than any other citizen in choosing a policy.

Consistent with this view, this book takes a positive economic approach by seeking to explain actual economic behavior. At the same time we consider several normative questions. For example, our discussion of monopoly shows how monopolistic firms may misallocate resources. Our analysis of incomplete property rights shows how these can cause goods to be misallocated as well. Each of these conclusions may suggest a change in policy (such as regulation of monopoly or full legal specification of property rights), but by pointing out the problems we are not necessarily recommending specific policies. Our goal is to show the consequences of undertaking any particular policy that might be proposed. Application 1.6: Economic Confusion? shows that there is far more agreement among economists about positive issues than there is about normative ones.

What You Will Learn from this Book

This book is divided into six parts. Each part explains a broad area of economic analysis in several closely related chapters. As you read each part, you will encounter a number of specific concepts, and you may have difficulty keeping all of them straight. Before starting an intensive review of the concepts, you should try to develop an overall sense of what the general purpose of the material is. The following brief descriptions may help you to do that. More extensive introductions accompany each part, which should help you put the material into perspective.

Part I introduces you to the study of microeconomics. Chapter 1 discussed some of the methodological issues arising in economic analysis. This chapter also reviewed the basic model of supply and demand developed by economists to explain how prices are determined, which is the framework for most of the analysis in this book. Chapter 2 reviews basic concepts of algebra, especially algebraic functions and graphs. These concepts are widely used in economics and are essential to this book.

Parts II and III examine the behavior of two important participants in the economic process. Part II develops in detail the economic theory of *individual behavior*. It explains how economists treat individuals' preferences and how these preferences affect decisions. Ultimately, this analysis leads to the concept of demand. Part III is concerned with *firms' behavior*. It focuses primarily on firms' costs and how firms' decisions affect costs; this leads to the concept of supply.

Part IV describes how prices are determined in perfectly competitive markets. These markets have so many buyers and sellers that no one of them has

APPLICATION 1.6
Economic Confusion?

To the general public, economists seem to belong to a confused profession. Your author has endured many conversations where economists bear the brunt of pointed jokes. Some of my favorites are the following:

Joke 1
If all the economists in the world were laid end-to-end, they would never reach a decision.
Joke 2
How many economists does it take to change a light bulb?
—Two, one to turn the bulb and one to say, "Turn it the other way."
Joke 3 (possibly true)
Harry Truman sought to hire a "one-handed" economist to head his Council of Economic Advisors. Repeatedly he was fed up with economists saying, "On the one hand . . . , but then, on the other hand. . . ."

Positive versus Normative Economics
These jokes convey the perception that economists never agree on anything. But that perception arises primarily from an inability to differentiate between the positive and normative arguments that various economists make. Economists (like everyone else) often disagree over political questions. They may, therefore, find themselves on the opposite sides of controversial policy questions. Economists may also differ on empirical matters. For instance, they may disagree about whether a particular effect is large or small. But on basic theoretical questions there is far less disagreement. Because most economists use the same tools, they tend to "speak the same language" and disagreements on positive questions are far less frequent.

Survey Results
This conclusion is supported by surveys of economists, a sampling of which are described in Table 1. The table shows a high degree of agreement among U.S., Swiss, and German economists about relatively positive questions such as the effects of tariffs or of rent controls.

Table 1
Percent of Economists Agreeing with Various Propositions in Three Nations

Proposition	U.S.A.	Switzer- land	Germany
Tariffs reduce economic welfare	95	87	94
Flexible exchange rates are effective for international transactions	94	91	92
Rent controls reduce the quantity of housing	96	79	94
Government should redistribute income	68	51	55
Government should hire the jobless	51	52	35

Source: B. S. Frey, W. W. Pommerehue, F. Schneider, and G. Gilbert, "Consensus and Dissension among Economists: An Empirical Inquiry," *American Economic Review* (December 1984): 986–994. Percentages represent fraction "Generally Agreeing" or "Agree with Provisions."

There is considerably less agreement about broad normative questions such as whether the government should redistribute income or act as the employer of last resort. For these types of questions, economists' opinions are as varied as any other group of citizens'.

To Think About
1. Economists from the United States, Switzerland, and Germany may not reflect the views of economists from lower income countries. Do you think such economists might answer the questions in Table 1 differently? Would these differences be based on positive or normative analysis?
2. What is the difference between a (<u>fill in blank</u>) and an economist? (A prize is offered by the author for the best completion for this joke.)

any influence on prices. Because of this, it is possible to analyze these markets rather completely. Not only does Part IV provide such a complete description, but it also develops the notion of economic efficiency as a way of evaluating whether markets are operating properly. The models developed in this part therefore provide a convenient benchmark against which to measure other economic situations.

In Part V we examine situations in which firms have some power to influence the market price of their products. The simplest case of this is when a monopoly firm is the sole supplier to a market and therefore can choose any price that it wishes. Our analysis will show why this circumstance is economically inefficient. We then proceed to examine more complex cases involving only a few producers and show that these also raise important questions about the markets' operating efficiency.

Many of the issues that arise when we study the way that prices of goods are determined also arise when we study the way in which prices paid to factors of production (wages of labor, rent on capital and land, and so forth) are determined. Part VI shows how the models developed previously can be adapted to the study of factor pricing. Because people get their incomes from renting out the labor and capital they possess, a study of these markets is a necessary part of the study of any economic system.

Finally, Part VII looks at a few problems that tend to extend beyond interactions between suppliers and demanders. Such problems as environmental pollution or the need to provide for a common defense may not be solvable through market mechanisms, and some sort of government action may be required. Our analysis in Part VII focuses on the reasons for such needs and on some of the difficulties that can arise in attempting to meet them.

Three Recurring Themes

Although we will describe many different economic models in this book, most of them are based on the same common elements. You will find that these elements are repeated in many different situations.

■ Using the Optimization Assumption to Explain Behavior

In order to develop economic models of behavior, we need to make some assumptions about why individuals and firms do what they do. Usually we will assume that these economic actors are working toward some goal and that they will choose to undertake actions that best achieve that goal. You have already seen one example of this approach—the profit maximization assumption. By adopting this assumption, it is possible to develop many implications about how firms will behave and to test those implications with data from the real world. Throughout this book we will be making similar assumptions about the motives of all of the economic actors we are looking at. We will see that such assumptions can provide many insights about how resources are ultimately allocated by these actors.

■ Describing a Market Equilibrium

Since Marshall's model of supply and demand is at the heart of many of the models we will examine in this book, it is not surprising that his concept of a market equilibrium is a crucial one. The establishment of equilibrium prices results in a situation in which buyers and sellers are both satisfied with what is happening. Such a situation will tend to persist until something changes it. And, as we saw in our application on U.S.-Soviet grain dealings, frequently it is possible to predict what a new equilibrium will be when something does change. This approach is repeated in many of the models we will examine. We first describe an equilibrium where supply and demand are in balance. Then we show how things change if the equilibrium is disturbed.

■ The Benefits of Free Exchange

Adam Smith's ideas about the beneficial effects of the "invisible hand" of market forces are alive and well today. Many recent governmental initiatives such as the deregulation of airlines in the United States or the selling-off of nationalized firms in the United Kingdom have been significantly motivated by just such ideas. Indeed, whole economies, such as those in Eastern Europe or in Latin America, are increasingly subjected to market forces. Throughout this book we will be encountering additional examples that further illustrate what Smith had in mind. Of course, as we will also illustrate, in some cases free exchange may lead to undesirable results—unregulated disposal of toxic wastes and the production of acid rain are results of some free market activities that could hardly be claimed beneficial. Our models will attempt to explain such undesirable results as well.

These three themes are found in practically all of microeconomics. Since they apply to a broad range of economic questions, you will be encountering them in many different forms throughout this book. In many respects these themes summarize the fundamental ways in which economists think about the world.

Summary

This chapter provides you with the background to begin your study of microeconomics. Much of this material should be familiar to you from your introductory economics course, but that should come as no surprise. In many respects the study of economics repeatedly investigates the same questions with an increasingly sophisticated set of tools. This course gives you some more of these tools. In establishing the basis for that investigation, this chapter reminds you of several important ideas:

- Economics is the study of allocating scarce resources among possible uses. Because resources are scarce, choices have to be made on how they will be used. Economists develop theoretical models to explain these choices.

- The most commonly used model of the allocation of resources is the model of supply and demand developed by Alfred Marshall in the latter part of the nineteenth century. The model shows how prices are determined by creating an equilibrium between the amount people want to buy and the amount firms are willing to produce. If supply and demand curves shift, new prices are established to restore equilibrium to the market.

- Marshall's model of supply and demand is a "partial equilibrium" model because it looks at only one market. Models of many markets are complicated by the number of relationships among the various markets.

- The production possibility frontier provides a simple illustration of the supply conditions in two markets. The curve clearly shows the limits imposed on any economy because resources are scarce. Producing more of one good means that less of something else must be produced. This reduction in output elsewhere is a measure of the opportunity cost involved in such additional production.

- Proving the validity of economic models is difficult and sometimes controversial. Occasionally the validity of a model can be determined by whether it is based on reasonable assumptions. More often, however, models are judged by how well they explain actual economic events.

Review Questions

1. We define economics to be the "study of the allocation of scarce resources among alternative end uses." Give some examples of this definition as applied to natural resources. How do you know these resources are scarce? What are some of the alternative end uses to which these might be put? Can you think of any resources that are not scarce? Do issues arise in choosing how to use non-scarce resources?

2. In many economic problems time is treated as a scarce resource. Describe how problems in using time meet our definition of "economics." Can you think of something that is different about using time than about using physical resources?

3. In Application 1.1 we described some biological research on foraging behavior. For the case of hawks, say, describe which scarce resources are being allocated by the hawk's decisions and illustrate some of the alternative uses that might be

made of those resources. Provide a similar analysis for some other foraging animal (a deer, a squirrel, or a whale, for example).

4. Provide a formal economic analysis of why honeybees find it in their interest to leave some nectar in each flower they visit. Can you think of any human activities that produce a similar outcome?

5. Classical economists struggled with the "Water-Diamond Paradox," which seeks an explanation for why water (which is very useful) has a low price, whereas diamonds (which are not particularly important to life) have a high price. How would Smith explain the relative prices of water and diamonds? Would Ricardo's concept of diminishing returns pose some problem for this explanation? Can you resolve matters by using Marshall's model of supply and demand? Is water "very useful" to the demanders in Marshall's model?

6. Economists use the term "equilibrium" to reflect a balancing of forces such that no party has any reason to change his or her behavior. Explain why an equilibrium price represents a balancing of forces. How do you know that each economic actor is content with the outcome? Can you think of any analogies to the notion of market equilibrium in noneconomic contexts?

7. Use the information from Application 1.3 to construct a simple supply-demand graph of the U.S. wheat market during the period described. Show how shifts in the demand curve for U.S. wheat can be used to explain the major price moves described in Application 1.3. What additional information would you need to decide whether this model is really adequate for explaining the wheat market during that period? Discuss some of the complications in the market that would not be accounted for by a simple supply-demand model.

8. Because Friedman's model of a pool player is based on clearly simplistic assumptions (most players do not explicitly know the laws of physics that apply to the game), it must be verified by empirical observations. How would you go about devising such a test of his model? What kind of evidence might refute the model?

9. Our discussion of economic sanctions against Iraq in Application 1.4 did not explicitly mention the markets for exports and imports with Iraq. Develop a simple supply-demand analysis of these two markets and describe how the implementation of sanctions would affect domestic prices in each of them. What incentives do these price changes set up for economic actors who might be willing to break the sanctions?

10. The following conversation was heard among four economists discussing whether the minimum wage should be increased:

Economist A: "Increasing the minimum wage would reduce employment of minority teenagers."

Economist B: "Increasing the minimum wage would represent an unwarranted interference with private relations between workers and their employers."

Economist C: "Increasing the minimum wage would raise the incomes of some unskilled workers."

Economist D: "Increasing the minimum wage would benefit higher wage workers and would probably be supported by organized labor."

Which of these economists is using positive analysis, and which is using normative analysis in arriving at his or her conclusions? Which of these predictions might be tested with empirical data? How might such tests be conducted?

Problems

1.1   The following data represent 5 points on the supply curve for orange juice:

Price ($1 per gallon)	Quantity (Millions of gallons)
1	100
2	300
3	500
4	700
5	900

   a. Graph these points with price on the vertical (Y) axis, and quantity on the horizontal (X) axis.
   b. Do these points seem to lie along a straight line? If so, what is that line?
   c. Use the equation calculated in part b to state how much will be supplied when $P = 0$ or when $P = 6$.

1.2   The following data represent 5 points on the demand curve for orange juice:

Price ($1 per gallon)	Quantity (Millions of gallons)
1	700
2	600
3	500
4	400
5	300

   a. Graph these points with price on the vertical (Y) axis, and quantity on the horizontal (X) axis.
   b. Do these points seem to lie along a straight line? If so, which line?
   c. Use the equation calculated in part b to state how much orange juice will be demanded when $P = 0$ or when $P = 6$.

1.3   Marshall defined an equilibrium price as one at which the quantity demanded equals the quantity supplied.

    a. Using the data provided in problems 1.1 and 1.2 show that P = 3 is the equilibrium price in the orange juice market.

    b. Explain using these data why P = 2 or P = 4 are not equilibrium prices.

    c. Graph your results and show that the supply-demand equilibrium resembles that shown in Figure 1.2.

    d. Suppose the demand for orange juice were to increase so that people want to buy 300 million more gallons at every price listed. How would that change the data in problem 1.2? How would it shift the demand curve you drew in part c?

    e. What is the new equilibrium price in the orange juice market given this increase in demand? Show this new equilibrium in your supply-demand graph.

1.4   Suppose that a freeze in Florida reduces orange juice supply by 300 million gallons at every price listed in problem 1.1.

    a. How would this shift in supply affect the data in problem 1.1? How would it affect the algebraic supply curve calculated in that problem?

    b. Given this new supply relationship together with the demand relationship shown in problem 1.2, what is the equilibrium price in this market?

    c. Explain why P = 3 is no longer an equilibrium in the orange juice market. How would the participants in this market know P = 3 is no longer an equilibrium?

    d. Graph your results for this supply shift.

1.5   How can you tell using data on price and quantity whether a rising price was caused by a shift in demand or a shift in supply? Explain using simple supply-demand graphs.

1.6   Application 1.2 suggests that low official prices for Soviet housing did not reflect all of the costs that a Soviet apartment seeker might have paid. Use a supply-demand graph to show why a renter would have been willing to pay more than the official price for an apartment. What would have determined the full price (including actual rent, bribes, and waiting time costs) that a buyer would have ultimately paid?

1.7   The following data show the production possibilities for a hypothetical economy during one year.

Output of X	Output of Y
1000	0
800	100
600	200
400	300
200	400
0	500

    a. Plot these points on a graph. Do they appear to lie along a straight line? What is that straight line production possibility frontier?

    b. Explain why output levels of X = 400, Y = 200 or X = 300, Y = 300 are inefficient. Show these output levels on your graph.

    c. Explain why output levels of X = 500, Y = 350 are unattainable in this economy.

    d. What is the opportunity cost of an additional unit of X output in terms of Y output in this economy? Does this opportunity cost depend on the amounts being produced?

1.8   Suppose an economy has a production possibility frontier characterized by the equation

$$X^2 + 4Y^2 = 100.$$

    a. In order to sketch this equation, first compute its intercepts. What is the value of X if Y = 0? What is the value of Y if X = 0?

    b. Calculate three additional points along this production possibility frontier. Graph the frontier and show that it has a general elliptical shape.

    c. Is the opportunity cost of X in terms of Y constant in this economy or does it depend on the levels of output being produced? Explain.

    d. How would you calculate the opportunity cost of X in terms of Y in this economy? Give an example of this computation.

*1.9   Suppose consumers in the economy described in problem 1.8 wish to consume X and Y in equal amounts.

    a. How much of each good should be produced to meet this goal? Show this production point on a graph of the production possibility frontier.

    b. Assume that this country enters into international trading relationships and decides to produce only good X. If it can trade one unit of X for one unit of Y in world markets, what possible combinations of X and Y might it consume?

    c. Given the consumption possibilities outlined in part b, what final choice will the consumers of this country make?

    d. How would you measure the costs imposed on this country by international economic sanctions that prevented all trade and required the country to return to the position described in part a?

1.10   Use supply and demand analysis to illustrate the trends in natural resource prices discussed in Application 1.5. Which curve seems to have shifted most during the 1980s? Does it make sense to say that resources have become more plentiful during the 1980s? Or have they become scarcer? Or do such terms have any precise economic meaning at all?

---

*Denotes a problem that is rather difficult. Brief solutions to all of the odd numbered problems can be found at the end of the book.

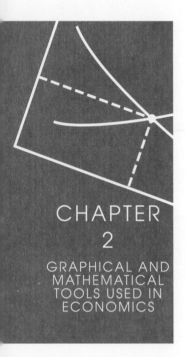

Mathematics began to be widely used in economics near the end of the nineteenth century. For example, Marshall's *Principles of Economics*, published in 1890, included a lengthy mathematical appendix that developed his arguments more systematically than the book itself. Today, mathematics is indispensable for economists. They use it not to hide behind symbols or to make their arguments hard to understand, but to show their results precisely. Just as the physical sciences use mathematics, economists use it to move logically from the basic assumptions of a model to deriving the results of those assumptions. Without mathematics, this process would be both more cumbersome and less accurate.

The models we discuss in this book are based on mathematical arguments. Sometimes these arguments are presented step by step, and in other cases they are discussed in a less rigorous, more literary way. Although the mathematics we use here is no more complex than basic algebra, some of the theories themselves are based on more advanced mathematics. That level of mathematics may be presented in footnotes, but more often you will be instructed to go to more advanced works.

This chapter reviews some of the basic concepts of algebra. We then discuss a few issues that arise in applying those concepts to the study of economics. We use the tools introduced here throughout the rest of the book.

Functions of One Variable

The basic elements of algebra are called **variables.** These are usually labeled X and Y and may be given any numerical value. Sometimes the values of one variable (Y) may be related to those of another variable (X) according to a specific functional relationship. This relationship is denoted by the **functional notation:**

$$Y = f(X). \qquad [2.1]$$

This is read, "Y is a function of X," meaning that the value of Y depends on the value given to X. For example, if we make X calories eaten per day and Y body weight, then Equation 2.1 shows the relationship between the amount of food intake and an individual's weight. The form of Equation 2.1 also shows causality. X is an **independent variable** and may be given any value. On the other hand, the value of Y is completely determined by X; Y is a **dependent variable.** The functional notation in Equation 2.1 shows that "X causes Y."

The exact functional relationship between X and Y may take on a wide variety of forms. The two most common ones are the following:

1. Y is a *linear function* of X. In this case

$$Y = a + bX, \qquad [2.2]$$

where a and b are constants that may be given any numerical value. For example, if a = 3 and b = 2, Equation 2.2 would be written as

$$Y = 3 + 2X. \qquad [2.3]$$

We could give Equation 2.3 an economic interpretation. For example, if we make Y the labor costs of a firm and X the number of labor hours hired, then the form of Equation 2.3 could record the relationship between costs and workers hired. In this case there is a fixed cost of $3 (when X = 0, Y = $3), and the wage rate is $2 per hour. A firm that hired 6 labor hours, for example, would incur total labor costs of $15 [= 3 + 2(6) = 3 + 12]. Table 2.1 illustrates some other values for this function for various values of X.

2. Y is a *quadratic function* of X. In this case

$$Y = a + bX + cX^2, \qquad [2.4]$$

where a, b, and c are constants that may be given any numerical value. One specific example of a quadratic function would make a = −5, b = 6, and c = −1; Equation 2.4 would then be written as

$$Y = -5 + 6X - X^2. \qquad [2.5]$$

Variables

The basic elements of algebra, usually called X, Y, and so on, that may be given any numerical value in an equation.

Functional notation

A way of denoting the fact that the value taken on by one variable (Y) depends on the value taken on by some other variable (X) or set of variables.

Independent variable

In an algebraic equation, a variable that is unaffected by the action of another variable and may be assigned any value.

Dependent variable

In algebra, a variable whose value is determined by another variable or set of variables.

	Linear Function		Quadratic Function
X	**Y = f(X) = 3 + 2X**	**X**	**Y = f(X) = –5 + 6X – X²**
–3	–3	–3	–32
–2	–1	–2	–21
–1	1	–1	–12
0	3	0	–5
1	5	1	0
2	7	2	3
3	9	3	4
4	11	4	3
5	13	5	0
6	15	6	–5

Table 2.1
Values of X and Y
for Linear and
Quadratic Functions

We could also give an economic interpretation to Equation 2.5. Suppose we make Y the output of corn on an acre of land and X the amount of fertilizer applied to that land. In this case, the ability of fertilizer to increase corn output declines as more fertilizer is added. This decline can be easily seen later when we illustrate the graph of this equation in Figure 2.4.

Sometimes it may be useful to look at the relationship between X and Y for several different values of X. Table 2.1 lists the values for Y for the integral values of X from −3 to +6 for both the linear and quadratic functions. Of course, many more values of X (including fractional values) could have been included in this table, and you should be able to compute the value for Y for any preassigned value of X.

Graphing Functions of One Variable

When we write down the functional relationship between X and Y, we are summarizing all there is to know about that relationship. In principle, this book, or any book that uses mathematics, could be written using only these equations. Graphs of some of these functions, however, are very helpful. Graphs not only make it easier for us to understand certain arguments, they also can take the place of a lot of the mathematical notation that must be developed. For these reasons, this book relies heavily on graphs to develop its basic economic models. Here we will look at a few simple graphing techniques.

A graph is simply one way to show the relationship between two variables. Usually the values of the dependent variable (Y) are shown on the vertical axis, and the values of the independent variable (X) are shown on the

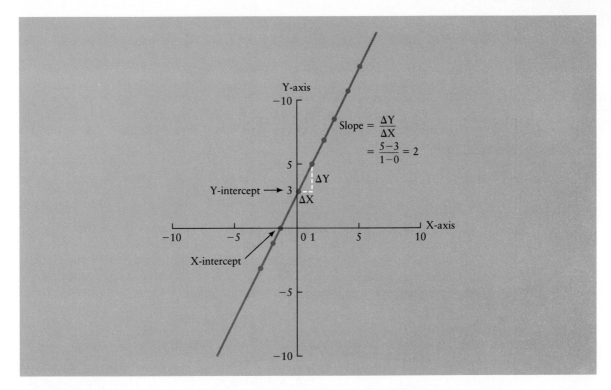

The Y-intercept is 3, when X=0, Y=3. The slope of the line is 2: an increase in X by 1 will increase Y by 2.

Figure 2.1
Graph of the Linear Function Y = 3 + 2X

horizontal axis.[1] Figure 2.1 uses this form to graph Equation 2.3. Although we use heavy dots to show only the points of this function that are listed in Table 2.1, the graph represents the function for every possible value of X. The graph of Equation 2.3 is a straight line, which is why this is called a **linear function**. In Figure 2.1, X and Y can take on both positive and negative values. The variables used in economics generally take on only positive values, and therefore we only have to use the upper right-hand (positive) quadrant of the axes.

Linear function
An equation that is represented by a straight-line graph.

Linear Functions: Intercepts and Slopes

Two important features of the graph in Figure 2.1 are its slope and its **intercept** on the Y-axis. The Y-intercept is the value of Y when X is equal to 0. For

Intercept
The value of Y when X equals zero.

[1] In economics this convention is not always followed. Sometimes a dependent variable is shown on the horizontal axis as, for example, in the case of demand and supply curves. In that case the independent variable (price) is shown on the vertical axis and the dependent variable (quantity) on the horizontal axis.

example, as we can see in Figure 2.1, when X = 0, Y = 3; this means that 3 is the Y-intercept.[2] In the general linear form of Equation 2.2,

$$Y = a + bX,$$

the Y-intercept will be Y = a, since this is the value of Y when X = 0.

We define the **slope** of any straight line to be the ratio of the change in Y to the change in X for a movement along the line. The slope can be defined mathematically as

$$\text{Slope} = \frac{\text{Change in Y}}{\text{Change in X}} = \frac{\Delta Y}{\Delta X},$$

Slope

The direction of a line on a graph. Shows the change in Y that results from a unit change in X.

where the Δ ("delta") notation simply means "change in." For the particular function shown in Figure 2.1, the slope is equal to 2. We can clearly see from the dashed lines, representing changes in X and Y, that a given change in X is met by a change of twice that amount in Y. Table 2.1 shows the same result— as X increases from 0 to 1, Y increases from 3 to 5. Consequently

$$\text{Slope} = \frac{\Delta Y}{\Delta X} = \frac{5 - 3}{1 - 0} = 2.$$

It should be obvious that this is true for all the other points in Table 2.1. Everywhere along the straight line, the slope is the same. Generally, for any linear function, the slope is given by b in Equation 2.2.[3] The slope of a straight line may be positive (as it is in Figure 2.1) or it may be negative, in which case the line would run from upper left to lower right.

A straight line may also have a slope of 0, which is a horizontal line. In this case the value of Y is constant; changes in X will not affect Y. The function would by Y = a + 0X, or Y = a. This equation is represented by a horizontal line (parallel to the X-axis) through point a on the Y-axis.

■ Slope and Units of Measurement

The slope of a function depends on the units in which X and Y are measured. For example, a study of a family's consumption of oranges might reveal that the number of oranges (Y) purchased in a week is equal to 3 + 2X, where X is the family's income measured in hundreds of dollars per week. Consequently, $\Delta Y / \Delta X = 2$: that is, a $100 increase in income one week causes 2 more oranges to be purchased. If income (X) is measured in single dollars, the relationship is Y = 3 + .02X and $\Delta Y / \Delta X = .02$. In this case, although the interpretation of this slope is the same (a $100 increase in income still increases orange

---

[2] One can also speak of the X-intercept of a function, which is defined as that value of X for which Y = 0. For Equation 2.3 it is easy to see that Y = 0 when X = −3/2, which is then the X-intercept. The X-intercept for the general linear function in Equation 2.2 is given by X = −a/b, as may be seen by substituting that value into the equation.

[3] In calculus, mathematicians call the slope of a function at a particular point "the derivative" and denote this concept by dY/dX where the d means the change in Y brought about by a very small change in X. For the general linear Equation 2.2, dY/dX = b.

purchases by 2 per week), the numerical value of the slope is very different. Similarly, if Y were measured in dozens of oranges per week and X in hundreds of dollars, the relationship would be Y = ¼ + ⅙ X. An increase in family income of $100 still increases orange purchases by 2 (⅙ of a dozen), but now the slope is different again. Clearly, one must be very careful when discussing *the* slope of a function to know how the variables are measured. In later chapters we look at some methods that help solve this "units" problem.

■ Changes in Slope

Quite often in this text we are interested in changing the parameters (that is, a and b) of a linear function. We can do this in two ways: we can change the Y-intercept, or we can change the slope. Figure 2.2 shows the graph of the function

$$Y = -X + 10. \qquad\qquad [2.6]$$

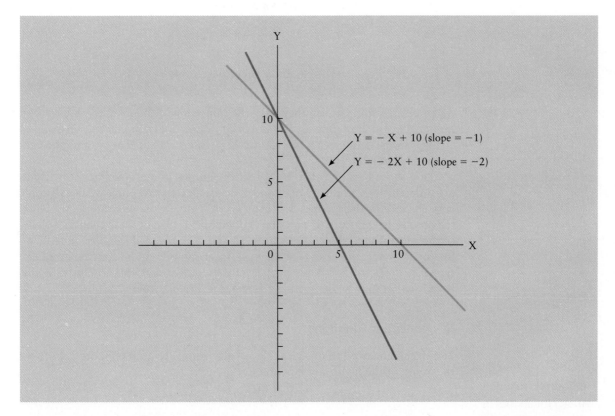

When the slope of a linear function is changed but the Y-intercept remains fixed, the graph of the function rotates about the Y-intercept.

Figure 2.2
Changes in the Slope of a Linear Function

This linear function has a slope of -1 and a Y-intercept of $Y = 10$. Figure 2.2 also shows the function

$$Y = -2X + 10. \hspace{2cm} [2.7]$$

We have doubled the slope of Equation 2.6 from -1 to -2 and kept the Y-intercept at $Y = 10$. This causes the graph of the function to become steeper and to rotate about the Y-intercept. In general, a change in the slope of a function will cause this kind of rotation without changing the value of its Y-intercept. Since a linear function takes on the value of its Y-intercept when X $= 0$, changing the slope will not change the value of the function at this point.

■ Changes in Intercept

Figure 2.3 also shows a graph of the function $Y = -X + 10$. It shows the effect of changes in the constant term, that is, the Y-intercept only, while the slope stays at -1. Figure 2.3 shows the graphs of

$$Y = -X + 12 \hspace{2cm} [2.8]$$

and

$$Y = -X + 5. \hspace{2cm} [2.9]$$

All three lines are parallel; they have the same slope. Changing the Y-intercept only makes the line shift up and down. Its slope does not change. Of course, changes in the Y-intercepts also cause the X-intercepts to change, and you can see these new intercepts.

You should also be able to see that the graphs of any two linear functions are different only in their slopes and Y-intercepts. In this book we usually discuss changes in their slopes and changes in Y-intercepts separately. Although the economic context will vary, the mathematical form of these changes will be of the general type shown in Figures 2.2 and 2.3. These graphs are quite helpful for showing the effects of changes in economic circumstances. Application 2.1: Property Tax Assessment uses these linear concepts to illustrate one such use that may be depressingly familiar to home owners.

■ Nonlinear Functions

Nonlinear functions of one variable are also simple to graph. Figure 2.4 shows the graph of the **quadratic function** in Equation 2.5:

$$Y = -5 + 6X - X^2. \hspace{2cm} [2.10]$$

Quadratic function

An equation that includes terms in X^2 and (possibly) X.

Heavy dots again show the points listed in Table 2.1, although the function could also, with a bit of effort, be computed for fractional values of X as well as for the integral values shown in the table. The Y-intercept is the constant

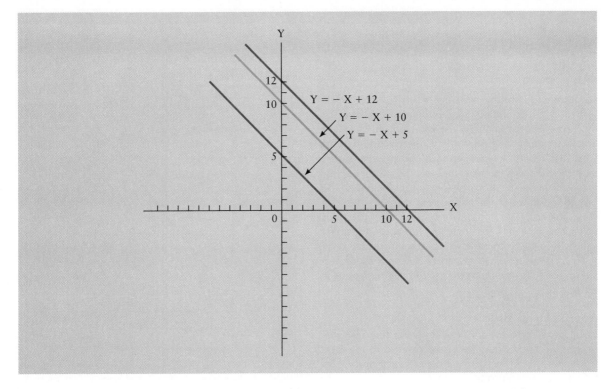

When the Y-intercept of a function is changed, the graph of the function shifts up or down and is parallel to the other graphs.

Figure 2.3
Changes in the Y-Intercept of a Linear Function

---

term (-5) in Equation 2.5.[4] In general, unlike linear functions, the slope of a nonlinear function is not the same everywhere.

   We define the slope of a nonlinear function at some particular point as the slope of the straight line that is tangent to the function at that point. For example, the slope of the function in Figure 2.4 at the point X = 1, Y = 0 is given by the slope of the line AA. The slope at the point X = 3, Y = 4 is given by the slope of the line BB; at the point X = 5, Y = 0, the slope is given by the line CC. When the function reaches its highest point (at X = 3, Y = 4), the slope of the function is 0. To the left of this highest point the graph has a positive slope, and to the right of it the slope is negative. We can define the slopes

---

[4] The X-intercepts (the values of X for which Y = 0) are called the "roots" of the quadratic function. They may be found by using the quadratic formula, which states that if Y = a + bX + cX², the roots are given by

$$X = \frac{-b \pm \sqrt{b^2 - 4ac}}{2c}.$$

You should be able to show that this formula provides the roots X = 1 and X = 5 for the example shown in the text.

APPLICATION 2.1

Property Tax Assessment

Property taxes are the most important source of local revenues in the United States. In most communities the taxes pay for schools, the local police force, the fire department, and so forth. Conceptually, figuring what a property owner owes in taxes is a simple matter—the town assessors multiply the tax rate by the market value of the property. A major problem with this procedure, however, is that current market values for most properties are not known because properties only rarely change hands. To come up with accurate market values, localities increasingly turn to sophisticated computer methods to assess properties. These methods provide a good illustration of the use of linear functions in economics.

A Simple Linear Model

Local property assessors begin by collecting information on all houses that were recently sold in the area. With these data they can estimate a relationship between sales price (Y) and a relevant characteristic of the house, say, its square footage (X). Such a relationship might be stated as

$$Y = \$10,000 + \$50X. \tag{1}$$

This equation means that a house with zero square footage (X = 0) should sell for $10,000 (because of the value of its land) and each square foot of living space adds $50 to the value of the house. Using the square footage of a house, the assessor can predict its current value by using Equation 1. This procedure is shown in Figure 1. According to the figure, a house with 2,000 square feet of living space would have a market value of $110,000, and one with 3,000 square feet would be worth $160,000.

Valuing Other Features of Homes

Of course, assessors must take into account more features of a house than just square footage. Suppose current sales suggest that a view is worth $30,000 in the current housing market. Assuming Equation 1 reflects the values of houses without views, the values for houses with views can be computed by:

Figure 1

Relationship between the Floor Area of a House and Its Market Value

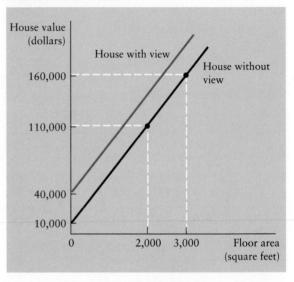

Using data on recent house sales, real estate appraisers can calculate a relationship between floor area (X, measured in square feet) and market value (Y). The entire relationship shifts upward by $30,000 if a house has a nice view.

$$Y = \$30,000 + \$10,000 + \$50X = \\ \$40,000 + \$50X. \tag{2}$$

Using data on recent house sales, real estate appraisers can calculate a relationship between floor area (X, measured in square feet) and market value (Y). The entire relationship shifts upward by $30,000 if a house has a nice view. This relationship is also shown in Figure 1. You can now use this figure to predict that 2,000 and 3,000 square foot houses with views are worth $140,000 and $190,000, respectively. Using similar procedures allows the assessor to evaluate all possible types of houses.

To Think About

1. Suppose spectacular views are more valuable in large houses than in small ones. How would this effect be represented with algebra?
2. Do you think that using these mathematical methods for assessment ends people's disputes over their tax bills?

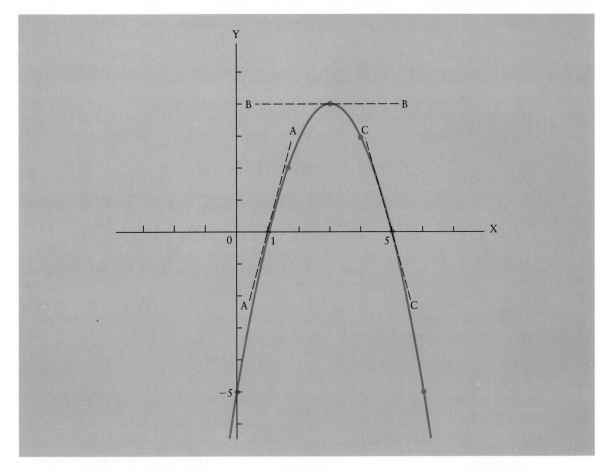

The slope of a nonlinear curve at any point is the slope of a line tangent to the curve at that point. For example, at the point X = 3, Y = 4, the slope of the diagrammed function is 0. This is the slope of the line BB.

Figure 2.4
Graph of a
Quadratic Function

---

of much more complex curves in the same way by looking at the slope of the straight line tangent to the curves.[5]

Whenever a function reaches its maximum value, the slope of the function generally will be 0 at that point. To use a mountain as an illustration, the slope of the ground at the mountaintop must be 0. Otherwise you would not be on the top, since walking in the appropriate direction will put you higher. Only if the slope is 0 will you be unable to go higher. Since throughout this book we are interested in maximum (that is, highest) points, this mountain example is very helpful to keep in mind.

---

[5] In elementary calculus it is shown that the slope of Y = f(X) at some point is given by the value of the derivative of this function at that point. For Equation 2.5, $dY/dX = -2X + 6$. At X = 1 the slope is +4, at X = 3 it is 0, and at X = 5 the slope is −4. The function reaches its maximum value when the derivative (and the slope) is equal to 0.

The fact that the slope of a function (or of its graph) must be 0 at a maximum point is very important in economics. The marginalist ideas in Chapter 1 grew directly out of this mathematical law. As long as the slope of a function is positive, increasing X will increase Y also. If Y is crop yield and X is fertilizer, adding fertilizer will increase yields if the slope of the graph is positive. The law of diminishing returns, however, implies that this slope will decline as fertilizer use (X) increases. If the slope becomes zero, adding X will not raise crop yields at all—the marginal value of fertilizer is zero. Application 2.2: The Changing U.S. Income Tax Structure illustrates these marginal ideas in the context of recent tax "simplification" initiatives.

Functions of Two or More Variables

Economists are usually concerned with functions of more than just one variable, since there is almost always more than a single cause of an economic outcome. To see the effects of many causes, economists must work with functions of several variables. A two-variable function might be written in functional notation as

$$Y = f(X, Z). \qquad [2.11]$$

This equation shows that Y's values depend on the values of two independent variables, X and Z. For example, an individual's weight (Y) depends not only on calories eaten (X), but also on how much the individual exercises (Z). Increases in X increase Y but increases in Z decrease Y. The functional notation in Equation 2.11 hints at the possibility that there might be trade-offs between eating and exercise. In Chapter 3 we will start to explore such trade-offs because they are central to the choices that both individuals and firms make.

■ A Simple Example

In general, we could have Y depend on the values of more than two variables, but a simple two-variable function can be used to explain most of the relevant facts about how multiple variable functions work. Suppose the relationship between Y, X, and Z is given by

$$Y = X \cdot Z. \qquad [2.12]$$

The form of this particular function is widely used in economics. Later chapters use a closely related form to show the utility (Y) that an individual receives from using two goods (X and Z) and also to show the production relationship between an output (Y) and two inputs (say, labor, X, and capital, Z). Here, however, we are interested mainly in this function's mathematical properties.

Some values for the function in Equation 2.12 are recorded in Table 2.2. Two important facts are shown by this table. First, even if one of the variables

X	Z	Y	
1	1	1	**Table 2.2**
1	2	2	Values of X, Z, and Y
1	3	3	that Satisfy the
1	4	4	Relationship Y = X • Z
2	1	2	
2	2	4	
2	3	6	
2	4	8	
3	1	3	
3	2	6	
3	3	9	
3	4	12	
4	1	4	
4	2	8	
4	3	12	
4	4	16	

is held constant (say, at X = 2), changes in the other independent variable (Z) will cause the value of the dependent variable (Y) to change. The value of Y increases from 4 to 6 as Z rises from 2 to 3, even though X is held constant. In economic terms, this illustrates the "marginal" influence of variable Z. Second, several different combinations of X and Z will result in the same value of Y. For example, Y = 4 if X = 2, Z = 2 or if X = 1, Z = 4 (or, indeed, for an infinite number of other X, Z combinations if fractions are used). Using this equality of values of Y for a number of X, Z combinations, functions of two variables can be graphed rather simply.

Graphing Functions of Two Variables

We would need to use three dimensions to graph a function of two variables completely: one axis for X, one for Z, and one for Y. Drawing three-dimensional graphs in a two-dimensional book is very difficult. Not only must an artist be good enough to be able to show depth in only two dimensions, but the reader must have enough imagination to read the graph as a three-dimensional model. Since economists are not necessarily good artists (and some would argue because economists lack imagination), they graph these functions another way that is much like the techniques mapmakers use.

Mapmakers are also confined to working with two dimensional drawings. They use **contour lines** to show the third dimension. These are lines of equal altitude that outline the physical features of the territory being mapped. For example, a contour line labeled "1,000 feet" on a map shows all those points of land that are 1,000 feet above sea level. By using a number of contour lines, mapmakers can show the heights and steepness of mountains and the depths

Contour lines

Lines in two dimensions that show the sets of values of the independent variables that yield the same value for the dependent variable.

APPLICATION 2.2

The Changing U.S. Income Tax Structure

The mathematical concept of slope and the economic idea of marginalism are clearly related because both refer to change in one variable brought about by a small change in some other variable. We can see this relationship in the determination of income taxes.

Progressive Income Taxation

Many governments use income taxes as their principal source of revenue, and most of the rate schedules for those taxes are *progressive;* that is, the proportion of income paid in taxes is greater for people with high incomes than for people with low incomes. Marginal tax rates (that is, the rate of tax on the last dollar earned) increase with increasing income levels; it is this feature that leads to progressivity.

　　The top half of Table 1 shows federal income taxes owed by taxpayers at various income levels under rates that prevailed for married couples in 1980. Marginal tax rates, which are shown in the second column of the table, were steeply progressive rising from 21 percent for a couple with a taxable income of $10,000 to 59 percent for someone earning $100,000. The top marginal tax rate in 1980 was 70 percent for couples with incomes over $215,000. The third and fourth columns of Table 1 show the effects of these rates on taxes owed. Because some income is excluded from taxes for all taxpayers and because marginal tax rates apply only to the last dollar earned, average tax rates always fall below marginal tax rates. Still, as judged by the percent of taxable income paid in taxes, the federal income tax was quite progressive in 1980.

A Graphical Presentation

These features of the U.S. tax structures are shown graphically in Figure 1. In this figure, the curve OT shows the relationship between taxable income and tax liabilities under the 1980 rate schedules. Increasing marginal tax rates are reflected by the increasing slope of the OT curve. Average tax rates, on the other hand, can be calculated from the curve as the slope of a ray through

Table 1

Federal Income Tax Liabilities in 1980 and 1986

Taxable Annual Income	Marginal Tax Rate (Percent)	Taxes Owed	Average Tax Rate (Percent)
Liabilities under 1980 Schedule			
$ 10,000	21	$ 1,719	17.2
25,000	32	5,721	22.8
50,000	49	16,444	32.9
100,000	59	44,004	44.0
Liabilities under 1986 Schedule			
$ 10,000	15	$ 1,500	15.0
25,000	15	3,750	15.0
50,000	33	11,100	22.2
100,000	33	27,600	27.6

Note: Figures apply to a married couple taking the standard deduction. Tax liabilities apply to taxable income, not gross income, which is larger.
Source: Author's tax forms, courtesy the Internal Revenue Service.

the origin to the appropriate point on OT. The slope of the ray OA, for example, shows that the average tax rate for a couple with a taxable income of $50,000 is 32.9 percent (= $16,444/$50,000). If we drew rays similar to OA for higher income levels, these would be steeper than OA, thereby showing how average tax rates increase. Similarly, for incomes less than $50,000, rays through the origin would be flatter than OA showing that lower income couples paid lower average tax rates. Elsewhere in this book we will frequently use this method to illustrate the relationship between marginal magnitudes (as reflected by the slope of a curve) and average magnitudes (as reflected by the slopes of rays through the origin).

The Reagan Tax Reforms

High marginal tax rates that prevailed as of 1980 were one of the principal targets of tax policy under the

Figure 1
Relationship between Taxable Income and
Tax Liability

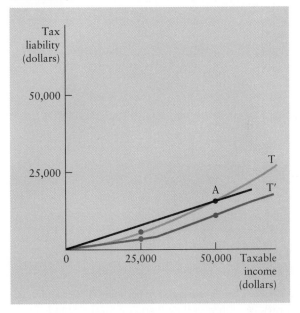

The curve OT shows the relationship between taxable income and federal income taxes owed that prevailed in 1980. The Tax Reform Act of 1986 lowered both marginal and average rates of income taxation, shifting the curve to OT′.

Reagan administration. It was argued that such high rates harmed individuals' incentives to work and to save and that such rates encouraged tax avoidance and evasion. Starting with the Economic Recovery Act of 1981, Congress and the President agreed on a phased-in program of reductions in marginal (and average) tax rates with the hope of improving U.S. economic performance. The final installment of the Reagan tax reductions was implemented as the Tax Reform Act of 1986. When fully implemented (by 1989), this Act specified a very simple tax schedule with much lower marginal rates: Incomes between 0 and $30,000 were to be taxed at 15 percent whereas incomes over $30,000 were to be taxed at 33 percent. For example, a couple with an income of

$50,000 would pay $11,100 in tax—$4,500 on the first $30,000 and $6,600 on the next $20,000. Hence, both the marginal tax rate (33 percent) and the average tax rate (22.2 percent = $11,100/$50,000) were much lower for such a couple than they had been in 1980.[1]

The final effects of these reductions are illustrated in the bottom half of Table 1 and by the curve OT′ in Figure 1. Notice especially how the simple two-bracket form for the schedule specified in 1986 resulted in two linear segments in the Tax curve OT′. The kink in the curve at $30,000 reflects the change in marginal tax rates at that income level. Of course, there remains considerable controversy over whether these reductions really did prompt people to work and save more. Additionally, the effects of the reductions seem to have contributed to the burgeoning budget deficits of the late 1980s. In many places in this book, therefore, we will continue to examine the effects of taxation (and especially the changes made during the 1980s) on economic behavior.

To Think About

1. Income tax *progressivity* is usually judged by the ratio of tax liability to income for various income levels. Does an income tax need to have increasing marginal rates to be progressive under this definition? Is the post-1989 income tax schedule much less progressive than the one that prevailed in the early 1980s? Can you develop a geometric analysis of the relationship between a progressive income tax and a set of increasing marginal rates?

2. The income tax schedules in this example are applied to "taxable income," but the definition of this concept also has changed over time. How would adoption of an increasingly broad definition of taxable income affect the tax schedules illustrated? How would such a change affect conclusions about the progressivity of the tax system?

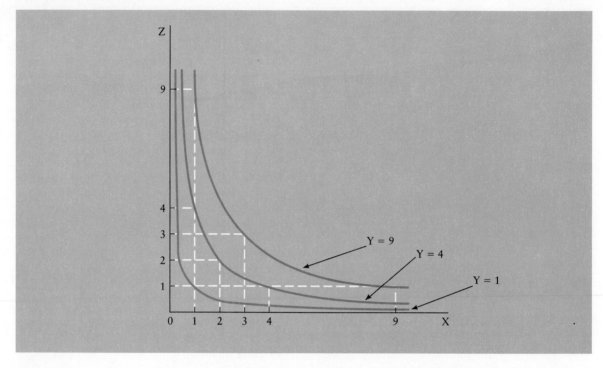

Figure 2.5
Contour Lines for
Y = X · Z

Contour lines for the function Y = X · Z are rectangular hyperbolas. They can be represented by making Y equal to various supplied values (here Y = 1, Y = 4, and Y = 9), and then graphing the relationship between the independent variables X and Z.

of valleys and ocean trenches. In this way they add the third dimension to a two-dimensional map.

Economists also use contour lines; that is, lines of equal "altitude." Equation 2.12 can be graphed in two dimensions (one dimension for the values of X and another dimension for values of Z), with contour lines to show the values of Y, the third dimension. This equation is graphed in Figure 2.5, with three contour lines: one each for Y = 1, Y = 4, and Y = 9.

Each of the contour lines in Figure 2.5 is a rectangular hyperbola. The contour line labeled "Y = 1" is a graph of

$$Y = 1 = X \cdot Z,$$
[2.13]

"Y = 4" is a graph of

$$Y = 4 = X \cdot Z,$$
[2.14]

and the line labeled "Y = 9" is a graph of

$$Y = 9 = X \cdot Z.$$
[2.15]

Some of the values along these contour lines are shown in Table 2.2. It would be easy to compute other points on the curves. Other contour lines for the function could also be drawn by making Y equal to the desired level and graphing the resulting relationship between X and Z. Since we can give Y any value we want, an infinite number of contour lines can be drawn. In this way we can show the original function in Equation 2.12 as accurately as we want without resorting to three dimensions. One practical application of this type of graph is discussed in Application 2.3: Oil Pipelines.

Simultaneous Equations

Another mathematical concept that is often used in economics is **simultaneous equations.** When two variables (say, X and Y) are related by two different equations, it is sometimes, though not always, possible to solve these equations together for a single set of values for X and Y that satisfies both of the equations. For example, it is easy to see that the two equations

$$X + Y = 3$$
$$X - Y = 1 \qquad\qquad\qquad [2.16]$$

have a unique solution of

$$X = 2$$
$$Y = 1. \qquad\qquad\qquad [2.17]$$

These equations operate "simultaneously" to determine the solutions for X and Y. One of the equations alone cannot determine each variable—the solution depends on both of the equations.

■ Changing Solutions for Simultaneous Equations

It makes no sense in these equations to ask how a change in, say, X would affect the solution for Y. There is only one solution for X and Y from these two equations. As long as both equations must hold, the values of neither X nor Y can change. Of course, if the equations themselves are changed, then their solution will also change. For example, the equation system

$$X + Y = 5$$
$$X - Y = 1 \qquad\qquad\qquad [2.18]$$

is solved as

$$X = 3$$
$$Y = 2. \qquad\qquad\qquad [2.19]$$

Changing just one of the parameters in Equation 2.16 gives us an entirely different solution set.

Simultaneous equations

A set of equations with more than one variable that must be solved together for a particular solution.

APPLICATION 2.3

Oil Pipelines

The amount of crude oil that can be put through a pipeline depends on the diameter of the pipe and the force with which the oil is pumped. Although there are a number of other engineering issues involved, a simple mathematical model of pipeline throughput closely resembles the algebraic example discussed in the text. Specifically, if we make Y the amount of oil pumped (measured in thousands of barrels per day), X the pumping force applied (in thousands of horsepower), and Z the pipe diameter (in inches), the approximate relationship is[1]

$$Y = 4 \sqrt{X \cdot Z}. \qquad [1]$$

This equation makes clear that there are many ways to obtain a throughput of, say, 50,000 barrels per day. A 12-inch pipeline requires about 13,000 horsepower to pump this amount. A 16-inch pipeline needs only 10,000 horsepower to pump the same amount. These combinations are illustrated in Figure 1, which shows a portion of the Y = 50 contour line for Equation 1. This contour line is a graph of the equation

$$Y^2 = 2,500 = 16X \cdot Z$$
$$156.25 = X \cdot Z. \qquad [2]$$

Other contour lines for higher and lower levels of oil pipeline throughput can be calculated in the same manner.

The importance of this kind of information to pipeline planners should be obvious. Knowing that they can achieve pipeline throughput a number of different ways, they can figure out how to do so in the least costly way by taking account of the prices of pipe and pumps, for example. In Chapter 9 we examine in considerable detail the general issue of input choices and how they are affected by input prices. Because they illustrate the options open to a firm, contour lines similar to the one

Figure 1

Alternative Combinations of Pumping Force and Pipeline Diameter That Allow a Throughput of 50,000 Barrels per Day

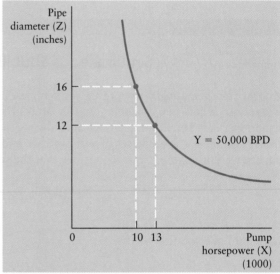

Using the relationship between output (Y), pumping force (X), and pipeline diameter (Z), we can draw a contour line for Y = 50 (thousand barrels per day). This curve shows that there are a number of ways to achieve this same level of throughput.

shown in Figure 1 will play an important role in our analysis.

To Think About

1. Suppose a pipeline firm wished to move 50,000 barrels of crude oil per day as cheaply as possible. What would the firm need to know in order to decide what size pipeline to build? Can you illustrate this choice in Figure 1?
2. Suppose pipeline throughput depends not only on pipe diameter and horsepower, but also on the nature of the terrain (whether the pipeline goes uphill or downhill). How might this be reflected in Equation 1? How would it alter Figure 1?

[1] This relationship is adapted from L. Cookenboo, *Crude Oil Pipelines and Competition in the Petroleum Industry* (Cambridge, Mass.: Harvard University Press, 1955).

■ Graphing Simultaneous Equations

These results are illustrated in Figure 2.6. The two equations in the set in Equation 2.16 are straight lines that intersect at the point (2,1). This point is the solution to the two equations since it is the only one that lies on both lines. Changing the constant in the first equation of this system gives us a different intersection for Equation 2.18. In that case the lines intersect at point (3, 2), and that is the new solution. Even though only one of the lines shifted, both X and Y take on new solutions.

The similarity between the algebraic graph in Figure 2.6 and the supply and demand graphs in Figures 1.2 and 1.3 is striking. The point of intersection of two curves is called a "solution" in algebra and an "equilibrium" in economics, but in both cases we are finding the point that satisfies both relationships. The shift of the demand curve in Figure 1.3 clearly resembles the change in the simultaneous equation set in Figure 2.6. In both cases the shift in one of the curves results in new solutions for both of the variables. Marshall's analogy of the blades of the supply and demand "scissors" determining market price and quantity can be seen in the algebraic notion of simultaneous systems and their solutions. Throughout this book we will be using such graphs to

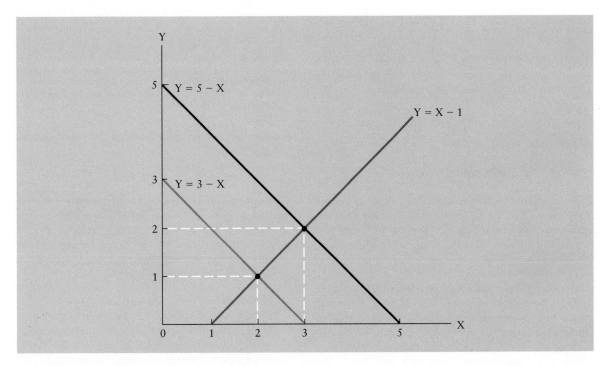

The linear equations X + Y = 3 (Y = 3 − X) and X − Y = 1 (Y = X − 1) can be solved simultaneously to find X = 2, Y = 1. This solution is shown by the point of intersection of the graphs of the two equations. If the first equation is changed (to Y = 5 − X), the solution will also change (to X = 3, Y = 2).

Figure 2.6
Solving Simultaneous Equations

APPLICATION 2.4

Oil and the Kuwait Invasion

Because crude oil is traded in a vast international market, disturbances in one part of this market rapidly affect prices throughout the world. A simple simultaneous model of supply and demand can be used to illustrate the effects that the Iraqi invasion of Kuwait had on this market.

A Simple Short-Run Solution

A simple model[1] of the demand for crude oil might be

$$Q_D = 75 - P \qquad [1]$$

where Q_D is crude oil consumed (in millions of barrels per day) and P is the market price of crude oil (technically, the dollar price per barrel of Saudi Arabian light crude). Supply might be represented by

$$Q_S = 54 + .4P. \qquad [2]$$

Market Equilibrium

Equilibrium in the crude oil market can be found by equating quantity supplied to quantity demanded:

$$Q_D = Q_S$$

which yields

$$P = 15 \text{ and } Q_D = Q_S = 60$$

These equilibrium solutions (a price of $15 per barrel and production of 60 million barrels per day) are approximately the values that prevailed in the world market in 1989. Figure 1 shows this initial market equilibrium.

The Kuwait Invasion

The Iraqi invasion of Kuwait, coupled with the United Nations boycott of Iraqi oil, reduced available world production by approximately 4 million barrels per day. This shifts the supply curve represented by Equation 2 to

$$Q_S = 54 + .4P - 4 = 50 + .4P.$$

As before, the new equilibrium can be found by solving

Figure 1

Effect of the Kuwait Invasion on Oil Prices

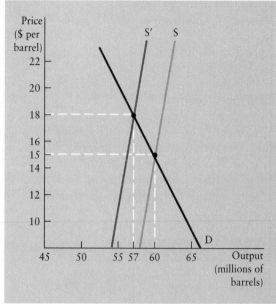

The Iraqi invasion of Kuwait shifted the supply curve for crude oil leftward by 4 million barrels per day. This increased market price from $15 to $18 per barrel. The price rise encouraged an increase in oil supply of 1 million barrels per day elsewhere.

this equation together with the original demand equation giving

$$P = 17.9 \text{ and } Q = 57.1.$$

This new equilibrium is also shown in Figure 1. The reduction in oil supply raised the equilibrium price from $15 to nearly $18 per barrel. Notice, however, that total production declined by only about 3 million barrels per day. The rise in price prompted other producers to produce 1 million additional barrels per day.

To Think About

1. Would you expect the price change from the cutback in Iraq and Kuwait supplies to be larger or smaller over the long term?
2. A large part of world oil output is controlled by OPEC. How would you expect that to affect the simple analysis used in this application?

[1] Although the model presented here is greatly simplified, its parameters are generally consistent with some of the more extensive studies of the supply and demand for crude oil we will examine in later chapters. All data are taken from U.S. Department of Energy, *Annual Energy Review*.

show how markets arrive at equilibrium outcomes that satisfy both supply and demand relationships simultaneously. Application 2.4: Oil and the Kuwait Invasion provides a first glimpse of this sort of analysis.

Special Features of Mathematics in Economics

A few peculiarities arise when the mathematical tools described in this chapter are applied to economic problems. First, as we mentioned before, practically all the variables used in economic analysis can take on only positive values. Economists talk about prices, quantities of output, and quantities of factors of production. In most situations these variables are either positive or zero; a negative price or quantity would have no meaning. Most graphs in this book show only the positive quadrant and its axes, where both of the variables are always nonnegative.

A second peculiarity is the economist's tendency to "reverse" the axes in a graph by putting the dependent variable on the horizontal axis. The supply and demand graphs in Figures 1.2, 1.3, and 1.4 show this arrangement. Economists usually assume that price is the independent variable in a supply and demand situation and that individuals and firms react to this price by choosing the quantities they will demand and the quantities they will produce, respectively. As we show later in Part 4, economists use the vertical axis to record the independent variable (price) in these relations and the horizontal axis to record the dependent variable (quantity).

Of course, the nature of an equation is not affected by which variables are put on which axes. The equation

$$Y = 2 + 2X \qquad\qquad [2.20]$$

is identical to the equation

$$X = \tfrac{1}{2}Y - 1 \qquad\qquad [2.21]$$

in that the same set of points satisfies both equations. Nevertheless, the equations are written differently (for example, the slope of Equation 2.21 is the reciprocal of the slope of Equation 2.20), and you should keep this departure from standard conventions in mind.

Summary

This chapter reviews material that should be familiar to you from prior math classes. What we have done here is to go over some basic algebra and show how simple functions can be graphed. Some of the results presented here that will be used throughout the rest of this book are listed on the following page:

- Linear equations have graphs that are straight lines. These lines are described by their slopes and by their intercepts with the Y-axis.

- Changes in the slope cause the graph of a linear equation to rotate about its Y-intercept. Changes in the Y-intercept cause the graph to shift in a parallel way.

- Nonlinear equations have graphs that have curved shapes. The most common shapes are parabolas and hyperbolas.

- Economists often use functions of two or more variables because economic outcomes have many causes. These functions can sometimes be graphed in two dimensions by using contour lines.

- Simultaneous equations determine solutions for two (or more) variables that satisfy all of the equations. An important use of such equations is to show how supply and demand curves determine equilibrium prices. For that reason, such equations are widely encountered in economics.

Review Questions

1. Using mathematics presents a number of advantages for economists in their construction of models of the economy. What are some of those advantages? In what ways does the use of mathematical models help avoid mistakes in model construction? Can you think of disadvantages in using mathematics? Are certain mistakes more likely in mathematical models than would be the case with less formal ways of constructing economic theories?

2. When we use the functional notation $Y = f(X)$, we mean that for each possible value of X there is precisely one value of Y. What does this imply about the graphs of functions? Can you think of graphs that cannot be represented by simple functions (how about a circle, for example)? Can you think of any economic situations in which a functional representation might not be appropriate—that is, can you think of economic activities where a single value for X might be consistent with several different values for Y?

3. If a graph of a linear function has a positive slope, what does this imply about the qualitative relationship between X and Y—do increases in X increase or decrease Y? Which of the following linear relationships have positive slopes?

    a. $Y = 3 + 5X$.
    b. $Y = 3 - 5X$.
    c. $Y + 5X = 3$.
    d. $Y - 5X = 3$.
    e. $-Y + 5X = 3$.
    f. $-Y - 5X = 3$.

    Answer this question also for the case of negatively sloped linear functions. Describe the qualitative relationship between two variables whose graph is a negatively sloped line, and indicate which of the listed functions have negative slopes.

4. Application 2.1 shows how a property tax assessment formula based on square footage might be generalized to take account of a good view. How might that formula be generalized further to take account of other factors such as a land-scaped yard or a swimming pool? Would a graphical description of the effects of such factors resemble the graph shown in Figure 1 in the application?

5. Following on question 4, how might property tax assessment formulas be ad-justed for "interactions" between the values of characteristics of houses? Suppose, for example, that each square foot of a house were more valuable if the house had a good view than if it did not. How would you reflect this fact al-gebraically and in a graph?

6. Explain why the economic notion of a "marginal" effect is reflected by the alge-braic concept of slope. Write down a functional representation that summarizes each of the following economic relationships, indicate what a graph of the rela-tionship might look like, and suggest how the slope of that relationship might be interpreted in marginal terms:

Dependent Variable	Independent Variable
a. Quantity produced	Labor hired
b. Total cost	Units of output
c. Revenue received	Units of output
d. Happiness (utility)	Ice cream eaten
e. Taxes paid	Income
f. Fish caught	Fishing lines used

7. A logical extension of the Tax Reform Act of 1986 (see Application 2.2) would be to adopt a single marginal tax rate (say, 40 percent) together with the exclu-sion of a certain minimal income (say, the first $10,000) from taxation. How would you graph such a tax schedule? Suppose the government desired that someone with a $50,000 taxable income would pay the same amount of tax un-der such a simplified tax schedule as under the 1986 act. If the income exemption were kept at $10,000, what would the marginal tax rate have to be to collect these revenues?

8. Suppose we tried to write down a functional representation of a contour map. This might be done by specifying

$$Y = \text{Altitude} = f(\text{latitude, longitude}) = f(X, Z).$$

Hence, given the coordinates of any location (in terms of latitude and longitude), we could use f to calculate the altitude of this place. Interpret the following alge-braic ideas for the function f in terms of physical movements over the actual con-tour map:

a. An increase in X holding Z constant.
b. An increase in Z holding X constant.
c. The increase in Y that results from increasing X (or Z) alone.

d. The increase in Y that results from increasing X and Z by the same amounts.

e. The implication of discovering that any small changes in X or Z always re-duce Y. In physical terms, what kind of a place is this on the map and in the real world the map represents?

f. The implication of discovering that any small changes in X or Z always in-crease Y. What kind of a place is this?

g. Finding a particular set of changes in X and Z that always keep Y constant. Would these map coordinates provide a good route for a railroad through this territory?

9. Explain why the following statement is nonsense: "In a pair of simultaneous equations, the relationship between X and Y can be found by finding two solu-tions and then joining them with a straight line. For example, the two solutions found in the text, (2,1) and (3,2), show that whenever X is increased by 1, Y will also increase by 1."

10. "In supply and demand graphs it is not possible to predict how much equilib-rium price will rise when the demand curve shifts up just by knowing the vertical shift in the curve. If demanders decided they were willing to pay $1 per bushel more for any given quantity of wheat, the demand curve would shift uniformly upward by $1. But the equilibrium price of wheat would probably rise by less than $1." Explain why this is so intuitively and illustrate your intuition with a suitable graph. Demonstrate cases in which price would rise by $1, by $.50, and in which price would not rise at all.

Problems

2.1   Consider the equation

$$Y = 15 + 3X.$$

a. If $X = 0$, what is the value of Y?

b. If $Y = 0$, what is the value of X?

c. Calculate Y for $X = 3$ and for $X = 4$. What do you conclude about the relationship between changes in Y and changes in X?

d. Graph the equation.

e. Graph the equation for

$$Y = 20 + 3X$$

and answer parts a through c for this equation.

f. Graph the equation

$$Y = 15 + 5X$$

and answer parts a through c for this equation.

g. Briefly describe why your answers to parts a through c differ for these three examples.

2.2   Consider the equation

$$Y = X^2 - 6X + 8.$$

a. If $X = 0$, what is the value of Y?
b. For what values of X does $Y = 0$?
c. If $X = 3$, what does Y equal? Can Y ever be less than this amount?
d. Graph the equation.
e. Using calculus it can be shown that the slope of the equation at any point is given by

$$\text{Slope} = 2X - 6.$$

Show that this slope is negative for $X < 3$ and positive for $X > 3$.
f. Explain intuitively why Y takes on its minimum value at $X = 3$ and why the slope of the equation is zero there.

2.3   The demand for potatoes is given by

$$Q_D = 40 - 2P + .001I,$$

where Q_D = Quantity of potatoes in millions of pounds
    P = Price of potatoes in cents per pound
    I = Average income in dollars.

a. If $I = 10,000$, graph the demand curve for potatoes. How many potatoes are demanded at a price of 0? How many are demanded at a price of 10 cents per pound? At what price does $Q_D = 0$?
b. Suppose now $I = 20,000$. How would your answers to part a change? Graph your results.
c. Suppose the government imposes an excise tax of 10 cents per pound on potatoes. Now

$$P = Pp + 10,$$

where P is the price paid by potato consumers and Pp is the price received by producers. If producers charge 10 cents per pound and $I = \$10,000$, how many potatoes will be demanded? If producers charge 0, how many will be demanded? At what producer price will potato demand go to zero? Graph the new demand curve and compare it to your results from part a.

2.4   The supply curve for flounder is given by

$$Q_S = -100 + 5P \text{ (for } Q_S > 0),$$

where Q_S is the quantity of flounder supplied in tons and P is the wholesale price of flounder received by producers in cents per pound.

a. Graph the flounder supply curve. At what price will producers actually start supplying flounder to the market?

b. Suppose the government imposes a 25 percent tax on flounder production. Hence

$$P_M = 1.25P,$$

where P_M is the market price of flounder. What will be the market supply curve for flounder (with Q_S as a function of P_M)? At what market price will any flounder be produced? Graph your results and compare them to your graph for part a.

2.5 This problem involves solving demand and supply equations together to determine price and quantity.

a. Consider a demand curve of the form

$$Q_D = -2P + 20,$$

where Q_D is the quantity demanded of a good and P is the price of the good. Graph this demand curve. Also draw a graph of the supply curve

$$Q_S = 2P - 4,$$

where Q_S is the quantity supplied. Be sure to put P on the vertical axis and Q on the horizontal axis. Assume that all the Q's and P's are nonnegative for parts a, b, and c. At what values of P and Q do these curves intersect— that is, where does $Q_D = Q_S$?

b. Now suppose that individuals demand four more units of output at each price—that the demand curve shifts to

$$Q_{D'} = -2P + 24.$$

Graph this new demand curve. At what values of P and Q does the new demand curve intersect the old supply curve—that is, where does $Q_{D'} = Q_S$?

c. Now, finally, suppose the supply curve shifts to

$$Q_{S'} = 2P - 8.$$

Graph this new supply curve. At what values of P and Q does $Q_{D'} = Q_{S'}$? You may wish to refer back to this simple problem when we discuss shifting supply and demand curves in later sections of this book.

2.6 a. Graph the demand curve

$$Q_D = -4P + 32.$$

At what value of P does $Q_D = 0$? At $P = 0$ what is Q_D?

b. Now graph the demand curve

$$Q_{D'} = -2P + 16.$$

Again, at what value of P does $Q_{D'} = 0$; what is $Q_{D'}$ when $P = 0$? Call this value Q^*.

c. Referring back to the demand curve Q_D, what are demanders willing to pay for Q*? Call this price P*. What is the product P* times Q*? Can you give an economic interpretation to this figure?

d. Now consider all possible products of P times Q where both P and Q lie on the demand curve Q_D. Show that P* times Q* is the largest value of these products.

We consider an example similar to this one in Chapter 8 when we discuss the concept of marginal revenue.

2.7   Taxes in Oz are calculated according to the formula

$$T = .1I^2,$$

where T represents thousands of dollars of tax liability and I represents income measured in thousands of dollars. Using this formula, answer the following questions:

a. How much in taxes is paid by individuals with incomes of $10,000, $30,000, and $50,000? What are the average tax rates for these income levels? At what income level does tax liability equal total income?

b. Graph the tax schedule for Oz. Use your graph to estimate marginal tax rates for the income levels specified in part a. Also show the average tax rates for these income levels on your graph.

c. Marginal tax rates in Oz can be estimated more precisely by calculating tax owed if persons with the incomes in part a get one more dollar. Make this computation for these three income levels. Compare your results to those obtained from the calculus-based result that for the Oz tax function its slope = .02I.

2.8   Consider the function

$$Y = \sqrt{X \cdot Z}$$

where X > 0, Z > 0. Draw the contour lines (in the positive quadrant) for this function for Y = 4, Y = 5, and Y = 10. What do we call the shape of these contour lines? Where does the line 20X + 10Z = 200 intersect the contour line Y = 50? (Hint: As in Application 2.3, it may be easier to graph the contour lines for Y^2 here.)

*2.9   Using the function $Y = \sqrt{X \cdot Z}$ from the previous problem, find that combination of X and Z for which Y is as large as possible and which also satisfies the following linear equations. Graph your results using contour lines for Y. (Hint: For this problem the slope of Y contour lines is given by $-Z/X$.)

a. 2X + Z = 20.
b. X + Z = 20.
c. X + 2Z = 40.
d. X + 5Z = 100.
e. 2X + Z = 40.
f. X + Z = 40.

---

*Denotes a problem that is rather difficult. Answers to all odd-numbered problems appear at the end of the book.

"Utility is that principle which approves or disapproves every action whatsoever according to the tendency it . . . (has) to augment or diminish . . . happiness . . ."

Jeremy Bentham

Introduction to the Principles of Morals and Legislation, 1789

Part 2 examines how economists look at people's demand for the goods they buy. Our main goal in this part is to develop Marshall's demand curve for a product and to show why this demand curve is likely to be downward sloping.

Chapter 3 describes how economists treat the consumer's decision problem. We first define the concept of utility, which represents a consumer's preferences. The second half of the chapter discusses how people decide to spend their incomes on different goods to get the greatest satisfaction possible—that is, to "maximize" their utility.

Chapter 4 investigates how people change their choices when their income changes or as prices change. This is the first example in the book of "comparative statics" analysis. In this analysis we compare two situations to see how the choices in these situations differ.

Chapter 5 shows how individual demand curves can be "added up" to make market demand curves. These curves are basic to the price determination process.

Chapter 6 applies the theory of individual choice developed in Chapters 3 through 5 to three additional economic topics. First, the model of utility maximization is used to show how welfare improvements can be measured. Second, the utility-maximization model is used to analyze price indices, such as the gross domestic product (GDP) price deflator and the Consumer Price Index (CPI). Finally, the utility-maximization model is used to look at trading between individuals.

In Chapter 7, the last chapter of Part 2, we look at how people act in uncertain or risky situations. In this application of the utility-maximization model we show why people dislike risk and are usually willing to "pay" something to avoid it.

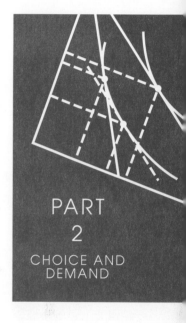

PART
2
CHOICE AND
DEMAND

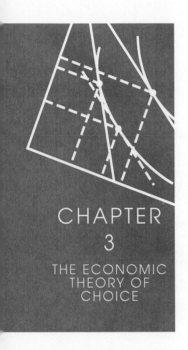

CHAPTER
3

THE ECONOMIC
THEORY OF
CHOICE

An economic system is nothing more than a collection of people and a set of institutions (such as firms or government agencies) that people operate. Economists therefore place the study of individuals' behavior at the center of their models. People's desires are assumed to have a strong effect in determining what goods are demanded and ultimately produced by any economy. People also decide what levels of productive services (labor and capital) they will supply, and, through their political activities, people influence the government's decisions.

These roles cannot be separated from one another. Any decision a person makes as a consumer, say, to buy a new car, will affect his or her decisions as a provider of resources (to save less or to work harder to pay for the car) and also his or her decisions as a voter (he or she may now favor government spending for new or better highways on which to drive the new car). Modern microeconomics examines people's choices in all of these roles.

Definition of Utility

Economists have developed a general model to study all of an individual's decision problems. This model formalizes the concept of preferences and shows how restrictions imposed by income, time, and other factors affect actual choices that are made. More than anything else, this conceptual apparatus underlies the economists' thinking about people's decisions—it is the fundamental economic **theory of choice.**

People's preferences can be modeled using the concept of **utility,** which is defined as the satisfaction that a person receives from his or her activities. This concept is very broad, and in the next few sections we define it more precisely. We use the simple case of a single consumer who receives utility from just two commodities. We will eventually analyze how that person chooses to allocate income between these two goods, but first we need to develop a better understanding of utility itself.

■ *Ceteris Paribus* Assumption

To identify all the factors affecting a person's feelings of satisfaction would be a lifelong task for an imaginative psychologist; to measure these factors precisely would probably be impossible. Economists focus on basic, quantifiable economic factors and look at how people choose among them. Economists clearly recognize that nonmeasurable factors (aesthetics, love, security, envy, and so forth) affect behavior, but they develop models in which these kinds of factors are held constant and are not specifically analyzed.

Much economic analysis is based on this *ceteris paribus* (other things being equal) **assumption.** We can simplify the analysis of a person's consumption decisions by assuming that satisfaction is affected only by choices made among the options being considered and that other effects on satisfaction remain constant. In this way we can isolate the economic factors that affect consumption behavior. This narrow focus is not intended to imply that other things that affect utility are unimportant; we are conceptually holding these other factors constant so that we may study consumption choices in a simplified setting.

■ Utility from Consuming Two Goods

This chapter concentrates on an individual's problem of choosing the quantities of two goods (which for most purposes we will call simply "X" and "Y") to consume. We assume that the person receives utility from these goods and that we can show this utility in functional notation (see Chapter 2) by

$$\text{Utility} = U(X, Y; \text{other things}). \qquad [3.1]$$

This notation indicates that the utility an individual receives from consuming X and Y over some period of time depends on the quantities of X and Y

■ Theory of choice
The interaction of preferences and income that causes people to make the choices they do.

■ Utility
The pleasure, satisfaction, or need fulfillment that people get from their economic activity.

■ Ceteris paribus assumption
In economic analysis, holding all other factors constant so that only the factor being studied is allowed to change.

consumed and on "other things." These other things might include easily quantifiable items such as the amounts of other kinds of goods consumed, the number of hours worked, or the amount of time spent sleeping. They might also include such unquantifiable items as love, security, and feelings of self-worth. These other things appear after the semicolon in Equation 3.1 because we assume that they are held constant while we examine the individual's choice between X and Y. If one of the other things should change, the utility from some particular amounts of X and Y might be very different than it was before.

For example, several times in this chapter we consider the case of a person choosing how many hamburgers (Y) and soft drinks (X) to consume during one week. Although our example uses seemingly trivial commodities, the analysis is quite general and will apply to any two goods. In analyzing the hamburger–soft drink choices, we assume that all other factors affecting utility are held constant. The weather, the person's preferences for hamburgers and soft drinks, the person's exercise pattern, and everything else are assumed not to change during the analysis. If the weather, for instance, were to become warmer, we might expect soft drinks to become relatively more desirable, and we wish to eliminate such effects from our analysis, at least for the moment. We usually write the utility function in Equation 3.1 as

$$\text{Utility} = U(X,Y) \tag{3.2}$$

with the understanding that many other things are being held constant. All economic analyses impose some form of *ceteris paribus* assumption so that the relationship between a selected few variables can be studied. You should try to identify the *important* things that are being held constant in this book as we explore various simplified models of choice.

■ Measurability of Utility

The first economists to deal with the concept of utility thought that it might be measurable. Some early psychological experiments on people's responses to electrical stimuli gave rise to the mistaken belief that all individual reactions were not only quantifiable but also of the same general type. If utility were measurable, many economic questions could be easily answered. Firms could understand and predict individual consumer behavior and thereby experience less uncertainty in their business, or the government could, if it wished, produce a "fair" distribution of goods (and utility) among people. Perhaps it is for the best that such accurate measures of preferences have proved impossible to obtain.

The obstacles to measuring utility have proved to be of two major types. The first concerns what to use for a unit of measurement. We have no very good psychological idea of what a *util* (that is, a unit of utility) might be. There is also no way of determining how one person's utils compare to another's. When asked, "On a scale of 1 to 10, how happy are you?" for example, people respond in very different ways. Application 3.1: The Pursuit of Happiness illustrates some of the problems that researchers have had in making such measurements.

APPLICATION 3.1

The Pursuit of Happiness

Even though the problems in measuring utility seem formidable, imaginative social scientists have not been shy about attempting to do so. The nineteenth-century psychologists Weber and Fechner, for example, conducted numerous experiments in which subjects were given mild electrical shocks. The pair found that individuals tended to experience discomfort in relation to the proportionate increase in the current applied rather than in relation to the absolute increase. An increase of 5 volts was clearly discernable at low levels of voltage, but at higher levels the increase was barely noticeable. Although, thankfully, such experiments are now widely regarded as inappropriate, Weber and Fechner's observation of what appeared to be diminishing returns continues to influence thinking about utility. For example, recent research has tended to focus on whether a dollar of extra income is worth less (in terms of extra utility) to a rich person than to a poor person.

Does Money Buy Happiness?

One approach to studying the relationship between income and utility relies on survey questions that ask people how happy they are. Sometimes respondents are asked whether they are "very happy," "fairly happy," or "not very happy," whereas in other cases they are asked to indicate their happiness on a scale of 1 to 10. Although many economists regard such questions as hopelessly vague, the survey responses do, nevertheless, show certain regularities.[1] The clearest finding is that people with higher incomes, not surprisingly, report that they are happier than do those with lower incomes. There is also some evidence that the fraction who report that they are "very happy" tends to level off at about 60 percent. At some point increasing amounts of income don't seem to add very much to reported happiness. Happiness may also be, to some extent, a relative concept. There seems to be little difference in reported happiness between middle-income people in high- and low-income countries, even though middle-income people in high-income countries have much higher incomes in absolute terms. Similarly, people, on average, apparently haven't become a lot happier in the United States during the past thirty years, even though average incomes have risen substantially. Hence, although there is a sense in which money seems to "buy" happiness, the exact relationship is not a simple one.

The Pursuit of Poverty

The relationship between an individual's purchasing power and his or her feelings of well-being is also reflected in attempts to measure what it means to say that someone is "poor." For example, since the 1960s, the U.S. government has regularly published an official count of the number of families living in poverty. In doing so, it calculates the income required to purchase a specific set of necessities. Numerous disputes have arisen over defining exactly what such a set of necessities should include. A more subjective approach has been taken by several European researchers who base their definition of poverty on survey responses to the question "What do you think is the minimum income needed to 'get along'?" These researchers have found that there is some consensus in various European countries about what it takes to "get along," but that respondents' answers tend to be significantly affected by their own incomes.[2] High-income people think it takes more income to "get along" than do low-income people. And, for some reason, people in France tend to believe it requires a much higher income to "get along" than do people in Germany.

To Think About

1. Why worry about the relationship between income and utility? Because a higher income makes it possible for a person to consume bundles of goods that were previously unaffordable, isn't he or she necessarily better off? Isn't that all we need to know?

2. Sometimes people are said to be poor if they have to spend more than, say, 25 percent of their income on food, or if they spend more than 35 percent on housing. What does such an approach implicitly assume about the relationship between income and purchases of these goods?

[1] For a summary of some of this evidence, see Richard A. Easterlin, "Does Economic Growth Improve the Human Lot?" in *Nations and Households in Economic Growth*, Paul A. David and Melvin W. Reder, eds. (New York: Academic Press, 1974): 89–126.

[2] See A. J. M. Hagenaars, *The Perception of Poverty* (Amsterdam: North Holland Publishing Company, 1986).

A second difficulty that arises in measuring utility in the study of individuals' choices concerns the *ceteris paribus* assumption. In simple psychological experiments it may be possible to hold everything constant except the stimulus under question (that is, to provide an adequate experimental "control"). In economics, however, the myriad factors that affect a person's economic choices are impossible to list and quantify. To hold some of them constant in order to measure the utility people get from various choices is out of the question.

Consequently, we must expect much less than measurability from a utility theory. All that can be assumed is that people rank the options open to them in some consistent way. If we were talking about consumption behavior, for example, we would assume that the individual can rank all possible combinations of goods that he or she might consider. To say that the utility of one set of goods, A, is greater than that of another set, B, only means that A is preferred to B. We cannot say how much A is preferred to B, since a hard-and-fast measure of utility is beyond our grasp. For example, we may be able to assert that a person prefers a roast beef dinner to a fried chicken dinner, but we cannot say that he or she is "5 percent happier" with the roast beef or that the chicken provides "7 fewer utils." There are many things we can say about individual choices despite this problem, however. Most observable economic behavior can be explained without having to measure utility.

Assumptions about Utility

What do we mean by saying that people's preferences are "consistent"? How do we describe the transactions that people are willing to make? Can these preferences (utility) be shown graphically? In this section we will explore these questions as we begin our study of economists' model of choice.

■ Basic Properties of Preferences

Although we cannot expect to be able to measure utility, we might expect people to express their preferences in a reasonably consistent manner. Between two consumption bundles, A and B, we might expect a person to be able to state clearly either "I prefer A to B," or "I prefer B to A," or "A and B are equally attractive to me." We do not expect the individual to be paralyzed by indecision, but rather to be able to say precisely how he or she feels about any potential consumption possibilities. This rules out such situations as the mythical jackass, who, finding himself midway between a pile of hay and a bag of oats, starved to death because he was unable to decide which way to go. Formally, we are assuming preferences are **complete**—that people can always make a choice between any two options presented to them.

In addition to expecting people to be able to state preferences clearly and completely, we might also expect people's preferences not to be self-

Complete preferences

The assumption that an individual is able to state which of any two options is preferred.

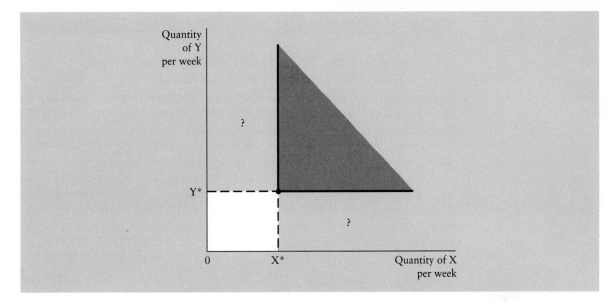

The gray area represents those combinations of X and Y that are unambiguously preferred to the combination X*, Y*. This is why goods are called "goods"; individuals prefer having more of any good rather than less. Combinations of X and Y in the white area are inferior to the combination X*, Y* whereas those in the questionable areas may or may not be superior to X*, Y*.

Figure 3.1
More of a Good Is
Preferred to Less

---

contradictory. We do not expect a person to make statements about his or her preferences that conflict with each other. In other words, we assume that preferences are **transitive**. If a person says, "I prefer A to B," and "I prefer B to C," then he or she can be expected to say, "I prefer A to C." A person who instead states the contrary (that is, "I prefer C to A") would appear to be hopelessly inconsistent. We wish to rule out such inconsistency from our analysis.

■ More Is Better: Defining an Economic "Good"

A third assumption we make about individual preferences is that a person prefers more of a good to less. In Figure 3.1 all points in the gray area are preferred to the amounts X* of good X and Y* of good Y. Movement from point X*, Y* to any point in the shaded area is an unambiguous improvement, since in this area the individual can obtain more of one good without taking less of another. This idea of preferences is implicit in our definition of an "economic good" as an item that yields positive benefits to people.[1] That is, more of a good is, by definition, better. Combinations of goods in the white area of Figure 3.1 are definitely inferior to X*, Y* since they offer less of *both* goods.

■
**Transitivity of
preferences**
The property that if A
is preferred to B, and
B is preferred to C,
then A must be
preferred to C.

---

[1] Later in this chapter, we briefly describe a theory of "bads"—items for which less is preferred to more. Such items might include toxic wastes, mosquitoes, or for this author, lima beans.

████████████████████████████

Voluntary Trades and Indifference Curves

How people feel about getting more of some good when they must give up an amount of some other good is probably the most important aspect of preferences. The areas identified with question marks in Figure 3.1 are difficult to compare to X*, Y* since they involve more of one good and less of the other. Whether a move from X*, Y* into these areas would increase utility is not clear. To be able to look into this situation, we need some additional tools. Since giving up units of one commodity (for example, money) to get back additional units of some other commodity (say, candy bars) is what gives rise to trade and organized markets, these new tools provide the foundation for the economic analysis of demand.

■ Indifference Curves

Indifference curve

All the combinations of goods or services that provide the same level of utility.

To study voluntary trades we will introduce the concept of an **indifference curve.** Such a curve shows all those combinations of two goods that provide the same utility to an individual; that is, the individual is "indifferent" about which particular combination on the curve he or she actually has. For example, Figure 3.2 records the quantity of soft drinks consumed by an individual in one period on the horizontal axis and the quantity of hamburgers consumed in the same period on the vertical axis. The curve U_1 in Figure 3.2 includes all those combinations of hamburgers and soft drinks with which the individual is equally happy. For example, the curve shows that the individual would be just as happy with six hamburgers and two soft drinks per week (point A) as with four hamburgers and three soft drinks (point B) or with three hamburgers and four soft drinks (point C). The points on U_1 all provide the same level of utility to the individual, and therefore he or she does not have any particular reason for preferring any point on U_1 to any other point.

The indifference curve U_1 is similar to a contour line on a map (discussed in Chapter 2) in that it shows those combinations of hamburgers and soft drinks that provide an identical "altitude" (that is, amount) of utility. Points to the northeast of U_1 promise a higher level of satisfaction and are preferred to points on U_1. Point E (five soft drinks and four hamburgers) is preferred to point C because it provides more of both goods. As in Figure 3.1, our definition of goods assures that combination E is preferred to combination C. Similarly, our assumption of transitivity assures that combination E is also preferred to combinations A, B, and D and to all other combinations on U_1.

Combinations of hamburgers and soft drinks that lie below U_1, on the other hand, are less desirable to the individual since they offer less satisfaction. Point F offers less of both goods than does point C. The fact that the indifference curve U_1 has a negative slope (that is, the curve runs from the upper left portion of the figure to the lower right portion) indicates that if an individual

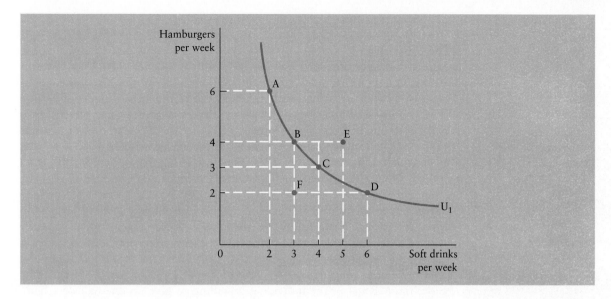

The curve U_1 shows the combinations of hamburgers and soft drinks that provide the same level of utility to an individual. The slope of the curve shows the trades an individual will freely make. For example, in moving from point A to point B, the individual will give two hamburgers to get one additional soft drink. In other words, the marginal rate of substitution is approximately 2 in this range. Points below U_1 (such as F) provide less utility than points on U_1. Points above U_1 (such as E) provide more utility than U_1.

Figure 3.2
Indifference Curve

is forced to give up some hamburgers, he or she must receive additional soft drinks to remain equally well-off. This type of movement along U_1 represents those trades that a person might freely make. Knowledge of U_1 therefore eliminates the ambiguity associated with the questionable areas we showed in Figure 3.1.

■ **Indifference Curves and the Marginal Rate of Substitution**

What happens when an individual moves from point A (six hamburgers and two soft drinks) to point B (four hamburgers and three soft drinks)? The individual remains equally well-off since the two commodity bundles lie on the same indifference curve. The individual will voluntarily give up two of the hamburgers that were being consumed at point A in exchange for one additional soft drink. The slope of the curve U_1 between A and B is therefore approximately $-\frac{2}{1} = -2$. That is, Y (hamburgers) declines two units in response to a one-unit increase in X (soft drinks). We call the absolute value of this slope the **marginal rate of substitution (MRS)**. Hence, we would say that the MRS (of soft drinks for hamburgers) between points A and B is 2: the individual is willing to give up two hamburgers in order to get one more soft drink.

■
**Marginal rate of
substitution (MRS)**

The rate at which an individual is willing to reduce consumption on one good when he or she gets one more unit of another good while remaining equally well-off. The negative of the slope of an indifference curve.

■ Diminishing Marginal Rate of Substitution

The MRS varies along the curve U_1. For points such as A the individual has quite a few hamburgers and is relatively willing to trade them away for soft drinks. On the other hand, for combinations such as those represented by point D, the individual has an abundance of soft drinks and is reluctant to give up any more hamburgers to get more soft drinks. The increasing reluctance to trade away hamburgers follows the notion that the consumption of any one good (here soft drinks) can be pushed too far. This characteristic can be seen by considering the trades that take place in moving from point A to B, from point B to C, and from point C to D. In the first trade two hamburgers are given up to get one more soft drink—the MRS is 2 (as we have already shown). The second trade involves giving up one hamburger to get one additional soft drink. In this trade, the MRS has declined to 1, reflecting the individual's increased reluctance to give up hamburgers to get more soft drinks. Finally, for the third trade, from point C to D, the individual is willing to give up a hamburger only if two soft drinks are received in return. In this final trade, the MRS is ½ (the individual is willing to give up one-half of a hamburger to get one more soft drink), which is a further decline from the MRS of the previous trades.

■ Balance in Consumption

Our conclusion of a diminishing MRS is based on the idea that people prefer balanced consumption bundles to unbalanced ones.[2] This assumption is illustrated precisely in Figure 3.3, where the indifference curve U_1 from Figure 3.2 is redrawn. Our discussion here concerns the two extreme consumption options A and D. In consuming A the individual receives six hamburgers and two soft drinks; the same satisfaction could be received by consuming D (two hamburgers and six soft drinks). Now consider a bundle of commodities (say, G)

---

[2] If we assume utility is measurable, we can provide an alternative analysis of a diminishing MRS. To do so we introduce the concept of the marginal utility of a good X (denoted by MU_X). Marginal utility is defined as the extra utility obtained by consuming one more unit of good X. The concept is meaningful only if utility can be measured and is not as useful as the MRS. If the individual is asked to give up some Y (ΔY) to get some additional X (ΔX), the change in utility is given by

$$\text{Change in utility} = MU_Y \cdot \Delta Y + MU_X \cdot \Delta X. \qquad [i]$$

It is equal to the utility gained from the additional X less the utility lost from the reduction in Y. Since utility does not change along an indifference curve, we can use Equation (i) to derive

$$\frac{-\Delta Y}{\Delta X} = \frac{MU_X}{MU_Y}. \qquad [ii]$$

Along an indifference curve, the negative of its slope is given by MU_X/MU_Y. That is, by definition, the MRS. Hence we have

$$MRS = MU_X/MU_Y. \qquad [iii]$$

For example, if an extra hamburger yields two utils ($MU_Y = 2$) and an extra soft drink yields four utils ($MU_X = 4$), MRS = 2 since the individual will be willing to trade away two hamburgers to get an additional soft drink. If it is assumed that MU_X falls and MU_Y increases as X is substituted for Y, Equation (iii) shows that MRS will fall as we move counterclockwise along U_1.

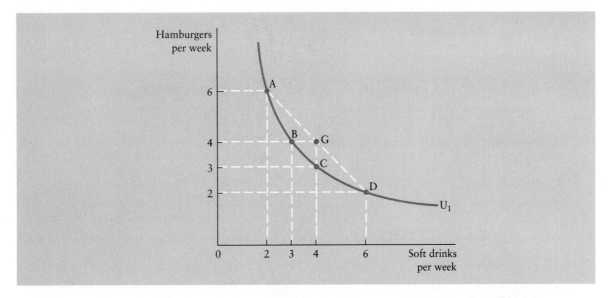

The consumption bundle G (four hamburgers, four soft drinks) is preferred to either of the extreme bundles A and D. This is a result of the assumption of a diminishing MRS. Because individuals become progressively less willing to give up hamburgers as they move in a southeasterly direction along U_1, the curve U_1 will have a convex shape. Consequently all points on a straight line joining two points such as A and D will lie above U_1. Points such as G will be preferred to any of those on U_1.

Figure 3.3
Balance in
Consumption
Is Desirable

"between" these extremes. With G (four hamburgers and four soft drinks) the individual obtains a higher level of satisfaction (point G is northeast of the indifference curve U_1) than with either of the extreme bundles A or D.

The reason for this increased satisfaction should be geometrically obvious. All of the points on the straight line joining A and D lie above U_1. Point G is one of these points (as the figure shows, there are many others). As long as the indifference curve obeys the assumption of a diminishing MRS, it will be convex; any bundle that represents an "average" between two equally attractive extremes will be preferred to those extremes. The assumption of a diminishing MRS reflects the notion that people prefer some variety in consumption.

Indifference Curve Maps

Although Figures 3.2 and 3.3 each show only one indifference curve, the positive quadrant contains many such curves, each one corresponding to a different level of utility. Since every combination of hamburgers and soft drinks must yield some level of utility, every point must have one (and only one) indifference curve passing through it. These curves are, as we said earlier, similar

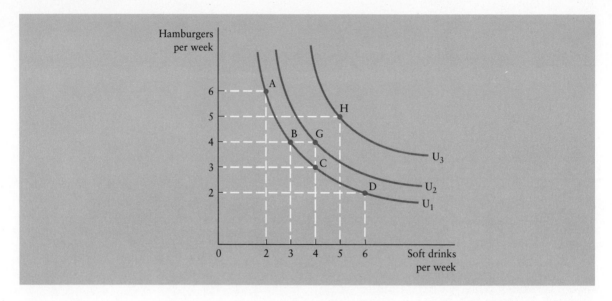

Figure 3.4
Indifference Curve Map for Hamburgers and Soft Drinks

The positive quadrant is full of indifference curves, each of which reflects a different level of utility. Three such curves are illustrated. Combinations of goods on U_3 are preferred to those on U_2, which in turn are preferred to those on U_1. This is simply a reflection of the assumption that more of a good is preferred to less, as may be seen by comparing points C, G, and H.

Indifference curve map

A contour map that shows the utility an individual obtains from all possible consumption options.

to the contour lines that appear on topographical maps in that they each represent a different "altitude" of utility. In Figure 3.4 three of these curves have been drawn and are labeled U_1, U_2, and U_3. These are only three of the infinite number of curves that characterize an individual's entire **indifference curve map.** Just as a map may have many contour lines (say, one for each inch of altitude), so too the gradations in utility may be very fine, as would be shown by very closely spaced indifference curves. For graphic convenience, our analysis generally deals with only a few indifference curves that are relatively widely spaced.

The labeling of the indifference curves in Figure 3.4 has no special meaning except to indicate that utility increases as we move from combinations of goods on U_1 to those on U_2 and then to those on U_3. As we have repeatedly pointed out, there is no precise way to measure the level of utility associated with, say, U_2. Similarly, we have no way of measuring the amount of extra utility an individual receives from consuming bundles on U_3 instead of U_2. All we can assume is that utility increases as the individual moves to higher indifference curves. That is, the individual would prefer to be on a higher curve rather than on a lower one. This map tells us all there is to know about this person's preferences. Economists have made many attempts to examine such preferences directly. Some of these studies are described in Application 3.2: Measuring Preferences.

APPLICATION 3.2
Measuring Preferences

Although most economic analyses of demand focus on actual buying behavior, some researchers have attempted to study consumers' preferences directly. For economists, such studies have tended to look at whether choices seem to be made in a rational way. On the other hand, marketing researchers have been more interested in whether information on preferences can be used to design better (and more profitable!) products. Here we look briefly at both types of analyses.

Transitivity Analysis
Economists who wish to examine the rationality of consumers' choices have usually focused on the transitivity assumption. In one experimental approach, for example, A. A. Weinstein examined how individuals ranked 10 everyday consumption items ranging from $3 in cash, to three Beatles records, to a 15-inch pizza.[1] A violation of transitivity would occur if, for example, someone reported preferring the cash to the Beatles records and the records to the pizza, but that he or she preferred pizza to cash. Among adults, Weinstein found few (less than 7 percent) intransitivities. The author did find, however, that younger people (notably children ages 9 through 12) exhibited considerably more intransitivities (about 20 percent of choices made). This led him to conclude that consistency in choices may to some extent be an acquired skill.

Studies of actual consumption data are also broadly consistent with the notion of transitivity. In a detailed study of families' food purchases over a four-year period in Michigan, for example, relatively few intransitive choices were found.[2] Those that did occur seemed to be related to family circumstances. Families where both spouses were employed tended to have relatively larger numbers of intransitivities whereas families with many children (and large food demands) tended to have fewer. Such observations suggest that rationality required to exhibit consistent, transitive preferences may to some extent be costly to families. So a varying degree of "optimal irrationality" may sometimes be observed.

Marketing Trade-Off Analysis
Market researchers wish to know how consumers feel about the attributes of goods. By understanding what attributes are valued by consumers and what kinds of trade-offs consumers might willingly make, researchers may be able to design better products. Information guiding this design is usually gathered from surveys or from small "focus group" discussions in which representative consumers are asked to state what they think of possible product attributes.

For example, the Marriott Hotel Corporation gathers together small groups of consumers and provides each with a set of index cards indicating various combinations of room size, reservation conveniences, hotel features (such as pools or saunas), and room service offerings. Sample members are then asked to choose combinations of such attributes that are roughly comparable in desirability.[3] In that way the company can design its hotels to better meet customer preferences. Similar techniques are used by computer makers when deciding what features to include on new models and by automobile firms to decide which options packages to offer with their new models.

To Think About
1. Do people have to learn to behave "rationally"? Don't young children, even babies, seem to know exactly what they want? If that is so, how do you explain the fact that children seem to make a fairly large number of inconsistent choices? How do you explain the fact that adults exhibit any such inconsistencies?
2. Describe how the market researchers' notion of trade-off analysis reflects the economists' notion of indifference curve analysis. What information would a firm need to decide which of two options packages that consumers judged equally desirable should actually be produced?

---

[1] A. Weinstein, "Transitivity of Preferences," *Journal of Political Economy* (March/April 1968): 307–311.
[2] A. Y. C. Koo and Georg Haverkamp, "Structure of Revealed Preference: Some Preliminary Evidence," *Journal of Political Economy* (July/August 1972): 724–744.
[3] This example is taken from Alex Hiam, *The Vest Pocket CEO* (Englewood Cliffs, NJ: Prentice Hall, 1990): 270–272.

■ Illustrating Particular Preferences

To illustrate some of the ways in which indifference curve maps might be used to reflect particular kinds of preferences, Figure 3.5 shows four special cases.

A Useless Good Panel a of Figure 3.5 shows an individual's indifference curve map for food (on the horizontal axis) and smoke grinders (on the vertical axis). Since smoke grinders are totally useless, increasing purchases of them does not increase utility. Only by getting additional food does this person enjoy a higher level of utility. The vertical indifference curve U_2, for example, shows that utility will be U_2 as long as this person has 10 units of food no matter how many smoke grinders he or she has.

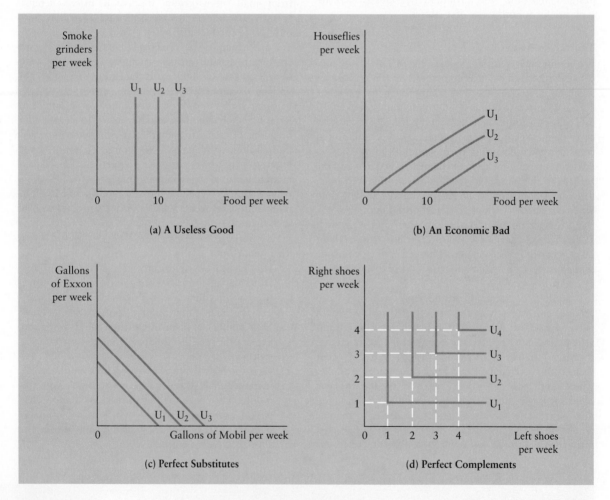

(a) A Useless Good

(b) An Economic Bad

(c) Perfect Substitutes

(d) Perfect Complements

Figure 3.5
**Illustrations of
Specific Preferences**

The four panels in this figure show indifference curve maps that record the specific nature of the relationship between two goods.

An Economic Bad   The situation illustrated in Panel a of Figure 3.5 implicitly assumes that useless goods cause no harm—having more smoke grinders causes no problem since one can always throw them away. In some cases, however, such free disposal is not possible, and additional units of a good can cause actual harm. For example, Panel b of Figure 3.5 shows an indifference curve map for food and houseflies. Holding food consumption constant at 10, utility declines as the number of houseflies increases. Because additional houseflies reduce utility, an individual might even be willing to give up some food (and buy flypaper instead, for example) in exchange for fewer houseflies.

Perfect Substitutes   Our illustrations of convex indifference curves in Figures 3.2 through 3.4 reflected the assumption that diversity in consumption is desirable. If, however, the two goods we were examining were essentially the same (or at least served identical functions), we could not make this argument. In Panel c of Figure 3.5, for example, we show an individual's indifference curve map for Exxon and Mobil gasoline. Since this individual is unconvinced by television advertisements, he or she has adopted the sensible proposition that all gallons of gasoline are virtually identical. Hence, he or she is always willing to trade one gallon of Exxon for a gallon of Mobil—the MRS along any indifference curve is 1.0. The straight-line indifference curve map in Panel c of Figure 3.5 reflects the perfect substitutability between these two goods.

Perfect Complements   In Panel d of Figure 3.5, on the other hand, we illustrate a situation in which two goods go together. This individual prefers to consume left shoes (on the horizontal axis) and right shoes (on the vertical axis) in pairs. If, for example, he or she currently has three pairs of shoes, additional right shoes provide no more utility (compare this to the situation in Panel a). Similarly, additional left shoes alone provide no additional utility. An extra pair of shoes, on the other hand, does increase utility (from U_3 to U_4) since this individual likes to consume these two goods together. Any situation in which two goods have such a strong complementary relationship to one another would be described by a similar map of L-shaped indifference curves.

   Of course, these simple examples only hint at the variety in types of preferences that can be illustrated by indifference curve maps. Later in this chapter we will encounter other examples that help to explain observed economic behavior. Because indifference curve maps reflect people's basic preferences about the goods they might select, such maps provide an important first building block for developing a theory of economic choice.

Utility Maximization: An Initial Survey

Economists assume that when a person is faced with a choice from among a number of possible options, he or she will choose the one that yields the highest utility—utility maximization. As Adam Smith remarked more than two centuries ago, "We are not ready to suspect any person of being defective in selfishness."[3] In other words, economists assume that people know their own minds and make choices consistent with their preferences. This section surveys in general terms how such choices might be made.

■ Choices Are Constrained

The most interesting feature of the utility-maximization problem is that people are constrained in what they can buy by the size of their incomes. Of those combinations of goods that an individual can afford, he or she will choose the one that is most preferred. This most preferred bundle of goods may not provide complete bliss; it may even leave this person in misery. It will, however, reflect the best use of limited income. All other combinations of goods that can be bought with that limited income would leave him or her even worse off. It is the limitation of income that makes the individual's problem of choice an economic one of allocating a scarce resource (the limited income) among alternative end uses. Application 3.3: Irrational Behavior illustrates how general the economist's notion of making the best of one's situation is.

■ The Basic Result

Consider the following trivial problem: How should an individual choose to allocate income among two goods (hamburgers and soft drinks) if he or she is to obtain the highest level of utility possible? Answering this question provides fundamental insights into all of microeconomics. The basic result can easily be stated at the outset. In order to maximize utility given a fixed amount of income to spend on two goods, an individual will spend the entire amount and will choose a combination of goods for which the marginal rate of substitution between the two goods is equal to the ratio of those goods' market prices.

The reasoning behind the first part of this proposition is straightforward. Because we assume that more is better, an individual will spend the entire amount budgeted for the two items. The only alternative here is throwing the money away, which is obviously less desirable than buying something.

The reasoning behind the second part of the proposition can be seen with our hamburger–soft drink example. Suppose that an individual is currently consuming some combination of hamburgers and soft drinks for which the MRS is equal to 1; he or she is willing to do without one hamburger in order to get an additional soft drink. Assume, on the other hand, that the price of hamburgers is $1.00 and that of soft drinks is $.50. The ratio of their prices is $.50/$1.00 = ½. The individual is able to obtain an extra soft drink in the market by giving up only one-half of a hamburger. In this situation the individual's MRS is not equal to the ratio of the goods' market prices, and we can show that some other combination of goods provides more utility.

Suppose this person consumes one less hamburger. This frees $1.00 in purchasing power. He or she can now buy one more soft drink (at a price of $.50)

---

[3] Adam Smith, *The Theory of Moral Sentiments* (1759; reprint, New Rochelle, N.Y.: Arlington House, 1969), p. 446.

APPLICATION 3.3
Irrational Behavior

The assumption that people seek to maximize their utility is essentially a belief that individuals act in a "rational" way to achieve certain ends. To many non-economists such an assumption seems preposterous. Instead, it is argued that people are "irrational" because they make unsystematic decisions dominated as much by whim and ignorance as by any sort of rational thought process. Of course, much purportedly irrational behavior merely represents differences in tastes. Although some people may claim it is irrational for consumers to eat at McDonald's, economists wish to make no such value judgment. Here instead we are interested in the type of behavior that suggests that people make decisions that are not in their own best interest.

Self-Imposed Constraints

One type of behavior that might be termed irrational occurs when individuals impose additional constraints on their own actions. People participate in compulsory savings plans (such as Christmas Clubs) that pay very low rates of interest; they pay to join stop-smoking clinics to break the cigarette habit; and they hide the key to the freezer to make sure they stay on a diet. Such behavior seems irrational because these people are voluntarily subjecting themselves to what would appear to be unnecessary constraints. Theoretical examinations of the notion of "self control," however, have shown why such behavior is indeed rational.[1] Introducing constraints for a specific purpose allows individuals to attain long-term goals, such as saving for a college education, stopping smoking, or losing weight, while maintaining considerable discretion in day-to-day decisions.

Criminal Behavior

Economists differ from many other social scientists by viewing much criminal behavior (particularly property crimes such as burglary, robbery, and auto theft) as fundamentally rational. Rather than viewing criminals as psychotic, economists treat them as utility maximizers who are responding to the deterrents they face. For example, in one study of how various factors affect crime rates, Isaac Ehrlich found that each 1 percent increase in the likelihood that someone committing a property crime will be caught was associated with a 0.8 percent reduction in such crimes. Ehrlich also found that each 1 percent increase in the severity of the penalty imposed on a convicted felon reduced the rate of property crime by nearly 1 percent.[2] Even for the types of crimes that seem least subject to rational economic calculation (such as aggravated assault), Ehrlich found evidence that the deterrents faced by criminals had an impact on observed crime rates.

Altruism

The fact that people give money to charity, to their own children, or even to strangers also seems to contradict the notion of rationality. Both economists and sociobiologists have given considerable attention to such altruistic behavior (which also characterizes some animal species) and have concluded that it is indeed rational from a broader perspective. The economist Gary Becker, for example, showed that altruists can actually make themselves better-off by giving to others, and that such behavior will tend to persist from one generation to the next.[3] He also demonstrated the interesting finding that altruistic behavior can be used to control the "rotten" kids in the family. Such behavior, therefore, has the potential for increasing utility.

To Think About

1. How might you explain the following types of purportedly irrational behavior (a) never shopping for bargains; (b) refusing to use a seat belt; (c) living in an unsafe neighborhood; (d) smoking; and (e) drinking too much alcohol?
2. What types of irrational behavior do you engage in? (If in doubt, ask your parents or roommate.)

---

[1] See, for example, R. H. Thaler and H. M. Shefrin, "An Economic Theory of Self-Control," *Journal of Political Economy* (April 1981): 392–406.

[2] Isaac Ehrlich, "Participation in Illegitimate Activities: A Theoretical and Empirical Investigation," *Journal of Political Economy* (May/June 1973): 550.

[3] For a collection of Becker's writing, see Gary Becker, *The Economic Approach to Human Behavior* (Chicago: The University of Chicago Press, 1976). See also James Coleman, *Foundations of Social Theory* (Cambridge, MA: Harvard University Press, 1990).

and is now as well-off as before since the MRS was assumed to be 1. However, $.50 (= $1.00 − $.50) is still unspent that can now be spent on either soft drinks or hamburgers (or some combination of the two). Such additional consumption clearly makes the individual better-off than in the initial situation.

Our numbers here were purely arbitrary. Whenever the individual selects a combination of goods for which the MRS differs from the price ratio, a similar beneficial change in spending patterns can be made. This reallocation will continue until the MRS is brought into line with the price ratio, at which time maximum utility is attained. We now present a more formal proof of this.

Graphic Analysis of Utility Maximization

To develop a graphic demonstration of the process of utility maximization, we will begin by showing how to illustrate an individual's **budget constraint.** This constraint shows which combinations of goods are affordable. It is from among these that the individual can choose the bundle that provides the most utility.

Budget constraint

The limit that income places on the combinations of goods and services that an individual can buy.

The Budget Constraint

Figure 3.6 shows the combinations of two goods (which we will call simply X and Y) that an individual with a fixed amount of money to spend can afford. If all available income is spent on good X, the number of units that can be purchased is recorded as X_{max} in the figure. If all available income is spent on Y, Y_{max} is the amount that can be bought. The line joining X_{max} to Y_{max} represents the various mixed bundles of goods X and Y that can be purchased using all the available funds. Points in the shaded area below the budget line are also affordable, but these leave some portion of funds unspent, so these points would usually not be chosen.

The downward slope of the budget line shows that the individual can afford more X only if Y purchases are cut back. The precise slope of this relationship depends on the unit prices of the two goods. If Y is expensive and X is cheap, the line will be relatively flat since choosing to consume one less Y will permit the purchasing of many units of X (an individual who decides not to purchase a new designer suit can instead choose to purchase many pairs of socks). Alternately, if Y is relatively cheap per unit and X is expensive, the budget line will be steep. Reducing Y consumption does not permit very much more of good X to be bought. All of these relationships can be made clearer by using a bit of algebra.

An Algebraic Approach

Suppose that the individual has I dollars to spend on either good X or good Y. Suppose also that P_X represents the price of good X and P_Y the price of good Y.

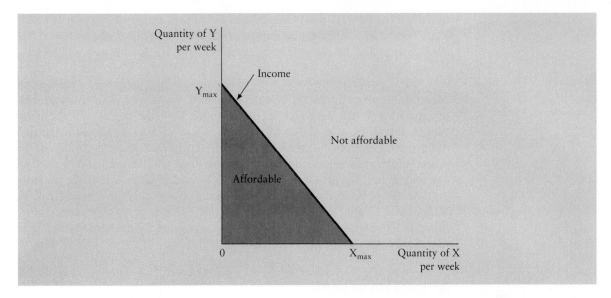

Quantity of Y
per week

Income

Y_{max}

Not affordable

Affordable

0 X_{max} Quantity of X
per week

Those combinations of X and Y that the individual can afford are shown in the shaded triangle. If, as we usually assume, the individual prefers more than less of every good, the outer boundary of this triangle is the relevant constraint where all of the available funds are spent on either X or Y. The slope of this straight boundary is given by $-P_X/P_Y$.

Figure 3.6
Individual's Budget
Constraint for
Two Goods

The total amount spent on X is given by the price of X times the amount purchased ($P_X \cdot X$). Similarly, $P_Y \cdot Y$ represents total spending on good Y. Since the available income must be spent on either X or Y we have

Amount spent on X + Amount spent on Y = I

or

$$P_X \cdot X + P_Y \cdot Y = I. \qquad [3.3]$$

Equation 3.3 is an algebraic statement of the budget line shown in Figure 3.6. To make the relationship clearer we can solve this equation for Y so that the budget line has the standard form for a linear equation ($Y = a + bX$) discussed in Chapter 2. This solution of Equation 3.3 gives

$$Y = -\left(\frac{P_X}{P_Y}\right)X + \frac{I}{P_Y}. \qquad [3.4]$$

Although the two representations of the budget constraint say exactly the same thing, the relationship between Equation 3.4 and Figure 3.6 should be somewhat clearer. It is obvious from that equation that if the individual chooses to spend all available funds on Y (that is, if X = 0), he or she can buy I/P_Y units. If hamburgers cost $1.00 each and this person has decided to spend his or her $10.00 income only on hamburgers, it is clear that 10 can be bought. That point is the Y-intercept in the figure, which we previously called Y_{max}. Similarly, a slight manipulation of the budget equation shows that if Y = 0, all income will be devoted to X purchases, and the X-intercept will be I/P_X. If \$10.00 is spent only on soft drinks, 20 (= \$10.00 ÷ \$.50) can be bought. Again, this point is labeled X_{max} in the figure. Finally, the slope of the budget constraint is given by the ratio of the goods' prices, $-P_X/P_Y$. This shows the ratio at which Y can be given up to get more X in the market. In the hamburger–soft drink case, the slope would be $-\frac{1}{2}$ (= -\$.50 ÷ \$1.00) showing that the opportunity cost of one soft drink is half a burger. More generally, as we noted before, if P_X is low and P_Y is high, the slope will be small and the budget line will be flat. On the other hand, a high P_X and a low P_Y will make the budget line steep. As for any linear relationship, the budget constraint can be shifted to a new position by changes in its Y-intercept or by changes in its slope. In Chapter 4 we will use this fact to examine how changes in income or in the prices of goods affect an individual's choices.

■ Utility Maximization

The individual can afford all bundles of X and Y that fall within the shaded triangle in Figure 3.6. From among these, this person will choose the one that offers the greatest utility. The budget constraint can be used together with the individual's indifference curve map to show this utility-maximization process. Figure 3.7 illustrates the procedure. The individual would be irrational to choose a point such as A; he or she can get to a higher utility (that is, higher than U_1) level just by spending some of the unspent portion of his or her income. Similarly, by reallocating expenditures the individual can do better than point B. This is the case in which the MRS and the price ratio differ, and the individual can move to a higher indifference curve (say, U_2) by choosing to consume less Y and more X. Point D is out of the question because income is not large enough to permit the purchase of that combination of goods. It is clear that the position of maximum utility will be at point C where the combination X^*, Y^* is chosen. This is the only point on indifference curve U_2 that can be bought with I dollars, and no higher utility level can be bought. C is a point of tangency between the budget constraint and the indifference curve. Therefore all funds are spent and

$$\text{Slope of budget constraint} = \text{Slope of indifference curve} \qquad [3.5]$$

or (neglecting the fact that both slopes are negative)

$$P_X/P_Y = \text{MRS}. \qquad [3.6]$$

The result is proved. For a utility maximum the MRS should equal the ratio of the prices of the goods. The diagram shows that if this condition is not ful-

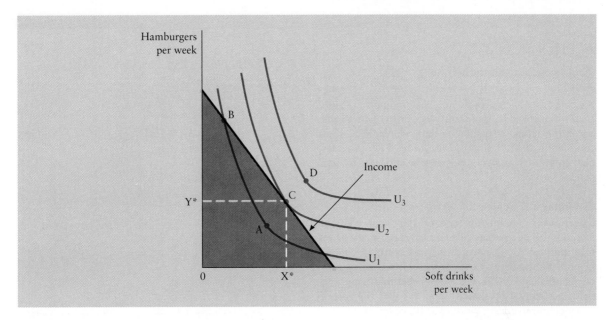

Point C represents the highest utility that can be reached by this individual, given the budget constraint. The combination X*, Y* is therefore the rational way for this person to use the available purchasing power. Only for this combination of goods will two conditions hold: all available funds will be spent; and the individual's psychic rate of trade-off (MRS) will be equal to the rate at which the goods can be traded in the market (P_X/P_Y).

Figure 3.7
Graphic
Demonstration of
Utility Maximization

filled, this person could be made better off by reallocating expenditures.[4] You may wish to try several other combinations of X and Y that the individual can afford in order to show that they provide a lower utility level than does combination C. In Application 3.4: Rationing and Black Markets, we examine a case in which people may not have such complete freedom in how they spend

[4] If we use the results of note 2 on the assumption that utility is measurable, Equation 3.6 can be given an alternative interpretation. Since

$$P_X/P_Y = MRS = MU_X/MU_Y \qquad [i]$$

for a utility maximum, we have

$$\frac{MU_X}{P_X} = \frac{MU_Y}{P_Y}. \qquad [ii]$$

The ratio of the extra utility from consuming one more unit of a good to its price should be the same for each good. Each good should provide the same extra utility per dollar spent. If that were not true, total utility could be raised by reallocating funds from a good that provided a relatively low level of marginal utility per dollar to one that provided a high level. For example, suppose that consuming an extra hamburger would yield 5 utils (units of utility) whereas an extra soft drink would yield 2 utils. Then each util costs $.20 (= $1.00 ÷ 5) if hamburgers are bought and $.25 (= $.50 ÷ 2) if soft drinks are bought. Clearly hamburgers are a cheaper way to buy utility. So this individual should buy more hamburgers and fewer soft drinks until each is an equally costly way to get utility.

APPLICATION 3.4

Rationing and Black Markets

Because economic goods do not exist in quantities sufficient to satisfy all human wants, they must always be allocated in some way among individuals. The most common method of allocation is through the price system. At times, however, goods may be allocated by nonmarket means.

Government Rationing

Government rationing is one of the most common methods of nonmarket allocation. Because a society may not wish to allocate goods by price for ideological or humanitarian reasons (as is the case with rice allotments in China) or because of the belief that temporary shortages should be shared by all (as was the case in many countries during World War II), governments may choose to ration existing stocks of goods equally.

Figure 1 illustrates such a situation. Given market prices and income, the individual wishes to consume the combination X^*, Y^*. If rationing limits the quantity of X available to any individual to an amount X_R (which must still be purchased at the prevailing price), that preferred point will be unattainable. From the figure it is clear that point B provides the maximum utility given this additional constraint. Rationing of X has reduced the individual's utility from U_2 to U_1.

Two aspects of the solution pictured in Figure 1 might be highlighted. First, rationing has an effect on the individual's choices only if $X_R < X^*$. If $X_R > X^*$, rationing is, for this person, ineffective. Because it is likely that X^* will be greater the higher an individual's income, the probability that rationing will effectively limit choices is greater for high-income persons than for low-income persons. For example, rations of meat in England during World War II provided only half the amount usually eaten by high-income families, but virtually all of peacetime consumption for low-income families.

Black Markets

A second feature of this problem concerns the stability of the rationed solution. Since the unrationed optimal choice (A) provides more utility than does the rationed choice (B), there is an incentive for the individual to find some way of moving from B to A. The appearance of

Figure 1
The Effect of Rationing Is to Reduce Utility

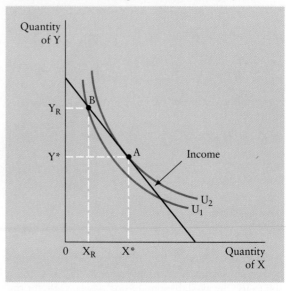

Rationing that allows an individual to purchase only X_R reduces utility (if $X_R < X^*$) from U_2 to U_1. Rationing is more likely to affect the choices of high-income consumers than of low-income consumers.

black markets in rationed commodities attests to the strength of this incentive. Such markets were relatively uncommon during World War II because of strong social pressures against them. But in peacetime situations, such markets flourish. Widespread "scalping" of World Series or rock concert tickets, for example, arises because the tickets are usually rationed by nonmarket means (first come, first served). Figure 1 suggests that high-income individuals would be more likely to make such black market purchases because they would have more to gain by doing so. When a low-income person sells his or her World Series tickets to a high-income person at an inflated price, both people gain.

To Think About

1. Governments that opt for rationing usually choose an equal allotment of the rationed good. Is that the best (utility maximizing) use of scarce resources?
2. Are the black markets that almost always arise in situations of rationing undesirable?

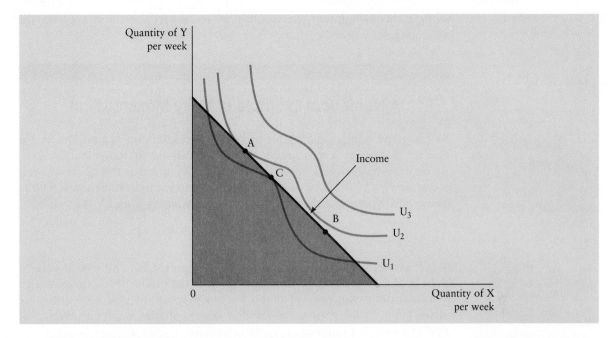

If indifference curves do not obey the assumption of a diminishing MRS, not all points of tangency (points for which MRS = P_X/P_Y) may truly be points of maximum utility. In this example, tangency point C is inferior to many other points that can also be purchased with the available funds.

Figure 3.8
Example of an Indifference Curve Map for which the Tangency Condition Does Not Ensure a Maximum

their incomes. We will show why this results in a lower level of utility than when they do have this freedom.

■ Importance of the Diminishing Marginal Rate of Substitution

If the individual is to maximize utility subject to a budget constraint, he or she must choose consumption bundles that exhaust income and whose MRS is equal to P_X/P_Y. Points of maximum satisfaction are characterized by a tangency between an individual's indifference curve map and the budget constraint. Not every such point of tangency must provide maximum satisfaction, however, as Figure 3.8 illustrates. Here a point of tangency (C) is inferior to a point of nontangency (B). The true maximum is, as it must be, at another point of tangency (A). The failure of the tangency condition to produce an unambiguous maximum can be attributed to the peculiar shape of the indifference curves in Figure 3.8. If the indifference curves are shaped like those in Figure 3.7 and elsewhere, no such problem can arise: if the MRS is assumed always to be diminishing, the condition of tangency assures a true maximum.

Without this assumption, we would have to be very careful in applying the tangency rule.

A Numerical Example of Utility Maximization

We can give a numerical example of utility maximization if we assume for the moment that utility is measurable. Again suppose that an individual is choosing between hamburgers (Y) and soft drinks (X) and that the prices of these goods are $P_Y = \$1.00$, $P_X = \$.50$. Assume also that the individual has $10.00 to spend. Finally, suppose that the utility from consuming X and Y is given by

$$\text{Utility} = U(X, Y) = \sqrt{XY}. \qquad [3.7]$$

We are assuming not only that utility can be measured but also that its value is given by the square root (denoted by $\sqrt{\ }$) of the product of X times Y. This particular utility function is suitable for our purposes because its indifference curves (contour lines) have the familiar convex shape (see, for example, the pipeline example examined in Application 2.3).

Table 3.1 lists several possible ways in which this person might spend $10.00 and calculates the utility associated with each choice. For example, if the individual buys six hamburgers and eight soft drinks (totally exhausting the $10.00), utility will be 6.9 (= $\sqrt{48}$). The other entries in the table all cost $10.00, but they yield very different levels of utility. Of those combinations listed, the bundle Y = 5, X = 10 yields the most utility, and that would seem to be how this fast-food gourmet should spend the $10.00.

Figure 3.9 confirms this view. Since the budget constraint is

$$\$.50X + \$1.00Y = \$10.00, \qquad [3.8]$$

the Y-intercept is 10 (= $10.00 ÷ $1.00), and the X-intercept is 20 (= $10.00 ÷ $.50). The slope of this line (–½) again shows that the opportunity cost of one

Table 3.1 Alternative Combinations of Hamburgers (Y) and Soft Drinks (X) that Can Be Bought with $10.00 (When P_Y = $1.00, P_X = $ .50) and the Utility of Each Combination	Hamburgers Y	Soft Drinks X	$U(X, Y) = \sqrt{XY}$
	0	20	$\sqrt{0} = 0$
	1	18	$\sqrt{18} = 4.2$
	2	16	$\sqrt{32} = 5.7$
	3	14	$\sqrt{42} = 6.5$
	4	12	$\sqrt{48} = 6.9$
	5	10	$\sqrt{50} = 7.1$
	6	8	$\sqrt{48} = 6.9$
	7	6	$\sqrt{42} = 6.5$
	8	4	$\sqrt{32} = 5.7$
	9	2	$\sqrt{18} = 4.2$
	10	0	$\sqrt{0} = 0$

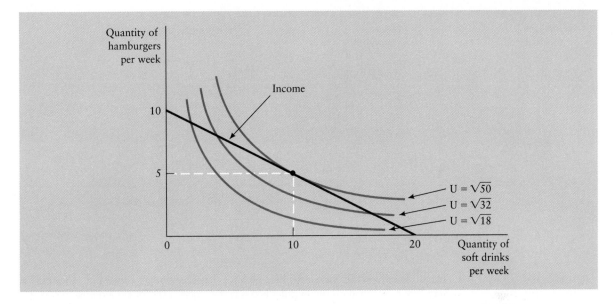

If P_X = \$.50, P_Y = \$1.00, and I = \$10.00, then the utility-maximizing choice for X and Y is X* = 10, Y* = 5. At this point, the budget constraint is just tangent to the indifference curve U = $\sqrt{XY}$ = $\sqrt{50}$ (or X · Y = 50), and this is the highest utility level obtainable.

Figure 3.9
Graphic of the Utility-Maximization Example

soft drink is ½ of a hamburger. As shown in Figure 3.9, the individual with this budget constraint can just reach the indifference curve U = $\sqrt{50}$ at the single point Y = 5, X = 10. Any other choices that cost \$10.00 or less yield a lower utility. At the point Y = 5, X = 10 the budget constraint is just tangent to the indifference curve;[5] the MRS is equal to the ratio of the goods' prices.

Using the Model of Choice

This simple model of utility maximization can be used to explain a number of common observations. Figure 3.10, for example, provides an illustration of why people with the same purchasing power choose to spend this in different ways. In all three panels of Figure 3.10 the budget constraints facing each individual are the same. However, Hungry Joe in Panel a of the figure has a clear preference for hamburgers. He chooses to spend his \$10 almost exclusively on burgers. Thirsty Teresa, on the other hand, chooses to spend most of her \$10 on soft drinks. She does buy two hamburgers, however, because she feels some need for solid food. Extra thirsty Ed, whose situation is shown in Panel c of Figure 3.10, wants a totally liquid diet. He gets the most utility from spending

---

[5] This indifference curve is a graph of XY = 50. Hence it is similar to the contour lines graphed in Chapter 2.

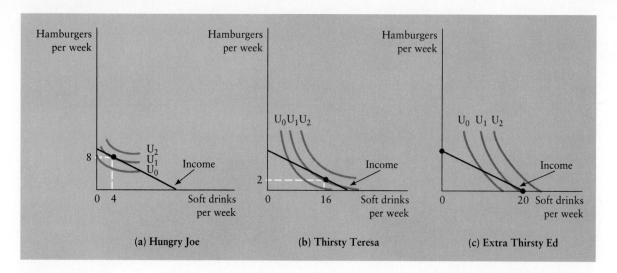

Figure 3.10
Differences in Preferences Result in Differing Choices

The three individuals illustrated here all have the same budget constraint. They choose very different consumption bundles because they have differing preferences for the two goods.

his entire $10 on soft drinks. Even though he would in some circumstances buy hamburgers, in the current case he is so thirsty that the opportunity cost of giving up a soft drink to do so is just too high.[6]

Figure 3.11 presents again the four specific indifference curve maps that were introduced earlier in this chapter. Now we have superimposed a budget constraint on each one and indicated the utility-maximizing choice by E. Some obvious implications can be drawn from these illustrations. Panel a makes clear that a utility-maximizing individual will never buy a useless good. Utility is as large as possible by consuming only food. There is no reason for this person to incur the opportunity cost involved in consuming any smoke grinders. A similar result holds for Panel b—there is no reason for this person to spend anything on houseflies (assuming there is a store that sells them).

In Panel c the individual buys only Exxon even though Exxon and Mobil are perfect substitutes. The relatively steep budget constraint in the figure indicates that Mobil is the more expensive of the two brands so this person opts to buy only Exxon. Since the goods are virtually identical, the utility-maximizing decision is to buy only the least expensive brand. People who buy only generic versions of prescription drugs or who buy all their brand name household staples at a discount supermarket are exhibiting a similar type of behavior.

Finally, the utility-maximizing situation illustrated in Panel d of Figure 3.11 shows that this person will only buy shoes in pairs. Any departure

---

[6] For example, suppose that with Y = 0, X = 20 the marginal utility of one more hamburger is 5 utils whereas for one more soft drink it is 3 utils. Then even when Ed is consuming only soft drinks, an extra util costs $.20 if he buys hamburgers, but only $.17 (= $.50 ÷ 3) if he buys soft drinks. Soft drinks are still the best buy for this thirsty person.

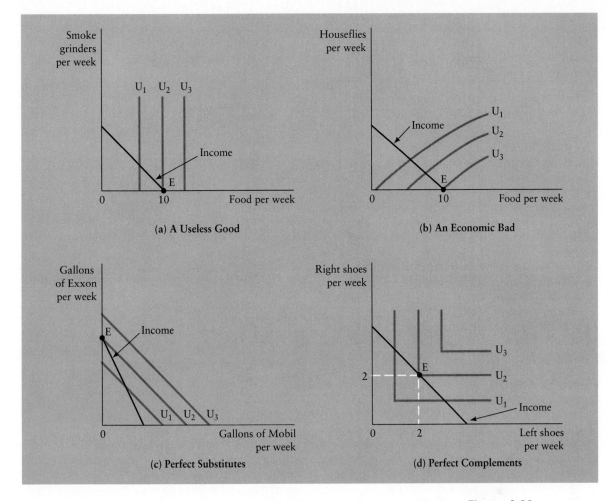

(a) A Useless Good

(b) An Economic Bad

(c) Perfect Substitutes

(d) Perfect Complements

The four panels in this figure repeat the special indifference curve maps from Figure 3.5. The resulting utility-maximizing positions (denoted by E in each panel) reflect the specific relationships among the goods pictured.

Figure 3.11
Utility-Maximizing
Choices for Special
Types of Goods

from this pattern would result in buying extra left or right shoes that alone provide no utility. In similar circumstances involving complementary goods, people also tend to purchase those goods together. Other items of apparel (gloves, earrings, socks, and so forth) are also bought mainly in pairs. Most people have preferred ways of concocting the beverages they drink (coffee and cream, gin and vermouth) or of making sandwiches (peanut butter and jelly, ham and cheese). And people seldom buy automobiles, stereos, or washing machines by the part. Rather, they consume these complex goods as fixed packages made up of their various components.

Application 3.5: Kinked Budget Constraints and Frequent-Flyer Programs pursues the types of analysis in Figure 3.11 a bit further. It shows how some

APPLICATION 3.5

Kinked Budget Constraints and Frequent-Flyer Programs

The budget constraints we have encountered in this chapter are graphed using straight lines implying that the prices of both goods are unaffected by how much the consumer buys. In cases where consumers may receive quantity discounts or may have to pay "excessive use" fees, this assumption is no longer valid, and the budget constraint may not have such a simple shape.

Quantity Discounts and the Budget Constraint

The case of a quantity discount is illustrated in Figure 1. Here consumers who buy less than X_D pay full price and face the usual budget constraint. Purchases in excess of X_D entitle the buyer to a lower price (on the extra units), and this results in a flatter budget constraint beyond X_D. The constraint, therefore, has a "kink" at X_D.[1] Effects of this kink on consumer choices are suggested by the indifference curve U_1, which is tangent to the budget constraint at both point A and point B. This individual is indifferent between consuming relatively little of X or a lot of X. A slightly larger quantity discount could tempt this consumer definitely to choose the larger amount of X. Notice that such a choice entails not only consuming low price units of X but also buying more X at full price in order to receive the discount.

Frequent-Flyer Programs

All major airlines sponsor frequent-flyer programs. These entitle customers to accumulate mileage with the airline at reduced fares. Because unused-seats revenues are lost forever, they utilize such programs to tempt consumers to travel more. Any additional full-fare travel that the programs may generate provides extra profits for the airline.

Some economists argue that frequent-flyer plans reduce competition among airlines by constraining a particular consumer to the airline on which he or she

Figure 1
Kinked Budget Constraint Resulting from a Quantity Discount

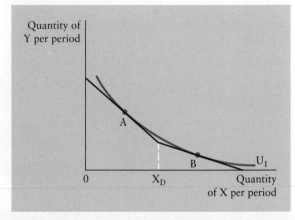

A quantity discount for purchases greater than X_D results in a kinked budget constraint. This consumer is indifferent between consuming relatively little X (Point A) or a lot of X (Point B).

maintains such a plan.[2] Of course, consumers are free to join a number of plans and some airlines give credit for travel on other airlines. Hence, the overall effect of the plans may simply be to fill seats that would have gone empty, with no effect on full-fare prices.

To Think About

1. Some medical insurance plans cover drug costs only to the extent that they exceed, say, $10 per month. How would such a plan affect an individual's budget constraint and his or her drug purchase decisions?

2. Suppose frequent-flyer coupons were transferrable among people. How would this affect Figure 1 and, more generally, the overall viability of the program?

---

[1] For a number of other illustrations of the relevance of kinked constraints, especially regarding analyzing tax systems, see Robert Moffitt, "The Econometrics of Kinked Budget Constraints," *Journal of Economic Perspectives* (Spring 1990): 119–139.

[2] For a discussion, see Andrew Kleit, "Competition Without Apology," *Regulation* (Summer 1991): 68–75.

commonly observed spending patterns can be explained using the simple choice model.

Generalizations

Although the previous examples studied only the individual's problem in choosing between two specific goods, the approach is quite general. In any situation in which people must make choices that are constrained by their economic circumstances, a very similar analysis could be used. The result that utility-maximizing individuals will equate the MRS between two goods to those goods' prices carries over directly to more complex cases.[7] Because economics is in many respects the study of how choices are made when scarcity is present, this model of choice lies behind many of the approaches taken by economists to study real-world questions.

One common graphing procedure for dealing with many goods might be mentioned. Often we wish to study a person's decisions about only one particular good and are not concerned with his or her decisions about any other specific goods. In this case we could record the good that is the object of attention on the horizontal (X) axis and treat all other goods as one single commodity shown on the vertical (Y) axis. That is, good Y is treated as a **composite good** that includes spending on everything except the good being explicitly examined. In this way, the standard two-dimensional analysis of choice is more general than might first appear to be the case.[8] In Chapter 4 we use this technique on several occasions.

Composite good

Combining expenditures on several different goods whose relative prices do not change into a single good for convenience in analysis.

Summary

This chapter covers a lot of ground. In it we have seen how economists explain the kinds of choices people make and the ways in which those choices are constrained by economic circumstances. The chapter has been rather tough going in places. The theory of choice is one of the most difficult parts of any study of microeconomics, and it is unfortunate that it usually comes at the very start of the course. But that placement clearly shows why the topic is so important.

---

[7] To examine such many-good cases requires the use of advanced mathematics since graphical techniques cannot be easily adapted to many dimensions. A relatively simple treatment of these mathematical derivations can be found in Walter Nicholson, *Microeconomic Theory: Basic Principles and Extensions,* 5th ed. (Ft. Worth, TX: The Dryden Press, 1992), Chapter 3. For a more complex discussion, see Paul A. Samuelson, *Foundations of Economic Analysis* (Cambridge, Mass.: Harvard University Press, 1947), Chapter 5.

[8] To make this convention rigorously correct requires that we assume that the relative prices of all the goods that constitute "everything else" are not changing during the analysis. Then it is possible to view the individual's choice problem as one of deciding how much income to devote to the purchase of X and how much to devote to everything else. For a discussion, see Nicholson, *Microeconomic Theory,* pp. 174–176.

Practically every model of economic behavior we will study starts with the building blocks introduced in this chapter.

Our principal conclusions in this chapter are:

- Economists use the term "utility" to refer to the satisfaction that people derive from their economic activities. Usually only a few of the things that affect utility are examined in any particular analysis. All other factors are assumed to be held constant so that a person's choices can be studied in a simplified setting.

- Utility can be represented by an indifference curve map. Each indifference curve shows those bundles of goods that the individual considers to be equally attractive. Higher levels of utility are represented by higher indifference curve "contour" lines.

- The slope of indifference curves shows how individuals are willing to trade one good for another while remaining equally well-off. The negative of this slope is called the "marginal rate of substitution" (MRS), since it shows the degree to which an individual is willing to substitute one good for another in his or her consumption choices.

- People are limited in what they can buy. Economists refer to such limits as "budget constraints." When a person is choosing between two goods, his or her budget constraint is usually a straight line. The negative of the slope of this line represents the price ratio of the two goods—it shows what one of the goods is worth in terms of the other in the marketplace.

- If individuals are to obtain the maximum possible utility from their limited incomes, they should spend all the available funds and should choose a bundle of goods for which the MRS is equal to the price ratio of the two goods. Such a utility maximum is shown graphically by a tangency between the individual's budget constraint and the highest indifference curve that his or her income can afford.

Review Questions

1. Our notion of utility is an "ordinal" one for which it is assumed that people can rank combinations of goods as to their desirability, but that they cannot assign a unique numerical (cardinal) categorization of the goods that identifies by "how much" one combination is preferred to another. For each of the following ranking systems, describe whether an ordinal or cardinal ranking is being used:
(a) military or academic ranks; (b) prices of vintage wines; (c) rankings of vintage wines by the French Wine Society; (d) press rankings of the "Top Ten" football teams; (e) results of the current U. S. Open Golf Championships (which are contested using stroke play); (f) results of early U.S. Open Golf Championships (which were conducted using match play).

2. Our discussion of actual food consumption patterns in Application 3.2 suggests that some particularly harried individuals may exhibit intransitivities in their choices. Under what conditions might people find it in their interest to demonstrate some irrationality in their choices of food items? Would these situations necessarily violate the assumption of utility maximization?

3. What kind of behavior would an economist consider truly "irrational"? Can you think of choices that people make that are not truly in their best interest, broadly conceived?

4. Explain why using the concept of the marginal rate of substitution (MRS) to describe voluntary trades does not require us to adopt any specific way to measure utility. Why is the MRS that an individual exhibits measured independently of how his or her utility might be measured?

5. Show that no two of an individual's indifference curves can intersect. What assumptions about behavior would be violated if two such curves did intersect? (Hint: Why can't two different contour lines [e.g., one for 100 feet and one for 150 feet] intersect on a topographic map?)

6. Sometimes an individual who has chosen a utility-maximizing combination of goods is said to have achieved an "equilibrium" in his or her decision problem. Why is this described as an equilibrium? What forces are being balanced in the individual's mind? In what sense will the equilibrium tend to persist until something changes?

7. Using the marginal utility interpretation of the utility-maximization process that is described in footnotes 2, 4, and 6 of this chapter, explain why the individual's decision problem can be described as "deciding how to get the biggest bang for his or her bucks." Use this to explain what it means to say that something "costs too much."

8. How might you draw an indifference curve map that illustrates the following ideas?

   a. Margarine is just as good as the high-priced spread.
   b. Things go better with Coke.
   c. A day without wine is like a day without sunshine.
   d. Popcorn is addictive—the more you eat, the more you want.
   e. If he doesn't wear English Leather, he wears nothing at all.
   f. It takes two to tango.

9. Application 3.4 illustrates how rationing of a commodity may reduce utility. Develop a similar graphic analysis to show why requiring the purchase of some particular amount of an item would have the same effect.

10. Suppose an individual consumes three items: steak, lettuce, and tomatoes. If we were interested only in examining this person's steak purchases, we might group lettuce and tomatoes into a single composite good called "salad." How would you define this good? What would this person's budget constraint for steak and salad be? What would it mean to say that "the relative price of salad has risen"?

Problems

3.1 Suppose a person has $8.00 to spend only on apples and oranges. Suppose apples cost $.40 each and oranges cost $.10 each.

   a. If this person buys *only* apples, how many can be bought?
   b. If this person buys *only* oranges, how many can be bought?
   c. If the person were to buy 10 apples, how many oranges could be bought with the funds left over?
   d. If the person consumes one less apple (that is, nine), how many more oranges could be bought? Is this rate of trade-off the same no matter how many apples are relinquished?
   e. Write down the algebraic equation for this person's budget constraint, and graph it showing the points mentioned in parts a through d (using graph paper would improve the accuracy of your work).

3.2 Suppose the person faced with the budget constraint described in problem 3.1 has preferences for apples (A) and oranges (O) given by

$$\text{Utility} = \sqrt{A \cdot O}.$$

   a. If A = 5 and O = 80, what will utility be?
   b. If A = 10, what value for O will provide the same utility as in part a?
   c. If A = 20, what value for O will provide the same utility as in parts a and b?
   d. Graph the indifference curve implied by parts a through c.
   e. Given the budget constraint from problem 3.1, which of the points identified in parts a through c can be bought by this person?
   f. Show through some examples that every other way of allocating income provides less utility than does the point identified in part e. Graph this utility-maximizing situation.

3.3 Oliver D. Dancefloor gets his utility by going to discos or rock concerts. His utility function is $U = \sqrt{D \cdot C}$, where D = the number of discos and C = the number of concerts he attends in a month. Draw the contour lines (in the positive quadrant) for this function for utility levels of 4, 5, and 10 (that is, for U = 4, U = 5, and U = 10). What do we call the shape of these contour lines? (Hint: Here it may be easier to graph U^2 rather than U.)

3.4 Assume Oliver D. Dancefloor has the utility function described in problem 3.3. If concert tickets are $4, the cover charge at the disco is $2, and Oliver's monthly entertainment budget is $64, what is his budget constraint? Where does this line intersect the indifference curve for $U = \sqrt{128}$? Does this seem to be the highest utility possible given the budget constraint?

3.5 Ms. Caffeine enjoys coffee (C) and tea (T) according to the function U(C, T) = 3C + 4T. What does her utility function say about her MRS of coffee for tea? What do her indifference curves look like? If coffee and tea cost $3 each and Ms. Caffeine has $12 to spend on these products, how much coffee and tea should she buy to maximize her utility? Draw the graph of her indifference curve map and her budget constraint, and show that the utility-maximizing point occurs only on the T-axis where no coffee is bought. Would she buy any coffee if she had more money to spend? How would her consumption change if the price of coffee fell to $2?

3.6 Mr. A derives utility from martinis in proportion to the number he drinks, U(M) = M. Mr. A is very particular about his martinis, however: he only enjoys them made in the exact proportion of two parts gin (G) to one part vermouth (V). Graph Mr. A's indifference curve in terms of G and V for various levels of martini consumption. (Hint: Does Mr. A have an MRS of G for V?) Show that regardless of the prices of the two ingredients, Mr. A will never alter the way he mixes martinis. Graph this result.

3.7 Assume consumers are choosing between housing services (H) measured in square feet and consumption of all other goods (C) measured in dollars.

a. Show the equilibrium position in a diagram.
b. Now suppose the government agrees to subsidize consumers by paying 50 percent of their housing cost. How will their budget line change? Show the new equilibrium.
c. Show in a diagram the minimum amount of income supplement the government would have to give individuals instead of a housing subsidy to make them as well-off as they were in part b.

*3.8 Suppose low-income people have preferences for nonfood consumption (NF) and for food consumption (F). In the absence of any income transfer programs, a person's budget constraint is given by

$$NF + P_FF = I,$$

where P_F is the price of food relative to nonfood items and NF and I are measured in terms of nonfood prices (that is, dollars).

a. Graph the initial utility-maximizing situation for this low-income person.
b. Suppose now that a food stamp program is introduced that requires low-income people to pay C (measured in terms of nonfood prices) in order to receive food stamps sufficient to buy F* units of food (presumably $P_FF^* >$ C). Show this person's budget constraint if he or she participates in the food stamp program.
c. Show graphically the factors that will determine whether the person chooses to participate in the program.
d. Show graphically what it will cost the government to finance benefits for the typical food stamp recipient. Show also that some people might reach a higher utility level if this amount were simply given with no strings attached.

*3.9 Suppose individuals derive utility from two goods, housing (H) and all other consumption (C). Show that if the government requires individuals to buy more housing than they would freely choose (say, by setting minimum housing standards), such a policy may reduce utility. Which group would you expect to

---

*Denotes a problem that is rather difficult.

suffer the greatest losses of utility from such a policy? (Hint: Use the analysis from Application 3.4.)

3.10 Recently, some electric companies have adopted "excess use charges" that increase the cost of electric power after a certain minimum amount of kilowatt hours per month has been used.

a. How does such a charge affect the individual's budget constraint? Illustrate the new constraint with a graph.
b. Which electricity consumers will be unaffected by this new charge? Which will probably change their behavior?
c. Show why it seems likely that many consumers will choose to use precisely the amount of electricity at which excess use charges begin.

This chapter studies how people change their choices when conditions change. In particular, we will study how changes in income or changes in the price of a good affect the amount that people choose to consume. We will compare the new choices with those that were made before conditions changed. This kind of investigation is sometimes called comparative statics analysis because it compares two utility-maximizing choices. A result of this approach will be to construct the individual's demand curve for a good. This curve shows how the individual responds to different prices for the good.

You need to be careful about two aspects of this kind of approach. First, the *ceteris paribus* assumption is important here. We are changing only one thing that affects choices at a time; everything else is being held constant. In particular, we are assuming that people's preferences do not change. In graphic terms, we will be keeping the individual's indifference curve map unchanged and studying the effects of shifting the budget constraint to alternative positions.

Second, you should understand that the general notion of "changing conditions" is only a beginning for our investigation. Ideally, we would like to explain why economic conditions change. Instead of supposing that, for example, the price of potatoes has risen, we will eventually be more interested in finding out *why* the price of potatoes has risen.

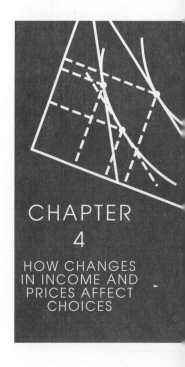

CHAPTER
4

HOW CHANGES
IN INCOME AND
PRICES AFFECT
CHOICES

Demand Functions

Chapter 3 showed that the quantities of X and Y that an individual chooses depend on the person's preferences (that is, on the shape of the indifference curve map) and on the budget constraint. If we knew a person's preferences and all of the economic forces that affect his or her choices, we could predict how much of each good would be chosen. We can summarize this conclusion using the **demand function** for some particular good, say, X:

■

Demand function

A representation of how quantity demanded depends on prices, income, and preferences.

$$\text{Quantity of X demanded} = d_X(P_X, P_Y, I; \text{preferences}). \qquad [4.1]$$

This functional notation contains the three elements that determine what the individual can buy—the prices of X and Y and the person's income (I)—as well as a reminder that choices are also affected by preferences for the goods. These preferences appear to the right of the semicolon in Equation 4.1 because for most of our analysis we assume that preferences do not change. People's basic likes and dislikes are assumed to be developed through a lifetime of experience. They are unlikely to change as we examine their reactions to relatively short-term changes in their economic circumstances caused by changes in commodity prices or incomes.

The quantity demanded of good Y depends on these same general influences and can be summarized by

$$\text{Quantity of Y demanded} = d_Y(P_X, P_Y, I; \text{preferences}). \qquad [4.2]$$

Preferences again appear to the right of the semicolon in Equation 4.2 because we assume that the person's taste for good Y will not change during our analysis. Here we are interested only in examining how choices change when economic conditions change.

■ Homogeneity

One important result that follows directly from Chapter 3 is that if the prices of X and Y and income (I) were all to double (or to change by any identical percentage), the same quantities of X and Y would be demanded. The budget constraint

$$P_X X + P_Y Y = I \qquad [4.3]$$

is identical to the budget constraint

$$2P_X X + 2P_Y Y = 2I. \qquad [4.4]$$

Graphically, Equations 4.3 and 4.4 are exactly the same lines. Consequently, both budget constraints are tangent to the individual's indifference curve map at precisely the same point. The quantities of X and Y the individual chooses when faced by the constraint in Equation 4.3 are exactly the same as when the individual is faced by the constraint in Equation 4.4.

Hence, we have shown an important result: the quantities an individual demands depend only on the relative prices of goods X and Y and on the "real" value of income. Proportional changes in the prices of X and Y and in income change only the units we count in (such as dollars instead of cents). They do not affect the quantities demanded. Individual demands are said to be **homogeneous** for identical proportional changes in all prices and income.[1] People are not hurt by general inflation of prices if their incomes increase in the same proportion. They will be on exactly the same indifference curve both before and after the inflation. Only if inflation increases some incomes faster or slower than prices change does it then have an effect on budget constraints, on the quantities of goods demanded, and on people's well-being.

■
Homogeneous demand function
Quantity demanded does not change when prices and income increase in the same proportion.

Changes in Income

As a person's total income rises, assuming prices don't change, we might expect the quantity purchased of each good also to increase. This situation is illustrated in Figure 4.1. As income increases from I_1 to I_2 to I_3, the quantity of X demanded increases from X_1 to X_2 to X_3, and the quantity of Y demanded increases from Y_1 to Y_2 to Y_3. Budget lines I_1, I_2, and I_3 are all parallel because we are changing only income, not the relative prices of X and Y. Remember the slope of the budget constraint is given by the ratio of the two goods' prices, and these prices are not changing in this analysis. Increases in income do, however, make it possible for this person to consume more; and this increased purchasing power is reflected by the outward shift in the budget constraint and an increase in overall utility.

■ Normal Goods

In Figure 4.1 both good X and good Y increase as income increases. Goods that follow this tendency are called **normal goods.** Most goods seem to be normal goods—as their incomes increase, people tend to buy more of practically everything. Of course, as Figure 4.1 shows, the demand for some "luxury"

■
Normal good
A good that is bought in greater quantities as income increases.

---

[1] Technically, a function f(X, Y) is said to be homogeneous of degree zero in X and Y if f(tX, tY) = f(X, Y) for any t > 0. Doubling X and Y for a function homogeneous of degree zero leaves the value of f unchanged. This is precisely the case for demand functions.

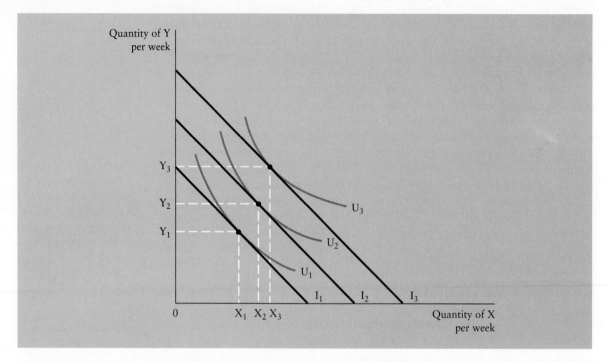

Figure 4.1
Effect of Increasing Income on Quantities of X and Y Chosen

As income increases from I_1 to I_2 to I_3, the optimal (utility-maximizing) choices of X and Y are shown by the successively higher points of tangency. The budget constraint shifts in a parallel way because its slope (given by the ratio of the goods' prices) does not change.

goods (such as Y) may increase rapidly when income rises, but the demand for "necessities" (such as X) may grow less rapidly. The relationship between income and the amounts of various goods purchased has been extensively examined by economists as Application 4.1: Engel's Law shows.

■ Inferior Goods

Inferior good

A good that is bought in smaller quantities as income increases.

The demand for a few unusual goods may decrease as a person's income increases. Some examples of these goods are "rotgut" whiskey, potatoes, and secondhand clothing. This kind of good is called an **inferior good.** How the demand for an inferior good responds to rising income is shown in Figure 4.2. The good Z is inferior because the individual chooses less of it as his or her income increases. Although the curves in Figure 4.3 continue to obey the assumption of a diminishing MRS, they exhibit inferiority. Good Z is inferior only because of the way it relates to the other goods available (good Y

APPLICATION 4.1

Engel's Law

Probably the most famous sample data illustrating the relationship between income and the consumption of certain goods are those used by the Prussian economist, Ernst Engel (1821–1896), in his original studies of household behavior. An abbreviated set showing the spending patterns of Belgian families in 1853 is shown in Table 1. Engel drew one major conclusion from these data: The proportion of income spent on food declines as income rises. This hypothesis has come to be known as Engel's law, and it has been verified in hundreds of studies. Cross-country comparisons also show that, on average, people in less-developed countries spend more of their income on food than people in richer industrial countries and, over time, the percentage of income spent on food also tends to decline as incomes rise. For example, in nineteenth-century America, people spent nearly 50 percent of their income on food. Today, as we show in Table 2, that figure has fallen to about 15 percent.

Engel was cautious about drawing conclusions from the other data in his table. Even today, no other laws of consumption are believed to be as true as Engel's law of food consumption. For example, according to the data, shelter expenses seem to be a constant fraction of income. Whether housing spending is really proportional to income has been hotly debated for many years, particularly as to how property taxes affect various income groups.

Recent Data

Table 2 updates Engel's data for the United States in 1988. Although there have been vast changes since 1853 in the types of goods that people consume (which means the categories in the two tables are not directly comparable), some of Engel's conclusions remain valid. Most importantly, Engel's law continues to hold. People with higher incomes still spend proportionally less of their income on food than do people with lower incomes. The overall rise in incomes since the nineteenth century is due to the huge increases in spending on "other goods." The necessities of life (food, clothing, shelter) now occupy a less important portion of the individual's budget than they did in the previous century.

Table 1

Percentage of Total Expenditures on Various Items by Belgian Families in 1853

Expenditure Item	Annual Income		
	$225–$300	$450–$600	$750–$1,000
Food	62.0%	55.0%	50.0%
Clothing	16.0	18.0	18.0
Lodging, light, and fuel	17.0	17.0	17.0
Services (education, legal, health)	4.0	7.5	11.5
Comfort and recreation	1.0	2.5	3.5
Total	100.0	100.0	100.0

Source: Reproduced in A. Marshall, *Principles of Economics,* 8th ed. (London: Macmillan & Co., Ltd., 1920), p. 97. Some items have been aggregated.

Table 2

Percentage of Total Expenditures on Various Items by U.S. Families in 1988

Expenditure Item	Annual Income		
	$12,000	$25,000	$65,000
Food	16.7%	15.2%	12.5%
Clothing	5.3	5.8	6.2
Lodging, light and fuel	32.6	30.3	29.6
Other expenditures	45.4	48.7	51.7
Total	100.0%	100.0%	100.0%

Source: Statistical Abstract of the United States, 1991, Table 718

To Think About

1. What does this discussion of Engel's law suggest about using food expenditures to measure poverty?
2. In recent years the percentage of income devoted to food people eat away from home has been rising. Does this trend contradict Engel's law?

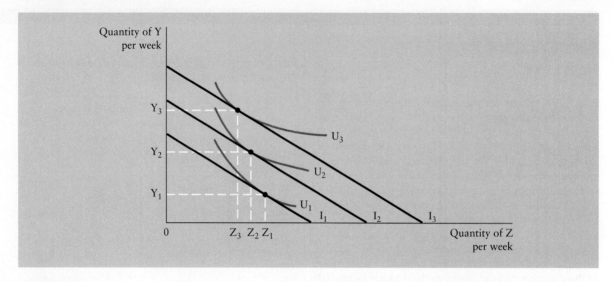

Figure 4.2
Indifference Curve
Map Showing
Inferiority

Good Z is inferior because the quantity purchased declines as income increases. Y is a normal good (as it must be if only two goods are available), and purchases of it increase as total expenditures increase.

here), not because of its own qualities. Purchases of rotgut whiskey decline as income increases, for example, because an individual is able to afford more expensive goods (such as Jack Daniel's). Inferior goods are probably quite rare. Application 4.2: Are Children Inferior? exhibits a common pitfall that makes some goods appear to be inferior when they really are not.

Changes in a Good's Price

■

Substitution effect

The part of the change in quantity demanded that is caused by substitution of one good for another. A movement along an indifference curve.

Examining how a price change affects the quantity demanded of a good is more complex than looking at the effect of a change in income. Changing the price geometrically involves not only changing the intercept of the budget constraint but also changing its slope. Moving to the new utility-maximizing choice means moving to another indifference curve and also changing the MRS.

When a price changes, it has two different effects on people's choices. With the **substitution effect,** even if the individual stays on the same indifference curve, consumption has to be changed to equate MRS to the new price

APPLICATION 4.2

Are Children Inferior?

One decision that seems to involve an inferior good is the decision to have children. Table 1 lists U.S. birthrates and average annual earnings (adjusted to 1990 dollars) for census years from 1890 to 1990. During that period, except for a temporary increase in the years after World War II, birthrates fell rather sharply. At the same time, average real incomes nearly quadrupled. As Americans become richer they seem to demand fewer children. This pattern is also found in most other countries throughout the world. Does it mean that children are "inferior" goods?

Economists are reluctant to accept at face value these data that seem to show a pattern of inferiority. They look for other explanations for the observed pattern. Most commonly, economists argue in this case that many other factors besides the decline in the birthrate accompany rising income levels. In reality, interpreting the relationship between income and birthrates is more difficult than it at first appears, because it is not a *ceteris paribus* relationship.

Quality versus Quantity

Economist Gary Becker was one of the first to point out that a couple's decision to have children really has two dimensions: a decision about how many to have (quantity) and a series of decisions about how much money to spend on their upbringing (quality).[1] As people earn more money, it seems likely that they will be more interested in the quality dimension of their child rearing. They may spend more money to buy braces, violin lessons, finance college educations, and so forth. They may even choose to have fewer children. Hence, the data on number of children may be entirely consistent with the notion that children are "normal" goods.

The Price of Children

Another view of the data on birthrates considers how the cost of having children changes with increasing levels of affluence. This view argues that costs rise rapidly pri-

Table 1
U.S. Birthrates and Earnings since 1890

Year	Birthrate per 1,000 Population	Average Annual Earnings in 1990 Dollars
1890	33.7	$ 6,678
1900	32.3	7,162
1910	30.1	7,780
1920	27.7	8,588
1930	21.3	9,953
1940	19.4	11,268
1950	24.1	15,195
1960	23.7	20,134
1970	18.4	24,172
1980	15.9	24,546
1990	15.9	25,020

Source: Computed from various series in *U.S. Historical Statistics from Colonial Times to 1970* and *U.S. Statistical Abstract*, 1991.

marily because of the opportunity cost of the wages that are no longer earned by parents who stay home to provide child care. In the United States during the past hundred years, for example, it is argued that rising wages for women have sharply increased the opportunity cost of childbearing, and that this is one reason why birthrates have fallen. Once this cost is taken into account, many researchers find that the direction of the relationship between income and birthrate is reversed.[2]

To Think About

1. Many less developed countries have attempted to control the size of their populations by adopting stringent birth control programs. Might economic growth be a more successful way to limit population growth?

2. How do income tax rates affect couples' decisions to have children? Might such taxes have different effects depending on which family member we examine?

[1] Gary S. Becker, "An Economic Analysis of Fertility," in *Demographic and Economic Change in Developed Countries*, National Bureau Conference Series 11 (Princeton, N.J.: Princeton University Press, 1960).

[2] A great deal of this evidence is reviewed in T. W. Schultz, ed., "New Economic Approaches to Fertility," *Journal of Political Economy* (March/April 1973).

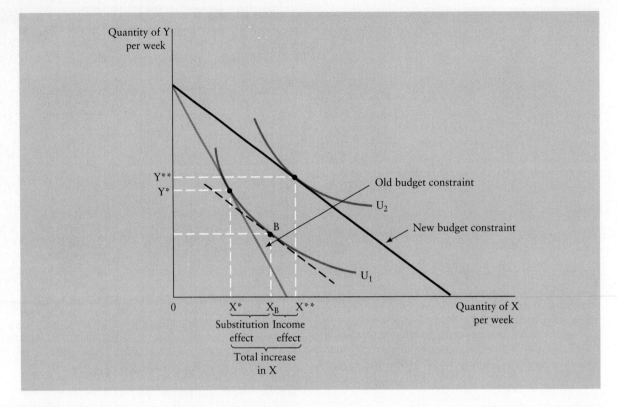

Figure 4.3
Income and
Substitution Effects
of a Fall in Price

When the price of X falls, the utility-maximizing choice shifts from X*, Y* to X**, Y**. This movement can be broken down into two effects: first, a movement along the initial indifference curve to point B where the MRS is equal to the new price ratio (the substitution effect); second, a movement to a higher level of utility, since real income has increased (the income effect). Both the substitution and income effects cause more X to be bought when its price declines. The Y-intercept is the same for both budget constraints because both P_Y and I are held constant.

■
Income effect
The part of the change in quantity demanded that is caused by a change in real income.

ratio of the two goods. With the **income effect,** because the price change also changes "real" purchasing power, people will move to a new indifference curve that is consistent with their new purchasing power. We now look at these two effects of price changes in several different situations.

■ Substitution and Income Effects from a Fall in Price

Let's look first at how the quantity consumed of good X changes in response to a fall in its price. This situation is illustrated in Figure 4.3. Initially the individual maximizes utility by choosing the combination X*, Y*. Suppose that the price of X falls. The budget line now shifts outward to the new budget constraint as shown in the figure. Remember that the budget constraint meets the Y-axis at the point where all available income is spent on good Y. But, since neither the person's income nor the price of good Y has changed here, this Y-intercept is the same for both constraints. The new X-intercept is to the right of the old one because the lower price of X means that, with the lower price, more of it can now be bought. The flatter slope of the budget constraint shows us that the relative price of X to Y (that is, P_X/P_Y) has fallen.

Substitution Effect   With this change in the budget constraint, the new position of maximum utility is at X^{**}, Y^{**}. There the new budget line is tangent to the indifference curve U_2. The movement to this new set of choices is the result of two different effects. First, the change in the slope of the budget constraint would have motivated the individual to move to point B even if the person had stayed on the original indifference curve U_1. The dashed line in Figure 4.3 has the same slope as the new budget constraint, but it is tangent to U_1 because we are holding "real" income (that is, utility) constant. A relatively lower price for X causes the individual to move from X^*, Y^* to B if he or she is not better-off as a result of the lower price. This movement is a graphic demonstration of the substitution effect. Even though the individual is no better-off, the change in price still causes a change in consumption choices.

Income Effect   The further move from B to the final consumption choice X^{**}, Y^{**} is identical to the kind of movement we described in Figure 4.1 for changes in income. Because the price of X has fallen, but nominal income (I) has stayed the same, the individual has a greater "real" income and can afford a higher utility level (U_2). If X is a normal good, the individual will now demand more of it. This is the income effect that arises from a decline in the price of X. As is clear from the figure, both the substitution effect and the income effect cause the individual to choose more X when the price of X declines.

The Effects Combined   People do not actually move from X^*, Y^* to point B and then to X^{**}, Y^{**} when the price of good X falls. We never observe the point B; only the two actual choices of X^*, Y^* and X^{**}, Y^{**} are reflected in this person's behavior. But the analysis of income and substitution effects is still valuable because it shows that a price change affects the quantity demanded of a good in two conceptually different ways.

We can use the hamburger–soft drink example from Chapter 3 to show these effects at work. Suppose that the price of soft drinks falls to $.25 from the earlier price of $.50. This price change will increase the individual's purchasing power. Whereas earlier 20 soft drinks could be bought with an income of $10.00, now 40 of them can be bought. The price decrease shifts the budget constraint outward and increases utility. The individual now will choose some different combination of hamburgers and soft drinks than before, if only because the previous choice of five hamburgers and ten soft drinks (under the old budget constraint) now costs only $7.50—there is $2.50 left unspent, and this person will choose to do something with it.

In making the new choices, the individual is influenced by two different effects. First, even if we hold constant the individual's utility by somehow compensating for the positive effect the price change has on utility, the individual will still act so that the MRS is brought into line with the new price ratio (now one hamburger to four soft drinks). This compensated response is the substitution effect. Even with a constant real income the individual will still choose more soft drinks and fewer hamburgers since the opportunity cost of eating a burger is now higher than before.

In actuality, real income has also increased; in order to assess the total effect of the price change on the demand for soft drinks, we must also investigate the effect of the change in purchasing power. Because the individual's real income has increased, this (assuming soft drinks are normal goods) would be another reason to expect soft drink purchases to increase.

■ Substitution and Income Effects from an Increase in Price

We can use a similar analysis to see what happens if the price of good X increases. The budget line in Figure 4.4 shifts inward because of an increase in the price of X. The Y-intercept for the budget constraint again does not change since neither income nor P_Y has changed. The slope of the budget constraint is now steeper, however, because X costs more than it did before.

The movement from the initial point of utility maximization (X*, Y*) to the new point X**, Y** is again caused by two forces. First, even if the individual stayed on the initial indifference curve (U_2), he or she would substitute Y for X and move along U_2 to point B. At this point the dashed line (with the same slope as the new budget constraint) is just tangent to the indifference curve U_2. The movement from X*, Y* to B along U_2 is the substitution effect. However, because purchasing power is reduced by the increase in the price of X (the amount of income remains constant, but now X costs more), the person must move to a lower level of utility, which is the income effect of the higher price. In Figure 4.4 both the income and substitution effects work in the same direction and cause the quantity demanded of X to fall in response to an increase in its price.

■ Summary of Substitution and Income Effects

In conclusion, then, how does the quantity demanded of X change graphically in response to changes in its price (P_X)? Because of the substitution effect, the quantity demanded of X always moves in a direction opposite to the direction of the price change. A decrease in P_X lowers the price ratio (P_X/P_Y). To reestablish the tangency condition for utility maximization, the MRS must also fall. In order to reduce the MRS, the person will choose more X and less Y by moving in a southeasterly direction along the indifference curve. Consequently, the quantity of X increases as a result of the substitution effect. This result is a direct consequence of the assumption (introduced in Chapter 3) of a diminishing MRS. Similarly, an increase in the price of X raises the price ratio (P_X/P_Y). The

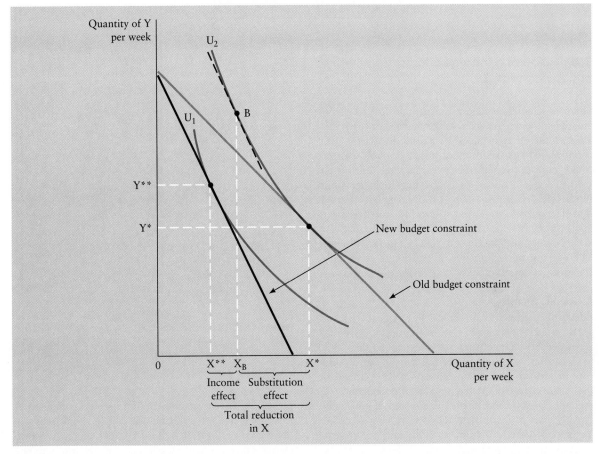

When the price of good X increases, the budget constraint shifts inward. The movement from the initial utility-maximizing point (X*, Y*) to the new point (X**, Y**) can be analyzed as two separate effects. The substitution effect causes a movement to point B on the initial indifference curve (U₂). The price increase would also create a loss of purchasing power. This income effect causes a consequent movement to a lower indifference curve. The income and substitution effects together cause the quantity demanded of X to fall as a result of the increase in its price. Again, the Y-intercept of the budget constraint is not affected by the change in the price of X.

Figure 4.4
Income and
Substitution Effects
of an Increase
in Price

individual moves to a point on the indifference curve with a higher MRS. This means choosing more Y and less X; the quantity demanded of X decreases.

Substitution effects are only part of the story. To determine the total effect of a change in P_X on the quantity demanded of X, we must also consider income effects. Now the analysis may become somewhat more complex. A change in the price of good X affects an individual's real income, and we must analyze how this income change effects quantity demanded. When X is a normal good (that is, the quantity demanded of X increases as income increases), income effects reinforce substitution effects: again, price and quantity move in

APPLICATION 4.3

Substitution and Income Effects of a Carbon Tax

There is scientific evidence that the release of carbon dioxide and other gasses from the burning of fossil fuels has had the effect of modestly raising the earth's temperature.[1] The possibility that this "greenhouse effect" could increase dramatically over the next century has led to greater concern for controlling such emissions. At the 1992 Earth Summit in Rio de Janiero, nations signed a general agreement to seek to stabilize greenhouse gas emissions. One proposed way to do that is by taxing carbon use. By one estimate, a tax rate of about $17 per ton of carbon would be enough to stabilize emissions at approximately 1990 levels.[2]

A Graphic Analysis

Effects of a carbon tax on choices by a typical consumer are illustrated in Figure 1. The rise in price of fossil fuels (good X) shifts the consumer's budget constraint from I to I', causing fossil fuel use to fall from X_1 to X_2. One way to measure the dollar value of taxes collected on this figure is to look at the amount of other goods (Y) that are foregone once the tax is imposed. If consumers buy X_2 units of fossil fuels, they would be able to buy Y_3 units of other goods without the tax, but only Y_2 units with the tax. The distance $Y_3 - Y_2$ measures the transfer in purchasing power represented by the carbon tax.

Welfare Effects of the Tax

To avoid the complex question of how wisely the government spends its tax revenues, a customary assumption in theoretical analysis is to presume that these revenues are simply given back to all taxpayers as a rebate. Because the amount of the rebate for the typical taxpayer is given by the distance $Y_3 - Y_2$, the budget constraint after such a rebate becomes I''. Notice that even with this rebate, the consumer cannot reach the

Figure 1

Substitution and Income Effects from a Carbon Tax

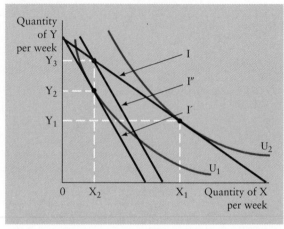

A tax on fossil fuels (X) would shift the budget constraint from I to I' and would reduce consumption from X_1 to X_2. Even a full rebate of the tax proceeds (I'') would not permit this individual to reach his or her original utility level (U_2).

pretax indifference curve, U_1. The rebate compensates for the income effect of the tax, but the consumer still obtains lower overall welfare because of the substitution of other goods for fossil fuel use. According to one set of estimates, the dollar value of this utility loss from a carbon tax might amount to about $100–$300 per year for a typical family.[3]

To Think About

1. A large carbon tax on fossil fuels would probably affect many prices. Which prices might be affected the most, and which the least?
2. How do you know that the utility level provided with budget constraint I'' is lower than that provided by I (that is, U_2)?

---

[1] Chapter 22 contains a more complete discussion of the economics of environmental control measures. Application 22.4 looks further at the greenhouse effect.

[2] These figures are taken from D. W. Jorgenson, D. T. Slesnick, and P. J. Wilcoxen, "Carbon Taxes and Economic Welfare," *Brookings Papers on Economic Activity, Microeconomics* (1992): 393–431. As described in the comments that follow this article, some economists believe these estimates are too optimistic and that much larger taxes may be required to achieve stable levels of emissions.

[3] Ibid., 426. In Chapter 6 we describe how such calculations might be made.

opposite directions. For example, a decrease in P_X causes real income to rise, and the person will choose to consume more X (since X is a normal good). The substitution effect is reinforced by the income effect. Similarly, when P_X increases, real income falls, and the quantity of X demanded falls; this also reinforces the substitution effect. For normal goods, then, income and substitution effects reinforce each other. Both cause the price of X and the quantity demanded of X to move in opposite directions. That was the case in both Figures 4.3 and 4.4. Our analysis of substitution and income effects is therefore consistent with the idea that a person will buy more of a good whose price has fallen. This will provide the basis for our development of demand curves later in this chapter. Using substitution and income effects also clarifies many important issues about the effects of price changes on individual welfare. Application 4.3: Substitution and Income Effects of a Carbon Tax illustrates why it is important to recognize both effects of a price change.

■ Substitution and Income Effects for an Inferior Good

We cannot predict exactly the effect of a price change on consumption of an inferior good. The income and substitution effects of a change in such a good's price have opposite effects on the quantity demanded. Because inferior goods are relatively rare, we will only look briefly at this case.

Figure 4.5 shows the income and substitution effects from an increase in P_X when X is an inferior good. As the price of X rises, the substitution effect causes the individual to choose less X. This substitution effect is represented by a movement from the initial point X^*, Y^* to point B in the initial indifference curve, U_2. This movement is exactly the same as in Figure 4.4 for a normal good. Because P_X has increased, however, the individual now has a lower real income and must move to a lower indifference curve, U_1. The individual will choose X^{**}, Y^{**}. At X^{**} more X is chosen than at point B. This happens because good X is an inferior good: as real income falls, the quantity demanded of X increases rather than declines as it would for a normal good. In Figure 4.5, however, X^{**} is less than X^*; less X is ultimately demanded in response to the rise in its price. In our example here the substitution effect is strong enough to outweigh the "perverse" income effect of an inferior good's price change.

■ Giffen's Paradox

If the income effect of a price change is strong enough, the change in P_X and the resulting change in the quantity demanded of X actually could move in the same direction. Legend has it that the English economist Robert Giffen observed this paradox in nineteenth-century Ireland—when the price of potatoes rose, people reportedly consumed more of them. This peculiar result can be explained by looking at the size of the income effect of a change in the price of potatoes. Potatoes were not only inferior goods but also used up a large portion of the Irish people's income. An increase in the price of potatoes therefore reduced real income substantially. The Irish were forced to cut back on other luxury food consumption in order to buy more potatoes. Even though this

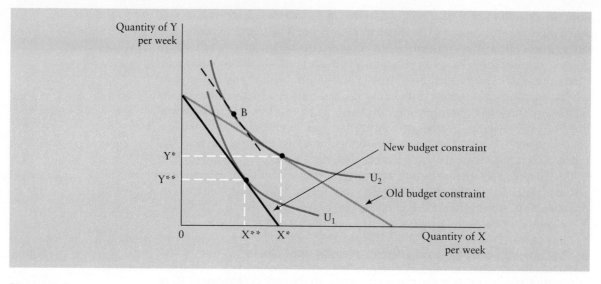

Figure 4.5
Income and
Substitution Effects
for an Inferior Good

When the price of X increases, the substitution effect causes less X to be demanded (as shown by a movement to point B on the indifference curve U_2). However, because good X is inferior, the lower real income brought about by its price increase causes the quantity demanded of X to increase from B to X^{**}. In this particular example, the substitution effect outweighs the income effect and X consumption still falls (from X^* to X^{**}).

rendering of events is historically implausible, the possibility of an increase in the quantity demanded in response to the price increase of a good has come to be known as **Giffen's paradox.**[2]

Giffen's paradox

A situation in which the increase in a good's price leads people to consume more of the good.

Giffen's paradox is probably quite rare in the real world—not only must the good be inferior, but the (perverse) positive income effect from a price rise must be strong enough to outweigh the negative substitution effect. A strong income effect will not usually exist unless the good makes up a large part of the individual's expenditures (as with potatoes in nineteenth-century Ireland). We can therefore conclude that price and quantity demanded of a good will usually move in opposite directions, even when the good is inferior. That is, Giffen's paradox will not occur except in unusual circumstances.

The Lump-Sum Principle

Application 4.3 provided an initial introduction to one of the most important illustrations of our analysis of the effects of price changes: how taxation af-

---

[2] A major problem with this explanation is that it disregards Marshall's observation that both supply and demand factors must be taken into account when analyzing price changes. If potato prices increased because of a decline in supply due to the potato blight, how could *more* potatoes possibly have been consumed? Also, since many Irish people were potato farmers, the potato price increase should have increased real income for them. For a detailed discussion of these and other fascinating bits of potato lore, see G. P. Dwyer and C. M. Lindsey, "Robert Giffen and the Irish Potato," *American Economic Review* (March 1984): 188–192.

fects individual welfare. Of course, it seems obvious (if we don't consider the government services that taxes provide) that paying taxes must reduce a person's utility because purchasing power is reduced. But, through the use of income and substitution effects, we can show that the size of this welfare loss will depend on how the tax is structured. Specifically, taxes that are imposed on general purchasing power will have smaller welfare costs than will taxes imposed on a narrow selection of commodities. This "lump-sum principle" lies at the heart of the study of the economics of taxation.

■ A Graphical Analysis

A graphical proof of the lump-sum principle is presented in Figure 4.6. Initially, the individual has I dollars to spend and chooses to consume X^* and Y^*. This combination yields utility level U_3. A tax on good X alone would raise its price, and the budget constraint would become steeper. With that budget constraint (shown as line I' in the figure), a person would be forced to accept a lower utility level (U_1) and would choose to consume the combination X_1, Y_1.

Suppose now that the government decided to institute a general income (purchasing power) tax that raised the same revenue as this single-good excise tax. This would shift the individual's budget constraint to I''. The fact that I'' passes through X_1, Y_1 shows that both taxes raise the same amount of

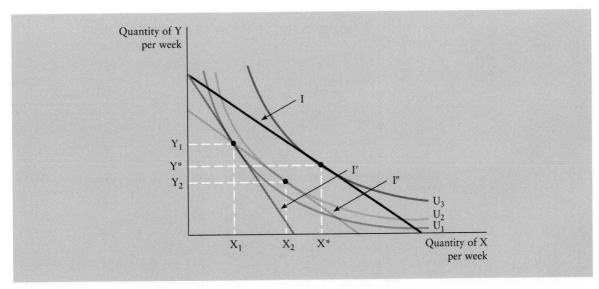

An excise tax on good X shifts the budget constraint to I'. The individual chooses X_1, Y_1 and receives utility of U_1. A lump-sum tax that collects the same amount shifts the budget constraint to I''. The individual chooses X_2, Y_2 and receives more utility (U_2).

Figure 4.6
The Lump-Sum Principle

revenue.[3] However, with the income tax budget constraint I″, the person will choose to consume X_2, Y_2 (rather than X_1, Y_1). Even though the individual pays the same tax bill in both instances, the combination chosen under the income tax yields a higher utility (U_2) than does the tax on a single commodity.

An intuitive explanation of this result is that a single-commodity tax affects people's well-being in two ways: It reduces general purchasing power (an income effect) and it directs consumption away from the taxed commodity (a substitution effect). An income tax incorporates only the first effect, and, with equal tax revenues raised, individuals are better off under it than under a tax that also distorts consumption choices.

■ Generalizations

More generally, the demonstration of the lump-sum principle in Figure 4.6 suggests that the utility loss associated with the need to collect a certain amount of tax revenue can be kept to a minimum by taxing goods for which substitution effects are small. By doing so, taxes will have relatively little welfare effect beyond their direct effect on purchasing power. On the other hand, taxes on goods for which there are many substitutes will cause individuals to alter their consumption plans in major ways. This additional distortionary effect raises the overall utility cost of such taxes to consumers.[4] In Application 4.4: The Lump-Sum Principle in Practice, we look at a few implications of these observations for actual tax and transfer policies.

Changes in the Price of Another Good

Figures 4.3, 4.4, and 4.5 show that a change in the price of X will also have an effect on the quantity demanded of the other good (Y). In Figure 4.3, for example, a decrease in the price of X causes not only the quantity demanded of X to increase, but the quantity demanded of Y to increase as well. We can explain this result by looking at the substitution and income effects on the demand for Y associated with the decrease in the price of X.

---

[3] Algebra shows why this is true. With the sales tax (where the tax rate is given by t) the individual's budget constraint is

$$I = I' = (P_X + t) X_1 + P_Y Y_1.$$

Total tax revenues are given by

$$T = tX_1.$$

With an income tax that collected the same revenue, after-tax income is

$$I'' = I - T = P_X X_1 + P_Y Y_1,$$

which shows that I″ passes through the point X_1, Y_1 also.

[4] These ideas are pursued a bit further in Chapters 6 and 13, which show how the welfare costs of taxes might be measured.

APPLICATION 4.4
The Lump-Sum Principle in Practice

The lump-sum principle provides a convenient base case that can be used to evaluate a variety of real-world schemes for taxing and transferring income. All taxes reduce purchasing power and utility, and all transfers increase purchasing power and utility. Utility losses from taxes are smallest when taxes are taken as a lump sum; utility gains from transfers are greatest when transfers are provided in a lump-sum way. Of course, actual tax or transfer programs will probably depart from pure lump-sum principles, thereby creating some utility shortfalls.

Tax Policy Applications

The most commonly proposed real-world approximation to a lump-sum tax is a general tax on income. Because such a tax affects a person's after-tax wage, however, it is not really a lump sum reduction in purchasing power. Rather, as we discuss in more detail in Chapter 20, a tax on income affects an individual's decision about how much to work and perhaps other decisions as well, such as whether or not to seek out tax-avoiding strategies. An income tax, especially one with high marginal rates, may, therefore, involve significant utility costs. For example, in an important 1981 study, J. Hausman found that the average taxpayer lost about 22 percent more utility under the then existing U.S. progressive income tax than he would have lost by paying lump-sum taxes of an equal magnitude.[1] Movement toward a more simplified rate structure during the 1980s (see Application 2.2) probably has reduced these costs to a modest extent.

Transfer Policy Applications

The argument presented in the text for positive taxes applies to negative taxes (that is, income subsidies) as well. A general income subsidy is a cheaper way of raising utility than is the provision of a good at below-market prices. For example, in T. Smeeding's 1977 report on the antipoverty effects of various transfer programs, it was shown that $1 of existing subsidies for food, housing, and medical care was worth considerably less than $1 in cash to the individuals who received the subsidies.[2] Specifically, the author found that one dollar of food subsidies was worth about 88 cents; $1 of housing subsidies about 56 cents; and $1 of medical care subsidies about 68 cents. The author, therefore, concluded that the ability of such programs to increase the overall well-being of poor people was considerably lessened by providing subsidies for specific goods rather than cash. Overall, the fraction of total assistance provided in cash declined substantially during the 1980s, whereas the fraction provided through food and medical care subsidies rose rapidly. Hence, transfer programs' effectiveness in increasing utility has probably declined over time.[3]

To Think About

1. What kinds of taxes seem to come closest to the lump-sum principle? That is, which taxes seem to least distort the economic choices people make? Should we make more use of such taxes? Or are there good reasons to have some taxes (for example, taxes on cigarettes) that do distort people's choices?

2. If direct income grants are more effective in raising people's utility than subsidies on particular goods, why does the government operate so many subsidy programs (that is, food, housing, medical care, legal services, and education subsidies, to name just a few)? Couldn't these all be "cashed out" to provide a great deal more utility to the low income people for whom they are intended? Or, are there good reasons to retain subsidies on specific goods?

---

[1] Jerry A. Hausman, "Labor Supply," in Henry J. Aaron and Joseph H. Pechman, *How Taxes Affect Economic Behavior* (Washington, D.C.: Brookings Institution, 1981): 54.
[2] Timothy M. Smeeding, "The Antipoverty Effectiveness of In-Kind Transfers," *Journal of Human Resources* 12, no. 3 (Summer 1977): 365.

[3] This statement disregards possible effects of cash benefits on the labor market choices of the poor. For a discussion, see R. Moffitt, "Incentive Effects of the U.S. Welfare System: A Review," *Journal of Economic Literature* (March 1992): 1–61.

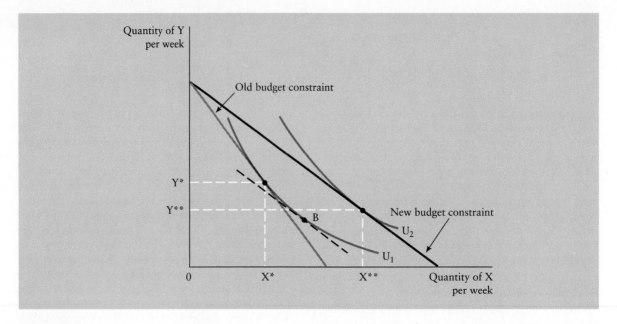

Figure 4.7
Effect on the
Demand for Good Y
of a Decrease in the
Price of Good X

In contrast to Figure 4.3, the quantity demanded of Y now declines (from Y* to Y**) in response to a decrease in the price of X. The relatively flat indifference curves cause the substitution effect to be very large. Moving from X*, Y* to point B means giving up a substantial quantity of Y for additional X. This effect more than outweighs the positive income effect (from B to X**, Y**), and the quantity demanded of Y declines. So, purchases of Y may either rise or fall when the price of X falls.

First, as we see in Figure 4.3, the substitution effect caused less Y to be demanded. In moving along the indifference curve U_1 from X*, Y* to point B, X is substituted for Y because the lower ratio of P_X/P_Y required an adjustment in the MRS. In this figure the income effect of the decline in the price of good X is strong enough to reverse this result. Because Y is a normal good, and real income has increased, more Y is demanded: the individual moves from point B to X**, Y**. Here Y** exceeds Y*, and the total effect of the price change is to increase the demand for Y.

A slightly different set of indifference curves (that is, different preferences) could have shown different results. Figure 4.7 shows a relatively flat set of indifference curves where the substitution effect from a decline in the price of X is very large. In moving from X*, Y* to point B, a large amount of X is substituted for Y. The income effect on Y is not strong enough to reverse this large substitution effect. In this case the quantity of Y finally chosen (Y**) is smaller than the original amount. The effect of a decline in the price of one good has on the quantity demanded of some other good is ambiguous; it all depends on what the person's preferences, as reflected by his or her indifference curve map, look like. We have to examine carefully income and substitution effects that (at least in the case of only two goods) work in opposite directions.

Using our hamburger–soft drink example, we have already discussed the substitution and income effects that a fall in the price of soft drinks (from $.50 to $.25) will have on the number of soft drinks bought. What happens to the number of hamburgers chosen? The substitution effect predicts that fewer hamburgers will be purchased. Since hamburgers are now relatively more expensive than they were before soft drink prices fell, the initial level of utility can be achieved at lower cost by drinking more soft drinks and eating fewer hamburgers.

The total effect of the soft drink price decrease on hamburger purchases also depends on the income effect of the price change, however. As a result of the decrease in the price of soft drinks, the person has a higher real income and may buy more soft drinks and more hamburgers. This total effect of the price change on hamburger purchases is therefore ambiguous. The substitution effect works to decrease hamburger purchases, whereas the income effect works to increase such purchases. The final result depends on how the individual feels about the two goods.

■ Substitutes and Complements

Economists use the terms substitutes and complements to describe the way people look at the relationships between goods. Complements are goods that go together in the sense that people will increase their use of both goods simultaneously. Examples of complements might be coffee and cream, fish and chips, peanut butter and jelly, or brandy and cigars. Substitutes, on the other hand, are goods that replace one another. Tea and coffee, hamburgers and hot dogs, or wheat and corn are some goods that are substitutes for each other.

Whether two goods are substitutes or complements of each other is primarily a question of the shape of people's indifference curves. The market behavior of individuals in their purchases of goods helps to discover these relationships. Two goods are **complements** if an increase in the price of one causes a decrease in the quantity consumed of the other. For example, an increase in the price of coffee might cause not only the quantity demanded of coffee to decline, but also the demand for cream to decrease because of the complementary relationship between cream and coffee. Similarly, coffee and tea are **substitutes** because an increase in the price of coffee might cause the quantity demanded of tea to increase, as tea replaces coffee in use.

How the demand for one good relates to the price increase of another good is a result of both income and substitution effects. It is only the combined gross result of these two effects that we can observe. Including both income and substitution effects of price changes in our definitions of substitutes and complements can sometimes lead to problems, however. For example, it is theoretically possible for X to be a complement for Y and at the same time for Y to be a substitute for X. This perplexing state of affairs has led some economists

■
Complements
Two goods such that when the price of one increases, the quantity demanded of the other falls.

■
Substitutes
Two goods such that if the price of one increases, the quantity demanded of the other rises.

APPLICATION 4.5

Gas Prices and Automobiles

Gasoline and automobiles provide an important example of complementary goods. Over the past twenty years, there have been periods of both rapidly rising and rapidly falling gasoline prices. These trends have significantly influenced the demand for automobiles, and, perhaps more important, variations in the kinds of cars purchased.

Empirical Studies

In order to examine the influence of gasoline prices on individuals' decisions, it is important to choose a time frame for the analysis. Over the short term, changes in gasoline prices may have relatively little impact. People own particular types of cars and are more or less locked into specific travel patterns. Primarily, people just complain about higher gas prices, or they express happiness about lower ones. Over the longer term, however, people can alter their commuter patterns (they can join ride pools, for example); they can take more or fewer vacations, and they can change the kinds of cars they own. These differing reactions are reflected in Table 1, which shows estimated responses to a 50 percent increase in the price of gasoline in the United States. This is approximately the level of increase both in 1973–1974 and in 1979–1980. It is estimated that this price increase causes a decrease in gasoline consumption of about 15 percent over the short term. Roughly half of that adjustment was caused by a reduction in the number of miles driven. The other half came from an increase in the number of miles per gallon experienced by the total fleet of cars in the United States. The small mileage improvement probably results from better automobile maintenance and lower highway speeds rather than significantly improved mile-per-gallon ratings of the individual cars.

In the long run, older, low-mileage cars may be traded in for more fuel efficient models, in which case the mileage effect becomes substantial. Table 1 indicates that a 50 percent increase in gasoline price would cause a 24 percent increase in miles per gallon (say, from an average of 20 miles per gallon to about 25 miles per gallon) in the long term. In response to higher prices, people buy more fuel-efficient cars.

Table 1

Estimated Reaction of U.S. Consumers to a 50 Percent Rise in the Retail Price of Gasoline

Time Period	Reduction in Miles Driven	Increase in Miles per Gallon	Total Change in Consumption
Short term	−7%	+8%	−15%
Long term	−4	+24	−28

Source: Calculated from figures given in Carol A. Dahl, "Consumer Adjustment to a Gasoline Tax," *Review of Economics and Statistics* (August 1979): 427–431.

Evidence from the Automobile Market

Actual car sales provide clear support for these suggestions. In 1970 only about 18 percent of total U.S. automobile sales were of small (compact or subcompact) cars. By 1980 this figure had increased to more than 50 percent, mainly in response to the four-fold increase in gasoline prices during the period. If rapidly rising imports of Japanese automobiles are included, the shift toward small cars becomes even more dramatic. After 1980, however, gasoline prices began to stabilize and then started to fall in real terms. As a result, small car sales were curtailed as U.S. buyers shifted back toward purchasing full-size automobiles. By the early 1990s small cars had fallen to about 40 percent of all U.S. car sales. Even former small-car makers such as Toyota and Nissan began exporting large, luxury cars such as the Lexus and the Infinity to eager American buyers.

To Think About

1. During the 1970s, the federal government implemented "corporate fuel economy standards" that U.S. automakers were required to meet; the standards were subsequently raised every few years. Can you think of any reasons why the government should require people to buy more fuel-efficient cars than they themselves would choose to buy?

2. For individuals who own many durable goods that use a lot of electricity, such as refrigerators and air conditioners, how would you expect rising electricity prices to affect their demands for these products?

to favor a definition of substitutes and complements that looks only at the direction of substitution effects.[5] We do not make that distinction in this book. In Application 4.5: Gas Prices and Automobiles, we take a brief look at some of the complex relationships between gas prices and the cars people drive.

Construction of Individual Demand Curves

We have now completed our discussion of how the individual's demand for good X is affected by various changes in economic circumstances. We started by writing the demand function for good X as

$$\text{Quantity of X demanded} = d_X(P_X, P_Y, I; \text{preferences}).$$

Then we examined how changes in each of the economic factors P_X, P_Y, and I might affect an individual's decision to purchase good X. The principle purpose of this examination has been to permit us to derive individual demand curves and to analyze those factors that might cause a demand curve to shift its position. This section shows how a demand curve can be constructed. The next section analyzes why this curve might shift.

An **individual demand curve** shows the *ceteris paribus* relationship between the quantity demanded of a good (say, X) and its price (P_X). Not only are preferences held constant under the *ceteris paribus* assumption (as they have been throughout our discussion in this chapter), but the other economic factors in the demand function (that is, the price of good Y and income) are also held constant. In demand curves we are limiting our study to only the relationship between the quantity of a good chosen and changes in its own price.

Figure 4.8 shows how we can construct a person's demand curve for good X. In Panel a the individual's indifference curve map is drawn using three different budget constraints in which the price of X decreases. These decreasing prices are P'_X, P''_X, and P'''_X. The other economic factors that affect the position of the budget constraint (the price of good Y and income) do not change. In graphic terms, all three constraints have the same Y-intercept. The successively lower prices of X rotate this constraint outward. Given the three separate budget constraints, the individual's utility-maximizing choices of X are given by X', X", and X'''. These three choices show that the quantity demanded of X increases as the price of X falls.

The information in Panel a in Figure 4.8 can be used to construct the demand curve shown in Panel b. The price of X is shown on the vertical axis, and the quantity chosen continues to be shown on the horizontal axis. The demand curve (d_X) is downward sloping, showing that when the price of X falls, the

■

Individual demand curve

A graphic representation of the relationship between the price of a good and the quantity of it demanded by a person, holding all other factors constant.

---

[5] For a slightly more extended treatment of this subject, see Walter Nicholson, *Microeconomic Theory: Basic Principles and Extensions*, 5th ed. (Fort Worth, TX: The Dryden Press, 1992), pp. 170–174. For a complete treatment, see J. R. Hicks, *Value and Capital* (London: Cambridge University Press, 1939), Chapter 3 and the mathematical appendix.

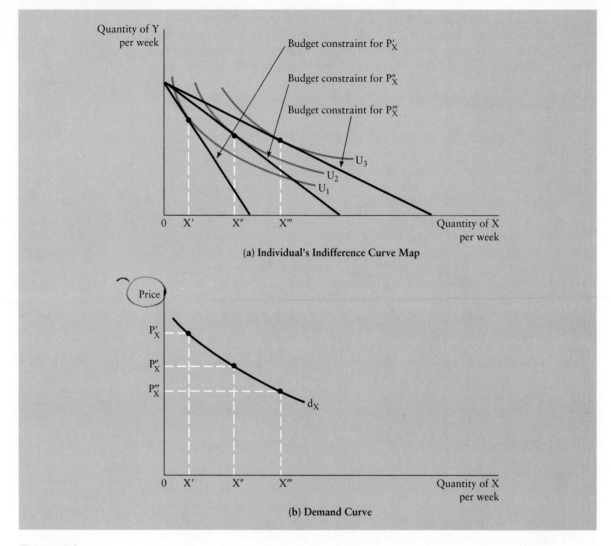

Figure 4.8
Construction of
an Individual's
Demand Curve

In Panel a the individual's utility-maximizing choices of X and Y are shown for three successively lower prices of X. In Panel b this relationship between P_X and X is used to construct the demand curve for X. The demand curve is drawn on the assumption that the price of Y and money income remain constant as the price of X varies.

quantity demanded of X increases. As we have shown, this increase represents both the substitution and income effects of the price decline.

■ Shape of the Demand Curve

The precise shape of the demand curve is determined by the income and substitution effects that occur when the price of X changes. An individual's demand curve may be either rather flat or quite steeply sloped, depending on the nature of his or her indifference curve map. If X has many close substitutes, the indifference curves will be nearly straight lines (such as those shown in Figure 4.7), and the substitution effect from a price change will be very large. The quantity of X chosen may fall substantially in response to a rise in its price; consequently the demand curve will be relatively flat. For example, consider a person's demand for one particular brand of cereal (say, the famous Brand X). Because any one brand has many close substitutes, the demand curve for Brand X will be relatively flat. A rise in the price of Brand X will cause people to shift easily to other kinds of cereal, and the quantity demanded of Brand X will be reduced significantly.

On the other hand, the individual's demand curve for some goods may be steeply sloped. That is, price changes will not affect consumption very much. This might be the case if the good has no close substitutes. For example, consider a person's demand for water. Because water satisfies many unique needs, it is unlikely that it would have any substitutes when the price of water rose, and the substitution effect would be very small. However, since water does not use up a large portion of a person's total income, the income effect of the increase in the price of water would also not be large. The quantity demanded of water probably would not respond greatly to changes in its price; that is, the demand curve would be nearly vertical.

As a third possibility, consider the case of food. Because food as a whole has no substitutes (although individual food items obviously do), an increase in the price of food will not induce important substitution effects. In this sense, food is similar to our water example. However, food is a major item in a person's total expenditures, and an increase in its price will have a significant effect on purchasing power. It is possible, therefore, that the quantity demanded of food may be reduced substantially in response to a rise in food prices because of this income effect. The demand curve for food might be flatter (that is, demand reacts more to price) than we might expect if we thought of food only as a "necessity" with few, if any, substitutes.[6]

Shifts in an Individual's Demand Curve

The individual's demand curve summarizes the *ceteris paribus* relationship between the price of X and the quantity demanded of X. The income and substitution effects of changes in that price cause the person to move along his or her demand curve. If one of the factors (the price of Y, income, or preferences) that we have so far been holding constant were to change, the entire curve would shift. The demand curve remains fixed only while the *ceteris paribus* assumption is in effect. Figure 4.9 shows the kinds of shifts that might take place. In

---

[6] For this reason sometimes it is convenient to talk about demand curves that reflect only substitution effects. These compensated demand curves are constructed on the assumption that any effect of a price change on the individual's purchasing power is automatically compensated for. Hence, real income rather than nominal income is being held constant. In Chapter 6 we will briefly examine this concept.

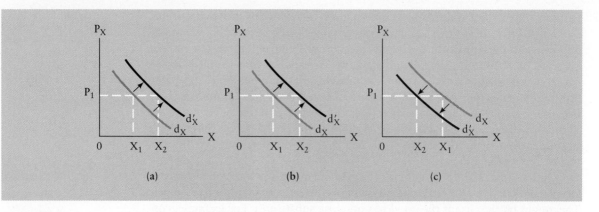

Figure 4.9
Shifts in an
Individual's
Demand Curve

In Panel a the demand curve shifts outward because the individual's income has increased. More X is now demanded at each price. In Panel b the demand curve shifts
outward because the price of Y has increased, and X and Y are substitutes for the individual. In Panel c the demand curve shifts inward because of the increase in the price of
Y: that is, X and Y are complements.

Panel a the effect on good X of an increase in income is shown. Assuming that
good X is a normal good, an increase in income causes more X to be demanded at each price. At P_1, for example, the quantity of X demanded rises
from X_1 to X_2. This is the kind of effect we described early in this chapter
(Figure 4.1). When income increases, people buy more X even if its price has
not changed, and the demand curve shifts outward. Panels b and c in Figure 4.9 record two possible effects that an increase in the price of Y might have
on the demand curve for good X. In Panel b, X and Y are assumed to be substitutes—for example, coffee (X) and tea (Y). An increase in the price of tea
causes the individual to substitute coffee for tea. More coffee (that is, good X)
is demanded at each price than was previously the case. At P_1, for example,
coffee demand increases from X_1 to X_2.

On the other hand, suppose X and Y are complements—for example, coffee (X) and cream (Y). An increase in the price of cream causes the demand
curve for coffee to shift inward. Because coffee and cream go together, less coffee (that is, good X) will now be demanded at each price. This shift in the demand curve is shown in Panel c—at P_1, coffee demand falls from X_1 to X_2.

Changes in preferences might also cause the demand curve to shift. For
example, a sudden warm spell would undoubtedly shift the entire demand
curve for soft drinks outward. More drinks would be demanded at each price
because now the individual's desire for them has increased. Similarly, increased
environmental consciousness during the 1980s and 1990s vastly increased the
demand for items such as recycling containers and reusable packaging.
Application 4.6: Fads, Seasons, and Health Scares explores a few other reasons
why demand curves might shift.

APPLICATION 4.6
Fads, Seasons, and Health Scares

The theoretical notion that changes in preferences can influence the demand for products incorporates a wide variety of possible cultural and psychological influences. Let's look at a few.

Fads
Products such as Hula Hoops, Cabbage Patch Dolls, Rubik's Cubes, and Super Mario Brothers games all experienced extremely rapid growth in demand when they were initially introduced, followed by an equally rapid loss of interest by consumers. The widespread use of a product among consumers actually generates additional demand until a saturation point is reached. Then, demand falls precipitously. Such temporary bursts of demand (sometimes termed *bandwagon effects*) arise because of the interdependence among individual's preferences—everyone wants to be part of the latest craze. This recurring pattern in the product fad's purchasing illustrates that there is a rather stable demand for such products. Predicting exactly what will catch on is a mystery, however.

Seasonality
Seasonal goods are the polar opposites of fad products when it comes to predictability. Everyone knows that the demand for wedding cakes increases in June, that turkeys are mostly consumed at Thanksgiving, and that Christmas trees are bought in December. Seasonality also affects the demand for less familiar items. A famous study of New England fishing, for example, found that the demand for scrod (New Englandese for small cod) regularly increased by about 13 percent during Lent because of the dietary restrictions imposed during this period by the Catholic Church upon its members.[1] Flounder and haddock also experienced similar increases in demand during this time of the year. All of these seasonal patterns show that preferences are formed through a variety of long-term historical and cultural influences. This is one reason why economists tend to treat them as being stable over short periods.

Health Scares
Some of the more rapid shifts in demand in recent years have been associated with changing perceptions by consumers about the health risks associated with various products. Concern about the risks of smoking, for example, has resulted in a long-term reduction in the number of smokers in the United States since the Surgeon General's report on the subject was released in 1964 (see Application 17.4). Concern about cholesterol has led to similar long-term declines in individuals' demands for beef, eggs, and dairy products.

Health concerns have also had dramatic short-term effects on demand. A 1982 incident in Chicago in which cyanide tablets were inserted into a few Tylenol bottles reduced the demand for that product by more than 50 percent. Finding two cyanide-injected grapes in 1988 caused the demand for Chilean fruits to drop dramatically. Other short-term effects occur when new studies published practically weekly purport to show that certain products cause cancer. This often creates an immediate drop in the demand of these products, until, at least, the next contradicting studies are published.

People's concerns about their health have also spurred demand for other products. One example was the oat bran craze of the late 1980s. Following preliminary evidence that oat bran might help individuals control their cholesterol levels, bakeries everywhere began producing oat bran muffins. Even sales of Cheerios (where "Os" stand for oats) rose dramatically for a period of time. Ultimately, however, the scientific case for eating oat bran became somewhat less compelling, and demand leveled off.

To Think About
1. Does demand predictability affect the profits firms might earn on a product? Why might turkeys or Christmas trees yield relatively small profits, whereas fad products often are quite profitable? (See Part 4 for a further analysis.)
2. Do you think people often overreact to health scares? Are there any cases of underreactions you can think of? How would you differentiate between the types of risks in these two situations?

---

[1] F. W. Bell, "The Pope and the Price of Fish," *American Economic Review* (December 1968): 346–350.

■   Be Careful in Using Terminology

It is important that we keep the distinction between the shift in a demand curve and movement along a stationary demand curve clearly in mind. Changes in the price of X lead to movements along the demand curve for good X. Changes in other economic factors (such as a change in income, a change in another good's price, or a change in preferences) cause the entire demand curve for X to shift. If we wished to see how a change in the price of steak would affect a person's steak purchases, we would use a single demand curve and study movements along it. On the other hand, if we wanted to know how a change in income would affect the quantity of steak purchased, we would have to study the shift in the position of the entire demand curve.

To keep these matters straight, economists must speak carefully. The movement downward along a stationary demand curve in response to a fall in price is called an **increase in quantity demanded**. A shift outward in the entire curve is an **increase in demand**. A rise in the price of a good causes a **decrease in quantity demanded** (a move along the demand curve), whereas a change in some other factor may cause a **decrease in demand** (a shift of the entire curve to the left). It is important to be precise in using those terms; they are not interchangeable.

■
Increase or decrease in quantity demanded

The increase or decrease in quantity demanded caused by a change in the good's price. Graphically represented by the movement along a demand curve.

■
Increase or decrease in demand

The change in demand for a good caused by changes in the price of another good, income, or preferences. Graphically represented by a shift of the entire demand curve.

Summary

This chapter uses the model of individual choice to examine how people react to changes in income or prices. We have come to five major conclusions about the factors that affect the demand for a good:

- Proportionate changes in all prices and income will not affect choices because such changes do not shift the budget constraint.

- When income alone increases, the demand for a good will increase unless that good is inferior.

- A change in the price of a good has substitution and income effects that together cause changes in consumption choices. Except in the unlikely case of Giffen's paradox, a reduction in a good's price will cause more of it to be demanded. An increase in price will cause less of the good to be demanded.

- A change in the price of one good will usually affect the demand for other goods. If two goods are complements, an increase in the price of one will reduce the demand for the other. If the goods are substitutes, an increase in the price of one will increase the demand for the other.

- The demand for a good is also affected by preferences. Preferences are usually held constant under the *ceteris paribus* assumption in theoretical analysis, but changes in preferences can cause important shifts in real-world demand curves.

Probably the most important tool developed in this chapter is the individual's demand curve, which shows the relationship between the quantity demanded of a product and its price (when all other influences are held constant). Demand curves are usually drawn downward sloping. They shift if one of the factors held constant (income, other prices, preferences) changes. In Chapter 5 we show how individual demand curves can be combined to come up with the market demand curve, which helps to determine market prices.

Review Questions

1. Explain why the homogeneity of demand functions requires that the demand for a good remain unchanged if all prices *and* income were to double. What would happen to the budget constraint if all prices doubled but income did not? Suppose income doubled but prices remained unchanged?

2. Suppose an individual consumes only two goods, X and Y, and that the prices of these goods are fixed. How would the set of utility-maximizing points traced out by successively higher incomes look if

   a. the individual always split his or her income equally between X and Y?
   b. X were a luxury, Y a necessity?
   c. Y were a luxury, X a necessity?
   d. an unchanging amount of X were bought as income expanded above some minimal amount?
   e. X were an inferior good? (Can Y be inferior here too?)

3. Suppose an individual always spends half his or her income on food. How will changes in the price of food affect the quantity of food consumed? How will changes in the price of food affect total spending on food? How large an increase in income would be needed to offset the effect of a 10 percent increase in the price of food?

4. An individual always buys left and right shoes in pairs. Explain why a sale on right shoes will have an income effect but no substitution effect on his or her left and right shoe purchases.

5. Suppose an individual doesn't care what brand of toothpaste he or she buys. Show graphically why he or she will always buy the cheapest brand.

6. Is the following statement true or false? Explain.
   "Every Giffen good must be inferior, but not every inferior good exhibits the Giffen paradox."

7. Suppose that an individual never changes the quantity of water he or she consumes when the price of water changes. How would you illustrate this situation

with a graph? Does this imply water is an inferior good? How do income and substitution effects work in this case?

8. When coffee prices rise, an individual buys more tea but fewer coffee mugs. Explain the substitution and income effects of the price change on these two goods.

9. Does the theory of consumer choice require that an individual's demand curve for a good be downward sloping? In what case would a demand curve be vertical? When might it be positively sloped?

10. Explain whether the following events would result in a move along an individual's demand curve for popcorn or in a shift of the curve. If the curve would shift, in what direction?

    a. An increase in the individual's income.
    b. A decline in popcorn prices.
    c. An increase in prices for pretzels.
    d. A reduction in the amount of butter included in a box of popcorn.
    e. The presence of long waiting lines to buy popcorn.
    f. A sales tax on all popcorn purchases.

Problems

4.1   Ms. Boring maximizes her utility by spending her entire income on goods A, B, and C (whose prices stay constant in this problem). Ms. Boring makes $300 per week and purchases 10 units of good A, 10 units of good B, and 10 units of good C. When Ms. Boring's income rises to $400 per week, she buys 9 units of good A, 17 units of good B, and 14 units of good C. Finally, Ms. Boring gets another pay increase to $500 per week and purchases 8 units of good A, 26 units of good B, and 16 units of good C.

    a. Using the above information, graph the relationship between income and purchases of goods A, B, and C.
    b. Explain the nature of each good: is it normal or inferior? A luxury or necessity?

4.2   Elizabeth M. Suburbs makes $200 a week at her summer job and spends her entire weekly income on new sweaters and designer jeans since these are the only two items that provide utility to her. Furthermore, Elizabeth insists that for every sweater she buys, she must also buy a pair of jeans (without the jeans, the new sweater is worthless). Therefore, she buys the same number of sweaters and jeans in any given week.

    a. If jeans cost $20 and sweaters cost $20, how many will Elizabeth buy of each?
    b. Suppose that the price of jeans rises to $30 a pair. How many sweaters and jeans will she buy?
    c. Show your results by graphing the budget constraints from parts a and b.

Also draw Elizabeth's indifference curves and show her utility maximizing choices.

d. To what effect (income or substitution) do you attribute the change in amounts purchased between parts a and b?

4.3   Mr. Wright, a clothing salesman, is forced by his employer to spend at least $50 of his weekly income of $200 on clothing. Show that his utility level is lower than if he could freely allocate his income between clothing and other goods.

4.4   Pete Moss buys 100 units of fertilizer and 80 units of grass seed along with quantities of other goods. The price of fertilizer rises by $.40 per unit, and the price of grass seed drops by $.50 per unit; other prices and Pete's income remain unchanged. Will Pete buy more, less, or the same amount of fertilizer? Explain. (Hint: How do the price changes affect Pete's budget constraint?)

4.5   If a person consumes only two goods, potatoes and automobiles, and potatoes exhibit Giffen's paradox, how does an increase in the price of potatoes affect the quantity of automobiles purchased? What happens to total spending on each of the two goods?

4.6   Show that if there are only two goods (X and Y) to choose from, whether they are substitutes or complements will depend on whether the substitution or income effect is larger. Illustrate each case with a carefully drawn graph.

*4.7   David N. gets $3 per month as an allowance to spend any way he pleases. Since he only likes peanut butter and jelly sandwiches, he spends the entire amount on peanut butter (at $.05 per ounce) and jelly (at $.10 per ounce). Bread is provided free of charge by a concerned neighbor. David is a particular eater and makes his sandwiches with exactly 1 oz. of jelly and 2 oz. of peanut butter. He is set in his ways and will never change these proportions.

a. How much peanut butter and jelly will David buy with his $3 allowance in a week?

b. Suppose the price of jelly were to rise to $.15 per ounce. How much of each commodity would be bought?

c. By how much should David's allowance be increased to compensate for the rise in the price of jelly in part b?

d. Graph your results of parts a through c.

e. In what sense does this problem only involve a single commodity, peanut butter and jelly sandwiches? Graph the demand curve for this single commodity.

f. Discuss the results of this problem in terms of the income and substitution effects involved in the demand for jelly.

4.8   As in Application 4.3, suppose the government imposes an excise tax on gasoline and rebates all proceeds to taxpayers.

a. Show that the size of the average tax rebate will generally not be large enough to permit the average consumer to return to his or her pretax utility level.

---

*Denotes a problem that is rather difficult.

b. Show that if gasoline and other goods are used in fixed proportion (that is, that there are no substitutes for gasoline), the tax rebate is just sufficient to return to the original equilibrium.

*4.9 Each year Sam Mellow grows 200 units of wheat and 100 units of sunflower seeds for his own consumption and for sale to the outside world. Wheat and sunflower seeds are the only two items that provide utility to Sam. They are also his only source of income. Sam cannot save his proceeds from year to year.

a. If the price of wheat is $2 per unit and sunflower seeds sell for $10 per unit, Sam chooses to sell 20 units of the sunflower seeds he produces while retaining 80 units for his own use. Show Sam's utility-maximizing situation and indicate both his initial production levels and the amount of additional wheat he will buy with the proceeds from his sunflower seed sales.

b. Suppose sunflower seed prices fall to $6 per unit while wheat prices remain unchanged. Will Sam be made better- or worse-off by this price decline? Or is the situation ambiguous? Explain carefully using a graphic analysis. Show that if Sam is to be made better-off by the price decline, he must become a seller of wheat and a buyer of sunflower seeds.

c. Explain using the terms "income effect" and "substitution effect" why the analysis in part b differs from the usual case in which a price decline always increases an individual's utility level.

Hint: To start this problem show that Sam's budget constraint always passes through the point Wheat = 200, Sunflower seeds = 100.

*4.10 The Jones family spends all its income on food and shelter. It derives maximum utility when it spends 2/3 of its income on shelter and 1/3 on food.

a. Use this information to calculate the demand functions for shelter and food. Show that these are homogeneous in all prices and incomes.

b. Graph the demand curves for shelter and food for the Jones family if their family income is $12,000.

c. Show how the demand curves for shelter and food would shift if income rose to $15,000.

d. Explain why a change in food prices does not affect shelter purchases in this problem.

*Denotes a problem that is rather difficult.

Chapter 4 demonstrated how an individual's demand curve for a good can be constructed using his or her indifference curve map. This demand curve generally will be downward sloping, and the curve will shift when factors such as income and other prices change. Chapter 5 describes how individual demand curves are "added up" to create the market demand curve for a good. Market demand curves reflect the actions of many people and show how these actions are affected by market price.

We also will define a few ways of measuring market demand. We introduce the concept of elasticity and show how we can use it to record the extent to which the quantity demanded of a good changes in response to changes in income and prices. The final section of the chapter reviews some empirical evidence relating to real-world demand curves. We show how this evidence can be used to predict changes in people's decisions when economic circumstances change.

CHAPTER
5

MARKET
DEMAND AND
ELASTICITY

Market Demand Curves

The **market demand** for a good is the total quantity of the good demanded by all potential buyers. The **market demand curve** shows the relationship between this total quantity demanded and the market price of the good, when all other factors are held constant. The market demand curve's shape and position are determined by the shape of individuals' demand curves for the product in question. Market demand is nothing more than the combined effect of many people's economic choices.

■ Construction of the Market Demand Curve

Figure 5.1 shows the construction of the market demand curve for good X when there are only two buyers. For each price, the point on the market demand curve is found by summing the quantities demanded by each individual. For example, at a price of P_x^*, individual 1 demands X_1^*, and individual 2 demands X_2^*. The total quantity demanded at the market at P_x^* is therefore the sum of these two amounts: $X^* = X_1^* + X_2^*$. Consequently the point X^*, P_x^* is one point on the market demand curve D. The other points on the curve are plotted in the same way. The market curve is simply the horizontal sum of each individual's demand curve. At every possible price, we ask how much is demanded by each person, and then we add up these amounts to arrive at the quantity demanded by the whole market. The demand curve summarizes

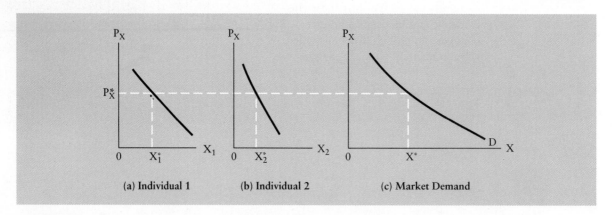

(a) Individual 1   (b) Individual 2   (c) Market Demand

Figure 5.1

Constructing a Market Demand Curve from Individual Demand Curves

A market demand curve is the horizontal sum of individual demand curves. At each price the quantity demanded in the market is the sum of the amounts each person demands. For example, at P_x^* the demand in the market is $X_1^* + X_2^* = X^*$.

the *ceteris paribus* relationship between the quantity demanded of X and its price. If other factors do not change, the position of the curve will remain fixed and will reflect how people as a group respond to price changes.

■ Shifts in the Market Demand Curve

Why would a market demand curve shift? We already know why individual demand curves shift. To discover how some event might shift a market demand curve, we must first find out how this event causes individual demand curves to shift and then compare the sum of these new demand curves with the old market demand. In some cases the direction of a shift in the market demand curve is reasonably predictable. For example, using our two-buyer case, if both of their incomes increase and both regard X as a normal good, then each person's demand curve would shift outward. Hence, the market demand curve would also shift outward. At each price more would be demanded in the market because each person could afford to buy more. This situation in which a general rise in income increases market demand is illustrated in Figure 5.2. Application 5.1: Consumption and Income Taxes shows how this notion can be used to study the effects of tax cuts although, as is often the case in economics, the story is not quite as simple as it appears to be.

In some cases the direction that a market demand curve shifts may be ambiguous. For example, suppose that one person's income increases but a second person's income decreases. The location of the new market demand curve now depends on the relative shifts in the individual demand curves that these

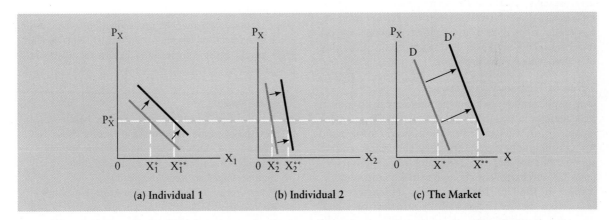

(a) Individual 1   (b) Individual 2   (c) The Market

An increase in income for each individual causes the individual demand curve for X to shift out (assuming X is a normal good). For example, at P_X^*, individual 1 now demands X_1^{**} instead of X_1^*. The market demand curve shifts out to D'. X* was demanded at P_X^* before the income increase. Now X^{**} (= $X_1^{**} + X_2^{**}$) is demanded.

Figure 5.2
Increases in Each Individual's Income Cause the Market Demand Curve to Shift Outward

APPLICATION 5.1

Consumption and Income Taxes

Individuals' ability to use their incomes to purchase goods is obviously affected by the taxes they must pay. Because of the income tax withholding system that applies to practically all earnings, workers never see their entire gross pay, but instead receive a net, after-tax amount. Hence, it seems clear that after-tax (disposable) income is the figure that is most relevant to consumer decisions. In this application, we will examine that relationship and show that the connection between taxes and consumption may be more complicated than first appears to be the case.

The Permanent-Income Hypothesis

In the 1950s, Milton Friedman was one of the first economists to recognize that a person's consumption decisions are not based simply on his or her current income.[1] Rather, Friedman argued, such decisions are based on a long-term view of a person's purchasing power. Temporary increases or decreases in income have little effect on consumer spending, which is determined by only slowly changing habits. Instead, temporary income fluctuations will be reflected in increases or decreases in savings. Friedman's notion, then, is that the individual's demand (and therefore the market demand) for goods is based on a long-term, permanent concept of income. This concept is used in practically all studies of actual consumption decisions.

Effects of Temporary Tax Changes

One implication of the permanent-income hypothesis is that changes in taxes that are only temporary, say, for only one year, will have little or no effect on the demand for consumption goods. The available data tend to support this presumption. For example, a temporary income tax surcharge was imposed by the Nixon administration in 1968 to 1969 but most researchers have found that the tax had practically no effect on actual consumer spending. Similarly, in mid-1975 during the Ford administration, a temporary rebate of 1974 taxes

was enacted, also having no apparent effect on purchases of goods and services.

The Reagan Tax Cuts

President Reagan entered office with the expressed intention of cutting income taxes. By August 1981, one of the largest tax reductions in history became law. These tax cuts were to be permanent. But the Reagan tax cuts were phased-in over a three-year period and were not to become fully effective until 1984. Some economists have argued that the Reagan tax program should be regarded as a permanent cut in income taxes in 1981 even though it was accompanied by a series of temporary tax surcharges in 1981, 1982, and 1983. In this view, then, Friedman's permanent income hypothesis would predict a big increase in consumer spending in 1981 because people would only respond to the permanent reductions the Reagan plan promised.

Unfortunately for economic theory, things don't seem to have worked out that way. Several statistical studies of the Reagan tax cuts have concluded that the permanent cuts had virtually no effect until they were fully implemented in 1984.[2] It seems that people were skeptical about whether the rate reductions would really come into effect, or whether the President and the Congress would reverse themselves before they were fully phased-in.

To Think About

1. If consumers' spending decisions are based on a long-term notion of permanent income, how do they cope with short-term fluctuations in their incomes? Aren't they constrained by their actual incomes in what they can spend?
2. What types of spending decisions do you think are based on long-term income prospects? Which types probably respond to short-term income fluctuations?

---

[1] Milton Friedman, *A Theory of the Consumption Function* (Princeton, N.J.: Princeton University Press, 1957).

[2] See, for example, A. S. Blinder and A. Deaton, "The Time Series Consumption Function Revisited," *Brookings Papers on Economic Activity*, no. 2 (1985):465–511.

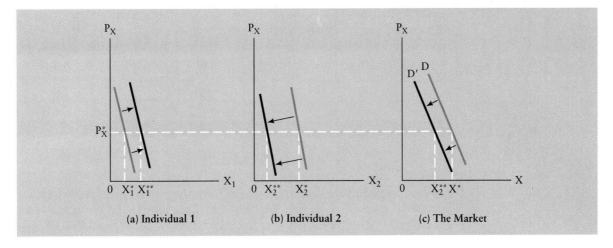

(a) Individual 1   (b) Individual 2   (c) The Market

Individual 1's income has increased, but individual 2's has decreased. The net result of these changes is to shift the market demand curve inward to D'.

Figure 5.3
Effect of Income
Changes Depends
on Their Distribution

income changes cause. Figure 5.3 shows the market demand curve shifting to a different position because of different income changes for our two buyers. Individual 2's demand curve shifts inward more than individual 1's shifts outward. The net result of these shifts is to shift the market demand curve inward to D'.

What holds true for our simple two-person example also applies to much larger groups of demanders—perhaps even to the entire economy. In this case, the market demand summarizes the behavior of all possible consumers. If personal income in the United States as a whole were to rise, the effect on the market demand curve for pizza would depend greatly on whether the income gains went to people who love pizza or to people who never touch it. If the gains went to pizza lovers, the U.S. market demand for pizza would shift outward significantly. It would change little if the income gains went to pizza haters.

A change in the price of some other good (Y) will also affect the market demand for X. If the price of Y rises, for example, the market demand curve for X will shift outward if most buyers regard X and Y as substitutes. On the other hand, an increase in the price of Y will cause the market demand curve for X to shift inward if most people regard the two goods as complements.

■ A Word on Notation and Terms

Often in this book we will be looking at only one market. In order to simplify the notation, we use the letter Q for the quantity of a good demanded (per week) in this market, and we use P for its price. When we draw a demand curve in the Q, P plane, we will assume that all other factors affecting demand are held constant. This is, income, the price of other goods, and preferences are assumed not to change. If one of these factors should change, the demand curve would probably shift. As was the case for individual demand curves, the term "change in quantity demanded" is used for a movement along a given market demand curve, and the term "change in demand" is used for a shift in the entire curve.

Elasticity

Economists frequently need to show how changes in one variable, say, A, affect some other variable, say, B. They ask, for example, how much does a change in the price of electricity affect the quantity of it demanded, or how does a change in income affect total expenditures on automobiles? One problem in determining these kinds of effects is that economic goods are measured in different units. For example, steak is typically sold per pound, whereas oranges are sold per dozen. A $.10 per pound rise in the price of steak might cause consumption of it to fall by two pounds per week, and a $.10 per dozen rise in the price of oranges might cause orange purchases to fall by one-half dozen per week. When two goods are measured in different units, we cannot make a simple comparison between them to determine which item is more responsive to changes in its price.

In order to make these comparisons, economists use the concept of **elasticity.** In general, the elasticity of variable B with respect to changes in variable A is defined as the percentage change in B brought about by a 1 percent change in A. Elasticity is unit-free—it compares one percentage to another, and the units disappear. In our oranges and steak example, a 1 percent rise in the price of steak might lead to a 2 percent decline in the quantity bought, whereas a 1 percent rise in the price of oranges might lead to only a 1 percent decline in the quantity bought. Steak purchases in this example are more responsive to price than orange purchases are. The fact that steak and oranges are measured in different units is no longer a problem because we can use percentage changes, which do not depend on how units of the good are measured.

Elasticity

The measure of the percentage change in one variable brought about by a 1 percent change in some other variable.

Price Elasticity of Demand

Although there are many different applications of elasticity in this book, probably the most important is the **price elasticity of demand.** Changes in P (the price of a good) will lead to changes in Q (the quantity of it purchased), and the price elasticity of demand measures this relationship. Specifically, the price elasticity of demand ($e_{Q,P}$) is defined as the percentage change in quantity in response to a 1 percent change in price. In mathematical terms,

Price elasticity of demand

The percentage change in the quantity demanded of a good in response to a 1 percent change in its price.

$$\text{Price elasticity of demand} = e_{Q,P} = \frac{\text{Percentage change in Q}}{\text{Percentage change in P}}. \quad [5.1]$$

Value of $e_{Q,P}$ at a Point on Demand Curve	Terminology for Curve at This Point	Table 5.1 Terminology for the Ranges of $e_{Q,P}$
$e_{Q,P} < -1$	Elastic	
$e_{Q,P} = -1$	Unit elastic	
$e_{Q,P} > -1$	Inelastic	

This elasticity records how Q changes in percentage terms in response to a percentage change in P. Because P and Q move in opposite directions (except in the rare case of Giffen's paradox), $e_{Q,P}$ will be negative.[1] For example, a value of $e_{Q,P}$ of -1 means that a 1 percent rise in price leads to a 1 percent decline in quantity, whereas a value of $e_{Q,P}$ of -2 means that a 1 percent rise in price causes quantity to decline by 2 percent.

■ Values of the Price Elasticity of Demand

A distinction is often made among values of $e_{Q,P}$ that are less than, equal to, or greater than -1. Table 5.1 lists the terms used for each value. For an elastic curve ($e_{Q,P}$ is less than -1), a price increase causes a more than proportional quantity decrease. If $e_{Q,P} = -3$, for example, each 1 percent rise in price causes quantity to fall by 3 percent. For a unit elastic curve ($e_{Q,P}$ is equal to -1), a price increase causes a decrease in quantity of the same proportion. For an inelastic curve ($e_{Q,P}$ is greater than -1), price increases proportionally more than quantity decreases. If $e_{Q,P} = -\frac{1}{2}$, a 1 percent rise in price causes quantity to fall by only $\frac{1}{2}$ of 1 percent. In general then, if a curve is elastic, its price affects quantity significantly; if the curve is inelastic, price has little effect on quantity demanded.

■ Price Elasticity and the Shape of the Demand Curve

We often classify the market demand for goods by their price elasticities of demand. For example, the quantity of medical services demanded is undoubtedly very inelastic. The market demand curve here may be almost vertical, showing that the quantity demanded is not responsive to price changes. On the other hand, price changes will have a greater effect on the quantity demanded of a particular kind of candy bar (the demand is elastic). Here the market demand curve would be relatively flat. If market price were to change even slightly, the quantity demanded would change significantly because people would buy other kinds of candy bars.

---

[1] Sometimes the price elasticity of demand is defined as the absolute value of the definition in Equation 5.1. Using this definition, elasticity is never negative; curves are classified as elastic, unit elastic, or inelastic depending on whether $e_{Q,P}$ is greater than, equal to, or less than 1. You need to recognize this distinction since there is no consistent use in economic literature.

■ Price Elasticity and the Substitution Effect

The discussion of income and substitution effects in Chapter 4 gives us some theoretical basis for judging what the size of the price elasticity for particular goods might be. Goods with many close substitutes (brands of breakfast cereal, small cars, brands of electronic calculators, and so on) are subject to large substitution effects from a price change. For these kinds of goods we can presume that demand will be relatively elastic ($e_{Q,P} < -1$). On the other hand, goods with few close substitutes (water, insulin, and salt, for example) have small substitution effects when their price changes. Demand for such goods will probably be inelastic with respect to price changes ($e_{Q,P} > -1$; that is, $e_{Q,P}$ is between 0 and −1). Of course, as we mentioned previously, price changes also create income effects on the quantity demanded of a good, which we must consider to completely assess the likely size of overall price elasticities. Still, because the price changes for most goods have only a small effect on individuals' real incomes, the existence (or nonexistence) of substitutes is probably the principal determinant of price elasticity.

■ Price Elasticity and Time

Making substitutions in consumption choices may take time. To change from one brand of cereal to another may only take a week (to finish eating the first box), but to change from one type of home heating fuel to another may take years since a new heating system must be installed. We already have seen in Application 4.5: Gas Prices and Automobiles how trends in gasoline prices may have little short-term impact because people already own their cars and have relatively fixed travel needs. Over a longer term, however, there is clear evidence that people will change the kinds of cars they drive in response to gasoline prices. In general then, it might be expected that substitution effects and the related price elasticities would be larger the longer the time period that people have to change their behavior. In some situations, therefore, it is important to make a distinction between short-term and long-term price elasticities of demand, since the long-term concept may show much greater responses to price change. In Application 5.2: Brand Loyalty, we look at a few cases where this distinction can be quite important.

■ Price Elasticity and Total Expenditures

The price elasticity of demand can be used to evaluate how total expenditures on a good change in response to a price change. Total expenditures on a good are found by multiplying the good's price (P) times the quantity purchased (Q). If demand is elastic, a price increase will cause total expenditures to fall. When demand is elastic, a given percentage increase in price is more than counterbalanced in its effect on total spending by the resulting large decrease in quantity demanded. For example, suppose people are currently buying 1 million automobiles at $10,000 each. Total expenditures on automobiles amount to $10 billion. Suppose also that the price elasticity of demand for automobiles is −2. Now, if the price increases to $11,000 (a 10 percent increase), the quantity

APPLICATION 5.2
Brand Loyalty

One reason that substitution effects are larger over long-term intervals than over short-term ones is because individuals develop spending habits that do not change easily. For example, when faced with a variety of brands consisting of the same basic product, individuals may develop a loyalty to a particular brand, purchasing it on a regular basis. This behavior makes sense because the individual does not need to reevaluate products on a continuous basis. Thus, decision-making costs are reduced. Brand loyalty also reduces the likelihood of brand substitutions even when there are short-term price differentials. Over the long term, however, price differences can tempt buyers into trying other brands and thereby switch their loyalties.

Automobiles

The competition between American and Japanese automakers provides a good example of changing loyalties. Prior to the 1980s, Americans exhibited considerable loyalty to U.S. automobiles. Repeat purchases of the same brand were a common pattern. Japanese automobiles originally made inroads into the American market on a price basis. The lower prices of Japanese cars eventually convinced Americans to buy them. Being satisfied with their experiences, by the 1980s, many Americans developed a loyalty to Japanese brands. This loyalty was encouraged, in part, by large differences in quality between Japanese and U.S. brands that became especially wide in the mid-1980s. Although U.S. automakers seem to have closed the quality gap in the early 1990s, lingering loyalty to Japanese autos has made it difficult to regain market share. By one estimate, U.S. cars would have to sell for approximately $1,600 less than their Japanese counterparts in order to encourage buyers of Japanese cars to switch.[1]

Wines

Although wine is produced in many areas of the world, some high-quality wines are associated with particular regions (France or California) and have few substitutes. But most modestly-priced wines, regardless of region, can be easily substituted. Brand loyalties and other factors, however, may slow the substitutions that otherwise would be made in response to differing relative prices. For example, during the period from 1985 to 1988, Australian wine sold in the United States at prices $2 to $3 per bottle less than similar U.S. wines. Eventually these price differences tempted some Americans to try Australian wines, which proved to be good substitutes for U.S. wines. Since 1987, sales of Australian wines in the United States have grown rapidly.

A similar situation, with an unusual twist, arose regarding Chilean wines. Traditionally, Chilean wines have been of good quality and have sold at prices well below comparable U.S. wines. But concern about the nature of the authoritarian government in Chile contributed to the unwillingness of some buyers to try this wine. In 1990, this negative, political attribute associated with Chilean wines ceased to be a factor as a new democratic government replaced the dicatorial government of General Pinochet. Within two years, the large price differences caused considerable substitutions in wine buyers' behavior, resulting in a market shift in purchases toward Chilean wines.

To Think About

1. Does the speed with which price differences erode brand loyalties depend on the frequency with which products are bought? Why might differences between short-term and long-term price elasticities be much greater for brands of automobiles than for brands of toothpaste?
2. How might the erosion of brand loyalties affect price differences? Can two products that are considered to be close substitutes sell at very different prices? Explain.

---

[1] F. Mannering and C. Winston, "Brand Loyalty and the Decline of American Automobile Firms," *Brookings Papers on Economic Activity, Microeconomics* (1991):67–113.

APPLICATION 5.3
The States' Take from Gambling

The gambling industry and its taxation by states provides an example of an elastic demand. Betting on horses is big business in the United States, and many states obtain substantial revenues by taxing pari-mutuel wagering. New York and other states operate off-track betting (OTB) parlors, which are also taxed. Because such *take-outs* (taxes) effectively raise the price of gambling, states must pay close attention to how increases in taxes affect the total amount bet. If the demand for gambling is very elastic with respect to the states' take, too high of a tax will divert many would-be bettors to illegal gambling where prices are lower. Also, more than thirty states currently operate lotteries. In this case, taxes are collected by awarding lottery players considerably less than the total amount bet, also raising the price to players.

Some Elasticity Estimates
A 1979 article by D. B. Suits provides some evidence of this elasticity.[1] One case that Suits examined concerned a major reduction in federal taxes in 1974 on gambling in Nevada. Following the tax reduction, bets placed in Nevada on out-of-state horse races nearly doubled. Increases in betting on sporting events were even larger. From these experiences as well as information about track wagering in other states, Suits concluded that the demand for gambling was price elastic—the price elasticity was at least −1.6 and perhaps as large as −2.

States' Experiences with This Elastic Demand
The findings that the demand for gambling is quite sensitive to the price that gamblers must pay in taxes have been reflected in states' experiences in taxing horse racing. In one study of wagering in southern California, for example, W. D. Morgan and J. D. Vasche found that the state take-out rate of nearly 16 percent in 1978 was not optimal from the state government's point of view.[2] They argued that a lower rate (about 12 percent) would have generated enough additional attendance and wagering at thoroughbred racing to raise state revenues. As for any elastic demand curve, a reduction in price would have increased total revenues.

State Lotteries
The relatively high-price elasticity of demand for gambling also affects the way states design their lotteries. For example, most states have a "3-digit numbers" game, which only offers a 500-to-1 payoff; the state takes 50¢ of every $1 bet. Some states have found that increases in the payoff rate (reduction in the state's take) not only increase total numbers played, but is also profitable for the state. Massachusetts, for example, moved to a 700-to-1 payoff in its numbers game for this reason. Studies show that "Lotto" games are subject to high elasticities of demand, also. An interesting consequence of this is that the rollover of jackpot totals, when there is no winner, essentially lowers the price of winning and generates substantial, additional play as prize amounts grow.[3] Finally, studies of "instant-winners" lottery games find that winners of small amounts usually reinvest these winnings in more tickets—a response that practically guarantees an elastic response to increases in payoff rates.

To Think About
1. Do people recognize that states tax their betting at the track or in a lottery? Isn't gambling by its very nature an irrational, emotional activity not really subject to very careful economic calculations? Is this just one more example of carrying economic analysis too far?
2. The relatively elastic demand for gambling reported here implies that there must be close substitutes for such activities. What are these substitutes? How will the demand for them respond to states' tax policies?

---

[1] D. B. Suits, "The Elasticity of Demand for Gambling," *Quarterly Journal of Economics* (February 1979):155–162.
[2] W. D. Morgan and J. D. Vasche, "Horseracing Demand, Pari-mutuel Taxation and State Revenue Potential," *National Tax Journal* (June 1979):185–194.

[3] For a discussion, see C. T. Clotfelter and P. J. Cook, "On the Economics of State Lotteries," *Journal of Economic Perspectives* (Fall 1990):105–119.

If Demand Is	In Response to an Increase in Price, PQ Will → total $ spent	In Response to a Decrease in Price, PQ Will	Table 5.2 Relationship between Price Changes and Changes in Total Expenditure
Elastic	Fall	Rise	
Unit elastic	Not change	Not change	
Inelastic	Rise	Fall	

purchased would fall to 800,000 cars (a 20 percent fall). Total expenditures are now $8.8 billion. Because demand is elastic, the price increase causes total expenditures to fall. This example can be easily reversed to show that if demand is elastic, a price fall will cause total expenditures to increase. The extra sales generated by the price decline more than compensate for the reduced price in this case. In Application 5.3: The States' Take from Gambling, we examine how this possibility is related to state-tax receipts on gambling.

If demand is unit elastic ($e_{Q,P} = -1$), total expenditures stay the same when prices change. A movement of P in one direction causes an exactly opposite proportional movement in Q, and the total price-times-quantity stays fixed. Even if prices fluctuate substantially, total spending on a good with unit elastic demand never changes.

Finally, when demand is inelastic, a price rise will cause total expenditures to rise. A price rise in an inelastic situation does not cause a very large reduction in quantity demanded, and total expenditures will increase. For example, suppose people buy 100 million bushels of wheat per year at a price of $3 per bushel. Total expenditures on wheat are $300 million. Suppose also that the price elasticity of demand for wheat is −0.5 (demand is inelastic). If the price of wheat rises to $3.60 per bushel (a 20 percent increase), quantity demanded will fall by 10 percent (to 90 million bushels). The net result of these actions is to increase total expenditures on wheat to $324 million. Because the quantity of wheat demanded is not very responsive to changes in price, total revenues are increased by a price rise. This same example could also be reversed to show that, in the inelastic case, total revenues are reduced by a fall in price. Application 5.4: The Paradox of Agriculture illustrates how inelastic demand can sometimes result in surprising conclusions.

These relationships between price elasticity and total expenditures are summarized in Table 5.2. You should think through the logic of each entry in the table to obtain a working knowledge of the elasticity concept. These relationships are used many times in later chapters.

Demand Curves and Price Elasticity

The relationship between a particular demand curve and the price elasticity it exhibits is relatively complicated. Although it is common to talk about *the* price elasticity of demand for a good, this usage conveys the false impression that price elasticity necessarily has the same value at every point on the demand

APPLICATION 5.4

The Paradox of Agriculture

Demand for most agricultural products is relatively inelastic; even sharp changes in price have little effect on the quantity of food that people demand. This gives rise to what is sometimes called the *paradox of agriculture*. During periods of drought, crops are reduced and farm prices (and farmers' incomes) rise substantially. Bad weather for the crops sometimes ends up being good for farmers. Similarly, good weather results in bumper crops and much lower agricultural prices, which may ultimately be a disaster for farmers' incomes. Because of the nature of the demand for agricultural products, the notions of *good* and *bad* weather can be paradoxical from a farmer's point of view.

The Paradox in Historical Perspective

Table 1 shows this paradox clearly with data on farm output and prices over several years. Prior to the 1980s, these data show that when agricultural output expanded rather rapidly (in 1951 to 1954, in 1966 to 1967, and in 1975 to 1977), prices tended to fall more than proportionally. When output fell in 1972 to 1974, prices rose substantially. Real farm income followed the trends in farm prices, falling when prices fell and rising when prices rose.

The data in the table do not identify all of the factors that affected farm prices during these periods. For example, the explosion in agricultural prices during 1972 to 1974 was probably caused more by an unusually large sale of grain to the Soviet Union (see Application 1.3) than by the rather slight fall in U.S. output. Still, the data clearly show the importance of the relatively inelastic nature of agricultural demand.

The Paradox during the 1980s

Two factors have tended to obscure the paradox of agriculture during the 1980s. First, many farm products increasingly are traded on a worldwide basis. Simply looking at data from the United States will not explain important influences of supply and demand patterns in foreign markets. Second, during the 1980s, government payments to farmers have grown rapidly. In such a situation, it is very difficult to determine patterns of supply and demand from actual data.

Despite these problems, agricultural markets continue to display some paradoxical results deriving from the inelasticity of demand. Consider the drought of 1988, one of the most severe on record. During the early summer of 1988, television reporters made repeated trips to the U.S. Midwest pointing with great concern to crops withering on the ground from lack of rainfall. But these reporters missed half of the story. Because of the drought, grain prices exploded. Corn prices, for example, rose from $2.35 per bushel in April, to nearly $3.60 in mid-June. By the end of the year, as initial scares about the severity of the drought subsided, corn prices were nearly 50 percent higher than the previous year. Although some farmers were clearly devastated by the drought, total net farm income proved to be quite healthy—nearly one-third higher in 1988 than in 1986.[1]

To Think About

1. This example suggests that farmers as a whole benefit from poor weather because they receive higher prices for their crops. How does that notion square with the more commonsense idea that farmers are impoverished by droughts?
2. Would farmers be better-off if the prices of their crops did not fluctuate so much?

Table 1

The Paradox of Agriculture during Four Recent Periods

| Period | Percentage Change in | | |
	Farm Output	Farm Prices	Real Farm Income
1951–1954	+5.3%	−19.0%	−24.9%
1966–1967	+5.3	−5.7	−14.6
1972–1974	−3.6	+53.6	+39.6
1975–1977	+4.4	−4.5	−35.5

Source: Calculated from *Economic Report of the President, 1981,* Tables B-92, 94, and 95.

[1] *Statistical Abstract of the United States* (1991), Table 1130.

curve. A more accurate way of speaking is to say that "at current prices, the price elasticity of demand is . . ." and, thereby, leave open the possibility that the elasticity may take on some other value at a different point on the demand curve. In some cases, this distinction may be unimportant because the price elasticity of demand is essentially the same over the range of demand being examined. In other cases, the distinction may be important, especially when large movements along a demand curve are being considered.

■ Linear Demand Curves and Price Elasticity

Probably the most important illustration of this warning about elasticities occurs in the case of a linear (straight-line) demand curve. As one moves along such a curve, the price elasticity of demand is always changing value. At high price levels, demand is elastic; that is, a fall in price increases quantity purchased more than proportionally. At low prices, on the other hand, demand is inelastic; a further decline in price has relatively little proportional effect on quantity.

This result can be most easily shown with a numerical example. Figure 5.4 illustrates a straight-line (linear) demand curve for, say, Walkman cassette tape players. In looking at the changing elasticity of demand along this curve, we will assume it has the specific algebraic form

$$Q = 100 - 2P, \qquad\qquad [5.2]$$

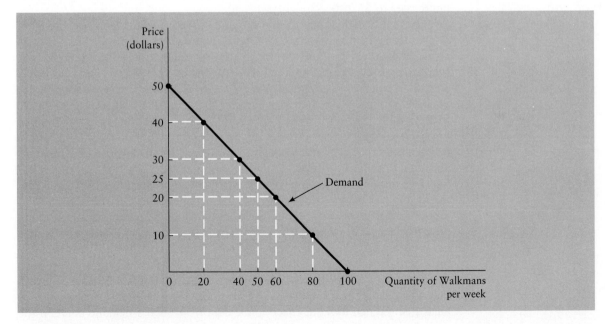

A straight-line demand curve is elastic in its upper portion, inelastic in its lower portion. This relationship is illustrated by considering how total expenditures change for different points on the demand curve.

Figure 5.4
Elasticity Varies along a Linear Demand Curve

	Price (P)	Quantity (Q)	Total Expenditures (P · Q)
	$50	0	$0
	40	20	800
	30	40	1,200
	25	50	1,250
	20	60	1,200
	10	80	800
	0	100	0

Table 5.3
Price, Quantity, and Total Expenditures on Walkmans for the Demand Function Q = 100 − 2P

(Handwritten annotations in left margin: 25, 33, 20, 25, 100)

where Q is the quantity of players demanded per week and P is their price. The demonstration would be the same for any other linear equation we might choose. Table 5.3 shows a few price–quantity combinations that lie on the demand curve, and these points are also reflected in Figure 5.4. Notice, in particular, that the quantity demanded is zero for prices of $50 or greater.

Table 5.3 also records total expenditures on Walkmans (P · Q) represented by each of the points on the demand curve. These expenditures are also represented by the areas of the various rectangles in Figure 5.4. For prices of $50 or above, total expenditures are $0. No matter how high the price, if nothing is bought, expenditures are $0. As price falls below $50, total expenditures increase. At P = $40, total expenditures are $800 ($40 · 20), and for P = $30, the figure rises to $1,200 ($30 · 40).

For relatively high prices, the demand curve in Figure 5.4 is elastic; a fall in price causes enough additional sales to increase total expenditures. This increase in total expenditures begins to slow as price drops still further. In fact, total expenditures reach a maximum at a price of $25. When P = $25, Q = 50 and total expenditures on tape players are $1,250. For prices below $25, reductions in price cause total expenditures to fall. At P = $20, expenditures are $1,200 ($20 · 60), whereas at P = $10, they are only $800 ($10 · 80). At these lower prices the increase in quantity demanded brought about by a further fall in price is simply not large enough to compensate for the price decline itself, and total expenditures fall.

This relationship is quite general. At relatively high prices on a linear demand curve, demand is elastic ($e_{Q,P} < -1$). Demand is unit elastic ($e_{Q,P} = -1$) at a price halfway between $0 and the price at which demand drops to nothing (given by P = $50 in the prior example). Hence, demand is unit elastic at a price of P = $25. Below that price demand is inelastic. Further reductions in price actually reduce total revenues.

Because of this property of linear demand curves, it is particularly important when using them to note clearly the point at which price elasticity is to be measured.[2] When looking at economic data from such a demand curve, if the price being examined has not changed very much over the period being analyzed, the distinction may be relatively unimportant. But, if the analysis is be-

---

[2]The changing price elasticity along a linear demand curve can be shown algebraically as follows: Assume a demand curve of the form (continued on p.135)

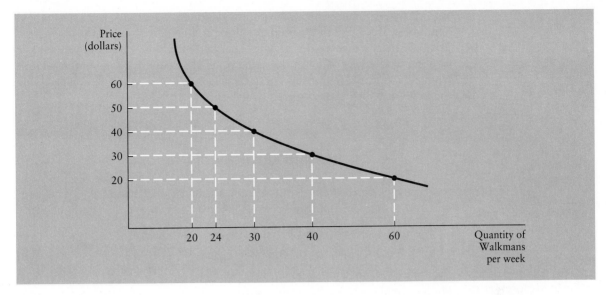

This hyperbolic demand curve has a price elasticity of demand of –1 along its entire length. This is shown by the fact that total spending on Walkmans is the same ($1,200) everywhere on the curve.

Figure 5.5
A Unitary Elastic
Demand Curve

ing conducted over a period of substantial price change, the possibility that elasticity may have changed should be considered.

■ A Unitary Elastic Curve

Suppose that instead of being characterized by Equation 5.2, the demand for Walkman tape players took the form

$$Q = \frac{1,200}{P}. \qquad [5.3]$$

As shown in Figure 5.5, the graph of this equation is a hyperbola—it is not a straight line. In this case, $P \cdot Q = 1,200$ regardless of the price. This can be

---

(*continued from p.134*)

$$Q = a - bP \qquad [i]$$

because

$$e_{Q,P} = \frac{\dfrac{\Delta Q}{Q}}{\dfrac{\Delta P}{P}} = \frac{\Delta Q}{\Delta P} \cdot \frac{P}{Q}.$$

For the case of the demand curve in equation (i),

$$e_{Q,P} = -b \cdot \frac{P}{Q}. \qquad [ii]$$

For large P, P/Q is large and $e_{Q,P}$ is a large negative number. For small P, P/Q is small and $e_{Q,P}$ is a small negative number. Equation [ii] provides a convenient way to compute $e_{Q,P}$: use two points on the demand curve to derive the curve's slope, b, then multiply by P/Q for the point being examined. Alternatively, equation [ii] can be used to derive –b (the slope of the demand curve) if $e_{Q,P}$, P, and Q are known.

verified by examining any of the points identified in Figure 5.5. Since total expenditures are constant everywhere along this hyperbolic demand curve, the price elasticity of demand is always −1. Therefore, this is one simple example of a demand curve that has the same price elasticity along its entire length.[3] Unlike the linear case, for this curve there is no need to worry about specifying the point at which elasticity is to be measured.

Income Elasticity of Demand

Income elasticity of demand

The percentage change in the quantity demanded of a good in response to a 1 percent change in income.

Another type of elasticity is the **income elasticity of demand** ($e_{Q,I}$). This concept records the relationship between income changes and change in quantity demanded:

$$\text{Income elasticity of demand} = e_{Q,I} = \frac{\text{Percentage change in Q}}{\text{Percentage change in I}}. \qquad [5.4]$$

For a normal good, $e_{Q,I}$ is positive since increases in income lead to increases in purchases of the good. For the unlikely case of an inferior good, on the other hand, $e_{Q,I}$ would be negative, implying that increases in income lead to decreases in quantity purchased.

Among normal goods, whether $e_{Q,I}$ is greater than or less than 1 is a matter of considerable interest. Goods for which $e_{Q,I} > 1$ might be called luxury goods, in that purchases of these goods increase more rapidly than income. For example, if the income elasticity of demand for automobiles is 2, then a 10 percent increase in income will lead to a 20 percent increase in automobile purchases. On the other hand, as Engel's law suggests, food probably has an income elasticity of much less than 1. If the income elasticity of the demand for food were 0.5, for example, then a 10 percent rise in income would result in only a 5 percent increase in food purchases.[4] Considerable research has been done to determine the actual values of income elasticities for various items, and we discuss the results of some of these studies in the final section of this chapter.

Cross-Price Elasticity of Demand

In Chapter 4 we showed that a change in the price of one good will affect the quantity demanded of most other goods. To measure such effects, economists

---

[3] More generally, if demand takes the form:

$$Q = aP^b \ (b < 0) \qquad [i]$$

the price elasticity of demand is given by b. This elasticity is the same everywhere along such a demand curve. Equation 5.3 is a special case of equation (i) for which

$$e_{Q,P} = b = -1. \qquad [ii]$$

[4] It seems obvious that not every good can have an income elasticity greater than 1. People cannot, in total, increase all of their expenditures proportionally more than their income increases because they are bound by budget constraints. In general, it can be shown that goods for which $e_{Q,I} > 1$ must be roughly balanced by those for which $e_{Q,I} < 1$.

use the **cross-price elasticity of demand.** This concept records the percentage change in quantity demanded (Q) that results from a 1 percentage point change in the price of some other good (call this other price P′). That is,

$$\text{Cross-price elasticity of demand} = e_{Q,P'} = \frac{\text{Percentage change in Q}}{\text{Percentage change in P}'}. \quad [5.5]$$

If these goods are substitutes, the cross-price elasticity of demand will be positive since the price of one good and the quantity demanded of the other good will move in the same direction. For example, the cross-price elasticity for changes in the price of tea on coffee demand might be 0.2. Each 1 percentage point increase in the price of tea results in a 0.2 percentage point rise in the demand for coffee since coffee and tea are substitutes in people's consumption choices. A fall in the price of tea would cause the demand for coffee to fall also since people would choose to drink tea rather than coffee.

If two goods are complements, the cross-price elasticity will be negative showing that the price of one good and the quantity of the other good move in opposite directions. The cross-price elasticity of doughnut prices on coffee demand might be, say, −1.0. This would imply that a 1 percent increase in the price of doughnuts would cause the demand for coffee to fall by 1 percent. When doughnuts are more expensive, it becomes less attractive to drink coffee since many people like to have a doughnut with their morning coffee. A fall in the price of doughnuts would raise coffee demand since, in that case, people will choose to consume more of both complementary products. As for the other elasticities we have examined, considerable empirical research has been conducted to try to measure actual cross-price elasticities of demand.

Cross-price elasticity of demand

The percentage change in the quantity demanded of a good in response to a 1 percent change in the price of another good.

Empirical Studies of Demand

Economists have for many years studied the demand for all sorts of goods. Some of the earliest studies generalized from the expenditure patterns of a small sample of families.[5] More recent studies have examined a wide variety of goods to estimate both income and price elasticities. Although it is not possible for us to discuss in detail here the statistical techniques used in such studies, we can show in a general way how these economists proceeded.

■ Estimating Demand Curves

The first important problem faced in any empirical investigation is how to implement the *ceteris paribus* assumption. In studying the relationship between the price of a good and the quantity demanded, for example, our theory requires that we hold income, other prices, and preferences constant. Otherwise, if income and other prices are not held constant, observed combinations of P

---

[5]For an interesting survey of some of the early empirical work in demand analysis, see George J. Stigler, "The Early History of Empirical Studies of Consumer Behavior," *Journal of Political Economy* (April 1954):95–113.

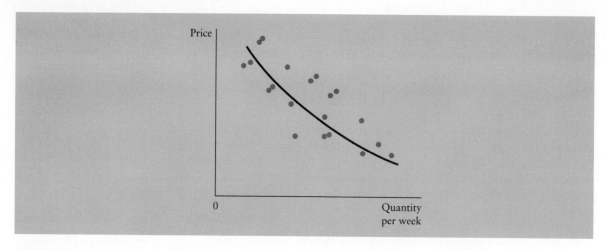

Figure 5.6
Fitting a Demand Curve to Empirical Observations

The points show various combinations of P and Q. It is important that these points be observed while holding constant the other factors that affect the demand for Q. Otherwise they will not lie on a single demand curve.

and Q will lie on many different demand curves rather than on the single curve we are trying to measure. Ideally, we would find several people to study who are identical in every respect except that each faces a different price for the good in question. We could then plot the price and quantity chosen on a graph such as that shown in Figure 5.6. If we were sure that our individuals were, in fact, identical, the points in Figure 5.6 would indeed reflect the *ceteris paribus* influence of price on quantity.

Of course, in practice it is impossible for us to impose the *ceteris paribus* assumption in this way. Finding a group of identical people is probably impossible, and in most cases, there is little variation in the prices people pay for the things they buy. It may be possible in the experimental sciences (such as biology) to isolate a single factor, but economists usually rely on the real world for their data. They must then use statistical techniques to impose the *ceteris paribus* assumption. The most widely used technique is *multiple regression analysis*.[6] Although we will not examine this technique here, it was used to estimate all of the elasticities we will discuss below.

Once the problem of the *ceteris paribus* assumption has been resolved, how do we decide which curve to use to fit the data points? Since a large number of possible curves could represent the points in Figure 5.6, we must develop some criteria for choosing which of them is the best. Again, this is a statistical problem that we cannot investigate in detail here. Usually the decision depends on which curve comes closest to the observed points and which curve seems most intuitively plausible.

---

[6]Multiple regression analysis, instead of looking at only the simple relationship $Q = a + bP$, attempts to estimate a relationship of the form $Q = a + bP + cI + dP' +$ other terms. Once this relationship is estimated, all the terms other than P can be held constant while the partial relationship between Q and P is examined. This is precisely what is required by the *ceteris paribus* assumption.

■ Some Income and Price Elasticity Estimates

Table 5.4 lists a few income and price elasticities of demand that economists have estimated. Although these estimates come from many sources, they do have certain similarities. The income elasticities for necessities (food and medical services) are considerably below those for luxuries (automobiles), as we might expect from the way purchases of these types of goods respond to income changes. A second observation is that most of the price elasticities are fairly low (although, as we expected, they are all negative). Price changes do not induce substantial proportional changes in quantities demanded.

A few of the elasticities in Table 5.4 are worth looking at more closely. For example, the table suggests that the demand for electricity is price elastic over the long term. One result of this fact is that rising energy prices during the 1970s and 1980s led to a significant slowing in the growth of demand for

	Price Elasticity	Income Elasticity	
			Table 5.4 Representative Price and Income Elasticities of Demand
Food	−0.21	+0.28	
Medical Services	−0.22	+0.22	
Housing			
Rental	−0.18	+1.00	
Owner occupied	−1.20	+1.20	
Electricity	−1.14	+0.61	
Automobiles	−1.20	+3.00	
Beer	−0.26	+0.38	
Wine	−0.88	+0.97	
Marijuana	−1.50	0.00	
Cigarettes	−0.35	+0.50	
Abortions	−0.81	+0.79	
Transatlantic air travel	−1.30	+1.40	
Imports	−0.58	+2.73	
Money	−0.40	+1.00	

Sources: Food: H. Wold and L. Jureen, *Demand Analysis* (New York: John Wiley & Sons, Inc., 1953):203. Medical Services: income elasticity from R. Andersen and L. Benham, "Factors Affecting the Relationship between Family Income and Medical Care Consumption"; price elasticity from G. Rosenthal, "Price Elasticity of Demand for Short-Term General Hospital Services"; both in *Empirical Studies in Health Economics,* Herbert Klarman, ed. (Baltimore: Johns Hopkins Press, 1970). Housing: income elasticities from F. de Leeuw, "The Demand for Housing," *Review of Economics and Statistics* (February 1971); price elasticities from H. S. Houthakker and L. D. Taylor, *Consumer Demand in the United States* (Cambridge, Mass.: Harvard University Press, 1970):166–167. Electricity: R. F. Halvorsen, "Residential Demand for Electricity," unpublished Ph.D. dissertation, Harvard University, December 1972. Automobiles: Gregroy C. Chow, *Demand for Automobiles in the United States* (Amsterdam: North Holland Publishing Company, 1957). Beer and Wine: J. A. Johnson, E. H. Oksanen, M. R. Veall, D. Fritz, "Short-Run and Long-Run Elasticities for Canadian Consumption of Alcoholic Beverages," *Review of Economics and Statistics* (February 1992):64–74. Marijuana: T. C. Misket and F. Vakil, "Some Estimates of Price and Expenditure Elasticities among UCLA Students," *Review of Economics and Statistics* (November 1972):474–475. Cigarettes: F. Chalemaker, "Rational Addictive Behavior and Cigarette Smoking," *Journal of Political Economy* (August 1991):722–742. Abortions: M. H. Medoff, "An Economic Analysis of the Demand for Abortions," *Economic Inquiry* (April 1988):253–259. Transatlantic Air Travel: J. M. Cigliano, "Price and Income Elasticities for Airline Travel," *Business Economics* (September 1980):17–21. Imports: M. D. Chinn, "Beware of Econometricians Bearing Estimates," *Journal of Policy Analysis and Management* (Fall 1991):546–567. Money: "Long-Run Income and Interest Elasticities of Money Demand in the United States," *Review of Economics and Statistics* (November 1991):665–674. Price elasticity refers to interest rate elasticity.

electric power. This decrease in demand caused a number of utility companies to cancel large power plant projects as they discovered that historical patterns significantly overstated the actual growth in electricity demand.

For housing, the finding that income elasticity of demand equals or exceeds 1 has interesting implications for the fairness of property taxation. If spending on housing increases more rapidly than income, a proportional tax on housing values will actually be relatively progressive because people with higher incomes will pay proportionally more in taxes than low-income people. The commonsense notion that property taxes are regressive because housing is a necessity is erroneous once one looks at the actual data.

Finally, the relatively high price elasticities for marijuana, alcoholic beverages, and cigarettes might be noted. These imply that taxes or (what amounts to the same thing) legal restrictions on the sale of such items will reduce consumption significantly. Of course, as we described in Application 4.4, the imposition of taxes on elastically demanded items will create a significantly larger burden on consumers than will a similar tax on an inelastically demanded item. But, in these cases the desire to tax may be related to concerns that extend beyond economics. In Application 5.5: National Health Insurance, we pursue the subject of price elasticities of demand a bit further by showing how they have played a major role in the debate about an important question of public policy.

■ Some Cross-Price Elasticity Estimates

Table 5.5 shows a few cross-price elasticity estimates that economists have derived. All of the pairs of goods illustrated are probably substitutes, and the positive estimated values for the elasticities confirm that view. The figure for the relationship between butter and margarine is the largest in Table 5.5. Even in the absence of health issues, the competition between these two spreads on the basis of price is clearly very intense. Natural gas prices have an important effect on electricity sales since they help to determine how people will heat their homes. The elasticity presented in the table was derived in ways that permitted such long-run responses to be captured. The final entry in the table suggests that coffee and tea are not particularly close substitutes. Although economics teachers (including your author) persist in using these commodities as examples of substitutes, apparently relative prices play only a minor role in determining which of them people choose to drink.

Table 5.5 Representative Cross-Price Elasticities of Demand	Demand for	Effect of Price of	Elasticity Estimate
	Butter	Margarine	1.53
	Electricity	Natural gas	.50
	Coffee	Tea	.15

Sources: Butter: Dale M. Heien, "The Structure of Food Demand: Interrelatedness and Duality," *American Journal of Agricultural Economics* (May 1982):213–221. Electricity: G. R. Lakshmanan and W. Anderson, "Residential Energy Demand in the United States," *Regional Science and Urban Economics* (August 1980): 371–386. Coffee: J. Huang, J. J. Siegfried, and F. Zardoshty, "The Demand for Coffee in the United States, 1963–77," *Quarterly Journal of Business and Economics* (Summer 1980):36–50.

APPLICATION 5.5
National Health Insurance

Most developed countries have some form of national health insurance. In the United States, the elderly are covered under the Medicare program and many of the poor receive Medicaid. In recent years, a number of more comprehensive health-care plans have been proposed. These plans vary greatly in cost, with a price tag of more than $200 billion per year for some of the more generous plans. A principal determinant of a plan's cost is the precise mix of services that it covers. Very basic plans cover only hospital stays and physicians' costs for major illnesses, whereas more extensive plans cover a wide variety of additional services, such as family counseling or dental care. An important question in choosing among such plans is how their adoption will affect the demand for specific medical services. Because insurance lowers the out-of-pocket cost to patients (who don't have to pay for services as they use them), there is certain to be some increase in demand. The empirical question is how large that increase might be.

Low Elasticities for Hospital and Doctors' Visits
The estimated price elasticity of demand for medical services given in Table 5.4 is −.22. This figure might be a starting point in predicting the effect of insurance on demand for medical services. This value indicates, as might be expected, that the demand for most medical services is quite inelastic. There probably would be some expansion in demand as effective prices fall because of insurance coverage, but this increase would be fairly small. For example, in a study of patients' responses to actual out-of-pocket costs for medical services, J. P. Newhouse and C. E. Phelps found very low (between 0 and −.10) price elasticities of demand for the lengths of stays in hospitals and for office visits to physicians.[1] These services, then, would show relatively little increase in demand if they were included in national health-insurance plans.

Some Elastically Demanded Services
On the other hand, several researchers have found much larger price elasticities for services such as dental care, ophthalmological care, and psychiatric counseling. These services may have a somewhat greater discretionary element to their consumption. For these items, a substantial increase in demand as a result of insurance coverage might be expected. Suggestions for ways of limiting this increase in demand have ranged from outright exclusion of such services from national health-insurance plans to cost sharing by patients using the services.

Consider, specifically, the case of dental care. Existing research on such care concludes that it is quite price responsive. For some elective services, such as dental examinations or regular teeth cleanings, the price elasticity of demand may be as large as −1 or larger.[2] For this reason, many private dental-insurance plans exclude regular periodic services from coverage or require that patients incur a minimum deductible amount before part of their costs are covered. Similar exclusions and copayment provisions occur in the Medicare and Medicaid programs and in dental coverage in other countries' health-insurance plans. Although proposing limits to coverage can sometimes be political suicide, it seems likely that those interested in the further development of national health insurance in the United States will find it necessary to take peoples' reactions to limited coverage, as well as the costs, into account.

To Think About
1. Does the relatively high price elasticity of demand for some medical services imply that these services are not really necessary? Should health-care planners use elasticity estimates as a guide for the kinds of services people really need?
2. Isn't the use of demand concepts in the health-care field inappropriate because a great deal of medical demand is determined by physicians, not by patients? Is there any reason for physicians to take the price of a service into account when deciding what to prescribe? Does the model of a utility-maximizing consumer have any validity in this case?

---

[1]J. P. Newhouse and C. E. Phelps, "Price and Income Elasticities for Medical Care Services," in *The Economics of Health and Medical Care,* M. Perlman, ed. (New York: John Wiley & Sons, 1974):139–161.

[2]See W. G. Manning and C. E. Phelps, "The Demand for Dental Care," *The Bell Journal of Economics* (Autumn 1979):503–525.

Summary

In this chapter, we have constructed a market demand curve by adding up the demands of many consumers. This curve shows the relationship between the market price of a good and the amount that people choose to purchase of that good, assuming all the other factors that affect demand do not change. The market demand curve is a basic building block for the theory of price determination. We will be using the concept frequently throughout the remainder of this book. You should therefore keep in mind the following points about this concept:

- The market demand curve represents the summation of the demands of a given number of potential consumers of a particular good. The curve shows the *ceteris paribus* relationship between the market price of the good and the amount demanded by all consumers.

- Factors that shift individual demand curves also shift the market demand curve to a new position. Such factors include changes in incomes, changes in the prices of other goods, and changes in people's preferences.

- The price elasticity of demand provides a convenient way of measuring the extent to which market demand responds to price changes. Specifically, the price elasticity of demand shows the percentage change in quantity demanded in response to a 1 percent change in market price. Demand is said to be elastic if a 1 percent change in price leads to a greater than 1 percent change in quantity demanded. Demand is inelastic if a 1 percent change in price leads to a smaller than 1 percent change in quantity.

- There is a close relationship between the price elasticity of demand and total expenditures on a good. If demand is elastic, a rise in price will reduce total expenditures. If demand is inelastic, a rise in price will increase total expenditures.

- Other elasticities of demand are defined in a way similar to that used for the price elasticity. For example, the income elasticity of demand measures the percentage change in quantity demanded in response to a 1 percent change in income.

- The price elasticity of demand is not necessarily the same at every point on a demand curve. For a linear demand curve, demand is elastic for high prices and inelastic for low prices.

- Economists have estimated elasticities of demand for many different goods based on real-world data. A major problem in making such estimates is to devise ways of holding constant all other factors that affect demand so that the points being used lie on a single demand curve.

Review Questions

1. In the construction of the market demand curve shown in Figure 5.1, why is a horizontal line drawn at the prevailing price, P_x^*? What does this assume about the price facing each person? How are people assumed to react to this price?

2. Explain how the following events might affect the market demand curve for prime filet mignon:

   a. A fall in the price of filet mignon because of a decline in cattle prices.
   b. A general rise in consumers' incomes.
   c. A rise in the price of lobster.
   d. Increased health concerns about cholesterol.
   e. An income tax increase for high-income people used to increase welfare benefits.
   f. A cut in income taxes and welfare benefits.

3. Why is the price elasticity of demand negative for a normal good? If the price elasticity of demand for automobiles is less than the price elasticity of demand for medical care, which demand is more elastic? Give a numerical example.

4. "Gaining extra revenue is easy for any producer—all it has to do is raise the price of its product." Do you agree? Explain when this would be true, when it would not be true.

5. Develop an intuitive proof of why the price elasticity of demand varies along a linear demand curve. What would the elasticity be near the price intercept (where $Q = 0$)? What would it be near the quantity intercept (where $P = 0$)?

6. Explain the relationship between the income elasticity of demand for an item and the fraction of income spent on that item. How can the income elasticity of demand be used to predict what will happen to the fraction of income spent on a good as income rises?

7. J. Trueblue always spends one-third of his income on American flags. What is the income elasticity of his demand for such flags? What is the price elasticity of his demand for flags?

8. Table 5.4 reports an estimated price elasticity of demand for electricity of -1.14. Explain what this means with a numerical example. Does this number seem large? Do you think this is a short- or long-term elasticity estimate? How might this estimate be important for owners of electric utilities or for bodies that regulate them?

9. Table 5.5 reports that the cross-price elasticity of demand for electricity with respect to the price of natural gas is 0.50. Explain what this means with a numerical example. What does the fact that the number is positive imply about the relationship between electricity and natural gas use?

10. What are some of the influences on the demand for housing that should be controlled for if you were trying to estimate a demand curve for housing? What would happen if you didn't control for these? How might shifts in the supply curve for housing interfere with your ability to identify a single demand curve? Illustrate your discussion with the appropriate graphs.

Problems

5.1 Suppose the demand curve for flyswatters is given by

$$Q = 500 - 50P$$

where Q is the number of flyswatters demanded per week and P is the price in dollars.

a. How many flyswatters are demanded at a price of $2? How about a price of $3? $4? Suppose flyswatters were free; how many would be bought?
b. Graph the flyswatter demand curve. Remember to put P on the vertical axis and Q on the horizontal axis. To do so, you may wish to solve for P as a function of Q.
c. Suppose during July the flyswatter demand curve shifts to

$$Q = 1,000 - 50P.$$

Answer parts a and b for this new demand curve.

5.2 Suppose that the demand curve for garbanzo beans is given by

$$Q = 20 - P$$

where Q is thousands of pounds of beans bought per week and P is the price in dollars per pound.

a. How many beans will be bought at $P = 0$?
b. At what price does the quantity demanded of beans become zero?
c. Calculate total expenditures $(P \cdot Q)$ for beans for each whole dollar price between the prices identified in parts a and b.
d. What price for beans yields the highest total expenditures?
e. Suppose the demand for beans shifted to $Q = 40 - 2P$. How would your answers to parts a through d change? Explain the differences intuitively and with a graph.

5.3 Consider the three demand curves

$$Q = \frac{100}{P} \qquad \text{[i]}$$

$$Q = \frac{100}{\sqrt{P}} \qquad \text{[ii]}$$

$$Q = \frac{100}{P^{3/2}}.$$ [iii]

a. Use a calculator to compute the value of Q for each demand curve for P = 1 and for P = 1.1.
b. What do your calculations show about the price elasticity of demand at P = 1 for each of the three demand curves?
c. Now perform a similar set of calculations for the three demand curves at P = 4 and P = 4.4. How do the elasticities computed here compare to those from part b? Explain your results using footnote 3 of this chapter.

5.4 The market demand for potatoes is given by

$$Q = 1,000 + 0.3I - 300P + 200P'$$

where

Q = Annual demand in pounds

I = Average income in dollars per year

P = Price of potatoes in cents per pound

P' = Price of rice in cents per pound.

a. Suppose I = $10,000 and P' = $.25; what would be the market demand for potatoes? At what price would Q = 0? Graph this demand curve.
b. Suppose I rose to $20,000 with P' staying at $.25. Now what would the demand for potatoes be? At what price would Q = 0? Graph this demand curve. Explain why more potatoes are demanded at every price in this case than in part a.
c. If I returns to $10,000 but P' falls to $.10, what would the demand for potatoes be? At what price would Q = 0? Graph this demand curve. Explain why fewer potatoes are demanded at every price in this case than in part a.

5.5 Tom, Dick, and Harry constitute the entire market for scrod. Tom's demand curve is given by
$$Q_1 = 100 - 2P$$

for P ≤ 50. For P > 50, $Q_1 = 0$. Dick's demand curve is given by

$$Q_2 = 160 - 4P$$

for P ≤ 40. For P > 40, $Q_2 = 0$. Harry's demand curve is given by

$$Q_3 = 150 - 5P$$

for P ≤ 30. For P > 30, $Q_3 = 0$. Using this information, answer the following:

a. How much scrod is demanded by each person at P = 50? At P = 35? At P = 25? At P = 10? And at P = 0?

b. What is the total market demand for scrod at each of the prices specified in part a?

c. Graph each individual's demand curve.

d. Use the individual demand curves and the results of part b to construct the total market demand for scrod.

5.6　Suppose the quantity of good X demanded by individual 1 is given by

$$X_1 = 10 - 2P_X + 0.01I_1 + 0.4P_Y,$$

and the quantity of X demanded by individual 2 is

$$X_2 = 5 - P_X + 0.02I_2 + 0.2P_Y.$$

a. What is the market demand function for total X $(= X_1 + X_2)$ as a function of P_X, I_1, I_2, and P_Y?

b. Graph the two individual demand curves (with X on the horizontal axis, P_X on the vertical axis) for the case $I_1 = 1,000$, $I_2 = 1,000$, and $P_Y = 10$.

c. Using these individual demand curves, construct the market demand curve for total X. What is the algebraic equation for this curve?

d. Now suppose I_1 increases to 1,100 and I_2 decreases to 900. How would the market demand curve shift? How would the individual demand curves shift? Graph these new curves.

e. Finally, suppose P_Y rises to 15. Graph the new individual and market demand curves that would result.

5.7　Assume that $e_{X,P_X} = -2$, $e_{X,P_Y} = .5$, and $e_{X,I} = .8$.

a. If originally $P_X = \$10$, $P_Y = \$10$, average $I = \$20,000$, and total consumption of good X is 1,000 units, how much of good X will be consumed when P_X rises to $10.10?

b. If P_Y rises to $10.10 instead and P_X stays at $10, how will consumption of good X be affected?

c. Now assume that P_X and P_Y stay constant at $10 but average I rises by $200. How will consumption of good X be affected?

5.8　The market demand for cashmere socks is given by

$$Q_c = 1,000 + .5I - 400P_c + 200P_w$$

where

Q_c = Annual demand in number of pairs

I = Average income in dollars per year

P_c = Price of one pair of cashmere socks

P_w = Price of one pair of wool socks.

Given that $I = \$20,000$, $P_c = \$10$, and $P_w = \$5$, determine e_{Q_c,P_c}, e_{Q_c,P_w}, and $e_{Q_c,I}$ at this point. (Hint: Use Footnote 2 of this chapter.)

5.9   Suppose ham and cheese are pure complements—they are always used in the ratio of one slice of ham to one slice of cheese to make a sandwich. Suppose also that ham and cheese sandwiches are the only goods that consumers can buy and that bread is free.

   a. Show that if the price of a slice of ham equals the price of a slice of cheese, the price elasticity of demand for ham is −½.
   b. Show that if the price of a slice of ham equals the price of a slice of cheese, the cross-price elasticity of a change in the price of cheese on ham consumption is also −½.
   c. How would your answers to parts a and b change if a slice of ham cost twice as much as a slice of cheese?

5.10   For the linear demand curve shown in Figure A show that the price elasticity of demand at any given point (say, point E) is given by minus the ratio of distance X to distance Y in the figure. (Hint: Use footnote 2 of this chapter.) Explain how this result provides an alternative way of showing how elasticity varies along a linear demand curve.

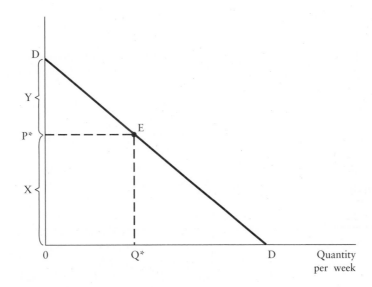

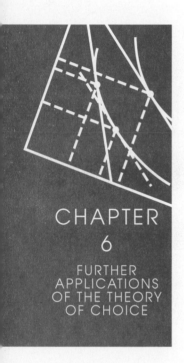

CHAPTER
6

FURTHER
APPLICATIONS
OF THE THEORY
OF CHOICE

In Chapters 4 and 5, we used the utility-maximization model of people's consumption choices to develop the market demand curve. Although this is probably the model's most important application, it is by no means the only one. Because the notion of utility maximization is a very general theory of how choices are made, it can be applied to a wide variety of economic issues. This chapter looks at a few of these additional applications. All of these involve using our previous model to examine whether certain economic events make people better-off or worse-off.

We begin with the development of a different type of demand curve that illustrates only the substitution effects that arise from price changes; any effects of price changes on a person's real purchasing power are compensated for by the way the curve is constructed. We use this curve to show how the effects of price changes on people's welfare can actually be measured. Our second related application concerns the properties of *index numbers*. We show how the consumer choice model can be used to investigate the accuracy of these measurements. Finally, this chapter concludes with a discussion of the gains from trade. We use the utility-maximization model to show how voluntary trading between two people can make both of them better-off.

Compensated Demand Curves

As we pointed out when we developed the individual demand curve (Figure 4.8), utility changes as we move along the curve. As P_X falls, the individual is made increasingly better-off as shown by the increase in utility from U_1 to U_2 to U_3. This happens because the demand curve is drawn on the assumption that nominal income and other prices are held constant; hence, a decline in P_X makes the individual better-off by increasing his or her real purchasing power. Although this is the most common way to impose the *ceteris paribus* assumption in developing a demand curve, it is not the only way. An alternative approach holds the individual's utility constant while examining reactions to changes in P_X. The derivation is illustrated in Figure 6.1. There we hold utility

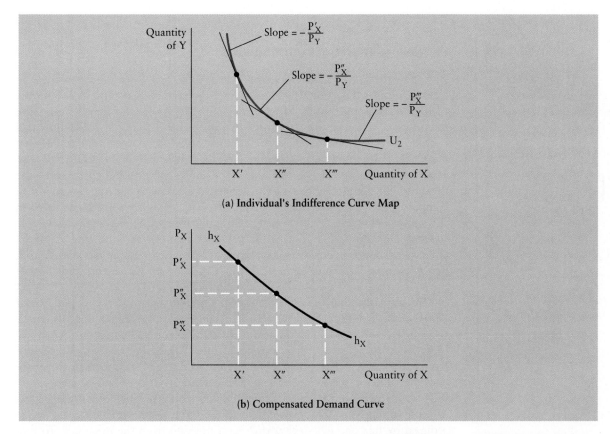

(a) Individual's Indifference Curve Map

(b) Compensated Demand Curve

The curve h_X shows how the quantity of X demanded changes when P_X changes, holding P_Y and *utility* constant. That is, the individual's income is "compensated" so as to keep utility constant. Hence h_X reflects only the substitution effects of changing prices.

Figure 6.1
Construction of a Compensated Demand Curve

constant (at U_2) while successively reducing P_X. The various budget constraints in Figure 6.1 reflect reductions in this person's nominal income just large enough to keep him or her on U_2.

In other words, the effects of the price change on purchasing power are "compensated" so as to prevent the individual's welfare from increasing as a result of the price decline. If we were to examine increases in P_X instead, such compensation would be positive. The individual's income would have to be increased to permit him or her to stay on U_2. The resulting **compensated demand curve**, therefore, shows this individual's reactions to price changes of a good on the assumption that all other prices and utility are held constant. Movements along such curves reflect only substitution effects because all of the income effects arising from price changes have been adjusted for. Compensated demand curves for individuals can be added up in much the same way we did in the previous chapter to get market demand curves. For our discussion, we will use only compensated demand curves for the market as a whole.

■ **Compensated demand curve**

A demand curve drawn on the assumption that other prices and utility are held constant. Income effects of price changes are compensated for along the curve, and it reflects only substitution effects.

■ **Welfare Effects of Price Changes**

Although the compensated demand curve is probably not used as widely in economics as is the ordinary (Marshallian) demand curve, it still has a number of important applications. Most of these involve using the curve to measure the dollar costs or benefits to people of various price changes. To see how this is done, consider the compensated demand curve for video games illustrated in Figure 6.2. Suppose that initially the price of games is P_0 and people choose to consume a quantity of Q_0. If the price of games were to fall (because of the invention of better electronic chips) to P_1, we know, from our discussion in Chapter 4, that people would be better-off. But can we attach a dollar value to this increase in welfare? In a variety of applications it is important to be able to do so. For example, it is sometimes claimed that one valuable spin-off of the U.S. space program was the development of cheaper computer chips (and, hence, cheaper electronic games). A full evaluation of the benefits and costs of the space program should take these welfare gains into account.

To develop such a dollar estimate, remember how the compensated demand curve in Figure 6.1 was constructed. For movements along the curve, individuals' utility was held constant by making suitable adjustments to their incomes in response to price changes. Hence a measure of the welfare gain from lower priced electronics is provided by the size of the income compensation that takes place in response to the decline in price. That is, when price falls from P_0 to P_1 in Figure 6.2, individuals would normally be made better-off, but along the compensated demand curve their purchasing power is reduced by just enough so that they gain nothing from the price fall. To find a dollar value for the welfare gain, therefore, we must measure this income compensation.

Suppose the price of computer games had fallen by just a very small amount, say, to P_0'. If this change were small enough, we could treat Q as remaining unchanged at Q_0. People would therefore save $(P_0 - P_0') \cdot Q_0$ in their

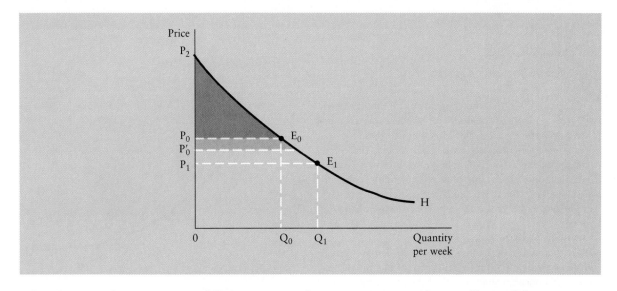

When the price of computer games falls from P_0 to P_1 the area $P_0E_0E_1P_1$ provides an estimate of the real income that people gain. The area $P_2E_0P_0$ provides an estimate of how much people would spend for the right to purchase Q_0 computer games at a price of P_0 rather than doing without the games. This represents the consumer surplus available from people's current expenditure plans.

Figure 6.2
Use of the Market Compensated Demand Curve to Measure Welfare Gains or Losses

game purchases—an amount that can be measured by the lightly shaded area in Figure 6.2. This is the amount of income that people could spend on something else and represents the amount of compensation required to keep them from being made better-off by the price decline.

By continuing to drop the price of computer games in small increments, the additional compensation rectangles shown in Figure 6.2 could be computed. Adding these up provides our measure of the total income adjustment required to compensate for the total price decline. If we used very small rectangles, it is clear that this total area would be given by $P_0E_0E_1P_1$. This then is our measure of the welfare gain from the fall in price.

This result is quite general: changes in welfare that are caused by changes in prices can be given an approximate[1] dollar value by finding the area under the compensated demand curve that is bounded by the extent of the price change. In Application 6.1: The Excess Burden of a Tax, for example, we show how this measure can be used to appraise the true burden of a tax on a

---

[1] The word *approximate* is used here for two reasons. First, the compensated demand curve concept for an individual involves some ambiguity about exactly what level of utility should be used to construct the curve; the location of the compensated demand curve depends on the utility level assumed in its construction. Second, the use of a market compensated demand curve assumes away many important problems about how compensation should be made to specific individuals when prices change. For a discussion of these issues, see Walter Nicholson, *Microeconomic Theory: Basic Principles and Extensions,* 5th ed. (Ft. Worth: The Dryden Press, 1992), Chapter 5.

APPLICATION 6.1

The Excess Burden of a Tax

In Chapter 4, we showed that most commodity taxes will affect individuals' welfare not only because they reduce purchasing power, but also because they provide incentives to change behavior. Such taxes, therefore, impose an excess burden relative to lump-sum taxes that affect only purchasing power. By using the compensated demand curve, we can show this effect in a very simple way and provide a way to measure such costs.

A Graphic Analysis

Figure 1 again shows the compensated demand curve for video games. With a current price of P_0, individuals choose to consume quantity Q_0. If the government were to institute a tax of t per computer game (as a way of collecting revenue and possibly saving players from a wasted life), the price of the game would rise[1] to $P_0 + t$ and purchases would be reduced to Q_2. The total welfare loss to consumers of this price rise would be given by area $AE_2E_0P_0$. Tax receipts, which are given by area AE_2BP_0, constitute a portion of this loss. But the value of this loss exceeds tax revenues by the size of the triangular area E_2E_0B. This triangular area represents the excess burden of the tax; it is a loss of consumer welfare that is not captured by the tax collector.

Measuring Excess Burden

If the shape of the compensated demand curve is known, measuring the excess burden associated with a particular tax is a simple matter. Information regarding the size of the price change brought about by the tax and the reduction in demand the price change causes (this can be computed if the price elasticity of the compensated demand curve is known) can be used to evaluate the size of the triangular area in Figure 1.

Unfortunately, providing an exact measure can run into many pitfalls in attempting to define the compensated demand curve for a good. Still, economists have not been shy about putting forth estimates. In one recent set of articles about the excess burden involved in taxing wages, for example, various researchers calculated that the excess burden associated with raising

Figure 1
Excess Burden of a Tax

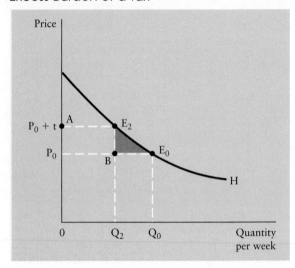

Imposition of a tax on video games raises their price to $P_0 + t$ and reduces quantity bought to Q_2. The welfare loss from this price change is given by the area $AE_2E_0P_0$ under the compensated demand curve, H. This amount exceeds total tax collections, which are given by area AE_2BP_0.

income taxes in the United States could constitute between 15 and 50 percent of the amount of tax revenues collected.[2] Hence, these estimates suggest that the welfare losses associated with taxation are not trivial.

To Think About

1. Cigarettes and alcohol taxes are frequently supported because they will (1) reduce consumption of these "sinful" items; and (2) because they may involve relatively little excess burden. Are these two rationales for taxes consistent with each other?

2. Some authors differentiate between the *average* excess burden of a tax (total excess burden as a percentage of taxes collected) and the *marginal* excess burden (the extra excess burden from raising a tax as a percentage of extra taxes collected). Explain why the marginal excess burden of a tax will usually exceed the average excess burden.

---

[1] In Chapter 13 we will want to amend this analysis by allowing for supply effects in the video games market.

[2] For a summary, see E. K. Browning, "On the Marginal Welfare Cost of Taxation," *American Economic Review* (March 1987): 11–23.

consumer good. The concept has a number of other applications that we will encounter at several places later in the book.

■ Consumer Surplus

Using these observations also provides a way to estimate how much a particular good is worth to people. In the video game illustration in Figure 6.2, for example, we know that people are currently spending $P_0 \cdot Q_0$ for such games. If the price of games were to rise to P_2, demand would fall to zero, and individuals would require an income compensation represented by area $P_2 E_0 P_0$ to retain the same utility level they enjoyed before the price rise. Relative to a situation where they consume no video games, therefore, the value of current consumption is given by area $P_2 E_0 Q_0 0$—that is, by the entire area under the compensated demand curve up to consumption level Q_0. This represents the sum of what people actually spend on games ($P_0 E_0 Q_0 0$) plus the compensation they would demand in order to voluntarily reduce consumption to zero ($P_2 E_0 P_0$).

What this shows, then, is that individuals tend to value the consumption of a good more highly than simply what they spend on it. Although they willingly spend $P_0 \cdot Q_0$ for computer games, they would need some additional compensation to get them to do without the games completely. This extra compensation (given by area $P_2 E_0 P_0$ in Figure 6.2) is sometimes called **consumer surplus.** It represents the extra value people get from being able to consume a good that is in excess of what they actually pay for it. In later chapters, we will show how the consequences of many economic activities for people's welfare can often be judged by whether the activities cause consumer surplus to increase or decrease. Application 6.2: Valuing Clean Air provides an introduction to this type of reasoning.

Consumer surplus

The extra value individuals receive from consuming a good over what they pay for it. What people would be willing to pay for the right to consume a good at its current price.

Index Numbers

Economists frequently need to average many different trends into a single number. In measuring *the* rate of inflation, for example, some method must be found for averaging the different price trends of a wide variety of commodities. Calculating changes in the real quantity of production (that is, changes in real gross national product) means finding some way to add up changes in the quantities produced of a number of different goods. Although these kinds of constructions are often viewed as tedious exercise in number crunching, the development of **index numbers** raises several interesting conceptual issues. As a second application of the model of utility maximization, we examine a few of these issues. We focus mainly on the problems that arise in constructing the Consumer Price Index as a measure of inflation, because these are representative of the issues involved in all index number constructions.

Index number

An average of many different trends into one number.

APPLICATION 6.2

Valuing Clean Air

In recent years, a variety of environmental laws have been passed to clean up the nation's air, water, and land. Many of these actions are quite expensive with costs running into the billions of dollars. In order to determine whether such costs are warranted, economists have devised some ingenious procedures for evaluating the benefits that environmental regulations provide.

Estimating a Demand Curve

One method economists use to evaluate improvements is to look at how environmental factors affect measurable values in related markets. For example, by looking at the *ceteris paribus* relationship between air pollution levels in various locations and the prices of houses in these locations, it is possible to infer the amount that people will pay (in terms of more expensive houses) to avoid dirty air. One study of six metropolitan areas found that home owners were willing to pay between $30 and $80 more for a house in order to avoid one extra microgram of suspended particulates per cubic meter of air.[1] Using this information, it is possible to compute a (compensated) demand curve for clean air illustrated by the form shown in Figure 1. In this figure, the vertical axis shows the price homebuyers seem willing to pay to avoid air pollution and the horizontal axis shows the quantity of clean air purchased. Here clean air is measured by the number of suspended particles and ranges from very dirty (100 micrograms per cubic meter) to very clean (0 micrograms per cubic meter). National average figures are reflected by point E on the demand curve: homebuyers pay about $44 to avoid one extra microgram of particulates and *consume* air containing an average of about 55 micrograms of suspended particulates per cubic meter.[2]

Consumer Surplus and the Value of Clean Air

Figure 1 shows that on average individuals are spending $1,980 (= $44 times a reduction of 45 micrograms of particulates) extra in housing costs to avoid dirty air. But this reflects only part of the value of cleaner air to

Figure 1
Compensated Demand Curve for Clean Air

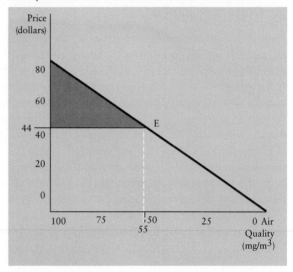

When making housing decisions, individuals show a willingness to pay $44 in extra housing costs to avoid one microgram of suspended particulates per cubic meter. This results in an average reduction in particulates of 45 mg per cubic meter. At E, consumers pay $1,980 for cleaner air and receive consumer surplus of $810 (the shaded area in the figure).

consumers. At point E, individuals also receive a consumer surplus represented by the shaded triangle in the figure. This represents the total additional amount that consumers would be willing to pay rather than being forced to live with dirty air. The value represented by this triangle is $810 (= [80 − 44] · [45] ÷ 2). This value can be multiplied by the total number of households to estimate the total current value of clean air.

To Think About

1. What is the total value of completely clean air for the typical individual illustrated in Figure 1? How might this figure be used to evaluate environmental clean-up activities?
2. Does the use of a linear demand curve in Figure 1 seem reasonable? What does the curve imply about individuals' willingness to tolerate dirty air (more than 100 mg/m³)?

[1] R.B. Palmquist, "Estimating the Demand for Characteristics of Housing," *Review of Economics and Statistics* (August 1989): 394–404. Prices have been updated to 1992 levels.
[2] Using footnote 2 of Chapter 5, it can be shown that the implied price elasticity of demand for clean air at point E is −1.22—a figure consistent with those summarized in M. L. Cropper and W. E. Oates, "Environmental Economics: A Survey," *Review of Economic Literature* (June 1992): 675–790.

The Consumer Price Index

One of the principal measures of inflation in the United States is provided by the **Consumer Price Index (CPI)**, which is published monthly by the U.S. Department of Labor. To construct the CPI, the Bureau of Labor Statistics first defines a typical market basket of commodities purchased by consumers in a base year (1982 is the year currently used). Then data are collected every month about how much this market basket of commodities currently costs the consumer. The ratio of the current cost to the bundle's original cost (in 1982) is then published as the current value of the CPI. The rate of change in this index between two periods is reported to be the rate of inflation.

This construction can be clarified with a simple two-good example. Suppose that in 1982 the typical market basket contained X^{82} of good X and Y^{82} of good Y. The prices of these goods are given by P_X^{82} and P_Y^{82}. The cost of this bundle in the 1982 base year would be written as

$$\text{Cost of bundle in 1982} = B^{82} = P_X^{82} \cdot X^{82} + P_Y^{82} \cdot Y^{82}. \qquad [6.1]$$

To compute the cost of the same bundle of goods in, say, 1993, we must first collect information on the goods' prices in that year (P_X^{93}, P_Y^{93}) and then compute

$$\text{Cost of bundle in 1993} = B^{93} = P_X^{93} \cdot X^{82} + P_Y^{93} \cdot Y^{82}. \qquad [6.2]$$

Notice that now, the quantities purchased in 1982 are being valued at 1993 prices. The CPI is defined as the ratio of the costs of these two market baskets:

$$\text{CPI (for 1993)} = \frac{B^{93}}{B^{82}}. \qquad [6.3]$$

The rate of inflation can be computed from this index. For example, if a market basket of items that cost \$100 in 1982 costs \$150 in 1993, the value of the CPI would be 1.50, and we would say there had been a 50 percent increase in prices over this eleven-year period.[2] It might be said that people would need a 50 percent increase in 1982 income to enjoy the same standard of living in 1993 that they had in 1982. Cost-of-living adjustments in Social Security benefits and in many job agreements are calculated in precisely this way.

The CPI and True Inflation

The problem with the above calculation is that it assumes that people who are faced with 1993 prices will continue to demand the same basket of commodities that they consumed in 1982. The analysis makes no allowance for

> ### Consumer Price Index (CPI)
>
> The current value of the market basket of goods and services purchased by a typical household compared to a base year value of the same market basket.

---

[2] Frequently, index numbers are multiplied by 100 to avoid computation to several decimal places. Instead of reporting the CPI as 1.50, a value of 150 would be reported. Each figure shows a 50 percent gain in the index over the base period.

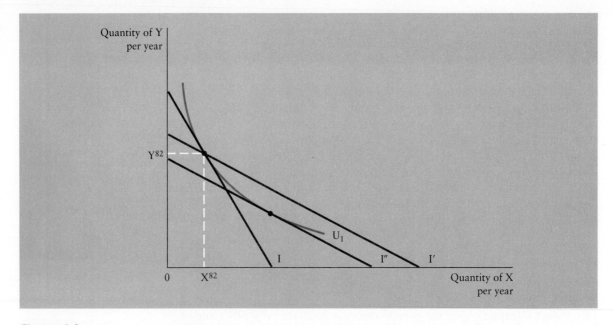

Figure 6.3
Substitution Bias
of the Consumer
Price Index

In 1982 with income I the typical consumer chose X^{82}, Y^{82}. If this market basket is used to construct a price index when different relative prices prevail, the basket's cost will be given by I'. This cost exceeds what is actually required to permit the consumer to reach the original level of utility, I".

substitutions among commodities in response to changing prices. The calculation may overstate the decline in purchasing power that inflation has caused, because it takes no account of how people will seek to get the most utility for their dollars when prices change.

In Figure 6.3, for example, a typical individual initially is consuming X^{82}, Y^{82}. Presumably this choice provides maximum utility (U_1), given his or her budget constraint in 1982 (which we call I). Suppose that by 1993 relative prices have changed in such a way that P_X/P_Y falls—that is, assume that good X becomes relatively less expensive. Using these new prices, the CPI calculates what X^{82}, Y^{82} would cost. This cost would be reflected by the budget constraint I', which is flatter than I (to reflect the changed prices) and passes through the 1982 consumption point. As the figure makes clear, the erosion in purchasing power that has occurred is overstated. With I' our typical individual could now reach a higher utility level than could have been attained in 1982.

A true measure of inflation would be provided by evaluating an income level, say, I", which reflects the new prices but just permits the individual to remain on U_1. By failing to take account of the substitutions in consumption that people might make in response to changed prices (they would consume more X and less Y in moving along U_1), the CPI has exaggerated the true decline in purchasing power that people have experienced. In Application 6.3:

APPLICATION 6.3

Substitution Biases and Cost-of-Living Allowances

Several economists have tried to estimate the extent to which a fixed market basket-type price index overstates the true rate of price increase because it fails to consider the types of substitutions individuals make in response to changing relative prices. Table 1 reports the results of one such study by S. D. Braithwait. In this study, the author compared the actual performance of the U.S. Consumer Price Index over the period of 1958 to 1973 to the performance of an estimated true cost-of-living index that takes account of substitution in consumption. As the table shows, the actual CPI rose 47.5 percent during the 15-year interval being examined (from 100 to 147.5), whereas the true index rose only 46.0 percent. Hence, over the entire period the CPI tended to overstate inflation by about 1.5 percent by failing to consider substitution among items in the market basket.

Inflation in Particular Items

For major consumption categories within the CPI, rather different patterns emerged. In the case of food and clothing, little substitution tended to occur among specific items within each category in response to changing relative prices, so the bias was quite small—less than 1 percent over the entire period. In the recreation and entertainment category, on the other hand, substitution was more prevalent. Hence, the bias was larger, amounting to nearly one-half a percentage point per year. By failing to account for individuals' shifting demands among items such as televisions, spectator events, and use of hotels and motels, the CPI tended to exaggerate the general inflation rate for the goods in this category. The rapid growth in consumption of services since 1973 implies that the bias in the CPI may have grown larger in more recent years, perhaps reaching as much as 0.2–0.3 percent per year.

Cost-of-Living Allowances

These conceptual difficulties with the CPI shed light on the nature of the cost-of-living allowances (COLAs) that characterize many government programs and some private labor contracts. Perhaps the most interesting

Table 1
Estimated Substitution Bias in the Consumer Price Index, 1958–1973

Category	Actual CPI (1958 = 100)	True Cost-of-Living Index (1958 = 100)
Food	156.1	155.4
Clothing	149.3	148.5
Shelter	136.8	135.8
Transportation	134.0	132.5
Personal services	172.6	168.1
Recreation	146.9	139.9
Total consumption	147.5	146.0

Source: S. D. Braithwait, "The Substitution Bias of the Laspeyres Price Index: An Analysis Using Estimated Cost of Living Indices," *American Economic Review* (March 1980): 80.

feature of these allowances is the degree to which they provide full compensation for inflation as measured on the CPI. Under the U.S. Social Security retirement program, for example, such compensation is complete; each year benefits are adjusted upward by the full rate of change in the CPI. For most private labor contracts, however, COLAs provide a much smaller adjustment for inflation. During 1990, for example, such allowances compensated for only about half of the actual inflation that workers experienced. One interpretation of this finding is that workers, in their contract negotiations, exhibit less of a need to assure the ability to purchase a fixed market basket of items than do retired individuals. Therefore, they are willing to consider trading-off what may prove to be excessive inflation protection against other items in the negotiations.

To Think About

1. The Bureau of Labor Statistics revises the weights used in the CPI about every 10 years. How would you decide what the time interval should be?

2. How should new or improved goods be handled in constructing the CPI? What would be the consequences of disregarding quality improvements when computing the CPI?

Substitution Biases and Cost-of-Living Allowances, we show how large this error can be.

This problem of determining a more precise measure of inflation is not an easy one to solve. Without knowing an individual's actual preferences, there is no precise way to know how much real purchasing power has been eroded through price changes. An individual's actual spending patterns may not provide sufficient information. For example, using the 1993 market basket to calculate the CPI leads to the same sort of problems that are illustrated in Figure 6.3. Economists have experimented with a variety of more sophisticated indices of price change, but none of these has proven to be completely satisfactory.[3] Some care must always be taken in interpreting the CPI (and other index number) statistics.

■ Index Number Problems

The difficulties in constructing the CPI are fairly typical of a broad class of problems in developing any index numbers that average together various economic magnitudes. Whenever trends in two or more different commodities must be averaged to form a single index, some sort of weighting scheme is always necessary. In the case of the CPI, the quantities of various goods in the 1982 market basket are used to average together the prices for goods X and Y in various years. Calculating real inflation-adjusted gross national product figures reverses this process with a set of base prices to value the physical quantities of commodities produced in successive years; that is, the calculation implicitly assumes that the base year prices will continue to apply in every year. Application 6.4: International Comparisons of Real Income contains some examples of the pitfalls involved in this sort of calculation. In all such computations, the precise weights that are chosen can have a major impact on the final averages obtained. But, that choice (as in the case of the CPI) will always be arbitrary to some extent. To study the properties of such calculations requires the development of an economic model of the concepts being measured to help establish standards of accuracy. The study of index numbers is therefore another major area in economics in which issues of measurement are closely linked to the underlying theory of choice.

Gains from Voluntary Trade

Our final application of the theory of choice is to show that two people can be made better-off through voluntary trading with each other. Two-person trades need not have a winner and a loser, but can be mutually beneficial. For example, everyone participates in voluntary trading when he or she gives up an amount of money to buy something (say, a candy bar) that is valued more

---

[3] For a detailed treatment of index numbers and their associated problems, see R. G. D. Allen, *Index Numbers in Theory and Practice* (London: Macmillan Co., 1975).

APPLICATION 6.4
International Comparisons of Real Income

A problem similar to the substitution bias in the CPI arises in comparing real income (or GDP) between two countries. Ideally, data are available on the quantities of various goods produced in each country. The problem, however, is choosing what prices to use in adding up these quantities into a real income measure. Two solutions might be adopted. First, we could use the prices that actually prevail in each country: for example, to compare U.S. and Colombian real GDP, we could use U.S. prices to compute U.S. GDP and Colombian prices to compute Colombian GDP. Next we would use some exchange rate to convert Colombian pesos into U.S. dollars (or vice versa). Changes in this exchange rate could then have a major effect on how countries rank. For example, the rapid increase in the value of the Japanese yen in the late 1980s caused per capita GDP in Japan to exceed U.S. GDP, although most observers believed Japanese standards of living were actually quite a bit lower.

Using Common Prices

A second solution is to use only one nation's prices to evaluate GDP in both countries. For example, both U.S. and Colombian GDP could be computed using U.S. prices for the quantities of goods. This approach, although it solves the exchange rate problem, raises another problem of its own. We can assume that Colombian consumers buy relatively few goods that are especially expensive in Colombia (household appliances, for example) and that U.S. consumers have similarly economized on items that are expensive in the United States (coffee, for example). If different goods are expensive in each country, this method may produce biases as some high U.S. prices (for coffee, say) will be applied to goods which Colombians consume in large amounts. Real Colombian income will be overstated.

Empirical Evidence

Table 1 shows data on various countries' per capita GDPs as a percentage of the per capita GDP in the United States. The table compares GDPs in two ways: in terms of each country's own prices and in terms of only U.S. prices. As you can see, which prices are used can make a big difference in the comparison. In the case of India, the lowest income country compared, per capita

Table 1
International Comparisons of Gross Domestic Product per Capita as a Percentage of the U.S. Level of GDP

	Own Domestic Prices	U.S. Prices
India	3.8%	7.9%
South Korea	8.2	15.3
Colombia	11.9	26.1
Hungary	36.0	51.7
Japan	54.5	66.0
United Kingdom	54.7	66.4
West Germany	65.0	79.8
United States	100.0	100.0

Source: I. B. Kravis et al., *International Comparisons of Real Product and Purchasing Power* (Baltimore: Johns Hopkins University Press, 1978), p. 219.

GDP is less than 4 percent of that in the United States when India's GDP is evaluated using India's own prices, but nearly 8 percent of the U.S. GDP when India's GDP is evaluated using U.S. prices. Colombia is another country whose relative position to the U.S. level is more than doubled by using U.S. rather than local prices. As the table seems to indicate, large differences may occur primarily for low-income countries, whereas they are less dramatic for high-income countries, such as Japan or Germany. Higher income countries' expenditure patterns are probably more like those in the United States than those of low-income countries, so the effect of using different prices should be less noticeable.

To Think About

1. Nonmarket transactions (such as trading among farmers or the revenue from illegal activities) are not included in GDP calculations. Would the poor nations look relatively richer if such transactions were included in GDP?

2. Would problems similar to those which arise in comparing GDP among countries arise in comparing the real incomes of people living in different parts of the United States?

highly than the cash—as it must be or it would not be bought. The seller also benefits from this transaction—the seller values the cash more highly than the candy bar since he or she is willing to make the sale. Although we begin by studying mutually beneficial transactions in a very simple setting, the results of our examination are quite general and reappear in various forms throughout this book. People's desires to make mutually beneficial transactions is in many ways what the study of markets is all about.

■ A Simple Exchange Situation

Let's begin by assuming that only two goods, our old favorites, hamburgers (which again we will call Y) and soft drinks (which we will call X) are available. Assume also that there are fixed total amounts of X = 15 and Y = 15. Person A starts out with X = 5 and Y = 10, and person B starts out with X = 10 and Y = 5. These initial quantities appear in the first columns of Table 6.1.

To look at voluntary trades away from this initial position, we need to know these people's preferences to determine what trades would make each of them better-off. Figure 6.4 presents indifference curve maps for our two traders, including the initial allocations of X and Y. At X = 5, Y = 10, person A has a marginal rate of substitution (MRS) of 2; because she has an abundance of hamburgers, she is willing to give up two of them to get one more soft drink. For person B, on the other hand, the MRS is ½; because she has quite a lot of soft drinks already, she is rather unwilling to give up hamburgers to get even more of them.

Suppose now that these two people reach an agreement under which person A trades one Y to person B for one X. Results of this trade are recorded in Table 6.1 and shown graphically in Figure 6.4. The striking fact of the trade is that it makes both people better-off. Person A now has X = 6 and Y = 9. Since she would have been as well-off as in her initial situation if the trade resulted in X = 6, Y = 8 (because her MRS is assumed to be 2), the post-trade allocation is clearly better—she still gets the same amount of X and more Y. Person B now has X = 9, Y = 6, which improves her utility. She would have been willing to accept X = 8, Y = 6 (with her assumed MRS of ½), but the proposed trade leaves her with one more X over what would have been acceptable. The proposed voluntary trade would make both people better-off.

A similar demonstration could be made anytime two people have combinations of goods that result in their having different marginal rates of substi-

	Initial Quantity		Quantity Traded		Final Quantity	
	X	Y	X	Y	X	Y
Person A	5	10	+1	−1	6	9
Person B	10	5	−1	+1	9	6

Table 6.1
A Trade in which
Both Parties Gain

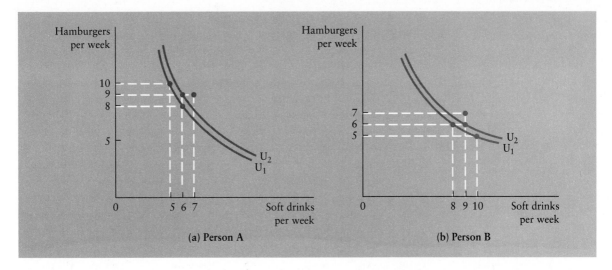

Person A starts with 10 units of Y and 5 units of X and has an MRS of 2. Person B starts with 10 units of X and 5 units of Y and has an MRS of ½. If person A trades one Y to person B for one X, each person will be on a higher indifference curve than in their initial situation. In other examples the actual distribution of the trading gains depends on the terms of trade that are established.

Figure 6.4
Both Individuals Gain from a Trade

tution (if MRSs were the same, there would be no gains to trade). If they agree to trade goods in some ratio that lies between these two MRSs, both will be made better-off.

■ Distribution of the Gains from Trade

Although both individuals may gain from a voluntary trading situation, the gains may sometimes be unevenly divided. We would not expect people to agree to a trade that actually resulted in lower utility (people might be forced into such trades; for example, a gun is an effective form of coercion for a mugger!). But, even in voluntary trades, one person may get the bulk of the gains. Two such situations are illustrated in Table 6.2. In case 1, our two people have decided to exchange Y for X in the ratio of two Y for one X. This trade leaves person A (with X = 6, Y = 8) precisely as well-off as before the trade. As shown in Figure 6.4, both the initial combination of goods and this new posttrade combination lie on the same indifference curve, U_1. Although person A doesn't lose from the trade, she doesn't gain anything either.

In this new trade, person B is the big winner. She now has X = 9, Y = 7, which, as Figure 6.4 shows, is not only preferred to her initial position, but also makes her better-off than in our first trading example.

Case 2 of Table 6.2 shows a trade in which person A gets the better deal. Now the two individuals have agreed to trade at a ratio of one Y for two X. After this trade person B is still on her initial indifference curve. Person A with

Table 6.2
Distribution of the
Gains from Trade
Depends on the
Terms of Trade

Case 1: 1 X trades for 2 Y—only person B gains.

	Initial Quantity		Quantity Traded		Final Quantity	
	X	Y	X	Y	X	Y
Person A	5	10	+1	−2	6	8
Person B	10	5	−1	+2	9	7

Case 2: 2 X trade for 1 Y—only person A gains.

	Initial Quantity		Quantity Traded		Final Quantity	
	X	Y	X	Y	X	Y
Person A	5	10	+2	−1	7	9
Person B	10	5	−2	+1	8	6

X = 7, Y = 9 is now better-off than in any of the previous cases. With these "terms of trade," person A is the only gainer from trading. In general, then, as this example suggests, most of the gains from trade accrue to the person whose MRS differs most from the terms of trade that are decided upon.

■ Edgeworth Box Diagram

Obviously, the numbers in this example were purely arbitrary. Any allocation in which the MRSs of two individuals differ and in which the individuals consume both goods can be shown to be inefficient in that these goods can be reallocated in an unambiguously better way; that is, a better allocation can be found. There may be many such allocations, however, and we can most easily demonstrate them by using a graphic device known as the *Edgeworth box,*[4] the construction of which is shown in Figure 6.5. The Edgeworth box has dimensions given by the total (fixed) quantities of the two goods (call these goods simply X and Y). The horizontal dimension of the box represents the total quantity of X available, whereas the vertical height of the box is the total quantity of Y. The point O_S is considered to be the origin for the first person (call her Smith). Quantities of X are measured along the horizontal axis rightward from O_S; quantities of Y, along the vertical axis upward from O_S. Any point in the box can be regarded as some allocation of X and Y to Smith. For example, at point E, Smith gets X_S^E and Y_S^E. The useful property of the

[4] Named for F. Y. Edgeworth (1854–1926), who in 1881 derived the concept of a contract curve in his *Mathematical Psychics: An Essay on the Application of Mathematics to the Moral Sciences* (New York: August M. Kelly, 1953).

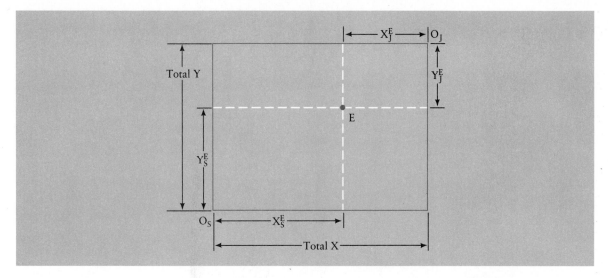

The Edgeworth box diagram permits all possible allocations of two goods (X and Y) to be visualized. If we consider the corner O_S to be Smith's "origin" and O_J to be Jones', then the allocation represented by point E would have Smith getting X_S^E and Y_S^E, and Jones would receive what is left over (X_J^E, Y_J^E). The purpose of this diagram is to discover which of the possible locations within the box are efficient.

Figure 6.5
Edgeworth Box
Diagram

Edgeworth box is that the quantities received by the second person (say Jones) are also recorded by point E. Jones simply gets that part of the total quantity that is "left over." In fact, we can regard Jones' quantities as being measured from the origin O_J. Point E therefore also corresponds to the quantities X_J^E and Y_J^E for Jones. Notice that the quantities assigned to Smith and Jones in this manner exactly exhaust the total quantities of X and Y available.

■ Mutually Beneficial Trades

Any point in the Edgeworth box represents an allocation of the available goods between Smith and Jones, and all possible allocations are contained somewhere within the box. To discover which of the allocations offer mutually beneficial trades, we must introduce preferences. In Figure 6.6 Smith's indifference curve map is drawn with origin O_S. Movements in a northeasterly direction represent higher levels of utility to Smith. In the same figure, Jones' indifference curve map is drawn with the corner O_J as an origin. We have taken Jones' indifference curve map, rotated it 180°, and fit it into the northeast corner of the Edgeworth box. Movements in a southwesterly direction represent increases in Jones's utility level.

Using these superimposed indifference curve maps, we can identify the allocations from which some mutually beneficial trades might be made. Any point for which the MRS for Smith is unequal to that for Jones represents such an opportunity. Consider an arbitrary initial allocation such as point E in

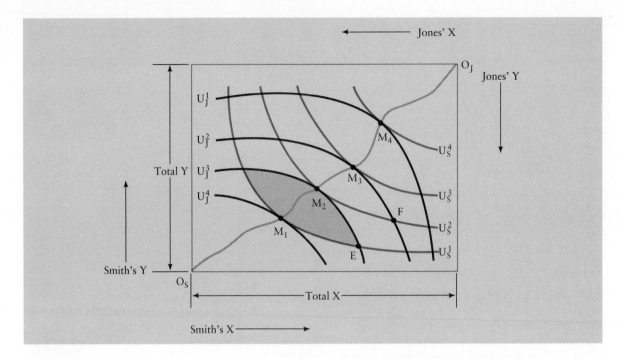

Figure 6.6
Edgeworth Box
Diagram of Pareto
Efficiency in
Exchange

The points on the curve O_S, O_J are efficient in the sense that at these allocations Smith cannot be made better-off without making Jones worse-off, and vice versa. An allocation such as E, on the other hand, is inefficient because both Smith and Jones can be made better-off by choosing to move into the shaded area. Notice that along O_S, O_J, the MRS for Smith is equal to that for Jones. The line O_S, O_J is called the *contract curve*.

Figure 6.6. This point lies on the point of intersection of Smith's indifference curve U_S^1 and Jones' indifference curve U_J^3. Obviously, the marginal rates of substitution (the slopes of the indifference curves) are not equal at E. Any allocation in the oval-shaped area in Figure 6.6 represents a mutually beneficial trade for these two people—they can both move to a higher level of utility by adopting a trade that moves them into this area.

■ Efficiency in Exchange

When the marginal rates of substitution of Smith and Jones are equal, however, such mutually beneficial trades are not available. The points M_1, M_2, M_3, and M_4 in Figure 6.6 indicate tangencies of these individuals' indifference curves, and movement away from such points must make at least one of the people worse-off. A move from M_2 to E, for example, reduces Smith's utility from U_S^2 to U_S^1 even though Jones is made no worse-off by the move. Alternatively, a move from M_2 to F makes Jones worse-off, but keeps the utility level of Smith constant. In general, then, these points of tangency do not offer the promise of additional mutually beneficial trading. Such points are

APPLICATION 6.5

The Gains from Trading among Nations

The analysis of the gains from trading between two individuals applies to far more complex trading situations as well. Consider, for example, the case of trading among nations. In this situation there may be gains to all parties from voluntary trade. A principle source of much of these gains derives from production considerations (as we discuss in Chapter 14), but some gains also arise because of the wider options that trade offers to consumers in the countries involved. This application combines these elements for nations' gains from trade.

Trade Restrictions

Most countries restrict international trade using tariffs, quotas, and various nonquantitative measures such as product safety laws. During the late 1970s, for example, tariff rates averaged about 11 percent in the major industrialized countries. Table 1 shows a series of estimates of how much trade would be created (and welfare improved) by elimination of such barriers, based on the Tokyo round of tariff negotiations in the late 1970s. For example, the complete elimination of tariffs would have resulted in a nearly $17 billion (in 1974 dollars) expansion in the annual level of trade among countries, and it is estimated that real income in those countries would have increased by about $2 billion. The estimated welfare gains reported in the table are probably substantial underestimates of the true gains. They do not take into account the side benefits of freer trade (a more efficient economy, greater technical advancement, better relations among nations, and so forth), nor of the fact that the gains are expected to occur each year into the future. Some researchers estimate that the overall true gains from reductions in trade restrictions may be actually $200 billion if tariffs and other barriers were completely eliminated.[1]

The effects of tariff reduction formulas proposed by the United States, Japan, and the European Economic Community (EEC), respectively, are also reported in Table 1. Although the welfare gains under these pro-

Table 1

Estimated Trade and Welfare Gains for Industrial Countries from the Tokyo Round of Tariff Reductions

Plan	Average Reduction	Additional Trade per Year ($ Billions)	Basic Welfare Gain per Year ($ Billions)
Complete elimination	100%	$16.9	$2.0
United States	65	11.0	1.7
Japan	46	8.0	1.6
European Economic Community	33	5.7	1.4

Source: W. R. Cline, N. Kawanaabe, T. O. M. Kronsjo, and T. Williams, *Trade Negotiations in the Tokyo Round* (Washington, D.C.: Brookings Institute, 1978).

posals are not as large as those for complete tariff elimination, they are nevertheless quite substantial. The different reduction formulas probably relate to different countries' domestic political situations. Differences in the formulas also relate to how specific goods would be treated under each proposal, and how the countries feel about expanding trade for those items. For example, the United States has generally advocated freer trade in agricultural products, whereas the EEC and Japan have tried to protect their farmers. The United States has tended to restrict trade in steel and automobiles, whereas Japan has sought to expand such trade.

To Think About

1. Does everyone gain from trade between nations? Who might lose in such trading?
2. Some authors claim that less developed countries do not gain very much from trade because prices are mainly determined by markets in the industrialized countries. Do you agree?

---

[1] Similar gains have been estimated for tariff reductions when a few countries form a free trade union. For a review, see R. E. Baldwin, "Are Economists' Traditional Trade Policy Views Still Valid," *Journal of Economic Literature* (June 1992): 804–829.

Pareto efficient allocation

An allocation of available resources in which no mutually beneficial trading opportunities are unexploited. That is, an allocation in which no one person can be made better-off without someone else being made worse-off.

Contract curve

The set of all efficient allocations of the existing goods in an exchange situation. Points off that curve are necessarily inefficient, since individuals can be made unambiguously better-off by moving to the curve.

called **Pareto efficient allocations** of resources after the Italian scientist Vilfredo Pareto (1878–1923) who pioneered in the development of the formal theory of exchange. Notice that the Pareto definition of efficiency does not require any interpersonal comparisons of utility; we never have to compare Jones's gains to Smith's losses or vice versa. Rather, individuals decide for themselves whether particular trades improve utility. For efficient allocations there are no such additional trades to which both parties would agree.

Contract Curve

The set of all the efficient allocations in an Edgeworth box diagram is called the **contract curve**. In Figure 6.6 this set of points is represented by the line running from O_S to O_J and includes the tangencies M_1, M_2, M_3, and M_4 (and many other such tangencies). Points off the contract curve (such as E or F) are inefficient, and mutually beneficial trades are possible. But, as its name implies, moving onto the contract curve exhausts all such mutually beneficial trading opportunities. A move along the contract curve (say, from M_1 to M_2) does not represent a mutually beneficial trade since there will always be a winner (Smith) and a loser (Jones).

In the case where the contract curve is interior to the Edgeworth box (as in Figure 6.6), individuals' MRSs will be equal along the contract curve. If preferences are such that for some efficient allocations some individuals choose not to consume all goods, corner solutions will arise in which rates of substitution are not necessarily equalized. Whatever their quantitative nature, all such efficient allocations are depicted on the contract curve. Some additional examples are illustrated in the problems in this chapter. Application 6.5: The Gains from Trading among Nations shows how voluntary trading among nations produces efficiency gains from international trade.

Summary

This chapter looks at three different applications of the notion that people make economic choices in a utility-maximizing way. Each of these applications shows how economists have tried to study a particular problem in the theory of choice, and each has important implications for a number of economic subjects. The principal conclusions that can be drawn from these applications are

- The individual's compensated demand curve shows the quantity that would be demanded at various prices if utility were held constant by compensating for the effects of price changes on real income. The curve summarizes only the substitution effects of price changes.

- Dollar values for the welfare effects of price changes can be approximated by areas under the compensated demand curve for the market as a whole.

One application of this is the notion of consumer surplus, which represents the total amount individuals would be willing to pay to continue with their current consumption plans rather than being forced to consume none of a good.

- Construction of economic index numbers is a complex process that involves selecting weights to be used in adding up different magnitudes. A primary reason that the construction of some index numbers is particularly difficult is that they seek to approximate individuals' preferences, which are essentially unmeasurable.

- Voluntary trade can make both of the parties involved better-off. The possibility for such mutually beneficial transactions occurs whenever two people's current consumption choices result in their having unequal marginal rates of substitution (MRS).

- The gains from trade may be unequally shared in any particular transaction. Generally, the closer the terms of trading are to an individual's MRS, the smaller that person's gains from trading will be.

- All efficient trading outcomes in a simple exchange situation can be illustrated using an Edgeworth box diagram. The set of such Pareto efficient allocations is called the contract curve. For points on the contract curve, one person can be made better-off only by making someone else worse-off.

Review Questions

1. Explain why the principal difference between the Marshallian (uncompensated) demand curve and the compensated demand curve arises from the definition of income being held constant in their derivation: For uncompensated demand curves, nominal income is held constant whereas for compensated demand curves, real income is held constant.

2. Show that compensated and Marshallian demand curves intersect at an individual's current price-quantity choice. Explain why, for a normal good, the Marshallian demand curve is more elastic at this point.

3. Consumer surplus shows the amount that people would be willing to pay to maintain their current consumption of a good rather than doing without it. Explain why the area shown in Figure 6.2 reflects this concept and differentiate between the total amount people pay for a good and the total value of that good to them.

4. Explain why a market basket-type price index (such as the CPI) yields an overestimate of true inflation because it disregards substitution effects. If people consumed items in fixed proportions, would such a price index be biased?

5. Suppose that the CPI were developed by defining a current market basket of goods and asking what this basket would have cost in *prior* years. Would this type of calculation also encounter a substitution bias? Can you think of any advantages or disadvantages to this approach?

6. Explain why the per capita GDP comparisons in Application 6.4 are subject to the same types of substitution biases as the CPI.

7. Could mutually beneficial trade occur if two individuals had exactly the same preferences? Could such trade occur if the individuals had the same preferences *and* the same initial holdings of the available goods?

8. Suppose David and Goliath decide to engage in voluntary exchange. Goliath, being much the larger of the two, demands that trade be conducted at his pre-trade MRS. Who gains the most from this demand? What advice might you give Goliath?

9. Can you think of a case where the contract curve in a two-good Edgeworth box diagram would be a single point? How about a case where the contract curve would consist of all points in the box?

10. Explain why, if traders start out with particular initial holdings of the goods in an Edgeworth box, not all points on the contract curve may be attainable through voluntary transactions. How will the final utility levels attained through such transactions tend to reflect the utility levels associated with the initial holdings? (Hint: If trading in Figure 6.6 starts at point E, what final allocations are possible?)

Problems

6.1 Irene consumes only pizza and chianti. She consumes these goods in fixed proportions: 2 slices of pizza for each bottle of chianti. Her current income is $100 per week.

 a. If pizza costs $1 per slice and chianti is $3 per bottle, how much of each good will Irene consume?
 b. If pizza costs $.50 per slice, how much of each good will Irene consume?
 c. Graph Irene's (uncompensated) demand curve for pizza. Why does this curve have a negative slope?
 d. Graph Irene's compensated demand curve for pizza for the utility level described in part a. Explain why the curve has the shape it has. (Hint: Does Irene's pizza demand exhibit any substitution effects?)
 e. Graph Irene's compensated demand curve for pizza for the utility level described in part b. How has this curve shifted from the position described in part d?
 f. Combine the graphs from parts c, d, and e. What do you conclude about the relationship between the compensated and uncompensated demand curves for a good? Explain why the curves intersect where they do.

6.2   Irving consumes only pizza and chianti, but, unlike Irene in problem 6.1, he is willing to substitute one of these goods for the other. Irving has a weekly income of $100. If pizza costs $1 per slice and chianti costs $3 per bottle, he chooses to consume 40 pizza slices and 20 bottles of chianti each week.

   a.   Graph Irving's budget constraint and show his utility-maximizing point.
   b.   Explain why both Irving's uncompensated demand curve for pizza and his compensated demand curve for pizza must pass through the point

$$\text{Price} = \$1, \quad \text{pizza} = 40.$$

   c.   If pizza prices fall to $.50 per slice but nothing else changes, Irving chooses to consume 68 slices per week. How many bottles of chianti will he consume?
   d.   Graph Irving's new budget constraint and his new utility-maximizing choices of pizza and chianti. Explain why Irving's utility has increased as a result of the fall in the price of pizza.
   e.   Does the point

$$\text{Price} = \$.50, \quad \text{pizza} = 68$$

lie on the same uncompensated demand curve for pizza that was described in part b?
   f.   Does the point described in part c lie on a different compensated demand curve than that described in part b? Explain.

6.3   Assume that martini drinkers always use a ratio of 10 units of gin to 1 unit of vermouth when mixing their cocktails. Assuming they spend all their income on martinis, show that real income calculations for martini drinkers will be the same regardless of whether base year or current year prices are used.

6.4   Suppose oil prices, natural gas prices, and coal prices always move together, with the price of a gallon of fuel oil being exactly equal to the price of 1,000 cubic feet of natural gas and 50 pounds of coal. Show that in this situation an index of fossil fuel (that is, oil, natural gas, and coal) prices will give the same estimate of inflation regardless of whether base year or current year quantities are used as weights.

6.5   The residents of Uurp consume only pork chops (X) and Coca-Cola (Y). The utility function for the typical resident of Uurp is given by

$$\text{Utility} = U(X, Y) = \sqrt{X \cdot Y}.$$

In 1992 the price of pork chops in Uurp was $1 each and Cokes were also $1 each. The typical resident consumed 40 pork chops and 40 Cokes (saving is impossible in Uurp). In 1993 swine fever hit Uurp, and pork chop prices rose to $4 with the Coke price remaining unchanged. At these new prices the typical Uurp resident consumed 20 pork chops and 80 Cokes.

   a.   Show that utility for the typical Uurp resident was unchanged between the two years.

    b. Show that using 1992 prices would indicate an increase in real income between the two years.

    c. Show that using 1993 prices would indicate a decrease in real income between the years.

    d. What do you conclude about the ability of these indices to measure changes in real income?

6.6   The nation of Oskago is a rocky island whose inhabitants are particularly hardworking and adept fishers. They are able to catch eight tons of fish per year, yet they can gather only four tons of coconuts per year. The going price for one coconut on the island is two fish. Nearby is the island paradise of Silveto whose lazy inhabitants catch only four tons of fish per year but gather eight tons of coconuts every year from the lush forests. On Silveto, the price of one fish is two coconuts. With the advent of lightweight boats, the possibility of cost-free trade now exists. Should the two island nations trade products? Why or why not?

6.7   Backyard Jack has a yard full of trees and firewood, but cannot grow very much corn due to poor sunlight. Sunshine Sophie, on the other hand, has wide open cornfields but little firewood to keep her warm. Jack starts out with 20 cords of firewood and only 5 bushels of corn and has an MRS (of firewood for corn) of 1/3. Sophie begins with 25 bushels of corn and only 10 cords of firewood and has an MRS of 2. How can both be made better-off through trade? Illustrate this situation with a graph.

*6.8   Smith and Jones are stranded on a desert island. Each has in her possession some slices of ham (H) and cheese (C). Smith is a very choosy eater and will eat ham and cheese only in the fixed proportions of 2 slices of cheese to 1 slice of ham. Jones is more flexible in her dietary tastes and has a utility function given by $U_J = 4H + 3C$. Total endowments are 100 slices of ham and 200 slices of cheese.

    a. Draw the Edgeworth box diagram that represents the possibilities for exchange in this situation. What is the only exchange ratio that can prevail in any equilibrium?

    b. Suppose that Smith initially had 40H and 80C. What would the equilibrium position be?

    c. Suppose that Smith initially had 60H and 80C. What would the equilibrium position be?

    d. Suppose that Smith (much the stronger of the two) decides not to play by the rules of the game. Then what could the final equilibrium position be?

*6.9   Suppose, as in problem 6.8, that there are only two individuals (Smith and Jones) and two goods (ham and cheese) in an exchange economy. As before, Smith chooses to consume ham and cheese in fixed proportions of 2C to 1H and Jones has flexible preferences and utility given by $U_J = 4H + 3C$. Initial endowments for Smith are H = 60, C = 80 and for Jones H = 40, C = 120.

---

*Denotes a problem that is rather difficult.

a. Graph the Edgeworth box diagram for this exchange economy and indicate all the mutually beneficial trades that might be made.

b. Explain why trades that result in Smith having H and C in other than fixed proportions are inefficient.

c. What is the contract curve for this economy? What portion of the curve might be attainable through voluntary trading starting from the initial endowments?

*6.10 One way to illustrate the idea that Smith likes good X relatively more than Jones does is to assume that for every consumption bundle, Smith's MRS exceeds Jones' MRS.

a. Illustrate the notion that Smith likes X more than Jones does on an indifference curve map.

b. What do the preferences in part a imply about the shape of the contract curve between Smith and Jones? (Hint: Would an even splitting of the goods be on the contract curve?)

c. Show that the contract curve in part b implies that at all efficient allocations X/Y for Smith exceeds X/Y for Jones.

*Denotes a problem that is rather difficult.

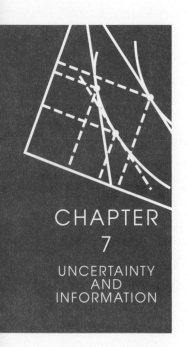

CHAPTER
7

UNCERTAINTY
AND
INFORMATION

S o far in this book, we have assumed that people's choices do not involve any degree of uncertainty; once they decide how to spend their income, they get what they have chosen. That is not always the way things work in many real-world situations, however. When you buy a lottery ticket, invest in shares of common stock, or play poker, what you get back is subject to chance. Many of the choices that people must make involve incomplete information (such as deciding which used car is a lemon and which isn't), and these choices must be made somewhat "in the dark." In this chapter, we will look at three questions raised by such economic problems involving uncertainty: (1) why do people generally dislike risky situations, (2) what can people do to avoid or reduce risks, and (3) how can the problem of uncertainty be treated more generally as the economics of information?

Probability and Expected Value

The study of individual behavior under uncertainty and the mathematical study of probability and statistics have a common historical origin in games of chance. For example, gamblers who try to devise ways of winning at blackjack and casinos trying to keep the game profitable as a business are a modern example of this. Two statistical concepts that originated from studying games of chance, *probability* and *expected value*, will be very important to our study of economic choices in uncertain situations.

The **probability** of an event happening is, roughly speaking, the relative frequency with which it will occur. For example, to say that the probability of a head coming up on the flip of a fair coin is $1/2$ means that if a coin is flipped a large number of times, we can expect a head to come up in approximately one-half of the flips. Similarly, the probability of rolling a "2" on a single die is $1/6$. In approximately one out of every six rolls, a "2" should come up. Of course, before a coin is flipped or a die is rolled, we have no idea what will come up, so each flip or roll has an uncertain outcome.

The **expected value** of a game with a number of uncertain outcomes (or prizes) is the size of the prize that the player will win on average. Suppose Jones and Smith agree to flip a coin once. If a head comes up, Jones will pay Smith \$1; if a tail comes up, Smith will pay Jones \$1. From Smith's point of view there are two prizes, or outcomes, (X_1 and X_2) in this game: if the coin is a head, $X_1 = +\$1$; if a tail comes up, $X_2 = -\$1$ (the minus sign indicates that Smith must pay). From Jones's point of view the game is exactly the same, except that the signs of the outcomes are reversed. The expected value of the game is then

$$\tfrac{1}{2}X_1 + \tfrac{1}{2}X_2 = \tfrac{1}{2}(\$1) + \tfrac{1}{2}(-\$1) = 0. \qquad [7.1]$$

The expected value of this game is zero. If the game were played a large number of times, it is not likely that either player would come out very far ahead.

Now suppose the prizes of the game were changed slightly so that, from Smith's point of view, $X_1 = \$10$, and $X_2 = -\$1$. Smith will win \$10 if a head comes up, but will lose only \$1 if a tail comes up. The expected value of this game is \$4.50:

$$\tfrac{1}{2}X_1 + \tfrac{1}{2}X_2 = \tfrac{1}{2}(\$10) + \tfrac{1}{2}(-\$1) = \$5 - \$.50 = \$4.50. \qquad [7.2]$$

If this game is played many times, Smith will certainly end up the big winner, averaging \$4.50 each time the coin is flipped. The game is so attractive that Smith might be willing to pay Jones something for the privilege of playing. She might even be willing to pay as much as \$4.50, the expected value, for a chance to play. Games such as the one in Equation 7.1 with an expected value of zero and games such as the one in Equation 7.2 that cost their expected values for the right to play (here \$4.50) are called actuarially **fair games.** If fair

Probability

The relative frequency with which an event occurs.

Expected value

The average outcome from an uncertain gamble.

Fair games

Games that cost their expected value.

APPLICATION 7.1

Blackjack Systems

The game of blackjack (or twenty-one) provides an illustration of the expected-value notion and its relevance to people's behavior in uncertain situations. Blackjack is a very simple game. Each player is dealt two cards (with the dealer playing last). The dealer asks each player if he or she wishes another card. The player getting a hand that totals closest to 21, without going over 21, is the winner. If the receipt of a card puts a player over 21, that player automatically loses.

Played in this way, blackjack offers a number of advantages to the dealer. Most important, the dealer, who plays last, is in a somewhat favorable position because other players can go over 21 (and therefore lose) before the dealer plays. Under the usual rules, the dealer has the additional advantage of winning ties. These two advantages give the dealer a margin of winning the game of about 6 percent on average. Players can expect to win 47 percent of all hands played, whereas the dealer will win 53 percent of the time.

Betting Systems

Because the rules of blackjack make it relatively unfair to players, casinos have gradually eased the rules in order to entice more people to play the game. At Las Vegas casinos, for example, dealers must play under fixed rules that allow no discretion depending on the individual game situation, and in the case of ties, rather than winning them, dealers must return bets to the players. These rules alter the fairness of the game quite a bit. By some estimates, Las Vegas casino dealers enjoy a blackjack advantage of as little as 0.1 percent, if that. In fact, in recent years a number of systems have been developed by players that they claim can even result in a net advantage for the player.[1] The systems involve card counting, systematic varying of bets, and numerous other strategies for special situations that arise in the game. Computer simulations of literally billions of potential blackjack hands have shown that careful adherence to a correct strategy can result in an advantage to the player of as much as 1 or 2 percent. Actor Dustin Hoffman illustrated these potential advantages by his character's remarkable ability to count cards in the 1989 movie, *Rainman*.

Casino's Response

It should come as no surprise that players' use of these blackjack systems is not particularly welcomed by those in Las Vegas. The casinos have made several rule changes (such as using multiple card decks to make card counting more difficult) in order to reduce system players' advantages. They have also started to refuse admission to known system players. Dustin Hoffman and Tom Cruise, in *Rainman*, were rudely ejected from the casino after their big win using these strategy systems. Recent books on blackjack systems have long sections on how players can avoid detection when counting cards.

All of this turmoil illustrates the importance of small changes in expected values for a game such as blackjack that involves many repetitions. System players pay little attention to the variability of outcomes on a single hand. Instead, they focus on improving the average outcome of many hours at the card table.

To Think About

1. If blackjack systems increase people's expected winnings, why doesn't everyone use them? Who do you expect would be most likely to learn how to use the systems?
2. Casinos make money by gearing their games of chance to result in a positive expected value for them. With many players they are, therefore, assured of making a profit. Explain how the house manages to win, on average, slot machine, craps, roulette, and stud poker games.

[1] For an amusing although slightly outdated introduction, see E. O. Thorpe, *Beat the Dealer,* new ed. (New York: Vintage Press, 1966).

games are played many times, the monetary losses or gains are expected to be rather small. Application 7.1: Blackjack Systems shows the importance of the expected-value concept in the game of blackjack, a game in which players and casinos struggle endlessly to gain an advantage.

Risk Aversion

Economists have found that when people are faced with a risky but fair situation, they will usually choose not to participate.[1] A major reason for this **risk aversion** was first identified by the Swiss mathematician Daniel Bernoulli in the eighteenth century.[2] In his early study of behavior under uncertainty, Bernoulli theorized that it is not the strictly monetary payoff of a game that matters to people. Rather, it is the expected utility (what Bernoulli called the *moral value*) associated with the game's prizes that is important for people's decisions. If the game's money prizes do not completely reflect utility, people may find that games that are fair in dollar terms are in fact unfair in terms of utility. Specifically, Bernoulli (and most later economists) assumed that the utility associated with the payoffs in a risky situation increases less rapidly than the dollar value of these payoffs. That is, the extra (or marginal) utility that winning an extra dollar in prize money provides is assumed to decline as more dollars are won.

■ **Risk aversion**
The tendency of people to refuse to accept fair games.

■ Diminishing Marginal Utility

This assumption is illustrated in Figure 7.1, which shows the utility associated with possible prizes (or incomes) from $0 to $15,000. The concave shape of the curve reflects the assumed diminishing marginal utility of these prizes. Although additional income always raises utility, the increase in utility resulting from an increase in income from $1,000 to $2,000 is much greater than the increase in utility that results from an increase in income from $14,000 to $15,000. It is this assumed diminishing marginal utility of income (which is in some ways similar to the assumption of a diminishing MRS introduced in Chapter 3) that gives rise to risk aversion. For example, a fair game that promises a gain of $1,000 when you win and a loss of $1,000 when you lose is not "fair" in utility terms. The $1,000 loss brings more pain than the $1,000 gain brings pleasure. Consequently, most people will refuse to play the game. People are more averse to playing fair games with big prizes than to playing fair games with small prizes for the same reason.

---

[1] The games we discuss here are assumed to yield no utility in their play other than the prizes. The observation that many people gamble at unfair odds (for instance, in the game of roulette there are 38 possible outcomes, but the house pays only 36 to 1 for a winning number) is not necessarily a refutation of risk aversion. These people can reasonably be assumed to derive some utility from the circumstances associated with the play of the game (perhaps playing the game makes them feel like James Bond). We try to differentiate the consumption aspect of gambling from the pure risk aspect.

[2] Bernoulli's original article is well worth reading in Daniel Bernoulli, "Exposition of a New Theory on the Measurement of Risk," *Econometrica* (January 1954): 23–36.

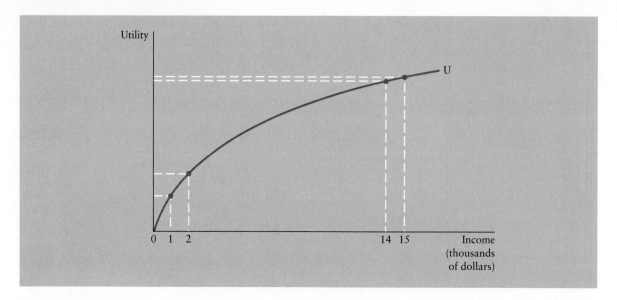

Figure 7.1
Relationship
between Income
and Utility

The curve U shows the utility of different levels of income (or prizes) from a game. On the assumption that the additional utility provided by an extra dollar of income declines as income increases, the curve will have the concave shape shown in the figure. This can be seen by comparing the utility gain associated with going from $1,000 to $2,000 to the gain associated with going from $14,000 to $15,000.

■ Graphic Analysis of Risk Aversion

Figure 7.2 illustrates risk aversion. The figure repeats the utility of income curve from Figure 7.1 and assumes that three options are open to this person. He or she may (1) retain the current level of income ($10,000) without taking any risk; (2) take a fair bet with a 50–50 chance of winning or losing $2,000; or (3) take a fair bet with a 50–50 chance of winning or losing $5,000. To examine the person's preferences among these options, we must compute the expected utility available from each.

The utility received by staying at the current $10,000 income is given by U_3. The U curve shows directly how the individual feels about this current income. The utility level obtained from the $2,000 bet is simply the average of the utility of $12,000 (which the individual will end up with by winning the game) and the utility of $8,000 (which he or she will end up with when the game is lost). This average utility is given by U_2.[3] Because it falls short of U_3, we can assume that the person will refuse to make the $2,000 bet. Finally, the utility of the $5,000 bet is the average of the utility from $15,000 and the utility from $5,000. This is given by U_1, which falls below U_2. In other words, the person likes the risky $5,000 bet even less than the $2,000 bet.

---

[3] Through simple geometry this average utility can be found by drawing the chord joining U($12,000) and U($8,000) and finding the midpoint of that chord. Since the vertical line at $10,000 is midway between $12,000 and $8,000, it will also bisect the chord.

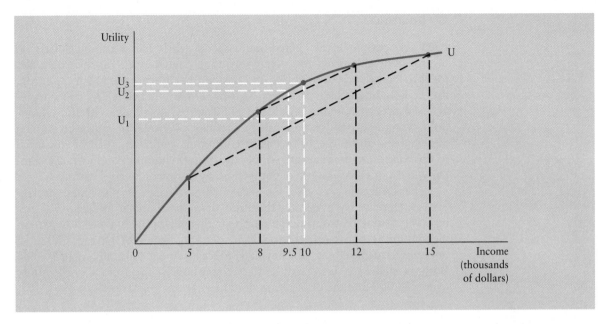

An individual characterized by the utility of income curve U will obtain a higher utility (U_3) from a risk-free income of $10,000 than from a 50–50 chance of winning or losing $2,000 ($U_2$). He or she will be willing to pay up to $500 to avoid having to take this bet. A fair bet of $5,000 provides even less utility (U_1) than the $2,000 bet.

Figure 7.2
Risk Aversion

Diminished marginal utility of income, as Figure 7.2 documents, means that people will be averse to risk. Among options with the same expected dollar values ($10,000 in all of our examples), people will prefer risk-free incomes to risky options. In fact, a person would be willing to give up some amount of certain income to avoid taking a risk. In Figure 7.2, for example, a risk-free income of $9,500 provides the same utility as the $2,000 gamble ($U_2$). The individual is willing to pay up to $500 to avoid taking that risk. There are a number of ways this person might spend these funds to reduce the risk or avoid it completely. In the next section, we will look at a few of them.

Methods for Reducing Risk

In many situations taking risks is unavoidable. Even though driving a car or eating a meal at a restaurant subjects an individual to some uncertainty about what will actually happen, short of becoming a hermit, there is no way all risks can be avoided. Our analysis in the previous section suggests, however, that people will generally be willing to pay something to reduce these risks. In this section, we examine two methods for doing so—insurance and diversification. In the final section of this chapter, we look at more general issues involved in acquiring information to reduce risks.

■ Insurance

Each year people in the United States spend nearly half a trillion dollars on insurance of all types. Most commonly, they buy coverage for their own life, for their home and automobiles, and for their health-care costs. But, insurance can be bought (perhaps at a very high price) for practically any risk imaginable. For example, many people in California buy earthquake insurance, outdoor swimming pool owners can buy special coverage for injuries to falling parachutists, and surgeons or basketball players can insure their hands. In all of these cases, individuals are willing to pay a premium to an insurance company in order to be assured of compensation if something goes wrong.

The underlying motive for insurance purchases is illustrated in Figure 7.3. Here we have repeated the utility of income curve from Figure 7.2, but now we assume that during the next year this person with a $10,000 current income (and consumption) faces a 50 percent chance of having $4,000 in unexpected medical bills, which would reduce his or her consumption to $6,000. Without insurance this person's utility could be U_1—the average of the utility from $10,000 and the utility from $6,000.

Fair insurance

Insurance for which the premium is equal to the expected value of the loss.

Fair Insurance　This person would clearly be better-off with an actuarially **fair insurance** policy for his or her health-care needs. Such a policy would cost $2,000—the expected value of what insurance companies would have to pay each year in health claims. A person who bought the policy would be assured of $8,000 in consumption. If he or she bought the policy and stayed well, income would be reduced by the $2,000 premium. If this person suffered the illness, the insurance company would pay the $4,000 in medical bills, but this person would have paid the $2,000 premium so consumption would still be $8,000. As Figure 7.3 shows, the utility from a certain income of $8,000 ($U_2$) exceeds that attainable from facing the world uninsured, so the policy represents a desirable use for funds.

Unfair Insurance　No insurance company can afford to sell insurance at actuarially fair premiums. Not only do such companies have to pay benefits, but they must also maintain records, collect premiums, and investigate claims to assure they are not fraudulent. Hence, a would-be insurance purchaser can always expect to pay more than an actuarially fair premium. Still, a buyer may decide that the risk reduction that insurance provides is worth the extra charges. In the health-care illustration in Figure 7.3, for example, this person would be willing to pay up to $2,500 for health insurance since the risk-free consumption stream of $7,500 that buying such "unfair" insurance would yield provides as much utility (U_1) as does facing the world uninsured. Of course, even a desirable product such as insurance can become too expensive. At a price of $3,500, the utility provided with full insurance (U_0) falls short of what would be obtained from facing the world uninsured. In this case, this person is better-off taking the risk of paying his or her own medical bills than accepting such an actuarially unfair insurance premium.

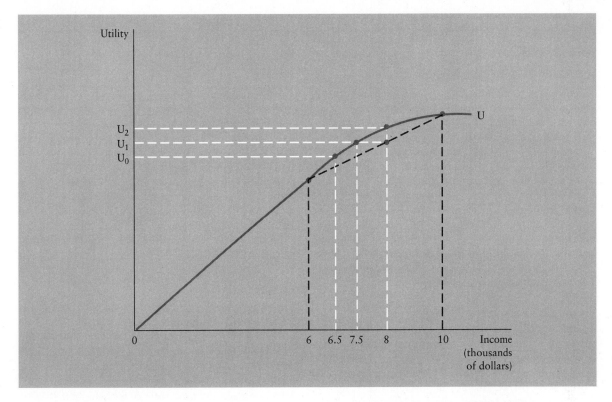

A person with $10,000 in income who faced a 50–50 chance of $4,000 in medical bills would have an expected utility of U_1. With fair insurance (which costs $2,000) utility would be U_2. Even unfair insurance costing $2,500 would still yield the same utility (U_1) as facing the world uninsured. But a premium of $3,500, which provides a utility of only U_0, would be too costly.

Figure 7.3
Insurance
Reduces Risk

Uninsurable Risks   The preceding discussion shows that risk-averse individuals will always buy insurance against risky outcomes unless insurance premiums exceed the expected value of a loss by too much. Three types of factors may result in such high premiums and thereby cause some risks to become uninsurable. First, some risks may be so unique or difficult to evaluate that an insurer may have no idea how to set the premium level. Determining an actuarially fair premium requires that a given risky situation must occur frequently enough so that the insurer can both estimate the expected value of the loss and rely on being able to cover expected payouts with premiums from individuals who do not suffer losses. For rare or very unpredictable events such as wars, nuclear power plant mishaps, or invasions from Mars, would-be insurers may have no basis for establishing insurance premiums and therefore will refrain from offering any coverage.

Two other reasons for absence of insurance coverage relate to the behavior of the individuals who want to buy insurance. In some cases these individuals

APPLICATION 7.2
The Savings and Loan Fiasco

During the latter part of the 1980s hundreds of savings and loan institutions (S & Ls) filed for bankruptcy in the United States. Ultimately these failures may cost taxpayers as much as $150 billion to reimburse depositors in these institutions. The popular trend is to blame either ineffectual regulators or greedy S & L executives for the fiasco. Although a careful review of the history of the situation does, indeed, reveal that a number of unsavory characters participated in the failures, the underlying economic causes of the problems are much less titillating. At its core, the S & L debacle was actually a straightforward example of the *moral hazard* inherent in all insurance contracts.

Federal Deposit Insurance
To examine the moral hazard involved in the S & L situation, it is important to begin with an understanding of federal deposit insurance. The National Housing Act of 1934 created the Federal Savings and Loan Insurance Corporation (FSLIC) to provide insurance coverage to small depositors at federally-chartered savings and loan institutions. Starting in the mid-1970s, regulatory controls on these institutions were relaxed and availability of FSLIC insurance was made more widespread. Most important, a 1980 law extended federal deposit insurance to accounts as large as $100,000. Actions like these throughout the early 1980s implied that the FSLIC intended to insure virtually all accounts, regardless of size. Other laws relaxed restrictions on the types of investments S & L institutions could make in order to allow them to be more competitive with other types of banks.

Incentives Created by These Changes
The changes in the general economic environment within which S & Ls operated provided a perverse set of incentives to S & L managers and depositors. For managers, there were obvious incentives to make the newly-permitted riskier types of loans. Because riskier loans provided higher yields, managers could offer depositors higher interest rates, thereby enabling their institutions to grow rapidly. Depositors who might have worried about the safety of their funds in earlier times now had virtually complete deposit insurance to allay their fears. A would-be depositor simply had to read an advertisement in the newspaper for high-yielding S & L deposits and send in his or her money with no questions asked. FSLIC insurance eliminated the need for any careful analysis of the risks involved, since presumably there were none.

Moral Hazard
In economic terms, this situation is a clear example of moral hazard. Insurance coverage of risky S & L deposits encouraged depositors to behave in ways that they would not have under previous regulations. Their reactions to insurance availability actually increased the likelihood of incurring the risk they were being insured against (bankruptcy of their S & Ls). By 1986, the FSLIC had become insolvent, requiring ever-increasing infusions of taxpayers' money for bailout purposes.[1] The 1990 recession further exacerbated the problem as risky loan policies left S & Ls with vast holdings of failed real-estate developments. Sales of these developments at rock-bottom prices by the government have yielded only a small fraction of the government's ultimate liability to depositors.

To Think About
1. Suppose (contrary to fact) that the cost of FSLIC insurance were based on the riskiness of an S & L's loan practices. How would this mitigate the moral hazard of deposit insurance?
2. Why does the government offer deposit insurance in the first place? Is government-provided insurance preferable to a private insurance plan that S & Ls might devise for themselves?

---

[1] See E. J. Kane, *The S & L Insurance Mess* (Washington, D.C.: The Urban Institute Press, 1989).

may know more about the likelihood that they will suffer a loss than does an insurer. Those who expect large losses will buy insurance whereas those who expect small ones will not. This **adverse selection** will result in the insurer paying out more in losses than expected unless the insurer finds a way to control who buys the policies offered. As we will see in the next section, in the absence of such controls, no insurance would be provided even though people would willingly buy it.

The behavior of individuals once they are insured may also affect the possibility for insurance coverage. If having insurance makes people more likely to incur losses, insurers' premium calculations will be incorrect, and again they may be forced to charge premiums that are too unfair in an actuarial sense. For example, if people who have insurance on the cash they carry in their pockets are far more likely to lose it through carelessness than those who do not have insurance, insurance premiums to cover such losses may have to be very high. Insurance against accidental losses of cash will not be available on any reasonable terms. Application 7.2: The Savings and Loan Fiasco illustrates an especially spectacular example of this type of so-called **moral hazard**.

■ Diversification

A second way for risk-averse individuals to reduce risk is by diversifying. This is the economic principle underlying the adage, "Don't put all your eggs in one basket." By suitably spreading risk around, it may be possible to raise utility above that provided by following a single course of action. This possibility is illustrated in Figure 7.4, which shows the utility of income for an individual with a current income of $10,000 who must invest $4,000 of that income in risky assets.

For simplicity, assume there are only two such assets, shares of stock in company A or company B. One share of stock in either company costs $1, and the investor believes that the stock will rise to $2 if the company does well during the next year; if the company does poorly, however, the stock will be worthless. Each company has a 50–50 chance of doing well. How should this individual invest the $4,000? At first it would seem that it doesn't matter since the two companies' prospects are identical. But, if we assume the company's prospects are unrelated to one another, it is possible to show that holding both stocks will reduce this person's risks.

Suppose the individual decides to plunge into the market by investing only in 4,000 shares of company A. Then he or she has a 50 percent chance of having $14,000 at the end of the year and a 50 percent chance of having $6,000. This undiversified investment strategy will therefore yield a utility of U_1.

Let's consider a diversified strategy in which the investor buys 2,000 shares of each stock. There are now four possible outcomes depending on how each company does. These are illustrated in Table 7.1 together with the individual's income in each of these eventualities. Each of these outcomes is equally likely. Notice that the diversified strategy only achieves very good or very bad results when both companies do well or poorly, respectively. In half the cases illustrated, the gains in one company's shares balance the losses in the other's, and

■
Adverse selection

When buyers and sellers have different information, market outcomes may exhibit adverse selection—the quality of goods or services traded will be biased toward market participants with better information.

■
Moral hazard

The effect that having insurance has on the behavior of the insured.

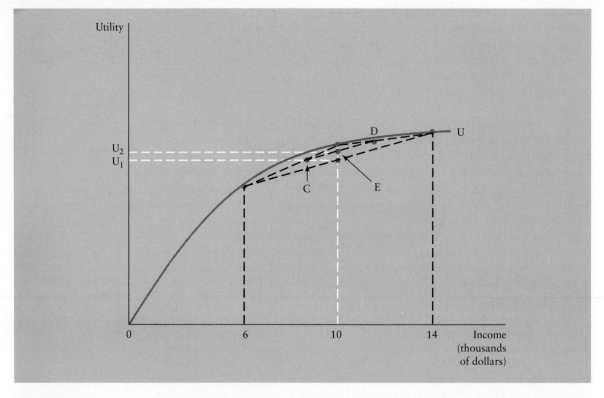

Figure 7.4
Diversification
Reduces Risk

Here an investor must invest $4,000 in risky stocks. If he or she invests in only one stock, utility will be U_1. Although two unrelated stocks may promise identical returns, investing in both of them can, on average, reduce risk and raise utility to U_2.

the individual ends up with the original $10,000. The diversified strategy, although it has the same expected value ($10,000) as the single stock strategy, is less risky.

Illustrating the utility gain from this reduction in risk requires a bit of ingenuity because we must average the utilities from the four outcomes shown in Table 7.1. We do so in a two-step process. Point C in Figure 7.4 represents the average utility for the case where company B does poorly (the average

Table 7.1
Possible Outcomes
from Investing in
Two Companies

		Company B's Performance	
		Poor	Good
Company A's	Poor	$ 6,000	$10,000
Performance	Good	10,000	14,000

of the utility from $6,000 and $10,000) whereas point D represents the average utility when company B does well ($10,000 and $14,000). The final average of points C and D is found at point E, which represents a utility level of U_2. Because U_2 exceeds U_1, it is clear that this individual has gained from diversification.

The conclusion that spreading risks through **diversification** can increase utility applies to a number of situations. The reasoning in our simple illustration can be used, for example, to explain why individuals opt to buy mutual funds that invest in many stocks rather than choosing only a few stocks on their own (see Application 7.3: Mutual Funds). It also explains why people invest in many kinds of assets (stocks, bonds, cash, precious metals, real estate, and durable goods such as automobiles) rather than in only one. Individuals may also choose to diversify their earnings stream by obtaining skills that can be used in many kinds of jobs or by choosing jobs whose success does not depend on the fortunes of a single product. In all of these cases, our analysis shows that individuals will not only obtain higher utility levels because of the risk reduction from diversification, but that they might even be willing to pay something (say, mutual fund fees or educational costs) to obtain these gains.

■
Diversification
The spreading of risk among several options rather than choosing only one.

The Economics of Information

In a sense, all individual behavior in uncertain situations can be regarded as a response to a lack of information. If people knew that a coin were going to come up a head, or knew how their investments would fare next year, they would be better-off. They may even be willing to pay for additional information to reduce uncertainty, and probably will do so as long as the expected gains from this information exceed its cost. For example, someone trying to decide whether to buy a used car may pay an impartial mechanic to evaluate the car's condition before buying it; someone wishing to buy a color television may check around to find the best price. They may also consult *Consumer Reports* magazine, which gives its subscribers detailed information on various consumer goods. Similarly, farmers may use information about the weather to make decisions about what to grow and when to harvest their crops. In this section, we will look briefly at a model that can be used to study such activities.

■ A Utility-Maximizing Model

Many of the issues that arise in studying the economics of information can be examined by using a simple utility-maximizing model similar to the one we presented in Chapters 3 to 6. The basic outline of the model is presented in Figure 7.5. For this model, an individual is assumed to face two possible outcomes (sometimes called *states of the world*), but he or she does not know which outcome will occur. The individual's consumption in the two states is

APPLICATION 7.3

Mutual Funds

One of the most convenient ways for individuals to invest in common stocks is by purchasing mutual fund shares. Mutual funds pool money from many investors to buy shares in several different companies. For this service, individuals pay an annual management fee of about 1 to 2 percent of the value of the money they have invested.

Diversification and Riskiness of Funds

Although mutual fund managers often sell their services on the basis of their supposed superiority in picking stocks, the diversification that funds offer probably provides a better explanation of why individuals choose them. Any single investor who tried to purchase shares in, say, one hundred different companies would find that most of his or her funds would be used for brokerage commissions with little money left over to buy the shares themselves. Because mutual funds deal in large volume, brokerage commissions are lower. It then becomes feasible for an individual to own a proportionate share in the stocks of many companies. For the reasons illustrated in Figure 7.4, this diversification reduces risk.

Still, investing in stocks generally is a risky enterprise, so mutual fund managers offer products that allow investors to choose the amount of risk they are willing to tolerate. Money market and short-term bond funds tend to offer little risk; balanced funds (which consist of both common stocks and bonds) are a bit riskier; growth funds offer the greatest risk. On average, the riskier funds have tended to yield a somewhat higher return for investors. For example, one well-known study of mutual fund performance during the 1960s found that each 10 percent increase in riskiness resulted in an increase in average total yield from the funds of about one percentage point.[1]

Portfolio Management

Managers of mutual funds can reduce riskiness further by the choices they make when purchasing specific stocks. Our numerical illustration of the benefits of diversification assumed that the returns on the shares of the two companies were independent of each other; it was that fact which resulted in the benefits from diversification. Further benefits in terms of risk reduction can be achieved if mutual fund managers find investments whose returns tend to move in opposite directions (that is, when one does well, the other does not and vice versa). For example, some fund managers may choose to hold some of their funds in mining companies because precious metal prices tend to rise when stock prices fall. Another way to achieve this balancing of risk is to purchase stocks from companies in many countries. Such global mutual funds and international funds (which specialize in securities from individual countries) have grown rapidly in recent years. More generally, fund managers may even be able to develop complex strategies involving short sales or stock options that allow them to hedge their returns from a given investment even further. Recent financial innovations such as standardized put and call options, stock index options, interest rate futures, and a bewildering variety of computer-program trading schemes illustrate the increasing demand for such risk reduction vehicles.

To Think About

1. Most studies of mutual fund performance conclude that managers cannot consistently exceed the average return in the stock market as a whole. Why might you expect this result? (See also Chapter 15.) What does it imply about investors' motives for buying mutual funds?

2. Some mutual funds are managed by computer so as to have a performance that precisely duplicates the performance of a particular stock market average (e.g., the Standard and Poor 500 Stock Average). Why would an investor want to buy such a fund? Alternatively, given that such index funds tend to have low management costs, why would an investor buy any other kind of fund?

---

[1] M. Jensen, "Risk, the Pricing of Capital Assets, and the Evaluation of Investment Performance," *Journal of Business* (April 1969).

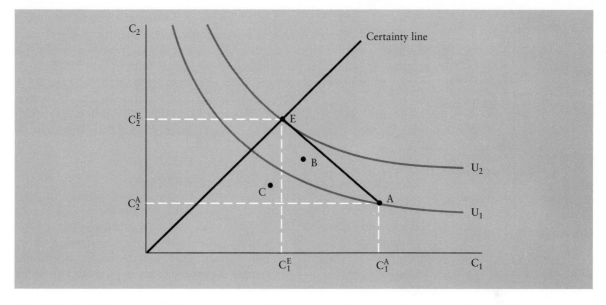

The individual faces two possible situations and the axes record consumption under each of them. If insurance costs are reflected by the slope of AE, this person will opt for complete insurance ($C_1 = C_2$) and raise utility to U_2. Opportunities to acquire information may either raise utility (point B) or reduce utility (point C).

Figure 7.5
Utility Maximization under Uncertainty

denoted by C_1 and C_2 and possible values for these are recorded on the axes in Figure 7.5. A particular risk such as point A in the figure promises C_1^A if state 1 occurs and C_2^A if state 2 occurs.

In the situation illustrated in Figure 7.5, this individual has considerably more consumption in state 1 than in state 2. If there were ways to give up some consumption from state 1 to increase consumption in state 2, this person might jump at the chance. He or she could then avoid the possibility of ending up impoverished should state 2 occur. Insurance, as we learned in the previous section, is one mechanism that might be used for this purpose. By paying an insurance premium, the individual reduces C_1 (consumption during a good time when things don't go wrong) in order to increase C_2 (consumption when things do go wrong). For example, if the terms at which insurance can be bought are reflected by the slope of the line AE, this person can increase utility from U_1 to U_2 by purchasing complete insurance and moving to point E where $C_1 = C_2$. This outcome is similar to the complete insurance solution examined in Figure 7.3. In other words, by paying a premium of $C_1^A - C_1^E$, this person has assured enough additional consumption when things go wrong ($C_2^E - C_2^A$) that consumption is the same no matter what happens. Buying complete insurance has allowed this person to obtain C_1^E (which equals C_2^E) with certainty.[4]

---

[4] The set of points for which $C_1 = C_2$ is labeled the "certainty line" to indicate that consumption is the same no matter what happens. For a discussion of the conditions under which a utility-maximizing individual will buy complete insurance, see W. Nicholson, *Microeconomic Theory: Basic Principles and Extensions*, 5th ed. (Fort Worth, TX: The Dryden Press, 1992):256–262.

There are many other ways in which the individual pictured in Figure 7.5 might improve his or her situation. For example, if insurance were more costly than indicated by the slope of the line AE, some utility improvement might still be possible. In this case, the budget line would be flatter than AE (because more expensive insurance means that obtaining additional C_2 requires a greater sacrifice of C_1) and this person could not attain utility level U_2. He or she might not opt for complete insurance, selecting instead a point where C_1 still exceeded C_2. But achieving a utility level greater than U_1 might be possible.

■ Balancing the Gains and Costs of Information

Another way that this person might better his or her situation would be to gather additional information. The key question, of course, is whether such activities are worth the effort they may entail. Consulting *Consumer Reports* when buying a new automobile might make sense because the cost is low and the potential gains (in terms of getting a better car for one's money) may be significant. Similarly, investing in a few phone calls to discount stores may be worth the time before buying an expensive appliance. On the other hand, visiting every store in town to find a lower-priced candy bar clearly carries the information search too far.

These ideas can also be illustrated with the model presented in Figure 7.5. For an individual initially facing the prospects represented by point A, the issue is whether acquiring information will raise utility above U_1. Because most information is costly to obtain, gathering it will usually result in a lower consumption in favorable situations. Reading *Consumer Reports* or checking around for low prices won't improve consumption prospects if you would have chosen correctly in any case; moreover, the magazine or phone calls cost both time and money. But, gathering the information will probably raise C_2 because the information makes it possible to be a wiser consumer when things go wrong. Point B, for example, represents a utility-improving investment in information acquisition. For that point, the sacrifice of C_1 is more than compensated for by the rise in C_2, and utility rises above U_1. An investment in information that yielded point C would be a poor one, however. Even though the information does have value (C_2 rises), its cost in terms of C_1 is too great and utility would fall below U_1. Again, visiting every store in town in search of a cheaper candy bar is a poor use of time. The individual, in terms of cost, has little use for this information. However, as Application 7.4: The Value of Accurate Weather Forecasts to Raisin Growers illustrates, in many cases it is better to be informed than to be uninformed.

■ Asymmetry of Information

Figure 7.5 suggests two observations about acquiring information. First, the level of information that an individual acquires will depend on how much the information costs. Unlike market prices for most goods (which are usually assumed to be the same for everyone), there are many reasons to believe that

APPLICATION 7.4

The Value of Accurate Weather Forecasts to Raisin Growers

Accurate weather forecasts are crucial in many situations in which decisions are made based on the weather. People must make decisions about where to spend their vacations or whether to go to a baseball game; commuters must decide how they will get to work in bad weather; builders must schedule their outside work to take advantage of good weather; and ski-slope operators must decide whether or not to turn on their artificial snow machines. One of the most important examples of the impact of weather on production is agriculture. Anticipated rainfall affects a number of decisions, such as which crop to plant, when to harvest, and whether to use the sun or indoor facilities for crop drying.

The Raisin Industry

These calculations are particularly important in the raisin industry of the San Joaquin Valley in California. Raisins are produced by sun-drying grapes in the early fall. If conditions for drying are expected to be unfavorable, the grapes can be crushed instead to produce wine, although this may be somewhat less profitable. A farmer who opts for drying raisins takes a considerable risk because rain could virtually destroy the raisin crop (leaving the grapes with only a scrap value if sold to a distillery). Weather forecasting, therefore, plays a major role in growers' decisions: A fall forecast of rain could prompt many to sell their grapes for wine, whereas a sunny forecast probably would cause many raisin farmers to try and make it through the integral 21-day drying period.

The Value of Information

In an important study, Lester Lave estimated the value that more accurate weather forecasts would have for raisin growers.[1] He first carefully outlined all of the relevant decisions that growers make as the fall harvest approaches and calculated how each decision depends on the expected weather. He then compared the expected profits under average (but uncertain) weather patterns with the profits that might be yielded if the likelihood of rain could be accurately forecast over a three-week period. Using this procedure, Lave estimated that improved forecasting accuracy would increase raisin growers' profits by about $91 per acre. Applied to all acres planted in 1960, this figure yielded an estimate of over $20 million for the value of better weather information to the industry as a whole.[2] Even for this relatively small segment of the economy, the value of information can be substantial.

To Think About

1. How can better weather forecasts make raisin growing more profitable? Better forecasts, after all, don't bring better weather, so why should it matter if growers know what the weather will be? How can better forecasts have any economic value at all?

2. Most weather forecasting in the United States is done by the U.S. Weather Service, a government agency. If weather forecasts are so valuable, why don't private firms buy their own forecasts just as they buy other productive services? What kinds of weather forecasts would you think would be most likely to be provided through private markets? Which kinds through the government?

---

[1] Lester B. Lave, "The Value of Better Weather Information to the Raisin Industry," *Econometrica* (January/April 1963): 151–164.
[2] Lave also pointed out that the increased raisin production brought about through better information may cause raisin prices to fall, making this kind of aggregate estimate an overestimate for the industry as a whole. Lower prices would benefit consumers, however, so Lave's estimates may understate the social value of better forecasts.

APPLICATION 7.5

Safe Driver Insurance Policies

The notion that actuarially fair insurance can increase the utility of risk-averse individuals implies that individuals who face very different probabilities of loss should pay different insurance premiums. The difficulty faced by insurers in this situation is in estimating an individual's probability of loss so that insurance can be correctly priced. When insurers possess less information than do insurance buyers, adverse selection may undermine the entire insurance market.

A Theoretical Model

This possibility is illustrated in Figure 1, which assumes that two individuals initially face identical consumption prospects represented by point A. If person 1 has a relatively low risk of incurring state 2, costs of insurance will be low and this individual's budget constraint is given by AE. If insurance is fairly priced, this risk-averse individual would choose to fully insure by moving to point E on the certainty line. For person 2, losses are more likely. Fair insurance costs are represented by AF. This person too might choose to be fully insured by moving to point F. If the insurance company cannot tell how risky a particular customer is, however, this twin solution is unstable. Person 2 will recognize that he or she can gain utility by purchasing a policy intended for person 1. The additional losses this implies means that the insurer will lose money on policy AE and will have to increase its price, thereby reducing person 1's utility. Whether there is a final solution to this type of adverse selection is a complex question. It is possible that person 1 may choose to face the world uninsured rather than buy an unfairly priced policy.[1]

Safe Driver Policies

Traditionally insurers have used accident data to devise group rating factors that assign higher premium costs to groups such as young males and urban dwellers, who tend to be more likely to have accidents. Recently, however, this rate-setting procedure has come under attack as unfairly lumping both safe and unsafe drivers

Figure 1
Adverse Selection in Insurance Markets

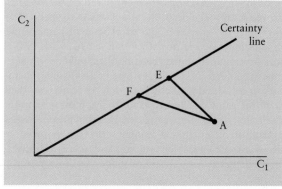

Two individuals face identical consumption prospects at A. Low-risk individuals can buy insurance at a rate reflected by AE, high-risk individuals must pay the rate reflected by AF. If insurers cannot distinguish among individuals, high-risk people will choose AE type policies and cause them to be unprofitable. Low-risk individuals will be made worse off by the absence of such policies.

together. A 1989 ballot initiative in California, for example, sharply limited the use of rating factors by requiring them to be primarily individual-based rather than group-based. Because data on individuals is hard to obtain and not very good at predicting accidents, the main result has been to force rates together for all groups. The main beneficiary of the law seems to have been young male drivers in Los Angeles. Figure 1 suggests that individuals in safer groups (females and rural California residents) may have been the losers.

To Think About

1. How are low-risk individuals made worse off by adverse selection?
2. Can you think of other types of rules where risk ratings might differ among individuals? How would you decide which group of risk differences should be reflected in rates and which should not?

---

[1] For a discussion, see M. Rothschild and J. Stiglitz, "Equilibrium in Competitive Insurance Markets: An Essay on the Economics of Imperfect Information," *Quarterly Journal of Economics* (November 1976):629–650.

information costs may differ significantly among individuals. Some people may possess specific skills relevant to information acquisition (they may be trained mechanics, for example), whereas others may not possess such skills. Some individuals may have other types of experiences that yield valuable information while others may lack that experience. For example, the seller of a product will usually know more about its limitations than will a buyer since the seller knows precisely how the good was made and what possible problems might arise. Similarly, large-scale repeat buyers of a good may have greater access to information about it than do first-time buyers. Finally, some individuals may have invested in some types of information services (for example, by having a computer link to a brokerage firm or by subscribing to *Consumer Reports*) that make the cost of obtaining additional information lower than for someone without such an investment.

Differing preferences provide a second reason why information levels may differ among buyers of the same good. Some people may care a great deal about getting the best buy. Others may have a strong aversion to seeking bargains and will take the first model available. As for any good, the trade-offs that individuals are willing to make are determined by the nature of their preferences.

The possibility that information levels will differ among people raises a number of difficult problems about how markets operate. Although it is customary to assume that all buyers and sellers are fully informed, in a number of situations this assumption is untenable. In Chapter 15, we will explore some of the general consequences of such asymmetry of information for markets as a whole. In Application 7.5: Safe Driver Insurance Policies, we look at one specific case where these differences can pose major problems in adverse selection for insurance companies.

Summary

In this chapter, we have briefly surveyed the economic analysis of individual behavior in uncertain situations. From that survey we reached several conclusions that have relevance throughout the study of microeconomics.

- In uncertain situations individuals are concerned with the expected utility associated with various outcomes. If individuals have a diminishing marginal utility for income, they will be risk averse. That is, they will generally refuse bets that are actuarially fair in dollar terms but result in an expected loss of utility.

- Risk-averse individuals will purchase insurance that allows them to avoid participating in fair bets. Even if the premium is somewhat unfair (in an actuarial sense), they will still buy insurance in order to increase utility.

- Diversification among several uncertain options may reduce risk. Such risk spreading may sometimes be costly, however.

- New information is valuable because it may permit individuals to make new choices that increase expected utility.

- Individuals may face differing costs of obtaining information and may therefore acquire different amounts of it.

Review Questions

1. What does it mean to say we expect a fair coin to come up heads about half the time? Would you expect the fraction of heads to get closer to exactly 0.5 as more coins are flipped? Explain how this law of large numbers applies to the risks faced by casinos or insurance companies.

2. Why does the assumption of diminishing marginal utility of income imply risk aversion? Can you think of other assumptions that would result in risk-averse behavior but would not require the difficult-to-verify notion of diminishing marginal utility?

3. Why does the purchase of fair insurance provide a certain, nonrandom income to the buyer? Why must all insurance premiums be somewhat unfair in a statistical sense? What determines whether a person will purchase insurance at an unfair premium?

4. Explain why the presence of imperfect information in insurance markets can result in adverse selection. Why does adverse selection pose a problem for insurance companies in their rate setting?

5. "The term *moral hazard* is entirely inappropriate since it maligns individuals' reactions to economic incentives provided by insurance that in other circumstances are regarded as perfectly normal." Do you agree? Explain.

6. The diversification example illustrated in Table 7.1 and Figure 7.4 requires that returns on the two stocks be independent. Explain what "independent" means in this context and why independence of returns provides opportunities for diversification. Why would such opportunities be limited if the returns on the stocks in the example moved together?

7. "The model in Figure 7.5 differs from other models because the individual does not ultimately consume both C_1 and C_2; rather these are the two possible outcomes from one random event." Explain exactly how this model does differ from the one in Chapters 3 and 4 and provide a simple example of how Figure 7.5 might apply to an actual situation.

8. What benefits do individuals derive from obtaining additional information? Explain why the marginal value to additional information declines as a person becomes more fully informed.

9. Explain why the marginal cost of acquiring additional information increases. Can you think of a personal example that illustrates this situation?

10. Why do the observations in questions 8 and 9 suggest that individuals have a utility-maximizing amount of information? Why is some ignorance optimal?

Problems

7.1 Suppose a person must accept one of three bets.

> Bet 1: Win $100 with probability 1/2; lose $100 with probability 1/2.
> Bet 2: Win $100 with probability 3/4; lose $300 with probability 1/4.
> Bet 3: Win $100 with probability 9/10; lose $900 with probability 1/10.

a. Show that all of these are fair bets.
b. Graph each bet on a utility of income curve similar to Figure 7.2.
c. Explain carefully which bet will be preferred and why.

7.2 Two fast food restaurants are located next to each other and offer different procedures for ordering food. The first offers five lines leading to a server, whereas the second has a single line leading to five servers, with the next person in the line going to the first available server. Use the assumption that most individuals are risk averse to discuss which restaurant will be preferred.

7.3 Show that if an individual's utility of income function is convex (rather than concave as shown in Figure 7.1), he or she will prefer fair gambles to income certainty and may even be willing to accept somewhat unfair gambles. Do you believe this sort of risk-taking behavior is common? What factors might tend to limit its occurrence?

7.4 A person purchases a dozen eggs and must take them home. Although making trips home is costless, there is a 50 percent chance that all of the eggs carried on one trip will be broken during the trip.
This person considers two strategies:

> Strategy 1: Take all 12 eggs in one trip.
> Strategy 2: Make two trips, taking 6 eggs in each trip.

a. List the possible outcomes of each strategy and the probabilities of these outcomes. Show that, on average, 6 eggs make it home under either strategy.
b. Develop a graph to show the utility obtainable under each strategy.
c. Could utility be improved further by taking more than two trips? How would the desirability of this possibility be affected if additional trips were costly?

7.5 Jimmy the Greek is seen to place an even money $100,000 bet on the Bulls to win their NBA Championship final with the Suns. If Jimmy has a logarithmic utility of wealth function and if his current wealth is $1,000,000, what must he believe the minimum probability is that the Bulls will win?

7.6 Suppose there is a 50–50 chance that a risk-averse individual with a current wealth of $20,000 will contract a debilitating disease and suffer a loss of $10,000.

a. Calculate the cost of actuarially fair insurance in this situation and use a utility of wealth graph (such as shown in Figure 7.1) to show that the individual will prefer fair insurance against this loss to accepting the gamble uninsured.
b. Suppose two types of insurance policies were available:

1. A fair policy covering the complete loss.
2. A fair policy covering only half of any loss incurred.

Calculate the cost of the second type of policy and show that the individual will generally regard it as inferior to the first.

c. Suppose individuals who purchase cost-sharing policies of the second type take better care of their health, thereby reducing the loss suffered when ill to only $7,000. In this situation, what will be the cost of a cost-sharing policy? Show that some individuals may now prefer this type of policy. (This is an example of the moral hazard problem in insurance theory.)

*7.7 It is known that parking in an illegal space in downtown Podunk leads to a 50 percent chance of getting a $10 parking ticket.

a. Graph the individual's decision to park in this space. Show that, unless the space provides substantial convenience, the individual will not choose to park there.
b. Podunk is considering increasing its parking fine to $20. Show that this would reduce the utility of parking in the illegal space further.
c. The police chief of Podunk argues that increasing patrols to ensure that any violator is caught (that is, to ensure that there is a 100 percent likelihood of getting a $10 ticket if one parks in the illegal space) would be more effective at deterring illegal parking than increasing the fine. Would you agree? Graph your results.

*7.8 Ms. Fogg is planning an around-the-world trip. The utility from the trip is a function of how much she spends on it (Y) given by

$$U(Y) = \log Y.$$

Ms. Fogg has $10,000 to spend on the trip. If she spends all of it, her utility will be

$$U(10,000) = \log 10,000 = 4.$$

(In this problem we are using logarithms to the base 10 for ease of computation.)

a. If there is a 25 percent probability that Ms. Fogg will lose $1,000 of her cash on the trip, what is the trip's expected utility?
b. Suppose that Ms. Fogg can buy insurance against losing the $1,000 (say, by purchasing traveler's checks) at an actuarially fair premium of $250. Show

---

*Denotes a problem that is rather difficult.

that her utility is higher if she purchases this insurance than if she faces the chance of losing the $1,000 without insurance.

   c. What is the maximum amount that Ms. Fogg would be willing to pay to insure her $1,000?

   d. Suppose that people who buy insurance tend to become more careless with their cash than those who don't, and assume that the probability of their losing $1,000 is 30 percent. What will be the actuarially fair insurance premium? Will Ms. Fogg buy insurance in this situation?

7.9   Losing one's watch can be quite traumatic. Not only does the loss entail giving up an attractive piece of wristwear, but it also can result in missing important engagements.

   a. Use a diagram similar to Figure 7.5 to show an individual's consumption possibilities in the two states: (1) keep watch; and (2) lose watch.

   b. What are some of the things a person might do to move toward the certainty line in your diagram? What would determine whether these actions were undertaken or not?

   c. If it were possible to buy watch loss insurance that guaranteed an immediate replacement upon loss, how might this raise utility? Indicate this possibility on your diagram.

   d. Suppose blue-eyed people are more likely to lose their watches than are brown-eyed people, but that otherwise such individuals are identical. If insurance companies could tell the color of people's eyes, show how the situations of blue-eyed and brown-eyed people would differ.

   e. What difficulties might arise if insurance companies could not know the color of people's eyes, but each individual knows the color of his or her own eyes (and therefore the likelihood of watch loss)?

7.10 Suppose Molly Jock wishes to purchase a high-definition television to watch the 1996 Olympic Greco-Roman wrestling competition. Her current income is $20,000, and she knows where she can buy the television she wants for $2,000. She has heard the rumor that the same set can be bought at Crazy Eddie's (recently out of bankruptcy) for $1,700, but is unsure if the rumor is true. Suppose this individual's utility is given by

$$\text{Utility} = \ln(Y)$$

where Y is her income after buying the television.

   a. What is Molly's utility if she buys from the location she knows?

   b. What is Molly's utility if Crazy Eddie's really does offer a lower price?

   c. Suppose Molly believes there is a 50–50 chance that Crazy Eddie does offer the lower-priced television, but it will cost her $100 to drive to the discount store to find out for sure (the store is far away and has had its phone disconnected). Is it worth it to her to invest the money in the trip? (Hint: To calculate the utility associated with part c, simply average Molly's utility from the two states: (1) Eddie offers the television; (2) Eddie doesn't offer the television.)

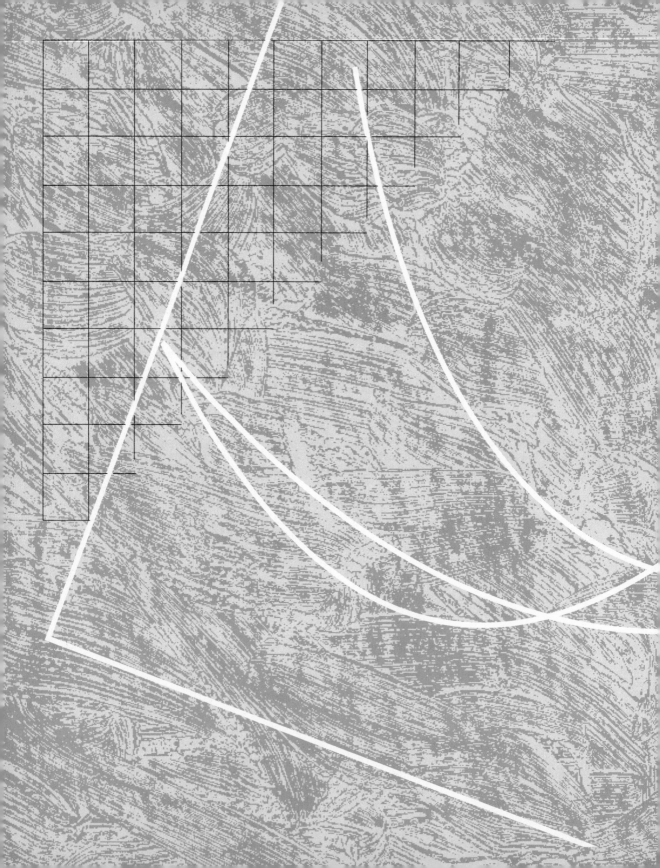

> "The laws and conditions of production partake of the character of physical truths. There is nothing arbitrary about them."

J. S. Mill

Principles of Political Economy, 1848

Part 3 considers the production and supply of economic goods. The institutions that are engaged in this process are called firms. They may be large, complex organizations, such as IBM or the U.S. Defense Department, or they may be quite small, such as "mom and pop" stores or self-employed farmers. The organizations may also have different goals—IBM may pursue maximum profits, while the U.S. Defense Department may be interested in the protection it can provide with the overall size of its budget. Whatever goals they pursue, all firms must make choices about what inputs they will use and the level of output they will supply. Part 3 looks at these choices.

To be able to produce any output, firms must hire many inputs (labor, capital, natural resources, and so forth). Because these inputs are scarce, they have costs associated with their use. Our goal in Chapters 8 and 9 is to develop curves that relate the costs of these inputs to the level of the firm's output. In Chapter 8 we introduce the firm's production function, which shows the relationship between inputs used and the level of output that results. Once the relationship between inputs and outputs is known, the costs of needed inputs can be determined for various levels of output, as shown in Chapter 9.

Chapter 10 uses the cost curves developed in Chapter 9 to discuss firms' supply decisions. It concludes with a detailed analysis of the supply decisions of profit-maximizing firms.

Chapter 11 looks at a few additional applications of the theory of the firm. The chapter is specifically concerned with the types of agreements (that is, "contracts") that exist between firms and their employees and managers.

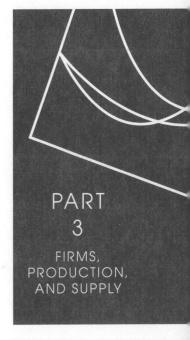

PART
3

FIRMS, PRODUCTION, AND SUPPLY

CHAPTER
8
PRODUCTION

I n Chapters 8 and 9, we describe the relationship between the level of production in a firm and the input costs the firm incurs. This description of costs provides the basis for our analysis of firms' supply decisions—the principal topic of Part 3. Chapter 8 begins this process with an analysis of the physical aspects of production. We show how economists conceptualize the relationship between the inputs a firm uses and the output it thereby obtains.

Production Functions

The purpose of any **firm** is to turn inputs into outputs: General Motors combines steel, glass, workers' time, and hours of assembly line operation to produce automobiles; farmers combine their labor with seed, soil, rain, fertilizer, and machinery to produce crops; and colleges combine professors' time with books and (hopefully) hours of student study to produce educated students. Because economists are interested in the choices that firms make to accomplish their goals, and because they wish to avoid many of the intricacies involved in actual production decisions, they have developed a rather abstract model of production. In this model the relationship between inputs and outputs is formalized by a **production function** of the form

$$Q = f(K,L,M \ldots), \qquad [8.1]$$

where Q represents the output of a particular good[1] during a period, K represents the machine (that is, capital) use during the period, L represents hours of labor input, and M represents raw materials used. The form of the notation indicates the possibility of other variables affecting the production process. The production function, therefore, summarizes what the firm knows about mixing various inputs to yield output.

For example, this production function might represent a farmer's output of wheat during one year as being dependent on the quantity of machinery employed, the amount of labor used on the farm, the amount of land under cultivation, the amount of fertilizer and seeds used, and so forth. The function shows that, say, 100 bushels of wheat can be produced in many different ways. The farmer could use a very labor-intensive technique that would require only a small amount of mechanical equipment (as tends to be the case in China). The 100 bushels could also be produced using large amounts of equipment and fertilizer with very little labor (as in the United States). A great deal of land might be used to produce the 100 bushels of wheat with less of the other inputs (as in Brazil or Australia); or relatively little land could be used with great amounts of labor, equipment, and fertilizer (as in British or Japanese agriculture). All of these combinations are represented by the general production function in Equation 8.1. For any possible combination of land, equipment, labor, and other inputs, the function records the maximum wheat output that can be produced from those given inputs. The important question about the production function from an economic point of view is how the firm chooses the individual levels of Q, K, L, and M. We take this question up in detail in the next several chapters.

Firm

Any organization that turns inputs into outputs.

Production function

The mathematical relationship between inputs and outputs.

---

[1] Sometimes the output for a firm is defined to include only its "value added"; that is, the value of raw materials used by the firm is subtracted to arrive at a net value of output for the firm.

■ A Simplification

We will simplify the production function here by assuming that the firm's production depends on only two inputs: capital (K) and labor (L). Hence, our simplified production function is now

$$Q = f(K,L). \qquad [8.2]$$

Our decision to focus on capital and labor is arbitrary. Most of our analysis here will hold true for any two inputs that might be investigated. For example, if we wished to examine the effects of rainfall and fertilizer on crop production, we could use those two inputs in the production function while holding other inputs (quantity of land, hours of labor input, and so on) constant. In the production function that characterizes a school system, we could examine the relationship between the "output" of the system (say, academic achievement) and the inputs used to produce this output (such as teachers, buildings, and learning aids). The two general inputs of capital and labor are used here for convenience, and we will frequently show these inputs on a two-dimensional graph.

Marginal Physical Productivity

■
Marginal physical productivity

The additional output that can be produced by one more unit of a particular input while holding all other inputs constant.

The first question we might ask about the relationship between inputs and outputs is how much extra output can be produced by adding one more unit of an input to the production process. The **marginal physical productivity** of an input is defined as the quantity of extra output provided by employing one additional unit of that input while holding all other inputs constant. For our two principal inputs of capital and labor, the marginal physical product of labor (MP_L) is the extra output obtained by employing one more worker while holding the level of capital equipment constant. Similarly, the marginal physical productivity of capital (MP_K) is the extra output obtained by using one more machine while holding the number of workers constant.

As an illustration of these definitions, consider the case of a farmer hiring one more person to harvest a crop while holding all other inputs constant. The extra output produced by this person is the marginal physical productivity of labor input. The concept is measured in physical quantities such as bushels of wheat, crates of oranges, or heads of lettuce. We might, for example, observe that 25 workers on a farm are able to produce 10,000 bushels of wheat per year, whereas 26 workers (with the same land and equipment) can produce 10,200 bushels. The marginal physical product of the 26th worker is 200 bushels per year.

■ Diminishing Marginal Physical Productivity

We might expect the marginal physical productivity of an input to depend on how much of that input is used. For example, workers cannot be added indef-

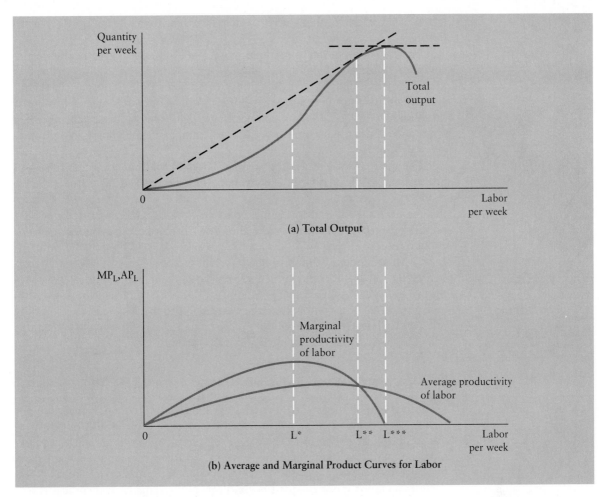

(a) Total Output

(b) Average and Marginal Product Curves for Labor

These curves show how the average and marginal productivity of labor curves can be derived from the total output curve. The total output (TP_L) curve in Panel a represents the relationship between labor input and output, on the assumption that all other inputs are held constant. In Panel b, the slope of this curve shows the marginal productivity of labor (MP_L), and the slope of a chord joining the origin to a point on the TP_L curve gives the average productivity of labor (AP_L).

Figure 8.1
Constructing Average and Marginal Productivity of Labor Curves from the Total Product Curve

initely to the harvesting of oranges (while keeping the amount of equipment, fertilizer, and so forth fixed) without the marginal productivity eventually deteriorating. This possibility is illustrated in Figure 8.1. The relationship between the quantity of a particular input (labor) and total output is recorded in Panel a of Figure 8.1. At low levels of labor usage, output increases rapidly as additional labor is added. However, because *other inputs are held constant,* the ability of additional labor to generate additional output eventually begins to deteriorate. Finally, at L*** output reaches its maximum level. Any labor added beyond this point actually decreases output. Beyond L*** additional laborers get in each other's way to such an extent that total output begins to decline.

The total output curve in Panel a of Figure 8.1 shows graphically the assumption that labor's marginal physical productivity eventually declines as more labor is added to the production process while other inputs are held constant. This assumption is extremely important in economic analysis. It is based on the notion that the inputs that are being held fixed (such as machinery or land) will eventually become "overutilized," and a decline in marginal productivity will set in.

The nineteenth century philosopher Thomas Malthus used these ideas to argue that if additional labor is constantly added to a fixed supply of land, the productivity of labor in food production eventually must diminish.[2] Because the quantity of land is absolutely fixed in the long run, Malthus predicted that population growth would outpace the growth in food production (with not enough food for everyone). This led to economics being called the "dismal science." Most modern economists believe that Malthus did not adequately recognize the possibilities for added capital equipment and technical advances that would prevent the decline of labor's productivity in agriculture. Nevertheless, the basic observation that the marginal productivity of labor (or any other factor) declines when *all other inputs and technology* are held constant is still recognized as an empirically valid proposition.

■ Marginal Physical Productivity Curve

From the total labor productivity curve in Panel a of Figure 8.1, several other productivity curves can be constructed. The marginal physical product of labor is simply the slope of the total output curve, since this slope shows how output expands as additional labor is added. In Panel b in Figure 8.1, the marginal product curve (MP_L) is drawn. This curve reaches a maximum at L^* and declines as labor input is added beyond this point. This movement is a reflection of the assumption of a diminishing marginal product of labor. MP_L is equal to 0 at the point L^{***} at which total output reaches a maximum. Beyond L^{***} further additions of labor input actually reduce output. In other words, MP_L is negative in this range. Production will not take place beyond L^{***} since using more labor (which is presumably costly) will result in less output for the firm.

■ Average Physical Productivity

"Labor productivity" usually means average productivity. When it is said that a certain industry has experienced productivity increases, this is taken to mean that output per unit of labor input has increased. In Application 8.1: Average

---

[2] A somewhat facetious "proof" of the diminishing marginal productivity of labor input argues that if it were not true, the entire world food supply could be grown in a single flowerpot if a sufficient quantity of labor were applied to the pot. Because this situation is obviously absurd, the marginal productivity of labor must diminish after some point.

APPLICATION 8.1
Average Productivity in Steel Production

The steel industry offers a case in which average labor productivity is fairly easy to measure and trends in labor productivity have played an important role in affecting the success of the domestic steel industry. During the late 1960s and early 1970s, the average productivity of labor in steel production grew very slowly in the United States relative to experiences in other countries. At the start of this period, each 100 hours of labor input yielded approximately 7 tons of steel in the United States. By 1975 this figure had increased only to approximately 8 tons. Japan, on the other hand, started the period with an average productivity of only about 5 tons per 100 labor hours, but by 1975 its figures were virtually on a par with those of the United States. Most observers attribute this outcome to the rapid adoption of new steel-making techniques in Japan. Manufacturers in the United States had made large investments in facilities in the 1950s, but were either unwilling or unable to invest in better facilities in subsequent decades.

Consequences of the Trends
The major result of these productivity trends was that by the mid-1970s Japan had become the world's lowest-cost steel producer. Between 1967 and 1977 Japanese steel exports tripled, increasing demands for tariff protection by American producers. In response, the U.S. government instituted fair price standards with the purpose of stemming Japanese imports. Gradually these standards evolved into "Voluntary Restraint Agreements" (VRAs) with Japan and other low-cost producers that were intended to give U.S. producers some "breathing room" within which to adopt better methods of production.[1] Although the VRAs lapsed in early 1992, domestic producers have continued to seek relief from expanding competition from countries experiencing rapid productivity gains such as South Korea and Brazil. In Chapter 13 we will see how to evaluate the large costs these VRAs imposed on American consumers.

Recent Experiences
Despite the continued protectionist plans, foreign challenges seem to have effectively prompted U.S. steel makers to improve their technical performance. Throughout the 1980s average productivity in steel production grew rapidly, averaging over 5 percent growth per year. This was the best productivity performance of any major U.S. industry during this time.[2] By the end of the decade, average productivity stood at about 14 tons per hundred labor hours, an increase of 75 percent over the mid-1970's number. A principal reason for the improved performance was the closing of outmoded production facilities, coupled with the development of smaller, more flexible production facilities with electric furnaces. By the 1990s, U.S. production had stabilized at about 11 percent of world output, and U.S. steel exports had actually risen a bit.

To Think About
1. Are the figures reported for average labor productivity in steel production here a correct reflection of the definitions developed in the text? What other inputs have been changing throughout the period studied? How would these changes affect the curves shown in Figure 8.1?

2. Some authors argue that Japan had an "advantage" in adopting new techniques for making steel because most of its older facilities were destroyed during World War II. Does this argument make sense? Are there reasons why a firm with older facilities might delay in scrapping them when a better technology comes along?

---

[1] For a discussion, see R. W. Crandall, *The U.S. Steel Industry in Recurrent Crisis* (Washington, D.C., Brookings Institution, 1981).

[2] See *Statistical Abstract of the United States (1991)*, Table 670.

Productivity in Steel Production, for example, we use this measure to look at some issues involving the production of steel. Because average productivity is easily measured (say, as so many tons of steel per hour of labor input), it is often used as a measure of efficiency.

It is a simple matter to derive average productivity relationships from the total product curve. This is also done in Figure 8.1. By definition the **average productivity** of any input (say, labor) is the ratio of total output produced to the quantity of the input employed. That is,

Average productivity
The ratio of total output produced to the quantity of a particular input employed.

$$\text{Average productivity of labor} = AP_L = Q/L. \qquad [8.3]$$

Geometrically, the value of the average productivity of labor for any quantity of labor input is the slope of the chord drawn from the origin in Panel a in Figure 8.1 to the relevant point on the total output curve. This is true since the slope of such a chord is simply Q/L. By drawing a series of chords through the origin to various points on the total output curve, the average product of labor curve (AP_L) can be constructed. This curve is shown in Panel b in Figure 8.1. It can be seen that the average and marginal productivities of labor are equal at L^{**}. For this level of labor input, the chord through the origin in Panel a in Figure 8.1 is just tangent to the total output curve. The slope of the chord is equal to the slope of TP_L so average and marginal productivities of labor are equal.

Also at L^{**} the average productivity of labor is at its maximum value. This feature of the curve can be demonstrated as follows: for levels of labor input less than L^{**}, the marginal productivity of labor (MP_L) exceeds its average productivity (AP_L). Consequently, adding one more worker will raise the average productivity of all workers since the increased output from hiring this additional worker exceeds that produced by the average worker previously. A good example of this is a baseball team with a team batting average of .260. If the team acquires a .300 hitter, the team average will rise. For labor input greater than L^{**}, the average productivity of labor falls. Beyond L^{**}, labor's average productivity exceeds its marginal productivity, so AP_L is falling. Adding a worker to the production process causes output to rise by less than the average that previously prevailed. Consequently, the average productivity of labor will fall. In our baseball analogy, adding a .200 hitter to the team will indeed cause the team average to fall.

We have shown that to the left of L^{**} the AP_L curve is rising; to the right of L^{**} it is falling. Therefore, the average productivity of labor reaches its maximum value at L^{**}. Labor added beyond this point will cause the average productivity of labor to fall.

■ Physical Productivity Curves and the *Ceteris Paribus* Assumption

Figure 8.1 records all the available information about the way in which varying labor input (or any other single input) affects output. It is important to remember the assumption that lies behind the construction of these curves: all possible inputs, other than labor, are being held constant at some specified levels. The marginal productivity curve records the *ceteris paribus* productivity of additional units of labor input, and the average productivity curve similarly records the *ceteris paribus* average productivity of various levels of labor input. If the firm were to hire more of some other input (say, more machines), all of the curves pictured in Figure 8.1 would move to new positions. For example, if a farmer were to double the land under cultivation and the use of machinery to work that land, we would expect both the marginal and the average productivity curves for labor to shift upward and to the right. With increased levels of complementary inputs, more labor can be used before diminishing returns begin to appear.

The *ceteris paribus* assumption limits the applications of the curves in Figure 8.1. Most firms change the levels of both labor *and* machines in response to changes in economic circumstances. We will therefore never observe a neat tracing of a single total productivity of labor curve, but rather a series of Q, L points that lie on a number of different curves. Because of these differences, it may sometimes be difficult to interpret data on average productivity as Application 8.2: Sources of the Japanese Advantage in Automobile Production illustrates for the case of international comparisons of productivity in automobile production.

Isoquant Maps

One way to picture an entire production function in two dimensions is to look at its **isoquant map**. We can again use a production function of the form $Q = f(K,L)$, using capital and labor as convenient examples of any two inputs that might happen to be of interest. To show the various combinations of capital and labor that can be employed to produce a particular output level, we use an **isoquant** (from the Greek *iso*, meaning equal). For example, all those combinations of K and L that fall on the curve labeled "Q = 10" in Figure 8.2 are capable of producing 10 units of output per period. This single isoquant records the many alternative ways of producing 10 units of output. One combination is represented by point A. A firm could use L_A and K_A to produce 10 units of output. Alternatively, the firm might prefer to use relatively less capital and more labor, and would therefore choose a point such as B. The isoquant clearly demonstrates that a firm can produce 10 units of output in many different ways just as the indifference curves in Part 2 showed that many different bundles of goods yield the same utility.

There are infinitely many isoquants in the K–L plane. Each isoquant represents a different level of output. The isoquants record successively higher levels of output as we move in a northeasterly direction since using more of each of the inputs will permit output to increase. Two other isoquants (for Q = 20 and Q = 30) are also shown in Figure 8.2. They record those combinations of inputs that can produce the specified level of output. You may notice the similarity between an isoquant map and the individual's indifference curve map discussed in Part 2. Both are "contour" maps which show the "altitude" (that

Isoquant map

A contour map of a firm's production function.

Isoquant

A curve that shows the various combinations of inputs that will produce the same amount of output.

APPLICATION 8.2
Sources of the Japanese Advantage in Automobile Production

In 1979, Japan overtook the United States as the world's largest producer of automobiles. Imports of Japanese cars topped 2 million per year in 1983 and have remained high ever since. The story of the changing auto buying behavior of Americans provides a major focus for several applications in this book. The following discussion takes a look at production.

Labor Productivity
By most estimates, the Japanese enjoy a considerable productivity advantage. In terms of average labor productivity, for example, it is estimated to take about 40 labor hours to produce a small car in Japan versus about 65 hours in the United States. Similar differentials have been found in total vehicle production costs.[1] Unlike the steel case (Application 8.1), however, it is not possible to trace these productivity differences to any specific types of capital equipment. Automobiles are far more complex products than steel, and explanations for productivity differences are likely to be equally complex.

Differences in Production Methods
Some of the productivity differences between U.S. and Japanese producers may be related to production methods. Because most Japanese cars and pickup trucks are about the same size, many types of vehicles can be produced on the same assembly lines. U.S. producers tend to use many more assembly lines to accommodate their greater variability in vehicle size. In addition, automating production (through the use of robots, for example) is, therefore, somewhat easier in Japan.

There are also differences in the way auto production is organized in the United States and Japan. Although firms in both countries tend to buy many components of cars from independent suppliers, in Japan the suppliers are better integrated with the assembly firms. Information and engineering staffs are more widely shared so that redesigning is needed less frequently. This relationship also leads to higher levels of quality control.

Differences in Industrial Relations
In addition to these technical differences, some observers have also suggested that Japanese industrial relations practices may aid productivity. Because many workers effectively cannot be fired, usually belong to a company union, and obtain a large portion of their pay in terms of year-end bonuses, they may feel a greater attachment to their firm than in the United States where relations between labor and management are more adversarial. Some evidence that Japanese labor relations practices may be significant factors is provided by experiences with Japanese-run automobile plants (for example, the Honda assembly plant in Marysville, Ohio) in the United States. In these plants, labor productivity appears to be only slightly lower than for the same firms in Japan and higher than productivity in U.S. firms. There is no general agreement about the causes of such productivity differences, however.

To Think About
1. Why would auto producers in Japan and in the United States use different methods to make cars? Because there are no great secrets surrounding auto production (U.S. and Japanese engineers frequently visit each others' factories), why wouldn't firms everywhere adopt the same production functions?
2. If Japanese industrial relations practices really do make workers more productive, how would you reflect this with a production function? Is "good labor relations" a separate input? If so, why don't all firms practice better labor relations?

---

[1] M. A. Fuss and L. Waverman, *Costs and Productivity in Automobile Production* (Cambridge, U.K.: Cambridge University Press, 1992): 61.

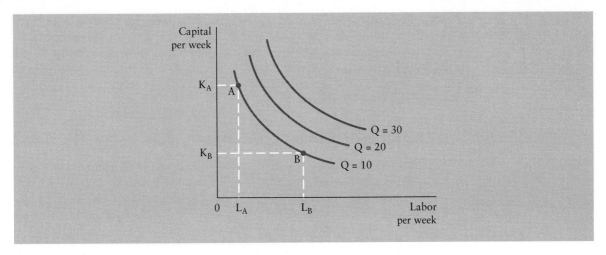

Isoquants record the alternative combinations of inputs that can be used to produce a given level of output. The slope of these curves shows the rate at which L can be substituted for K while keeping output constant. The negative of this slope is called the (marginal) rate of technical substitution (RTS). In the figure, the RTS is positive, and it is diminishing for increasing inputs of labor.

Figure 8.2
Isoquant Map

is, utility or output) associated with various input combinations. For isoquants, however, the labeling of the curves is measurable (an output of 10 units has a quantifiable meaning), and we are more interested in the shape of these curves than we were in the exact shape of indifference curves.

■ Rate of Technical Substitution

The slope of an isoquant shows how one input can be traded for another while holding output constant. Examining this slope gives some information about the technical possibilities for substituting labor for capital. Because of this, the slope of an isoquant (or, more properly, its negative) is called the **marginal rate of technical substitution (RTS)** of labor for capital. More precisely, the RTS is defined as the amount by which capital input can be reduced while holding quantity produced constant when one more unit of labor input is used. Mathematically,

$$
\begin{aligned}
\text{Rate of technical substitution} & \\
\text{(of labor for capital)} &= \text{RTS (of L for K)} \\
&= -(\text{Slope of isoquant}) \qquad [8.4] \\
&= -\frac{\text{Change in capital input.}}{\text{Change in labor input}} \\
& \quad \text{(holding Q constant)}
\end{aligned}
$$

Marginal rate of technical substitution (RTS)

This shows the amount by which one input can be reduced while holding output constant when one more unit of another input is added. The negative of the slope of an isoquant.

The particular value of this trade-off rate will depend not only on the level of output but also on the quantities of capital and labor being used. Its value depends on the point on the isoquant map at which the slope is to be measured. At a point such as A in Figure 8.2, relatively large amounts of capital can be given up if one or more units of labor are employed—at point A, the RTS is a high positive number. On the other hand, at point B the availability of an additional unit of labor does not permit a very large reduction in capital input, and the RTS is relatively small.

■ The RTS and Marginal Productivities

We can use the RTS concept to discuss the likely shape of a firm's isoquant map. Most obviously, it seems clear that the RTS should be positive; that is, each isoquant should have a negative slope. If the quantity of labor employed by the firm increases, the firm should be able to reduce capital input and still keep output constant. Since labor presumably has a positive marginal productivity, the firm should be able to get by with less capital input when more labor is used. If increasing labor actually required the firm to use more capital, it would imply that the marginal productivity of labor (or of capital[3]) is negative, and no firm would be willing to hire an input with a negative marginal physical productivity. All isoquants that are actually observed should therefore be negatively sloped, showing that there is a trade-off between capital and labor input use.

■ Diminishing RTS

The isoquants in Figure 8.2 are drawn not only with a negative slope (as they should be) but also as convex curves. Along any one of the curves the RTS is *diminishing*. For a high ratio of K to L, the RTS is a large positive number indicating that a great deal of capital can be given up if one more unit of labor is employed. On the other hand, when a lot of labor is already being used, the RTS is low, signifying that only a small amount of capital can be traded for an additional unit of labor if output is to be held constant. This shape seems intuitively reasonable: the more labor (relative to capital) that is used, the less labor can substitute for capital. The diminishing RTS shows that a particular input can be pushed too far. Firms will not want to use "only labor" or "only machines" to produce a given level of output.[4] They will choose a more balanced input mix that uses at least some of each input. In Chapter 9, we will see

---

[3] This result can be shown formally by recognizing that the RTS is equal to the ratio of the marginal productivity of labor to the marginal productivity of capital. That is,

$$\text{RTS (of L for K)} = MP_L/MP_K,$$

since this value of marginal productivities shows how L can be traded for K while holding Q constant. For example, if $MP_L = 2$ and $MP_K = 1$, the RTS will be 2, since the extra output produced by hiring one more unit of labor input can replace the production of two units of capital. Given this result, it is clear that if the RTS is negative (that is, if an isoquant has a positive slope), either MP_L or MP_K must be negative.

[4] An incorrect, but possibly instructive, argument (based on footnote 3 of this chapter) might proceed as follows. In moving along an isoquant, more labor and less capital are being used. Assuming that each factor exhibits a diminishing marginal productivity, it might be argued that MP_L would decrease (since the quantity of labor has increased) and that MP_K would increase (since the quantity of capital has decreased). Consequently, the RTS (= MP_L/MP_K) should decrease. The fallacy in this argument is that *both* factors are changing together. It is not possible to make such simple determinations about changes in marginal productivities when two inputs are changing, since the marginal productivity concept requires that all other inputs be held constant.

exactly how an optimal (that is, minimum cost) mix of inputs might be chosen. Application 8.3: Engineering and Economics illustrates how isoquant maps can be developed from actual production information.

Returns to Scale

Because production functions represent tangible, measurable productive processes, economists pay considerable attention to the form of these functions. The shape and properties of a firm's production function are important for a variety of reasons. Using such information, a firm may decide how its research funds might best be spent on developing technical improvements. Or, public policymakers might study the form of production functions to argue that laws prohibiting very large-scale firms would harm economic efficiency. In this section we develop some terminology to aid in examining such issues.

■ Adam Smith on Returns to Scale

The first important question we might ask about production functions is, how does the quantity of output respond to increases in all inputs together? For example, suppose all inputs were doubled. Would output also double, or is the relationship not quite so simple? Here we are asking about the **returns to scale** exhibited by a production function, a concept that has been of interest to economists ever since Adam Smith intensively studied (of all things) the production of pins in the eighteenth century. Smith identified two forces that come into play when all inputs are doubled (for a doubling of scale). First, a doubling of scale permits a greater "division of labor." Smith was intrigued by the skill of people who made only pin heads, or who sharpened pin shafts, or who stuck the two together. He suggested that efficiency might increase—production might more than double—as greater specialization of this type becomes possible.

    Smith did not envision that these benefits to large-scale operations would always be available, however. He recognized that large firms may encounter inefficiencies in managerial direction and control if scale is dramatically increased. Coordination of production plans for more inputs may become more difficult when there are many layers of management and many specialized workers involved in the production process.

■ A Precise Definition

Which of these two effects of scale is more important is an empirical question. To investigate this question, economists need a precise definition of returns to scale. A production function is said to exhibit *constant returns to scale* if a doubling of all inputs results in a precise doubling of output. If a doubling of all inputs yields less than a doubling of output, the production function is said to exhibit *decreasing returns to scale*. If a doubling of all inputs results in more than a doubling of output, the production function exhibits *increasing returns to scale*.

> **■**
> **Returns to scale**
> The rate at which output increases in response to proportional increases in all inputs.

APPLICATION 8.3

Engineering and Economics

One way economists manage to derive production functions for a specific good is through the use of information provided by engineers. An illustration of how engineering studies might be used is provided in Figure 1. Here engineers have developed three processes (A, B, and C) for producing a given good. Process A uses a higher ratio of capital to labor than does process B, and process B uses a higher ratio than does process C. Each process can be expanded as much as desired by duplicating the basic machinery involved. The points a, b, and c on each respective ray show a particular output level, say, Q_0. By joining these points we obtain the Q_0 isoquant, with points between each ray reflecting proportionate use of two techniques.

Solar Hot Water Heating

This method was used by G. T. Sav to examine the production of domestic hot water by rooftop solar collectors.[1] Because solar systems require backup hot water generators for use during periods of reduced sunlight, Sav was especially interested in the proper way to integrate the two processes. Sav used engineering data to develop an isoquant map showing the trade-off between fuel use and system capital requirements. He showed that isoquant maps differ in various regions of the United States, with the productivity of solar collectors obviously depending upon the amount of sunlight available in the different regions.

Energy and Capital

More generally, the engineering approach has been used to examine the relationship between energy use and firms' capital input choices. A number of engineering studies suggest that energy and capital substitute for each other in the design of industrial equipment; to economize on energy usage generally requires more sophisticated machinery.

Although the substitutability between energy and capital seems clear on the engineering level, economists

Figure 1
Construction of an Isoquant from
Engineering Data

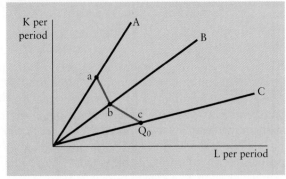

The rays A, B, and C show three specific industrial processes. Points a, b, and c show the level of operation of each process necessary to yield Q_0. The Q_0 isoquant reflects various mixtures of the three processes.

have sometimes found that energy and capital appear to complement each other in production; levels of the two inputs seem to rise and fall together. For example, some economists have claimed that recent poor productivity performances in certain countries (see Application 8.5) may have resulted from rising energy prices, which deterred both energy and capital use. Reconciling these economic observations with the underlying engineering reality has proved to be a challenging matter for economists.[2]

To Think About

1. In the late 1970s, the U.S. government offered large tax incentives to people who installed solar collectors. Would these incentives affect the technology used to produce domestic hot water? Do the incentives seem to be a good idea?
2. Engineers sometimes talk about the energy efficiency of an industrial process. Many systems (such as home heating plants) produce output at rates well below 40 percent efficiency. What does this fact suggest about capital energy substitutability?

[1] G. T. Sav, "The Engineering Approach to Production Functions Revisited: An Application to Solar Processes," *The Journal of Industrial Economics* (September 1984): 21–35.

[2] For one such reconciliation, see E. R. Berndt and D. O. Wood, "Engineering and Econometric Interpretations of Energy–Capital Complementarity," *American Economic Review* (June 1979): 342–353.

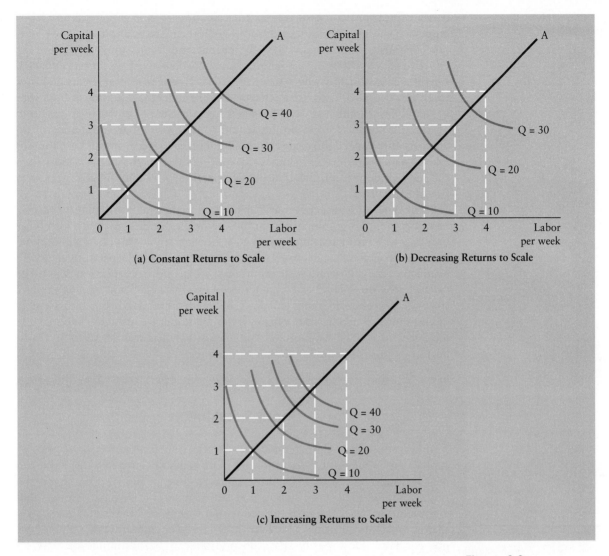

(a) Constant Returns to Scale

(b) Decreasing Returns to Scale

(c) Increasing Returns to Scale

In Panel a an expansion in both inputs leads to a similar, proportionate expansion in output. This is constant returns to scale. In Panel b an expansion in inputs yields a less than proportionate expansion in output, illustrating decreasing returns to scale. Panel c shows increasing returns to scale—output expands proportionately faster than inputs.

Figure 8.3
Isoquant Maps Showing Constant, Decreasing, and Increasing Returns to Scale

■ Graphic Illustrations

These possibilities are illustrated in the three graphs of Figure 8.3. In each case production isoquants for Q = 10, 20, 30, and 40 are shown, together with a ray (labeled 0A) showing a uniform expansion of both capital and labor inputs.

Panel a illustrates constant returns to scale. There, as both capital and labor inputs are successively increased from 1 to 2, then 2 to 3, and then 3 to 4, output expands proportionally. That is, output and inputs move in unison. In Panel b, by comparison, the isoquants get further apart as output expands. This is a case of decreasing returns to scale—an expansion in inputs does not result in a proportionate rise in output. For example, the doubling of both capital and labor inputs from 1 to 2 units is not sufficient to increase output from 10 to 20. That increase in output would require more than a doubling of inputs. Finally, Panel c illustrates increasing returns to scale. In this case the isoquants get closer together as input expands—a doubling of inputs is more than sufficient to double output. Large-scale operation would in this case appear to be quite efficient.

The types of scale economies experienced in the real world may, of course, be rather complex combinations of these simple examples. A production function may exhibit increasing returns to scale over some output ranges and decreasing returns to scale over other ranges. Or, some aspects of a good's production may illustrate scale economies, whereas other aspects may not. For example, the production of computer chips exhibits significant scale economies since the process of making chips can be highly automated. But the assembly of chips into electronic components is more difficult to automate and may exhibit few such scale economies. Application 8.4: Returns to Scale in Transportation illustrates similar complex possibilities.

Input Substitution

Another important characteristic of a production function is how "easily" capital can be substituted for labor, or, more generally, how any one input can be substituted for another. This characteristic depends more on the shape of a single isoquant than on the whole isoquant map. So far we have assumed that a given output level can be produced with a variety of different input mixes—that is, we assumed firms could substitute labor for capital while keeping output constant. How easily that substitution can be accomplished may, of course, vary. In some cases the substitution can be made easily and quickly in response to changing economic circumstances. Mine owners found it relatively easy to automate in response to rising wages for miners, for example. In other cases firms may have little choice about the input combination they must use. Producers of operas have little chance to substitute capital (scenery) for labor (singers). Economists can measure this degree of substitution very technically, but for us to do so here would take us too far afield.[5] We can look at one special case in which input substitution is impossible, which will show us the kinds of problems in substitution that economists have noted.

---

[5] Formally, the ease of input substitution is measured by the *elasticity of substitution,* which is defined as the ratio of the percentage change in K/L to the percentage change in the RTS along an isoquant. See K. J. Arrow et al., "Capital–Labor Substitution and Economic Efficiency," *Review of Economics and Statistics* (August 1961): 225–250.

APPLICATION 8.4
Returns to Scale in Transportation

The possibility of increasing returns to scale significantly influences the ways goods are transported from place to place. To illustrate this point, we look at cargo ships and railroads in order to see some of the complications involved.

Cargo Ships

Oceangoing ships effectively illustrate the importance of the returns-to-scale concept for practical decision making. We can see easily why ships might exhibit increasing returns to scale using a geometric example. Picture a ship as an empty cube. If the lengths of the four sides and top and bottom of the cube are doubled, its overall surface area will increase fourfold. The volume of the cube, on the other hand, will increase eightfold. A doubling of inputs (in this case, the size of the ship's hull) will more than double its carrying capacity.

A closer examination of specific types of ships reveals substantial problems with increases in size. Loading and unloading cargo from very large ships can be a difficult and costly process: Larger cranes are needed, interior handling equipment must be used in the large holds, and goods must sometimes be moved substantial distances just to get them off the ship. The geometric allure of large ships must be tempered somewhat by logistical problems of cargo handling. A 1978 study by J. O. Jansson and D. Schneerson illustrates these considerations quite clearly.[1] Jansson and Schneerson showed that a 50 percent increase in the carrying capacity of a cargo ship on average increases the ship's capital cost by only about 25 percent. Ships' operating costs are increased even less (for example, a ship, no matter how large, needs only one captain). On the other hand, the authors found that a 50 percent increase in carrying capacity tends to increase capital costs associated with cargo handling by nearly 90 percent. Shipping firms must make very careful calculations in deciding how to trade off these advantages and disadvantages of very large-sized vessels.

Railroads

It is also reasonable to expect that freight railroads may experience increasing returns to scale, at least up to a point. One of the principal logistical problems faced by railroads is the assembling and scheduling of trains. As the traffic over a given stretch of track increases, it becomes possible to utilize both specialized trains (only coal cars, for example) and frequent scheduling (particularly important for perishable cargo). These benefits extend only so far, however. As traffic density increases over a fixed-rail network, maintenance expenses rise and traffic management (signals and siding controls) becomes more complex. By one estimate, annual traffic densities greater than about 8 million tons per track mile encounter diminishing returns precisely because of these logistical difficulties.[2] Few U.S. railroads approach such high levels of operations, though.

To Think About

1. Why might the optimal size of a ship change over time as economic conditions change? For example, what factors might have led oil companies to opt to start building very large crude oil carriers (VLCCs) in the early 1970s, whereas before they had used smaller vessels?

2. Do you think that other forms of transportation such as trucking or air cargo experience similar types of increasing returns to scale to those examined here? How might these be similar to ships and railroads? How do they differ?

---

[1] J. O. Jansson and D. Schneerson, "Economies of Scale of General Cargo Ships," *Review of Economics and Statistics* (May 1978): 291–296.

[2] See T. Keeler, *Railroads, Freight and Public Policy* (Washington, D.C., The Brookings Institution, 1983).

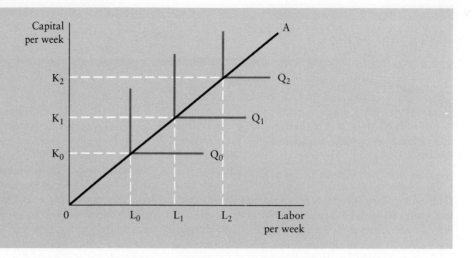

Figure 8.4
Isoquant Map with
Fixed Proportions

The isoquant map shown here has no substitution possibilities. Capital and labor must be used in fixed proportions if neither is to be redundant. For example, if K_1 machines are available, L_1 units of labor should be used. If L_2 units of labor are used, there will be excess labor since no more than Q_1 can be produced from the given machines. Alternatively, if L_0 laborers were hired, machines would be in excess to the extent $K_1 - K_0$.

■ Fixed-Proportions Production Function

Figure 8.4 demonstrates a case where no substitution is possible. This case is rather different from the ones we have looked at so far. Here the isoquants are L-shaped, indicating that machines and labor must be used in absolutely fixed proportions. Every machine has a fixed complement of workers that cannot be varied. For example, if K_1 machines are in use, L_1 workers are required to produce output level Q_1. Employing more workers than L_1 will not increase output with K_1 machines, since the Q_1 isoquant is horizontal beyond the point K_1, L_1. In other words, the marginal productivity of labor is zero beyond L_1. On the other hand, using fewer workers would result in excess machines. If only L_0 workers were hired, for instance, only Q_0 units could be produced, but these units could be produced with only K_0 machines. When L_0 workers are hired, there is an excess of machines of an amount given by $K_1 - K_0$.

Fixed-proportions production function

A production function in which the inputs must be used in a fixed ratio to one another.

The production function whose isoquant map is shown in Figure 8.4 is called a **fixed-proportions production function**. Both inputs will be fully employed only if a combination of K and L that lies along the ray 0A, which passes through the vertices of the isoquants, is chosen. Otherwise one input will be excessive in the sense that it could be cut back without restricting output. If a firm with such a production function wishes to expand, it must increase all inputs simultaneously so that none of the inputs are excessive.

The fixed-proportions production function has a wide variety of applications to real-world production techniques. Many machines do require a fixed complement of workers; more than these would be excessive. For example, consider the combination of capital and labor required to mow a lawn. The lawn mower needs one person for its operation, and a worker needs one lawn mower in order to produce any output. Output can be expanded (that is, more grass can be mowed at the same time) only by adding capital and labor to the productive process in fixed proportions. Many production functions may be of this type, and the fixed-proportions model is in many ways appropriate for production planning.[6]

■ The Relevance of Input Substitutability

The ease with which one input can be substituted for another is of considerable interest to economists. They can use the shape of an isoquant map to see the relative ease with which different industries can adapt to the changing availability of productive inputs. For example, over the past hundred years the output of the American economy has shifted markedly away from agricultural production and toward manufacturing and service industries. This shift moved certain factors of production (notably labor) out of agriculture and into other industries. If production were relatively flexible in terms of input substitutability, the inputs formerly used in agriculture could be easily accommodated in the manufacturing and service industries. On the other hand, if production were closer to fixed proportions, the inputs might not be absorbed in exactly the proportions released by agriculture, and unemployment might result.

■ An Illustration

To show this possibility, suppose that the capital–labor ratio in manufacturing is two to one; that is, it takes two machines to equip one worker. Suppose, on the other hand, that the capital–labor ratio in agriculture is one to one. If demand shifts so that agricultural production must be reduced and manufacturing output increased, problems will arise. The reduction in agricultural output will release capital and labor in the ratio of one to one. However, manufacturing can absorb capital and labor only in the ratio of two to one. It needs two machines from the agricultural sector in order to be able to employ one more worker. Half of the workers released by the agricultural sector will be unemployed. On the other hand, the released labor might easily have been absorbed if the capital–labor ratio in manufacturing could be changed. To assess the effects on inputs of a shift in demand, we need to know how flexible production techniques are and how markets work to accommodate the inflexibility that does exist.

---

[6] The lawn mower example points up another possibility. Presumably there is some leeway in choosing what size and type of lawn mower to buy. Any device, from a pair of clippers to a gang mower, might be chosen. Prior to the actual purchase, the capital–labor ratio in lawn mowing can be considered variable. Once the mower is purchased, however, the capital–labor ratio becomes fixed.

Changes in Technology

A production function reflects firms' technical knowledge about how to use inputs to produce outputs. When firms improve their production techniques, the production function changes. This kind of technical advancement occurs constantly as older, outmoded machines are replaced by more efficient ones that embody state-of-the-art techniques. Workers too are part of this technical progress as they become better educated and learn special skills for doing their jobs. Today, for example, steel is made far more efficiently than in the nineteenth century both because blast furnaces and rolling mills are better and because workers are better trained to use these facilities.

The production function concept and its related isoquant map are important tools for understanding the effect of technical change. Formally, technical progress represents a shift in the production function, such as that illustrated in Figure 8.5. In this figure the isoquant Q_0 summarizes the initial state of technical knowledge. That level of output can be produced using K_0, L_0, or any of

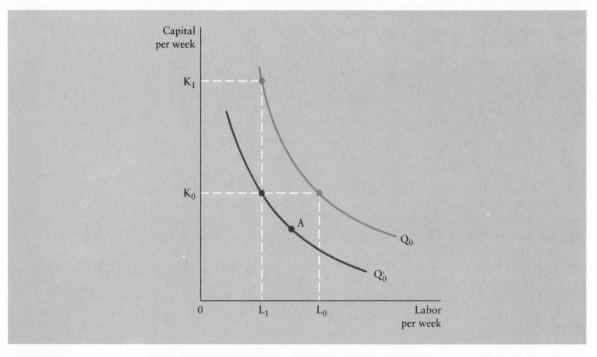

Figure 8.5
Technical Change

Technical progress shifts the Q_0 isoquant inward to Q_0'. Whereas previously it required K_0, L_0 to produce Q_0, now, with the same amount of capital, only L_1 units of labor are required. This result can be contrasted to capital–labor substitution in which the required labor input for Q_0 also declines to L_1 as more capital (K_1) is used.

a number of input combinations. With the discovery of new production techniques, the Q_0 isoquant shifts toward the origin—the same output level can now be produced using smaller quantities of inputs. If, for example, the Q_0 isoquant shifts inward to Q_0', it is now possible to produce Q_0 with the same amount of capital as before (K_0) but with much less labor (L_1). It is even possible to produce Q_0 using both less capital and less labor than previously by choosing a point such as A. **Technical progress** represents a real savings on inputs and (as we shall see in the next chapter) a reduction in the costs of production.

■ Technical Progress versus Input Substitution

We can use Figure 8.5 to show an important distinction between true technical advancement and simple capital–labor substitution. With technical progress, the firm can continue to use K_0, but it produces Q_0 with less labor (L_1). The average productivity of labor rises from Q_0/L_0 to Q_0/L_1. Even in the absence of technical improvements the firm could increase the average productivity of labor by choosing to use K_1 units of capital. This substitution of capital for labor would also have caused the average productivity of labor to rise from Q_0/L_0 to Q_0/L_1. This rise would not mean any real improvement in the way goods are made, however. In studying productivity data, especially data on output per worker, we must be careful that the changes being observed represent technical improvements rather than capital–labor substitution. Application 8.5: The Worldwide Productivity Decline illustrates this distinction.

Technical progress
A shift in the production function that allows a given output level to be produced using less inputs.

A Numerical Example

Additional insights about the nature of production functions can be obtained by looking at a simple numerical example. Although this example is obviously unrealistic (and, hopefully, a bit amusing), it does reflect many aspects of actual production processes.

■ The Production Function

Suppose we looked in detail at the production process used by the fast food chain, Hamburger Heaven (HH). The production function for each outlet in the chain is

$$\text{Hamburgers per hour} = Q = 10 \sqrt{KL} \qquad [8.5]$$

where K represents the number of grills used and L represents the number of workers employed during an hour of production. One aspect of this function is that it exhibits constant returns to scale.[7] Table 8.1 shows this fact by looking

---

[7] Since this production function can be written $Q = 40K^{1/2}L^{1/2}$, it is a "Cobb–Douglas" function with constant returns to scale (since the exponents sum to 1.0). See problem 8.7.

APPLICATION 8.5

The Worldwide Productivity Decline

Since the early 1970s rates of productivity growth seem to have declined in most industrialized countries. One simple measure of this decline is the data on growth rates in per capita GDP shown in Table 1. In all of the countries listed in the table, growth rates during the 1973 to 1986 period were only about half what they were in the earlier period. More detailed studies of productivity growth reach a similar conclusion. In the United States, for example, growth in *total factor productivity* (a measure that controls for growth rates in all inputs, not just labor alone) averaged about 1.5 percent per year prior to 1973 and only about 0.5 percent after.

Possible Explanations

Many explanations have been made for the worldwide productivity decline. One author lists at least 10 proposed explanations, ranging from fairly straightforward suggestions about lagging research and development spending resulting in fewer new major technical advances, to more conjectural possibilities such as the notion that workers "don't want to work hard any more."[1]

Four specific explanations have interested economists the most. First is the question of whether the high rates of inflation during the 1970s and early 1980s contributed to poor productivity by making it more difficult for business managers to plan their production activities. A second related explanation focuses on changing energy prices after 1973 and how they affected firms' use of capital (this explanation is discussed in Application 8.3). Third, a number of authors have pointed to increasing government regulation of the economy (particularly in the environmental and health areas) as a possible cause of lagging productivity growth. In this view, much investment currently yields output (e.g., clean air) that is not included in GDP statistics. Finally, some authors have suggested that the shift in most industrialized economies from goods toward services production may have caused growth to decline since service jobs cannot be easily automated. Despite voluminous

Table 1
Annual Growth Rates in per Capita GDP for Selected Countries (Percent)

	1955–1973	1973–1986
United States	2.0	1.3
Canada	3.0	2.0
France	4.6	1.9
Germany	4.2	2.0
Italy	4.9	2.0
Japan	8.8	3.1
United Kingdom	2.5	0.9

Source: International Financial Statistics (Washington, D.C.: International Monetary Fund, 1988).

research, there is no general agreement about the importance of each of these explanations.

Policies to Spur Productivity Gains

Similarly, there is no agreement about what kinds of policies might reverse the productivity decline. In the United States, for example, much interest has focused on improving schools (George Bush billed himself as the "education President") and on encouraging investment in research (President Clinton's economic plan contains a number of R&D tax breaks). Whether such actions will have any important economic effect on productivity growth remains to be seen, however.

To Think About

1. Explain why figures for growth in "total factor productivity" are smaller than the figures for growth in labor productivity. Which of the measures do you think is more appropriate for judging improvements in technology? Which is better for judging how much workers should be paid?
2. How would you judge whether environmental and safety regulation played a role in the recent productivity decline? How would you evaluate the disadvantages of such a decline if it were possible to measure it?

---

[1] M. N. Baily, "What Has Happened to Productivity Growth?" *Science* (October 24, 1986): 443–451.

Grills (K)	Workers (L)	Hamburgers per Hour	
1	1	10	**Table 8.1**
2	2	20	Hamburger
3	3	30	Production Exhibits
4	4	40	Constant Returns
5	5	50	to Scale
6	6	60	
7	7	70	
8	8	80	
9	9	90	
10	10	100	

Source: Equation 8.5.

Grills (K)	Workers (L)	Hamburgers per Hour(Q)	AP_L (=Q/L)	MP_L	
4	1	20.0	20.0	—	**Table 8.2**
4	2	28.3	14.1	8.3	Total Output,
4	3	34.6	11.5	6.3	Average
4	4	40.0	10.0	5.4	Productivity, and
4	5	44.7	8.9	4.7	Marginal
4	6	49.0	8.2	4.3	Productivity with
4	7	52.9	7.6	3.9	Four Grills
4	8	56.6	7.1	3.7	
4	9	60.0	6.7	3.4	
4	10	63.2	6.3	3.2	

Source: Equation 8.5 and use of definitions for AP_L, MP_L.

at input levels for K and L ranging from 1 to 10. As both workers and grills are increased together, hourly hamburger output rises proportionally. To increase the number of hamburgers it serves, HH must simply duplicate its kitchen technology over and over again.

■ Average and Marginal Productivities

To show the average and marginal productivity relationships for HH we must hold one input constant and vary the other one. Suppose that HH has 4 grills (K = 4, a particularly easy number of which to take a square root). In this case

$$Q = 10\sqrt{4 \cdot L} = 20\sqrt{L} \qquad [8.6]$$

and this provides a simple relationship between output and labor input. Table 8.2 shows this relationship. Notice two things about the table. First, the average productivity of labor declines as more hamburger flippers are employed.

	Hamburgers per Hour (Q)	Grills (K)	Workers (L)
Table 8.3 Construction of the Q = 40 Isoquant	40	16.0	1
	40	8.0	2
	40	5.3	3
	40	4.0	4
	40	3.2	5
	40	2.7	6
	40	2.3	7
	40	2.0	8
	40	1.8	9
	40	1.6	10

Source: Equation 8.10.

Since K is fixed, this undoubtedly occurs because the flippers get in each other's way as they become increasingly crowded around the four grills. Second, notice that the productivity of each additional worker hired also declines and is below the average productivity. Hiring added workers drags down average productivity because of the diminishing returns arising from the fixed number of grills. Even though HH's production exhibits constant returns to scale when both K and L can change, holding one input constant yields the expected declining average and marginal productivities.

■ The Isoquant Map

The overall production technology for HH is best illustrated by its isoquant map. Here we will show how to get one isoquant, but any others desired could be computed in exactly the same way. Suppose HH wants to produce 40 hamburgers per hour. Then its production function becomes

$$Q = 40 \text{ hamburgers per hour} = 10 \sqrt{KL} \qquad [8.7]$$

or

$$4 = \sqrt{KL} \qquad [8.8]$$

or

$$16 = K \cdot L. \qquad [8.9]$$

Table 8.3 shows a few of the K, L combinations that satisfy this equation. Clearly there are many ways to produce hamburgers ranging from using a lot of grills with workers dashing among them to using many workers gathered around a few grills. All possible combinations are reflected in the "Q = 40" isoquant in Figure 8.6. Other isoquants would have exactly the same shape showing that HH has many substitution possibilities in the ways it actually chooses to produce its heavenly burgers.

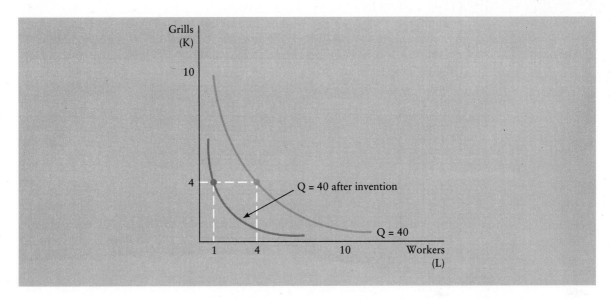

The Q = 40 isoquant comes directly from Table 8.3. Technical progress causes this iso-quant to shift inward. Previously it took 4 workers with 4 grills to produce 40 ham-burgers per hour. With the invention, it takes only 1 worker working with 4 grills to achieve the same output.

Figure 8.6
Technical Progress in Hamburger Production

Technical Progress

The possibility for scientific advancement in the art of hamburger production can also be shown in this simple case. Suppose that genetic engineering leads to the invention of self-flipping burgers so that the production function becomes

$$Q = 20\sqrt{K \cdot L}. \qquad [8.10]$$

We can compare this new technology to that which prevailed previously by re-calculating the Q = 40 isoquant:

$$Q = 40 = 20\sqrt{KL} \qquad [8.11]$$

or

$$2 = \sqrt{KL} \qquad [8.12]$$

or

$$4 = KL. \qquad [8.13]$$

The combinations of K and L that satisfy this equation are shown by the "Q = 40 after invention" isoquant in Figure 8.6. One way to see the overall ef-fect of the invention is to calculate average labor productivity in these two cases. With 4 grills, Figure 8.6 shows that it took 4 workers under the prior technology to produce 40 hamburgers per hour. Average productivity was 10 hamburgers per hour per worker. Now a single worker can produce 40 hamburgers per hour because each burger flips itself. Average productivity is 40 hamburgers per hour per worker. This level of average labor productivity could have been attained under the old technology, but this would have required using 16 grills and would have been considerably more costly.

Summary

Chapter 8 shows how economists conceptualize the process of production. We introduced the notion of a production function, which records the relationship between input use and output, and we showed how this function can be illustrated with an isoquant map. Several features of the production function are explicitly discussed in the chapter:

- The marginal productivity of any input is the extra output that can be produced by adding one more unit of that input while holding all other inputs constant. The marginal productivity of an input declines as more of that input is used.

- The possible input combinations that a firm might use to produce a given level of output are shown on an isoquant. The slope of the isoquant is called the rate of technical substitution (RTS)—it shows how one input can be substituted for another while holding output constant.

- "Returns to scale" refers to the way in which a firm's output responds to proportionate increases in all inputs. If a doubling of all inputs causes output to more than double, there are increasing returns to scale. If such a doubling of inputs causes output to less than double, returns to scale are decreasing. The middle case, when output exactly doubles, is constant returns to scale.

- In some cases it may not be possible for the firm to substitute one input for another. In these cases, the inputs must be used in fixed proportions. Such production functions will have L-shaped isoquants.

- Technical progress will shift the firm's entire isoquant map. A given output level can be produced with fewer inputs.

Review Questions

1. Provide a brief description of the production function for each of the following firms. What is the firm's output? What inputs does it use? Can you think of any special features of the way production takes place in the firm?

a. An Iowa wheat farm
b. An Arizona vegetable farm
c. U.S. Steel Corporation
d. A local arc welding firm
e. Sears
f. Joe's Hot Dog Stand
g. The Metropolitan Opera
h. The Metropolitan Museum of Art
i. The National Institute of Health
j. Dr. Smith's private practice
k. Paul's lemonade stand.

2. Why are firms' isoquant maps and individuals' indifference curve maps basically the same idea? What are the most important ways in which these concepts differ?

3. On a firm's isoquant map, what is held constant along a single isoquant? What does the slope of an isoquant show? Why would you never expect a firm to operate in a region of its isoquant map where the slope of the isoquants is positive?

4. Much discussion of productivity focuses on "output per worker." Is this an average or a marginal productivity notion? Which of these concepts do you think is most relevant to a firm's hiring decisions?

5. Contrast the notions of diminishing marginal productivity and diminishing returns to scale. Why do economists believe production usually exhibits diminishing marginal productivity for inputs but not necessarily diminishing returns to scale? Could a production function exhibit diminishing marginal productivities for *every* input and still exhibit either constant or increasing returns to scale?

6. Answer question 5 for two specific production functions:

a. A fixed-proportions production function;
b. A Cobb–Douglas production function of the form

$$Q = \sqrt{K \cdot L}$$

(see problems 8.4, 8.7, and 8.8 for a discussion of this case).

7. "Most purported cases of diminishing returns to scale actually arise because one input is held constant. These therefore represent a misuse of the notion of returns to scale and should instead be viewed as an illustration of diminishing marginal productivities." Do you agree? Explain the theoretical notion of *returns to scale* and describe some of the problems in using the precise definition of the term in real-world situations.

8. Explain why a firm with a fixed-proportions production function would not be able to substitute one input for another while holding output constant. By analogy to consumer theory, what would an isoquant map that illustrated very easy substitution look like?

9. Could a fixed-proportions production function exhibit increasing or decreasing returns to scale? What would its isoquant map look like in these cases?

10. Explain why it is difficult to differentiate between technical progress and capital-labor substitution as a cause of changes in the average productivity of labor. How might a measure of "total factor productivity" ameliorate this problem?

Problems

8.1   Imagine that the production function for beer cans is given by

$$Q = 6K + 4L$$

where

Q = Output of beer cans per hour
K = Capital input per hour
L = Labor input per hour.

a. Assuming capital is fixed at $K = 6$, how much L is required to produce 60 beer cans per hour? To produce 100 per hour?
b. Now assume that capital input is fixed at $K = 8$; what L is required to produce 60 beer cans per hour? To produce 100 per hour?
c. Graph the $Q = 60$ and $Q = 100$ isoquants. Indicate the points found in parts a and b. What is the RTS along the isoquants?

8.2   Frisbees are produced according to the production function

$$Q = 2K + L$$

where

Q = Output of frisbees per hour
K = Capital input per hour
L = Labor input per hour.

a. If $K = 10$, how much L is needed to produce 100 frisbees per hour?
b. If $K = 25$, how much L is needed to produce 100 frisbees per hour?
c. Graph the $Q = 100$ isoquant. Indicate the points on that isoquant defined in parts a and b. What is the RTS along this isoquant? Explain why the RTS is the same at every point on the isoquant.
d. Graph the $Q = 50$ and $Q = 200$ isoquants for this production function also. Describe the shape of the entire isoquant map.
e. Suppose technical progress resulted in the production function for frisbees becoming

$$Q = 3K + 1.5L.$$

Answer parts a through d for this new production function and discuss how it compares to the previous case.

8.3 Digging clams by hand in Sunset Bay requires only labor input. The total number of clams obtained per hour (Q) is given by

$$Q = 100\sqrt{L}$$

where L is labor input per hour.

a. Graph the relationship between Q and L.
b. What is the average productivity of labor in Sunset Bay? Graph this relationship and show that AP_L diminishes for increases in labor input.
c. It can be shown that the marginal productivity of labor in Sunset Bay is given by

$$MP_L = 50/\sqrt{L}.$$

Graph this relationship and show that $MP_L < AP_L$ for all values of L. Explain why this is so.

*8.4 The production of barstools (Q) is characterized by a production function of the form

$$Q = K^{1/2} \cdot L^{1/2} = \sqrt{K \cdot L}.$$

a. What is the average productivity of labor and capital for barstool production (AP_L will depend on K, and AP_K will depend on L)?
b. Graph the AP_L curve for K = 100.
c. For this particular function it can be shown that $MP_L = \frac{1}{2} AP_L$, and $MP_K = \frac{1}{2} AP_K$. Using that information, add a graph of the MP_L function to the graph calculated in part b (again for K = 100). What is unusual about this curve?
d. Sketch the Q = 10 isoquant for this production function.
e. Using the results from part c together with footnote 3 of this chapter, what is the RTS on the Q = 10 isoquant at the points: K = L = 10; K = 25, L = 4; and K = 4, L = 25? Does this function exhibit a diminishing RTS?

*8.5 Suppose the production function for widgets is given by

$$Q = KL - .8K^2 - .2L^2$$

where Q represents the annual quantity of widgets produced, K represents annual capital input, and L represents annual labor input.

a. Supposing K = 10, graph the total and average productivity of labor curves. At what level of labor input does this average productivity reach a maximum? How many widgets are produced at that point?
b. Again assuming that K = 10 and using the information that the MP_L curve is a straight line with an intercept of 10 (for L = 0), graph this curve. At what level of labor input does $MP_L = 0$?
c. Suppose capital inputs were increased to K = 20. How would your answers to parts a and b change?

---

*Denotes a problem that is rather difficult.

8.6 Power Goat Lawn Company uses two sizes of mowers to cut lawns. The smaller mowers have a 24-inch blade and are used on lawns with many trees and obstacles. The larger mowers are exactly twice as big as the smaller mowers and are used on open lawns where maneuverability is not so difficult. The two production functions available to Power Goat are:

	Output per Hour (Square Feet)	Capital Input (No. of 24" Mowers)	Labor Input
Large mowers	8,000	2	1
Small mowers	5,000	1	1

a. Graph the Q = 40,000 square feet isoquant for the first production function. How much K and L would be used if these factors were combined without waste?
b. Answer part a for the second function.
c. How much K and L would be used without waste if half of the 40,000 square foot lawn were cut by the method of the first production function and half by the method of the second? How much K and L would be used if three-fourths of the lawn were cut by the first method and one-fourth by the second? What does it mean to speak of fractions of K and L?
d. On the basis of your observations in part c, draw a Q = 40,000 isoquant for the combined production functions.

8.7 The production function

$$Q = K^a L^b$$

where $0 \leq a, b \leq 1$ is called a Cobb–Douglas production function. This function is widely used in economic research. Using the function, show that

a. The barstool production function in problem 8.4 is a special case of the Cobb–Douglas.
b. If a + b = 1, a doubling of K and L will double Q.
c. If a + b < 1, a doubling of K and L will less than double Q.
d. If a + b > 1, a doubling of K and L will more than double Q.
e. Using the results from parts b–d, what can you say about the returns to scale exhibited by the Cobb–Douglas function?

*8.8 For the Cobb–Douglas production function in problem 8.7, it can be shown (using calculus) that

$$MP_K = aK^{a-1}L^b$$

$$MP_L = bK^a L^{b-1}.$$

If the Cobb–Douglas exhibits constant returns to scale (a + b = 1), show that

a. Both marginal productivities are diminishing;
b. The RTS for this function is given by

$$RTS = \frac{bK}{aL}.$$

c. The function exhibits a diminishing RTS.

8.9 The production function for puffed rice is given by

$$Q = 100 \sqrt{KL}$$

where Q is the number of boxes produced per hour, K is the number of puffing guns used each hour, and L is the number of workers hired each hour.

a. Calculate the Q = 1,000 isoquant for this production function and show it on a graph.
b. If K = 10, how many workers are required to produce Q = 1,000? What is the average productivity of puffed rice workers?
c. Suppose technical progress shifts the production function to

$$Q = 200 \sqrt{KL}.$$

Answer parts a and b for this case.

8.10 Capital and labor are used in fixed proportions to produce airline flights—it takes two operators (pilots) and one plane for each trip made. Technical and safety problems make it impossible for a single pilot to fly a plane.

a. What is the output of this production process and what do the isoquants look like?
b. Suppose an airline hired 30 pilots and 10 planes during a particular period. Explain both graphically and in words why this might be a foolish thing to do.
c. Suppose progress in avionic equipment made it possible for a single pilot to handle each plane. How would that shift the isoquant map described in part a? Would this raise the average productivity of labor in this industry? Would it raise the average productivity of capital (planes)? Explain.

CHAPTER
9

COSTS

Now that we have developed concepts to describe the technical aspects of production, we can calculate the costs associated with productive activities. This chapter answers two basic questions about costs. First, how should the firm choose its inputs to produce any given level of output as cheaply as possible? Second, how does this process of cost minimization differ between the short run when the firm has rather limited flexibility and the long run when responses can be much more flexible? We are still not considering the crucial issue of how a firm chooses the level of output it will supply. That topic will be studied in Chapter 10.

Basic Concepts of Costs

At least three different concepts of costs can be distinguished: opportunity cost, accounting cost, and economic cost. For economists the most general of these is **opportunity cost** (sometimes called *social cost*). Because resources are limited, any decision to produce more of one good means doing without some other good. When an automobile is produced, for example, an implicit decision has been made to do without 15 bicycles, say, that could have been produced using the labor, chrome, and glass that goes into the automobile. The opportunity cost of one automobile is 15 bicycles.

Because it is often inconvenient to express opportunity costs in terms of physical goods, we sometimes choose monetary units instead. The price of a car may often be a good reflection of the costs of the goods that were given up to produce it. We could then say the opportunity cost of an automobile is $10,000 worth of other goods. This may not always be the case, however. If something were produced with resources that could not be usefully employed elsewhere, the true opportunity cost of this good's production would be close to 0, even though the resources may have been paid something.

Although the concept of opportunity cost is fundamental to all economic analysis, it may be too theoretical to be of practical use to firms. Our two other concepts of cost are directly related to the firm's choices. **Accounting cost** stresses out-of-pocket expenses, historical costs of machines and depreciation related to them, and other bookkeeping entries. **Economic cost** (which draws, in obvious ways, on the idea of opportunity cost), on the other hand, is defined as the payment required to keep a resource in its present employment, or the remuneration that the resource would receive in its next best alternative use.

To look at how the economic definition of cost might be applied in practice and how it differs from accounting ideas, we now consider the economic costs of three specific inputs: labor, capital, and the services of entrepreneurs.

■ Labor Costs

Economists and accountants view labor costs in much the same way. To the accountant, expenditures on wages and salaries are current expenses and therefore are costs of production. Economists regard such payments as an *explicit cost:* labor services (worker-hours) are purchased at some hourly **wage rate** (which we will denote by w), and it is assumed that this rate is the amount that workers would earn in their next best alternative employment. If a firm hires a worker at, say, $10 per hour, we usually assume that this figure represents about what the worker would earn elsewhere.

■ Capital Costs

In the case of capital services (machine-hours), accounting and economic definitions of costs differ greatly. Accountants, in calculating capital costs, use the

■
Opportunity cost
The cost of a good or service as measured by the alternative uses that are forgone by producing the good or service.

■
Accounting cost
The concept that goods or services cost what was paid for them.

■
Economic cost
The cost concept that goods or services cost the amount required to keep them in their present use: the amount that they would be worth in their next best alternative use.

■
Wage rate (w)
The cost of hiring one worker for one hour.

historical price of a particular machine and apply some (more or less) arbitrary depreciation rule to determine how much of that machine's original price to charge to current costs. For example, a machine purchased for $1,000 and expected to last 10 years might be said to "cost" $100 per year, in the accountant's view. Economists, on the other hand, regard the historical price of a machine as a **sunk cost**. Once such a cost has been incurred, there is no way to get it back. Since sunk costs do not reflect forgone opportunities, economists instead focus on the *implicit cost* of a machine as being what someone else would be willing to pay for its use. Thus, the cost of one machine hour is the **rental rate** for that machine in the best alternative use. By continuing to use the machine, the firm is implicitly forgoing the rental rate someone else would be willing to pay for its use. We will use v to denote this rental rate for one machine-hour. This is the rate that the firm must pay for the use of the machine for one hour regardless of whether the firm owns the machine (in which case it is an implicit cost) or rents the machine from someone else (in which case it is an explicit cost).

Sunk cost

Expenditure that once made cannot be recovered.

Rental rate (v)

The cost of hiring one machine for one hour.

■ Entrepreneurial Costs

The owner of a firm is entitled to whatever is left from the firm's revenues after all costs have been paid. To an accountant all of this excess would be called "profits" (or "losses" if costs exceed revenues). Economists, however, ask whether owners (or entrepreneurs) also encounter opportunity costs by being engaged in a particular business. If so, their entrepreneurial services should be considered an input to the firm, and some cost should be imputed to that input. For example, suppose a highly skilled computer programmer starts a software firm with the idea of keeping any (accounting) profits that might be generated. The programmer's time is clearly an input to the firm, and a cost should be imputed for it. Perhaps the wage that the programmer might command if he or she worked for someone else could be used for that purpose. Hence, some part of the accounting profits generated by the firm would be categorized as entrepreneurial costs by economists. Residual economic profits would be smaller than accounting profits. They might even be negative if the programmer's opportunity costs exceeded the accounting profits being earned by the business. Application 9.1: Economic Costs of Home Owning looks at these ideas as they relate to home ownership—a subject for which differences in economists' and accountants' cost definitions matter quite a lot.

■ Using Economic Costs

In this book, not surprisingly, we shall use economists' definition of cost for all inputs that the firm uses. Focusing on this definition is not meant to imply that accountants' concepts are irrelevant to economic behavior. Indeed, bookkeeping methods are integrally important to any manager's decision-making process because they can greatly affect the rate of taxation to be applied against profits. They also have the desirable property of being readily available

APPLICATION 9.1

Economic Costs of Home Owning

In examining differences between accounting and economic notions of cost, consider the following claim: "Rent is just money down a rat hole; it will never be seen again. The same money spent on mortgage payments is an investment. Once your mortgage is paid off, housing costs will be much cheaper." Although this claim is frequently made by prudent parents to their spendthrift children, it is simply wrong. It confuses the notion of the out-of-pocket costs of home ownership with the true economic costs of that ownership. Once a mortgage is paid off, out-of-pocket expenses are indeed reduced. But someone who has a substantial investment in a house incurs an opportunity cost in terms of the interest these funds could have earned in other investments. Even though this opportunity cost is implicit rather than explicit, it will still influence home owning behavior.

Profitability Calculation

Consider the consequences of owning and renting homes in southern California in the late 1980s. At that time, a $200,000 home could be rented for about $2,000 per month, or $24,000 per year. The owner of such a home might have incurred maintenance, taxes, and other expenses of $15,000 per year, so in terms of explicit costs, renting to someone else appears to be a profitable enterprise. From an accounting point of view, renting the home out provides a profit of $9,000 per year to the owner (see Table 1). But had the owner been able to invest the $200,000 value of the house at the prevailing bank interest rate of about 8 percent, this sum would have earned $16,000 per year in interest. This forgone interest is an opportunity cost of home-owning. Economic profits are therefore –$7,000.

Effects of Inflation

Why should property owners in southern California be willing to rent homes to someone else at a loss? The answer is that they expect the value of their homes to increase. Even a rather small annual rate of appreciation in house prices (say, 5 percent) would turn owning

Table 1

Alternative Views of the Profitability of Owning Rental Housing

Accounting View		Economic View	
Rental income	$24,000	Rental income	$24,000
Less:		Less:	
Costs (maintenance and depreciation)	15,000	Explicit costs (maintenance and depreciation)	15,000
Accounting profit	$ 9,000	Implicit costs (forgone interest)	16,000
		Loss before capital gain	–7,000
		Capital gain	10,000
		Economic profit	$ 3,000

rental property into a profitable activity. The $10,000 capital gain on a house (5% of $200,000) following its sale would result in net economic profits of $3,000. Hence, owners are willing to rent "at a loss" in the belief that the returns on their housing investments will result in a true overall profit. If the potential for gains were reduced (as they were in the early 1990s when increases in property values stalled), we would expect rents to more closely approximate economic costs. For example, if house prices were expected to rise only 2 percent per year, an owner would have to obtain $27,000 in annual rental fees simply to break even.

To Think About

1. "Burning the mortgage papers" is a popular custom once the mortgage on a house has been paid off. Does paying off a mortgage have any economic significance? Should people try to get their mortgage paid off as quickly as possible? Is it better to live in a debt-free house?

2. Sometimes older people are said to be "house poor," meaning that too large a portion of their total assets is tied up in their house. What problems does being house poor pose for older people? Is there a solution to this problem?

sources of data. Since the "economic costs" of General Motors are seldom calculated, it is usually necessary to use some accounting concepts for empirical work. Economists' definitions, however, do have the desirable features of being broadly applicable to all firms and of forming a conceptually consistent system.[1]

■ Two Simplifying Assumptions

We will make two simplifying assumptions about the inputs a firm uses. First, we will assume, as before, that there are only two inputs: homogeneous labor (L, measured in labor-hours) and homogeneous capital (K, measured in machine-hours). Entrepreneurial services will be assumed to be included in capital input. That is, it will be assumed that the primary opportunity costs faced by a firm's owner are those associated with the capital the owner provides.

A second assumption will be that the inputs to the firm are hired in perfectly competitive markets. Firms can buy (or sell) all the labor or capital services they want at the prevailing rental rates (w and v). In graphic terms the supply curve for these resources that the firm faces is horizontal at the prevailing factor prices.

■ Economic Profits and Cost Minimization

Given these simplifying assumptions, total costs for the firm during a period can be represented by

$$\text{Total costs} = TC = wL + vK, \tag{9.1}$$

where, as before, L and K represent input usage during the period. Assuming the firm produces only one output, its total revenues are given by the price of its product (P) times its total output [Q = f(K,L), where f(K,L) is the firm's production function]. **Economic profits** (π) are then the difference between total revenues and total economic costs:

Economic profits

The difference between a firm's total revenues and its total economic costs.

$$\pi = \text{Total revenues} - \text{Total costs} = PQ - wL - vK$$
$$= Pf(K,L) - wL - vK. \tag{9.2}$$

In general, then, Equation 9.2 shows that the economic profits obtained by a firm are simply a function of the amount of capital and labor employed. If, as we will assume in many places in this book, the firm seeks maximum profits, we might study its behavior by examining how it chooses K and L so as to do so. This would, in turn, lead to a theory of the "derived demand" for capital and labor inputs—a topic we take up explicitly in Chapter 19.

Here, however, we wish to develop a theory of costs that is somewhat more general and might apply to firms that are necessarily profit maximizers. Hence

---

[1]In fact, in recent years accountants have moved toward economists' definitions. For example, the conceptual model of economic costs has been applied to several topics in depreciation accounting.

we begin our study of costs by finessing a discussion of output choice for the moment. That is, we assume that for some reason the firm has decided to produce a particular output level (say, Q_1). The firm's revenues are therefore fixed at PQ_1. Now we wish to examine how the firm might choose to produce Q_1 at minimal costs. The precise connection between such a cost-minimizing choice and the assumption of profit maximization will be illustrated in Chapter 10.

Cost-Minimizing Input Choice

In order to minimize the cost of producing Q_1, a firm should choose that point on the Q_1 isoquant which has the lowest cost. To do so it should choose that input combination for which the marginal rate of technical substitution (RTS) of L for K is equal to the ratio of the inputs' costs, w/v. It should operate where the rate at which K can be substituted for L in the productive process is equal to the rate at which they can be traded in the marketplace. To see why this is so intuitively, let's ask what would happen if a firm chose an input combination for which this was not true. Suppose the firm is producing output level Q_1 using K = 10, L = 10, and the RTS is 2 at this point. Assume also that w = $1, v = $1, and hence that w/v = 1, which is unequal to the RTS of 2. At this input combination the cost of producing Q_1 is $20, which is not the minimal input cost. Q_1 can also be produced using K = 8 and L = 11; the firm can give up two units of K and keep output constant at Q_1 by adding one unit of L. At this input combination the cost of producing Q_1 is only $19. A proof similar to this one can be demonstrated any time the RTS and the ratio of the input costs differ. Therefore, we have shown that to minimize total cost the firm should produce where the RTS is equal to the ratio of the prices of the two inputs.

■ Graphic Presentation

This cost-minimization principle is demonstrated graphically in Figure 9.1. The isoquant Q_1 shows all the combinations of K and L that are required to produce Q_1. We wish to find the least costly point on this isoquant. Using Equation 9.1 we can see that those combinations of K and L that keep total costs constant lie along a straight line with slope −w/v.[2] Consequently, all lines of equal total cost can be shown in Figure 9.1 as a series of parallel straight lines with slopes −w/v. There lines of equal total cost are shown in Figure 9.1: $TC_1 < TC_2 < TC_3$. It is clear from the figure that the minimum total cost for producing Q_1 is given by TC_1 where the total cost curve is just tangent to the isoquant. The cost-minimizing input combination is L^*, K^*.

---

[2]For example, if TC = $100, Equation 9.1 would read 100 = wL + vK. Solving for K gives K = −w/vL + 100/v. Hence, the slope of this total cost line is −w/v, and the intercept is 100/v (which is the amount of capital that can be purchased with $100).

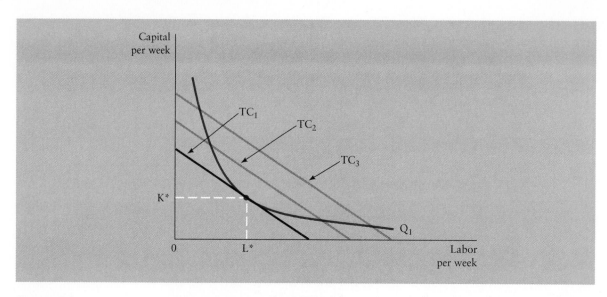

Figure 9.1
Minimizing the Costs
of Producing Q_1

A firm is assumed to choose capital (K) and labor (L) to minimize total costs. The condition for this minimization is that the rate at which L can be substituted for K (while keeping $Q = Q_1$) should be equal to the rate at which these inputs can be traded in the market. In other words, the RTS (of L for K) should be set equal to the price ratio w/v. This tangency is shown here in that costs are minimized at TC_1 by choosing inputs K^* and L^*.

We have therefore shown that for a cost minimum the slope of the isoquant should equal $-w/v$. At that point of tangency the rate at which the firm is technically able to trade L for K (the RTS) is equal to the rate at which the firm can trade L for K in the market.[3]

The Firm's Expansion Path

We can perform an analysis such as the one we just performed for any level of output by a firm. For each Q we would find that input combination that mini-

---

[3]An alternative interpretation can be made using the result from note 3 of Chapter 8 that

$$\text{RTS (of L for K)} = \frac{MP_L}{MP_K}.$$

Hence, cost minimization requires

$$\text{RTS} = \frac{MP_L}{MP_K} = \frac{w}{v},$$

or, using the final two equations

$$\frac{MP_L}{w} = \frac{MP_K}{v}.$$

To minimize cost the firm should choose K and L so that the marginal productivity per dollar spent is the same for all inputs used. If the firm were to spend an extra dollar on inputs, it could get the same amount of extra output regardless of which input it hired.

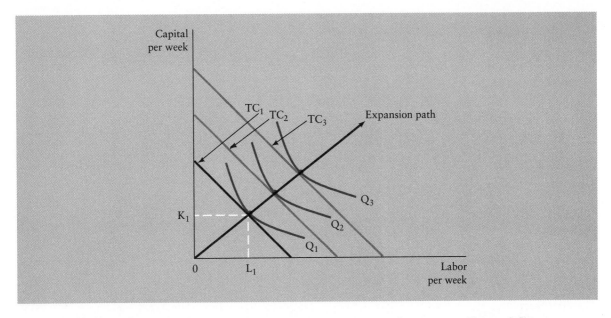

The firm's expansion path is the locus of cost-minimizing tangencies. On the assumption of fixed input prices, the curve shows how input use increases as output increases.

Figure 9.2
Firm's Expansion Path

mizes the cost of producing Q. If input costs (w and v) remain constant for all amounts the firm chooses to use, we can easily trace out this locus of cost-minimizing choices, as shown in Figure 9.2. This ray records the cost-minimizing tangencies for successively higher levels of Q. For example, the minimum cost for producing output level Q_1 is given by TC_1, and inputs K_1 and L_1 are used. Other tangencies in the figure can be interpreted in a similar way. The locus of these tangencies is called the firm's **expansion path** because it records how input use expands as output expands while holding the prices of the inputs constant. The expansion path need not necessarily be a straight line. The use of some inputs may increase faster than others as output expands. Which inputs expand more rapidly will depend on the shape of the production isoquants.

Expansion path
The locus of cost-minimizing input combinations a firm will choose to produce various levels of output (when the prices of inputs are held constant).

Cost Curves

The firm's expansion path shows how minimum-cost input use increases when the level of output expands. The path allows us to develop the relationship between output levels and total input costs. Cost curves that reflect this relationship are fundamental to the theory of supply. Figure 9.3 illustrates four possible shapes for this cost relationship. Panel a reflects a situation of constant returns to scale. In this case, as Figure 8.3 showed, output and required

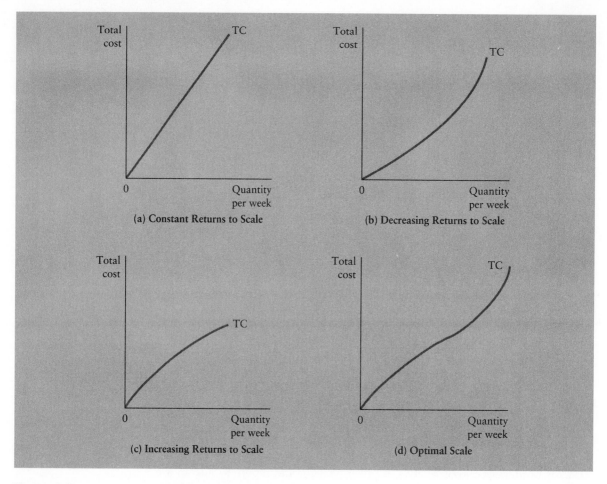

Figure 9.3
Possible Shapes of
the Total Cost Curve

The shape of the total cost curve depends on the nature of the production function. Panel a represents constant returns to scale: as output expands, input costs expand proportionately. Panels b and c show decreasing returns to scale and increasing returns to scale, respectively. Panel d represents costs where the firm has an "optimal scale" of operations.

input use are proportional to one another. A doubling of output requires a doubling of inputs. Assuming input prices do not change, the relationship between output and total input costs is also directly proportional—the total cost curve is simply a straight line that passes through the origin (since no inputs are required if Q = 0).[4]

Panels b and c in Figure 9.3 reflect the cases of decreasing returns to scale and increasing returns to scale, respectively. With decreasing returns to scale,

---

[4]A technical property of constant returns to scale production functions is that the RTS depends only on the ratio of K to L, not on the scale of production. For given input prices, the expansion path is a straight line, and cost-minimizing inputs expand proportionally along with output. For an illustration, see the numerical example later in this chapter.

successively larger quantities of inputs are required to increase output, and input costs rise rapidly as output expands. This possibility is shown by the convex total cost curve in Panel b. With increasing returns to scale, on the other hand, successive input requirements decline as output expands. In that case the total cost curve is concave, as shown in Panel c. In this case considerable cost advantages result from large-scale operations.

Finally, Panel d in Figure 9.3 demonstrates a situation in which the firm experiences ranges of both increasing and decreasing returns to scale. Such a situation might arise if the firm's production process required a certain "optimal" level of internal coordination and control by its managers. For low levels of output this control structure is underutilized, and expansion in output is easily accomplished. At these levels the firm would experience increasing returns to scale—the total cost curve is concave in its initial section. As output expands, however, the firm must add additional workers and capital equipment, which perhaps need entirely separate buildings or other production facilities. The coordination and control of this larger scale organization may be successively more difficult, and diminishing returns to scale may set in. The convex section of the total cost curve in Panel d reflects that possibility.

The four possibilities in Figure 9.3 illustrate most of the types of relationships between a firm's output and its input costs that arise from the desire to minimize costs. The cost information shown in Figure 9.3 can also be depicted on a per-unit-of-output basis. Although this depiction adds no new details to the information implicit in the total cost curves, it will be quite useful when we analyze the supply decision in the next chapter.

■ Average and Marginal Costs

Two per-unit-of-output cost concepts are average and marginal costs. **Average cost** (AC) measures total costs per unit. Mathematically,

$$\text{Average cost} = AC = \frac{TC}{Q}. \tag{9.3}$$

This is the per-unit-of-cost concept with which people are most familiar. If, for example, a firm has total costs of \$100 in producing 25 units of output, it is quite natural to consider the cost per unit to be \$4. Equation 9.3 reflects this common averaging process.

For economists, however, average cost is not necessarily the most meaningful cost-per-unit figure. In Chapter 1, we introduced Marshall's analysis of demand and supply. In his model of price determination, Marshall focused on the cost of the last unit produced since it is that cost that influences the supply decision. To reflect this notion of incremental cost, economists have developed the concept of **marginal cost** (MC). By definition then,

$$\text{Marginal cost} = MC = \frac{\text{Change in TC}}{\text{Change in Q}}. \tag{9.4}$$

That is, as output expands, total costs increase, and the marginal cost concept measures this increase only *at the margin*. For example, if producing 24 units

■ Average cost

Total cost divided by output: a common measure of cost per unit.

■ Marginal cost

The additional cost of producing one more unit of output.

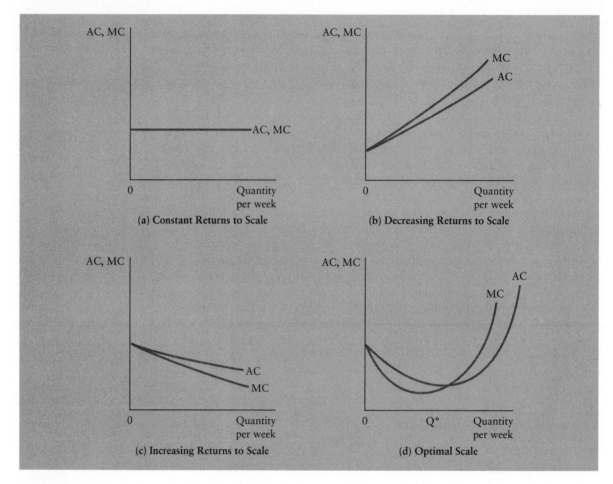

Figure 9.4
Average and Marginal Cost Curves

The average and marginal cost curves shown here are derived from the total cost curves in Figure 9.3. The shapes of these curves depend on the nature of the production function.

costs the firm $98, but producing 25 units costs it $100, the marginal cost of the 25th unit is $2: to produce that unit the firm incurs an increase in cost of only $2. This example shows that the average cost of a good ($4) and its marginal cost ($2) may be quite different. This possibility has a number of important implications for pricing and overall resource allocation.

■ Marginal Cost Curves

Now that we have defined costs on a per-unit basis, we can show them graphically. Figure 9.4 compares average and marginal costs for the four total cost relationships shown in Figure 9.3. As our definition makes clear, marginal costs are reflected by the slope of the total cost curve since (as we discussed in

Chapter 2) the slope of any curve shows how the variable on the vertical axis (here total cost) changes for a unit change in the variable on the horizontal axis (here quantity). In Panel a of Figure 9.3 the total cost curve is linear—it has the same slope throughout. In this case, marginal cost (MC) is constant. No matter how much is produced, it will always cost the same to produce *one more unit*. The horizontal MC curve in Panel a of Figure 9.4 reflects this fact.

In the case of a convex total cost curve (Panel b in Figure 9.3), marginal costs are increasing. The total cost curve becomes steeper as output expands, so at the margin, the cost of one more unit is becoming greater. The MC curve in Panel b in Figure 9.4 is positively sloped reflecting these increasing marginal costs.

For the case of a concave total cost curve (Panel c in Figure 9.3), this situation is reversed. Since the total cost curve becomes flatter as output expands, marginal costs fall. The marginal cost curve in Panel c in Figure 9.4 has a negative slope.

Finally, the case of first concave, then convex total costs (Panel d in Figure 9.3) yields a U-shaped marginal cost curve in Figure 9.4. Initially marginal costs fall because the coordination and control mechanism of the firm is being utilized more efficiently. Diminishing returns eventually appear, however, and the marginal cost curve turns upward. The MC curve in Panel d in Figure 9.4 reflects the general idea that there is some optimal level of operation for the firm—if production is pushed too far, very high marginal costs will be the result. We will make this idea of optimal scale more precise as we study average costs.

■ Average Cost Curves

Developing average cost (AC) curves for each of the cases in Figure 9.4 is relatively simple. The average and marginal cost concepts are identical for the very first unit produced. If the firm produced only one unit, both average and marginal cost would be the cost of that one unit. Graphing the AC relationship begins at the point where the marginal cost curve intersects the vertical axis. For Panel a in Figure 9.4, marginal cost never varies from its initial level. It always costs the same amount to produce one more unit, and AC must also reflect this amount. If it always costs a firm $4 to produce one more unit, both average and marginal costs are $4. Both the AC and MC curves are the same horizontal line in Panel a in Figure 9.4.

In the case of convex total costs, rising marginal costs also result in rising average costs. Since the last unit produced is becoming more and more costly as output expands, the overall average of such costs must be rising. Because the first few units are produced at low marginal costs, however, the overall average will always be somewhat less than the high marginal cost of the last unit produced. In Panel b in Figure 9.4 the AC curve is upward sloping, but it is always below the MC curve.

In the case of concave total costs, the opposite situation prevails. Falling marginal costs cause average costs to fall as output expands, but the overall average also reflects the relatively high marginal costs of producing the first few units. As a consequence, the AC curve in Panel c in Figure 9.4 is negatively sloped and always lies above the MC curve. Falling average cost in this case is, as we shall see in Chapter 16, a principal force leading to relatively large-scale operations for firms with such increasing returns to scale technologies.

The case of a U-shaped marginal cost curve represents a combination of the two preceding situations. Initially falling marginal costs cause average costs to decline also. For low levels of output, the configuration of average and marginal cost curves in Panel d in Figure 9.4 resembles that in Panel c. Once the marginal costs turn up, however, the situation begins to change. As long as marginal cost is below average cost, average cost will continue to decline since the last good produced is still less expensive than the prior average. When MC < AC, producing one more unit pulls AC down. Once the rising segment of the marginal cost curve cuts the average cost curve from below, however, average costs begin to rise. Beyond point Q* in Panel d in Figure 9.4, MC exceeds AC. The situation now resembles that in Panel b and AC must rise.[5] Average costs are being pulled up by the high cost of producing one more unit. Since AC is falling to the left of Q* and rising to the right of Q*, average costs of production are lowest at Q*. In a sense, Q* represents an "optimal scale" for a firm whose costs are represented in Panel d in Figure 9.4. Later chapters show that this output level plays an important role in the theory of price determination. Application 9.2: Findings on Long-Run Costs looks at how average cost curves can be used to determine which industries might find large-scale firms more appropriate. Application 9.3: Costs for Airlines and Trash Collection then looks more closely at the average costs of two particular industries and describes how they are affected by the different ways in which production is organized.

Distinction between the Short Run and the Long Run

It has been traditional in economics to distinguish between the **short run** and the **long run** for firms. These terms denote the length of time over which a firm may make decisions. As we will see, this distinction is quite useful for studying market responses to changed conditions. For example, if only the short run is considered, the firm may need to treat some of its inputs as fixed, because it may be technically impossible to change those inputs on short notice. If a time interval of only one week is involved, the size of a firm's factory would have to be treated as absolutely fixed. Similarly, an entrepreneur who is committed to a particular business in the short run would find it impossible (or extremely costly) to change jobs—in the short run, the entrepreneur's input to the production process is essentially fixed. Over the long run, however, neither of those inputs needs to be considered fixed, since a firm's plant size can be altered and an entrepreneur can indeed quit the business.

Short run

The period of time in which a firm must consider some inputs absolutely fixed in making its decisions.

Long run

The period of time in which a firm may consider all of its inputs to be variable in making its decisions.

---

[5]An analogy may help here. If, on your most recent quiz (that is, your "marginal" quiz) you received a lower grade than your previous average, that average must be falling. On the other hand, if your most recent quiz score exceeded your previous average, the average must be rising. When the marginal and average grades are identical, your average will not change.

APPLICATION 9.2

Findings on Long-Run Costs

Economists have investigated long-run cost curves for many industries. Most studies of long-run cost curves have found that average cost curves have a modified L-shape, such as the one shown in Figure 1.

Some Evidence

Table 1 reports the results of representative studies of long-run average cost curves for a variety of industries. Entries in the table represent the long-run average cost for a firm of a particular size (small, medium, or large)

Table 1
Long-Run Average Cost Estimates

Industry	Firm Size		
	Small	**Medium**	**Large**
Aluminum	166.6%	131.3%	100.0%
Automobiles	144.5	122.7	100.0
Electric power	113.2	101.1	101.5
Hospitals	129.6	111.1	100.0
Life insurance	113.6	104.5	100.0
Lotteries (state)	175.0	125.0	100.0
Sewage treatment	104.0	101.0	100.0
Trucking	100.0	102.1	105.6

Sources: Aluminum: J. C. Clark and M. C. Fleming, "Advanced Materials and the Economy," *Scientific American* (October 1986): 51–56. Automobiles: M. A. Fuss and L. Waverman, "Costs and Productivity Differences in Automobile Production" (Cambridge, U.K., Cambridge University Press, 1992). Electric power: L. H. Christensen and W. H. Greene, "Economies of Scale in U.S. Power Generation," *Journal of Political Economy* (August 1976): 655–676. Hospitals: H. A. Cohen, "Hospital Cost Curves," in *Empirical Studies in Health Economics*, H. F. Klarman, ed. (Baltimore: Johns Hopkins Press, 1970), 279–293. Life insurance: R. Geehan, "Returns to Scale in the Life Insurance Industry," *The Bell Journal of Economics* (Autumn 1977): 497–516. Lotteries: C. T. Clotfelter and P. J. Cook, "On the Economics of State Lotteries," *Journal of Economic Perspectives* (Fall 1990): 105–119. Sewage treatment: M. R. J. Knapp, "Economies of Scale in Sewage Purification and Disposal," *Journal of Industrial Economics* (December 1978): 163–183. Trucking: R. Koenka, "Optimal Scale and the Size Distribution of American Trucking Firms," *Journal of Transport Economics and Policy* (January 1977): 54–67.

Figure 1
Long-Run Average Cost Curve Found in Many Empirical Studies

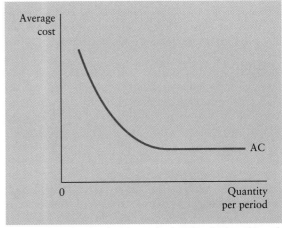

In most empirical studies the AC curve has been found to have this modified L-shape.

as a percentage of the minimal average cost firm in the industry. For example, the data for hospitals indicate that small hospitals have average costs that are about 29.6 percent greater than average costs for large ones.

The costs of most other industries seem to be similar to those illustrated in Figure 1. Average costs are lower for medium and large firms than for smaller ones; that is, there appears to be a "minimum efficient scale" (termed, appropriately, MES, in the field of industrial organization) of operation for firms in these industries. However, in several cases the average cost advantages are not great. And for at least one industry (trucking), smaller firms seem to operate with lower average costs.

To Think About

1. Many of the industries listed in Table 1 seem to exhibit modest cost economies of large-scale operation. Why don't you think this seems to apply to trucking?

2. The average cost estimates in Table 1 typically refer to costs for an entire firm. Do you think a study of individual plants would show larger or smaller economies of scale?

APPLICATION 9.3
Costs for Airlines and Trash Collection

Economists have looked carefully at the cost structures of many industries. Here we look at two of these, airlines and trash collection, in a bit more detail.

Airlines

Average costs differ substantially among U.S. airlines. Measured on a cost-per-passenger mile basis, average costs of the lowest-cost major airline (Southwest) are about 58 percent of those for the highest-cost airline (USAir).[1] Differences in costs are also significant between major airlines and local commuter carriers—the cost-per-passenger mile is, on average, 38 percent higher for local carriers. Because airline cost data are readily available, economists have investigated a number of possible reasons for the cost differentials.

One set of explanations focuses on the nature of the airlines' routes. Airlines that fly longer average distances on each flight stage and airlines that operate a greater number of flights over their networks tend to have lower average costs. Such features permit airlines to spread the fixed costs they incur for terminals and other facilities over a larger output volume. Other technical factors explaining the differences in airlines' costs stem from the equipment they operate; on the whole, newer planes have much lower fuel and maintenance costs. Finally, some economists have argued that a significant portion of the differences in airlines' costs reflects managerial abilities. Several airlines have a reputation for poor management, even though they possess other low-cost characteristics. The wave of airline bankruptcies and takeovers in recent years may have been motivated, in part, by such managerial shortcomings.

Trash Collection

Refuse collection is a major municipal service carried out by both private and public enterprises. The question of scale economies plays an important role in deciding exactly how this service should be organized to achieve minimal costs. Two types of scale economies can be distinguished. First, operating a large number of trucks may reduce average costs if it were to reduce the costs of maintenance facilities and to allow for the purchase of specialized equipment. A number of studies have found that these scale economies are relatively insignificant, however, except at very-small firm sizes.

A second, more important source of economies in refuse collection stems from customer density. As density increases, multiple pickups from a single stop become possible, and collection times (and costs) fall dramatically. One study finds that each 10 percent increase in density of collection tonnage results in a 5 percent reduction in costs.[2]

These research findings on refuse collection costs have two implications for how the service might be organized. First, the absence of scale economies provides little support for the notion that collection should be done on a citywide basis. Contracting with several different firms instead would not result in increased costs. Second, offering exclusive contracts to refuse collectors to service entire areas (rather than permitting a free market of trash collection, resulting in overlapping routes) should minimize overall average costs of refuse collection by creating density economies.[3]

To Think About

1. Would you expect differences in airlines' costs to be eliminated by vigorous competition among firms? Could such competition affect stage lengths or network density? How about its effects on aircraft choice or managerial ability?
2. How is trash collected in your town? If it is done by the government, does there seem to be any cost advantages in doing so, or is this primarily a political decision? If your trash is collected by private firms, do they have overlapping routes despite the obvious inefficiencies involved?

---

[1]The figures in 1990 were $0.11 per passenger mile for Southwest, $0.19 for USAir. See S. Borenstein, "The Evolution of U.S. Airline Competition," *Journal of Economic Perspectives* (Spring 1992): 61.
[2]Peter Kemper and J. M. Quigley, *The Economics of Refuse Collection*

(Cambridge, Mass.: Ballinger Publishing Company, 1976): 53.
[3]See B. J. Stevens, "Scale, Market Structure and the Cost of Refuse Collection," *Review of Economics and Statistics* (August 1978): 438–448.

■ Short-Run Production Function

Probably the easiest method to introduce the distinction between the short run and the long run into our analysis of a firm's costs is to assume that one of the inputs is held constant in the short run. Specifically, we will assume that capital input is held constant at a level of K_1 and that (in the short run) the firm is free to vary only its labor input. The short-run production function now can be written as

$$Q = f(K_1, L). \qquad [9.5]$$

This notation explicitly shows that capital input may not vary. The firm still can change the level of Q only by altering its use of labor. We have already studied this possibility in Chapter 8, when we examined the marginal productivity of labor. Here we are interested in analyzing how changes in a firm's output level in the short run are related to changes in total costs. We can then contrast this relationship to the cost relationships studied earlier, in which both inputs could be changed. We will see that the diminishing marginal productivity that results from a fixed input causes costs to rise rapidly as output expands.

■ A Note on Input Flexibility

Any firm obviously uses far more than two inputs in its production process. The level of some of these inputs may be changed on rather short notice. Firms may ask workers to work overtime, hire part-time replacements from an employment agency, or rent equipment (such as power tools or automobiles) from some other firm. Other types of inputs may take somewhat longer to be adjusted; for example, to hire new, full-time workers is a relatively time-consuming (and costly) process, and ordering new machines designed to unique specifications may involve a considerable time lag. At the most lengthy extreme, entirely new factories can be built, new managers may be recruited and trained, and new raw material supplies can be developed. It would be impossible to cover all such variations of input types in any detail. Our analysis continues using only our two-input model holding the level of capital input fixed. This treatment should not be taken to imply that labor is a more flexible input than capital. We are considering only the distinction between fixed and variable inputs, and this approach enables us to do so. You could substitute any other inputs for capital and labor in the discussion that follows.

■ Short-Run Total Costs

Total cost for the firm continues to be given by

$$TC = vK + wL \qquad [9.6]$$

for our short-run analysis, but now capital input is fixed at K_1. To denote this fact, we will write

$$STC(K_1) = vK_1 + wL. \qquad [9.7]$$

Fixed costs

Costs associated with inputs that are fixed in the short run.

Variable costs

Costs associated with inputs that can be varied in the short run.

The addition of the S to our notation makes it clear that we are analyzing short-run costs, and the notation also records the level of capital that is being held constant. The two types of input costs in Equation 9.7 are given special names. The term vK_1 is referred to as (short-run) **fixed costs**; since K_1 is constant, these costs will not change in the short run. If the firm has 20 machines each of which rents for $500 per week, short-run fixed costs are $10,000 per week and cannot be varied. The term wL is referred to as (short-run) **variable costs,** since labor input can indeed be varied in the short run. Using the terms $SFC(K_1)$ for short-run fixed costs and $SVC(K_1)$ for short-run variable costs, we have

$$SFC(K_1) = vK_1$$

$$SVC(K_1) = wL \tag{9.8}$$

and therefore

$$STC(K_1) = SFC(K_1) + SVC(K_1). \tag{9.9}$$

Short-run total costs are now classified as being either fixed or variable. How do these short-run costs change as the firm's output changes?

■ Short-Run Fixed and Variable Cost Curves

In the short run, fixed costs are obviously fixed. They do not change as the level of output changes. This relationship is shown in Panel a in Figure 9.5. The $SFC(K_1)$ curve is a horizontal line representing the rental cost of the fixed amount of capital being employed.

Panel b in Figure 9.5 records one possible relationship between short-run variable costs and output. Initially the marginal productivity of labor is assumed to rise as labor is added to the production process. The fixed input of capital is initially "underutilized," and labor's marginal productivity rises as the amount of labor available to work with this fixed amount of capital increases. Because the marginal product of labor is increasing, short-run variable costs rise less rapidly than output expands—in its initial section, the $SVC(K_1)$ curve is concave. Beyond some output level, say, Q', however, the marginal product of labor will begin to decline. Because capital input is constant at K_1, the ability of labor to generate extra output will diminish; since the per-unit cost of labor is assumed to be constant, costs of production will begin to rise rapidly. Beyond Q' the $SVC(K_1)$ curve becomes convex to reflect this diminishing marginal productivity of labor. For output levels to the right of Q', existing capital inputs are now being "overutilized." The shape of the $SVC(K_1)$ curve in Panel b in Figure 9.5 is in general agreement with our hypotheses about the marginal productivity of labor in Figure 8.1. It is also quite similar to the case of U-shaped (long-run) marginal costs we discussed in the previous section.

■ Short-Run Total Cost Curve

We can now construct the short-run total cost curve by summing the two cost components in Figure 9.5. This total cost curve is shown in Figure 9.6, which

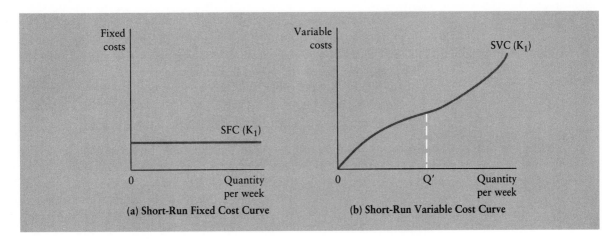

The curve SFC(K_1) in Panel a shows that fixed costs do not vary in the short run. They are determined by the fixed input of capital (here K_1) being used. Variable costs do change as the output increases. The shape shown in Panel b assumes that initially labor exhibits an increasing marginal productivity but that, after some point, the marginal productivity of labor diminishes, causing short-run costs to rise rapidly.

Figure 9.5
Fixed and Variable Costs in the Short Run

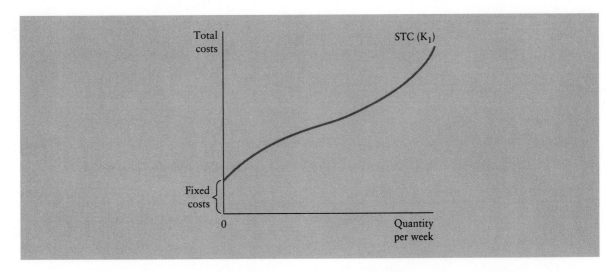

This curve summarizes the two curves shown in Figure 9.5. Short-run fixed costs determine the zero-output intercept for the curve, whereas the short-run variable cost curve determines the short-run total cost curve's shape.

Figure 9.6
Short-Run Total Cost Curve

has two important features. First, when output is 0, total costs are given by fixed costs, SFC(K_1). Since capital input is fixed, it must be paid its rental rate even if no production takes place. The firm cannot avoid these fixed costs in the short run. Contrary to the long-run case, therefore, the STC curve does not pass through the origin. The firm can, of course, avoid all variable costs simply by hiring no labor. A second important feature of Figure 9.6 is that the shape of the curve is determined solely by the shape of the short-run variable cost curve. The way that changes in output affect costs determines the shape of the curve. Because fixed costs are constant, they play no role in determining the shape of the $STC(K_1)$ curve other than determining its zero-output intercept.

■ Input Inflexibility and Cost Minimization

The total costs shown in Figure 9.6 are not the minimal costs for producing the various output levels shown. Because we are holding capital fixed in the short run, the firm does not have the flexibility in input choice that was assumed when we discussed cost minimization and the related long-run cost curves earlier in this chapter. Rather, to vary its output level in the short run, the firm will be forced to use "nonoptimal" input combinations: the RTS will not be equal to the ratio of the input prices.

This is shown in Figure 9.7. In the short run, the firm can use only K_1 units of capital. To produce output level Q_0, it must use L_0 units of labor, L_1 units of

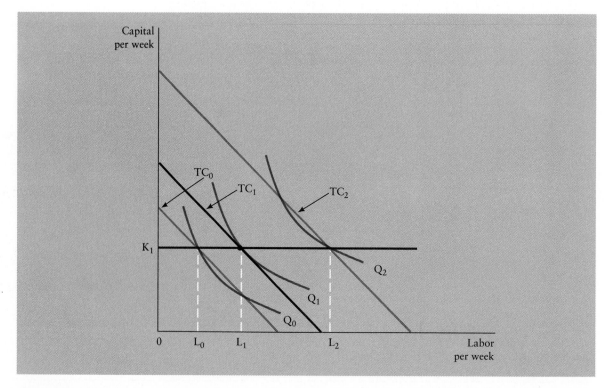

Figure 9.7
"Nonoptimal" Input
Choices Must
Be Made in the
Short Run

Because capital input is fixed at K_1 in the short run, the firm cannot bring its RTS into equality with the ratio of input prices. Given the input prices, Q_0 should be produced with more labor and less capital than it will be in the short run, whereas Q_2 should be produced with more capital and less labor than it will be.

labor to produce Q_1, and L_2 units to produce Q_2. The total costs of these input combinations are given by TC_0, TC_1, and TC_2, respectively. Only for the input combination K_1, L_1 is output being produced at minimal cost. Only at that point is the RTS equal to the ratio of the input prices. From Figure 9.7 it is clear that Q_0 is being produced with "too much" capital in this short-run situation. Cost minimization should suggest a southeasterly movement along the Q_0 isoquant, indicating a substitution of labor for capital in production. On the other hand, Q_2 is being produced with "too little" capital, and costs could be reduced by substituting capital for labor. Neither of these substitutions is possible in the short run. However, over the long run the firm will be able to change its level of capital input and will adjust its input usage to the cost-minimizing combinations. This flexible case was discussed earlier in this chapter when we assumed that both labor and capital could be varied.

Per-Unit Short-Run Cost Curves

Using the short-run total cost curve already derived, we can easily describe the per-unit short-run cost curves related to it. As for the long run, we define

$$\text{Short-run average cost} = SAC = \frac{STC(K_1)}{Q} \quad [9.10]$$

and

$$\text{Short-run marginal cost} = SMC = \frac{\text{Change in } STC(K_1)}{\text{Change in } Q}. \quad [9.11]$$

These short-run concepts are similar to those defined earlier for the long run in Equations 9.3 and 9.4 except that now they are based on total costs incurred with the level of capital input fixed at K_1. Because having capital fixed in the short run yields a total cost curve that has both concave and convex sections, the resulting short-run average and marginal cost relationships will also be U-shaped. These are illustrated in Figure 9.8.

As before, the curves not only are U-shaped, but the marginal cost curve (SMC) passes through the lowest point in the average cost curve (SAC) for exactly the same reason as in long-run curves. When SMC < SAC, average cost is falling since the last produced goods were relatively low in cost and lowered the average. Once SMC > SAC, however, the higher costs associated with successive increments of production pull up the average.

■ Short-Run Average Variable Costs

Although the SAC and SMC curves will be used frequently in our discussions of supply and price determination, one other short-run cost concept will be needed occasionally. Recall from Equation 9.9 that short-run costs are categorized as being either "fixed" or "variable." That is,

$$STC = SFC + SVC. \quad [9.12]$$

For simplicity we have omitted the notation of the level of capital being used in the short run. Using these two categories of short-run costs, we can break down short-run average cost into fixed and variable components by dividing Equation 9.12 by Q. That is,

$$\frac{STC}{Q} = SAC = \frac{SFC}{Q} + \frac{SVC}{Q}$$

$$= \text{Short-run average fixed cost} + \text{Short-run average variable cost}$$

$$= SAFC + SAVC. \tag{9.13}$$

Although the concept of average fixed cost is of little economic usefulness (since fixed costs never change), short-run average variable cost (SAVC) does enter the analysis on a few occasions. SAVC indicates the average "avoidable" costs that firms must incur to produce anything; unlike fixed costs, these costs are avoidable if the firm produces no output. In Chapter 10, we will show that avoidable costs clearly can affect firms' short-run production decisions. As shown in Figure 9.8, the SAVC curve looks very much like the SAC curve. SAVC always lies below SAC (the vertical difference being average fixed costs), but the two curves approach each other at high levels of output for which average fixed costs are quite small.[6]

■ Relationship between Short-Run and Long-Run Per-Unit Cost Curves

Implicit in the relationship between short-run and long-run total costs is a complex set of relations among the per-unit cost curves. Although it is possible to illustrate the precise relationship among all these curves, a detailed presentation is not essential here. For firms with U-shaped long-run average and marginal cost curves, one particular set of relationships is useful to us, however.

Figure 9.9 shows all of these cost relationships for such a firm. For this firm, long-run average costs reach a minimum at output level Q*, and as we have noted in several places, at this output level MC = AC. Also associated with Q* is a certain level of capital usage, K*. What we wish to do now is to examine the short-run average and marginal cost curves based on this level of capital input. We now look at the costs of a firm whose level of capital input is fixed at K* to see how costs vary in the short run as Q departs from its optimal level of Q*.

Our discussion about the total cost curves in Figure 9.7 shows that when the firm's level of capital input yields minimum costs for the output it wishes to produce, short-run and long-run total costs are equal. Average costs then are equal also. At Q*, AC is equal to SAC(K*). This means that at Q*, MC and

---

[6]The SMC and SAVC curves in Figure 9.8 have the same zero-output intercept. The marginal cost and the average variable costs of the first unit produced in the short run are equal. The zero-output intercept for short-run average total cost is undefined since for Q = 0 this represents positive fixed costs divided by zero.

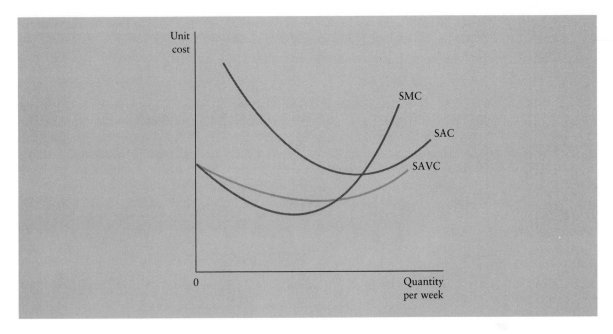

Short-run average and marginal cost curves are U-shaped because one input is held fixed in the short run. The figure illustrates short-run average variable costs (SAVC), which are also relevant to short-run production decisions.

Figure 9.8
Per-Unit, Short-Run Cost Curves

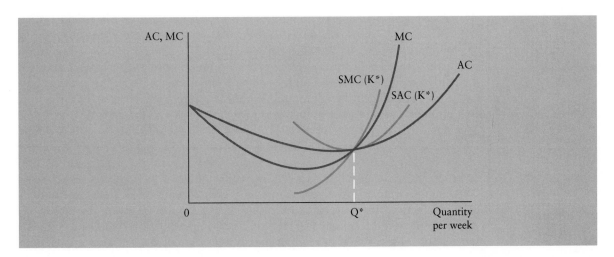

When long-run average cost is U-shaped and reaches a minimum at Q*, SAC and SMC will also pass through this point. For increases in output above Q* short-run costs are higher than long-run costs.

Figure 9.9
Short-Run and Long-Run Average and Marginal Cost Curves at Optimal Output Level

SMC(K*) are also equal, since both of the average cost curves are at their lowest points. At Q* in Figure 9.9 the following equality holds:

$$AC = MC = SAC(K^*) = SMC(K^*). \tag{9.14}$$

For increases in Q above Q*, short-run costs are higher than long-run costs. These higher per-unit costs reflect the inflexibility in the short run because some inputs are fixed. This inflexibility has important consequences for firms' short-run supply responses and for price changes in the short run. In Application 9.4: Airport Congestion Costs, we look at some cases where short-run costs rise rapidly as the traffic at airports increases.

Shifts in Cost Curves

We have shown how cost curves for a firm's output are derived from its cost-minimizing expansion path. Any change in economic conditions that affects this expansion path will also affect the shape and position of the cost curves. Two kinds of economic changes are likely to have such effects: changes in input prices and technological innovations.

■ Changes in Input Prices

A change in the price of an input will tilt the firm's total cost lines and alter its expansion path. A rise in wage rates will, for example, cause firms to produce any output level using relatively more capital and relatively less labor. To the extent that a substitution of capital for labor is possible (remember substitution possibilities depend on the shape of the isoquant map), the entire expansion path of the firm will rotate toward the capital axis. This movement in turn implies a new set of cost curves for the firm. A rise in the price of labor input has caused the entire relationship between output levels and costs to change. Presumably all cost curves would be shifted upward, and the extent of the shift would depend both on how "important" labor is in production and on how successful the firm is in substituting other inputs for labor. If labor is relatively unimportant or if the firm can readily shift to more mechanized methods of production, increases in costs resulting from a rise in wages may be rather small. On the other hand, if labor is a very important part of a firm's costs and input substitution is difficult (remember the case of lawnmowers), production costs may rise significantly.

■ Technological Innovation

New technologies can also have important effects on cost curves. Since technical advances alter a firm's production function (as discussed in Chapter 8), isoquant maps as well as the firm's expansion path will shift when technology

APPLICATION 9.4

Airport Congestion Costs

Although economists have had difficulty measuring sharply increasing marginal costs in many production situations, such increasing costs are shown quite clearly in transportation cases. For example, peak-load traffic places considerable demands on the capacity of highways, bridges, tunnels, and airports. The resultant traffic jams provide a vivid and often irritating example of rising marginal costs, consisting primarily of time delays.

Evidence from Airports

Economists have paid particular attention to congestion costs that arise during peak hours of airport use. Because most air travelers seem to want to arrive or depart in the early morning or late afternoon, these time periods pose the heaviest demands on airport facilities. Runway capacity is the primary limiting factor, as large numbers of planes must line up to take off or adopt circuitous flight paths while waiting to land. Airways also become more congested at peak travel times and air-traffic controllers impose significant waits on planes wishing to fly into busy air corridors (such as those in the Boston-Washington area). All of these delays create additional costs both in terms of extra fuel usage and in terms of passengers' time. Although the marginal cost of handling one extra flight is fairly low during off-peak hours (say $200–$300), time delays raise these costs as much as tenfold during peak times (to perhaps $3,000 per arriving flight). The increases are especially large for airports that handle wide-bodied jets (such as 747s) because time delays imposed on any one plane are experienced by a larger number of passengers.

Airport Pricing

Problems of airport congestion might be ameliorated by the adoption of landing-fee schedules that would prompt airlines to operate at off-peak hours. Existing pricing policies are not especially encouraging in that regard, however. Most landing fees are based on aircraft weight, with heavier planes paying higher fees. Such fees may approximate the cost of wear-and-tear on runways, but they are a poor measure of the complete marginal cost associated with a landing or takeoff. Because planes take about the same time on a runway regardless of their size, the costs of delays brought about by the arrival of an additional plane are largely unrelated to weight. Hence, existing pricing schedules vastly understate the costs imposed on others by small commuter-type planes, and may even overstate the full marginal costs of a large plane.[1] Pressures by commuter and general aviation firms have managed to block most moves toward congestion cost-based pricing, however.

To Think About

1. Sometimes critics of the economic approach to runway pricing claim that congestion costs are not "real costs" because they primarily consist of people's time. Why do economists view these as being as real as any other costs? (See Chapter 20 for a more complete discussion of the value of time.)

2. Use of urban highways during peak times involves congestion costs also. What is the nature of these costs? How might pricing schemes be developed to reflect these costs? Would such pricing schemes be more difficult to implement than runway pricing? Can you think of examples of peak-time pricing for highways or bridges?

---

[1]According to one set of estimates, commuter aircraft pay only about 10 percent of the landing fees that they would pay during peak hours under full marginal cost pricing. See S. A. Morrison, "The Equity and Efficiency of Runway Pricing," *Journal of Public Economics* (October 1987): 45–60.

changes. For example, an advance in knowledge might simply shift all isoquants toward the origin, with the result that any output level could then be produced with a lower level of input and a lower cost. Alternatively, technical change might be "biased" in that it might save only on the use of one input—if workers become more skilled, for instance, this would save only on labor input. Again the end result would be to alter isoquant maps, shift expansion paths, and finally affect the shape and location of a firm's cost curves. In Application 9.5: The Microelectronic Revolution, we look at a case where technical improvements have had a dramatic effect on costs.

Numerical Example

If you have the stomach for it, we can continue the numerical example we began in Chapter 8 to derive cost curves for Hamburger Heaven (HH). To do so, let's assume HH can hire workers at $5 per hour and that it rents all of its grills from the Hertz Grill Rental Company for $5 per hour. Hence, total costs for HH during one hour are

$$TC = 5K + 5L \qquad [9.15]$$

where K and L are the number of grills and the number of workers hired during that hour, respectively. To begin our study of HH's cost-minimization process, suppose the firm wishes to produce 40 hamburgers per hour. Table 9.1 repeats the various ways HH can produce 40 hamburgers per hour and uses Equation 9.15 to compute the total cost of each method. It is clear in Table 9.1 that total costs are minimized when K and L are each 4. With this employment of inputs, total cost is $40 with half being spent on grills ($20 = $5 × 4 grills)

Table 9.1 Total Costs of Producing 40 Hamburgers per Hour	Output (Q)	Workers (L)	Grills (K)	Total Cost (TC)
	40	1	16.0	$85.00
	40	2	8.0	50.00
	40	3	5.3	41.50
	40	4	4.0	40.00
	40	5	3.2	41.00
	40	6	2.7	43.50
	40	7	2.3	46.50
	40	8	2.0	50.00
	40	9	1.8	54.00
	40	10	1.6	58.00

Source: Table 8.2 and Equation 9.15.

APPLICATION 9.5

The Microelectronic Revolution

The development of semiconductor technology during the second half of the twentieth century is one of the most important examples of a cost-reducing technical innovation in history. By some estimates, the effect of the revolution has been the halving of the cost of computing power every two or three years since the early 1970s.

Hand-held Calculators

The first hand-held electronic calculators were introduced in the early 1970s. These simple, four-function (adding, subtracting, multiplying, and dividing) calculators cost about $100 to produce and, because of their novelty, sold for much more. Improvements in metal oxide semiconductors (MOS) occurred rapidly in the early 1970s, quickly reducing the costs associated with internal computations. In addition, the development of complex integrated circuits made it possible to tie a calculator's computation functions together with its display functions on a single chip. Manufacturing costs for calculators fell accordingly, reaching approximately $10 by 1975. Further cost reductions in calculator production came about later in the decade as improved, lower-power displays based on liquid crystal technology became available. What had been an expensive gadget for a few professionals eventually became a standard giveaway to anyone opening bank accounts.

Personal Computers

The dramatic declines in calculator production costs were repeated with regard to personal computers (PCs) during the 1980s. Improved processing chips, cheaper memory capabilities, and lower-cost hard disks all had the effect of lowering the costs and increasing the performance of desktop machines. By the end of the decade, low-cost PCs easily surpassed the performance characteristics of the best mainframe machines available ten years earlier.

Some of the most extensive studies of the declining costs of PCs and other computer equipment have been conducted by the Bureau of Economic Analysis (BEA) of the U.S. Commerce Department in their construction of the National Income and Products Accounts. Table 1 shows some of the resulting price indices during the mid-1980s. Overall, the price of all computer and peripheral equipment fell by about 60 percent between 1982 and 1987. The decline for personal computers alone was even larger. The techniques used to estimate these price changes are very similar to those described in Application 2.1: Property Tax Assessment. The agency estimates the implicit cost of various aspects of a computer (speed, memory, storage capacity, and so forth) in a base year, and then calculates what more modern computers would have cost at these implicit prices. The difference between this (high) price and the actual (lower) price at which PCs sold provides an estimate of the decline in prices, holding quality constant.[1]

To Think About

1. Most computers are used as "inputs" in other businesses. How would the price declines recorded in Table 1 affect the cost curves for these other firms?
2. In some cases (such as controlling robots and machine tools), the increasing availability of low-cost computer chips has permitted other equipment to perform better. How would you show this in a production function context?

Table 1

Price Indices for Computers 1982–1987
(1982 = 100)

Year	All Computers and Peripherals	Storage Devices	Displays	Personal Computers
1982	100.0	100.0	100.0	100.0
1984	64.4	64.4	68.0	60.5
1987	39.1	49.0	34.2	37.6

Source: Survey of Current Business (November 1988): 22.

---

[1]For a discussion, see D. W. Cartwright and S. D. Smith, "Deflators for Purchases of Computers in GNP," *Survey of Current Business* (November 1988): 22–23.

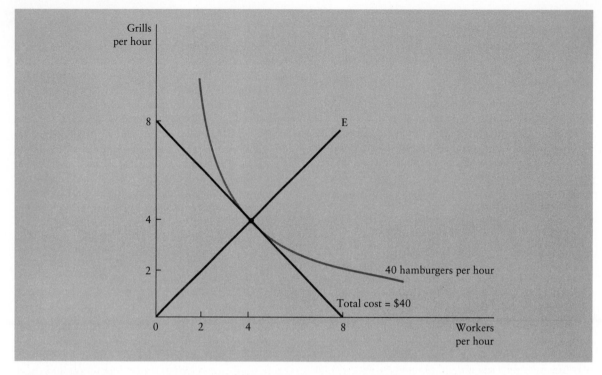

Figure 9.10
Cost-Minimizing
Input Choice for
40 Hamburgers
per Hour

Using four grills and four workers is the minimal cost combination of inputs that can be used to produce 40 hamburgers per hour. Total costs are $40.

and the other half being spent workers. Figure 9.10 shows this cost-minimizing tangency.

■ Long-Run Cost Curves

Because of the constant returns-to-scale nature of HH's production function, it is a simple matter to compute its expansion path; all of the cost-minimizing tangencies will resemble the one shown in Figure 9.10. Long-run minimization will always require K = L. Some of these input combinations are listed in Table 9.2 together with the total cost of each. Notice the simple relationship between total costs and quantity produced—total costs rise by exactly $10 for each 10 extra hamburgers produced. This result is shown graphically in Figure 9.11. HH's long-run total cost curve is a straight line through the origin and its long-run average and marginal costs are constant at $1 per burger. The very simple shapes shown in Figure 9.11 are a direct result of the constant returns-to-scale production function HH has.

Output (Q)	Workers (L)	Grills (K)	Total Cost (TC)	Table 9.2 Expansion Path for Hamburger Production
10	1	1	$10	
20	2	2	20	
30	3	3	30	
40	4	4	40	
50	5	5	50	
60	6	6	60	
70	7	7	70	
80	8	8	80	
90	9	9	90	
100	10	10	100	

Source: Table 8.1 and Equation 9.15.

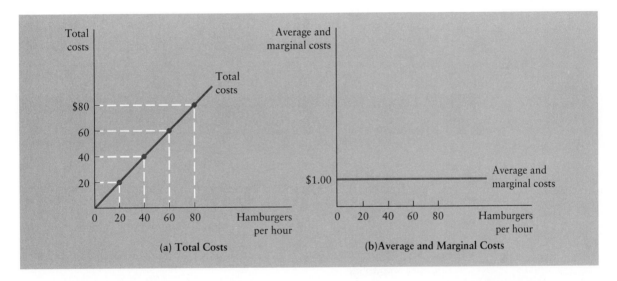

The total cost curve is simply a straight line through the origin reflecting constant returns to scale. Long-run average and marginal costs are constant at $1 per hamburger.

Figure 9.11
Total, Average, and Marginal Cost Curves

■ Short-Run Costs

If we hold one of HH's inputs constant, its cost curves have a more interesting shape. For example, with the number of grills fixed at 4, Table 9.3 repeats the labor input required to produce various output levels (see Table 8.3). Total costs of these input combinations are again computed from Equation 9.15 and shown in the table. Notice how the diminishing marginal productivity of labor for HH causes its costs to rise rapidly as output expands.

Table 9.3 Short-Run Costs of Hamburger Production	Output (Q)	Workers (L)	Grills (K)	Total Cost (STC)	Average Cost (SAC)	Marginal Cost (SMC)
	10	0.25	4	$21.25	$2.125	—
	20	1.00	4	25.00	1.250	$0.50
	30	2.25	4	31.25	1.040	0.75
	40	4.00	4	40.00	1.000	1.00
	50	6.25	4	51.25	1.025	1.25
	60	9.00	4	65.00	1.085	1.50
	70	12.25	4	81.25	1.160	1.75
	80	16.00	4	100.00	1.250	2.00
	90	20.25	4	121.25	1.345	2.25
	100	25.00	4	145.00	1.450	2.50

Source: Table 8.3, Equation 9.15, and footnote 7.

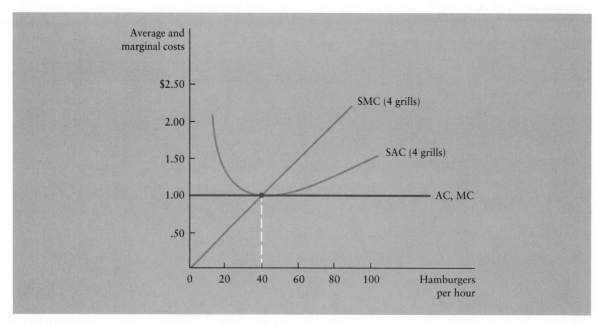

Figure 9.12
Short-Run and Long-Run Average and Marginal Cost Curves for Hamburger Heaven

For this constant returns to scale production function AC and MC are constant over all ranges of output. This constant average cost is $1 per unit. The short-run average cost curve does, however, have a general U-shape since the number of grills is held constant. The SAC curve is tangent to the AC curve at an output of 40 hamburgers per hour.

This is shown even more clearly by computing the short-run average and marginal costs implied by those total cost figures.[7] The marginal cost of the 100th hamburger amounts to a whopping $2.50 because of the four grill limitation in the production process.

Finally, Figure 9.12 superimposes the short-run average and marginal cost figures from Table 9.3 onto the long-run curve shown in Figure 9.11. Notice that SAC reaches its minimum value of $1 per hamburger at an output of 40 burgers per hour since that is the optimal output level for 4 grills. For increases in output above 40 hamburgers per hour, both SAC and SMC increase rapidly.[8]

Summary

This chapter shows how to construct the firm's cost curves. These curves show the relationship between the amount that a firm produces and the costs of the inputs required for that production. In later chapters we will see how these curves are important building blocks for developing the theory of supply. The primary results of this chapter are:

- To minimize the cost of producing any particular level of output, the firm should choose a point on the isoquant for which the rate of technical substitution (RTS) is equal to the ratio of the inputs' market prices.

- By repeating this cost-minimization process for every possible level of output, the firm's expansion path can be constructed. This shows the minimum cost way of producing any level of output. The firm's total cost curve can be calculated directly from the expansion path.

- The two most important unit cost concepts are average cost (that is, cost per unit of output) and marginal cost (that is, the incremental cost of the last unit produced). Average and marginal cost curves can be constructed directly from the total cost curve. The shape of these curves depends on the shape of the total cost curve.

- Short-run cost curves are constructed by holding one of the firm's inputs constant in the short run. These short-run costs will not generally be the lowest cost the firm could achieve if all inputs could be adjusted. Short-run costs also increase rapidly as output expands because the inputs that can be increased experience diminishing marginal productivities.

[7]Average costs shown in Table 9.3 were computed by dividing TC by Q. Because SMC is constantly changing, it cannot be approximated precisely from Table 9.3 and must instead be computed directly from the TC function using calculus. Total costs in this case can be found by substituting the production function into Equation 9.15 to obtain $STC = 20 + Q^2/80$. Differentiation yields $SMC = dTC/dQ = Q/40$ and this was used to provide the figures in the table.

[8]For some examples of how the cost curves in this example might shift, see Problems 9.9 and 9.10.

- Cost curves will shift to a new position whenever the prices of inputs change. Improvements in production techniques will also shift cost curves since the same output can then be produced with fewer inputs.

Review Questions

1. Trump Airlines is thinking of buying a new plane for its shuttle service. Why does the economist's notion of cost suggest that Trump should consider the plane's price in deciding whether it is a profitable investment, but that once bought, the plane's price is not directly relevant to Trump's profit-maximizing decisions? In such a case of "sunk costs," what cost should be assigned in deciding how to use the plane? (See Chapter 18 for further details on sunk capital costs.)

2. Farmer McDonald was heard to complain, "Although my farm is still profitable, I just can't afford to stay in this business any longer. I'm going to sell out and start a fast-food business." In what sense is McDonald using the word "profitable" here? Explain why his statement might be correct if he means profits in the accountant's sense, but would be dubious if he is referring to economic profits.

3. Explain why the assumption of cost minimization implies that the total cost curve must have a positive slope. An increase in output will always increase *total* cost.

4. Suppose a firm had a production function with linear isoquants, implying that its two inputs were perfect substitutes for each other. What would determine the firm's expansion path in this case? For the opposite case of a fixed-proportions production function, what would the firm's expansion path be?

5. Consider two possible definitions of marginal cost:

   a. The extra cost involved in producing one more unit of output.
   b. The cost of the last unit produced.

   Are these definitions identical? If not, which is more correct? Why might the other be misleading?

6. Explain why the average cost associated with any level of output can be depicted graphically as the slope of a chord joining the appropriate point on the TC curve to the origin. Use this fact to show why average and marginal costs are equal at the point of minimum average cost.

7. Late Bloomer is taking a course in microeconomics. Grading in the course is based on 10 weekly quizzes, each with a 100 point maximum. On the first quiz Late Bloomer receives a 10. In each succeeding week he raises his score by 10 points, scoring a 100 on the final quiz of the year.

   a. Calculate Late Bloomer's quiz average for each week of the semester. Why, after the first week, is his average always lower than his current week's quiz?
   b. To help Late Bloomer, his kindly professor has decided to add 40 points to the total of his quiz scores before computing the average. Recompute Late Bloomer's weekly averages given this professorial gift.

c. Explain why Late Bloomer's quiz averages now have a U-shape. What is his lowest average during the term?

d. Explain the relevance of this problem to the construction of cost curves. Why does the presence of a "fixed cost" of 40 points result in a U-shaped curve? Are Late Bloomer's average and marginal test scores equal at his minimum average?

8. Why does the assumption of cost minimization imply that short-run costs for any level of production must be at least as high as long-run costs? If long-run costs are lower, why can't the firm use the input mix required for these lower costs in the short run?

9. Why does the result of question 8 necessarily imply that short-run *average* costs must be at least as great as long-run *average* costs? Can the SAC curve ever be below the AC curve? Where are they equal?

10. Use Figure 9.1 to explain why a rise in the cost of an input must increase the total cost of producing any given output level. What does this result suggest about how such a price increase shifts the AC curve? Do you think it is possible to draw any definite conclusion about how MC would be affected?

Problems

9.1 A widget manufacturer has an infinitely substitutable production function of the form

$$Q = 2K + L.$$

a. Graph the isoquant maps for Q = 20, Q = 40, and Q = 60. What is the RTS along these isoquants?

b. If the wage rate (w) is $1 and the rental rate on capital (v) is $1, what cost-minimizing combination of K and L will the manufacturer employ for the three different production levels in part a? What is the manufacturer's expansion path?

c. How would your answer to part b change if v rose to $3 with w remaining at $1?

9.2 A stuffed wombat manufacturer determined that the lowest average production costs were achieved when eight wombats were produced at an average cost of $1,000 each. If the marginal cost curve is a straight line intersecting the origin, what is the marginal cost of producing the ninth wombat?

9.3 The long-run total cost function for a firm producing skateboards is

$$TC = Q^3 - 40Q^2 + 430Q$$

where Q is the number of skateboards per week.

a. What is the general shape of this total cost function?

    b. Calculate the average cost function for skateboards. What shape does the graph of this function have? At what level of skateboard output does average cost reach a minimum? What is the average cost at this level of output?

    c. The marginal cost function for skateboards is given by

$$MC = 3Q^2 - 80Q + 430.$$

    Show that this marginal cost curve intersects average cost at its minimum value.

    d. Graph the average and marginal cost curves for skateboard production.

9.4   Trapper Joe, the fur trader, has found that his production function in acquiring pelts is given by

$$Q = 2\sqrt{H}$$

where Q = the number of pelts acquired in a day and H = the number of hours Joe's employees spend hunting and trapping in one day. Joe pays his employees $8 an hour.

    a. Calculate Joe's total and average cost curves (as a function of Q).

    b. What is Joe's total cost for the day if he acquires four pelts? Six pelts? Eight pelts? What is Joe's average cost per pelt for the day if he acquires four pelts? Six pelts? Eight pelts?

    c. Graph the cost curves from part a and indicate the points from part b.

9.5   A firm producing hockey sticks has a production function given by

$$Q = 2\sqrt{K \cdot L}.$$

In the short run, the firm's amount of capital equipment is fixed at K = 100. The rental rate for K is v = $1, and the wage rate for L is w = $4.

    a. Calculate the firm's short-run total cost curve. Calculate the short-run average cost curve.

    b. The firm's short-run marginal cost curve is given by SMC = Q/50. What are the STC, SATC, and SMC for the firm if it produces 25 hockey sticks? Fifty hockey sticks? One hundred hockey sticks? Two hundred hockey sticks?

    c. Graph the SATC and the SMC curves for the firm. Indicate the points found in part b.

    d. Where does the SMC curve intersect the SATC curve? Explain why the SMC curve will always intersect the SATC at its lowest point.

9.6   Professor Smith and Professor Jones are going to produce a new introductory textbook. As true scientists they have laid out the production function for the book as

$$Q = \sqrt{SJ}$$

where Q = the number of pages in the finished book, S = the number of working hours spent by Smith, and J = the number of hours spent working by Jones.

Smith values his labor at $3 per working hour. He has spent 900 hours preparing the first draft. Jones, whose labor is valued at $12 per working hour, will revise Smith's draft to complete the book.

a. How many hours will Jones have to spend to produce a finished book of 150 pages? Of 300 pages? Of 450 pages?
b. What is the marginal cost of the 150th page of the finished book? Of the 300th page? Of the 450th page?

*9.7 An enterprising entrepreneur purchases two firms to produce widgets. Each firm produces identical products and each has a production function given by

$$Q_i = \sqrt{K_i \cdot L_i}$$

$$i = 1, 2.$$

The firms differ, however, in the amount of capital equipment each has. In particular, firm 1 has $K_1 = 25$, whereas firm 2 has $K_2 = 100$. The marginal product of labor is $MP_L = 5/(2\sqrt{L})$ for firm 1, and $MP_L = 5(\sqrt{L})$ for firm 2. Rental rates for K and L are given by $w = v = \$1$.

a. If the entrepreneur wishes to minimize short-run total costs of widget production, how should output be allocated between the two firms?
b. Given that output is optimally allocated between the two firms, calculate the short-run total and average cost curves. What is the marginal cost of the 100th widget? The 125th widget? The 200th widget?
c. How should the entrepreneur allocate widget production between the two firms in the long run? Calculate the long-run total and average cost curves for widget production.
d. How would your answer to part c change if both firms exhibited diminishing returns to scale?

9.8 Suppose a firm's constant returns to scale production function requires it to use capital and labor in a fixed ratio of two workers per machine to produce 10 units and that the rental rates for capital and labor are given by $v = 1$, $w = 3$.

a. Calculate the firm's long-run total and average cost curves.
b. Suppose K is fixed at 10 in the short run. Calculate the firm's short-run total and average cost curves. What is the marginal cost of the 10th unit? The 25th unit? The 50th unit? The 100th unit?

9.9 In the numerical example of Hamburger Heaven's production function in Chapter 8, we examined the consequences of the invention of a self-flipping burger which changed the production function to

$$Q = 20\sqrt{KL}.$$

*Denotes a problem that is rather difficult.

a. Assuming this shift does not change the cost-minimizing expansion path (which requires K = L), how are long-run total, average, and marginal costs affected? (See the numerical example at the end of this chapter.)

b. More generally, technical progress in hamburger production might be reflected by

$$Q = (1 + r)\sqrt{KL}$$

where r is the annual rate of technical progress (that is, a rate of increase of 3 percent would have r = .03). How will the year-to-year change in the average cost of a hamburger be related to the value of r?

9.10 In our numerical example, Hamburger Heaven's expansion path requires K = L because w (the wage) and v (the rental rate of grills) are equal. More generally, for this type of production function, it can be shown that

$$K/L = w/v$$

for cost minimization. Hence, relative input usage is determined by relative input prices.

a. Suppose both wages and grill rents rise to $10 per hour. How would this affect the firm's expansion path? How would long-run average and marginal cost be affected? What can you conclude about the effect of uniform inflation of input costs on the costs of hamburger production?

b. Suppose wages rose to $20, but grill rents stay fixed at $5. How would this affect the firm's expansion path? How would this affect the long-run average and marginal cost of hamburger production? Why does a multiplication of the wage by 4 result in a much smaller increase in average costs?

Chapter 9 looked at how firms minimize costs for any level of output. This chapter now focuses on how firms determine what level of output they will produce. Before we investigate that decision, we discuss briefly the nature of firms themselves and describe a few ways in which their output choices might be analyzed.

CHAPTER
10

PROFIT
MAXIMIZATION
AND SUPPLY

Nature of Firms

As we pointed out earlier, a firm is a collection of people who turn inputs into outputs. Different individuals supply different types of inputs, such as workers' skills and types of capital equipment, to the output process, and they expect to receive some type of reward for doing so. The relationships among these providers of inputs in a firm may be quite complicated. Each provider agrees to devote his or her input to production activities under a set of understandings about how the input is to be used and what benefit the provider will receive. In some cases these relationships are explicitly set down in contracts. Workers often negotiate contracts that specify in considerable detail what hours are to be worked, what rules of work are to be followed, and what rate of pay is to be received. Similarly, capital owners invest in a firm under a set of explicit legal principles about how the capital will be used and the compensation the owners will receive. In addition to these formal arrangements, there are many more implicit relationships among the people in a firm. For example, managers and workers follow certain procedures in making production decisions, and there are many implicit understandings about who has the authority to do what. Capital owners often delegate considerable authority to managers and workers to make decisions on their behalf. General Motors shareholders, for example, are never involved in the decision of how assembly line equipment will be used, though technically they own it. All of these explicit and implicit relationships among providers change through time in response to experiences and to events external to the firm. Much as a basketball team will try out new plays and defensive strategies, so too firms will alter the nature of their internal organizations in order to achieve better long-run results.[1]

■ Firms' Goals

These complicated relationships among the providers of inputs in a firm pose some problems for economists who wish to develop theoretical generalizations about how firms behave. In our study of demand theory, it made some sense to talk about choices by a rational consumer because we were examining decisions by only a single person. But for firms, many people may be involved in decisions, and any detailed study of such decisions may quickly become deeply mired in questions of psychology, sociology, and group dynamics.

Although some economists have adopted an "organizational behavior" approach to studying firms' decisions, that approach can be too cumbersome for general purposes. Instead, most economists treat the firm as a single decision-making unit, an approach that sweeps away all the complicated behavioral

---

[1]All of these points are examined in more detail in Chapter 11, which looks at the explicit and implicit contracts within firms.

issues about relationships among employees and capital owners. This approach often assumes that firms' decisions are made by a single dictatorial manager who rationally pursues some goal, usually the maximization of the firm's economic profits. This is the approach we will take in this chapter to develop the theory of a firm's supply behavior.

Profit Maximization

If firms pursue the goal of achieving the largest economic profits possible, by definition they seek to make the difference between total revenues and total economic costs as big as possible. Here we are using economic concepts of costs and profits. Accounting notions of profits may be relevant to questions about how the firm is taxed (Application 10.1: Corporate Profits, Taxes, and Leveraged Buyouts looks at this relationship), but, as we will show, maximizing economic profits is assumed to be the fundamental goal motivating actual behavior.

■ Marginalism

If firms are strict profit maximizers, they will make decisions in a marginal way. The manager-owner will adjust the things that can be controlled until it is impossible to increase profits further. The manager looks, for example, at the incremental (or marginal) profit from producing one more unit of output, or the additional profit from hiring one more laborer. As long as this incremental profit is positive, the manager will decide to produce the extra output or hire the extra laborer. When the incremental profit of an activity becomes zero, the manager has pushed the activity far enough—it would not be profitable to go farther.

■ The Output Decision

We can show this relationship between profit maximization and marginalism most directly by looking at the output level that a firm will choose to produce. A firm sells some level of output, Q, and from these sales the firm receives its revenues, R(Q). The amount of revenues received obviously depends on how much output is sold and on what price it is sold for. Similarly, in producing Q certain economic costs are incurred, TC(Q), and these also will depend on how much is produced. As in Chapter 9, economic profits (π) are therefore defined as

$$\pi = R(Q) - TC(Q). \tag{10.1}$$

APPLICATION 10.1

Corporate Profits, Taxes, and Leveraged Buyouts

Corporate income (or profit) taxes were first levied in the United States in 1909, about four years before the personal income tax was put into effect. In 1991 (a recession year where profits tended to be low), corporate income tax revenues amounted to more than $103 billion, or approximately 10 percent of total federal tax collections. Many people view the tax as a natural complement to the personal income tax. Because under U.S. law, corporations share many of the same rights as do individuals, it may seem only reasonable that corporations should be taxed in a similar way. Some economists, however, feel that the corporate profits tax seriously distorts the allocation of resources, both because of its failure to use an economic profit concept under the tax law and because a substantial portion of corporate income is taxed twice.

Definition of Profits

A large portion of what is defined as corporate profits under the tax laws is in fact a normal return to shareholders for the equity they have invested in the corporations. Shareholders expect a similar return from other investments they make; if they deposit their money in a bank they expect to be paid interest. Hence, some portion of corporate profits should be considered an economic cost of doing business because it reflects what owners have forgone by making an equity investment. If this cost were added to other corporate costs, correctly defined economic profits would be reduced substantially.

Effects of the Double Tax

The corporate profits tax is not so much a tax on profits as it is a tax on the equity returns of corporate shareholders. Such taxation may have two consequences. First, corporations will find it more attractive to finance new capital investments through loans and bond offerings (whose interest payments are an allowable cost) than through new stock issues (whose implicit costs are not an allowable cost under the tax law). A second ef-

fect occurs because a part of corporate income is double taxed—first when it is earned by the corporation and then later when it is paid out to shareholders in the form of dividends. Hence, the total rate of tax applied to corporate equity capital is much higher than that applied to other sources of capital. As a consequence, investors will be less willing to invest in corporate businesses than in other assets which are not subject to the corporate profits tax. A number of economists have found that such distortionary effects are rather large and have suggested ways in which the corporate profits tax might be changed so as to reduce them.[1]

The Leveraged Buyout Wave

Some observers have suggested that these peculiarities of the corporate income tax are partly responsible for the wave of leveraged buyouts (LBOs) that swept financial markets in the late 1980s. The basic principle of an LBO is to use borrowed funds to acquire most of the outstanding stock of a corporation. Essentially those involved in such a buyout are substituting a less highly taxed source of capital (debt) for a more highly taxed form (equity). Huge deals such as the $25 billion buyout of RJR-Nabisco by the Kohlberg, Kravis, Roberts company (see Application 11.5) may be an attempt to maximize the true economic profits that can be extracted from a business.

To Think About

1. Would the defects of the corporate profits tax be cured by taxing only economic profits? How could this be achieved in practice? Is it possible to redefine accounting concepts of costs to reflect economic concepts?

2. A popular slogan of some tax reformers is: "Corporations don't pay taxes, people do." Do you agree? If so, why do we have a separate corporate tax? Which "people" end up paying the tax?

---

[1]See C. E. McClure, *Must Corporate Income Be Taxed Twice?* (Washington, D.C.: Brookings Institution, 1979).

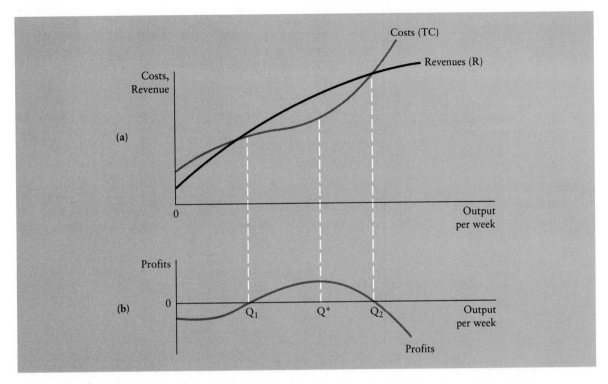

Since economic profits are defined as total revenues minus total economic costs, profits reach a maximum when the slope of the revenue function (marginal revenue) is equal to the slope of the cost function (marginal cost). In the figure this occurs at Q^*. Profits are zero at both Q_1 and Q_2.

Figure 10.1
Marginal Revenue Must Equal Marginal Cost for Profit Maximization

In deciding how much output to produce, the firm will choose the amount for which economic profits are as large as possible. This process is illustrated in Figure 10.1. There the curve $TC(Q)$ is drawn with the same general shape as the total cost curves we introduced in Chapter 9. The curve $R(Q)$, which represents total revenue, is drawn so that selling more output leads to greater revenues.[2] We can calculate profits by looking at the vertical distance between the $R(Q)$ and $TC(Q)$ curves, and profits are shown explicitly in the bottom panel of the figure. It is clear that profits reach a maximum at Q^*. For outputs either larger or smaller than Q^*, profits are lower than they are at Q^*. We wish to examine those conditions that must hold at Q^* for maximum profits.

---

[2]We will examine the exact shape of the $R(Q)$ curve when we reintroduce demand curves. For the moment, the curve $R(Q)$ is drawn so that increasing output leads to increasing revenues. In the case where the firm's decisions do not affect price, the $R(Q)$ curve would be the straight-line $R(Q) = P \cdot Q$, where P is the market price of the firm's output. Later in this chapter, we will make a distinction between output by a single firm (q) and in the market as a whole (Q), but we do not do so here.

■ The Marginal Revenue/Marginal Cost Rule

If we start from an output level below Q*, an increase in output brings in more additional revenue than producing this additional output costs. A firm interested in maximizing profits would never stop short of Q*. If a firm decided to increase its output level beyond Q*, it would reduce its profits. The additional revenues from increasing Q beyond Q* fall short of the additional costs incurred in expanding output. Consequently, at Q* the additional costs of producing an infinitesimal amount more are exactly equal to the additional revenues that this extra output will bring in. Economists would say that at Q*, *marginal cost* (we have already met this concept in Chapter 9) is equal to **marginal revenue** (the extra revenue provided by the sale of one more unit). In order to maximize profits, a firm should produce that output level for which the marginal revenue from selling one more unit of output is exactly equal to the marginal cost of producing that unit of output.[3] More succinctly,

■ **Marginal revenue**

The extra revenue a firm receives when it sells one more unit of output.

$$\text{Marginal revenue} = \text{Marginal cost} \qquad [10.2]$$

or

$$MR = MC. \qquad [10.3]$$

This principle is so important for the theory of the firm (and for the analysis of supply) that it deserves further elaboration. A firm might determine its maximum profits conceptually starting at an output level of zero and increasing output one unit at a time. As long as marginal revenue exceeds marginal cost, the firm should continue to increase output—each additional unit it produces will add something to its total profits. The firm can push things too far, however. Eventually marginal costs will start to rise. As soon as they equal marginal revenue, the firm has gone far enough. Further increases in output would reduce profits since the cost of producing more output would exceed the revenue it brings in. Whenever conditions change, the firm can conduct a similar conceptual experiment and thus decide on a new profit-maximizing output level.

■ Marginalism in Input Choices

So far we have developed a firm's marginal decision rules as they relate to output choices; we can make a similar argument for input choices as well. Hiring additional labor, for example, entails some increase in costs, and a profit-maximizing firm should balance the additional costs against the extra revenue brought in by selling the output produced by the extra labor. A similar analysis

---

[3]Geometry provides another way of visualizing this result. The distance between any two curves is greatest when the slopes of the curves are equal—if the slopes aren't equal, you can get farther apart by moving one way or the other. For the R(Q) and TC(Q) curves, this geometric fact again proves that profits are maximized when marginal revenue equals marginal cost since MR is the slope of the revenue curve and MC is the slope of the total cost curve.

holds for the firm's decision on the number of machines to rent. Additional machines should be hired only as long as their marginal contributions to profits are positive. As the marginal productivity of machines begins to decline, the ability of machines to yield additional revenue also declines. The firm will eventually reach a point at which the marginal contribution of an additional machine to profits is exactly zero—the extra sales generated precisely match the costs of the extra machines. The firm should not expand the rental of machines beyond this point. In Chapter 19, we will see how this application of marginalism leads to a theory of input demand. For the moment, our attention is centered on a firm's output choice and on the profit-maximizing condition: Marginal revenue equals marginal cost. Since we have already discussed the concept of marginal cost in detail, we now turn to the notion of marginal revenue.

Marginal Revenue

It is the revenue from selling one more unit of output that is relevant to a profit-maximizing firm. If a firm can sell all it wishes without affecting market price (that is, if the firm is a **price taker**), the market price will indeed be the extra revenue obtained from selling one more unit. In other words, if a firm's output decisions will not affect market price, marginal revenue is equal to price. We can easily demonstrate this result. Suppose a firm were selling 50 widgets at $1 each. Then total revenues would be $50. If selling one more widget does not affect price, that additional widget will also bring in $1, and total revenue will rise to $51. Marginal revenue from the 51st widget will be $1 (= $51 − $50). For a firm that cannot affect market price, we therefore have

$$MR = P. \qquad [10.4]$$

■ **Price taker**
A firm or individual whose decisions regarding buying or selling have no effect on the prevailing market price of a good or service.

■ Marginal Revenue for a Downward-Sloping Demand Curve

A firm may not always be able to sell all it wants at the prevailing market price. If it faces a downward-sloping demand curve for its product, it can sell more only by reducing its selling price. In this case marginal revenue will be less than market price. To see why, assume in our prior example that to sell the 51st widget the firm must reduce its price to $.99. Total revenues are now $50.49 (= $.99 × 51), and the marginal revenue from the 51st widget is only $.49 (= $50.49 − $50.00). Even though the 51st widget sells for $.99, the extra revenue obtained from selling the widget is a net gain of only $.49 (a $.99 gain on the 51st widget less a $.50 reduction in revenue from the first 50). When selling one more unit causes market price to decline, marginal revenue is less than market price:

$$MR < P. \qquad [10.5]$$

Table 10.1	Price (P)	Quantity (Q)	Total Revenue (P· Q)	Marginal Revenue (MR)
Total and Marginal Revenue for Cassette Tapes (Q = 10 – P)	$10	0	$ 0	
	9	1	9	$ 9
	8	2	16	7
	7	3	21	5
	6	4	24	3
	5	5	25	1
	4	6	24	−1
	3	7	21	−3
	2	8	16	−5
	1	9	9	−7
	0	10	0	−9

Firms that must reduce their prices to sell more of their products (that is, firms facing a downward-sloping demand curve) must take this fact into account in deciding how to obtain maximum profits.

■ A Numerical Example

The result that marginal revenue is less than price for a downward-sloping demand curve is illustrated with a numerical example in Table 10.1. There we have recorded the quantity of, say, tape cassettes demanded per week (Q), their price (P), total revenues from cassette sales (P · Q), and marginal revenue (MR) for a simple linear demand curve of the form

$$Q = 10 - P. \qquad [10.6]$$

Total revenue from tape sales reaches a maximum at $Q = 5$, $P = 5$. For $Q > 5$, total revenues decline. Increasing tape sales beyond 5 per week actually causes marginal revenue to be negative.

In Figure 10.2, we have drawn this hypothetical demand curve and can use the figure to illustrate the marginal revenue concept. Consider, for example, the extra revenue obtained if the firm sells four tapes instead of three. When output is three, the market price per tape is $7 and total revenues (P · Q) are $21. These revenues are shown by the area of the rectangle P*AQ*0. If the firm produces four tapes per week instead, price must be reduced to $6 to sell this increased output level. Now total revenue is $24, illustrated by the area of the rectangle P**BQ**0. A comparison of the two revenue rectangles shows why the marginal revenue obtained by producing the fourth tape is less than its price. The sale of this tape does indeed increase revenue by the price at which it sells ($6). Revenue increases by the area of the dark gray rectangle in Figure 10.2. But to sell the fourth tape, the firm must reduce its selling price from $7 to $6 on the first three tapes sold per week. That price reduction causes a fall in revenue of $3, shown as the area of the light gray rectangle in Figure 10.2.

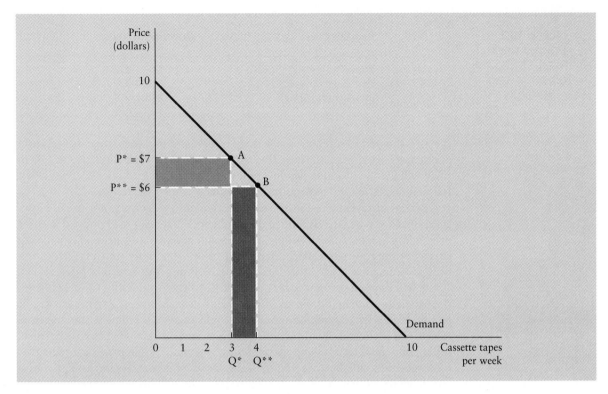

For this hypothetical demand curve, marginal revenue can be calculated as the extra revenue from selling one more tape. If the firm sells four tapes instead of three, for example, revenue will be $24 rather than $21. Marginal revenue from the sale of the fourth tape is therefore $3. This represents the gain of $6 from the sale of the fourth tape *less* the decline in revenue of $3 as a result of the fall in price for the first three tapes from $7 to $6.

Figure 10.2
Illustration of Marginal Revenue for the Demand Curve for Cassette Tapes (Q = 10 – P)

The net result is an increase in revenue of only $3 ($6 – $3) rather than the gain of $6 that would be assumed if only the sale of the fourth tape is considered in isolation. The marginal revenue for other points in this hypothetical demand curve could also be illustrated. In particular, if you draw the case of a firm producing eight tapes instead of seven, you will see that marginal revenue from the eighth tape is negative. Although the tape itself sells for $2, selling it requires the firm to reduce price by $1 on the other seven tapes it sells.

■ Marginal Revenue and Price Elasticity

In Chapter 5, we introduced the concept of the price elasticity of demand ($e_{Q,P}$), which we defined as

$$e_{Q,P} = \frac{\text{Percentage change in Q}}{\text{Percentage change in P}}.$$ [10.7]

	Demand Curve	Marginal Revenue
Table 10.2 Relationship between Marginal Revenue and Elasticity	Elastic ($e_{Q,P} < -1$)	MR > 0
	Unit elastic ($e_{Q,P} = -1$)	MR = 0
	Inelastic ($e_{Q,P} > -1$)	MR < 0

We also showed that the price elasticity of demand provides some information about how total expenditures (P · Q) change when price changes. A fall in price will increase total expenditures if demand is elastic ($e_{Q,P} < -1$), but such a fall will decrease total expenditures if demand is inelastic ($e_{Q,P} > -1$).

Marginal revenue is concerned with changes in quantity, not price. However, since for a negatively sloped demand curve increases in Q imply decreases in P, it is clear that the concepts of marginal revenue and price elasticity are closely related. In particular, attempting to sell one more unit may require a firm to reduce its price (if it doesn't, MR = P and the firm is a price taker). What will happen to total revenues (that is, to the product P · Q) depends on the elasticity of demand. From our previous discussion it is easy to see that if demand is elastic, selling one more unit will increase revenues: the marginal revenue of the last unit sold will be positive. Since demand is price responsive, selling one more unit will necessitate only a "small" fall in price; consequently total revenues will increase. On the other hand, if demand is inelastic, the firm will have to reduce the price substantially to be able to sell one more unit of output. This price decline will be so large that total revenues will be reduced by the sale: marginal revenue now is negative.[4] As an intermediate case, demand might be of unitary elasticity ($e_{Q,P} = -1$), in which case total revenues are constant. Selling one more unit will bring about a price decline of the exact magnitude necessary to keep P · Q constant. In that case the marginal revenue from the sale of one more unit is zero.

These relationships between marginal revenue and elasticity are summarized in Table 10.2. More generally, it can be shown that

$$MR = P\left(1 + \frac{1}{e_{Q,P}}\right), \qquad [10.8]$$

and all of the relationships in Table 10.2 can be derived from this basic equation.[5] For example, if demand is elastic ($e_{Q,P} < -1$), Equation 10.8 shows that MR is positive. Indeed, if demand is infinitely elastic ($e_{Q,P} = -\infty$), MR will equal price since, as we showed before, the firm is a price taker and cannot affect the price it receives.

---

[4]As long as marginal costs are positive, a profit-maximizing firm will not produce at a point on the demand curve for its products where demand is inelastic. In such a case, marginal revenue (negative) could not be equated to marginal cost (positive). In Chapters 15 and 16 we use this observation to show how the elasticity of demand may reflect something about market structure.

[5]The proof requires calculus. See Walter Nicholson, *Microeconomic Theory: Basic Principles and Extensions*, 5th ed. (Hinsdale, Ill.: The Dryden Press, 1992), p. 376.

As another use of Equation 10.8, suppose that a firm knew that the elasticity of demand for its product was −2. It might derive this figure from historical data that show that each 10 percent decline in its price has usually led to an increase in sales of about 20 percent. Now assume that the price of the firm's output is $10 per unit and the firm wishes to know how much additional revenue the sale of one more unit of output would yield. The additional unit of output will not yield $10 because the firm faces a downward-sloping demand curve: to sell the unit requires a reduction in its overall selling price. The firm can, however, use Equation 10.8 to calculate that the additional revenue yielded by the sale will be $5 [= $10 \cdot (1 + 1/−2) = $10 \cdot ½]. The firm will produce this extra unit if marginal costs are less than $5; that is, if MC < $5, profits will be increased by the sale of one more unit of output. Although firms in the real world may use more complex means to decide on the profitability of increasing sales (or of lowering prices), our discussion here illustrates the logic these firms must use. They must recognize how changes in quantity sold affect price (or vice versa) and how these price changes affect total revenues.

Marginal Revenue Curve

Any demand curve has a **marginal revenue curve** associated with it. It is sometimes convenient to think of a demand curve as an *average revenue curve* in that it shows the revenue per unit (in other words, the price) yielded at various output choices. The marginal revenue curve, on the other hand, shows the extra revenue provided by the last unit sold. In the usual case of a downward-sloping curve, the marginal revenue curve will lie below the demand curve since at any level of output, marginal revenue is less than price.[6] In Figure 10.3 we have drawn a marginal revenue curve together with the demand curve from which it was derived. For output levels greater than Q_1, marginal revenue is negative. As Q increases from 0 to Q_1, total revenues ($P \cdot Q$) increase. However, at Q_1 total revenues ($P_1 \cdot Q_1$) are as large as possible; beyond this output level, price falls proportionately faster than output rises.[7]

■ Shifts in Demand and Marginal Revenue Curves

In Chapter 5, we talked in detail about the possibility of a demand curve's shifting because of changes in factors such as income, other prices, or preferences. Whenever a demand curve shifts, its associated marginal revenue curve shifts with it. This should be obvious since the marginal revenue curve is always calculated by referring to a specific demand curve. In later analysis we

■ Marginal revenue curve

A curve showing the relation between the quantity a firm sells and the revenue yielded by the last unit sold. Derived from the demand curve.

---

[6]If demand is infinitely elastic (that is, if the demand curve is a horizontal line at some price), the average and marginal revenue curves coincide. Selling one more unit has no effect on price; therefore marginal and average revenue are equal.

[7]Another way of saying this is that beyond Q_1 demand is inelastic. See our discussion of elasticity along a linear demand curve in Chapter 5.

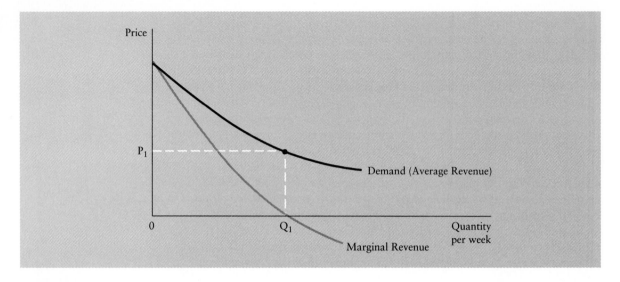

Figure 10.3
Marginal Revenue
Curve Associated
with a Demand
Curve

Since the demand curve is negatively sloped, the marginal curve will fall below the demand ("average revenue") curve. For output levels beyond Q_1, marginal revenue is negative. At Q_1 total revenue ($P_1 \cdot Q_1$) is a maximum; beyond this point additional increases in Q actually cause total revenues to fall because of the related declines in price.

will have to keep in mind the kinds of shifts that marginal revenue curves might make when we talk about changes in demand.

Some economists doubt that firms are able to make calculations about marginal revenue or marginal cost with any degree of accuracy. For this and other reasons, there is considerable controversy over the precise meaning of the profit-maximization hypothesis in its simplest form. Before examining that controversy, Application 10.2: Profit Maximization and Airline Deregulation shows the importance of marginal decisions to the behavior of the airline industry following deregulation.

Controversy over the Profit-Maximization Hypothesis

The marginalist, profit-maximizing approach to firm behavior has been criticized on two general grounds: (1) that real-world firms do not have suitable information to be able to maximize profits, nor would they particularly want to maximize profits if they had such information and (2) that there exist alternative, equally simple hypotheses that can better explain what firms do. The second of these criticisms is dealt with later in this chapter, where some other

APPLICATION 10.2

Profit Maximization and Airline Deregulation

Under the Airline Deregulation Act of 1978, a number of laws restricting U.S. airline operations were to be gradually phased out. Regulation of airline fares was reduced or eliminated entirely, and rules governing the assignment of airline routes were relaxed significantly. These dramatic changes in the legal environment under which airlines operated provided economists with an ideal opportunity to observe how firms respond to altered circumstances. In general, the responses were quite consistent with the profit-maximization hypothesis.

Marginal Revenue

A clear example of the airlines' attention to marginal revenue was their development of new fare structures following deregulation. Prices for standard coach fares dropped relatively little because these fares are usually paid by business people whose demands are relatively inelastic. Consequently, little, if any, extra airline revenues would have been earned by their attempting to lure additional coach-fare passengers into flying. For special discount fares, it was an entirely different story, however. Discount fares were generally targeted toward people with highly elastic travel demands (tourists, families traveling together, and so forth). In this case, large price reductions increased passenger demand significantly, thereby improving the passenger levels on many flights. Overall, the increased use of discount fares resulted in a 17 percent decline in the average price per passenger-mile flown.[1] The structure of the price declines ensured that they generated far more additional revenue for the airlines than would have an across-the-board fare cut of a similar magnitude. Whether airlines can continue such price discrimination in the new, more competitive environment is open to debate.

Marginal Cost

The airlines' attention to marginal costs in response to deregulation is also what might have been expected based on the profit-maximization hypothesis. Their fleets of aircraft could not be changed significantly in the short run, so airlines altered their route structures to coincide with those aircraft they already had. As Alfred Kahn has observed, from an economic point of view their planes represented "marginal costs with wings," which could easily be moved around once deregulation came.

Effects of such reallocations by airlines were readily apparent. Service in many small communities (previously required under Civil Aeronautics Board regulation) was curtailed. Flight lengths were generally brought into greater correspondence with the optimal operating characteristics of the aircraft. Many airlines adopted a hub-and-spoke procedure for connecting flights. More recently, a slowing in the growth of air traffic in the 1991 recession left many airlines with excess capacity in their wide-bodied planes (747s, DC-10s, and L1011s). Because the marginal costs of carrying additional passengers on those planes were quite low, fare discounting was aimed particularly toward flights on wide-bodied crafts. At times it has been cheaper to fly coast-to-coast than to fly from New York to Cleveland.

To Think About

1. Some critics of airline deregulation have charged that it has led to an airline industry of uncertain financial health and has caused airlines to skimp on safety-related maintenance to keep costs down. Does this really reflect profit maximization? How would a determined advocate of deregulation respond to these charges?

2. How do you think airline employees (pilots, cabin attendants, luggage handlers, and so forth) feel about deregulation? Might employees of successful airlines feel differently than employees of bankrupt ones?

---

[1]This figure and much of the analysis in this example are based on J. R. Meyer et al., *Airline Deregulation—The Early Experience* (Boston: Auburn House, 1981). See also S. Morrison and C. Winston, *Economic Effects of Airline Deregulation* (Washington, D.C.: The Brookings Institution, 1986).

simple motives that have been proposed as substitutes for profit maximization are mentioned. This section summarizes the arguments of the first type.[8]

■ Evidence on Profit Maximization

The empirical evidence on whether firms maximize profits is ambiguous. As we mentioned in Chapter 1, when firms answer questionnaires, they seldom rank profits as their only goal. Similarly they often say they lack sufficient information about their revenues or costs to make precise marginal choices. On the other hand, economists have found the profit-maximization hypothesis to be accurate in predicting certain aspects of firms' behavior. For example, many firms seem eager to enter into the most profitable industries, and large, stagnant firms often seek to diversify to increase profitability. Many firms have also adopted a "profit center" form of organization in which managers are judged by the profits their divisions earn.

Some of the attempts to reconcile this ambiguous evidence about profit maximization center on the question of the role of assumptions in economics. Many economists argue that one cannot judge the assumption of profit maximization either by *a priori* logic or by asking firms what they do. They feel the ultimate test is the predictive ability of the hypothesis. Remember Milton Friedman's analogy of the expert pool player who has no knowledge of the rules of physics that determine the movements of the balls on the table. Friedman argued that this ignorance on the part of the player does not prevent an observer from accurately predicting the player's behavior by applying physical principles.[9] Just as Molière's Monsieur Jourdain spoke prose all his life without knowing it, firms may in fact maximize profits despite the fuzziness of their responses to questions about their motives.

■ Survivorship Principle and the Market for Firms

A second set of reasons why economists tend to favor profit maximization as an explanation of firm behavior concerns competitive pressures. Profits represent a return to the owners of a firm. If the firm does not make the largest profits possible, owners may take their assets elsewhere. Indeed, in Chapter 12 we will see that competition itself can force all firms in an industry to operate with, at most, zero economic profits. If a firm opts not to follow the marginal rules, it will have negative profits. In that event, the owner will be even more likely to close down. Those firms that survive in such an environment will be those that do maximize profits. The **survivorship principle** states that we are likely to find only profit-maximizing firms in competitive markets.

Related to this principle is the fact that firms themselves can be bought and sold. Any firm that is not making maximum profits with its existing assets

■
Survivorship principle
The idea that in competitive markets only profit-maximizing firms are likely to survive.

---

[8]Further details on the material discussed here can be found in a series of debates between R. A. Lester and Fritz Machlup in the *American Economic Review* during the years 1946 and 1947.

[9]See Milton Friedman, "The Methodology of Positive Economics," in *Essays in Positive Economics* (Chicago: University of Chicago Press, 1953).

is a tempting target for an investor who believes he or she can do better. Like any economic goods, firms will gravitate toward those buyers who can do the most with them. This "market for corporate control" provides another force that encourages profit-maximizing behavior. The study of this market is one of the major new areas of research in the economics of business behavior, and we examine it in a bit more detail in the next chapter.

Alternatives to Profit Maximization

The debate over whether firms have enough information actually to maximize profits has caused economists to examine a number of other possible goals that may not be so hard for firms to achieve. Two of these are *revenue maximization* and *markup pricing*. These can be easily examined using the tools you already know.

■ Revenue Maximization

One alternative to profit maximization for firms is **revenue maximization.** This goal was first proposed by William J. Baumol who observed that most managerial incentives are tied to increases in sales revenues rather than to profits.[10] For example, higher salaries are paid to the managers of the largest corporations (with the highest dollar volume of sales) rather than to the managers of the most profitable ones. Other pieces of evidence also suggested to Baumol that revenue maximization might be the most important goal for firms. Often a firm's success is judged by the share of the market it commands. Firms that dominate the market may have a number of advantages over other firms, such as better credit with banks or greater consumer recognition of products.[11]

Figure 10.4 shows that a strictly revenue-maximizing firm would produce that quantity of output for which marginal revenue equals zero—the quantity Q^{**}. Output will be expanded as long as any additional revenue is obtainable. Baumol suggests that a firm may not go this far in pursuing sales volume to the exclusion of any consideration of cost, however. Instead, the firm's owners may require that some minimum amount of profits be earned. Baumol's firm would probably produce some quantity between that which a profit maximizer would produce (Q^* in Figure 10.4) and that which a revenue maximizer would produce (Q^{**} in Figure 10.4). Some of the issues involved in the conflict between profit maximization and sales maximization are reflected in Application 10.3: Textbook Royalties, which focuses on textbook pricing (a favorite topic of your author).

■ Revenue maximization

A goal for firms in which they work to maximize their total revenue rather than profits.

---

[10]A clear statement of this hypothesis is found in Chapter 6 of William J. Baumol, *Business Behavior, Value and Growth*, rev. ed. (New York: Harcourt, Brace & World, 1967).

[11]It has also been suggested that maintaining market share is a reasonable long-run profit-maximizing strategy in an uncertain market environment.

APPLICATION 10.3
Textbook Royalties

Most authors (including the author of this textbook) receive royalties based on total book sales. Royalty rates usually range between 10 and 20 percent of the sales price of a book, although some particularly popular authors may be able to negotiate a higher rate. Once a contract is signed, royalties are a fixed fraction of total revenues, so authors would like their publishers to price their books in such a way as to maximize this total revenue figure. That is, the authors would prefer the price to be set so that the quantity demanded will be that quantity for which marginal revenue is zero.

Potential Conflicts with Profits

Publishers, on the other hand, may not agree with their authors. They may wish to price their books so that the quantity demanded is the quantity for which marginal revenue is equal to marginal cost. As Figure 10.4 illustrates, this will usually result in a higher price for the book and a lower quantity sold than revenue-maximizing authors would prefer. Because publishers must be concerned with costs, they will not push sales revenues to the limit.

The potential conflict between authors and publishers may also arise in their wishes about inputs as well. Authors may prefer publishers to invest additional resources to sell books as long as those resources yield any new sales, regardless of what the resources cost the publishers. Authors prefer elaborate sales efforts, large customer service departments, and special book features like detailed graphic devices or ancillary readings. Publishers, on the other hand, will want to use these added inputs only if the additional revenues they generate exceed their costs. Conflicts about marketing of a text can be expected to occur frequently, with publishers again being more cost conscious than authors.

Textbook Contracts

This view of the author-publisher conflict may be too simplistic, however. The prevalence of revenue-based royalty contracts for textbook publishing suggests that these contracts provide benefits to both parties relative to other ways in which authors might be paid. In part, this occurs because there may be little difference between revenue maximization and profit maximization in the case of textbooks. Because the marginal cost of a book is very low once the type has been set, the difference between MR = 0 and MR = MC may be trivial.

More generally, the royalty rate specified in a contract is open to negotiation. Therefore, it may be in both the author's and the publisher's interest to adopt sales strategies that make total profits as large as possible. A royalty rate then can be chosen that gives the author a "fair" share of the profits. Also, strategies for profit maximization may be more complex than they appear to be. For example, because used copies are the main competitors of any new edition an author publishes, the overall pursuit of profit maximization may opt for lower prices (and greater sales volume) than simple calculations might imply. Similarly, some royalty contracts may include rates that rise as a book's sales increase, offering incentives to authors to produce a good product. As is often the case in economics, a deeper examination of the terms of an author's contract may suggest that they are more efficient for both parties than at first appears to be the case.

To Think About

1. Many textbook contracts also include an advance on royalties that are expected to be earned. How do such advances reduce the risks for authors? Why are publishers willing to make such payments? How would these affect textbook pricing decisions?
2. Many textbook ancillaries (workbooks, test banks, instructor's manuals, and so forth) have fixed-fee contracts, that is, the author is simply paid a fixed amount for the product. Why might authors and publishers adopt such contracts? How might the availability of ancillaries affect textbook pricing decisions?

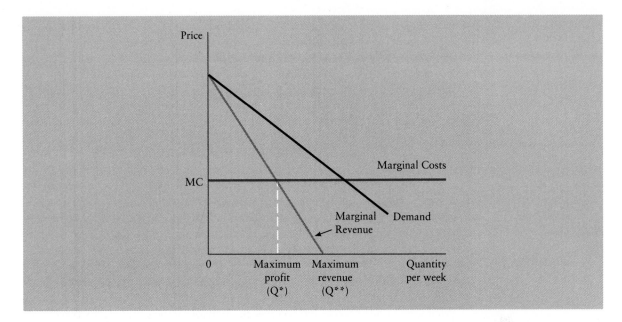

For simplicity we assume that each unit of output can always be produced at a cost of MC. A profit-maximizing firm will therefore produce output level Q*, for which MR = MC. If the firm pursues the goal of revenue maximization, however, it would proceed to output level Q**, since at this level of output marginal revenue is zero.

Figure 10.4

A Comparison of Profit Maximization and Revenue Maximization

■ Markup Pricing

Even when they do profess to seek profits, many firms use very different methods than those described in our analysis. The most common such management technique for seeking profits is **markup pricing.** This section compares this technique to the profit-maximization model we have developed.

The markup pricing technique works as follows. Management first computes the average total cost of producing some normal level of output. To this cost it then adds a profit "markup" to arrive at the good's selling price. Usually the profit markup is a fixed percentage of average costs, which means that the selling price is some multiple of average cost. With a markup of 50 percent, for example, firms would price their goods at 1.5 times average total cost. Unlike a revenue-maximizing firm, the firm that uses a markup pricing strategy is obviously paying some attention to costs. But is this firm actually maximizing profits?

A first distinction between profit maximizing and markup pricing is that the former requires firms to use marginal cost in their calculations whereas the latter requires them to use average total cost. As we showed in Chapter 9, if a firm is producing at the low point of its average total cost curve, average and marginal costs are equal. Markup pricing and profit maximization, at least

Markup pricing

Determining the selling price of a good by adding a percentage to the average cost of producing it.

with regard to the cost side of the calculation, may not be very different in this case, especially if firms have long-run average total cost curves that are horizontal over a broad range of output levels.

A second principal difference between profit-maximizing behavior and markup pricing is that markup pricing seems to take no account of demand. A profit maximizer must, as we have shown, consider the marginal revenue from selling one more unit of output. A firm using a markup over average cost would appear to make no such consideration. Only if firms' markup were in some way influenced by demand would this not be the case.

Several observations suggest that firms do indeed consider demand in deciding on a markup. For example, convenience stores have much higher markups on specialty or emergency items, such as deli foods or cold remedies, than on everyday items such as milk or soft drinks that can be bought anywhere. Hot dogs sold at ball games or amusement parks usually have a higher price than hot dogs sold by street vendors, which probably reflects the greater choices available to consumers of the street vendors' hot dogs. If firms using a markup pricing strategy are profit maximizers, the markup would be higher for goods that are inelastically demanded.[12] Application 10.4: Actual Markup Pricing Behavior shows that there is some evidence to support this possibility.

━━━━━━━━━━━━━━━━━━━━━━━━━━━━━━━

Short-Run Supply by a Price-Taking Firm

Short-run supply decisions by a price-taking firm are our final and most important illustration of the profit-maximizing assumption. Our analysis here leads directly into the study of market supply and price determination that we take up in the next part. Here we focus only on the profit-maximizing decisions of a single firm.

■ Profit-Maximizing Decision

By definition, a price-taking firm's output decision has no effect on the price it receives for its product. In this case, as we showed earlier in this chapter, market price is also the marginal revenue from selling one more unit. No matter how much the firm sells, it has no effect on this price. Under these assumptions the firm's desire to maximize profits then dictates that it should produce that

---

[12]A precise analysis of this result would use Equation 10.8 together with the MR = MC rule:

$$MC = MR = P\left(1 + \frac{1}{e}\right),$$

where e is the price elasticity of demand. If AC = MC, we have

$$\text{Markup} = \frac{P}{AC} = \frac{P}{MC} = \frac{e}{1 + e}.$$

If $e > -1$, demand is inelastic, and MR cannot be equal to MC; we need only examine elastic cases where $e < -1$. If demand is infinitely elastic ($e = -\infty$), then P/MC = 1 and there is no markup. As e gets closer to -1, the markup increases. If, for example, $e = -2$, the profit-maximizing markup is 2.0—price should be set at twice average and marginal cost.

APPLICATION 10.4
Actual Markup Pricing Behavior

Most available evidence concludes that major corporations take demand into account when pricing their products. Markups are broadly consistent with the notion of profit maximization.

Evidence for Major Corporations

In their classic study of the pricing policies of U.S. Steel Corporation, Kaplan, Dirlam, and Lanzillotti found that the markup on steel products varied inversely with the elasticity of demand for these products. Margins were high on steel rails, for example, because this was a product line in which U.S. Steel faced little competition. On the other hand, margins were low on stainless steel and tin plate, because these products faced strong competition from aluminum and lumber producers. The authors found analogous results with regard to pricing policies of many major corporations, including E. I. du Pont de Nemours, Standard Oil Company of New Jersey, and Aluminum Company of America.[1] Target profit margins seemed to be related to the elasticity of demand, just as profit maximization requires. Similarly, in a study of large Danish firms, B. Fog reported that many companies respond to questions about how profit margins are set by noting they will "charge what the traffic will bear" or that the "market conditions determine the price."[2] In other words, markups are determined in a profit-maximizing way.

Evidence from Retailing

In their study of retailing, R. M. Cyert and J. G. March spent considerable effort analyzing the feedback from the market for the pricing of a product. Even though the firm may set prices and profit margins without considering demand, the subsequent reaction of the market (which provides information on the true demand situation) causes the firm to adjust its prices accordingly. Cyert and March apply their model to a department store's markdown policy and conclude that the prices of items are adjusted over time to meet demand conditions.[3] Any experienced bargain hunter knows that retailers adjust the prices of unpopular items downward much more rapidly than they reduce the prices of "hot" items. Price changing such as this is consistent with the notion that markups are set with profit-maximization goals in mind.

Evidence over the Business Cycle

Markups also seem to vary over the business cycle, and this also is consistent with profit maximization. During recessions, demand is weak and buyers may readily shift their purchases among firms. When business conditions are strong, firms may possess somewhat increased market power. Profit maximization would, therefore, suggest that markups should vary systematically with overall business conditions; empirical evidence on the U.S. economy tends to support this supposition. Not only do markups seem to vary with general business conditions, but they also seem to be affected by other events that may affect overall product demand, such as military purchases by the government or even what political party is in power.[4]

To Think About

1. Profit markups are much higher in the prescription drug industry than in the fast food industry. Is this consistent with profit-maximizing behavior?
2. Are price markups a good measure of the overall profitability of an industry? Is a high ratio of price to average cost an indication that an industry would represent a desirable investment?

---

[1]A. D. H. Kaplan, J. B. Dirlam, and R. F. Lanzillotti, *Pricing in Big Business: A Case Approach* (Washington, D.C.: Brookings Institution, 1958), pp. 172–174.
[2]B. Fog, *Industrial Pricing Policies* (Amsterdam: North-Holland Publishing Co., 1960), p. 104. See especially Chapter 6.
[3]R. M. Cyert and J. G. March, *A Behavioral Theory of the Firm* (Englewood Cliffs, N.J.: Prentice-Hall, 1963), Chapter 7.
[4]See R. E. Hall, "The Relation Between Price and Marginal Cost in U.S. Industry," *Journal of Political Economy* (October 1988): 921–947.

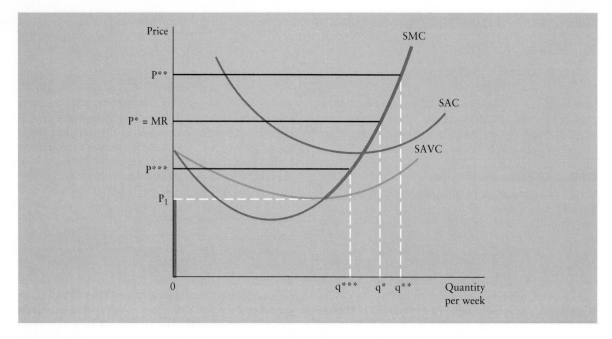

Figure 10.5
Short-Run Supply
Curve for a Price-
Taking Firm

In the short run a price-taking firm will produce the level of output for which SMC = P. At P*, for example, the firm will produce q*. The SMC curve also shows what will be produced at other prices. For prices below SAVC, however, the firm will choose to produce no output. The heavy colored lines in the figure represent the firm's short-run supply curve.

quantity for which marginal cost equals price. The short-run marginal cost curve is relevant to this decision in the short run.

Figure 10.5 shows the individual firm's short-run decision. The market price is given by P*. The demand curve facing the firm is therefore a horizontal line through P*. This line is labeled P* = MR as a reminder that this price-taking firm can always sell an extra unit without affecting the price. Output level q* provides maximum profits, since at q* price is equal to short-run marginal cost.[13] The fact that profits are positive can be seen by noting that at q* price exceeds average costs. The firm earns a profit on each unit sold. If price were below average cost (as is the case at q***), the firm would have a loss on each unit sold. If price and average cost were equal, profits would be zero. In later chapters, we will make considerable use of this way of showing profits per unit as the vertical gap between price and average cost.

A geometric proof that profits are at a maximum at q* would proceed as follows. For output levels slightly less than q*, price (P*) exceeds short-run marginal cost. Reducing output below q* would cut back more on revenues than on costs, and profits would fall. For output levels greater than q*, mar-

---

[13]From now on we will use a lowercase q to denote the individual firm's output. In Chapter 12, the uppercase Q is used to denote the output of the industry as a whole. Here, and throughout Parts 4–6, firms' supply will be shown in color in the graphs.

ginal costs exceed P*. Producing more than q* would now cause costs to rise more rapidly than revenues, and again profits would fall. This means that if a firm produces either more or less than q*, its profits will be lowered. Only at q* are profits at a maximum.

Notice that at q* the marginal cost curve has a positive slope. This is required if profits are to be a true maximum. If P = MC on a negatively sloped section of the marginal cost curve, this is not a point of maximum profits. Increasing output by one unit would yield more in revenues (the market price) than this production would cost (marginal cost would decline if the MC curve had a negative slope). Consequently, profit maximization requires both that P = MC and that at this point marginal cost is increasing.

■ The Firm's Supply Curve

The positively sloped portion of the short-run marginal cost curve is the **short-run supply curve for this price-taking firm,** since the curve shows how much the firm will produce for every possible market price. At a higher price of P**, for example, the firm will produce q** since it will find it in its interest to incur the higher marginal costs q** entails. With a price of P***, on the other hand, the firm opts to produce less (q***) since only a lower output level will result in lower marginal costs to meet this lower price. By considering all possible prices that the firm might face, we can see by the marginal cost curve how much output the firm should supply at each price.

■ The Shutdown Decision

For very low prices we have to be careful about this conclusion. Should market price fall below P_1, the profit-maximizing decision would be to produce nothing. Prices less than P_1 do not cover variable costs. There will be a loss on each unit produced in addition to the loss of all fixed costs. By shutting down production, the firm still must pay fixed costs, but it avoids the losses incurred on each unit produced. Since, in the short run, the firm cannot close down and avoid all costs, its best decision is to produce no output. On the other hand, a price only slightly above P_1 means the firm should produce some output. Even though profits may be negative (which they will be if price falls below short-run average total costs—the case at P***), as long as variable costs are covered, the profit-maximizing decision is to continue production. Fixed costs must be paid in any case, and any price that covers variable costs will provide some revenue as a partial offset to these fixed costs.[14]

■
Short-run supply curve for a price-taking firm
The positively-sloped section of a firm's SMC curve above the point of minimum SAVC. Shows the supply decisions of a price-taking firm.

---

[14]Some algebra may clarify matters. Since we know total costs equal the sum of fixed and variable costs,

$$TC = FC + VC,$$

profits are given by

$$\pi = TR - TC = P \cdot q - FC - VC.$$

If q = 0, variable costs are zero, so

$$\pi = -FC,$$

and the firm will only produce if $\pi > -FC$. But that means that

$$P \cdot q > VC \text{ or } P > VC/q = AVC.$$

APPLICATION 10.5

The Demise of OPEC and Drilling for Oil in the United States

Beginning in the early 1970s the Organization of Petroleum Exporting Countries (OPEC) came to exercise a dramatic effect on the world pricing of crude oil. Between 1970 and 1980 world oil prices increased more than 800 percent. In real inflation-adjusted terms the increase was somewhat less spectacular, but still amounted to a threefold increase in the relative price of crude oil. For oil well drillers throughout the world, the price increase provided a clear signal to produce more. In the United States, for example, even though the influence of OPEC was softened a bit by domestic price controls and restrictions on imports, drilling increased dramatically. As Table 1 shows, the number of wells drilled more than doubled between 1970 and 1980. Increasingly, these additional wells were drilled in high-cost locations (for example, in deep water offshore or in difficult environments such as Alaska).

Price Decline and Supply Behavior

The steep recession of 1982 and 1983, combined with vast new supplies of crude oil (in the North Sea and Mexico, for example), put considerable pressure on the OPEC pricing structure. By 1989, nominal crude oil prices had declined by about 30 percent from their highest levels. In real terms the decline was even sharper, falling nearly in half. U.S. drillers were quick to respond to these changing circumstances. As Table 1 shows, fewer than half the number of wells were drilled in 1989 as in 1981. In addition, drilling tended not to be in as costly locations as had previously been the case. Domestic drillers responded to lower prices by no longer incurring very high marginal costs in their drilling activities.

The decline in oil prices also prompted oil well operators to shut down some marginal operations. Many "stripper wells" (wells producing less than 10 barrels of oil per day), being relatively costly to operate, were shut down. In some cases, it was a simple matter to reopen these wells if prices rose, but in other cases the shutdowns were permanent since water could subsequently seep into depleted oil reservoirs.

Table 1
World Oil Prices and Oil Well Drilling Activity in the United States

Year	World Price per Barrel	Real Price per Barrel[a]	Number of Wells Drilled
1970	$3.18	$7.93	27,177
1980	$21.59	$25.16	62,011
1989	$15.85	$13.43	26,693

[a]Nominal price divided by producer price index for capital equipment, 1982 = 100. *Source: Statistical Abstract of the United States,* 1991. Various Tables.

Consequences of the Decline in Drilling

The decline in drilling activity in the late 1980s posed significant problems for suppliers to the oil exploration industry. For example, producers of high-strength oil pipe in Texas and Louisiana suffered huge financial losses because they were not able to sell enough pipe to keep their factories fully utilized. Similarly, firms in the business of supplying oil drilling teams with everything from food and clothing to candy and VCR movies also suffered from the slowdown. Many cities in Louisiana and Texas experienced sharp economic downturns as the effects of the drilling cutback spread. By 1988 the federal government had adopted special programs to aid workers affected by the cutback.[1]

To Think About

1. Are U.S. producers of crude oil accurately described as price takers? How many companies are there in this industry? Is a firm such as Exxon too large to be a price taker? Perhaps you'll need to look up some data on the oil industry to resolve these issues.

2. This example shows that there are many kinds of margins to consider in connection with marginal cost (for example, location and depth of drilling). What are some of the other factors that may influence the marginal cost of drilling for oil? Can you think of examples in other industries of how increasing marginal costs might occur along several dimensions?

[1]For a thorough discussion of drilling costs in the oil industry, see U.S. Congress Office of Technology Assessment, *U.S. Oil Production: The Effect of Low Prices,* Washington, D.C.: 1987.

For prices above P_1 the firm's short-run marginal cost curve shows how much output will be supplied. The price P_1 represents a **shutdown price**, however. If price falls below that level, nothing will be produced. The colored segment of the vertical axis up to P_1 reflects these zero-output decisions. Only when price rises above P_1 does the firm's marginal cost curve correctly show what will be supplied. Our later analysis of competitive markets makes considerable use of this short-run supply curve for price-taking firms. Application 10.5: The Demise of OPEC and Drilling for Oil in the United States illustrates the kinds of effects that changing prices can have on firms' willingness to incur various levels of marginal cost.

■
Shutdown price
The price below which the firm will choose to produce no output in the short run. Equal to minimum average variable cost.

Summary

In this chapter, we examine the assumption that firms seek to achieve maximum profits in making their decisions. Although some questions have been raised about whether firms have all of the information that would be required to make such decisions, we show that much available evidence supports the profit-maximizing approach to analyzing firm behavior. We also describe how a variety of market pressures may enforce profit maximization by firms. The profit-maximization assumption seems to provide a good foundation for our study of firm behavior. A number of conclusions follow from this assumption:

- In making output decisions a firm should produce the output level for which marginal revenue equals marginal cost. Only at this level of production is the cost of extra output, at the margin, exactly balanced by the revenue it yields.

- Similar marginal rules apply to the hiring of inputs by profit-maximizing firms. These are examined in Part 6.

- For a firm facing a downward-sloping demand curve, marginal revenue will be less than price. In this case the marginal revenue curve will lie below the market demand curve.

- The techniques of analyzing profit-maximizing firms can also be used to study firms that use other strategies, such as revenue maximization or markup pricing. In some cases, pursuit of such other strategies may be consistent with profit maximization.

- A firm whose decisions have no effect on the price of its product (a price taker) will maximize profits where price equals marginal cost. The marginal cost curve will be the supply curve for such a firm. If price falls below short-run average variable costs, however, the firm will choose to shut down and produce no output.

Review Questions

1. Why do economists assume firms seek maximum economic profits? Since accounting rules determine what the dollar value of profits actually is, why should firms be concerned with the economists' concept of cost? Which notion of profits do you believe is most important to entrepreneurs who are considering starting a business?

2. For its owners, a firm represents an asset that they own. Why would the pursuit of profit maximization by the firm make this asset as valuable as possible?

3. Explain whether each of the following actions would affect the firm's profit-maximizing decision by describing how it would affect the firm's marginal revenue function or its marginal cost function. Or, would the action have no effect on the firm's profit-maximizing decision?

   a. An increase in the cost of a variable input such as labor.
   b. A decline in the market price for a price-taking firm.
   c. Institution of a small fixed fee to be paid to the government for the right of doing business.
   d. Institution of a 50 percent tax on the firm's profits.
   e. Institution of a per-unit tax on each unit the firm produces.
   f. Receipt of a no-strings-attached grant from the government.
   g. Receipt of a subsidy per unit of output from the government.
   h. Receipt of a subsidy per worker hired from the government.

4. Why is the assumption of profit maximization sometimes referred to as the assumption of "marginal behavior"? Explain how such behavior might be reflected in a firm's choice of output. How would it be reflected in its hiring of inputs? How might it be reflected in decisions such as whether to package its product in a fancy box or whether to invest more in an advertising campaign?

5. What kind of demand curve does a price-taking firm face? For such a curve, what is the relationship between price and marginal revenue? Explain why an individual firm can be a price taker even though the entire market demand for its product may be downward sloping. Why would a firm believe that its output decisions have no effect on market prices?

6. Under what conditions would a firm face a downward-sloping demand curve for its own output? Explain why marginal revenue is less than price in such a situation. Is it possible that a firm can produce one more unit and sell that unit at a positive price, but still find that its total revenue has fallen?

7. If a firm faces a negatively sloped linear demand curve, at what output level does its marginal revenue reach zero? Why would a revenue-maximizing firm choose to produce such a level of output? Would this output level be greater or smaller than what would be produced by a profit-maximizing firm? Are there any situations in which the two output choices would be relatively close to each other?

8. Why might a firm choose to use markup pricing even if it were interested in profit maximization? Explain how a firm interested in maximum profits should choose its markup.

9. Why do economists believe short-run marginal cost curves have positive slopes? Why does this belief lead to the notion that short-run supply curves have positive slopes? What kind of signal does a higher price send to a firm with increasing marginal costs? Would a reduction in output ever be the profit-maximizing response to an increase in price for a price-taking firm?

10. Why might short-run variable costs also be called "avoidable" costs? How can such costs be avoided? Why is it impossible to avoid short-run fixed costs? Why are avoidable costs relevant to the short-run shutdown decision, but fixed costs are not? Would fixed costs be relevant to a firm's decision to stay in business over the long run? Suppose the firm had sunk costs incurred at the time the firm was started. Would these affect the decision to stay in business?

Problems

10.1 John's Lawn Mowing Service is a small business that acts as a price taker (MR = P). The prevailing market price of lawn mowing is $20 per acre. Although John can use the family mower for free (but see problem 10.2), he has other costs given by

$$\text{Total cost} = .1q^2 + 10q + 50$$

$$\text{Marginal cost} = .2q + 10$$

where q = the number of acres John chooses to mow in a week.

   a. How many acres should John choose to mow in order to maximize profit?
   b. Calculate John's maximum weekly profit.
   c. Graph these results and label John's supply curve.

10.2 Consider again the profit-maximizing decision of John's Lawn Mowing Service from problem 10.1. Suppose John's greedy father decides to charge John for the use of the family lawn mower.

   a. If the lawn mower charge is set at $100 per week, how will this affect the acres of lawns John chooses to mow? What will his profits be?
   b. Suppose instead that John's father requires John to pay 50 percent of his weekly profits as a mower charge. How will this affect John's profit-maximizing decision?
   c. If John's greedy father imposes a charge of $2 per acre for use of the family mower, how will this affect John's marginal cost function? How will it affect his profit-maximizing decision? What will his profits be now? How much will John's greedy father get?
   d. Suppose finally that John's father collects his $2 per acre by collecting 10 percent of the revenues from each acre John mows. How will this affect John's profit-maximizing decision? Explain why you get the same result here as for part c.

10.3 Suppose a farmer can sell all the corn that he or she can produce at a price of P. Show the total revenue curve for the farmer and demonstrate geometrically (using a graph similar to Figure 10.1) that in this case the profit-maximizing output level occurs where marginal cost is equal to P.

10.4 Widgets International faces a demand curve given by

$$q = 10 - P$$

and has a constant marginal and average cost of $3 per widget produced. Complete the following table for the various production levels.

q	P	TR (= P · q)	MR	MC	AC	TC	π
1							
2							
3							
4							
5							
6							
7							
8							
9							
10							

How many widgets will the firm produce in order to maximize profits? Explain briefly why this is so.

10.5 Suppose that a firm faces a demand curve that has a constant elasticity of −2. This demand curve is given by

$$q = 256/P^2.$$

Suppose also that the firm has a marginal cost curve of the form

$$MC = .001q.$$

a. Graph these demand and marginal cost curves.
b. Calculate the marginal revenue curve associated with the demand curve; graph this curve. (Hint: Use Equation 10.8 for this part of the problem.)
c. At what output level does marginal revenue equal marginal cost?

10.6 Suppose a firm faces the following demand curve:

$$q = 60 - 2P.$$

a. Calculate the total revenue curve for the firm (in terms of q).
b. Using a tabular proof, show that the firm's MR curve is given by
MR = 30 − q.
c. Assume also that the firm has an MC curve given by MC = .2q. What output level should the firm produce to maximize profits?
d. Graph the demand, MC, and MR curves and the point of profit maximization.

10.7 A firm faces a demand curve given by

$$q = 100 - 2P.$$

Marginal and average costs for the firm are constant at $10 per unit.

a. Use a graphic or tabular proof to show that, for this demand curve, MR = $50 - q$.

b. What output level should the firm produce to maximize profits? What are profits at that output level?

c. What output level should the firm produce to maximize revenues? What are profits at that output level?

d. Suppose the firm wishes to maximize revenues subject to the constraint that it earn $12 in profits for each of the 64 machines it employs. What level of output should it produce?

e. Graph your results.

* 10.8 Universal Widget produces high-quality widgets at its plant in Gulch, Nevada, for sale throughout the world. The cost function for total widget production (q) is given by

$$\text{Total costs} = .25q^2.$$

$$\text{Marginal costs} = .50q.$$

Widgets are demanded only in Australia (where the demand curve is given by $q = 100 - 2P$ and MR = $50 - q$) and Lapland (where the demand curve is given by $q = 100 - 4P$ and MR = $25 - q/2$). If Universal Widget can control the quantities supplied to each market, how many should it sell in each location in order to maximize total profits? What are these profits?

10.9 The town where John's Lawn Mowing Service is located (see problem 10.1) is subject to sporadic droughts and monsoons. During periods of drought, the price for mowing lawns drops to $15 per acre, whereas, during monsoons, it rises to $25 per acre.

a. How will John react to these changing prices?

b. Suppose that weeks of drought and weeks of monsoons each occur half the time during a summer. What will John's average weekly profit be?

c. Suppose John's kindly (but still greedy) father offers to eliminate the uncertainty in John's life by agreeing to trade him the weekly profits based on a stable price of $20 in exchange for the profits John actually makes. Should John take the deal?

d. Graph your results and explain them intuitively.

10.10 In order to break the hold of John's greedy father over his struggling son (problems 10.1 and 10.2), the government is thinking of instituting an income subsidy plan for the lad. Two plans are under consideration: (1) a flat grant of $200 per week to John; and (2) a grant of $4 per acre mowed.

a. Which of these plans will John prefer?

b. What is the cost of plan (2) to the government?

---

*Denotes a problem that is rather difficult.

CHAPTER
11

FURTHER
APPLICATIONS
OF THE THEORY
OF THE FIRM

Our analysis of the firm and its decisions in Chapter 10 was based on a very simple model in which the manager chooses levels of inputs and outputs with the sole goal of obtaining maximum profits. In this chapter, we move beyond this simple model by looking more closely at the internal operations of firms. We focus on the nature of firms and on the kinds of contracts that exist between firms and their workers and between firms' owners and hired managers. By so doing, we hope to provide a somewhat more detailed picture of how firms operate. The topics in this chapter represent some of the most important areas of current research in economics. Many economists believe that in order to understand such diverse topics as persistent unemployment, worker productivity, and corporate takeovers, a necessary first step is to develop a better understanding of the firm itself. A major purpose of this chapter, then, is to introduce some of the recent work related to these topics.

Why Do Firms Exist?

The wide variety of existing firms has prompted economists to speculate about the kinds of factors that might influence their organization. Ronald Coase laid out the basic principles of these investigations in a famous 1937 article.[1] To Coase, firms were an alternative to the marketplace as a way of organizing production. At one extreme, think of a situation in which all production is carried out by individuals. A person who wanted to, say, produce an automobile would buy the parts from thousands of independent suppliers, assemble these parts, and then turn the car over to someone else to sell. All transactions in such a situation would be among individuals who would each be very specialized producers. At the alternative extreme, all production in an economy might take place inside a single vast firm. This firm would coordinate the production of all automobiles, all automobile parts, and everything else through nonmarket, command and control directives. In such a world there would be no need for any market transactions involving intermediate goods.

To Coase, the location of an actual organization of production along this spectrum of possibilities was largely determined by cost considerations. Specifically, he argued that a firm's size and complexity would expand up to the point at which the costs involved in making additional transactions internally were exactly balanced by the costs involved in making the transactions through the market. In order to understand the size and scope of a firm's activities, we must therefore examine the relative significance of these various costs.

■ Advantages of the Market

Purchasing intermediate products in the marketplace offers a number of potential cost advantages to a firm. Because many firms buy from a single supplier, that supplier may be able to achieve economies of scale in production that would not be attainable if the firm tried to produce the input internally. For example, producers of personal computers (especially IBM "clones") purchase all of the principal internal electronics from one or two suppliers. Since electronic chip manufacturing involves substantial economies of scale whereas computer assembly does not, many computer producers are not integrated backward into the product of chips.

Uncertainties in the demand for a firm's product may also provide a good reason for the firm to purchase its inputs in the market. Since the input supplier can sell to many firms, it may be able to maintain a fairly smooth flow of production even though sales to any one user may be quite erratic. Small convenience stores, for example, depend on outside firms to supply them with a

[1] R. H. Coase, "The Nature of the Firm," *Economica* (November 1937): 386–405. For a more recent survey see O. E. Williamson, "The Modern Corporation: Origins, Evolution, Attributes," *Journal of Economic Literature* (December 1981): 1537–1568.

wide range of items they sell only occasionally ("peg-board" items such as scissors, labels, or playing cards) whereas they may develop their own supply of regularly demanded items such as milk or deli sandwiches.

Finally, reliance on markets for inputs may permit the firm to utilize the pressures of competition to restrain costs. It may have the option of taking its business elsewhere if a particular supplier becomes too costly. An integrated firm must instead try to keep its production costs down through various types of internal control mechanisms. Indeed, in some very large firms, competition between divisions may be initiated purposely to keep production costs in line. In many situations reliance on the marketplace serves this function automatically.

■ Advantages of Integration

Using the marketplace to acquire intermediate inputs for the firm also has many undesirable features, however. Purchasing inputs from someone else requires that the firm undertake some type of transaction, which may have costs associated with it. Thus the firm must find a suitable provider, negotiate contract terms, and arrange for the goods to be delivered. All of these costs may be reduced (or entirely eliminated) if the firm decides to produce the input internally. Of course, internal production requires that the firm spend something for monitoring and controlling the production process. An independent provider would incur similar costs, however, and with internal production a firm may be more certain that production quality standards are met. Overall then, integration of the production process might be expected to enable the firm to obtain significant savings in transactions costs.

The need for specialized equipment provides a second possible rationale for expanding the types of functions carried on within the firm. If a firm must utilize a machine that is useful only to it (perhaps because the equipment must fit into a unique location or use a particular type of fuel), then it is probably less costly for the firm to buy than to try to locate another firm willing to make the investment. Only in relatively rare instances will a supplier firm invest in equipment that is only useful to one buyer since that puts the supplier in a very risky position. In such a case, the supplier can be viewed as a "hostage" of the purchasing firm and may have to make contract concessions to it during the equipment's lifetime. Therefore, in general, suppliers will not invest in such specialized equipment, and firms will usually make such purchases for themselves.

A final, related way in which a firm may enlarge the scope of its activities in order to minimize transactions costs concerns the hiring of workers with specialized skills. If workers must learn special skills that are uniquely valuable to one firm (for example, computer programmers who know the machine language for a particular line of computers), it may be more beneficial for the firm to develop long-term contractual relationships with these workers than to purchase their services from some other firm. In that way, as we shall see in the next section, the firm can structure employment contracts that give the workers an incentive to stay with the firm. If the workers were employed by an outside supplier, they might have fewer incentives to continue to use their specialized skills for the benefit of the final producer.

■ Size and Scope of the Firm

These considerations suggest that the size and scope of a firm's activities are an important subject for economic analysis. Although it made sense to start our study of demand by defining the basic unit of analysis as the individual (or perhaps the family), defining the basic unit of analysis for supply decisions must necessarily involve some ambiguity. Ultimately, the definition of "the firm" is a fuzzy one that is determined by a constantly changing economic environment. Only a careful consideration of all the costs involved can provide an understanding of why the size of a firm changes over time. Application 11.1: Supplier Relations in Japan illustrates this dynamic process.

Contracts within Firms

Once the basic nature of a firm is decided upon, the activities of workers, managers, and suppliers of capital must be coordinated and controlled. This is accomplished through a series of contracts among these parties. In some cases the contracts may be explicitly written down—for example, the contract between the United Automobile Workers and General Motors runs for hundreds of pages. In many other instances, however, contracts may be in the form of implicit understandings about what the terms of employment are. Even though such contracts are not on paper, they may be very effective in assuring that the rights and responsibilities of the various parties are followed.

The modern study of the theory of the firm is primarily a study of these various contracts. The firm itself is a legal entity (in the United States, legally firms are treated as individuals) that usually represents one side of the contract, and workers, managers, and capital suppliers represent the other side. These parties face the problem of developing contracts that are desirable to everyone concerned. For example, contracts with workers must be desirable from the workers' point of view in terms of the wages paid and the working conditions provided, and desirable from the firm's point of view in terms of providing incentives for the workers to perform in a productive way. Creating such contracts may be a costly and tedious process even when nothing has to be explicitly written down. And the final solutions adopted may, at first glance, seem unusual or even counterproductive. But the contracting process is necessary for any firm, and there will usually be good reasons for the provisions that are chosen.

Contracts with Workers

Fewer than 20 percent of American workers are represented by unions with collective bargaining agreements. The fraction of workers covered by such formal arrangements is somewhat higher in other Western countries, but even in

APPLICATION 11.1

Supplier Relations in Japan

The forces that mold the actual organization of a firm can be illustrated by looking at the degree of "vertical integration" shown in various situations. Sometimes firms simply act as final assemblers, buying all the parts they need from other firms. Many makers of computers are final assemblers. These firms produce only the label they affix to the machines. On the other hand, a firm's activities may extend far back into the production process; they may not only produce the parts but also the basic raw materials needed to manufacture their products. Many U.S. manufacturing firms (most notably, automobile producers) operate such integrated firms.

Japanese Firms
Japanese firms are quite different from their U.S. counterparts in this regard. Instead of directly controlling the flow of materials, Japanese firms rely on a complex web of suppliers for much of what they need. Elaborate systems of coordination have been developed between the parent firm and its suppliers to assure that parts arrive on time and meet the necessary technical specifications. The "Kaban" system of using a constant rotating set of tags for parts has been highly developed as a way of assuring this coordination. Related procedures, such as "just-in-time" inventory management, help to assure that the inefficiencies inherent in dealing with many suppliers are kept to a minimum.

Reasons for the Japanese System
Although there are important historical reasons for the development of the Japanese system of supplier firms (many such arrangements began under the umbrella of a major bank, for example), the continued reliance on the system probably stems from its overall flexibility. By relying on many suppliers, a downstream firm can foster some degree of competition among them and can switch from one supplier to another as the quality of offerings changes. Relations with a specific supplier can be terminated on short-term notice if its parts are no longer needed. Of course, that possibility makes the suppliers'

business rather risky, but sometimes these risks are shared by the downstream firm by the nature of the pricing agreements reached. Downstream firms also share technical personnel with their suppliers both as a way of assuring quality control and as a way of allowing many suppliers to have access to people with special skills.[1]

The "Outsourcing" Controversy
Firms in the United States have not been oblivious to the advantages of Japanese-type supplier relationships. In recent years, for example, U.S. automobile firms have tended to close down some of their parts-making operations, relying on independent producers instead. The United Automobile Workers union has not been especially enthusiastic about this increased reliance on "outsourcing" since it has had a negative impact on their own members' jobs. In 1992, two major strikes over this issue at the General Motors Corporation virtually stopped production of the popular Saturn and Pontiac GrandAm models. Despite the labor friction, however, the company seems determined to continue the process of moving to a more flexible organizational structure.

To Think About
1. What types of firms would find vertical integration a desirable organization of a firm? Would simple products (for example, steel bars) or complex products (automobiles) be more susceptible to a hierarchical form of integration?
2. What economic pressures might make a firm change the way it is organized? Why do you think General Motors has chosen to emphasize the outsourcing option only recently?

---

[1]For a further discussion, see M. Aoki, "Toward an Economic Model of the Japanese Firm," *Journal of Economic Literature* (March 1990): 1–27.

these other countries most workers are not covered by this sort of explicit contract. Still, virtually all employees have clear understandings with their employers about what their duties are and how they will be paid. In Chapters 19 and 20 we will examine the theory of how wage levels are determined. Here we are not interested in the wage itself, but rather will focus on explicit and implicit employment contracts and show how they may affect the firm's costs and its supply decisions.

Job-Specific Skills and Long-Term Contracts

As workers hold a job longer, they learn to do it better. Anyone who has ever started a new job knows the feeling of being confused and perplexed when trying to fit into a new employment situation. A new worker's productivity may be negative for the first few weeks because he or she asks so many questions and makes so many mistakes that total firm output may actually decline for a while. Even after the chaos of orientation has ended, new workers may not be very productive until they learn what the job entails and how they can work most effectively with those around them. In economic terms, any new worker must learn a set of **job-specific skills,** and that learning process will be time-consuming and costly.

Job-specific skills
Skills learned on a job that enable a worker to do that specific job better.

Firms wish to reduce these costs as much as possible. The most direct way to do that is to adopt policies that encourage workers to stay with the firm. In Chapters 8 through 10 we were not concerned with this issue. Nothing in those chapters would have prevented a firm from hiring a different set of workers every hour as long as they all could be hired at the prevailing wage rate. In fact, however, such employee turnover would be very costly for firms both because of the expenses involved in hiring new employees (such as the paperwork) and because of the low productivity of new employees. Instead, firms will try to develop a longer-term relationship with their employees.

Effects on Employment Decisions

One consequence of such a long-term employment policy is that firms will be reluctant to vary the number of workers they hire in response to temporary fluctuations in the demand for their products. They may make short-run decisions that are not exactly the same as those we examined in Chapters 9 and 10. Figure 11.1 illustrates such a situation. Panel a of this figure shows a price-taking firm's isoquant map, and Panel b shows its short-run supply (and marginal cost) curve. Initially, the firm faces a market price of P_2 for its output and opts to produce at a level of q_2 per week as shown in Panel b. Assuming the firm has been producing q_2 for some time, it will have adjusted both its capital and labor inputs to their cost-minimizing levels K_2, L_2. These are shown in Panel a.

Suppose now that the market price of this firm's product falls temporarily to P_0—perhaps because a recession temporarily reduces the demand for most goods. How will the firm respond to this decline? According to our discussion in Chapter 10, the firm would reduce output to q_0 and reduce its hiring of labor to L_0 since capital is fixed at K_2 in the short run. Under our previous

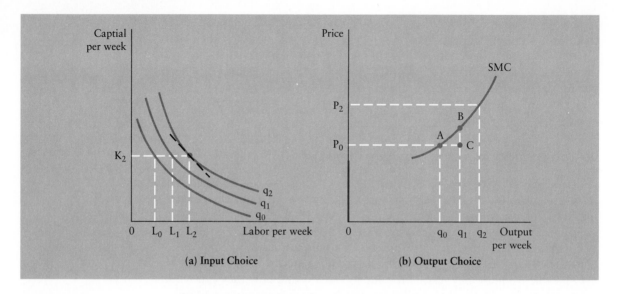

Figure 11.1
With Implicit Contracts, Output and Hiring Decisions May Be Less Flexible

With no costs associated with changing labor input, a firm faced with a decline in price from P_2 to P_0 would reduce output from q_2 to q_0 and reduce labor input from L_2 to L_0. If there were an implicit contract between the workers and the firm, hiring might only fall to L_1, and output to q_1. This would still be the most profitable output level since costs associated with reducing labor input to L_0 would exceed profits lost at q_1 (area ABC).

assumptions, this temporary cutback in hiring could be accomplished by the firm with no special problems.

If workers have unique job-specific skills, however, reducing employment in this way may be costly for the firm. Once a worker is laid off, he or she may seek another job. Job-specific skills already acquired would be lost to the firm making the layoff. Even if the worker ultimately is hired back by this firm once the price returns to P_2, he or she may still need to readjust to the work process. For these reasons, the firm may hesitate to reduce employment immediately in response to temporary declines in demand. It may, instead, reassign workers to nonproduction activities (for example, cleaning up the stockroom or doing preventive maintenance on machines), or it may continue to produce and add the surplus goods to inventory. The firm might also change work schedules, as discussed in Application 11.2: Short-Time Compensation and Layoffs.

In all of these cases the nature of the explicit or implicit contracts between workers and firms makes employment decisions far more complicated than our previous models assumed. Since a reduction of labor input to L_0 in Figure 11.1 may therefore be very costly, a more modest step might be taken. The firm could, for example, reduce hiring to L_1 and produce output level q_1. Such an output level would not provide maximum profits under our previous analysis of supply (see Panel b of Figure 11.1), but it may be more profitable than q_0 once all the costs associated with changing labor input are taken into account—that is, if the costs of reducing labor further exceed the profits lost

APPLICATION 11.2
Short-Time Compensation and Layoffs

When firms need to reduce the labor they employ, they have two options: they may reduce the number of hours each employee works, or they may lay off some employees completely. During recessions, firms use both of these methods to adjust their labor input. Firms in the United States seem more willing to use layoffs than do firms in other countries such as West Germany or Japan where hours reductions are much more common.

Disadvantages of Layoffs
The layoff-prone nature of the U.S. economy has been a concern to many economists both because of the problems that unemployment poses for laid-off workers and because of the inefficiencies that layoffs may cause. When employees are laid off, they may seek other jobs and may, if the layoff lasts for a while, lose some of their job skills. Rehiring workers following layoffs can be a costly process for the firm. Many of these inefficiencies could be avoided if firms reduced hours of work during recessions, which would keep the employment relationship largely intact.

Encouraging Hours Reductions
One policy that has been suggested to encourage employees and employers to choose hours reductions instead of layoffs is for workers on short time to receive unemployment benefits for the hours they do not work. Under the rules that prevail in most states unemployment benefits can be collected only if the worker is completely laid off. Some economists believe this policy encourages layoffs rather than hour reductions. As evidence they point to European countries where workers generally are able to collect benefits for hours reductions and where layoffs are much less prevalent. During the economic downturns of the mid-1970s and the early 1980s, for example, over 80 percent of labor force time lost in the United States resulted from layoffs, whereas only about 40 percent came from layoffs in western European countries. If these differences are caused by unemployment insurance laws, some policymakers have argued that perhaps the United States should consider adopting European practices.

Adoption of Short-Time Compensation by the States
California was the first state to adopt a short-time compensation provision in its unemployment insurance law in 1977. Since that time, about a dozen other states have followed suit. One study of the 1982 to 1983 recession found that firms that used short-time benefits reduced their layoffs by about 15 percent over what they would have been without the program.[1] For the relatively few firms that used it, the program did seem to be effective in preserving the long-term employment relationship for some workers. As the program becomes more widely understood, its use in future recessions may be even more substantial.

To Think About
1. Why should firms care whether or not their employees receive unemployment insurance benefits? Can't they make decisions on how to reduce their work forces without thinking about the workers' well-being? What does this example suggest about the relationship between employers and employees?
2. Unemployment insurance is financed by a tax on employers. In some cases tax rates are adjusted to reflect a firm's unemployment experiences. Would the way in which such rates are calculated have an effect on how firms react to a decline in their labor requirements?

---

[1]For a summary, see Stuart Kerachsky, Walter Nicholson, Edward Cavin, and Alan Hershey, "Work Sharing Programs: An Evaluation of Their Use," *Monthly Labor Review* (May 1986): 31–33.

when the output level is q_1 rather than q_0 (area ABC). Consequently, the firm's short-run supply (and hiring) decisions may be less responsive to temporary price changes than our simple models in Chapter 10 suggested.

■ Other Effects of Implicit Contracts

Long-term implicit contracts may affect other aspects of the worker-firm relationship. Both parties may find it attractive to adopt incentive schemes that encourage workers to stay with a firm rather than to switch jobs in response to other opportunities. Seniority-based wage systems are probably the most important example of the way in which workers are rewarded for staying with a firm. The widespread use of such systems, instead of systems in which compensation is based exclusively on an individual worker's productivity, illustrates how implicit contracts serve to tie workers and firms together as a team in order to develop an efficient overall organization of production.

Special types of nonwage compensation are also used to achieve this result. Pension benefits are usually based on length of service and often depend on the financial success of the firm as well. Some firms use bonus payments as a way of supplementing wages. This practice is quite common in Japan where wage bonuses may constitute as much as one-third of annual pay. Some authors argue that such bonuses give workers a more direct stake in the success of their firms. Employee stock ownership plans (ESOPs) may also encourage workers to be more productive in their current jobs by giving them a stake in the financial success of the firm.

These possible outcomes of the implicit contract between workers and the firm suggest that, at least in some cases, long-term employees will be paid more than it would cost the firm to hire replacements for them. In the interest of maintaining a long-term productive arrangement, the firm will pay an **efficient wage** higher than the prevailing market wage, w.[2] By itself, such an action would tend to raise costs, but if it succeeds in developing a more efficient enterprise, it may in fact reduce costs. The effect on the marginal cost curve illustrated in Figure 11.1 is therefore indeterminate.

■ Efficient wage

A wage above the market wage paid to encourage a worker to remain with a firm.

Contracts with Managers

In Chapter 10 we tended to treat the owner of a firm (that is, the owner of the firm's capital) and the manager of that firm as if they were the same person. This treatment makes the assumption of profit-maximizing behavior believable—a person who maximizes the profits in a firm that he or she owns will succeed in making as much income as possible from this ownership. The process of profit maximization is consistent with the process of utility maximization we studied in Part 2.

---

[2]One of the first economists to propose this efficient wage hypothesis was Joseph Stiglitz in "Wage Determination and Unemployment in L.D.C.'s: The Labor Turnover Model," *Quarterly Journal of Economics* (May 1974): 194–227.

For many firms, however, managers do not actually own the firm for which they work. Rather, there is a separation between the ownership of the firm and the control of its behavior by hired managers. In this case, a manager acts as an **agent** for the owner. Do agents perform in the ways that owners want—that is, do they maximize profits?

■ A Model of the Agent Relationship

Adam Smith understood the basic conflict between owners and managers. In *The Wealth of Nations* he observed that "the directors of . . . companies, being the managers of other people's money than of their own, it cannot well be expected that they should watch over it with the same anxious vigilance with which [owners] watch over their own."[3] From this observation Smith went on to look at the behavior of such famous British institutions as the Royal African Company, the Hudson's Bay Company, and the East India Company, which he used to illustrate some of the consequences of management by nonowners. His observations provide an important starting point for the study of modern firms.

The major issue raised by the use of manager-agents is illustrated in Figure 11.2. This figure shows the indifference curve map of a manager's preferences between the firm's profits (which are of primary interest to the owners) and various benefits (such as a fancy office or travel in the corporate jet or helicopter) that accrue mainly to the manager.[4] This indifference curve map has the same shape as those in Part 2 on the presumption that both profits and benefits provide utility to the manager.

To construct the budget constraint that the manager faces in seeking to maximize his or her utility, assume first that the manager is also the owner of this firm. If the manager chooses to have no special benefits from the job, profits will be π_{max}. Each dollar of benefits received by the manager reduces these profits by one dollar. The budget constraint will have a slope of -1, and profits will reach zero when benefits total π_{max}.

Given this budget constraint, the owner-manager maximizes utility by opting for profits of π^* and benefits of B^*. Profits of π^*, while less than π_{max}, still represent profit maximization in this situation since any other owner-manager would also wish to receive B^* in benefits. That is, B^* represents a true cost of doing business, and given these costs, the firm's manager really does maximize profits.

■ Conflicts in the Agent Relationship

Now suppose that the manager is not the only owner of this firm. Instead, assume that, say, one-third of the capital of the firm is owned by the manager and the other two-thirds are owned by outside investors who play no role in operating the firm. In this case the manager will act as if he or she no longer

[3]Adam Smith, *The Wealth of Nations*, 1776 Cannan Edition (New York: Modern Library, 1937), p. 700.
[4]Figure 11.2 is based on one presented in Michael C. Jensen and William H. Meckling, "Theory of the Firm: Managerial Behavior, Agency Costs and Ownership Structure," *Journal of Financial Economics* (January 1976): 78–133.

Agent
The role of making economic decisions for another party, e.g., the manager of a firm being hired to act for the owner.

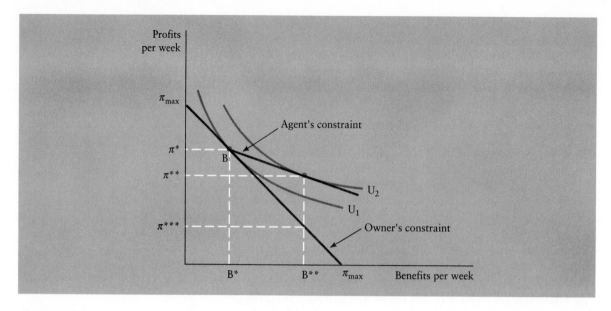

Figure 11.2

Incentives for a Manager Acting as an Agent for a Firm's Owners

If a manager were the sole owner of a firm, π^*, B^* would be chosen since this combination of profits and benefits provides maximum utility. If the manager only owns one-third of the firm, however, the perceived budget constraint will be flatter and B^{**}, π^{**} will be chosen.

faces a budget constraint that requires sacrificing one dollar of the profits for each dollar of benefits. Now a dollar of benefits costs the manager only $.33 in profits, since the other $.67 is effectively paid by the other owners in terms of reduced profits on their investment. Although the new budget constraint continues to include the point B^*, π^* (since the manager could still make the same decision a sole owner could), for benefits greater than B^* the slope of the budget constraint to the manager appears to be only $-1/3$; profits on the manager's portion of the business decline by only $.33 for each dollar in benefits received. Given this apparent budget constraint, the manager would choose point B^{**}, π^{**} to maximize his or her utility. Being only a partial owner of the firm causes the manager to choose a lower level of profits and a higher level of benefits than would be chosen by a sole owner.

Point B^{**}, π^{**} is not really attainable by this firm. Although the cost of one dollar of benefits appears to be only $.33 in profits for the manager, in reality, of course, the benefits cost one dollar to all the owners. When the manager opts for B^{**} in benefits, profits are π^{***}. The firm's owners are harmed by having to rely on an agency relationship with the firm's manager. It appears that the smaller the fraction of the firm that is owned by the manager, the greater the extent of the distortions that will be induced by this relationship.

The situation illustrated in Figure 11.2 is representative of a variety of principal-agent problems that arise in economics. Whenever one person (the principal) relies on another person (the agent) to make decisions, the motivation of this agent must be taken into account since the agent may make different decisions than the principal would. Examples of this relationship occur not only in the management of firms, but also in such diverse applications as hiring investment advisors (do they really put their clients' interest first?); relying on an automobile mechanic's assessment in ordering repairs; and buying clothes for a relative. In Application 11.3: Principals and Agents in Franchising and Medicine, we briefly examine two specific examples of the agency relationship.

■ Reactions of Owners and the Development of Management Contracts

The firm's owners would be unlikely to take the kind of behavior illustrated in Figure 11.2 lying down. They are being forced to accept lower profits than might be earned on their investments in exchange for manager-oriented benefits that provide no value to them personally. What can they do? Most obviously, they can refuse to invest in the firm if they know the manager will behave in this manner. In that event the manager would have two options. First, he or she could go it alone, financing the company completely with his or her own funds. The firm would then return to the owner-manager situation in which B^*, π^* is the preferred choice of benefits and profits. Alternatively, the manager may obtain outside financing to operate the firm if the operation is too expensive to finance alone. In this case the manager has to work out some sort of contractual arrangement with would-be owners to get them to invest.

Writing a contract under which managers pay completely for benefits out of their share of the profits is probably impossible for owners to do. Enforcing the provisions of such a contract would require constant supervision of the manager's activities—something the owners would prefer not to do since that would force them into a managerial role. Instead, they may try to develop less strict contracts that give managers an incentive to economize on benefits and thereby pursue goals closer to pure profit maximization. By offering such contract options as profit-sharing bonuses, stock option plans, and company-financed pensions, the owner may be able to give managers an incentive to be careful about the benefits they choose to take. As with labor contracts, the development of management contracts requires considerable give-and-take between the parties (owners and managers). The final agreement will be a compromise between owners' desires to incorporate incentives to encourage profit-maximizing behavior and the costs involved in writing the contract and monitoring that behavior. Real-world management contracts may be quite complex and may raise difficult legal questions. In Application 11.4: Stock Ownership, Manager Behavior, and Insider Trading, we look at some issues related to contracts that encourage managers to own stock in their companies.

The Market for Firms

So far we have discussed labor and management contracts as evolving from bargaining between the parties involved with the firm. Now we take a somewhat

APPLICATION 11.3
Principals and Agents in Franchising and Medicine

Problems in principal-agent relationships arise in economic situations as diverse as fast food operations and the provision of medical care. A closer examination shows that these situations have much in common.

Franchising

Many large businesses operate their local retail outlets through franchise contracts. The McDonald's Corporation, for example, does not actually own every place that displays the golden arches. Instead, local restaurants are usually owned by small groups of investors who have bought a franchise from the parent company. The problem for the parent company is to ensure that their franchisee agents operate in a proper manner.

Various provisions of franchise contracts help to ensure this result. McDonald's franchisees, for example, must meet certain food-quality and service standards and they must purchase their supplies (hamburgers, frozen fries, buns, napkins, and so forth) from firms that also meet standards set by the parent company. In return, the franchisee gets some management assistance and enjoys the reputation of the McDonald's trademark (together with its national advertising). More important, the franchisee gets to keep a large share of the profits generated by the local restaurant, thereby providing significant incentives to operate it efficiently. The existence of these incentives probably explains why McDonald's and other firms in fields such as electronic retailing, automobile sales, and gasoline service stations have opted for franchising rather than direct ownership—this form of contract is better suited for controlling the principal-agent problems that arise in these industries.[1]

Doctors and Patients

A similar set of problems occurs between physicians and their patients. When people are sick, they often have very little idea of what is wrong or what the most promising treatment is. They place themselves under a physician's care in the belief that the physician is better qualified to make decisions about the proper course of action. They physician then acts as an agent for the patient. But there are several reasons why a physician might not choose exactly what a fully informed patient would choose. The physician generally pays none of the patient's bills; to the physician the price of anything prescribed is essentially zero. Indeed, since the physician may in many instances also be the provider of care, he or she may even benefit from the services prescribed.

These aspects of the agent relationship between physicians and patients suggest that more medical care will be chosen by physicians for their patients than the patients will choose for themselves. A number of studies have gathered evidence on physician-induced demand, and most have reported relatively small but significant effects. For example, a 1978 study by Victor Fuchs of surgery found that the more surgeons located in a given geographic area, other things being equal, the more surgical operations were performed.[2]

Still, as for the franchise case, there are a number of elements in the physician-patient relationship that serve to bring the interests of the parties into line. Patients can choose not to follow a doctor's advice or to seek a second opinion. Physicians must guard their reputations and may sometimes be accountable to peer review boards. The implicit contract between physicians and patients may, therefore, be as effective as the explicit franchise contract in controlling outcomes of the principal-agent relationship.

To Think About

1. Many states have enacted laws that protect franchisees from their larger parent firms. Many states license auto dealerships and do not allow the establishment of new dealerships from the same parent if they would be unfair to existing firms. How would such restrictions affect the efficiency of franchise contracts?

2. Can you think of other explanations for Fuch's finding of a correlation between surgeons' locations and the number of operations performed? How would you devise a clear test for physician-induced demand?

---

[1] For a more complete discussion, see P. H. Rubin, "The Theory of the Firm and the Structure of the Franchise Contract," *Journal of Law and Economics* (April 1978): 223–233.

[2] Victor Fuchs, "The Supply of Surgeons and the Demand for Operations," *Journal of Human Resources*, vol. 13 supplement (1978): 35–56.

APPLICATION 11.4
Stock Ownership, Manager Behavior, and Insider Trading

An obvious way for a firm's owners to encourage managers to seek maximum profits is to give the managers a financial stake in the success of the business. For public corporations, this amounts to encouraging managers to own common stock. Many corporations have rather elaborate stock ownership incentives, especially for their top managers who are most involved in decision making. Some of these plans, such as stock options, offer personal tax benefits to the manager; they are a lower cost way of paying the manager (as opposed to paying them taxable wages) whether or not they provide any incentive to maximize the firm's profits. Other plans, such as those under which managers can buy shares at, say, 85 percent of market price with borrowed funds and no brokerage commissions, offer few direct tax advantages but do directly encourage profit maximization.

Evidence on Stock Purchase Plans

A 1985 study of 130 stock purchase plans provides some evidence of these plans' effects.[1] On average, these plans offered about 8 percent of the corporation's stock to its managers at a discount of 12 to 15 percent from market price. Practically all of the plans allowed the shares to be bought with borrowed funds, usually with the managers paying very low interest rates. Judging by the stock market's reaction, these plans were quite successful in encouraging managers' performance. Following announcement of the plans, the value of the firm's shares tended to rise by about 3 percent over the general market trend. Stock purchase plans for top managers were more effective in prompting such stock-price increases than were other plans, perhaps because investors believed it was more important to have top managers own a portion of the company.

Insider Trading

A particularly controversial question about managers' ownership of stock is whether they should be able to profit from transactions based on "insider" information they may have about their company. To many people the answer appears obvious—insider trading gives an unfair advantage to those doing it and the practice should be illegal. Several recent insider trading cases (such as those involving Ivan Boesky or Michael Milken) have been based on this common-sense idea.

To some economists, however, the case against insider trading is not so clear cut. They argue that permitting insiders to gain from what they know may be a good way to provide incentives to managers to maximize profits; that is, insider trading may act to control the principal-agent problem.[2] In addition, allowing insider trading provides market participants with an incentive to divulge new information quickly and this may help financial markets to operate more efficiently. So far, however, such "perverse" thoughts by economists have had little effect on the actual development of securities laws in the United States.

To Think About

1. If direct stock ownership by managers is desirable, why not require it as a condition of employment? What would be the effects of such a requirement? Would such a requirement necessarily be best for the firm in terms of overall efficiency of operations?
2. How would you define insider trading? Doesn't every stock trader know (or thinks he or she knows) something special? How, if at all, is the practice defined by U.S. laws? Do other countries have similar laws?

---

[1] Sanjai Bhagat, James A. Brickley, and Ronald C. Lease, "Incentive Effects of Stock Purchase Plans," *Journal of Financial Economics* (June 1985): 195–215.
[2] See, for example, F. H. Easterbrook, "Insider Trading as an Agency Problem," in *Principals and Agents: The Structure of Business*, J. W. Pratt and R. J. Zeckhauser, eds. (Boston: Harvard Business School Press, 1985): 81–100.

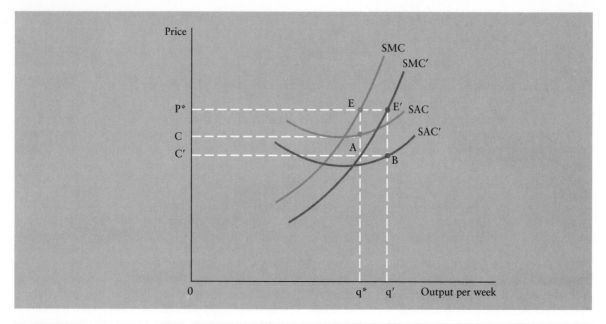

Figure 11.3
Inefficient Costs
Make the Firm a
Takeover Candidate

If the firm's costs (SMC, SAC) exceed those that a would-be buyer could achieve (SMC', SAC'), the firm may be acquired provided the increase in profits exceeds the costs of the acquisition.

broader view by considering the outside market pressures that affect these settlements. Specifically, we focus on the market for firms themselves—what has come to be called "the market for corporate control" in recent economic discussions. Our general goal is to show how the workings of this market help to weed out inefficient, high-cost contractual arrangements and thereby impose some discipline on the contracting process.

Two other types of market pressures on firms should be mentioned. First, any firm must be attentive to the markets for the inputs it hires. Labor contracts that are distinctly inferior to those offered elsewhere will make it impossible for the firm to attract workers. Similarly, inferior management contracts will severely restrict the firm's ability to attract the managers it wishes to hire. The economic operations of these markets is a topic we take up in Part 6. Second, firms must be attentive to the market for their product. If the firm's costs are too high, it may not be able to compete effectively with other producers. Competition in the product market provides a powerful regulator of firms' behavior, and we study that topic extensively in Part 4.

Profit Opportunities in the Market for Firms

The possible attractions of a firm to a would-be buyer are illustrated in Figure 11.3. The firm's short-run average and marginal cost curves are given by SAC and SMC.[5] With a market price of P* this firm will produce q* and, since price exceeds average cost, earn a modest profit.

Assume now that a would-be buyer believes that this firm is currently rather inefficient and could be operated at lower cost by a new management team. Specifically, assume this buyer believes that the firm could be operated with costs given by SAC' and SMC' if it were under new management. With these new costs, profits would be given by area P*E'BC' instead of P*EAC. Such larger profits offer a major incentive for the potential buyer to proceed with plans to purchase the firm. If the firm is privately owned, an offer may be made directly to these owners. If ownership of the firm is spread widely over a large number of shareholders, however, the buyer may make a public offer to these shareholders. In Application 11.5: Corporate Raiders and the RJR-Nabisco Takeover, we take a brief look at one of the more spectacular recent examples of such takeover efforts.

Buying an entire firm is a more complex transaction than, say, buying a loaf of bread. Often considerable capital may be required to make the transaction, necessitating complex borrowing arrangements with banks and the accompanying legal formalities. Takeovers may also involve some explicit short-term costs, such as the relocation of a firm's headquarters or the departure of highly skilled employees because they oppose the change. Existing management may make the purchase of their firm difficult by adopting various defensive ploys such as rigging the voting by shareholders or enlisting the government's assistance in opposing the takeover. As a result of these costs, it might be expected that only purchases that are quite profitable would proceed. Situations in which potential buyers would obtain only minor cost improvements over existing management would not produce sufficiently higher short-run profits to warrant incurring these costs. Instead, the normal workings of the marketplace (as we take up in the next part) will ensure that such inefficiencies are reduced over the long run.

Evidence from merger and takeover activity in the 1980s is consistent with this view. One extensive review of the research on this topic finds that shareholders of firms that were acquired in this way experienced a significant increase in the value of their investments.[6] Unsuccessful takeover attempts, on the other hand, actually resulted in a small loss for existing shareholders, perhaps because managers spent real resources fighting off the takeover.

It is possible that some of these gains from successful takeovers represent factors other than the lower operating costs illustrated in Figure 11.3. For example, as we discuss in Chapter 15, some of these gains may reflect monopoly profits that are garnered by the larger firms that result from a merger. But such monopoly gains probably occur in only a few cases, and these mergers are extensively regulated by antitrust law. It seems likely that a substantial portion of shareholders' profits do reflect some type of improved management efficiencies.

---

[5]Figure 11.3 uses short-run curves because, as our discussion in Chapter 12 will show, cost inefficiencies are substantially eliminated over the longer term by competition in the market for goods.

[6]G. A. Jarrell, J. A. Brickley, and J. M. Netter, "The Market for Corporate Control: The Empirical Evidence since 1980," *Journal of Economic Perspectives* (Winter 1988): 49–68.

APPLICATION 11.5

Corporate Raiders and the RJR-Nabisco Takeover

Corporate raiders are groups of investors who seek to take over the management of specific target firms primarily by using borrowed funds. The common principal fear about raiders appears to be that they will loot the target company. Many claim that raiders are solely interested in making a quick profit and leaving the surviving company in shambles.

Both economic logic and the actual evidence contradict this villainous view of corporate raiders. In theoretical terms, raiders have no reason to destroy a firm. Presumably they are purchasing a firm's assets because they believe the assets are worth more than currently valued in the market. If the raider were really set upon destroying the firm, some other potential buyer would step in to prevent this from happening.

An alternative view is that corporate raiders are performing a useful function by identifying poorly managed firms and promoting new management practices. For example, a 1985 study of the activities of six infamous corporate raiders by Clifford Holderness and Dennis Sheehan generally reaches this conclusion.[1] The authors show that announcement of stock purchases by these six influential investors significantly raised the market value of the target firms' shares, a finding inconsistent with the destructive raider notion. The authors then examine possible reasons for this market reaction and conclude that a major portion can be attributed to the investors' ultimate involvement in managing the company. That is, the value of the corporation was increased by the raider's activities in some measure because the raider represented the promise of better management.

The RJR-Nabisco Takeover

Perhaps the most notorious takeover battle over management practices was the 1988 fight for control of the RJR-Nabisco company.[2] Events were set in motion by the plan of the then chairman of RJR-Nabisco, Ross Johnson, to take the company private by borrowing funds to buy out the existing shareholders. Upon examining the situation, other would-be buyers quickly concluded that, under Johnson, the company had been poorly managed and that its underlying assets were undervalued in the market. The bidding for the company readily escalated and culminated in the purchase of the company for a record 25 billion dollars by the Wall Street firm of Kohlberg, Kravis, and Roberts. The previous management promptly retired to comfortable vacation houses with generous separation payments.

Although the KKR investors promised better management for RJR-Nabisco, the result remains doubtful. Because of the large amount of debt incurred in the takeover, the firm suffered large losses in 1989 and 1990 while it remained under private ownership. In 1991, KKR used a public stock offering to generate funds to pay off substantial portions of the firm's debts, restoring modest profitability to the company. Overall performance continued to be below historical norms established before the takeover battle, however.

To Think About

1. Some observers believe much corporate takeover activity is motivated by the desire to change a firm's capital structure by using more debt and less equity. Why might an investor do this? What are the advantages and disadvantages of using debt rather than equity finance?

2. Should the government seek to control takeover activity? What would be the gains and losses of curtailing such activity? What might have been the result of preventing the RJR-Nabisco takeover?

[1]Clifford G. Holderness and Dennis P. Sheehan, "Raiders or Saviors? The Evidence on Six Controversial Investors," *Journal of Financial Economics* (December 1985): 555–579.
[2]For a discussion of the history of this takeover, see B. Burrough and J. Helyar, *Barbarians at the Gate: The Fall of RJR-Nabisco.* New York, Harper and Row (1990). The book's discussions of RJR's lavish private air fleet, its employment of numerous sports stars on "Team Nabisco" (Frank Gifford, Bobby Orr, and Reggie Jackson, to name a few), and the "golden parachutes" given its executives are especially recommended.

Summary

This chapter surveys some recent topics in the theory of the firm. The main purpose of this survey is to show how the traditional theory can be applied to a number of new and exciting topics. The principal conclusions from this examination were:

- Firms can be regarded as comprising a set of contracts among workers, capital owners, and managers. The scope of a firm's activities will be affected by the relative costs of market versus internal transactions.

- Contracts with workers will reflect the firm-specific skills that are developed on the job. They promote long-term relationships and deter extensive short-term turnover of employees.

- Managers must act as agents for the firm's owners. In their decisions as managers they may pursue some goals that reduce the firm's profits and are therefore costly to the owners.

- Management contracts will be structured to control these agency problems. Such contracts may be costly for owners to develop and enforce.

- The market for firms will operate to ensure that the firm's contracts are relatively efficient. High-cost, inefficient firms may be acquired by another owner if the profits from such an acquisition exceed the costs involved in making the acquisition.

Review Questions

1. What is Coase trying to explain with his theory of the firm? Why do economists need such a theory? Why not just take the structure of firms as given by historical accident and analyze how they react to changes in prices of their inputs or outputs?

2. Usually we have been treating labor as "homogeneous." What does that term mean? When skills can be learned on the job, is the assumption realistic? How should labor of different skill levels be handled in the production function?

3. Do the comments about labor homogeneity in question 2 apply also to capital? Why might a firm's capital stock exhibit differing productivity depending on when it was acquired?

4. What are job-specific skills? Why should a firm pay higher wages to retain workers with such skills? If a firm does pay higher than the wage that workers could earn in their next best alternative employment, how should labor costs be defined?

5. Why might a firm opt to retain workers in response to a temporary decline in demand? If a firm behaves in this way during recessions, how will its average labor productivity react over the business cycle?

6. Explain how the slope and location of the manager's budget constraint were derived in Figure 11.2. What would the constraint look like if the manager did not own any of the firm? How would he or she choose benefits in this case? Does this solution seem likely?

7. How might managerial contracts be structured to take owners' interests into account? How will the market for managerial talent reflect owners' interests? According to economic theory, which managers should earn the highest wages?

8. Consider another agent relationship such as that between physicians and patients or between advisers and investors. Explain the motives of each party in these relationships. How do the motives suggest divergent behavior? What contractual devices are used to align the parties' interests more closely?

9. Explain why an active market for corporate control can enforce profit-maximizing behavior on firms. If a "raider" threatens to buy a firm, what precisely does he or she buy? Should the market for corporate control be considered one aspect of the overall market for capital investment?

10. "If the extra profits obtained by a company takeover come from reductions in costs, that is good for the economy. If they come from the ability to raise price and increase revenues, that is bad." Do you agree? Explain why a takeover might have either, both, or none of these effects.

Problems

11.1 How do costs associated with hiring new employees affect the marginal revenue–marginal cost rule for profit maximization? Explain carefully why this effect might depend on whether short-run or long-run marginal costs are used. Why might a firm respond differently to temporary and permanent changes in the price of its product?

* 11.2 One way of modeling the way firms adjust their work forces is to use a "stock-adjustment model" that assumes the change in labor hired between week $t - 1$ and week t $(L_t - L_{t-1})$ is a fraction of the difference between what the firm wants to hire (L_t^*) and what it hired last week (L_{t-1}). That is,

$$L_t - L_{t-1} = k(L_t^* - L_{t-1})$$

where k is some fraction less than one.

Suppose that a taxidermy shop has a short-run production function given by

$$q = \sqrt{L}$$

where q is the number of animals stuffed per week and L is hours of labor hired per week. Assume that the wage rate is $1 per hour and that short-run total costs are given by

$$STC = 200 + 10q^2.$$

Short-run marginal costs are given by

$$SMC = 20q.$$

---

*Denotes a problem that is rather difficult.

a. If the market price of q is $200 each, how many will be produced and how many workers will the firm wish to hire each week?

b. Suppose the firm starts in week 0 with 50 hours of workers' time used per week. If $k = \frac{1}{2}$, how many workers will be hired in week 1? How many animals will be stuffed?

c. Answer part b for week 2.

d. Graph the firm's output and labor hiring decisions for weeks 0 to 5.

e. How many weeks will it take for the firm to get within one hour of the desired labor input?

11.3   Suppose the production function for high-quality brandy is given by

$$q = \sqrt{K \cdot L}$$

where q is the output of brandy per week and L is labor hours per week. In the short run, K is fixed at 100, so the short-run production function is

$$q = 10\sqrt{L}.$$

a. If capital rents for 10 each and wages are $5 per hour, show that short-run total costs are

$$STC = 1,000 + .05q^2.$$

b. Given the short-run total cost curve in part a, short-run marginal costs are given by

$$SMC = .1q.$$

With this short-run marginal cost curve, how much will the firm produce at a price of $20 per bottle of brandy? How many labor hours will be hired per week?

c. Suppose that during recessions, the price of brandy falls to $15 per bottle. With this price, how much would the firm choose to produce and how many labor hours would be hired?

d. Suppose that the firm believes that the fall in the price of brandy will last for only one week, after which it will wish to return to the level of production in part a. Assume also that for each hour that the firm reduces its work force below that described in part a, it incurs a cost of $1. If it proceeds as in part c, will it earn a profit or a loss? Explain.

e. Is there some level of hiring other than that described in part c that will yield more profits for the firm during the temporary recession?

*11.4   United Airbags (A) and United Balloons (B) are two firms in the lighter-than-air parcel post business. For each the number of delivered packages per hour (q) is a simple function of the number of workers hired each hour (L):

$$q = 10L - L^2.$$

Wages of balloon pilots are determined by their opportunity costs of $40 per hour. Marginal costs are given by

$$MC = \frac{20}{\sqrt{25 - q}}.$$

Initially the competitive cost price of a delivered package is $10.

---

*Denotes a problem that is rather difficult.

a. If firm A is a profit maximizer, how many packages will it deliver and how many pilots will it hire?
b. If firm B wishes to adopt a revenue-sharing formula that also yields $40 per hour to pilots and results in the same level of employment as for firm A, what share of revenues should it pay to its pilots?
c. Suppose the price of delivered packages falls to $5; what will happen to hiring at firm A?
d. If the price of delivered packages falls to $5 and firm B maintains the revenue-sharing formula and employment levels calculated in part b, what will happen to pilots' wages? How might you expect firm B to adjust its contract to the lower price of delivered packages?

11.5 Suppose that Mr. Entrepreneur is the only decision maker in his firm. The profits of this firm depend solely on the amount of time Mr. Entrepreneur spends on the job:

$$\pi = f(H),$$

where H is the number of hours on the job. However, Mr. E, who is a harsh boss, gets on everyone's nerves if he is around too long. Hence π reaches a maximum long before H reaches 24 hours per day.

a. Graph this relationship between π and H.
b. Suppose also that Mr. E has a utility function for profits and leisure (L = 24 − H) of the form U = U(π,L); graph the indifference curve map for this function.
c. In this situation, will the number of hours of work corresponding to profit maximization be the same number that maximizes Mr. E's utility? What special condition must hold for this to be true? Is this condition "reasonable"?

11.6 Managers often receive liberal severance pay provisions in their contracts (these are sometimes called "golden parachutes"). Why would owners opt for such provisions? Once a manager is fired, he or she no longer can affect profits, so why should owners pay managers anything in such a situation?

11.7 United Frisbee produces high-quality, jeweled frisbees. The firm's short-run total costs are given by

$$STC = .01q^2 + 10,000$$

where q is the quantity of frisbees produced per week. Marginal costs are given by

$$SMC = .02q.$$

a. Suppose United can sell its frisbees at $30 each. How many will be produced and what will weekly profits be?
b. Suppose Ted Turnover, a famous corporate raider, can operate United at three-fourths the costs of the current management. What would the costs of the firm be in this situation? If frisbee prices remain at $30, how many would be produced and what would profits be?
c. How much more would Ted be willing to pay for United than would another buyer who could not achieve these cost efficiencies?

11.8   Suppose the managers of a firm could prevent a takeover by lobbying for a law to make such a takeover illegal. Under what conditions would managers choose to do this? Would such an expenditure be in the interest of the original owner of the firm? Are there conditions under which laws banning takeovers might make existing owners better off?

11.9   The Quickstitch Hospital Corporation (QHC) produces medical care that has two dimensions: quantity of care (Q) and quality of care (C), both measured on a regular weekly basis.

Weekly total costs for QHC are given by

$$TC = .1Q^2 + .2C^2 - 125$$

and marginal costs by

$$MC \text{ (of } Q) = .2Q$$

$$MC \text{ (of } C) = .4C.$$

Market prices of medical care are given by

$$P_Q = 10, P_C = 4.$$

a.   If QHC maximizes profits, how much of each dimension of care should it produce? What will the profits be?
b.   Suppose QHC adopts a nonprofit status and is run by the physicians it employs who argue that Q and C should always be equal and as large as possible. Given these physicians' preferences, how much Q and C will QHC produce? (Hint: If QHC is to be nonprofit, TR = TC; Q and C do not have integer values here.)

* 11.10   The United Cabbage Cooperative (UCC) produces cabbage (q) according to the production function

$$q = 2\sqrt{KL}.$$

In the short run, K is fixed at 100 and must be rented from the government at $1 per unit. The workers at UCC adopt an egalitarian compensation scheme, promising to pay each worker an equal share of the revenue left over after capital charges are paid.

a.   Show how total payments per worker depend on the number of workers at UCC (L) and on the market price UCC receives for its cabbages.
b.   If UCC wishes to choose L so as to maximize the amount of income each worker gets, show that this requires that it choose

$$L = 100/P^2.$$

(This requires calculus—you may wish to take it on faith.)
c.   Given the results from part b, calculate how much UCC will produce when P = 1 and when P = 2. What does UCC's supply curve look like?

---

*Denotes a problem that is rather difficult.

"By directing industry in such a manner as its produce may be of greatest value . . . (the manager) . . . is led by an invisible hand to promote . . . (the interest of) . . . society more effectively than he really intends to promote it."

Adam Smith

The Wealth of Nations, 1776

The four chapters in this part draw together our analyses of individual and firm behavior to describe how prices are determined. We do so using a particularly simple model of perfect competition. In this model we assume there are large numbers of both buyers and sellers who act as price takers; that is, economic actors on both sides of the market believe they cannot affect market prices, but can only respond to the signals these prices provide.

Chapter 12 describes the way prices are determined in a single competitive market. It examines how changes in the market price bring about an equilibrium between supply and demand in such a market and how that equilibrium price changes when conditions change. A major portion of the chapter is concerned with the role of economic profits in motivating firms' supply decisions and in encouraging firms to enter or leave the market.

Because the models developed in Chapter 12 are so widely used, Chapter 13 provides a brief summary of some of these applications. Indeed, these applications provide a starting point for examining many other topics in economics.

The analysis in Chapters 12 and 13 examines only a single market at a time. In Chapter 14 we expand the competitive model to show how many markets operate simultaneously. The purpose of the chapter is to describe a general equilibrium situation involving many competitive markets.

Finally, Chapter 15 completes our study of competitive markets by looking again at some of the problems caused by imperfect information in these markets. We will see that the absence of full information may make it impossible for markets to reach an equilibrium. Even when equilibrium prices can be found, the resulting allocation of resources may not be very desirable when information is imperfect.

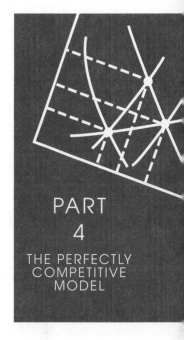

PART
4
THE PERFECTLY
COMPETITIVE
MODEL

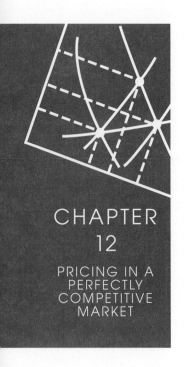

CHAPTER
12

PRICING IN A
PERFECTLY
COMPETITIVE
MARKET

This chapter discusses perfectly competitive price determination in a single market. The theory we develop here is an elaboration of Marshall's supply and demand analysis that we introduced in Chapter 1. We show how equilibrium prices are established and describe some of the factors that may tend to change such prices. In its final and complete form the competitive model we develop here is the most basic model of pricing used by economists. In Chapter 13, we will illustrate some of these applications.

Timing of a Supply Response

In the analysis of pricing it is important to decide the length of time that is to be allowed for a **supply response** to changing demand conditions. The establishment of equilibrium prices will be different if we are talking about a very short period of time during which supply is essentially fixed and unchanging or if we are envisioning a very long-run process in which it is possible for entirely new firms to enter a market. For this reason, it has been traditional in economics to discuss pricing in three different time periods: (1) the very short run, (2) the short run, and (3) the long run. Although it is not possible to give these terms an exact time length, the essential distinction among them concerns the nature of the supply response that is assumed to be possible. In the *very short run* there can be no supply response—quantity supplied is absolutely fixed. In the *short run,* existing firms may change the quantity they are supplying, but no new firms can enter the market. In the *long run,* firms can further change the quantity supplied, and completely new firms may enter an industry; this produces a very flexible supply response. This chapter discusses each of these different types of responses.

Supply response
The change in quantity of output in response to a change in demand conditions.

Pricing in the Very Short Run

In the very short run or **market period,** there is no supply response. The goods are already "in" the marketplace and must be sold for whatever the market will bear. In this situation price acts to ration demand. The price will adjust to clear the market of the quantity that must be sold. Although the market price may act as a signal to producers in future periods, it does not perform such a function in the very short run since current period output cannot be changed.

Figure 12.1 illustrates this situation. Market demand is represented by the curve D. Supply is fixed at Q^*, and the price that clears the market is P_1. At P_1 people are willing to take all that is offered in the market. Sellers want to dispose of Q^* without regard to price (for example, the good in question may be perishable and will be worthless if not sold immediately). The price P_1 balances the desires of demanders with the desires of suppliers. For this reason it is called an **equilibrium price.** In Figure 12.1, a price in excess of P_1 would not be an equilibrium price since people would demand less than Q^* (remember firms are always willing to supply Q^* no matter what the price). Similarly, a price below P_1 would not be an equilibrium price since people would then demand more than Q^*. P_1 is the only equilibrium price possible when demand conditions are those represented by the curve D.

Market period
A short period of time during which quantity supplied is fixed.

Equilibrium price
The price at which the quantity demanded by buyers of a good is equal to the quantity supplied of the good by sellers.

■ Shifts in Demand: Price as a Rationing Device

If the demand curve in Figure 12.1 shifted outward to D′ (perhaps because incomes increased, or because the price of some substitute increased), P_1 would

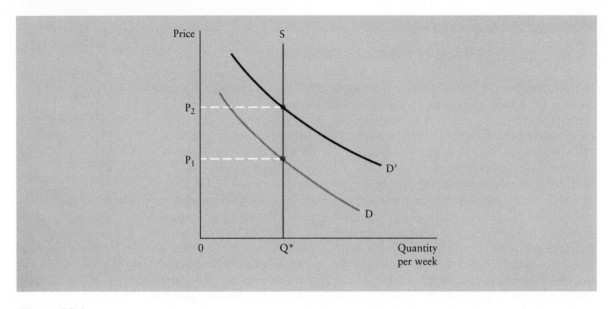

Figure 12.1
Pricing in the Very Short Run

When quantity is absolutely fixed in the very short run, price acts only as a device to ration demand. With quantity fixed at Q^*, price P_1 will prevail in the marketplace if D is the market demand curve. At this price, individuals are willing to consume exactly that quantity available. If demand should shift upward to D', the equilibrium price would rise to P_2.

no longer be an equilibrium price. With the demand curve D', far more than Q^* is demanded at the price P_1. Some people who wish to make purchases at a price of P_1 would find that not enough of the good is now available to meet the increase in demand. In order to ration the available quantity among all demanders, the price would have to rise to P_2. At that new price, demand would again be reduced to Q^* (by a movement along D' in a northwesterly direction as the price rises). Hence the price rise would restore equilibrium to the market. The curve labeled S (for "supply") in Figure 12.1 shows all the equilibrium prices for Q^* for any conceivable shift in demand. The price must always adjust to ration demand to exactly what supply is available. In Application 12.1: Auctions for Fish and Flowers, we look at auctions for two perishable items and show how this price-setting mechanism works in practice.

■ **Applicability of the Very Short-Run Model**

The model of the very short run is not particularly useful for most markets. Although the theory may adequately apply to some situations where goods are perishable, the far more common situation involves some degree of supply response to changing demand. It is usually presumed that a rise in price will prompt producers to bring additional quantity into the market. The next section looks at why firms would increase their output levels in the short run in response to a price increase.

APPLICATION 12.1

Auctions for Fish and Flowers

Auctions provide an important example of pricing in the very short run. In most cases the goods put up for bid at an auction must all be sold. Supply is fixed, and prices act only to allocate the available goods among auction participants. However, when perishable goods are being auctioned, market period analysis is even more directly relevant. This is because auctioneers cannot refuse to sell goods that do not attain what they consider suitable prices. Unlike art auctions where items are withdrawn if they don't meet "reserve prices," perishable goods must sell for whatever price the market will bear.

Fish Auctions

Auctions of freshly caught fish are conducted in practically every major fishing city in the world. Although the particular customs of these auctions differ among nations, the procedures are very similar. First, the auctions are conducted quickly. Because fresh fish must be sold rapidly to the final users, there is no time for middlemen to engage in lengthy haggling over prices. Consequently, highly organized, sometimes frantic auction methods have been developed. Second, although a variety of these auction methods are employed, all methods result in equilibrium prices being reached quickly and accurately. For example, the three most widely used bidding systems (the English ascending bid system, the Dutch descending bid system, and the Japanese simultaneous bid system) all seem to result in attaining the same equilibrium prices.

A final similarity among fish (and other) auctions throughout the world is the importance of market participants knowing the total quantity being sold on a particular day. Because fish demand is relatively inelastic, rather small differences in quantity supplied can result in great differences in the final prices agreed upon. Hence, market participants must know what the true supply situation is if they are to avoid serious mistakes. For example, a common practice in Manila and other Far East fish markets is for fishers at first to unload only part of their day's catch to make it appear that supply is small. By so doing, they hope that higher prices will be bid. Of course, buyers are generally aware of this strategy and may actually hire elaborate networks of spies to examine fishing boats in order to find out the true situation.

Flower Auctions

Fresh flowers are also often sold through auctions. Many of the flowers found in American supermarkets were originally sold at auctions in London or Amsterdam and flown to their final destination immediately after the sales. As in the case of fish, because flowers are perishable they must be sold quickly. Consequently, prices fluctuate rapidly in response to supply availability. One way in which flower sellers attempt to influence buyers' perceptions of supply is by setting "reservation" prices for their initial offerings of flowers. If these prices are not reached, the flowers are withdrawn from sale, thereby putting pressure on buyers to increase their bids for the next lot or face the prospect of going home empty-handed. The ploy is intended only to influence the price of future lots because (unlike art) the flowers withdrawn from an auction have no alternative value and are often destroyed. Success of this strategy, then, depends upon sellers being able to take advantage of their superior knowledge of the true supply situation.[1]

To Think About

1. Why do auctions succeed in arriving at equilibrium prices? If a price starts well below equilibrium, as in the American bidding system, why does the supply and demand model predict that price must rise to its equilibrium level before bidding stops?

2. This example illustrates two ways in which sellers may use their superior information to try to influence the outcomes of auctions. Can you think of other types of ploys they might use? What kinds of strategies might buyers use to get lower prices? How is the likely success of various strategies dependent on how informed the parties are?

---

[1]For a further discussion of these and other issues, see R. P. McAfee and J. McMillan, "Auctions and Bidding," *Journal of Economic Literature* (June 1987): 699–738.

Before beginning that analysis, we should understand that increases in quantity supplied need not come only from increased production. In a world in which some goods are durable (that is, last longer than a single market period), current owners of these goods may supply them in increasing amounts to the market as price rises. For example, even though the supply of Rembrandts is absolutely fixed, we would not draw the market supply curve for these paintings as a vertical line, such as that shown in Figure 12.1. As the price of Rembrandts rises, people (and museums) become increasingly willing to part with them. From a market point of view, the supply curve for Rembrandts will have an upward slope even though no new production takes place. A similar analysis would follow for many types of durable goods, such as antiques, used cars, 1950s baseball cards, or corporate shares, all of which are in nominally fixed supply. Here we are more interested in examining how demand and production are related, however, so we will not look at these other cases in detail.

Short-Run Supply

In analysis of the short run, the number of firms in an industry is fixed. It is assumed that firms are not flexible enough either to enter or to leave a given market. However, the firms currently operating in the market are able to adjust the quantity they are producing in response to changing prices. Because there are a large number of firms producing a homogeneous good, each firm will act as a price taker. The model of short-run supply by a price-taking firm in Chapter 10 is therefore an appropriate one to use here. That is, each firm's short-run supply curve is simply the positively sloped section of its short-run marginal cost curve above minimum average variable cost. Using this model to record individual firms' supply decisions, we can add up all of these decisions into a single market supply curve.

■ Construction of a Short-Run Supply Curve

The quantity of a good that is supplied to the market during some period is the sum of the quantities supplied by each firm. Since each firm considers the same market price in deciding how much to produce, the total supplied to the market will also depend on this price. This relationship between market price and quantity supplied is called a **short-run supply curve**.

Short-run supply curve

The relationship between market price and quantity supplied of a good in the short run.

Figure 12.2 illustrates the construction of the curve. For simplicity we assume there are only two firms, A and B. The short-run supply (that is, marginal cost) curves for firms A and B are shown in Panels a and b. The market supply curve shown in Panel c is the horizontal sum of these two curves. For example, at a price of P_1, firm A is willing to supply q_1^A, and firm B is willing to supply q_1^B. At this price the total supply in the market is given by Q_1, which is equal to $q_1^A + q_1^B$. The other points on the curve are constructed in an

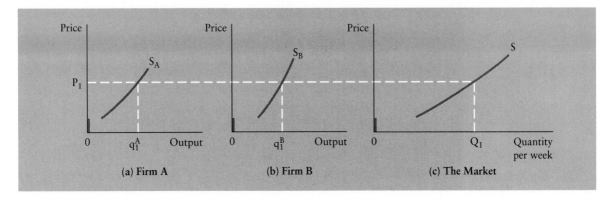

The supply (marginal cost) curves of two firms are shown in Panels a and b. The market supply curve in Panel c is the horizontal sum of these curves. For example, at P_1, firm A supplies q_1^A, firm B supplies q_1^B, and total market supply is given by $Q_1 = q_1^A + q_1^B$.

Figure 12.2
Short-Run Market
Supply Curve

identical way. Because each firm's supply curve slopes upward, the market supply curve will also slope upward. This upward slope reflects the fact that short-run marginal costs increase as firms attempt to increase their outputs. They will be willing to incur these higher marginal costs only at higher market prices.

■ Slope of the Supply Curve

Although the construction in Figure 12.2 uses only two firms, actual market supply curves represent the summation of many firms' supply curves. Again the market supply curve will have a positive slope because of the positive slope in each firm's underlying marginal cost curve. This market supply curve summarizes the short-run diminishing returns experienced by all firms, the prices of the inputs they use, and the profit-maximizing decisions that each firm makes.

There is a second reason why the short-run supply curve may have a positive slope. Although each firm takes input prices as given in making its decisions, those prices may not remain constant as output for the industry as a whole expands. It is possible that increases in industry output will increase the demand for scarce inputs, thereby bidding up the prices of those inputs. This might happen if firms use very specialized inputs and can hire more of them only by raising prices. For example, increasing sales of music videos in the 1980s increased the demand for big name stars. Rising salaries for those stars resulted in higher costs for firms that make these videos. These types of effects are called **external price effects**—they arise when expanding output raises input costs and therefore raises all firms' marginal costs. When these effects are present, the short-run market supply curve may be more steeply sloped than a simple summation of firms' marginal cost curves would suggest. Expansion in output raises firms' marginal costs both because of diminishing marginal productivity and because rising input prices may increase overall costs. The

■
External price effects

Effects that changes in the level of production of an industry have on the prices of inputs to that industry.

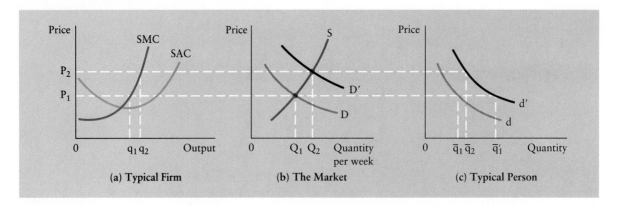

Figure 12.3
Interactions of Many Individuals and Firms Determine Market Price in the Short Run

Market demand curves and market supply curves are each the horizontal sum of numerous components. These market curves are shown in Panel b. Once price is determined in the market, each firm and each individual treat this price as fixed in their decisions. If the typical person's demand curve shifts to d′, market demand will shift to D′ in the short run, and price will rise to P_2.

short-run supply curve summarizes both effects, and, as we show in the next section, using that curve lets us see how these factors interact with market demand to determine price.

Short-Run Price Determination

We can now combine demand and supply curves to demonstrate how equilibrium prices are established in the short run. Figure 12.3 shows this process. In Panel b, the market demand curve D and the short-run supply curve S intersect at a price of P_1 and a quantity of Q_1. This price-quantity combination represents an equilibrium between the demands of individuals and the supply decisions of firms—the forces of supply and demand are precisely balanced. What firms supply at a price of P_1 is exactly what people want to buy at that price. This equilibrium will tend to persist from one period to the next unless one of the factors underlying the supply and demand curves should change.

■ Functions of the Equilibrium Price

Here the equilibrium price P_1 serves two important functions. First, this price acts as a signal to producers about how much should be produced. In order to maximize profits, firms will produce that output level for which marginal costs are equal to P_1. In the aggregate, then, production will be Q_1. A second function of the price is to ration demand. Given the market price of P_1, utility-maximizing individuals will decide how much of their limited incomes to spend on that particular good. At a price of P_1, total quantity demanded will be Q_1, which is precisely the amount that will be produced. This is what economists mean by an equilibrium price. No other price brings about such a balancing of supply and demand.

The implications of the equilibrium price (P_1) for a typical firm and for a typical person are shown in Panels a and c of Figure 12.3, respectively. For the typical firm, the price P_1 will cause an output level of q_1 to be produced. The firm earns a small profit at this particular price because price exceeds short-run average total cost. The initial demand curve d for a typical person is shown in Panel c. At a price of P_1, this person demands $\overline{q_1}$. Adding up the quantities that each person demands at P_1 and the quantities that each firm supplies shows that the market is in equilibrium. The market supply and demand curves are a convenient way of doing that addition.

■ Effect of an Increase in Market Demand

To study the nature of the short-run supply response, we can assume that many people decide they want to buy more of the good in Figure 12.3. The typical person's demand curve shifts outward to d′ and the entire market demand curve will shift. Panel b shows the new market demand curve, D′. The new equilibrium point is P_2, Q_2: at this point, supply-demand balance is reestablished. Price has now increased from P_1 to P_2 in response to the demand shift. The quantity traded in the market has also increased from Q_1 to Q_2.

The rise in price in the short run has served two functions. First, as shown in our analysis of the very short run, it has acted to ration demand. Whereas at P_1 a typical individual demanded $\overline{q_1'}$, now at P_2 only $\overline{q_2}$ is demanded.

The rise in price has also acted as a signal to the typical firm to increase production. In Panel a the typical firm's profit-maximizing output level has increased from q_1 to q_2 in response to the price rise. That is what economists mean by a short-run supply response: an increase in market price acts as an inducement to increase production. Firms are willing to increase production (and to incur higher marginal costs) because price has risen. If market price had not been permitted to rise (suppose, for example, government price controls were in effect), firms would not have increased their outputs. At P_1 there would have been an excess (unfilled) demand for the good in question. If market price is allowed to rise, a supply-demand equilibrium can be reestablished so that what firms produce is again equal to what people demand at the prevailing market price. At the new price P_2, the typical firm has also increased its profits. This increased profitability in response to rising prices is important to our discussion of long-run pricing later in this chapter.

Shifts in Supply and Demand Curves

In previous chapters we analyzed many of the reasons why either demand or supply curves might shift. Some of these reasons are summarized in Table 12.1.

Table 12.1 Reasons for a Shift in a Demand or Supply Curve	Demand	Supply
	Shifts outward (→) because • Income increases • Price of substitute rises • Price of complement falls • Preferences for good increase	Shifts outward (→) because • Input prices fall • Technology improves
	Shifts inward (←) because • Income falls • Price of substitute falls • Price of complement rises • Preferences for good diminish	Shifts inward (←) because • Input prices rise

You may wish to review the material in Chapter 5, "Market Demand," and Chapter 9, "Costs," to see why these changes shift the various curves. These types of shifts in demand and supply occur frequently in real-world markets. When either a supply curve or a demand curve does shift, equilibrium price and quantity will change. This section looks briefly at such changes and how the outcome depends on the shapes of the curves.

■ Short-Run Supply Elasticity

Some terms used by economists to describe the shapes of demand and supply curves need to be understood before we can discuss the effects of these shifts. We have already introduced the terminology for demand curves in Chapter 5. There we developed the concept of the price elasticity of demand, which shows how the quantity demanded responds to changes in price. When demand is elastic, changes in price have a major impact on quantity demanded. In the case of inelastic demand, however, a price change does not have very much effect on what people choose to buy. Firms' short-run supply responses can be described along the same lines. If an increase in price causes firms to supply significantly more output, we say that the supply curve is "elastic" (at least in the range currently being observed). Alternatively, if the price increase has only a minor effect on the quantity firms choose to produce, supply is said to be inelastic. More formally:

$$\text{Short-run supply elasticity} = \frac{\text{Percentage change in quantity supplied in short run}}{\text{Percentage change in price}}. \qquad [12.1]$$

■ Short-run elasticity of supply

The percentage change in quantity supplied in the short run in response to a 1 percent change in price.

For example, if the short-run supply elasticity is 2.0, each 1 percent increase in price results in a 2 percent increase in quantity supplied. Over this range, the short-run supply curve is fairly elastic. If, on the other hand, a 1 percent increase in price leads only to a 0.5 percent increase in quantity supplied, the **short-run elasticity of supply** is 0.5, and we would say that supply is inelastic. As we will see, whether short-run supply is elastic or inelastic can have a significant effect on market performance.

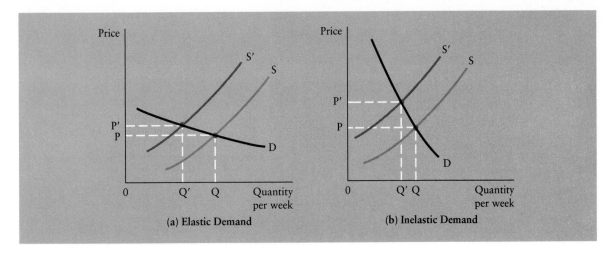

In Panel a the shift inward in the supply curve causes price to increase only slightly, whereas quantity contracts sharply. This results from the elastic shape of the demand curve. In Panel b, the demand curve is inelastic; price increases substantially with only a slight decrease in quantity.

Figure 12.4
Effect of a Shift in the Short-Run Supply Curve Depends on the Shape of the Demand Curve

■ Shifts in Supply Curves and the Importance of the Shape of the Demand Curve

A shift inward in the short-run supply curve for a good might result, for example, from an increase in the prices of the inputs used by firms to produce the good. Whatever the cause of the shift, its effect on the equilibrium levels of P and Q will depend on the shape of the demand curve for the product. Figure 12.4 illustrates two possible situations. The demand curve in Panel a is relatively price elastic; that is, a change in price substantially affects the quantity demanded. For this case, a shift in the supply curve from S to S′ will cause equilibrium prices to rise only moderately (from P to P′), whereas quantity is reduced sharply (from Q to Q′). Rather than being "passed on" in higher prices, the increase in the firms' input costs is met primarily by a decrease in quantity (a movement down each firm's marginal cost curve) with only a slight increase in price.[1]

This situation is reversed when the market demand curve is inelastic. In Panel b in Figure 12.4, a shift in the supply curve causes equilibrium price to rise substantially but quantity is little changed, because people do not reduce their demands very much if prices rise. Consequently, the shift upward in the supply curve is passed on to demanders almost completely in the form of higher prices.

---

[1]Notice, for example, that on the supply curve S′, the marginal cost of producing output level Q is considerably higher than the marginal cost of producing Q′.

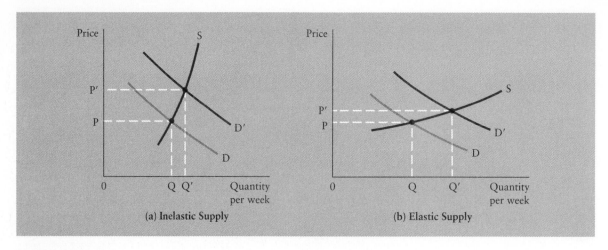

Figure 12.5

Effect of a Shift in the Demand Curve Depends on the Shape of the Short-Run Supply Curve

In Panel a supply is inelastic; a shift in demand causes price to increase greatly with only a small increase in quantity. In Panel b, on the other hand, supply is elastic; price rises only slightly in response to a demand shift.

■ Shifts in Demand Curves and the Importance of the Shape of the Supply Curve

We can also show that a given shift in a market demand curve will have different implications for P and Q depending on the shape of the short-run supply curve. Two illustrations are shown in Figure 12.5. In Panel a the supply curve for the good in question is relatively inelastic. As quantity expands, firms' marginal costs rise rapidly, giving the supply curve its steep slope. In this situation, a shift outward in the market demand curve (caused, for example, by an increase in income) will cause prices to increase substantially. On the other hand, the quantity increases only slightly. The increase in demand (and in Q) has caused firms to move up their steeply sloped marginal cost curves. The accompanying large increase in price serves to ration demand. There is little response in terms of quantity supplied.

Panel b in Figure 12.5 shows a relatively elastic short-run supply curve. This kind of curve would occur for an industry in which marginal costs do not rise steeply in response to output increases. For this case an increase in demand produces a substantial increase in Q. However, because of the nature of the supply curve, this increase is not met by great cost increases. Consequently, price rises only moderately.

These examples again demonstrate Marshall's observation that demand and supply together determine price and quantity. In Chapter 1, we mentioned his analogy—just as it is impossible to say which blade of a scissors does the cutting, so too it is impossible to attribute price solely to demand or to supply characteristics. Rather, the effect that shifts in either a demand curve or a supply curve will have depends on the shapes of both of the curves. In predicting the effects of shifting supply or demand conditions on market price and quantity in the real world, this simultaneous relationship must be considered. Application 12.2: Dairy Price Supports illustrates how this short-run model might be used to examine some of the problems with government price support schemes.

■ A Numerical Illustration

We can also illustrate changes in market equilibria with a simple numerical example. Suppose, as we did in Chapter 10, that the quantity of cassette tapes demanded per week (Q) depends on the price of tapes (P) according to the simple relation

$$\text{Demand: } Q = 10 - P. \qquad [12.2]$$

Suppose also that the short-run supply curve for tapes is given by

$$\text{Supply: } Q = P - 2 \text{ or } P = Q + 2. \qquad [12.3]$$

Figure 12.6 graphs these equations. As before, the demand curve (labeled D in the figure) intersects the vertical axis at P = $10. At higher prices no tapes are

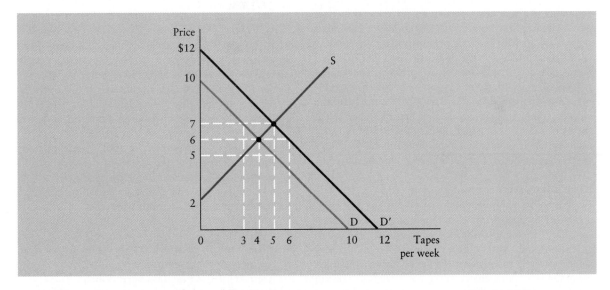

With the curves D and S, equilibrium occurs at a price of $6. At this price people demand four tapes per week, and that is what firms supply. When demand shifts to D', price will rise to $7 to restore equilibrium.

Figure 12.6
Demand and Supply Curves for Cassette Tapes

APPLICATION 12.2

Dairy Price Supports

Located throughout the United States are nearly 200,000 dairy farmers. These farmers comprise a powerful political force that encourages the enactment of a variety of laws favoring their industry. Three specific federal programs raise prices for these goods above the levels that would exist under a competitive equilibrium: (1) classification of milk into various grades and the specification of minimum prices for some of these grades; (2) government purchase of surplus butter and cheese; and (3) major restrictions on the importing of dairy products.

A Graphic Analysis

The implication of these actions can be illustrated in the simple short-run supply-demand diagram in Figure 1. In the absence of government programs, the market for dairy products would have an equilibrium price of P^* with quantity Q^* being purchased. The web of protective programs for the industry results in raising the price to P_R. At this higher price, consumers purchase Q_1, farmers produce Q_2, and there is a surplus of $Q_2 - Q_1$. These surplus products are bought through various government programs as a way of supporting the price P_R. The effect of the rise in prices from P^* to P_R is to reduce consumer surplus by area $P_R E' E P^*$. A part of this is converted to (short-run) profits for the industry (area $P_R E' A$), and there is a deadweight loss of consumer surplus (area $E'EA$). Costs of the price support plan for the government are represented by area $E'BQ_2Q_1$ (assuming all the surplus commodities must be bought). In dollar terms these costs can be quite high. During the 1980s, the government regularly bought about 10 percent of total dairy production at annual costs of $2 to 4 billion or more.

Some Consequences of the Programs

Government involvement in the dairy industry has led to a number of bizarre, and even humorous, consequences. In 1983, for example, the U.S. Department of Agriculture sponsored a vast "cheese giveaway" program under which virtually anyone near the delivery truck could get 10 pounds of free cheese. Because of crowd control problems, the program was quietly cancelled. In 1985, a complex deal was worked out to get rid of butter by selling a large quantity to the Soviet Union. In order to

Figure 1
Effect of Dairy Price Supports

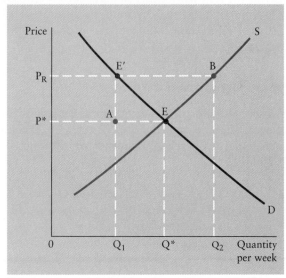

Various measures to help the dairy industry raise prices to P_R. There is a surplus of $Q_2 - Q_1$ which must be bought by the government at a cost of $E'BQ_2Q_1$.

avoid the political embarrassment of selling it to the Soviets at the world price (which was about one-half of what American consumers were paying), the United States instead gave the butter to New Zealand (a country with little need for surplus U.S. butter). The New Zealanders then made a tidy profit on the sale to the Soviets. At times the government has paid farmers not to produce milk (as it has also done on a larger scale with grain crops). The agriculture department even experimented with a "whole herd buyout" program under which dairy farmers could sell all of their cows to the government. Unfortunately, the farmers (and their cows) kept turning up elsewhere, perhaps to sell their herds to the government again at another location.

To Think About

1. Proponents of dairy price supports argue that they are needed to prevent ruinous competition. How would you evaluate this contention?

2. Figure 1 represents a short-run analysis. Would you expect the costs of such a program to be higher in the short run or in the long run? Explain.

Price	Supply Q = P − 2 Quantity Supplied (Tapes per Week)	Demand Case 1 Q = 10 − P Quantity Demanded (Tapes per Week)	Case 2 Q = 12 − P Quantity Demanded (Tapes per Week)
$10	8	0	2
9	7	1	3
8	6	2	4
7	5	3	5
6	4	4	6
5	3	5	7
4	2	6	8
3	1	7	9
2	0	8	10
1	0	9	11
0	0	10	12

Table 12.2
Supply and Demand Equilibrium in the Market for Cassette Tapes

□ New equilibrium.
■ Initial equilibrium.

demanded. The supply curve (labeled S) intersects the vertical axis at P = 2. This is the shutdown price for firms in the industry—at a price lower than $2 no tapes will be produced. As Figure 12.6 shows, these supply and demand curves intersect at a price of $6 per tape. At that price people demand four tapes per week, and firms are willing to supply four tapes per week. This equilibrium is also illustrated in Table 12.2, which shows the quantity of tapes demanded and supplied at each price. Only when P = $6 do these amounts agree. At a price of $5 per tape, for example, people want to buy five tapes per week, but only three will be supplied; there is an excess demand of two tapes per week. Similarly, at a price of $7 per tape there is an excess supply of two tapes per week.

If the demand curve for tapes were to shift outward, this equilibrium would change. For example, Figure 12.6 also shows the demand curve D′, whose equation is given by

$$Q = 12 - P. \qquad [12.4]$$

With this new demand curve, equilibrium price rises to $7 per tape, and quantity also rises to five tapes per week. This new equilibrium is confirmed by the entries in Table 12.2, which show that this is the only price that clears the market given the new demand curve. For example, at the old price of $6 there is now an excess demand for tapes, since the amount people want (Q = 6) exceeds what firms are willing to supply (Q = 4). The rise in price from $6 to $7 restores equilibrium both by prompting people to buy fewer tapes and by encouraging firms to produce more.

The Long Run

In perfectly competitive markets, supply responses are considerably more flexible in the long run than in the short run for two reasons. First, firms' long-run cost curves reflect the greater input flexibility that firms have in the long run. Second, the long run also allows firms to enter and exit an industry in response to profit opportunities. These actions have important implications for pricing. We begin our analysis of these various effects with a description of the long-run equilibrium for a competitive industry. Then, as we did for the short run, we will show how supply and prices change when conditions change.

■ Equilibrium Conditions

A perfectly competitive market is in equilibrium when no firm has an incentive to change its behavior. Such an equilibrium has two components: firms must be content with their output choices (that is, they must be maximizing profits), and they must be content to stay in (or out of) the market. We discuss each of these components separately.

■ Profit Maximization

As before, we assume that firms seek maximum profits. Because each firm is a price taker, profit maximization requires that the firm produce where price is equal to (long-run) marginal cost. This first equilibrium condition, $P = MC$, determines both the firm's output choice and its choice of inputs that minimize these costs in the long run.

■ Entry and Exit

A second feature of long-run equilibrium concerns the possibility of the entry of entirely new firms into the industry, or the exit of existing firms from that industry. The perfectly competitive model assumes that such entry and exit entail no special costs. Consequently, new firms will be lured into any market in which (economic) profits are positive. Similarly, firms will leave a market when profits are negative.

If profits are positive, the entry of new firms will cause the short-run industry supply curve to shift outward, since more firms are now producing than were in the industry previously. Such a shift will cause market price (and industry profits) to fall. The process will continue until no firm contemplating entering the industry would be able to earn an economic profit.[2] At that point,

---

[2]Remember, we are using the economic definition of profits here. These profits represent the return to the owner of a business in excess of that which is strictly necessary to keep him or her in the business.

entry by new firms will cease, and there will be an equilibrium number of firms in the industry. When the firms in an industry suffer short-run losses, some firms will choose to leave the industry, causing the supply curve to shift to the left. Market price will then rise, eliminating losses for those firms remaining in the industry.

■ Long-Run Equilibrium

For the purposes of this chapter we assume that all the firms in an industry have identical cost curves; that is, we assume that no single firm controls any special resources or technologies.[3] Because all firms are identical, the equilibrium long-run position requires every firm to earn exactly zero economic profits. In graphic terms, long-run equilibrium price must settle at the low point of each firm's long-run average total cost curve. Only at this point do the two equilibrium conditions hold: P = MC (which is required for profit maximization) and P = AC (which is the required zero-profit condition).

These two equilibrium conditions have rather different origins. Profit maximization is a goal of firms. The P = MC rule reflects our assumptions about firms' behavior and is identical to the output decision rule used in the short run. The zero-profit condition is not a goal for firms. Firms would obviously prefer to have large profits. The long-run operation of the market, however, forces all firms to accept a level of zero economic profits (P = AC) because of the willingness of firms to enter and to leave an industry. Although the firms in a perfectly competitive industry may earn either positive or negative profits in the short run, in the long run only a level of zero profits will prevail.[4]

Long-Run Supply: Constant Cost Case

Before we can discuss long-run pricing in detail, we must make some assumption about how the entry of new firms into an industry affects the costs of inputs. The simplest assumption is that entry has no external price effects. Hence, the per-unit costs of inputs to firms do not change. Under this assumption, no matter how many firms enter or leave an industry, every firm will retain exactly the same set of cost curves with which it started. There are many important cases for which this constant input cost assumption may not be made; we will analyze these cases later. For the moment, however, we wish to examine the equilibrium conditions for a **constant cost industry.**

■ Constant cost industry

An industry in which the entry or exit of firms has no effect on the cost curves of the firms in the industry.

---

[3]The important case of firms having different costs is discussed in Chapter 13. In that chapter we see that very low-cost firms can earn positive, long-run profits. These represent a return to the input that provides the firms' unique low cost (e.g., especially fertile land or a low-cost source of raw materials).

[4]These equilibrium conditions also point out what seems to be, somewhat imprecisely, an "efficient" aspect of the long-run equilibrium in perfectly competitive markets. The good under investigation will be produced at minimum average cost. We consider the issue of efficiency in more detail in the next two chapters.

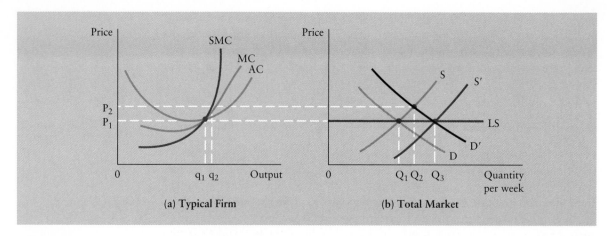

(a) Typical Firm   (b) Total Market

Figure 12.7

Long-Run Equilibrium for a Perfectly Competitive Industry: Constant Cost Case

An increase in demand from D to D′ will cause price to rise from P_1 to P_2 in the short run. This higher price will create profits in the industry and new firms will be drawn into the market. If the entry of these new firms has no effect on the cost curves of the firms in the industry, new firms will continue to enter until price is pushed back down to P_1. At this price economic profits are zero. The long-run supply curve LS will therefore be a horizontal line at P_1. Along LS, output is increased by increasing the number of firms that each produce q_1.

■ Market Equilibrium

Figure 12.7 demonstrates long-run equilibrium for a constant cost industry. For the market as a whole, in Panel b, the demand curve is labeled D and the short-run supply curve is labeled S. The short-run equilibrium price is therefore P_1. The typical firm in Panel a will produce output level q_1, since at this level of output price is equal to short-run marginal cost (SMC). In addition, with a market price of P_1, output level q_1 is also a long-run equilibrium position for the firm. The firm is maximizing profits since price is equal to long-run marginal cost (MC). When all possible variations in inputs are considered, q_1 remains the optimal level of output for a profit-maximizing firm. Panel a in Figure 12.7 also shows a second long-run equilibrium property: price is equal to long-run average total costs (AC). Consequently, economic profits are zero, and there is no incentive for firms either to enter or to leave the industry.

The market shown in Figure 12.7 is in both short-run and long-run equilibrium. Each firm is in equilibrium because it is maximizing profits, and the number of firms is stable because economic profits are zero. This equilibrium will tend to persist until either supply or demand conditions change.

■ A Shift in Demand

Suppose now that the market demand curve shifts outward to D′. If S is the relevant short-run supply curve for the industry, then in the short run, price will rise to P_2. The typical firm will, in the short run, choose to produce q_2, and will earn profits on this level of output. In the long run, these profits will attract new firms into the market. Because of the constant cost assumption, this entry of new firms will have no effect on input costs, and therefore the typical firm's cost curves will not shift. New firms will continue to enter the market until price is forced down to the level at which there are again no pure economic profits. The entry of new firms will therefore shift the short-run supply curve to S′ where the equilibrium price (P_1) is reestablished. At this new long-run equilibrium, the price-quantity combination P_1, Q_3 will prevail in the market. The typical firm will again produce at output level q_1, although now there will be more firms than there were in the initial situation.

■ Long-Run Supply Curve

By considering many such shifts in demand, we can examine long-run pricing in this industry. Our discussion suggests that no matter how demand shifts, economic forces that cause price always to return to P_1 will come into play. All long-run equilibria will occur along a horizontal line at P_1. Connecting these equilibrium points shows the long-run supply response of this industry. This long-run supply curve is labeled LS in Figure 12.7. For a constant cost industry of identical firms, the long-run supply curve is a horizontal line at the low point of the firms' long-run average total cost curves. Application 12.3: The Video Rental Market looks at a case where this is approximately true.

Shape of the Long-Run Supply Curve

In the previous section we pointed out that, contrary to the short-run case, long-run analysis has very little to do with the shape of the marginal cost curve. Rather, the zero-profit condition centers attention on the low point of the long-run average cost curve as the factor most relevant to long-run price determination. In the constant cost case the position of this low point does not change as new firms enter or leave the industry. Consequently, only one price can prevail in the long run regardless of how demand shifts. The long-run supply curve is horizontal at this price.

Once the constant cost assumption is abandoned, this need not be the case. If the entry of new firms causes average costs to rise, the long-run supply curve will have an upward slope. On the other hand, if entry causes average costs to decline, it is even possible for the long-run supply curve to be negatively sloped. We now discuss these possibilities.

■ The Increasing Cost Industry

The entry of new firms may cause the average cost of all firms to rise for several reasons. New firms may compete for scarce inputs, thus driving up their prices. New firms may impose external costs on existing firms (and on themselves) in the form of air or water pollution. And new firms may place strains

APPLICATION 12.3

The Video Rental Market

Prior to 1980, few Americans owned videocassette recorders (VCRs). Early VCRs were large, unreliable, and incorporated a variety of noncompatible, competing technologies. With the establishment of a common technical standard (VHS) and the advent of lower-cost electronics, VCR ownership grew rapidly. Whereas fewer than 1 percent of American families owned VCRs in 1980, by the end of the decade the number of owners had grown to over 70 percent. This huge growth vastly increased the demand for movie rentals on videotape.

Entry Conditions

Early video rental outlets were the beneficiaries of the increase in demand. Tapes rented for five dollars or more per night, so a typical tape could pay for itself after only a few rentals. At first, the industry was very profitable. Unfortunately for the early owners, however, there were no significant barriers to entry into the industry. Any would-be entrepreneur could rent space, build storage shelves and a checkout area, buy tapes, and get in on the action. Inputs used by the tape rental industry (primarily low-skilled labor and general purpose rental space) were readily available at prevailing market prices. Between 1982 and 1987, the number of tape rental outlets expanded nearly fourfold throughout the United States. Even grocery stores and mini-mart gasoline retailers began stocking video rentals. By the end of the decade, prices had fallen dramatically (to an average of about $1.50 per night) and new entry into the industry had largely ceased. Long-run equilibrium was established, with returns on investments in video rental outlets approximating profits earned in other businesses.

New Technology Again

The equilibrium, however, may not last long in the fast-moving home entertainment market. Cable television services also expanded rapidly during the 1980s, providing potentially serious competition to video rental outlets. Currently most of this competition is simply due to the expanding viewing options that cable TV offers.

With more than 40 or 50 channels to choose from, individuals can often stay at home and find something to watch rather than going to the trouble of renting a video. Pay-per-view events (such as major prize fights or NBC's ill-fated "Triple Cast" of the 1992 Olympics) further increase viewers' options.

Some cable outlets are starting to offer rental movies on a pay-per-view basis, which is perhaps the most detrimental blow to the video rental industry. No longer is there any need to visit a video rental store at all. The same dynamic forces of the electronics industry that gave rise to video rentals on every corner may ultimately lead to the industry's demise.

To Think About

1. One primary input to video rentals is, of course, movies to put on tape. What do you think the supply elasticity for tapes is? Might increasing demand for tape rentals lead to increasing prices for videotapes themselves, or is the tape industry itself also characterized by constant costs?

2. How has the growth of home video rentals affected movie theater attendance? Although it seems obvious that video renting should reduce theater demand, can you think of reasons why this effect might be relatively small? How do movie producers manage the release of their films in order to maximize their returns from both markets?

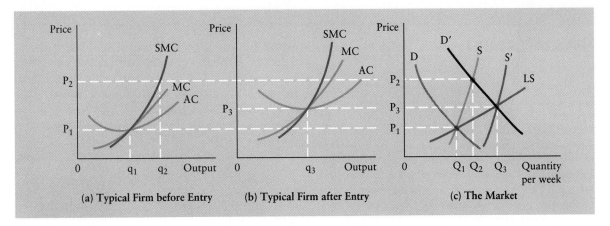

(a) Typical Firm before Entry (b) Typical Firm after Entry (c) The Market

Initially the market is in equilibrium at P_1, Q_1. An increase in demand (to D') causes price to rise to P_2 in the short run, and the typical firm produces q_2 at a profit. This profit attracts new firms into the industry. The entry of these new firms causes costs to rise to the levels shown in Panel b. With this new set of curves, equilibrium is reestablished in the market at P_3, Q_3. By considering many possible demand shifts and connecting all the resulting equilibrium points, the long-run supply curve LS is traced out.

Figure 12.8
An Increasing Cost Industry Has a Positively Sloped Long-Run Supply Curve

on governmental services (police forces, sewage treatment plants, and so forth), and these may show up as increased costs for all firms.

Figure 12.8 demonstrates market equilibrium in an **increasing cost industry**. The initial equilibrium price is P_1. At this price the typical firm in Panel a produces q_1, and total industry output, shown in Panel c, is Q_1. Suppose that the demand curve for the industry shifts outward to D'. In the short run, price will rise to P_2, which is where D' and the industry's short-run supply curve (S) intersect. At this price, the typical firm will produce q_2 and will earn a substantial profit. This profit attracts new entrants into the market and shifts the short-run supply curve outward.

Suppose that the entry of new firms causes the cost curves of all firms to rise. The new firms may, for example, compete for scarce inputs, driving up their prices. A typical firm's new (higher) set of cost curves is shown in Panel b of Figure 12.8. The new long-run equilibrium price for the industry is P_3 (here $P = MC = AC$), and at this price Q_3 is demanded. We now have two points (P_1, Q_1, and P_3, Q_3) on the long-run supply curve.[5] All other points on the curve can be found in an analogous way by considering all possible shifts in the demand curve. These shifts would trace out the long-run supply curve LS. Here LS has a positive slope because of the increasing cost nature of the industry. Therefore this positive slope is caused by whatever causes average costs to rise in response to entry. Most commonly, a positively sloped LS curve occurs because entry drives up input costs for all firms. The LS curve is somewhat flatter than the short-run supply curves, which indicates the greater flexibility in supply response that is still possible in the long run.

■
Increasing cost industry

An industry in which the entry of firms increases the costs of the firms in the industry.

[5]Figure 12.8 also shows the short-run supply curve associated with the point P_3, Q_3. This supply curve has shifted to the right because more firms are producing now than initially.

APPLICATION 12.4
Long-Run Supply Elasticities

Table 1 reports a number of long-run supply elasticity estimates that have been gathered from a variety of sources. Many of these concern natural resources; economists from the time of Thomas Malthus have been interested in the pricing effects of increasing demand for resources. Other estimates reported relate to crops and housing. In all cases, as we have shown, positive, non-infinite supply elasticities reflect the presence of increasing minimum average costs as output expands. As we now show, the reasons for such increases may be quite varied.

Agricultural Production

The estimated elasticities for agricultural products are "acreage elasticities." They reflect how acres planted in a particular crop respond to that crop's price. Assuming a constant yield per acre, we can translate them directly into the supply-elasticity concept. All of the reported elasticities are relatively low (less than 1.0). But all are positive, indicating that increases in prices do lead to increases in output. Of course, increases in agricultural output in recent years have come about mainly from improved technology (a shift in the supply curve). The data show that higher prices also lead to more land being planted. Rising opportunity costs associated with using that land for one crop rather than another probably explains the positively sloped supply curve.

Natural Resources

Two different types of supply elasticity are reported for natural resources in Table 1. For aluminum and chromium, the data refer to the relationship between annual production and market price. They show that the long-run supply of aluminum is nearly infinitely elastic at current market prices. This is due to the fact that additional alumina deposits are easy to develop using current technology. The supply elasticity for chromium is considerably lower, primarily because developing new deposits requires incurring much higher average costs than is the case for mining existing deposits.

For coal, natural gas, and oil, supply elasticities refer to the responsiveness of available reserves to price.

Table 1
Selected Estimates of Long-Run Supply Elasticities

Industry	Elasticity
Agricultural acreage:	
Cotton	0.67
Wheat	0.93
Corn	0.18
Aluminum	Nearly infinite
Chromium	0–3
Coal (eastern reserves)	15–30
Natural gas (U.S. reserves)	0.50
Oil (U.S. reserves)	.75–1.50

Sources: Agricultural acreage: M. Nerlove, "Estimates of the Elasticities of Supply of Selected Agricultural Commodities," *Journal of Farm Economics* (May 1956): 496–509. Aluminum and chromium: estimated from *Critical Materials Commodity Action Analysis* (Washington, D.C.: U.S. Department of the Interior, 1975). Coal: estimated from M. B. Zimmerman, "The Supply of Coal in the Long Run: The Case of Eastern Deep Coal" (Cambridge, Mass.: MIT Energy Laboratory Report No. MITEL 75-021, September 1975). Natural gas: J. D. Khazzoom, "The FPC Staff's Econometric Model of Natural Gas Supply in the United States," *The Bell Journal of Economics and Management Science* (Spring 1971). Oil: D. N. Epple, *Petroleum Discoveries and Government Policy* (Cambridge, Mass.: Marc Ballinger Publishing Company, 1984), Chapter 3.

The data show that coal reserves are far more price responsive than are oil and natural gas reserves. For oil and natural gas, most low-cost reserves have already been found. New reserves can be developed only at much higher costs. As for other natural resources, that result derives primarily from geology: Greater reserves of coal are easily within the reach of current mining methods.

To Think About

1. What does it mean to say some natural resources are scarcer than others? How is the formal concept of supply elasticity related to the more common-sense notion of scarcity?
2. The coal and oil supply elasticities in this example refer to finding reserves. How is this activity related to firms' decisions about how much coal or oil to produce from these reserves?

■ Long-Run Supply Elasticity

As we have just shown, the long-run supply curve for an industry is constructed by considering all possible shifts in the demand curve for the product. In order to predict the effects that such increases in demand will have on market price, it is therefore important to know something about the shape of the supply curve. A convenient measure for summarizing the shape of long-run supply curves is the **long-run elasticity of supply.** This concept records how proportional changes in price affect the quantity supplied, once all long-run adjustments have taken place. More formally:

$$\text{Long-run elasticity of supply} = \frac{\text{Percentage change in quantity supplied in long run}}{\text{Percentage change in price}} . \quad [12.5]$$

An elasticity of 10, for example, would indicate that a 1 percent increase in price would result in a 10 percent increase in the long-run quantity supplied. We would say that long-run supply is very price elastic: the long-run supply curve would be nearly horizontal. A principal implication of such a high price elasticity is that long-run equilibrium prices would not increase very much in response to outward shifts in the market demand curve.

A small supply elasticity would have a quite different implication. If the elasticity were only 0.1, for example, a 1 percent increase in price would increase quantity supplied by only 0.1 percent. In other words, the supply curve would be nearly vertical, and shifts outward in demand would result in rapidly rising prices without significant increases in quantity. Application 12.4. Long-Run Supply Elasticities uses this elasticity concept to describe evidence about the supply situation in various industries.

■ The Decreasing Cost Industry

Not all industries must exhibit constant or increasing costs. In some cases entry may reduce costs. The entry of new firms may provide a larger pool of trained labor to draw from than was previously available, which would reduce the costs of hiring new workers. The entry of new firms may also provide a "critical mass" of industrialization that permits the development of more efficient transportation, communications, and financial networks. Whatever the exact nature of the cost reductions, the final result is illustrated in the three panels of Figure 12.9. The initial market equilibrium is shown by the price quantity combination P_1, Q_1 in Panel c. At this price the typical firm in Panel a produces q_1 and earns exactly zero in economic profits. Now suppose market demand shifts outward to D'. In the short run, price will increase to P_2, and the typical firm will produce q_2. At this price level, positive profits are earned. These profits cause new firms to enter the market. If these entries cause costs to decline, a new set of cost curves for the typical firm might resemble those in Panel b. Now the new equilibrium price is P_3. At this price, Q_3 is demanded. By considering all possible shifts in demand, the long-run supply curve LS can be traced out. For this **decreasing cost industry** the long-run supply curve has a negative slope.

■
Long-run elasticity of supply

The percentage change in quantity supplied in the long run in response to a 1 percent change in price.

■
Decreasing cost industry

An industry in which the entry of firms decreases the costs of the firms in the industry.

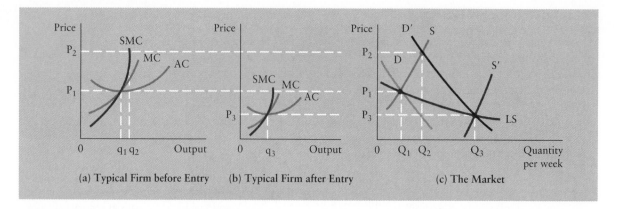

(a) Typical Firm before Entry   (b) Typical Firm after Entry   (c) The Market

Figure 12.9

A Decreasing Cost Industry Has a Negatively Sloped Long-Run Supply Curve

Initially the market is in equilibrium at P_1, Q_1. An increase in demand to D' causes price to rise to P_2 in the short run, and the typical firm produces q_2 at a profit. This profit attracts new firms to the industry. If the entry of these new firms causes costs to fall, a set of new cost curves might look like those in Panel b. With this new set of curves, market equilibrium is reestablished at P_3, Q_3. By connecting such points of equilibrium, a negatively sloped long-run supply curve LS is traced out.

■ **Infant Industries**

The possibility of a negatively sloped long-run supply curve is most commonly encountered in the case of newly-emerging, or "infant" industries. Initially, the costs of production of a new product may be very high. Few workers possess the skills needed to produce the good and procure other required inputs (such as communication networks or financing arrangements), which may be similarly underdeveloped. These difficulties are ameliorated as expanding production of the good yields a progressively larger pool of trained workers and a better developed set of necessary services. Likewise, the improved availability of inputs causes the costs of all firms within an infant industry to decline. For example, the development of the electronics industry in California's Silicon Valley or along Route 128 in Boston was undoubtedly aided by such cost-reducing economies stemming from the growing concentration of related firms in these areas.

Theoretical concepts about the ways that newly-established industries grow frequently have been applied to international trade policy. Because new industries have high costs, it is argued, they may not be able to compete against lower-cost, foreign competition. Given adequate protection (in the form of a tariff or quota) the domestic industry would grow, costs would fall, and eventually firms would be able to meet foreign competition. Although this argument undoubtedly has held some validity in times past (for example, protection of the U.S. textile industry in the early nineteenth century helped to make it the world's largest), today it is exploited by many industries simply wanting to be protected from foreign competitors. Application 12.5: Strategic Trade Policy looks at some current issues that surround this controversy.

APPLICATION 12.5

Strategic Trade Policy

Although the infant industry argument has been used for centuries to rationalize tariff protection, in recent years slightly different forms of the analysis have been used to justify an increasingly complex array of other protectionist measures. Generally these are categorized under the heading of "strategic trade policy" conveying the notion that government's "carefully targeted" policies help domestic firms achieve lower costs than their foreign rivals.[1] Here we look at two examples: (1) The European Airbus consortium; and (2) Japanese aid to the computer chip industry.

The European Airbus

In the 1970s, the governments of France, Germany, the United Kingdom, and Spain established Airbus Industries to compete with the U.S. companies Boeing and McDonnell Douglas in the production of wide-bodied airplanes. Together, these governments contributed about 20 to 30 percent of the costs of developing the A300 series of aircraft. Today, these models pose stiff sales competition for Boeing's line of 757 and 767 models.

The underlying rationale for the European government's assistance to Airbus rests on the observation that the early stages of developing new airplanes are very costly; alternative designs must be tested, special materials must be invented, and workers must be trained to perform to exacting specifications. However, costs decline dramatically as additional aircraft are produced, because fixed design costs then can be spread over more planes, and various kinks in the production process can eventually be worked out. In the absence of government subsidies, initial high costs might have deterred Airbus from entering the wide-body market, even though the firm could have become cost-competitive in the world market.

Computer RAM chips

Random Access Memory (RAM) chips are at the heart of modern desktop computers. The chips are produced by etching microcircuits on silicon wafers using various chemical baths. Considerable experience is needed to produce error-free versions of these complex chips, especially as engineers try to cram them with ever-increasing capacity. Throughout the 1970s, United States producers dominated the RAM market, claiming more than 70 percent of total sales. That situation began to change rapidly toward the end of the decade, as Japanese firms began to capture a large share of the market for the newly-developed 16K and 64K chips. How was Japan able to gain a foothold in this market given the experience (and lower costs) that U.S. firms had developed? Economists who have examined the record conclude that Japanese chip producers were able to gain a privileged position in their home market, largely protected from U.S. competition. Such protection resulted not from traditional tariffs or quotas on the importation of RAM chips, but, rather, was due to a web of close connections between Japanese computer firms (Fujitsu, Hitachi, NEC, and Toshiba) and the chip producers (who often were subsidiaries of the computer firms themselves). These linkages provided chip makers with the opportunity to achieve low-cost production methods without being forced to face outside competition from the outset. Indeed, a detailed simulation study of this market by R. E. Baldwin and P. R. Krugman concludes that, without this "breathing room," Japanese chip producers would never have entered the marketplace.[2] Because of their initial protection, Japanese firms have come to rival or even surpass U.S. firms in the worldwide marketplace for RAM chips.

To Think About

1. The Airbus case involves explicit government subsidies as a way to lower initial costs. Do you think U.S. producers such as Boeing and McDonnell Douglas received similar subsidies? Does the infant industry argument require that these subsidies eventually end?

2. In the RAM chip case, direct governmental subsidies were of minor importance. Who, then, subsidized the initial high costs of Japanese chip makers? Why were these subsidies made?

[1]See Paul R. Krugman, *Strategic Trade Policy and the New International Economics* (Cambridge, Mass.: MIT Press, 1986).
[2]R. E. Baldwin and P. R. Krugman, "Market Access and International Competition: A Simulation Study of 16K Random Access Memories," in R. Feenstra (ed.), *Empirical Studies of International Trade* (Cambridge, Mass.: MIT Press, 1988).

Summary

The model of pricing in perfectly competitive markets that we present in this chapter is probably the most widely used economic model. Even when markets do not strictly obey all of the assumptions of perfect competition, it is still frequently possible to use that model as a reasonable approximation of how such markets work. Some of the basic features of the perfectly competitive model that are highlighted in this chapter are

- The short-run supply curve in a perfectly competitive market represents the horizontal sum of the short-run supply curves for many price-taking firms. The upward slope of the short-run supply curve reflects these firms' increasing short-run marginal costs.

- Equilibrium prices are determined in the short run by the interaction of the short-run supply curve with the market demand curve. At the equilibrium price, firms are willing to produce precisely the amount of output that people want to buy.

- Shifts in either the demand curve or the supply curve will change the equilibrium price. The extent of such a change depends on the particular shape of the two curves.

- Economic profits will attract entrants into a perfectly competitive market in the long run. This entry will continue until economic profits are reduced to zero. At that point, the market price will equal long-run average cost, and each firm will be operating at the low point of its long-run average cost curve.

- Entry of new firms may have an effect on the cost of firms' inputs. In the constant cost case, however, input costs are not affected, so the long-run supply curve is horizontal. If entry raises input costs, the long-run supply curve is upward sloping. If entry reduces such costs, the long-run supply curve is downward sloping.

Review Questions

1. Explain how a market with a fixed supply (such as that shown in Figure 12.1) reaches an equilibrium price. How would market participants know that a non-equilibrium price was too high or too low? How might you use a graph such as this one to explain the way prices are established in an auction?

2. One assumption of a perfectly competitive market is that every firm faces the same, known price. How is this assumption reflected in Figure 12.2? Why do

economists believe markets for homogeneous goods may reasonably be assumed to exhibit the "law of one price"?

3. Why is the price for which quantity demanded equals quantity supplied called an "equilibrium price"? Suppose, instead, we viewed a demand curve as showing what price consumers are willing to pay and a supply curve as showing what price firms want to receive. Using this view of demand and supply, how would you define an "equilibrium quantity"?

4. "For markets with inelastic demand and supply curves, most short-run movements will be in prices, not quantity. For markets with elastic demand and supply curves, most movements will be in quantity, not price." Do you agree? Illustrate your answer with a few simple graphs.

5. Why would firms stay in an industry that only promised zero long-run profits? Why would firms ever want to enter such an industry? Wouldn't a firm's owners do better to invest somewhere else?

6. In long-run equilibrium in a perfectly competitive market, each firm operates at minimal average cost. Do firms also operate at minimum long-run average cost when such markets are out of equilibrium in the short run? Wouldn't firms make more in short-run profits if they opted always to produce that output level for which average costs were as small as possible?

7. What do economists assume about the long-run supply elasticities for the inputs used by a constant cost industry? In what situations would this assumption seem reasonable? When might it be unreasonable?

8. "Ultimately the long-run supply elasticity for an increasing cost industry is determined by the supply elasticities of the inputs it uses." Explain why this is so by comparing a case where a principal input (say, labor) is elastically supplied to a case where labor supply is inelastic.

9. Use your analysis from review question 8 to show that a decline in demand for a good that is produced by an increasing cost industry will have significant effects on inputs that are inelastically supplied to the industry. Why won't such a decline have a major negative effect on inputs that have elastic supplies or on the owners of the firms that may exit the industry?

10. "The existence of decreasing cost industries ultimately depends on the availability of inputs that also have negatively sloped supply curves. If firms themselves took actions that reduced costs, they would appropriate these cost reductions for themselves, and they would not spread to other firms." Do you agree? Or may some cost reductions not be fully appropriable by the firm that causes them?

Problems

12.1 Suppose the daily demand curve for flounder at Cape May is given by

$$Q_D = 1,600 - 600P$$

where Q_D is demand in pounds per day and P is price per pound.

a. If fishing boats land 1,000 pounds one day, what will the price be?
b. If the catch were to fall to 400 pounds, what would the price be?
c. Suppose the demand for flounder shifts outward to

$$Q_D' = 2,200 - 600P.$$

How would your answers to parts a and b change?
d. Graph your results.

12.2 Suppose, as in problem 12.1, the demand for flounder is given by

$$Q_D' = 1,600 - 600P,$$

but now assume that Cape May fishermen can, at some cost, choose to sell their catch elsewhere. Specifically, assume that the amount they will sell in Cape May is given by

$$Q_S = -1,000 + 2,000P \text{ for } Q_S \geq 0$$

where Q_S is the quantity supplied in pounds and P is the price per pound.

a. At least what price will flounder have to be if any is to be supplied to the Cape May market?
b. Given the demand curve for flounder, what will the equilibrium price be?
c. Suppose now, as in problem 12.1, demand shifts to
   $Q_D' = 2,200 - 600P.$
   What will be the new equilibrium price?
d. Explain intuitively why price will rise by less in part c than it did in problem 12.1.
e. Graph your results.

12.3 A perfectly competitive market has 1,000 firms. In the very short run each of the firms has a fixed supply of 100 units. The market demand is given by

$$Q = 160,000 - 10,000P.$$

a. Calculate the equilibrium price in the very short run.
b. Calculate the demand schedule facing any one firm in the industry. Do this by calculating what the equilibrium price would be if one of the sellers decided to sell nothing or if one seller decided to sell 200 units. What do you conclude about the effect of any one firm on market price?

12.4 Assuming the same conditions as in problem 12.3, suppose now that in the short run each firm has a supply curve that shows the quantity the firm will supply (q_i) as a function of market price. The specific form of this supply curve is given by

$$q_i = -200 + 50P.$$

Using this short-run supply response, supply new solutions to parts a and b in problem 12.3. Why do you get different solutions in this case?

12.5 Widgets, Inc. is a small firm producing widgets. The widget industry is perfectly competitive; Widgets, Inc. is a price taker. The short-run total cost curve for Widgets, Inc. has the form:

$$STC = 1/3 \; q^3 + 10q^2 + 100q + 48$$

and the short-run marginal cost curve is given by

$$SMC = q^2 + 20q + 100.$$

a. Calculate the firm's short-run supply curve with q (the number of widgets produced per day) as a function of market price (P).
b. How many widgets will the firm produce if the market price is P = 121? P = 169? P = 256? (Assume variable costs are covered.)
c. How much profit will Widgets, Inc. make when P = 121? P = 169? P = 256?

12.6 Suppose there are one hundred identical firms in the perfectly competitive note-card industry. Each firm has a short-run total cost curve of the form:

$$STC = 1/300q^3 + 0.2q^2 + 4q + 10,$$

and marginal cost is given by

$$SMC = .01q^2 + .4q + 4.$$

a. Calculate the firm's short-run supply curve with q (the number of crates of notecards) as a function of market price (P).
b. On the assumption that there are no interaction effects between costs of the firms in the industry, calculate the industry supply curve.
c. Suppose market demand is given by Q = −200P + 8,000. What will be the short-run equilibrium price-quantity combination?
d. Suppose everyone starts writing more research papers, and the new market demand is given by Q = −200P + 10,000. What is the new short-run price-quantity equilibrium? How much profit does each firm make?

*12.7 Suppose there are 1,000 identical firms producing diamonds and that the total cost curve for each firm is given by

$$TC = q^2 + wq$$

and marginal cost is given by

$$MC = 2q + w$$

where q is the firm's output level and w is the wage rate of diamond cutters.

a. If w = 10, what will be the firm's (short-run) supply curve? What is the industry's supply curve? How many diamonds will be produced at a price of 20 each? How many more diamonds would be produced at a price of 21?
b. Suppose that the wages of diamond cutters depend on the total quantity of diamonds produced and the form of this relationship is given by

$$w = .002Q$$

where Q represents total industry output, which is 1,000 times the output of the typical firm. In this situation show that the firm's marginal cost (and short-run supply) curve depends on Q. What is the industry supply curve? How much will be produced at a price of 20? How much more will be produced at a price of 21? What do you conclude about the shape of the short-run supply curve?

12.8 Wheat is produced under perfectly competitive conditions. Individual wheat farmers have U-shaped, long-run average cost curves that reach a minimum average cost of $3 per bushel when 1,000 bushels are produced.

a. If the market demand curve for wheat is given by

$$Q_D = 2,600,000 - 200,000P$$

where Q_D is the number of bushels demanded per year and P is the price per bushel, in long-run equilibrium what will be the price of wheat? How much total wheat will be demanded? How many wheat farms will there be?

b. Suppose demand shifts outward to

$$Q_D = 3,200,000 - 200,000P.$$

If farmers cannot adjust their output in the short run (that is, suppose the SMC curve is vertical), what will market price be with this new demand curve? What will the profits of the typical farm be?

c. Given the new demand curve described in part b, what will be the new long-run equilibrium? (That is, calculate market price, quantity of wheat produced, and the new equilibrium number of farms in this new situation.)

d. Graph your results.

* 12.9 Gasoline is sold through local gasoline stations under perfectly competitive conditions. All gasoline station owners face the same long-run average cost curve given by

$$AC = .01q - 1 + 100/q$$

and the same long-run marginal cost curve given by

$$MC = .02q - 1$$

where q is the number of gallons sold per day.

a. Assuming the market is in long-run equilibrium, how much gasoline will each individual owner sell per day? What are the long-run average cost and marginal cost at this output level?

b. The market demand for gasoline is given by

$$Q_D = 2,500,000 - 500,000P$$

---

*Denotes a problem that is rather difficult.

where Q_D is the number of gallons demanded per day and P is the price per gallon. Given your answer to part a, what will be the price of gasoline in long-run equilibrium? How much gasoline will be demanded and how many gas stations will there be?

c. Suppose that because of the development of solar-powered cars, the market demand for gasoline shifts inward to

$$Q_D = 2,000,000 - 1,000,000P.$$

In long-run equilibrium, what will be the price of gasoline, how much total gasoline will be demanded, and how many gas stations will there be?

d. Graph your results.

* 12.10 A perfectly competitive painted necktie industry has a large number of potential entrants. Each firm has an identical cost structure such that long-run average cost is minimized at an output of 20 units ($q_i = 20$). The minimum average cost is \$10 per unit. Total market demand is given by

$$Q = 1,500 - 50P.$$

a. What is the industry's long-run supply schedule?

b. What is the long-run equilibrium price (P*)? The total industry output (Q*)? The output of each firm (q_i*)? The number of firms? The profits of each firm?

c. The short-run total cost curve associated with each firm's long-run equilibrium output is given by

$$STC = .5q^2 - 10q + 200$$

where $SMC = q - 10$. Calculate the short-run average and marginal cost curves. At what necktie output level does short-run average cost reach a minimum?

d. Calculate the short-run supply curve for each firm and the industry short-run supply curve.

e. Suppose now painted neckties become more fashionable and the market demand function shifts upward to $Q = 2,000 - 50P$. Using this new demand curve, answer part b for the very short run when firms cannot change their outputs.

f. In the short run, use the industry short-run supply curve to recalculate the answers to part b.

g. What is the new long-run equilibrium for the industry?

---

*Denotes a problem that is rather difficult.

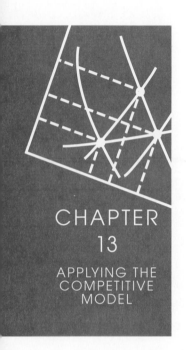

CHAPTER
13

APPLYING THE COMPETITIVE MODEL

I n Chapter 1, we encountered the educated parrot who became an economist by learning to say "Supply and Demand." Now that we have provided a detailed development of the basic supply-demand model that all economists use, it's time to show how it can be applied to a variety of real-world situations. Not only does the competitive model offer a good starting point for making predictions about how prices or quantities will change when conditions change, but, as we will see, the model also allows us to say quite a bit about who will be helped and who will be hurt by these changes. Of course, the competitive model of supply and demand is based on certain assumptions that may not hold in many circumstances. When these assumptions are violated it may be important to look at a situation differently, as we shall do in later chapters. For now, however, we focus on how the competitive model can be used to get a start on many different problems.

Consumer and Producer Surplus

In Chapter 6, we introduce the concept of **consumer surplus** as a way of illustrating part of the total value that people receive from consuming a good. Figure 13.1 illustrates this concept by showing the competitive equilibrium that might be established in, say, the market for fresh tomatoes. At the equilibrium price of P* individuals choose to consume Q* tomatoes. As we showed in Chapter 6, the total value to these buyers of their tomato purchases (relative to a situation where there were no tomatoes) is given by the area below the demand curve between 0 and Q*; that is, by area AEQ*0. For this value they pay an amount given by P*EQ*0 and hence receive a "surplus" (over what they pay) given by the gray shaded area AEP*. Possible happenings in the tomato market that change the size of this area clearly affect individuals' well-being.

Figure 13.1 also can be used to illustrate the surplus value received by tomato producers relative to a situation where no tomatoes are produced. This measure is based on the intuitive notion that the supply curve, S, shows the minimum price that producers would accept for each unit produced. At the market equilibrium P*,Q* producers receive total revenue of P*EQ*0. But under a scheme of selling one unit at a time at the lowest possible price, they would have been willing to produce Q* for a payment of BEQ*0. At Q*, therefore, they receive a **producer surplus** given by the colored area P*EB. To understand the precise nature of this surplus, we must again examine the short-run, long-run distinction in firms' supply decisions.

◼ Short-Run Producer Surplus

In Figure 13.1, the supply curve, S, is not referred to as either a short-run or a long-run supply curve. However, in Chapter 12, we showed that the upward slope of S (and hence the size of total producer surplus) has rather different causes in these two cases. In the short run, the market supply curve is the horizontal summation of all firms' short-run marginal cost curves. The curve's positive slope reflects the diminishing returns to fixed inputs that are encountered as output is increased. In this case, price exceeds marginal cost (as reflected by the supply curve) at all output levels, except Q*. Production of each of these "intra-marginal" units of output generates incremental profits for the firm. Firms' total short-run profits, then, are given by the sum of all of these profit increments (area P*EB) *less* short-run fixed costs, which must be paid no matter how much is produced. Short-run producer surplus (also area P*EB) therefore reflects the sum of both short-run profits and short-run fixed costs. It includes that part of total profits that is in excess of the profits firms would have if they chose to produce nothing (in which case they would suffer a loss equal to fixed costs). In this sense, short-run producer surplus mirrors consumer surplus, which measures what consumers would lose if nothing were produced.

◼
Consumer surplus
The extra value individuals receive from consuming a good over what they pay for it. What people would be willing to pay for the right to consume a good at its current price.

◼
Producer surplus
The extra value producers get for a good in excess of the opportunity costs they incur by producing it. What all producers would pay for the right to sell a good at its current market price.

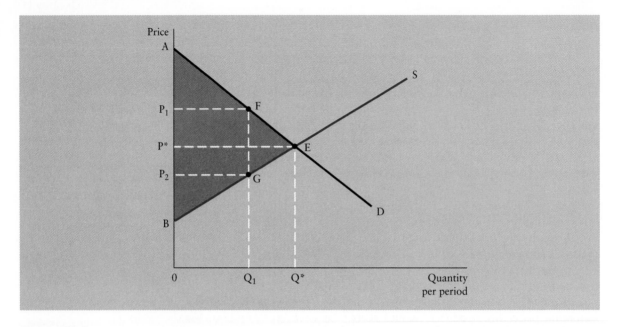

Figure 13.1
Competitive
Equilibrium and
Consumer/Producer
Surplus

At the competitive equilibrium (Q^*) the sum of consumer surplus (shaded gray) and producer surplus (shaded in color) is maximized. For an output level less than Q^*, say Q_1, there is a deadweight loss of consumer and producer surplus given by area FEG.

■ Long-Run Producer Surplus

In the long run, positively sloped supply curves arise because firms experience increasing costs. When the market is in equilibrium, each firm has zero profits and there are no fixed costs. Short-run producer surplus does not exist in this situation. Instead, long-run producer surplus now reflects the increasing payments being received by the firms' inputs as output expands. The area P^*EB in Figure 13.1 measures all of these increased payments relative to a situation in which the industry produces no output and its inputs therefore would receive much lower prices for their services.

■ Ricardian Rent

Long-run producer surplus can be most easily illustrated with a situation first described by David Ricardo in the early part of the nineteenth century.[1] Assume there are many parcels of land on which tomatoes might be grown.

[1]See David Ricardo, *The Principles of Political Economy and Taxation* (1817; reprinted London: J. M. Dent and Son, 1965), Chapters 2 and 32.

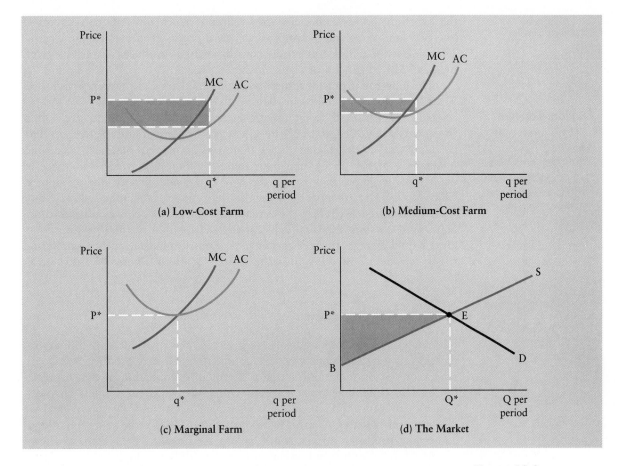

Low-cost and medium-cost farms can earn long-run profits (color shading) if these costs reflect ownership of unique resources. Total Ricardian rent represents producer surplus—area P*EB in Panel d. Sometimes Ricardian rents will be capitalized into resource prices.

Figure 13.2
Ricardian Rent

These range from very fertile land (low costs of production) to very poor, dry land (high costs). The long-run supply curve for tomatoes is constructed as follows. At low prices only the best land is used to produce tomatoes, and few are produced. As output increases, higher-cost plots of land are brought into production because higher prices make it profitable to grow tomatoes on this land. The long-run supply curve for tomatoes is positively sloped because of the increasing costs associated with using less fertile land.

Market equilibrium in this situation is illustrated in Figure 13.2. At an equilibrium price of P* both the low-cost and the medium-cost farms earn (long-run) profits. The "marginal farm" earns exactly zero economic profits. Farms with even higher costs stay out of the market because they would incur losses at a price of P*. Profits earned by the intra-marginal farms can persist in the long run, however, because they reflect a return to a unique resource—low-cost land. Free entry cannot erode these profits even over the long term. The sum of these long-run profits constitutes total producer surplus as given by area P*EB in Panel d of Figure 13.2.

The long-run profits illustrated in Figure 13.2 are sometimes referred to as **Ricardian rent.** They represent the returns obtained by the owners of unique resources (in this case, fertile tomato-growing land) in a marketplace. Often these rents will be "capitalized" into the prices of these resources; in short, fertile land will sell for higher prices than will poor land. Similarly, rich gold mines have higher prices than poor mines, favorably located retail space in malls rents for more than out-of-the-way space, and airport landing slots at Chicago's O'Hare are more valuable than slots at airports in the Yukon. All of these rents ultimately reflect the demand for the goods being produced. If demand were to shift, the total value of these rents (that is, total producer surplus) would change. In Application 13.1: Rent Capitalization of Commuting Costs, we show how the value of favorable locations ultimately shows up in house prices.

> ■ **Ricardian rent**
>
> Long-run profits earned by owners of low-cost firms. May be capitalized into the price of these firms' inputs.

■ Economic Efficiency

Our analysis of producer and consumer surplus also provides a preliminary indication of why economists believe competitive markets produce "efficient" allocations of resources. Although a thorough examination of that topic requires that we look at many markets (which we will do in the next chapter), here we can return to Figure 13.1 as a simple illustration. Any output level for tomatoes other than Q^* in this figure is inefficient in that the sum total of consumer and producer surplus is not as large as possible. If Q_1 tomatoes were produced, for example, a total surplus of area FEG would be forgone. At Q_1 demanders are willing to pay P_1 for another tomato, which would cost only P_2 to produce. That gap suggests that there exists a mutually beneficial transaction (such as producing one more tomato at a price of P^*) that could benefit both demanders (who would get the tomato for less than they were willing to pay) and suppliers (who would get more for the tomato than it would cost to produce). Only at Q^* are all such mutually beneficial transactions consummated and only then is the sum of consumer and producer surplus as large as possible.[2] Of course, a full discussion of efficiency in resource allocation will require us to be much more precise about the concepts we are using. However, it is helpful to use very simple supply models to illustrate the inefficiency of certain situations. Application 13.2: Missing Markets shows how this can be done in one common situation where trading is prevented by law, custom, or cost. More generally, much of the remainder of this chapter illustrates how changes in consumer or producer surplus can be used to judge the consequences of various policies for the economic welfare of market participants.

---

[2]Producing more than Q^* would also reduce total producer and consumer surplus since consumers' willingness to pay for extra output would fall short of the costs of producing that output.

APPLICATION 13.1
Rent Capitalization of Commuting Costs

One of the major ways suburban communities differ in their attractiveness to homebuyers is in their convenient location to places of work. Among houses with otherwise similar characteristics (for example, square feet of living space, air conditioning, lot size, and so forth), it would be expected that houses in easily accessible locations would command higher prices than those in locations requiring lengthy commuting. In other words, low commuting costs would be "capitalized" into the market prices of houses, just as in Ricardo's analysis—land's superior fertility and ability to earn rent would be reflected in its market value.

Evidence from the Housing Market
The question of how commuting costs are reflected in property values has been examined in a number of studies. In one of the most complete studies, J. P. Nelson focused on the Washington, D.C., metropolitan area for 1970.[1] By carefully controlling for the many other factors that influence the demand for housing, Nelson estimated that each minute of daily commuting time to major employment areas in Washington reduced house values by about $190. A home that sold for $50,000 in an area that involved about half an hour of commuting time would sell for about $44,300 in an area that required an hour commute. In fact, housing prices in metropolitan areas throughout the United States suggest that this type of price decline with respect to commuting costs may be quite common. Not only do prices seem to reflect automobile commuting times, but houses located near major railroad lines (say, in New York City, or suburbs in New Jersey or Connecticut) have higher prices than those located elsewhere.

The Value of Time
One way Nelson was able to check his estimate of the extent to which commuting costs were capitalized in house values was to calculate the implicit value that people placed on their own time. By assuming a certain number of commuting trips per year he was able to cal-culate an implicit value of commuting time of around $1.85 per hour (or about one-third of workers' average after-tax wage rates in 1970). That figure was quite consistent with a variety of other studies showing how individuals make choices among ways of getting to work that show an implicit time value of between one-third and one-half the market wage.

Capitalization of Other Amenities
This general procedure for using the value of an asset (here, houses) to study the capitalization of amenity values is quite common in empirical economics. We already encountered this technique in Application 6.2: Valuing Clean Air. There we showed that housing prices reflect the high costs of air pollution. Similar findings show the capitalization into house prices of the negative effects of airport noise, urban crime, and proximity to college fraternity houses. Prices for other durable assets have also been found to reflect capitalized cost differences. For example, used automobile prices reflect frequency-of-repair statistics for various models, and prices for used farm equipment reflect different brands' perceived reliability. In all of these cases, the initial price of these goods is irrelevant to the prices settled on in transactions of used goods, which will depend only on the benefits and costs of using the goods in the future.

To Think About
1. Some stores advertise that they have low prices because they don't have to pay "high downtown rents." Would Ricardo's analysis support this assessment? What elements of "price" in addition to out-of-pocket expenses should enter into a full analysis of why shoppers patronize various locations?

2. If buyers of durable assets have to pay prices that reflect all cost differences, would there ever be any pure economic profits in the long run? Wouldn't all firms' costs be the same once the costs of more productive durable assets were properly measured?

[1] J. P. Nelson, "Accessibility and the Value of Time in Commuting," *Southern Economic Journal* (January 1977): 1321–1329.

APPLICATION 13.2

Missing Markets

Our demonstration of the economic efficiency of voluntary market transactions requires that such markets, in fact, exist. Buyers and sellers need a "place" to conduct their trades. If the costs involved in establishing a market are high or if establishing such a market is not legally permitted, these trades will not occur and the resulting allocation of resources may be inefficient.

Transactions Costs

By referring to Figure 1, it is easy to see why high transactions costs may prevent the establishment of a market. The total gain per week from voluntary transactions in the market in Figure 1 is represented by area P_2EP_1. If the cost of conducting transactions (say, the rent on the building where the sales occur or the wages of an auctioneer hired to establish equilibrium prices) exceeds this amount, actors in this market would find it preferable to abstain from trading. None of this good will be produced and exchanged.

Instances of potentially high transactions costs deterring possible transactions are fairly common. For example, rental markets for such items as television sets, photographic equipment, or business suits are generally not very well developed. The costs involved in operating the rental outlet and assuring the item is returned in good condition probably exceed the potential value of rental transactions to traders. For other items such as automobiles or video cassettes, transactions costs are low relative to the value of potential rental transactions and for these goods, rental markets thrive.

Legal Market Restrictions—The Case of Directory Assistance

Sometimes the development of markets may be restricted by the law. For about two-thirds of the phone systems in the United States, it is illegal to charge for directory assistance even though the provision of this service obviously involves some costs. Contrary to the transactions costs case, this restriction leads to an overuse of directory assistance. Because the price of the service is set at zero, individuals will demand quantity Q_0. Area AQ_0E provides a measure of the value of inefficient transactions in directory assistance that occur as a result of failing to charge for the service—these are uses

Figure 1
Reasons for Missing Markets

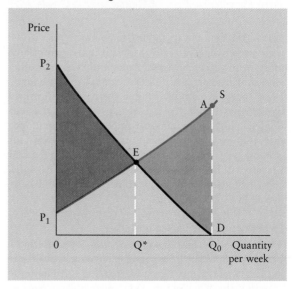

If transactions costs exceed the total gains from voluntary transactions (area P_2EP_1), no goods may be traded in a market. Requiring a zero price in a market will result in consumption of Q_0 and a welfare loss represented by area AQ_0E.

of directory assistance for which the value of the services received falls short of the cost of providing them.

A 1980 study of directory assistance usage suggests that these costs may be rather high.[1] Overall, the authors found that these costs in 1978 amounted to $750 million—more than half of the total cost of providing directory assistance to the jurisdictions that forbid its pricing. They also point out that most of these inefficient uses are made by relatively few customers (those who never use a phone book) and that the subsidy provided to these users may cause general phone service to be more expensive than it should be.

To Think About

1. If high transactions costs prevent all trading, should this situation be called "inefficient"? Is it better to devote resources to making the transactions, or simply forget the whole thing?
2. Might a zero-price regulation make sense if the costs of billing for directory assistance were high?

[1]A. Daly and T. Mayer, "Estimating the Value of a Missing Market: The Economics of Directory Assistance," *Journal of Law and Economics* (April 1980): 147–166.

■ Numerical Illustration

In Chapter 12, we looked at a hypothetical market for cassette tapes in which demand was represented by

$$Q = 10 - P \qquad\qquad\qquad [13.1]$$

and supply by

$$Q = P - 2. \qquad\qquad\qquad [13.2]$$

We showed that equilibrium in this market occurs at P* = $6 and Q* = 4 tapes per week. Figure 13.3 repeats Figure 12.6 by providing an illustration of this equilibrium. At point E consumers are spending $24 (= 6 · 4) per week for tapes. Total consumer surplus is given by the gray triangular area in the figure and amounts to $8 (= ½ of 4 · 4) per week. At E producers also receive revenues of $24 per week and gain a producer surplus of $8 per week as reflected by the colored triangle. Total consumer and producer surplus is therefore $16 per week.

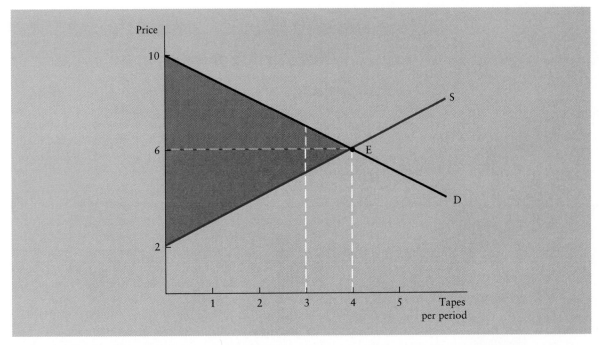

Equilibrium in the cassette tape market yields a price of $6 and a quantity of four tapes per week. Consumer surplus (shaded gray) and producer surplus (shaded in color) are each $8. An output of three tapes per week would reduce the sum of consumer and producer surplus from $16 to $15.

Figure 13.3
Efficiency in Tape Sales

The inefficiency of other potential tape output levels can also be illustrated with the help of Figure 13.3. If price remains at $6 but output is only three tapes per week, for example, consumers and producers each receive $7.50 per week of surplus in their transactions. Total consumer and producer surplus is $15 per week—a reduction of $1 from what it is at E. Total surplus would still be $15 per week with output of three tapes per week at any other price we might have chosen. Once output is specified, the price at which transactions occur affects the distribution of surplus between consumers and producers. But the transaction price does not affect the total amount of surplus, which is always given by the area between the demand curve and the supply curve.

Output levels greater than four tapes per week are also inefficient. For example, production of five tapes per week at a transaction price of $6 would again generate consumer surplus of $7.50 ($8 for the four tapes transaction less a loss of $.50 on the sale of the fifth tape, since the tapes sell for more than people are willing to pay). Similarly, a producer surplus of $7.50 would occur representing a loss of $.50 in the production of the fifth tape. Total surplus at this point is now $15 per week, one dollar less than at the market equilibrium. Again, the actual price assumed here doesn't matter—it is the fact that costs (reflected by the supply curve, S) exceed individuals' willingness to pay (reflected by the demand curve, D) for output levels greater than four tapes per week that results in the loss of total surplus value.

Price Controls and Shortages

Sometimes governments may seek to control prices at below equilibrium levels. Although adoption of such policies is usually claimed to be based on noble motives, frequently the controls deter long-run supply responses and create welfare losses for both consumers and producers. A simple analysis of this possibility is provided by Figure 13.4. Initially the market is in long-run equilibrium at P_1, Q_1 (point E). An increase in demand from D to D' would cause the price to rise to P_2 in the short run and encourage entry by new firms. Assuming this market is characterized by increasing costs (as reflected in the long-run supply curve, LS), price would fall somewhat as a result of this entry, ultimately settling at P_3. If these price changes were regarded as undesirable, the government could, in principle, prevent them by imposing a legally enforceable ceiling price of P_1. This would cause firms to continue to supply their previous output (Q_1) and, because at P_1 demanders now want to purchase Q_4, there will be a shortage, given by $Q_4 - Q_1$.

The welfare consequences of this price-control policy can be evaluated by comparing consumer and producer surplus measures prevailing under this policy to those that would have prevailed in the absence of controls. First, the buyers of Q_1 gain consumer surplus given by the gray area P_3CEP_1 because they can buy this good at a lower price than would exist in an uncontrolled market. This gain reflects a pure transfer from the level of producer surplus that would exist without controls. What current consumers have gained from the lower price,

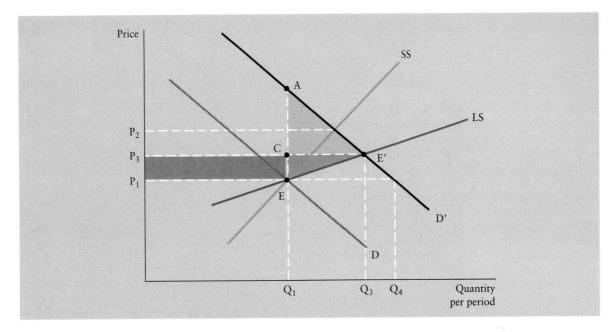

A shift in demand from D to D′ would raise price to P_2 in the short run. Entry over the long run would yield a final equilibrium of P_3, Q_3. Controlling the price at P_1 would prevent these actions and yield a shortage of $Q_4 - Q_1$. Relative to the uncontrolled situation, the price control yields a transfer from producers to consumers (shaded gray) and a deadweight loss of forgone transactions given by the two areas shaded in color.

Figure 13.4
Price Controls and Shortages

producers have lost. Though this transfer does not represent a loss of overall welfare, it does clearly affect the relative well-being of the market participants.

Second, the lightly colored area AE′C represents the value of additional consumer surplus that would have been attained without controls. Similarly, the darkly colored area CE′E reflects additional producer surplus available in the uncontrolled situation. Together these two areas (that is, area AE′E) represent the total value of mutually beneficial transactions that are prevented by the government policy of controlling price. This is, therefore, a measure of the pure welfare costs of that policy.

Finally, the welfare analysis associated with Figure 13.4 also provides some insights about the politics of any price control policy. Buyers who are able to get output Q_1 at a price of P_1 will be big supporters of the policy because they obtain substantial welfare benefits. Those benefits, however, come at the expense of producers of Q_1 who, because they earn less than they might, would likely oppose the policy. Both producers and consumers who wish to make transactions for amounts greater than Q_1 lose and they might also oppose the policy. They might, in fact, seek ways around the price controls by engaging in illegal transactions at prices higher than P_1. All of these likelihoods are supported by the analysis of Application 13.3: Rent Controls, which looks at perhaps the most widespread price-control policy.

APPLICATION 13.3

Rent Controls

During World War II, many American cities adopted controls on rent in order to stop rising prices that were occurring as a result of increased demand. Many cities (notably New York) and several European countries still maintain such controls. These are usually rationalized on the grounds that landlords (who are assumed to be rich) should not be allowed to exploit tenants (who are assumed to be poor). Without examining the facts behind such asserted principles of fairness (which are often incorrect), the economic implications of controls are clearly predicted by the competitive model: shortages will result.

Table 1 provides some evidence on shortages in the city of Stockholm during the 1950s. The data report the average period in months that families had to wait for an apartment. The data show that this period lengthened greatly during the 1950s as postwar increases in income sharply increased the demand for housing and rent controls retarded long-run supply responses. Existing tenants may have benefitted from lower rents, but substantial costs were imposed on families who had to wait more than three years to find a place of their own in which to live.

Rent Control and Housing Conditions

The effects of rent controls also show up in many other ways. In addition to the shortfall in the quantity of housing, the quality of housing may also deteriorate as landlords find it unprofitable to make repairs. For example, one study found that repair expenditures in 1967 on rent-controlled apartments in New York City averaged only about one-half of the expenditures on similar apartments that were not subject to rent controls.[1] Elective repairs (that is, those in excess of minimal requirements for health and safety) were particularly unlikely to be made in the rent-controlled apartments. Sometimes owners may simply give up. More than 2,000 rental units are abandoned in New York City each month for this reason. Indeed, the effects of rent control on the condition of housing have caused some economists to equate these ef-

Table 1

Waiting Time in Months for an Apartment in Stockholm

Year	Wait	Year	Wait
1950	9	1955	23
1951	15	1956	30
1952	21	1957	35
1953	24	1958	40
1954	26		

Source: S. Rydenfelt, "Rent Control Thirty Years On," in *Verdict on Rent Control* (London: Institute for Economic Affairs, 1972), p. 65.

fects to the devastation caused by bombing. Vietnamese Foreign Minister Nguyen Co Thach is reported to have said, "The Americans couldn't destroy Hanoi by bombing, but we have done the job by setting low rents."[2]

Rent Control and Tenants

Finally, tenants of rent-controlled apartments may sometimes take advantage of their possession of a good for which there is excess demand. It is a common practice in many cities to require that new tenants pay "key money" to existing tenants for the right to take over their leases. Or sometimes existing tenants will charge new tenants exorbitant prices for the curtain rods or the refrigerator. In this way, some of the mutually beneficial transactions that are prevented by rent controls end up being accomplished through illegal means.

To Think About

1. Why do communities vote for rent controls if their effects are so negative? Who gains and who loses from the controls? Do losers from rent control have as much political clout as the gainers?
2. Some cities with rent control also provide for "vacancy decontrol"—that is, rents can be raised on vacated apartments. How might existing tenants respond to such provisions? What would you expect to happen to the number of vacancies?

---

[1] George Sternlieb, *The Urban Housing Dilemma* (New York: Housing and Development Administration, 1972), p. 202.
[2] Quoted in *Fortune*, February 27, 1989, p. 134.

Tax Incidence

Another important application of the perfectly competitive model is to the study of the effects of taxes. Not only does the model permit an evaluation of how taxation alters the allocation of resources, but it also highlights the issue of who bears the actual burden of various taxes. By stressing the distinction between the legal obligation to pay a tax and the economic interactions that may shift that burden elsewhere, **tax incidence theory** helps to clarify the ways in which taxes actually affect individuals' well-being.

Figure 13.5 illustrates this approach by considering a "specific tax" of a fixed amount per unit of output that is imposed on all firms in a constant cost industry. Although legally the tax is required to be *paid* by the firm, this view of things may be quite misleading. To demonstrate this, we begin by noting that this tax can be analyzed as a shift downward in the demand curve facing this industry from D to D', where the vertical distance between the curves reflects the amount of the per unit tax, t. For any price that consumers pay (say, P) firms get to keep only P − t. It is that after-tax demand curve D', then, that is relevant to firms' behavior. Consumers continue to pay a "gross" price as reflected by the demand curve D. As we saw in Application 6.1, the tax creates a "wedge" between what consumers pay and what firms actually get to keep.

Tax incidence theory

The study of the final burden of a tax after considering all market reactions to it.

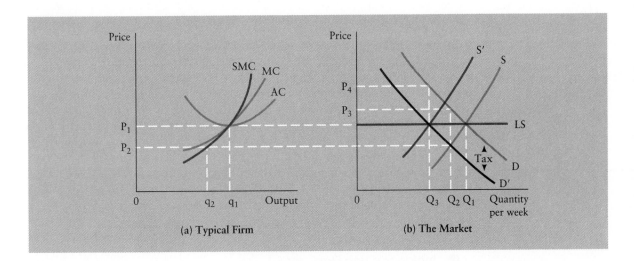

(a) Typical Firm   (b) The Market

A specific commodity tax of amount t lowers the after-tax demand curve to D'. With this "new" demand curve, Q_2 will be produced in the short run at an after-tax price of P_2. In the long run, firms will leave the industry and the price will return to P_1. The entire amount of the tax is shifted onto consumers in the form of a higher market price (P_4).

Figure 13.5
Effect of the Imposition of a Specific Tax on a Perfectly Competitive, Constant Cost Industry

The short-run effect of the tax is to shift the equilibrium from its initial position P_1, Q_1 to the point where the new demand curve D′ intersects the short-run supply curve S. That intersection occurs at output level Q_2 and an after-tax price to the firm of P_2. Assuming this price exceeds average variable costs, the typical firm will now produce output level q_2 at a loss. Consumers will pay P_3 for output level Q_2. By construction of the graph, $P_3 - P_2 = t$; so, in the short run, the tax is borne partially by consumers (who see the price they pay rise from P_1 to P_3) and partially by firms, which are now operating at a loss because they are receiving only P_2 (instead of P_1) for their output.

■ Long-Run Shifting of the Tax

In the long run, firms will not continue to operate at a loss. Some firms will leave the industry bemoaning the role of oppressive taxation in bringing about their downfall. The industry short-run supply curve will shift leftward as fewer firms remain in the market. A new long-run equilibrium will be established at Q_3 where the after-tax price received by firms still in the industry enables them to earn exactly zero in economic profits. Those firms remaining in the industry will return to producing output level q_1. The price paid by buyers in the market will now be P_4. In the long run the entire amount of the tax has been shifted into increased prices. Even though the firm ostensibly *pays* the tax, in fact the long-run burden is borne completely by the consumers of this good.[3]

■ Long-Run Incidence with Increasing Costs

In the more realistic case of increasing costs, both producers and consumers will pay a portion of this tax. Such a possibility is illustrated in Figure 13.6. Here the long-run supply curve (LS) has a positive slope because the costs of various inputs are bid up as industry output expands. Imposition of the tax, t, shifts the after-tax demand curve inward to D′ and this brings about a fall in net price over the long run from P_1 to P_2. Faced with the lower price, P_2, firms leave this industry, which has the effect of reducing some inputs' prices. Long-run equilibrium is reestablished at this lower net price and consumers now pay a gross price of P_3, which exceeds what they paid previously. Total tax collections are given by the gray area $P_3AE_2P_2$. These are partly paid by consumers (who pay P_3 instead of P_1) and partly by firms' inputs who are now paid based on a lower net price, P_2, instead of P_1.[4]

■ Incidence and Elasticity

A bit of geometric intuition suggests that the relative sizes of the price changes shown in Figure 13.6 will depend on the elasticities of the demand and supply

---

[3]Notice that owners of firms leaving the industry incur no long-run burden since they were initially earning zero economic profits, and, by assumption, can earn the same return elsewhere.

[4]Notice again that the firms' owners, per se, experience no losses here since they earned zero profits before the tax. Rather, the producer's share of the tax burden is borne by the owners of the inputs that now receive lower returns.

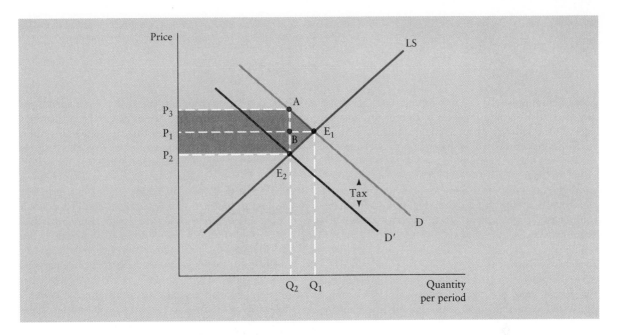

The initial equilibrium (E_1) is shifted to E_2 by the imposition of a tax. Total tax revenues (shaded gray) are partly paid by consumers, partly by producers. There is a deadweight loss (excess burden) from the tax shown by the area shaded in color.

Figure 13.6
Tax Incidence in an Increasing Cost Industry

curves. Intuitively, the actor with the more elastic response will be able more easily to "get out of the way" of the tax, leaving the actor with less elastic responses still in place to pay the most. We have already illustrated a special case of this principle in Figure 13.5. In that figure, the long-run elasticity of supply was infinite because of the constant-cost nature of the industry. Since the price received by firms (and by the inputs the firm employs) does not vary as output contracts as a result of the tax, the entire tax burden is shifted onto consumers. As demonstrated in Application 13.4: Cigarette Taxes, this outcome may be quite common in situations of some state or local taxes for which the good being taxed constitutes only a small portion of a larger national total.

More generally, if demand is relatively inelastic whereas supply is elastic, demanders will pay the bulk of a tax in the form of higher prices. Alternatively, if supply is relatively inelastic but demand is elastic, producers will pay most of the tax.[5] Indeed, in this case we can push the analysis further by noting that

---

[5]More precisely the fractional share of a specific tax paid by the supplier of a good is given by

$$\text{Share} = \frac{e^S}{e^S - e^D}$$

where e^S and e^D are the elasticities of supply and demand, respectively. For a proof, see W. Nicholson, *Microeconomic Theory: Basic Principles and Extensions,* 5th Ed. (Fort Worth: The Dryden Press, 1992), pp. 439–442.

APPLICATION 13.4

Cigarette Taxes

Most states impose excise taxes on cigarette sales. Usually these are specific taxes of a certain amount per pack. Our discussion of specific taxes suggests that virtually all these taxes will be passed on to consumers in the form of higher cigarette prices. The long-run supply curve for cigarettes in any state is nearly horizontal because increases in sales in a single state will not increase significantly industry-wide costs. Figure 13.5 probably represents the situation for state cigarette taxes fairly accurately.

Evidence on Incidence

Several studies of cigarette pricing have confirmed this theoretical prediction. For example, in 1981 Sumner and Ward found that about 93 percent of any change in a state's tax rate was quickly reflected in cigarette prices.[1] One reason suggested by the authors that the fraction is not exactly 100 percent (as predicted by our theory) is that additional consumers may choose to shop across state borders for their cigarettes when state tax rates change (many Massachusetts residents buy their cigarettes in New Hampshire, for example).

Another possible explanation is that under a specific tax, suppliers have an incentive to substitute quality for quantity in their activities, since only quantity is taxed. In the cigarette example, sellers may provide better service or more attractive displays. In the process, they will raise retailing costs; a change in selling techniques represents the profit-maximizing behavior a seller might take in response to the imposition of the unit tax.[2] The gap between price and cost may therefore narrow, making it appear that sellers are absorbing a portion of the tax.

Cigarette Taxes and Consumption

One rationale for taxing cigarettes, of course, is to deter consumption of these presumably harmful products. Because consumers pay virtually all of the tax, the effec-

tiveness of taxes as an anti-smoking policy depends primarily on the price elasticity of demand for cigarettes. Although most studies agree that this demand is rather inelastic in the short run, elasticities over the long run may be much higher. One important reason for the difference is the addictive nature of smoking. Because smoking in one year is highly complementary with smoking in another year, even a modest reduction in current cigarette use will have major long-term repercussions on future sales. Studies of smoking in the United States, Canada, and several European countries conclude that the long-run price elasticity of demand for cigarettes may be as great as $-.70$.[3] A price-based anti-smoking policy seems to be especially effective at deterring smoking by low-income individuals and teenagers. Higher-income individuals seem less influenced by prices, although anti-smoking educational efforts may be quite effective for this group.

To Think About

1. Could a local government impose a stiff tax on cigarettes if other local governments did not? Might a modest tax raise more revenues than a large one? What factors would determine the final outcome?
2. Why should the government seek to deter smoking through taxation? Isn't the decision to smoke up to the individual? Are there social reasons to deter smoking or are cigarette taxes just another case of government paternalism?

---

[1]M. T. Sumner and R. Ward, "Tax Changes and Cigarette Prices," *Journal of Political Economy* (December 1981): 1261–1265.
[2]For an example of how this differs from that of a tax on the value of sales, see Yoram Barzel, "An Alternative Approach to the Analysis of Taxation," *Journal of Political Economy* (December 1976): 1177–1197.

[3]See G. S. Becker, M. Grossman, and K. Murphy, "Rational Addiction and the Effect of Price on Consumption," *American Economic Review* (May 1991), pp. 237–241.

the producer's share will be paid primarily by those inputs which have inelastic supply curves because it is these inputs that will experience the greatest drop in price when demand for their services declines. For example, the producer's share of a tax on gold or silver would be largely paid by mine owners because the supply of mining land to this industry may be very inelastic. The supply of mining machinery or mine workers may be more elastic, however, because these inputs may have good alternative sources of employment. Hence, they would pay little of the tax. Of course, taking account of all of these repercussions of a tax in various markets is sometimes very difficult and simple models of supply and demand may not be up to the task. In Chapter 14, we will see how tax-incidence analysis can be explored even further using general equilibrium models that capture the operations of many markets simultaneously.

■ Taxation and Efficiency

Because taxation reduces the output of the taxed commodity, there will be a reallocation of production to other areas. This reallocation implies that some previously mutually beneficial transaction in the good will be forgone and that taxation will therefore reduce overall economic welfare. This loss can also be illustrated in Figure 13.6. The total loss in consumer surplus as a result of the tax is given by area $P_3AE_1P_1$. Of this area, P_3ABP_1 is transferred into tax revenues for the government and area AE_1B is simply lost. Similarly, the total loss of producer surplus is given by area $P_1E_1E_2P_2$ with area $P_1BE_2P_2$ being transferred into tax revenues and area BE_1E_2 being lost. From the point of view of the efficiency of resource allocation, the effect of the transfer into tax revenues (which amounts in total to area $P_3AE_2P_2$) is ambiguous. Whether this reduces the welfare of consumers and producers as a whole depends on how wisely government funds are spent—a thorny issue, to say the least. There is no ambiguity about the loss given by the colored area AE_1E_2. This is a **deadweight loss** for which there are no compensating gains. Sometimes (as we saw in Application 6.1) this loss is referred to as the "excess burden" of a tax; it represents the additional losses that consumers and producers suffer as a result of a tax, over and above the actual tax revenues paid.

The fact that all taxes involve some degree of excess burden has not, of course, proven to be a very convincing reason for shunning all taxes. Many government services provide significant benefits and must be somehow financed. Considerations of economic efficiency suggest that tax systems might be designed in a way so as to minimize excess burden, if possible. One way to do that is to tax goods for which either supply or demand is inelastic. In such cases, the resulting reduction in output will be small as will be the size of the excess burden triangle. These notions motivated the thinking of the nineteenth-century American economist, Henry George, to propose his "single tax" plan for a comprehensive tax on land only. He argued that such a tax would be the most efficient way to finance government because land itself is ultimately in inelastic supply.[6] While George's plan continues to have admirers (especially in

■
Deadweight loss
Losses of consumer and producer surplus that are not transferred to other parties.

---

[6]Henry George, *Progress and Poverty: An Inquiry into the Cause of Industrial Repression and the Increase of Want with Increase of Wealth* (New York: Henry George, 1881).

Canada and the United Kingdom), in practice it has proven to be very difficult to design taxes on "raw" land rather than on the improvements on the land (buildings, drainage, landscaping, and so forth) for which supply is more elastic. Indeed, the whole notion that land is the only inelastically supplied input might also be questioned since many types of labor (such as that of Tom Cruise, Michael Jordan, or Monica Seles) have an inelastic supply to one occupation.

■ Numerical Illustration

The effects of an excise tax can be illustrated by returning once again to our example of supply-demand equilibrium in the market for cassette tapes. Suppose the government implements a $2 per tape tax that the retailer adds to the sales price for each tape sold. In this case, the supply function for tapes remains

$$\text{Supply: } Q = P - 2 \qquad [13.3]$$

where P is now the net price received by the seller. Demanders, on the other hand, must now pay P + t for each tape so their demand function becomes:

$$\text{Demand: } Q = 10 - (P + t) \qquad [13.4]$$

or, since t = 2 here,

$$Q = 10 - (P + 2) = 8 - P. \qquad [13.5]$$

Notice, as we have shown graphically, that the effect of the tax is to shift the net demand curve (that is, quantity demanded as a function of the net price received by firms) inward. Equating supply and demand in this case yields

$$\text{Supply} = P - 2 = \text{Demand} = 8 - P \qquad [13.6]$$

or P* = 5, Q* = 3. At this equilibrium consumers pay $7 for each tape and total tax collections are $6 per week (= $2 per tape times three tapes per week). As we showed previously, an output of three tapes per week generates a total consumer and producer surplus of $15 per week of which $6 is now transferred into tax revenues. In this particular case, these revenues are half paid by firms (who see the net price fall from $6 to $5) and half by consumers (for whom the price rises from $6 to $7). In other cases, of course, one party or the other might bear a relatively greater burden (see Problem 13.6). Here the excess burden of taxation is $1 per week. This represents the loss in total consumer and producer surplus that is not collected in tax revenue. Again, this deadweight loss is shared equally in this example as shown in Figure 13.3.

■ Transactions Costs

Although we have developed this discussion in terms of tax incidence theory, models incorporating a wedge between buyers' and sellers' prices have a number of other applications in economics. Perhaps the most important of these concern costs associated with making market transactions. In some cases, these may be explicit. Most real estate transactions, for example, take place through a third-party broker, who charges a fee for the service of bringing buyer and seller together. Similar explicit transactions fees occur in the trading of stocks and bonds, boats and airplanes, and practically everything that is sold at auction. In all of these instances, buyers and sellers are willing to pay a fee to an agent or broker who facilitates the transaction. In other cases transactions costs may be largely implicit. Individuals trying to purchase a used car, for example, will spend considerable time and effort reading classified advertisements and examining vehicles. These activities amount to an implicit cost of making the transaction.

To the extent that transactions costs are on a per-unit basis (as they are in the real estate, securities, and auction examples), our previous taxation example applies exactly. From the point of view of the buyers and sellers, it makes little difference whether t represents a per-unit tax or a per-unit transactions fee, since the analysis of the fee's effect on the market will be the same. That is, the fee will be shared between buyers and sellers, depending on the specific elasticities involved. Output in these markets will also be lower than in the absence of such fees.[7]

A somewhat different analysis would hold, however, if transactions costs were a lump-sum amount per transaction. In that case individuals would seek to reduce the number of transactions made, but existence of the charge would not affect the total amount bought over the long term. For example, driving to the supermarket is mainly a lump-sum transaction cost on shopping for groceries. Existence of such a charge may not significantly affect the price of food items nor the amount of food consumed (unless it tempts people to grow their own). But the charge will cause individuals to shop less frequently, to buy larger quantities on each trip, and to hold larger inventories of food in their homes than would be the case in the absence of such a cost.

Trade Restrictions

Restrictions on the flow of goods in international commerce have effects similar to those we just examined for taxes. Impediments to free trade may reduce mutually beneficial transactions and cause a variety of transfers among the various parties involved. Once again the competitive model of supply and demand is frequently used to study these effects.

■ Gains from International Trade

Figure 13.7 illustrates the domestic demand and supply curves for a particular good, say, shoes. In the absence of international trade, the domestic equilibrium

---

[7]This analysis is restricted, however, by its failure to consider the possible benefits obtained from brokers. To the extent these services are valuable to the parties in the transaction, demand and supply curves will shift outward to reflect this value. Hence, output may actually expand from the availability of agents that facilitate transactions.

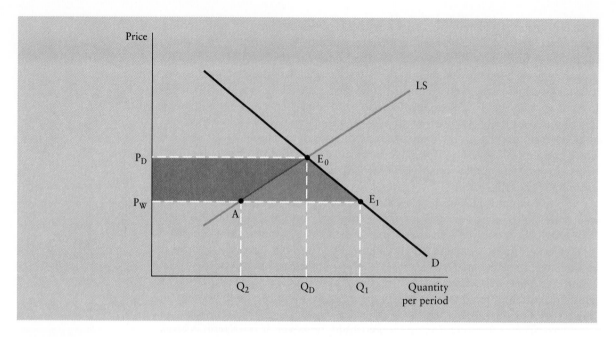

Figure 13.7
Opening of
International Trade
Increases Total
Welfare

Opening of international trade lowers price from P_D to P_W. At P_W domestic producers supply Q_2 and demanders want to buy Q_1. Imports amount to $Q_1 - Q_2$. The lower price results in a transfer from domestic producers to consumers (shaded gray) and a net gain of consumer surplus (shaded in color).

price of shoes would be P_D and quantity would be Q_D. Although this equilibrium would exhaust all mutually beneficial transactions between domestic shoe producers and domestic demanders, opening of international trade presents a number of additional options. If world shoe prices, P_W, are less than the prevailing domestic price, P_D, the opening of trade will cause prices to fall to this world level.[8] This drop in price will cause quantity demanded to increase to Q_1, whereas quantity supplied by domestic producers will fall to Q_2. Imported shoes will amount to $Q_1 - Q_2$. In short, what domestic producers do not supply at the world price are instead provided by foreign sources.

The shift in the market equilibrium from E_0 to E_1 causes a large increase in consumer surplus given by area $P_D E_0 E_1 P_W$. Part of this gain reflects a transfer from domestic shoe producers (area $P_D E_0 A P_W$, which is shaded in gray) and part represents an unambiguous welfare gain (the colored area $E_0 E_1 A$). The source of consumer gains here is obvious—buyers get shoes at a lower price than was previously available in the domestic market. As in our former analyses, losses of producer surplus are experienced by those inputs that give the long-run supply curve its upward slope. If, for example, the domestic shoe in-

[8]Throughout our analysis we will assume that this country is a price taker in the world market and can purchase all of the imports it wishes without affecting the price, P_W. If the country could affect world prices, there might be situations in which it could take advantage of this position by departing from free trade policies.

dustry experiences increasing costs because shoemaker wages are driven up as industry output expands, then the decline in output from Q_D to Q_2 as a result of trade will reverse this process, causing shoemaker wages to fall.

■ Tariff Protection

Shoemakers are unlikely to take these wage losses lying down. Instead, they will press the government for protection from the flood of imported footwear. Since the loss of producer surplus is experienced by relatively few individuals whereas consumer gains from trade are spread across many shoe buyers, shoe-makers may have considerably greater incentives to organize opposition to imports than consumers would have to organize to keep trade open. The result may be adoption of protectionist measures.

Historically, the most important type of protection employed has been a **tariff;** that is, a tax on the imported good. Effects of such a tax are shown in Figure 13.8. Now comparisons begin from the free trade equilibrium, E_1. Imposition of a per-unit tariff on shoes for domestic buyers of amount t raises the effective price to $P_W + t = P_R$. This price rise causes quantity demanded to fall from Q_1 to Q_3 whereas domestic production expands from Q_2 to Q_4. The total quantity of shoe imports falls from $Q_1 - Q_2$ to $Q_3 - Q_4$. Since each

Tariff

A tax on an imported good. May be equivalent to a quota or a nonquantitative restriction on trade.

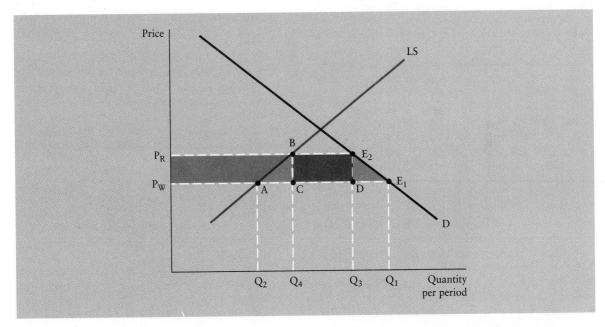

Imposition of a tariff of amount t raises price to $P_R = P_W + t$. This results in collection of tariff revenue (dark gray), a transfer from consumers to producers (light gray), and two triangles measuring deadweight loss (shaded in color). A quota has similar effects though in this case no revenues are collected.

Figure 13.8
Effects of a Tariff

APPLICATION 13.5

Voluntary Export Restraints on Automobiles

A variety of quantitative and nonquantitative restrictions on imports have essentially replaced tariffs as the principal impediment to world trade in recent years. "Voluntary" arrangements between countries to limit exports are one of the most popular of these arrangements. At various times United States' imports have been subject to such restrictions on steel products, nonrubber footwear, and a number of textile and apparel products. Probably the most significant such agreement is the voluntary export restraint (VER) negotiated with Japan in 1981 that limited imports of Japanese automobiles to 1.68 million per year. Figure 13.8 can be readily adapted to examine the effects of this policy.

Transfers from Consumers and Deadweight Losses

Mandatory restrictions of imports from distance AE_1 to BE_2 would have the same effect on import prices as did the tariff shown in Figure 13.8. The rise in price from P_W to P_R would, as before, cause a large transfer from consumers to domestic producers and a deadweight loss again given by the colored triangles in the figure. With quotas, however, there are no tariff revenues collected. Instead, this portion of consumer surplus will be transferred as "quota rents" to whomever obtains the rights to provide the restricted imports.

Economists have made a number of attempts to estimate these various effects of voluntary export restraints in the automobile industry.[1] The effects were probably most significant during the mid-1980s, since the quota was relaxed later in the decade and, at the same time, several Japanese firms built automobile assembly plants in the United States (whose output is exempt from the VERs). During the period of 1983 to 1986, however, it appears that the VERs raised average automobile prices by about $1,000 to $1,500. This resulted in an annual transfer of perhaps as much as $15 billion per year from consumers in the United States to domestic automobile producers. It also resulted in deadweight losses of about $1 billion per year. In all, these losses amounted to a significant fraction (about one-

third) of all the costs that trade protection imposed on American consumers in these years.

Quota Rents and Product Upgrading

Establishment of the VERs in automobiles allowed Japanese producers to receive higher prices for their imported cars than they would have otherwise. Division of these rents among specific Japanese auto companies was determined primarily by the Japanese government whose Ministry of International Trade and Industry allocated the quotas.[2] Generally, these allocations were based on historical market shares, so Toyota and Nissan were the major beneficiaries.

Since the VERs were stated as a fixed number of automobiles per year, Japanese makers had an incentive to seek further rents through the process of product upgrading. By increasing engine sizes and adding a variety of luxury equipment (such as fancy interiors or elaborate sound systems), these firms were able to increase further the profitability of each car sold. The process reached its natural conclusion with the flood of new Japanese luxury automobiles that hit U.S. markets in the late 1980s. Unfortunately for some domestic producers hoping to gain from the VERs (most notably, General Motors), consumers proved quite willing to buy Acura, Infiniti, and Lexus models instead of luxury American cars. Ultimately the VERs may have been detrimental to the firms they were intended to help.

To Think About

1. How would the sizes of the various transfers and deadweight losses created by VERs be affected by domestic demand and supply elasticities? For what kinds of goods would you expect losses to be greatest?

2. Product upgrading also seems to have characterized VERs in footwear and apparel. Why do firms find the upgrading option profitable? What might determine whether firms follow such a strategy or not?

---

[1]For a summary, see R. C. Feenstra, "How Costly is Protectionism?" *Journal of Economic Perspectives* (Summer 1992): 159–178.
[2]If the rights to import cars had been instead allocated by the U.S. government to domestic sales outlets (as had been the case with the oil import quota of the 1960s and 1970s), these firms would have garnered the quota rents.

imported pair of shoes is now subject to a tariff, total tariff revenues are given by the dark gray area, BE_2DC; that is, by $t(Q_3 - Q_4)$.

Imposition of the tariff on imported shoes creates a variety of welfare effects. Total consumer surplus is reduced by area $P_RE_2E_1P_W$. Part of this, as we have seen, is transferred into tariff revenues and part is transferred into increased domestic producer's surplus (area P_RBAP_W, shown in light gray). The two colored triangles BCA and E_2E_1D represent losses of consumer surplus that are not transferred to anyone; these are a deadweight loss from the tariff and are similar to the excess burden imposed by any tax. All of these areas can be measured if good empirical estimates of the domestic supply and demand curves for shoes are available.

■ Other Types of Trade Protection

In recent years, tariffs have come to play a much reduced role in international trade. They have been gradually negotiated downward under the General Agreement of Tariffs and Trade (GATT). The decline in tariffs has not necessarily meant a decline in protectionism, however. In their place are a number of restrictive measures including quotas, "voluntary" export restraints, and a series of nonquantitative restrictions such as those incorporated into seemingly beneficial health, safety, and environmental regulations. Many of these new types of restrictions can be illustrated by adapting the tariff diagram we have already developed in Figure 13.8.

A quota that limits imports to $Q_3 - Q_4$ would have effects that are very similar to those shown in the figure: market price would rise to P_R; a substantial transfer from consumers to domestic producers would occur (area P_RBAP_W); and there would be deadweight losses represented by the colored triangles. With a quota, however, no revenues are collected by the government, so the loss of consumer surplus represented by area BE_2DC must go elsewhere. In Application 13.5: Voluntary Export Restraints on Automobiles, we illustrate a case where these losses were largely captured by foreign auto producers, but other outcomes (such as windfall gains for the owners of import license) are also possible.

Nonquantitative restrictions such as inspection or testing requirements also impose cost and time delays that are often treated as an "implicit" tariff on imports. For example, imported aluminum baseball bats must be tested by officials of the Japanese Little League and in France imported VCRs must all pass through a single inspection station. Figure 13.8 can easily be adapted to illustrate the effects of these costly impediments to trade.

Summary

In this chapter we have shown how the competitive model of supply and demand can be used to investigate a wide range of actual economic activities and policies. Some of the general lessons from these applications include:

- The concepts of consumer and producer surplus provide useful ways of analyzing the effects of economic changes on the welfare of market participants. Changes in consumer surplus represent changes in the overall utility consumers receive from consuming a particular good. Changes in producer surplus represent changes in the returns producers receive.

- In the short run, producer's surplus represents the coverage of fixed costs plus whatever profits are received. In the long run, producer's surplus represents the extra returns that productive inputs enjoy relative to a situation where no output is produced.

- Ricardian rent is one type of producer surplus in which owners of low-cost firms receive long-run profits.

- Price controls involve both transfers between producers and consumers and losses of transactions that could benefit both consumers and producers.

- Tax incidence analysis concerns the determination of which economic actor ultimately bears the burden of a tax. In general this incidence will fall mainly on actors who exhibit inelastic responses to price changes. Taxes also involve deadweight losses that pose burdens in addition to the burden imposed by the actual tax revenues collected.

- Trade restrictions create both transfers between consumers and producers and deadweight losses of economic welfare. The effects of many types of trade restrictions can be modeled as being equivalent to a tariff.

Review Questions

1. Early in Chapter 1, we defined *economics* as "the study of the allocation of scarce resources among alternative end uses." How does the observation that a competitive equilibrium exhausts all mutually beneficial transactions relate to this definition? What "scarce resources" are being allocated by competitive markets? How are "alternative end uses" reflected by demand and supply curves?

2. "In the short run, firms may earn profits or losses, but, if they choose to produce anything, producer surplus will be positive." Explain this quote by discussing the role of fixed costs in differentiating between short-run profits and producer surplus.

3. "The size of producer surplus in the long run is ultimately determined by the elasticity of supply for the inputs to an industry." Use a series of graphs of both inputs' and goods' markets to explain this statement.

4. How can Ricardian rent persist in the long run? Doesn't the free entry assumption assume that any economic profits must be eroded over the long run?

5. Would price controls involve welfare losses even in the constant cost case? What economic process would such controls short circuit even in this case? Who would experience the welfare losses you describe?

6. Use a series of graphs to show that for a given demand curve the lower the elasticity of supply, the greater will be the burden of a specific tax paid by producers. Who actually absorbs this burden in the long run? How does this outcome depend on the supply elasticities for inputs?

7. Does a per-unit subsidy on the production of a good also result in an "excess burden"? Use a graphical analysis similar to Figure 13.6 to show that the allocation resulting from a per-unit subsidy also results in a deadweight loss.

8. Can a transactions charge ever be large enough to prevent all trading? What aspects of supply and demand conditions will help to determine whether a particular transactions charge is "too large"? Can you provide any real-world illustrations of this possibility?

9. Figure 13.8 shows that some part of the loss consumers suffer as a result of a tariff is transferred to domestic producers. Exactly how does this happen? Who gains from tariff protection?

10. Suppose that a nation institutes a costly inspection program on one of its imported goods. How would this affect equilibrium in the imported goods market? Explain how the various areas identified in Figure 13.8 should be interpreted in this circumstance.

Problems

13.1 Suppose that the demand for broccoli is given by

$$\text{Demand: } Q = 1,000 - 5P$$

where Q is quantity per year measured in hundreds of bushels and P is price in dollars per hundred bushels. The long-run supply curve for broccoli is given by

$$\text{Supply: } Q = 4P - 80.$$

a. Show that the equilibrium quantity here is $Q = 400$. At this output what is the equilibrium price? How much in total is spent on broccoli? What is consumer surplus at this equilibrium? What is producer surplus at this equilibrium?

b. How much in total consumer and producer surplus would be lost if $Q = 300$ instead of $Q = 400$?

c. Show how the allocation of the loss of total consumer and producer surplus between suppliers and demanders described in part b depends on the price at which broccoli is sold. How would the loss be shared if $P = 140$? How about if $P = 95$?

d. What would the total loss of consumer and producer surplus be if $Q = 450$ rather than $Q = 400$? Show that the size of this total loss also is independent of the price at which the broccoli is sold.

e. Graph your results.

13.2 The handmade snuffbox industry is composed of 100 identical firms, each having short-run total costs given by

$$STC = 0.5q^2 + 10q + 5$$

and short-run marginal costs by

$$SMC = q + 10$$

where q is the output of snuffboxes per day.

a. What is the short-run supply curve for each snuffbox maker? What is the short-run supply curve for the market as a whole?
b. Suppose the demand for total snuffbox production is given by

$$Q = 1,100 - 50P.$$

What will be the equilibrium in this marketplace? What will each firm's total short-run profits be?
c. Graph the market equilibrium and compute total producer surplus in this case.
d. Show that the total producer surplus you calculated in part c is equal to total industry profits plus industry short-run fixed costs.

*13.3 The perfectly competitive video tape copying industry is composed of many firms who can copy five tapes per day at an average cost of $10 per tape. Each firm must also pay a royalty to film studios and the per film royalty rate (r) is an increasing function of total industry output (Q) given by

$$r = .002Q.$$

a. Graph this royalty "supply" curve with r as a function of Q.
b. Suppose the daily demand for copied tapes is given by

$$Demand: Q = 1,050 - 50P.$$

Assuming the industry is in long-run equilibrium, what will be the equilibrium price and quantity of copied tapes? How many tape firms will there be? What will the per film royalty rate be? (Hint: Use P = AC. Now AC = 10 + .002Q)
c. Suppose that the demand for copied tapes increases to

$$Demand: Q = 1,600 - 50P.$$

Now, what is the long-run equilibrium price and quantity for copied tapes? How many tape firms are there? What is the per film royalty rate?
d. Graph these long-run equilibria in the tape market and calculate the increase in producer surplus between the situations described in parts b and c.
e. Use the royalty supply curve graphed in part a to show that the increase in producer surplus is precisely equal to the increase in royalties paid as Q expands incrementally from its level in part b to its level in part c.

---

*Denotes a problem that is rather difficult.

13.4 Consider again the market for broccoli described in problem 13.1.

    a. Suppose demand for broccoli shifted, outward to

$$\text{Demand: } Q = 1{,}270 - 5P.$$

    What would be the new equilibrium price and quantity in this market?

    b. What would be the new levels of consumer and producer surplus in this market?

    c. Suppose the government had prevented the price of broccoli from rising from its equilibrium level of problem 13.1. Describe how the consumer and producer surplus measures described in part b would be reallocated or lost entirely.

13.5 Returning once more to the broccoli market described in problem 13.1, suppose that the government instituted a $45-per-hundred bushel tax on broccoli.

    a. How would this tax affect equilibrium in the broccoli market?

    b. How would this tax burden be shared between buyers and sellers of broccoli?

    c. What is the excess burden of this tax?

13.6 Suppose the demand for broccoli in problem 13.5 had instead been

$$\text{Demand: } Q = 2{,}200 - 15P.$$

    a. Answer parts a and b of problem 13.5 for this alternative demand curve.

    b. Suppose now that the broccoli market is characterized by the original demand curve described in problems 13.1 and 13.5 but that the supply curve is

$$\text{Supply: } Q = 10P - 800.$$

    Answer parts a and b of problem 13.5 for this case.

    c. What do you conclude by comparing these three cases of tax incidence we have examined for the broccoli market?

13.7 Suppose that the government imposed a $3 tax on snuffboxes in the industry described in problem 13.2.

    a. How would this tax change the market equilibrium?

    b. How would the burden of this tax be shared between snuffbox buyers and sellers?

    c. Calculate the total loss of producer surplus as a result of the taxation of snuffboxes. Show that this loss equals the change in total short-run profits in the snuffbox industry. Why don't fixed costs enter into this computation of the change in short-run producer surplus?

*13.8 Suppose that the government institutes a $5.50-per-film tax on the film copying industry described in problem 13.3.

    a. Assuming that the demand for copied films is that given in part c of problem 13.3, how will this tax affect the market equilibrium?

    b. How will the burden of this tax be allocated between consumers and producers? What will be the loss of consumer and producer surplus?

*Denotes a problem that is rather difficult.

c. Show that the loss of producer surplus as a result of this tax is borne completely by the film studios. Explain your result intuitively.

13.9   The domestic demand for portable radios is given by

$$\text{Demand: } Q = 5{,}000 - 100P$$

where price (P) is measured in dollars and quantity (Q) is measured in thousands of radios per year. The domestic supply curve for radios is given by

$$\text{Supply: } Q = 150P.$$

a. What is the domestic equilibrium in the portable radio market?
b. Suppose portable radios can be imported at a world price of $10 per radio. If trade were unencumbered, what would the new market equilibrium be? How many portable radios would be produced domestically? How many portable radios would be imported?
c. If domestic portable radio producers succeeded in getting a $5 tariff implemented, how would this change the market equilibrium? How much would be collected in tariff revenues? How much consumer surplus would be transferred to domestic producers? What would the deadweight loss from the tariff be?
d. Graph your results.

13.10 How would your results from problem 13.9 be changed if the government reached an agreement with foreign suppliers to limit "voluntarily" the portable radios they export to 1,250,000 per year? Explain how this differs from the case of a tariff.

In Chapters 12 and 13 we developed a detailed model of how a single competitive market works. In this chapter we are interested in how a system of many competitive markets operates and whether this operation yields desirable results. Specifically, we will further develop our definition of what it means to allocate resources efficiently, and we will then examine whether competitive markets can achieve this goal.

We are examining a question first posed in the eighteenth century by Adam Smith, who saw in market forces an "invisible hand" that guides resources to their best use. Although the vast number of transactions that take place in an economy may seem like utter chaos, Smith viewed them as being quite orderly in moving resources to where they are most valued. A primary purpose of Chapter 14 is to investigate Smith's ideas rigorously and to show that, with some important limitations, his insights were essentially correct.

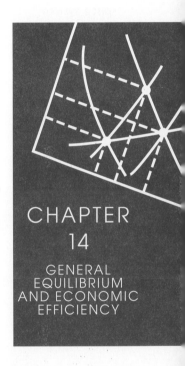

CHAPTER 14

GENERAL EQUILIBRIUM AND ECONOMIC EFFICIENCY

Perfectly Competitive Price System

Before starting our examination of Smith's invisible hand notion, we should describe the particular model of the economy we will be using. This model is a simple generalization of the supply-demand model of perfectly competitive price determination introduced earlier. Here we assume that all markets are of this type, and refer to this set of markets as a **perfectly competitive price system.** The assumption is that in this simple economy there is some large number of homogeneous goods. Included in this list of goods are not only consumption items but also factors of production (whose pricing is described later in Part 5). Each of these goods has an equilibrium price, established by the action of supply and demand.[1] At this set of prices, every market is cleared in the sense that suppliers are willing to supply the exact quantity that is demanded. We also assume that there are no transaction or transportation charges and that both individuals and firms have perfect knowledge of these prices. Both of these assumptions are examined in more detail in the next chapter.

Because we have assumed there are no transaction costs, each good in our model obeys the law of one price: a good trades at the same price no matter who buys it or which firm sells it. If one good were traded at two different prices, people would rush to buy the good where it was cheaper, and firms would try to sell all their output where the good was more expensive. These actions would tend to equalize the price of the good between the markets. This is why we may speak unambiguously of *the* price of a good.

The perfectly competitive model assumes that people and firms react to prices in specific ways:

1.   There are assumed to be a large number of people buying any one good. Each person takes all prices as given. Each adjusts his or her behavior to maximize utility, given the prices and his or her budget constraint. People may also be suppliers of productive services (for example, labor), and in such decisions they also regard prices as given.[2]
2.   There are assumed to be a large number of firms producing each good, and each firm produces only a small share of the output of any one good. In making input and output choices, firms are assumed to operate to maximize profits. The firm treats all prices as given when making these profit-maximizing decisions. The firm's activities, either as a supplier of goods or as a demander of factor inputs, have no effect on market prices.

These assumptions should be familiar. Our purpose here is to show how an entire economic system operates when all markets work in this way.

Perfectly competitive price system

An economic model in which individuals maximize utility, firms maximize profits, there is perfect information about prices, and every economic actor is a price taker.

---

[1]One aspect of this market interaction should be made clear from the outset. The perfectly competitive market only determines relative (not absolute) prices. For most of this chapter, we speak of relative prices. It makes no difference whether the prices of apples and oranges are $.10 and $.20, respectively, or $10 and $20. The important point in either case is that two apples can be exchanged for one orange in the market. At the end of this chapter we look briefly at how nominal (money) prices are determined.

[2]Since one price represents the wage rate, the relevant budget constraint is in reality a time constraint. This is the way we treat individuals' labor-leisure choices in Chapter 20.

An Illustration of General Equilibrium

A major distinction between this model and the perfectly competitive models we have used previously is that now we are interested in studying an entire system of many interconnected markets, not just a single market in isolation. That is, we wish now to take a "general equilibrium" view of the economy rather than the "partial equilibrium" approach used in Chapters 12 and 13. To illustrate this approach, Figure 14.1 shows the market for one good, say, tomatoes, and three of the many other markets related to it: (1) the market for tomato pickers; (2) the market for a related product—cucumbers; and (3) the

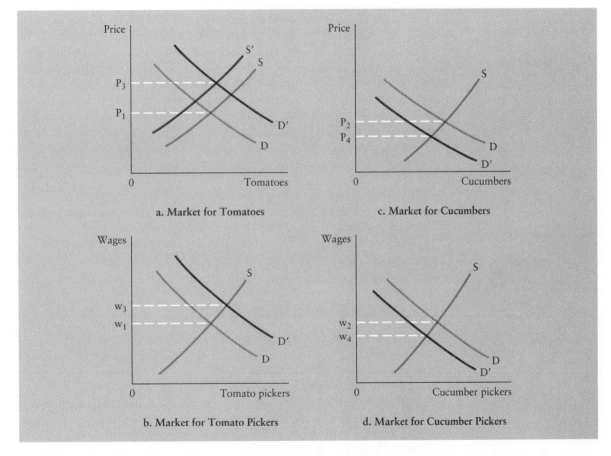

a. Market for Tomatoes

b. Market for Tomato Pickers

c. Market for Cucumbers

d. Market for Cucumber Pickers

Initially the market for tomatoes is in equilibrium (at P_1) as are the markets for tomato pickers, cucumbers, and cucumber pickers. An increase in demand for tomatoes will disturb these equilibria. Virtually all of the supply and demand curves will shift in the process of establishing a new general equilibrium.

Figure 14.1

The Market for Tomatoes and Several Related Markets

market for cucumber pickers. Suppose that initially all of these markets are in equilibrium as shown by the sets of shaded supply and demand curves in the four panels of Figure 14.1. That is, the equilibrium price of tomatoes is given by P_1, wages of tomato pickers by w_1, the price of cucumbers by P_2, and the wages of cucumber pickers by w_2. Since these prices act to equate the amount supplied and demanded in each of these markets, the general equilibrium shown in Figure 14.1 will persist from week to week until something happens to change it.

■ Disturbing the Equilibrium

Assume now that such a change does occur. Imagine a situation where the government announces that tomatoes have been found to cure the common cold, so everyone decides to eat more of them. An initial consequence of this discovery is that the demand for tomatoes will shift outward to D′. In our previous analysis this shift would cause the price of tomatoes to rise and that would be, more or less, the end of the story. Now, however, we wish to follow the repercussions of what has happened in the tomato market into the other markets shown in Figure 14.1. A first possible reaction would be in the market for tomato pickers. Since tomato prices have risen, the demand for labor used to harvest tomatoes will increase. The demand curve for labor in Panel b in Figure 14.1 will shift to D′. This will tend to raise wages of tomato pickers, which will, in turn, raise the costs of tomato growers. The supply curve for tomatoes (which, under perfect competition, just reflects growers' marginal costs) will shift to S′.

What happens to the market for cucumbers? Since people have an increased desire for tomatoes, they may reduce their demands for cucumbers because these tomato substitutes don't cure colds. The demand for cucumbers will shift inward to D′, and cucumber prices will fall. That will reduce the demand for cucumber workers, and the wage associated with that occupation will fall.

■ Reestablishing Equilibrium

We could continue this story indefinitely. We could ask how the lower price of cucumbers affects the tomato market. Or we could ask whether cucumber pickers, discouraged by their falling wages, might consider picking tomatoes, shifting the supply of labor curve in Panel b in Figure 14.1 outward. To follow this chain of events further or to examine even more markets related to tomatoes would add little to our story. Eventually we would expect all four markets in Figure 14.1 (and all the other markets we have not shown) to reach a new equilibrium, such as that illustrated by the solid supply and demand curves in the figure. Once all the repercussions have been worked out, the final result would be a rise in tomato prices (to P_3), a rise in the wages of tomato pickers (to w_3), a fall in cucumber prices (to P_4), and a fall in the wages of cucumber pickers (to w_4). This is what we mean then by a smoothly working system of perfectly competitive markets. Following any disturbance, all of the markets can eventually reestablish a new set of equilibrium prices at which quantity demanded is equal to quantity supplied in each market.[3] It is this model—or, as in Application 14.1: Modeling the Impact of Taxes with a Computer, a more complex form of this model involving hundreds, perhaps even millions of interconnected markets—that we will use to investigate the question of economic efficiency.

Efficiency in Production

In Chapter 13 we briefly described the notion of economic efficiency in one market. We start our analysis of efficiency in many markets by describing what it means to say that an economy with fixed amounts of resources has used these resources in a "technically efficient" way. To do this, we use the production possibility frontier concept first introduced in Chapter 1. We show here that an economy that is on its production possibility curve is allocating its resources in a technically efficient way. On the other hand, if production takes place inside the frontier, resources are being poorly allocated and moving them around would improve matters. Before we can show all of this, we first need to define technical efficiency.

■ Definition of Technical Efficiency

A major problem with defining efficient production is that any economy produces many different goods. For this reason it is impossible to talk about producing "as much total output as possible." There is simply no way to add together apples, oranges, automobiles, and aircraft carriers into something called output.[4] Instead, we adopt what at first may seem a relatively complicated definition. Under this definition an allocation of resources is said to be **technically efficient** if it is impossible to increase the output of one good without cutting back on the production of something else. Alternatively, resources are said to be allocated inefficiently if it is indeed possible, by moving resources around, to increase output of one good without sacrificing anything.

For example, suppose an economy produces only two products, wine and cloth. An allocation of resources under which more wine could be produced without having to reduce cloth output would be inefficient—there is no reason why the resources should not be shuffled around to yield more wine output. On the other hand, if increasing wine output meant cutting back on cloth output, the initial allocation would be technically efficient since output cannot be unambiguously increased. By using this definition it is never necessary to compare wine and cloth directly to decide whether or not resources are allocated

■

Technically efficient allocation of resources

An allocation of the available resources such that producing more of one good requires producing less of some other good.

---

[3]Actually, the question of whether many markets can establish a set of prices that brings equilibrium to each of them is a major and difficult theoretical question. For a simple discussion and some references, see Walter Nicholson, *Microeconomic Theory: Basic Principles and Extensions*, 5th ed. (Fort Worth, TX: The Dryden Press, 1992), pp. 482–489.

[4]Since we do not wish to introduce prices into our discussion of efficiency, it is not possible to add up different goods by valuing them at their market prices. The price system might be used to achieve economic efficiency, but prices cannot be used to define the concept itself.

APPLICATION 14.1

Modeling the Impact of Taxes with a Computer

In Chapter 13 we illustrated how the competitive model might be used to analyze the impact of taxes on a single market. A primary shortcoming of that approach is that it does not allow a very complete description of the various effects a tax may have. For example, we showed that an excise tax on a good is partly paid by consumers and partly paid by producers, with the respective shares being determined by elasticities of demand and supply. This conclusion tells us very little about who finally bears the burden of the tax. We have no idea how that burden is shared among different consumers of the good, nor do we know who finally pays the firms' share (it could be owners of the firms, workers in the firms, or some other input supplier). Simple models of supply and demand are just not rich enough in detail to answer such questions.

Computer and General Equilibrium Models

The development of large-scale computers and sophisticated programs to model the economy has changed this situation dramatically. Now it is possible to use general equilibrium models of the economy to obtain very detailed appraisals of the impact of taxes. Some of these models divide the economy into as many as 50 or more industries and equally many different types of consumers (depending on their incomes, where they live, and so on). A graphic representation of such models might look like Figure 14.1 but with more than 100 different markets represented. Coping with the information necessary to compute equilibrium prices in all of these markets without a computer would be impossible. Using the speed and accuracy of modern computers together with readily available software makes it a fairly simple process.

Results of General Equilibrium Models

These large general equilibrium models of the economy have yielded major and sometimes surprising conclusions about the effects of taxes on an economy. Generally, these effects are larger than those found using partial equilibrium methods.[1] One study of the entire tax system of the United Kingdom, for example, concluded that distortions introduced by that system resulted in a deadweight loss of 6 to 9 percent of total gross national product. The taxes also caused a transfer of nearly one-fourth of all income from high-income to low-income households. The study found that the British tax system imposed particularly heavy costs on its manufacturing industries—perhaps providing an explanation for recent poor industrial performance in that country. Studies of the U.S. tax system tend to reach similar, though perhaps not so dramatic, conclusions. For example, some researchers have reported that, at the margin, the U.S. tax system involves large efficiency losses. These studies suggest that moving to simpler tax schemes, such as a flat rate consumption tax, would reduce these losses substantially.

To Think About

1. Suppose the government were to institute a tax on each gallon of gasoline sold. How would you analyze the economic effects of this tax with a partial equilibrium model? What further repercussions of the tax would this simple model miss? How many markets do you think you should study to gain a fairly complete picture of the impact of the tax?

2. In most general equilibrium models of taxation the final results of who pays taxes are reported as how after-tax incomes of various groups of people are affected. There is no notion that firms pay any taxes at all. What do you make of this? How do you reconcile the common-sense (and politically popular) idea that firms do indeed pay taxes with the general equilibrium notion that ultimately only people pay taxes?

---

[1]For a summary of many of these models, see John B. Shoven and John Walley, "Applied General Equilibrium Models of Taxation and International Trade," *Journal of Economic Literature* (September 1984): 1007–1051.

efficiently. Rather, wine is compared only to wine (to see whether output of it has increased), and cloth is compared only to cloth.

■ Efficient Input Use and the Edgeworth Production Box

As a starting point in our discussion of technical efficiency in production, we treat the entire economy as a single firm that uses fixed amounts of two inputs, capital (K) and labor (L), to produce two different goods (called X and Y). The firm must decide only how to allocate the two inputs between producing X and producing Y. The firm will be operating efficiently if it is not possible for it to reallocate its inputs in such a way that output of X can be increased while keeping Y output constant.

A particularly useful device for studying this production problem is the **Edgeworth box diagram,** which we first introduced in our discussion of exchange in Chapter 6. The basics for constructing this diagram for the case of production are illustrated in Figure 14.2. Here the length of the box represents

■

Edgeworth box diagram

A graphic device for illustrating all of the possible allocations of two goods (or two inputs) that are in fixed supply.

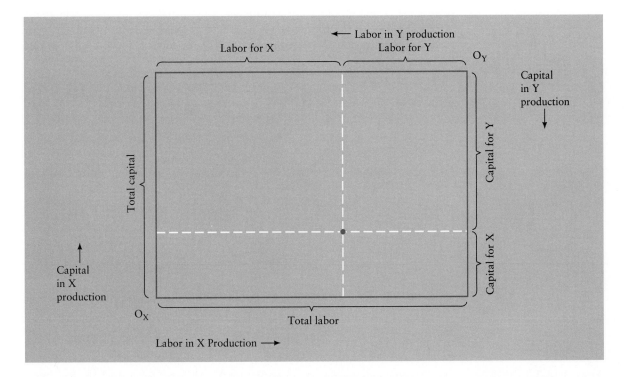

The dimensions of this diagram are given by the total quantities of labor and capital available. Quantities of these resources devoted to X production are measured from origin O_X; quantities devoted to Y are measured from O_Y. Any point in the box represents a fully employed allocation of the available resources to the two goods.

Figure 14.2
Construction of Edgeworth Box Diagram for Production

total labor hours and the height of the box represents total capital hours that are available in the economy. Now we let the lower left corner of the box represent the "origin" for measuring capital and labor devoted to production of good X. The upper right corner of the box represents the origin for resources devoted to Y. Using these conventions, any point in the box can be regarded as a fully employed allocation of the available resources between goods X and Y. Point A, for example, represents an allocation in which the indicated number of labor hours are devoted to X production together with a specified number of hours of capital. Production of good Y uses whatever labor and capital are left over. At point A, for example, Figure 14.2 shows the exact amount of labor and capital used in the production of good Y. Any point in the box has a similar interpretation. The Edgeworth box shows every possible way the available capital and labor might be used. Now we wish to discover which of these allocations are efficient.

■ Efficient Allocations

To discover these efficient allocations we must introduce the isoquant maps (see Chapter 8) for the two goods X and Y, since these show how much can be produced with various levels of capital and labor input. Figure 14.3 contains

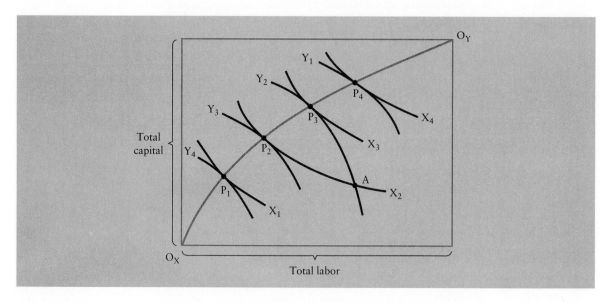

Figure 14.3
Box Diagram of
Efficiency in
Production

This diagram adds production isoquants for X and Y to Figure 14.2. It then shows technically efficient ways to allocate the fixed amounts of K and L between the production of the two outputs. The line joining O_X and O_Y is the locus of these efficient points. Along this line the RTS (of L for K) in the production of good X is equal to the RTS in the production of Y.

the isoquant map for good X using O_X as an origin. This isoquant map looks exactly like the ones we used before. For good Y, however, once again the trick of the Edgeworth box diagram is to use O_Y as an origin and rotate the usual diagram 180°. If you turn your book upside down, you will see that the isoquant map for good Y has the usual shape when viewed from that angle. We have put both of the isoquant maps on the same diagram, which will help us identify efficient allocations of labor and capital.

Our arbitrarily chosen point A is clearly not efficient. With capital and labor allocated in this way, Y_2 is produced together with X_2. By moving along the Y_2 isoquant to P_3, we can hold Y output constant and increase X output to X_3. Point A was not an efficient allocation since we were able to increase output of one good (X) without decreasing output of the other good (Y). Point A is inefficient because production of goods X and Y uses the available resources in the wrong combination, not because some of these resources were not used at all. Both point A and point P_3 represent fully employed allocations of the available resources. But, the allocation at point P_3 results in good X using more capital and less labor while Y uses more labor and less capital than at point A (check this for yourself!). This new allocation is a better way to use the available resources.

Which points in Figure 14.3 are the efficient ones? A bit of intuition should suggest to you that only points such as P_1, P_2, P_3, and P_4 are efficient. These represent allocations where the isoquants are tangent to each other. At any other point in the box diagram, the two goods' isoquants will intersect, and we can show inefficiency as we did for point A. At the points of tangency, however, this kind of unambiguous improvement cannot be made. In going from P_2 to P_3, for example, more X is being produced, but at the cost of less Y being produced, so P_3 is not more efficient than P_2—both of the points are efficient. Tangency of the isoquants for good X and good Y implies that their slopes are equal. That is, the RTS of capital for labor is equal in X and Y production. The curve joining O_X and O_Y that includes all of these points of tangency shows all of the efficient allocations of capital and labor. Points off this curve are inefficient in that unambiguous increases in output can be obtained by reshuffling inputs among the two goods. Points on O_X, O_Y are all efficient allocations, however. More X can be produced only by cutting back on Y production.

Production Possibility Frontier

We can use the information from Figure 14.3 to construct a production possibility frontier, which shows those alternative outputs of X and Y that can be produced with the fixed amounts of capital and labor. In Figure 14.4 the various efficient points from Figure 14.3 have been transferred onto a graph with X and Y outputs on the axes. At O_X, for example, no resources are devoted to

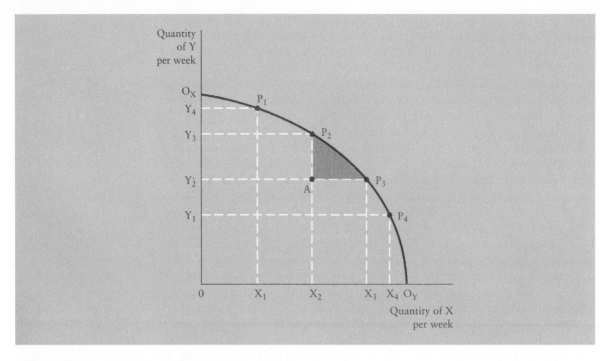

Figure 14.4
Production Possibility
Frontier Derived from
Figure 14.3

The production possibility frontier shows those alternative combinations of X and Y that can be efficiently produced by a firm with fixed resources. The curve can be derived from Figure 14.3 by varying inputs between the production of X and Y while maintaining the conditions for efficiency. The slope of the production possibility curve is called the rate of product transformation (RPT).

X production; consequently Y output is as large as possible using all of the available resources. Similarly, at O_Y, the output of X is as large as possible. The other points on the production possibility frontier (say, P_1, P_2, P_3, and P_4) are derived in an identical way.

The production possibility curve clearly exhibits the notion of technical efficiency we have been using. Any point inside the frontier is inefficient because output can be unambiguously increased. The allocation of K and L represented by point A, for example, is inefficient because output levels in the shaded area are both attainable and preferable to A. If you look again at Figure 14.3, you can see how the available resources might be reallocated to obtain those more efficient points.

■ Rate of Product Transformation

The slope of the production possibility frontier shows how X output can be substituted for Y output when total resources are held constant. For example, for points near O_X on the production possibility frontier, the slope is a small negative number, say, $-1/2$, implying that by reducing Y output by one unit, X output could be increased by two. Near O_Y, on the other hand, the slope is a large negative number, say, -5, implying that Y output must be reduced by five units to permit the production of one more X. The slope of the production possibility frontier shows the possibilities that exist for trading Y and X in production. We call this slope the **rate of product transformation** (RPT) of good X for good Y. This concept indicates the number of units by which Y output must be reduced in order to increase X output by one unit.

■
Rate of product transformation

The slope of the production possibility frontier that shows the opportunity costs involved in producing more of one good and less of some other good.

Shape of the Production Possibility Frontier

In Figure 14.4 we have drawn the production possibility frontier so that the RPT increases as X output increases. In moving clockwise along the frontier, progressively greater and greater amounts of Y must be given up in order to increase X output by one unit. Such a shape can be justified intuitively by arguing that increases in X (or Y) output encounter increasing costs. For output combinations near O_X, most resources are devoted to Y production. Some of these resources may be more suited to X production than they are to Y production. When X output is increased slightly, it is only reasonable to assume that these particular resources will be shifted into X output first. Such a shift will not reduce Y output very much, but it will increase X significantly. Near O_X, therefore, the RPT will be small. On the other hand, near O_Y, X output has been expanded greatly. To increase X further requires that resources be drawn out of Y production that are very good at producing Y but not good at producing X. Consequently, Y will have to be cut back significantly to get only one more unit of X. Near O_Y, the RPT will be high. An increasing RPT accords well with an intuitive idea that production of X exhibits increasing costs.

■ Rate of Product Transformation Is the Ratio of Marginal Costs

To show that the shape of the production possibility frontier in Figure 14.4 is rigorously justified, we can make use of the following result: the RPT (of X for Y) is equal to the ratio of the marginal cost of X (MC_X) to the marginal cost of Y (MC_Y). That is,

$$\text{RPT (of X for Y)} = \frac{MC_X}{MC_Y}. \qquad [14.1]$$

Although we will not prove this result mathematically here, we do provide an intuitive proof. Suppose only labor is used in the production of X and Y. Assume that, at some point on the production possibility frontier, the marginal cost of producing more X is 4 (that is, assume that it takes four units of labor input to produce an additional unit of X output). Suppose also that the marginal cost of Y (in terms of the additional labor required to produce one more unit) is 2. In this situation it is clear that, since the total supply of labor is fixed, two units of Y must be given up in order to free enough labor to produce one more unit of X. We would therefore say that the RPT (of X for Y) is 2. But this is simply the ratio of the marginal cost of X to the marginal cost of Y (that is, 4/2); at least for this simple case, Equation 14.1 holds. A more complete analysis would indicate that the equation holds even when many inputs are being used to produce X and Y.

■ Increasing Marginal Costs and the Shape of the Production Possibility Frontier

We are now in a position to show why the production possibility frontier has a concave shape. Such a shape is based on the presumption that the production of both X and Y exhibits increasing marginal costs. As production of either of these outputs is expanded, marginal costs are assumed to rise. Consider moving along the frontier in a clockwise direction. In so doing, the production of X is being increased, whereas that of Y is being decreased. By the assumption of increasing marginal costs, then, MC_X is rising while MC_Y falls. But, by Equation 14.1, this means that the RPT is rising as X is substituted for Y in production. The concave shape of the production possibility frontier is then justified by the assumption of increasing marginal costs.[5]

■ Production Possibility Frontier and Opportunity Cost

The reason we have given so much space to developing the concept of the production possibility frontier is that it is probably the single most important tool for studying technical efficiency in the production and supply of two goods. The curve clearly demonstrates that there are many combinations of goods that are technically efficient. The curve also shows that producing more of one good necessitates cutting back on the production of some other good. As we described in Chapter 1, this is precisely what economists mean by the term *opportunity cost*. The cost of producing more X can be most readily measured by the reduction in Y output that this entails. The opportunity cost of one more unit of X is therefore best measured as the RPT (of X for Y) at the prevailing point on the production possibility frontier. The increasing RPT for clockwise movements along the frontier shows in a general way how the opportunity cost of X increases as more of it is produced. In Application 14.2: Guns, Butter, and the Peace Dividend, we show that knowing something about such trade-off possibilities can be very important for public decision making.

---

[5]Even when both goods exhibit constant returns to scale, the production possibility frontier will be concave if the goods use K and L in different proportions. See W. Nicholson, *Microeconomic Theory: Basic Principles and Extensions*, 5th ed. (Fort Worth, TX: The Dryden Press, 1992), pp. 472–474.

APPLICATION 14.2

Guns, Butter, and the Peace Dividend

Traditionally when economics textbooks introduce the production possibility frontier, they label the axes "guns" and "butter" to record the notion that an economy can produce various combinations of defense ("guns") and nondefense ("butter") items. During wartime the economy reallocates resources toward guns, whereas in more peaceful periods a relatively larger share of resources is devoted to butter. Use of the production possibility frontier concept can be helpful in understanding the kinds of opportunity costs that might be incurred by such moves.

The 1960s Debate

In the early 1960s there was considerable interest in what the economic dislocations of disarmament might be. At that time, defense spending amounted to about 10 percent of U.S. gross national product, and a number of studies attempted to estimate what the effects of a fairly sharp reduction (say, cutting spending in half) might be. In many respects the issue was one of deciding how specialized the inputs devoted to defense were. If such input had uses that were highly specific to defense, the adjustment costs might be large since these inputs could not be easily employed elsewhere. If, on the other hand, inputs were easily transferable between sectors, opportunity costs of adjustment might be low.

These studies that were conducted in the early 1960s tended to conclude that for modest reductions in defense spending, adjustment costs would be relatively small.[1] Many products that are bought by the military can be readily sold to civilians (for example, food), and even for some goods that have solely defense uses (such as military aircraft), problems involved in converting to civilian production may have been rather minor. Only for highly-specialized industries such as ordinance or defense-related research and development did these researchers see substantial dislocations.

The Peace Dividend

From 1985 to 1991 the share of GNP devoted to military spending fell from about 6.5 percent to less than 5 percent (interestingly, about half of the 1960 level). With the breakup of the former Soviet Union, calls have been made to accelerate this decline, using the saved government revenues to fund a variety of domestic initiatives. Effects of this reallocation of production may raise more difficulties than were encountered in the 1960s, however, since resources devoted to defense may be more specialized than in the past. An increasing array of military goods have no obvious civilian counterparts (for example, antimissile defense systems), and practically all defense purchases have become more technically sophisticated. Research on cutbacks by defense firms supports this view. A large fraction of the reduction in defense-based employment consists of workforce reductions rather than transfers to the firms' civilian activities.[2] The economic dislocations posed by these reductions can be especially severe for the particular communities where defense employment is concentrated. Hence, a significant portion of the peace dividend resulting from the end of the Cold War may have to be used to ease the reallocation of resources this will require.

To Think About

1. If defense expenditures were reduced, what industries would be affected? Can you answer that question simply by asking what things the Defense Department would no longer buy? Or should you look further back in the chain of supply?
2. Currently, nearly half of all research and development expenditures in the United States are financed by the Defense Department. How might that affect the long-term growth of the economy? Do research and development innovations in defense result only in improved weapons or do they spill over into civilian sectors of the economy?

---

[1]For a summary, see Roger E. Bolton, ed., *Defense and Disarmament: The Economics of Transition* (Englewood Cliffs, NJ: Prentice-Hall, 1966).

[2]See J. Brauer and J. T. Maslin, "Converting Resources from Military to Non-Military Uses," *Journal of Economic Perspectives* (Fall 1992: 145–164).

An Efficient Mix of Outputs

The goal of an economic system is to satisfy human wants. Being technically efficient in production (that is, being on the production possibility frontier) may not be at all desirable if the "wrong" combination of goods is being produced. It does little good for an economy to be an efficient producer of yo-yos and xylophones if no one wants these goods. Similarly, an economy in which large amounts of resources are devoted to frivolous purposes by the government (say, erecting statues of the ruling leadership) may not be desirable even though production of statues itself uses the available resources in a technically efficient way. In order to assure overall **economic efficiency** in the allocation of resources, we need to tie people's preferences to the economy's productive abilities.

Economically efficient allocation of resources

A technically efficient allocation of resources in which the output combination also reflects people's preferences.

■ A Graphic Demonstration

Figure 14.5 illustrates the requirements for economic efficiency in the mix of outputs. It assumes that there are only two goods (X and Y) being produced and that there is just one person (or perhaps a number of identical people) in society. Those combinations of X and Y that can be produced in a technically efficient way lie along the production possibility frontier. By superimposing the typical person's indifference curve map on Figure 14.5, we see that only one point on the frontier provides maximum utility. This point of maximum utility is at E, where the frontier is tangent to the typical person's highest indifference curve, U_2. At this point of tangency the person's MRS (of X for Y) is equal to the technical RPT (of X for Y). This is the condition required for economic efficiency in the mix of outputs being produced. Point E is preferred to every other point on the production possibility frontier. In fact, for any other point, such as F, on the frontier, there exist points that are inefficient but that are preferred to F. In Figure 14.5 the technically inefficient point G is preferred to the technically efficient point F. From the typical person's point of view, it would be preferable to produce inefficiently than to consume the "wrong" combination of goods even though these are produced in a technically efficient way.

Figure 14.5 shows, at least for a simple case, how resources might be allocated efficiently in an economy that produces two goods. With this model we are now ready to examine how efficiency might be brought about through the operations of perfectly competitive markets.

Efficiency of Perfect Competition

We illustrate the economic efficiency of perfect competition in two steps. First, we provide a very brief proof of why firms' desires to minimize costs will result

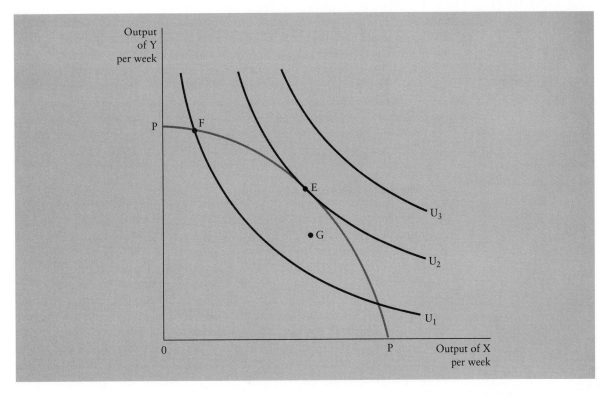

In this economy, the production possibility frontier represents those combinations of X and Y that can be produced. Every point on it is efficient in a technical sense. However, only the output combination at point E is a true utility maximum for the typical person. Only this point represents an economically efficient allocation of resources. At E that person's MRS is equal to the rate at which X can be traded for Y in production (the RPT).

Figure 14.5
Efficiency of
Output Mix

in their using an efficient mix of inputs; that is, we show that firms will produce in a technically efficient way on the production possibility frontier. Then, we present a more detailed proof of why competitive markets will result in the "right" final combination of goods being produced.

■ Efficiency in Input Use

If all inputs are traded in perfectly competitive markets, every firm will act as a price taker in making its decisions about which inputs to use. In this case, as we saw in Chapter 9, a firm will choose an input combination for which the rate of technical substitution (RTS) is equal to the ratio of the inputs' prices (w/v). But, since the producer of each good faces the same equilibrium input prices, w and v, the firms will all be equating their RTS to the same w/v. The desire to minimize costs will lead them to choose the same RTS, just what is required for efficiency. Since w and v are equilibrium prices of labor and capital, respectively, we also know that both inputs will be fully employed. If, in total, firms wished to have fewer workers than were available, the wage would fall to restore equilibrium between the quantity demanded and quantity supplied. Consequently, the workings of competitive markets for inputs ensure that both inputs are fully employed, and firms' desire to minimize costs ensures that they are efficiently employed among various uses. Smith's invisible hand (that is, competitive input markets) leads firms to one of the technically efficient allocations illustrated on the production possibility frontier in Figures 14.4 and 14.5.

■ Efficiency in Output Mix

A proof that the operations of competitive markets will also lead to an efficient choice of outputs is equally straightforward. Competitive markets will determine the equilibrium relative price for goods X and Y—we can call this equilibrium relative price P_X^*/P_Y^*. This price ratio is taken as given by both demanders and suppliers. For demanders, utility maximization (as we saw in Chapter 3) will lead each person to equate his or her marginal rate of substitution (MRS) to the equilibrium price ratio (P_X^*/P_Y^*). In maximizing profits, each competitive firm will produce where price equals marginal cost; that is, $P_X^* = MC_X$ and $P_Y^* = MC_Y$. But earlier in this chapter, we showed that the rate of product transformation between two goods (RPT) is given by the ratio of the good's marginal costs:

$$RPT = MC_X/MC_Y. \qquad [14.2]$$

Therefore, profit maximization will result in

$$RPT = MC_X/MC_Y = P_X^*/P_Y^*. \qquad [14.3]$$

Consequently, profit-maximizing firms equate the rate at which they can trade X for Y in production to P_X^*/P_Y^* just as people do in maximizing utility. The RPT of X for Y will equal the MRS and that, combined with the notion that demand must equal supply for each good, meets the requirements for economic efficiency described in Figure 14.5.

■ A Graphic Demonstration

Figure 14.6 illustrates this result. The figure shows the production possibility frontier for a two-good economy, and the set of indifference curves represents people's preferences for these goods. First, consider any initial price ratio P_X/P_Y. At this price ratio, firms will choose to produce the output combination X_1, Y_1. Only at this point on the production frontier will the ratio of the goods be equal to the ratio of their marginal costs (and equal to the RPT). Hence, only at X_1, Y_1 will competitive firms be maximizing profits. On the other hand, given the budget constraint represented by line C, individuals collec-

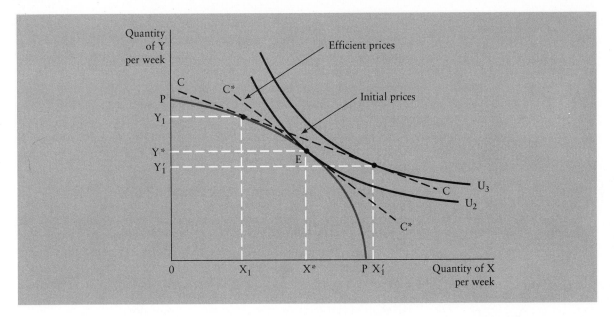

With an arbitrary initial price ratio, firms will produce X_1, Y_1; society's budget constraint will be given by line C. With this budget constraint, individuals demand X_1', Y_1'; that is, there is an excess demand for good X_1 $(X_1' - X_1)$ and an excess supply of good Y_1 $(Y_1 - Y_1')$. The workings of the market will move these prices toward their equilibrium levels P_x^*, P_y^*. At those prices, society's budget constraint will be given by the line C* and supply and demand will be in equilibrium. The combination X^*, Y^* of goods will be chosen, and this allocation is efficient.

Figure 14.6
How Perfectly Competitive Prices Bring about Efficiency

tively will demand X_1', Y_1'.[6] Consequently, at this price ratio there is an excess demand for good X (people want to buy more than is being produced), whereas there is an excess supply of good Y. The workings of the marketplace will cause P_X to rise and P_Y to fall. The price ratio P_X/P_Y will rise; the price line will move clockwise along the production possibility frontier. That is, firms will increase their production of good X and decrease their production of good Y. Similarly, people will respond to the changing prices by substituting Y for X in their consumption choices. The actions of both firms and individuals eliminate the excess demand for X and the excess supply of Y as market prices change.

Equilibrium is reached at X^*, Y^* with an equilibrium price ratio of P_X^*/P_Y^*. With this price ratio, supply and demand are equilibrated for both good X and

---

[6]It is important to recognize why the budget constraint has this location. Because P_X and P_Y are given, the value of total production is

$$P_X \cdot X_1 + P_Y \cdot Y_1.$$

This is the value of GNP in the simple economy pictured in Figure 14.6. Because of the "value of income = value of output" accounting identity, this is also the total income accruing to people in society. Society's budget constraint passes through X_1, Y_1 and has a slope of $-P_X/P_Y$. This is precisely the line labeled C in the figure.

good Y. Firms, in maximizing their profits, given P_X^* and P_Y^*, will produce X^* and Y^*. Given the income that this level of production provides to people, they will purchase precisely X^* and Y^*. Not only have markets been equilibrated by the operation of the price system, but the resulting equilibrium is also economically efficient. As we showed previously, the equilibrium allocation X^*, Y^* provides the highest level of utility that can be obtained given the existing production possibility frontier. Figure 14.6 provides a simple two-good general equilibrium proof that the results of supply and demand interacting in competitive markets can produce an efficient allocation of resources.

■ Prices, Efficiency, and Laissez-Faire Economics

We have shown that a perfectly competitive price system, by relying on the self-interest of people and of firms, and by utilizing the information carried by equilibrium prices, can arrive at an economically efficient allocation of resources. In a sense, this finding provides "scientific" support for the *laissez-faire* position taken by many economists. For example, Adam Smith's assertion that:

> The natural effort of every individual to better his own condition, when suffered to exert itself with freedom and security, is so powerful a principle that it is alone, and without any assistance, not only capable of carrying on the society to wealth and prosperity, but of surmounting a hundred impertinent obstructions with which the folly of human laws too often encumbers its operations. . . .[7]

has been shown to have considerable theoretical validity. As Smith noted, it is not the public spirit of the baker that provides bread for people to eat. Rather, bakers (and other producers) operate in their own self-interest in responding to market signals (Smith's invisible hand). In so doing, their actions are coordinated by the market into an efficient, overall pattern. The market system, at least in this simple model, imposes a very strict logic on how resources are used.

That efficiency theorem raises many important questions about the ability of markets to arrive at these perfectly competitive prices and about whether the theorem should act as a guide for government policy (for example, should governments avoid interfering in international markets as suggested by Application 14.3: Gains from Free Trade and Political Obstacles to Achieving Them?). The rest of this chapter makes a start toward answering this question, but this topic will generally occupy us for much of the remainder of this book.

Why Markets Fail to Achieve Economic Efficiency

Showing that perfect competition is economically efficient depends crucially on all of the assumptions that underlie the competitive model. In this section

---

[7]Adam Smith, *The Wealth of Nations* (1776; New York: Random House, Modern Library ed., 1937), p. 508.

we examine some of the conditions that may prevent markets from generating such an efficient allocation. We will show that many of these are quite likely to occur, although we generally delay our discussion on what to do about them until later chapters. The conditions that might interfere with perfect competition can be classed into four general groupings: *imperfect competition, externalities, public goods,* and *imperfect information.* We discuss each separately below.

■ Imperfect Competition

Imperfect competition in a broad sense includes all those situations in which economic actors (that is, buyers or sellers) exert some market power in determining price. The essential aspect of all such situations is that marginal revenue is different from market price since the firm is no longer a price taker. As we will show in Chapter 16, a profit-maximizing monopoly, by equating marginal revenue with marginal cost, will not produce where price is equal to marginal cost. Because of this behavior, relative prices will no longer accurately reflect relative marginal costs, and the price system no longer carries the information about costs necessary to ensure efficiency. Most of Part 5 in this book is concerned with investigating the consequences of this failure in the market for goods. Similar problems in input markets are briefly examined in Part 6.

■
Imperfect competition
A market situation in which buyers or sellers have some influence on the prices of goods or services.

■ Externalities

A price system can also fail to allocate resources efficiently when there are relationships among firms or between firms and people that are not adequately represented by market prices. Examples of such occurrences are numerous. Perhaps the most common is the case of a firm that pollutes the air with industrial smoke and other debris. This is called an **externality.** It is an effect of the firm's activities on people's well-being that is not taken directly into account through the normal operation of the price system. The basic problem with externalities is that firms' private costs no longer correctly reflect the social costs of production. In the absence of externalities, the costs a firm incurs accurately measure social costs. The prices of the resources the firm uses represent all the opportunity costs involved in production. When a firm creates externalities, however, there are additional costs—those that arise from the external damage. The fact that pollution from burning coal to produce steel causes diseases and general dirt and grime is as much a cost of production as are the wages paid to the firm's workers. Both types of costs should be considered in a full assessment of the social costs of steel production. However, the firm only responds to private input costs of steel production in deciding how much steel to produce. It disregards the social costs of its pollution. This results in a gap between market price and (social) marginal cost and therefore leads to a misallocation of resources.

■
Externality
The effect of one party's economic activities on another party that is not taken into account by the price system.

APPLICATION 14.3

Gains from Free Trade and Political Obstacles to Achieving Them

Following the Napoleonic Wars, high tariffs on grain imports were imposed by the British government. Debate over the effects of these "Corn Laws" dominated the politics of Great Britain during the period 1820 to 1845. A principal focus of the debate concerned the effect that elimination of tariffs would have on the welfare of British consumers and on the incomes of various groups in society. Here we examine the free trade question in both its historical context and in its more recent versions.

The Corn Laws Debate

The production possibility frontier in Figure 1 shows those combinations of grain (X) and manufactured goods (Y) that could be produced by English factors of production. Assuming (somewhat contrary to fact) that the Corn Laws completely prevented trade, market equilibrium would be at E with the domestic, pretrade price ratio shown in the figure. Removal of the tariffs would reduce this price ratio to the price ratio that prevailed in the rest of the world. Given that new ratio, England would produce combination A and consume combination B. Grain imports would amount to $X_B - X_A$ and these would be financed by export of manufactured goods equal to $Y_A - Y_B$. Overall utility would be increased by the opening of trade. Figure 1 illustrates that there may be substantial gains from trade.

By referring to the Edgeworth production box diagram that lies behind the production possibility frontier (Figure 14.3), it is also possible to analyze the effect of tariff reductions on factor prices. The movement from point E to point A in Figure 1 is similar to a movement from P_3 to P_1 in Figure 14.3. Production of X is decreased and production of Y is increased. Figure 14.3 shows the reallocation of capital and labor made necessary by such a move. If we assume that grain production is relatively capital intensive (that is, it uses a lot of land), the movement from P_3 to P_1 causes the ratio of land to labor to rise in both industries. This will, in turn, cause the relative price of land to fall (since effectively, each acre of land now has fewer workers on it). Figure 14.3 suggests that repeal of the Corn Laws would be harmful to land owners and helpful to workers. It is not surprising that landed interests fought repeal of these laws.

Modern Resistance to Trade

That trade policies may affect the relative incomes of various factors of production continues to exert a major influence on political debates about such policies. In the United States, for example, exports tend to be intensive in their use of skilled labor, whereas imports tend to be intensive in unskilled labor input. By analogy to our discussion of the Corn Laws, it might be expected that further movements toward free trade policies would result in rising relative wages for skilled workers and in falling relative wages for unskilled workers. It is not surprising that unions representing skilled workers (the Machinists, unions representing agricultural equipment workers, and the Petroleum and Atomic Workers) tend to favor free trade, whereas unions of unskilled workers (those in textiles, shoes, and related businesses) tend to oppose it.

Adjustment Costs

A careful study of Figure 1 indicates another reason why workers in firms that produce imported goods may be opposed to movement toward more open world trade. The reallocation of production from point E to point A in the figure requires that factors of production be transferred out of X (import) production into Y (export) production. Making such a reallocation may impose costs on workers. They may have to move to new communities, search for new jobs, or learn new skills. All of these activities are costly to the individuals involved. Even though society as a whole benefits from trade expansion (overall utility increases from U_2 to U_3), individual workers may not be so lucky.

Trade Adjustment Policy

In order to share the costs of adjusting to trade policies, most countries offer some sort of governmental assistance to trade-affected workers. As part of the Trade

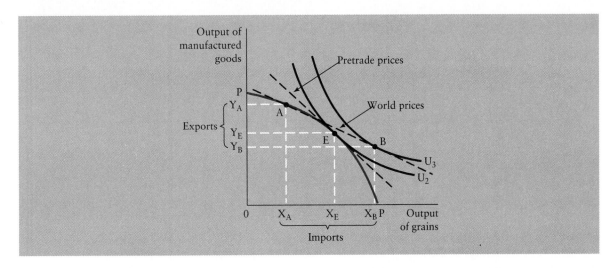

Reduction of tariff barriers on grain would cause production to be reallocated from point E to point A. Consumption would be reallocated from E to B. If grain production were relatively capital intensive, the relative price of capital would fall as a result of these reallocations.

Figure 1
Analysis of the Corn Laws Debate

Expansion Act of 1962, for example, the United States enacted a program of Trade Adjustment Assistance (TAA) to provide jobless benefits and other services to workers in industries affected by trade expansion. In 1974 all of these benefits were substantially liberalized.

Although early versions of the TAA program tended to consist mainly of cash benefits for laid-off workers, a series of amendments in 1981 and 1988 served to focus more directly on the adjustment services that the program offers. It was hoped that offering services such as job training, relocation benefits, or job search assistance would be an effective way of reducing adjustment costs. Designing appropriate services for a rapidly changing economic environment can be quite difficult. But the expanding importance of international trade in the world economy and the recent development of large free trade areas (such as that created in the 1992 North American Free Trade Agreement) suggests that the problem will grow in importance.[1]

To Think About

1. This example shows that the typical consumer gains from the opening of trade. Use Figure 1 to discuss under what circumstances these gains would be relatively large. When might they be small or nonexistent? Is it possible that the opening of the trade might actually make the typical consumer worse-off?

2. Figure 1 shows that a nation will tend to export goods that have a lower relative price domestically than they do in the international market (in this case, good Y). What factors will determine such differences in relative prices—that is, what factors determine a country's "comparative advantage" in international trade?

[1]For a further discussion see W. Corson, P. Decker, P. Gleason, and W. Nicholson, "International Trade and Worker Dislocation: Evaluation of the Trade Adjustment Assistance Program," *U.S. Department of Labor* (1992).

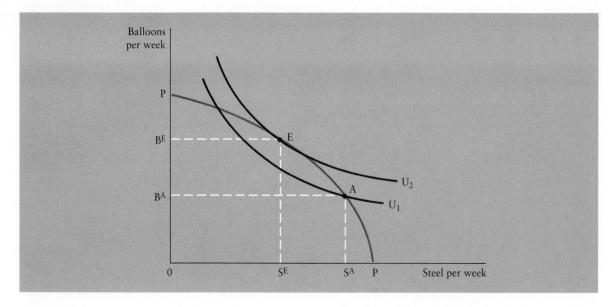

Figure 14.7
Externalities May
Cause an Inefficient
Allocation of
Resources

With an externality in steel production, firms choose to produce S^A units of steel and B^A units of balloons. Because of externalities involved in steel production, the market prices at A do not reflect individuals' true marginal rates of substitution. The allocation A is therefore inefficient and results in a lower utility level than does the efficient allocation E.

This result is illustrated in Figure 14.7. Again, in this figure, point E records an efficient allocation of resources at which the RPT is equal to the social MRS. Suppose now there is an externality in the production of good X, say, steel, but none in good Y, say, balloons. In this case, market prices do not lead economic agents to the efficient point E. Rather, firms choose to produce at point A where the RPT is equal to the ratio of equilibrium market prices. Although supply and demand are in equilibrium at these prices, such private decisions consider only the direct consumption values of steel and balloons: the steel-produced pollution is not taken into account. At point A the true MRS is less than the slope of the production possibility frontier, indicating that people are less willing to give up balloons to get more steel than is indicated by the market prices of those goods. The externality causes steel to be overproduced relative to the efficient allocation. Overall utility is reduced from U_2 to U_1 by this misallocation. In Chapter 22 we investigate a number of additional types of externalities and examine several ways in which the allocational problems they cause might be corrected.

■ **Public Goods**

A third and somewhat similar possible failure of the price system to yield an efficient allocation of resources stems from the existence of goods that can be provided to users at zero marginal cost and must be provided on a nonexclusive basis to everyone. Such goods include national defense, control of infectious diseases, provision of justice, and pest control. The distinguishing features of these goods are that providing benefits to one more person costs nothing and that they provide benefits to everyone. Once the goods are produced, it is impossible (or at least very costly) to exclude anyone from benefiting from them. In such a case price cannot equal marginal cost (which is zero) since then the fixed cost of providing the good would not be covered. There is also an incentive for each person to refuse to pay for the good in the hope that others will purchase it and thereby provide benefits to all. The pervasive nature of this incentive will ensure that not enough resources are allocated to public goods. To avoid this underallocation, communities (or nations) may decide to have the government produce these goods and finance this production through compulsory taxation. For that reason, such goods are frequently termed **public goods.** In Chapter 23 we treat the problems raised by public goods in detail.

■
Public goods
Goods that provide nonexclusive benefits to everyone in a group and that can be provided to one more user at zero marginal cost.

■ Imperfect Information

Throughout our discussion of the connection between perfect competition and economic efficiency, we have been implicitly assuming that the economic actors involved are fully informed. The most important kind of information they are assumed to have is a knowledge of equilibrium market prices. If for some reason markets are unable to establish these prices or if demanders or suppliers do not know what these prices are, the types of "invisible hand" results we developed may not hold. Consider, for example, the problem that any consumer faces in trying to buy a new television receiver. Not only does he or she have to make some kind of judgment about the quality of various brands (to determine what the available "goods" actually are) but this would-be buyer also faces the problem of finding out what various sellers are charging for a particular set. All of these kinds of problems have been assumed away so far by treating goods as being homogeneous and having a universally known market price. As we will see in the next chapter, if such assumptions do not hold, the efficiency of perfectly competitive markets is more problematic.

■ What to Do about These Problems

Any economic system will undoubtedly have examples of all four of these problems. Can solutions be found that still permit a competitive price system to do its job efficiently? Some solutions do seem possible. In Chapter 16, for example, we discuss several possible solutions to the allocational inefficiencies posed by monopolies. Similarly, in Chapter 22 we discuss solutions to the externality problem. In other cases, however, correcting problems with the competitive price system may be much more difficult. In Chapter 23, for example, we show how devising solutions to the public goods problem is particularly vexing. There seems to be no guarantee that if we leave the production of public goods to the political process (say, to be decided by voting in a democracy), this will result in the efficient amount of public goods being produced. In cases of imperfect information the route to achieving an efficient allocation of resources also may not be clear. Each problem requires a careful examination to see whether it is possible to devise solutions that help to improve allocational efficiency.

Efficiency and Equity

Equity
The fairness of the distribution of goods or utility.

So far in this chapter we have discussed the concept of economic efficiency and whether an efficient allocation of resources can be achieved through reliance on market forces. We have not mentioned questions of **equity** or fairness in the way goods are distributed among people. In this section we briefly take up this question. We show not only that it is very difficult to define what an equitable distribution of resources is, but also that there is no reason to expect that allocations that result from a competitive price system (or from practically any other method of allocating resources, for that matter) will be equitable.

Defining and Achieving Equity

A primary problem with developing an accepted definition of "fair" or "unfair" allocations of resources is that not everyone agrees as to what the concept means. Some people might call any allocation "fair" providing no one breaks any laws in arriving at it—these people would call only acquisition of goods by theft "unfair." Others may base their notions of fairness on a dislike for inequality. Only allocations in which people receive about the same levels of utility (assuming these levels could be measured and compared) would be regarded as fair. On a more practical level, some people think the current distribution of income and wealth in the United States is reasonably fair whereas others regard it as drastically unfair. Welfare economists have devised a number of more specific definitions, but these tend to give conflicting conclusions about which resource allocations are or are not equitable.[8] There is simply no agreement on this issue.

Equity and Voluntary Exchange

Even if everyone agreed on what a fair allocation of resources (and, ultimately, of people's utility) is, there would still be the question of how such a situation should be achieved. Can we rely on voluntary transactions among people to achieve fairness, or will something more be required? Our discussion of exchange in Chapter 6 shows why voluntary solutions may not always succeed.

---

[8]For a survey of these equity concepts, see Amartya Sen, "Social Choice Theory," in K. J. Arrow and M. D. Intriligator, *Handbook of Mathematical Economics*, vol. 3 (New York: North Holland Publishing Company, 1986), pp. 1106–1127.

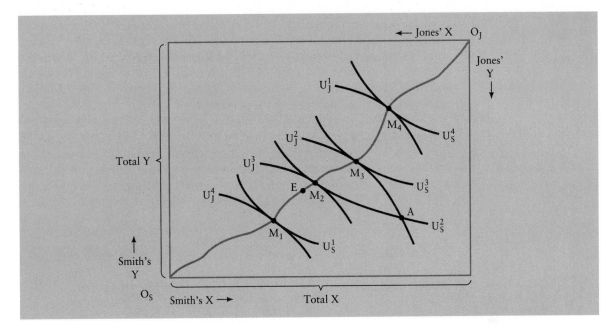

This Edgeworth box diagram for exchange is taken from Figure 6.6. Point E represents a "fair" sharing of the available goods (assuming that can be defined). If individuals' initial endowments are at point A, voluntary transactions cannot be relied on to reach point E since such an allocation makes Smith worse-off than at A.

Figure 14.8
Voluntary Transactions May Not Result in Equitable Allocations

Suppose, for example, that everyone agreed that the only fair allocation is one of equal utilities. Perhaps everyone remembers his or her childhood experiences in dividing up a cake or candy where equal shares seemed to be the only reasonable solution. This desired allocation might be represented by point E in the Edgeworth exchange box in Figure 14.8 (see Figure 6.6 also). On the other hand, suppose Smith and Jones start out at point A—at which Smith is in a fairly favorable situation. As we described previously, any allocation between M_2 and M_3 is preferable to point A because both people would be better-off by voluntarily making such a move. In this case, however, the point of equal utility (E) does not fall in this range. Smith would not voluntarily agree to a move to point E since that would make him or her worse-off than at point A. Smith would prefer to refrain from any trading rather than accept the "fair" allocation E. In the language of welfare economics, the **initial endowments** (that is, the starting place for trading) of Smith and Jones are so unbalanced that voluntary agreements will not result in the desired equal allocation of utilities. If point E is to be achieved, some coercion must be used to get Smith to accept it.

Initial endowments
The initial holdings of goods from which trading begins.

■ Equity, Efficiency, and Perfect Competition

Hence, any voluntary system of trading among people (such as occurs under perfect competition) will not necessarily result in an equitable allocation of the available resources. Initial endowments may be too skewed or the concept of equity may itself be too vague to permit such a result. There is no "invisible hand" guiding a competitive system toward equitable solutions. If we insist on equity (however defined), it may be necessary to opt for some governmental coercion (such as taxes to transfer income among people) to get people to agree to allocations they would not voluntarily accept.

Adopting coercive methods to achieve equity may involve problems too. For example, in several places in this book we have shown how taxes may affect people's behavior and result in efficiency losses that arise from this distortion. Using government's power to transfer income may therefore be a costly activity; achieving equity may involve some losses of efficiency. In Application 14.4: Equity in Policy Evaluation, we discuss some of the issues that arise in making these evaluations.

Money in the Perfectly Competitive Model

Thus far in this chapter, we have shown how competitive markets can establish a set of relative prices at which all markets are in equilibrium simultaneously. At several places we stressed that such competitive market forces determine only relative, not absolute, prices and that to examine how the absolute price level is determined we must introduce money into our models. Although a complete examination of this topic is more properly studied as part of macroeconomics, here we can briefly explore some questions of the role of money in a competitive economy that relate directly to microeconomics.

■ Nature and Function of Money

Money serves two primary functions in any economy: (1) it facilitates transactions by providing an accepted medium of exchange; and (2) it acts as a store of value so that economic actors can better allocate their spending decisions over time. Any commodity can serve as "money" provided it is generally accepted for exchange purposes and is durable from period to period. Today most economies tend to use government-created (fiat) money because the costs associated with its production (e.g., printing pieces of paper with portraits of past or present rulers or keeping records on magnetic tape) are very low. In earlier times, however, commodity money was common with the particular good chosen ranging from the familiar (gold and silver) to the obscure and even bizarre (sharks' teeth or, on the island of Yap, large stone wheels). Societies probably choose the particular form that their money will take as a result of a wide variety of economic, historical, and political forces.

■ Money as the Accounting Standard

One of the most important functions money usually plays is to act as an accounting standard. All prices are then quoted in terms of this standard. In

APPLICATION 14.4

Equity in Policy Evaluation

When public policies make some people better-off and other people worse-off, the problem of making judgments about equity is inescapable. Economists often adopt efficiency-based approaches to this problem by arguing that policy choices might be made in such a way as to make total national wealth as large as possible. Much of the analysis of shaded areas representing welfare gains and losses in Chapter 13 was based on this approach. Similarly, the approach in this chapter of using a representative individual's indifference curve may also implicitly involve an adding up of welfare gains. Such a "skirting" of the equity question has raised a number of concerns in the evaluation of public policies. Here we look at a few of these concerns.

The Issue of Standing

Our analysis of welfare effects in Chapter 13 implicitly assumed that only specific people's preferences were of significance. In the discussion of tariffs, for example, we only considered the welfare of domestic consumers and producers—any welfare effects on foreigners were disregarded. The question of whose benefits and costs are to matter in any particular analysis has come to be referred to by the legal term "standing." Individuals who are taken into account are said to have standing whereas those who are outside the analysis do not have standing.[1]

One intriguing aspect of the debate over standing concerns the question of criminal behavior. One goal of many social programs (such as job training, education, and substance abuse counseling) is to reduce crimes like auto thefts. Should the reduction in the value of stolen cars be considered a benefit of such programs? If criminals have standing, car thefts are simply a transfer (albeit, not a voluntary one) from one owner to another—from this point of view, reductions of such thefts would involve no benefits. On the other hand, if the utility gains from criminal activities are regarded as illicit, a reduction in auto thefts provides a net increase in welfare for car owners. The issue of standing can therefore have an important effect on the overall assessment of these types of programs.

Equity Weights

Computing the effect of various economic actions on total national wealth implicitly assumes that it is meaningful to add together the dollar amounts of gains and losses being incurred by different people. Some economists have argued that, because these people may have very different incomes, such a computation obscures actual welfare effects. Rather, they favor assigning equity weights under which dollar gains or losses to low-income people are weighted more heavy than are dollar gains or losses to high-income people. In this view, then, a tariff on French wine might actually improve welfare because the losers (high-income consumers) would have the dollar value of their losses weighted less than would the gainers (domestic wine producers, some of whom are poor farm workers).

Adoption of equity weights requires that a number of arbitrary assumptions be made and this approach has not been widely embraced by economists. The efficiency costs that would follow from basing policies on such an assessment might simply be too high to be acceptable to most people.[2] Instead, they prefer reliance on efficiency-based, net-wealth computations, perhaps supplemented with compensation and adjustment policies (such as those described in Application 14.3) to achieve equity ends.

To Think About

1. Can you think of any general principles for guidance in the standing question? Should foreign economic actors have standing? How about future generations? How about trees and wildlife (who may suffer losses from economic development policies)?
2. Can you think of a situation where the use of distributional weights would favor an excise tax over an untaxed situation? Under what general circumstances would such an outcome be more likely to occur?

---

[1]For a more complete discussion, see D. Whittington and D. MacRace, "The Issue of Standing in Cost-Benefit Analysis," *Journal of Policy Analysis and Management* (Summer 1986): 665–682.
[2]See A. C. Harberger, "On the Use of Distributional Weights in Social Cost-Benefit Analysis," *Journal of Political Economy* (April 1978): S87–S120. Harberger develops an example in which ice cream is to be shipped from a rich oasis to a poor one. Losses (from melting) of up to 98 percent of the amount shipped might still be socially beneficial given the distributional weights in his example.

general, relative prices will be unaffected by which good (or possibly basket of goods) is chosen as the accounting standard. For example, if one apple (good 1) exchanges for two plums (good 2):

$$\frac{P_1}{P_2} = \frac{2}{1},$$ [14.4]

and it makes little difference how those prices are quoted. If, for example, a society chooses clams as its monetary unit of account, an apple might exchange for four clams and a plum for two clams. If we denote clam prices of apples and plums by P_1' and P_2', respectively, we have

$$\frac{P_1'}{P_2'} = \frac{4}{2} = \frac{2}{1} = \frac{P_1}{P_2}.$$ [14.5]

We could change from counting in clams to counting in sharks' teeth by knowing that 10 sharks' teeth exchange for one clam. The price of our goods in sharks' teeth would be

$$P_1'' = 4 \cdot 10 = 40$$ [14.6]

and

$$P_2'' = 2 \cdot 10 = 20.$$

One apple (which costs 40 teeth) would still exchange for two plums which cost 20 teeth each.

Of course, using clams or sharks' teeth is not very common. Instead, societies usually adopt paper money as their accounting standard. An apple might exchange for half a piece of paper picturing George Washington (i.e., $.50) and a plum for one-fourth of such a piece of paper ($.25). Thus, with this monetary standard, the relative price remains two for one. Choice of an accounting standard does not, however, necessarily dictate any particular absolute price level. An apple might exchange for four clams or four hundred, but, as long as a plum exchanges for half as many clams, relative prices will be unaffected by the absolute level that prevails. But absolute price levels are obviously important, especially to individuals who wish to use money as a store of value. A person with a large investment in clams obviously cares about how many apples he or she can buy. Although a complete theoretical treatment of the price level issue is beyond the scope of this book, we do offer some brief comments here.

■ Commodity Money

In an economy where money is produced in a way similar to any other good (gold is mined, clams are dug, or sharks are caught), the relative price of money is determined like any other relative price—by the forces of demand

and supply. Economic forces that affect either the demand or supply of money will also affect these relative prices. For example, Spanish importation of gold from the New World during the fifteenth and sixteenth centuries greatly expanded gold supplies and caused the relative price of gold to fall. That is, the prices of all other goods rose relative to that of gold—there was general inflation in the prices of practically everything in terms of gold. Similar effects would arise from changes in any factor that affected the equilibrium price for the good chosen as money. Application 14.5: Exchange and Money in a POW Camp illustrates how the use of commodity money can arise in even the most trying of circumstances and how increases in this money can cause general inflation.

■ Fiat Money and the Monetary Veil

For the case of fiat money produced by the government, the analysis can be extended a bit. In this situation the government is the sole supplier of money and can generally choose how much it wishes to produce. What effects will this level of money production have on the real economy? In general, the situation would seem to be identical to that for commodity money. A change in the money supply will disturb the general equilibrium of all relative prices, and, although it seems likely that an expansion in supply will lower the relative price of money (that is, result in an inflation in the money prices of other goods), any more precise prediction would seem to depend on the results of a detailed general equilibrium model of supply and demand in many markets.

Beginning with David Hume, however, classical economists argued that money (especially fiat money) differs from other economic goods and should be regarded as being outside the real economic system of demand, supply, and relative price determination. In this view the economy can be dichotomized into a real sector in which relative prices are determined and a monetary sector where the absolute price level (that is, the value of fiat money) is set. Money, therefore, acts only as a "veil" for real economic activity; the quantity of money available has no effect on the real sector.[9]

Whether the classical dichotomy between the real and monetary sectors actually holds in the real world is an empirical question that cannot be resolved on theoretical grounds alone. Although a monetary sector can be incorporated into the standard competitive model of general equilibrium in ways that preserve the dichotomy, many of these are somewhat artificial and rely on rather restrictive assumptions. Discovering whether they still represent a reasonable approximation of the behavior of the economy (especially over the long term) is an important unresolved issue in macroeconomics.

---

[9]This leads directly to the quantity theory of the demand for money, first suggested by Hume:

$$D_M = \frac{1}{V} \cdot P \cdot Q,$$

where D_M is the demand for money, V is the velocity of monetary circulation (the number of times a dollar is used each year), P is the overall price level, and Q is a measure of the quantity of transactions (often approximated by real GDP). If V is fixed and Q is determined by real forces, a doubling of the supply of money will result in a doubling of the equilibrium price level.

APPLICATION 14.5
Exchange and Money in a POW Camp

Prisoner of war (POW) camps illustrate ways in which voluntary market-type arrangements may arise even in the most trying of circumstances. The basic goods available to prisoners in such situations are usually determined by what they are given by their captors and by what goods come through other sources (for example, the Red Cross). Very little actual production takes place. Still, as R. A. Radford shows in his famous article detailing his experiences as a POW during World War II, elaborate arrangements may develop for reallocating the available goods in more efficient ways.[1] Radford shows, for example, that most prisoners were given essentially the same set of basic necessities, but customary barter rates of exchange among these commodities rapidly developed to reflect the prisoners' preferences. Tins of jam typically traded for one-half pound of margarine, whereas tins of diced carrots were worth practically nothing in exchange.

Development of Monetary Institutions

Bartering one good for another involves a potential inefficiency. A person who wants to trade jam for margarine has to find someone willing to make the opposite trade. It is this problem that leads all modern societies to adopt money as a way of facilitating exchange. With a monetary system, one need not find someone willing to trade margarine for jam but can instead trade the jam for money and then use the money to buy margarine.

In the POW camps there was no money in the usual sense, but as Radford shows, cigarettes came to play this role. Every commodity had a customary price in terms of cigarettes, and relative cigarette prices reflected relative rates of exchange between commodities. During periods when many Red Cross packages were received, cigarette supplies rose, and there was a general inflation of goods' prices in terms of cigarettes. This reflects Hume's notion (see footnote 9) that general inflation may simply represent "too much money chasing too few goods." Similarly, Gresham's law (that bad money drives out good) was reflected by the fact that only relatively poor quality cigarettes were used for making transactions—the better ones were smoked.

Trade and Specialization

Radford also observed a form of international trade in the POW camps. Since French and British troops were imprisoned in separate areas, different prices developed for goods in these communities. Coffee, for example, was more highly valued in terms of cigarettes among French prisoners than among British prisoners. Risk-taking entrepreneurs who were willing to move between the camps (usually by bribing guards) could get "rich" by buying coffee from the British and selling it to the French. Because the French also used cigarettes as currency, such arbitrage activity was fairly easy to undertake.

To Think About

1. Suppose a POW camp's only source of jam was from monthly Red Cross packages. Would you expect sharp declines in jam prices just after the packages arrive? If you, as a prisoner, observed such a regular pattern, what would you do?

2. Some medical officers at the POW camps argued that use of cigarettes as money was unfair to smokers, since they might harm their health by selling their food rations for more cigarettes. The medical officers favored "price controls" on some food items. How would you evaluate this argument for price controls? How effective do you think such controls would be?

---

[1] R. A. Radford, "The Economic Organization of a POW Camp," *Economics* (November 1945): 189–201.

Summary

We began this chapter with a description of a general equilibrium model of a perfectly competitive price system. In that model, relative prices are determined by the forces of supply and demand, and everyone takes these prices as given in their economic decisions. We then arrive at the following conclusions about such a method for allocating resources:

- Profit-maximizing firms will use resources in a technically efficient way to produce goods because each cost-minimizing firm chooses a combination of inputs for which the RTS is equal to the ratio of the inputs' prices. Firms will therefore operate on the production possibility frontier.

- Profit-maximizing firms will also produce an economically efficient mix of outputs. The workings of supply and demand will ensure that the technical rate at which one good can be transformed into another in production (the rate of product transformation—RPT) is equal to the rate at which people are willing to trade one good for another (the MRS). Adam Smith's invisible hand brings considerable coordination into seemingly chaotic market transactions.

- Factors that interfere with the ability of prices to reflect marginal costs under perfect competition will prevent an economically efficient allocation of resources. Such factors include imperfect competition, externalities, and public goods. Imperfect information about market prices may also interfere with the efficiency of perfect competition.

- Under perfect competition there are no forces to ensure that voluntary transactions will result in equitable final allocations. Achieving equity (if that term can be adequately defined at all) may require some coercion to transfer income. Such interventions may involve costs in terms of economic efficiency.

- A perfectly competitive price system establishes only relative prices. Introduction of money into the competitive model is needed to show how nominal prices are determined. In some cases the amount of money (and the absolute price level) will have no effect on the relative prices established in competitive markets.

Review Questions

1. Why should an economist who is only interested in one market be concerned about general equilibrium relationships? Can't he or she just study shifts in

supply or demand in this single market without worrying about what is happening elsewhere? Provide a specific example of how omitting general equilibrium feedback effects might cause an analyst to make mistakes in his or her examination of a single market.

2. How does the approach to economic efficiency taken in Chapter 13 relate to the one taken here? How is the possible inefficiency in Figure 13.1 related to that in Figure 14.6?

3. Why are allocations on the production possibility frontier technically efficient? What is technically inefficient about allocations inside the frontier? Do inefficient allocations necessarily involve any unemployment of factors of production? In the model introduced in this chapter, would unemployment be technically inefficient?

4. Why does the rate of product transformation indicate relative opportunity costs? Why do economists expect the opportunity cost of X to increase as the output of X increases? Suppose the RPT were constant. What would the production possibility curve look like in this case and what would that assume about the marginal costs of X and Y production?

5. Suppose two countries had differing production possibility frontiers and were currently producing with different RPTs. If there were no transportation or other charges associated with international transactions, how might world output be increased by having these firms alter their production plans? Develop a simple numerical example of these gains for the case where both countries have linear production possibility frontiers (with different slopes). Interpret this result in terms of the concept of "comparative advantage" from the theory of international trade.

6. Use a simple two-good model of resource allocation (such as that in Figure 14.5) to explain the difference between technical efficiency and economic (or allocative) efficiency. Would you agree with the statement that "economic efficiency requires technical efficiency, but many technically efficient allocations are not economically efficient"? Explain your reasoning with a graph.

7. How can you read the capital-labor ratio in the production of each good from the Edgeworth box diagram in Figure 14.3? Why does this particular figure indicate that good X has a higher capital-labor ratio in its production than does good Y? Explain how a reduction in X output and an increase in Y output might affect the demand for capital in this economy. Since the supply of capital is fixed, how might such a shift in demand affect the price of capital? How is this related to the British Corn Laws debate described in Application 14.3?

8. In Chapter 12 we showed how a shift in demand or supply could be analyzed using a model of a single market. How would you illustrate an increase in the demand for good X in the general equilibrium model pictured in Figure 14.6? Why would such a shift in preferences cause the relative price of X to rise? What would happen to the market for good Y in this case? How would you conduct a similar comparative statics analysis of an improvement in the technology for producing good X?

9. Relative prices convey information about both production possibilities and people's preferences. What exactly is that information and how does its availability help attain an efficient allocation of resources? In what ways does the presence of monopoly or externalities result in price information being "inaccurate"?

10. In most of the theoretical examples in this book, prices have been quoted in dollars or cents. Is this choice of currency crucial? Would most examples be the same if prices had been stated in pounds, marks, or yen? Or, would it have mattered if the dollars used were "1900 dollars" or "1990 dollars"? How would you change the endless hamburger–soft drink examples, say, to phrase them in some other currency? Would such changes result in any fundamental differences? Or, do most of the examples in this book seem to display the classical dichotomy between real and nominal magnitudes?

Problems

14.1 Suppose the production possibility frontier for cheeseburgers (C) and milk-shakes (M) is given by

$$C + 2M = 600.$$

a. Graph this function.
b. Assuming that people prefer to eat two cheeseburgers with every milkshake, how much of each product will be produced? Indicate this point on your graph.
c. Given that this fast food economy is operating efficiently, what price ratio (P_C/P_M) must prevail?

14.2 Consider an economy with just one technique available for the production of each good, food and cloth:

Good	Food	Cloth
Labor per unit output	1	1
Land per unit output	2	1

a. Supposing land is unlimited but labor equals 100, write and sketch the production possibility frontier.
b. Supposing labor is unlimited but land equals 150, write and sketch the production possibility frontier.
c. Supposing labor equals 100 and land equals 150, write and sketch the production possibility frontier. (Hint: What are the intercepts of the production possibility frontier? When is land fully employed? Labor? Both?)
d. Explain why the production possibility frontier of part c is concave.
e. Sketch the relative price of food as a function of its output in part c.
f. If consumers insist on trading four units of food for five units of cloth, what is the relative price of food? Why?

g. Explain why production is exactly the same at a price ratio of $P_F/P_C = 1.1$ as at $P_F/P_C = 1.9$.

h. Suppose that capital is also required for producing food and cloth and that capital requirements per unit of food are 0.8 and per unit of cloth 0.9. There are 100 units of capital available. What is the production possibility curve in this case? Answer part e for this case.

*14.3 Suppose the production possibility frontier for guns (X) and butter (Y) is given by

$$X^2 + 2Y^2 = 900.$$

a. Graph this frontier.

b. If individuals always prefer consumption bundles in which $Y = 2X$, how much X and Y will be produced?

c. At the point described in part b, what will be the RPT and what price ratio will cause production to take place at that point? This slope should be approximated by considering small changes in X and Y around the optimal point.

d. Show your solution on the figure from part a.

14.4 The country of Extrenum produces only skis (S) and waterskis (W), using capital (K) and labor (L) as inputs. The production functions for both S and W are fixed proportions. It takes two units of labor and one unit of capital to produce a pair of skis. Waterskis, on the other hand, require one unit of labor and one unit of capital. If the total supply of labor is 150 units and the total supply of capital is 100 units, construct the production possibility curve for this economy. Are all inputs fully employed at every point on the production possibility curve? How do you explain any unemployment that might exist?

*14.5 Robinson Crusoe obtains utility from the quantity of fish he consumes in one day (F), the quantity of coconuts he consumes that day (C), and the hours of leisure time he has during the day (H) according to the utility function:

$$\text{Utility} = F^{1/4}C^{1/4}H^{1/2}.$$

Robinson's production of fish is given by

$$F = \sqrt{L_F}$$

(where L_F is the hours he spends fishing), and his production of coconuts is determined by

$$C = \sqrt{L_C}$$

(where L_C is the time he spends picking coconuts). Assuming that Robinson decides to work an eight-hour day (that is, $H = 16$), graph his production possibility curve for fish and coconuts. Show his optimal choices of those goods.

---

*Denotes a problem that is rather difficult.

14.6 Suppose two individuals (Smith and Jones) each have 10 hours of labor to devote to producing either ice cream (X) or chicken soup (Y). Smith's demand for X and Y is given by

$$X_S = .3I_S/P_X$$

$$Y_S = .7I_S/P_Y$$

whereas Jones' demands are given by

$$X_J = .5I_J/P_X$$

$$Y_J = .5I_J/P_Y$$

where I_S and I_J represent Smith's and Jones' incomes, respectively (which come only from working).

The individuals do not care whether they produce X or Y and the production function for each good is given by

$$X = 2L$$

$$Y = 3L$$

where L is the total labor devoted to production of each good. Using this information, answer the following:

a. What must the price ratio, P_X/P_Y, be?
b. Given this price ratio, how much X and Y will Smith and Jones demand? (Hint: Set the wage equal to 1 here so that each person's income is 10.)
c. How should labor be allocated between X and Y to satisfy the demand calculated in part b?

*14.7 In the country of Ruritania there are two regions, A and B. Two goods (X and Y) are produced in both regions. Production functions for region A are given by

$$X_A = \sqrt{L_X}$$

$$Y_A = \sqrt{L_Y}.$$

L_X and L_Y are the quantity of labor devoted to X and Y production, respectively. Total labor available in region A is 100 units. That is,

$$L_X + L_Y = 100.$$

Using a similar notation for region B, production functions are given by

$$X_B = 1/2\sqrt{L_X}$$

$$Y_B = 1/2\sqrt{L_Y}.$$

---

*Denotes a problem that is rather difficult.

There are also 100 units of labor available in region B:

$$L_X + L_Y = 100.$$

a. Calculate the production possibility curves for regions A and B.
b. What condition must hold if production in Ruritania is to be allocated efficiently between regions A and B (assuming that labor cannot move from one region to the other)?
c. Calculate the production possibility curve for Ruritania (again assuming that labor is immobile between regions). How much total Y can Ruritania produce if total X output is 12? (Hint: A graphic analysis may be of some help here.)

14.8 There are 200 pounds of food on an island that must be allocated between two marooned sailors. The utility function of the first sailor is given by

$$\text{Utility} = \sqrt{F_1}$$

where F_1 is the quantity of food consumed by the first sailor. For the second sailor, utility (as a function of food consumption) is given by

$$\text{Utility} = 1/2\sqrt{F_2}.$$

a. If the food is allocated equally between the sailors, how much utility will each receive?
b. How should food be allocated between the sailors to assure equality of utility?
c. Suppose that the second sailor requires a utility level of at least 5 to remain alive. How should food be allocated so as to maximize the sum of utilities subject to the restraint that the second sailor receive that minimum level of utility?
d. What other criteria might you use to allocate the available food between the sailors?

*14.9 Suppose that there are two individuals in an economy. Utilities of those individuals under five possible social states are shown in the following table.

State	Utility 1	Utility 2
A	50	50
B	70	40
C	45	54
D	53	50.5
E	30	84

The individuals do not know which number (1 or 2) they will be assigned when the economy begins operating. They are uncertain about the actual utility they will receive under the alternative social states. Which social state will be pre-

---

*Denotes a problem that is rather difficult.

ferred if an individual adopts the following strategies in his or her voting behavior to deal with this uncertainty?

a. Choose that state that assures the highest utility to the least well-off person.
b. Assume that there is a 50–50 chance of being either individual and choose that state with the highest expected utility.
c. Assume that, no matter what, the odds are always unfavorable in that there is a 60 percent chance of having the lower utility and a 40 percent chance of higher utility in any social state. Choose the state with the highest expected utility given these probabilities.
d. Assume that there is a 50–50 chance of being assigned either number, and that each individual dislikes inequality. Each will choose that state for which:

$$\text{Expected utility} - |U_1 - U_2|$$

is as large as possible (where the | . . . | notation denotes absolute value).
e. What do you conclude from this problem about the social choices under a veil of ignorance as to an individual's specific identity in society?

14.10 Return to problem 14.6 and now assume that Smith and Jones conduct their exchanges in paper money. The total supply of such money is $60 and each individual wishes to hold a stock of money equal to $1/4$ of the value of transactions made per period.

a. What will the money wage rate be in this model? What will the nominal prices of X and Y be?
b. Suppose the money supply increases to $90, how will your answers to part a change? Does this economy exhibit the classical dichotomy between its real and monetary sectors?

This appendix introduces the mathematical tool of linear programming and uses this tool to demonstrate some additional relationships between the efficient use of resources and the pricing of those resources. Since a detailed treatment of linear programming is beyond the scope of this book, our analysis here is brief.[1]

APPENDIX
TO
CHAPTER
14

LINEAR
PROGRAMMING,
PRICING OF
INPUTS, AND
DUALITY

The Problem

To illustrate some of the basic concepts of linear programming, we will look at one simple example. In this example, an economy is assumed to have fixed amounts of various productive inputs, and a central planner must choose how to allocate these inputs to the production of two goods, cars and pickup trucks. In order to avoid having to study the demand for these goods, we assume that prices of cars and pickups are determined outside of our model and do not change. We assume that the price of each truck (P_T) is $12,000 and that the price of each car (P_C) is $15,000. The sole goal of the central planner in our simply economy is to allocate the available resources to car and truck production so that the total value of output is as large as possible. That is, the goal is to choose car output (C) and truck output (T) so that

$$\text{Total value} = TV = P_T \cdot T + P_C \cdot C$$
$$= 12,000 \cdot T + 15,000 \cdot C \qquad \text{[14A.1]}$$

is as large as possible given available resources.

■ A Graphic Demonstration

Before we approach the solution to this problem using linear programming, the general kind of answer we will get can be demonstrated very simply. The most direct way to proceed is by using a graphic analysis. In Figure 14A.1 the production possibility frontier is drawn for the economy. The curve PP represents those combinations of cars and pickup trucks that can be produced given the inputs available. Our goal is to choose that point on the PP frontier that provides maximum revenues. This maximization process is shown in the figure. The several parallel straight lines (labeled TV_1, TV_2, TV_3) record those combinations of cars and trucks that provide equal value. The combinations lying along TV_3 provide more in total value than those on TV_2, which in turn provide more value than do those on TV_1. The slope of these lines is given by

$$-P_T/P_C \ (= -\$12,000/\$15,000 = -4/5)$$

since this ratio of prices tells how cars can be traded for trucks in the market while keeping the total value for output constant.

[1]For an interesting though fairly difficult survey of linear programming techniques, see Robert Dorfman, P. A. Samuelson, and R. M. Solow, *Linear Programming and Economic Analysis* (New York: McGraw-Hill, 1958).

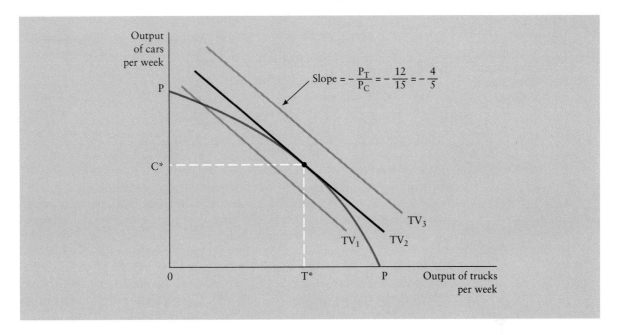

PP represents the feasible combinations of cars and trucks that can be produced with available resources. If a central planner wishes to maximize the total value of production (TV), the combination C*, T* should be produced. At this output combination, the RPT (of trucks for cars) is equal to the ratio of these goods' prices (P_T/P_C).

Figure 14A.1
Value Maximization in a Hypothetical Economy

The total value of cars and trucks produced is as large as possible when output combination C*, T* is chosen. This combination produces total revenues of TV_2, and it is the only combination that is capable of providing this amount. All other feasible output combinations on PP provide less total value than does this optimal choice. At C*, T* the production possibility frontier is exactly tangent to the total value line TV_2. This type of result should be familiar to you from Chapter 14. At the optimal point, the rate at which cars can technically be traded for trucks is equal to the rate at which these two goods are willingly traded by buyers in the market. In other words, the rate of product transformation (of trucks for cars) is equal to the price ratio (P_T/P_C).

A Linear Programming Statement of the Problem

Linear programming is a mathematical technique that is particularly suited to solving a problem like the one illustrated in Figure 14A.1. The technique was developed as a systematic way to find the maximum values of linear functions (such as Equation 14A.1) when the variables in these functions—in our case, car and truck production—are constrained in the values they can take on. In

Linear programming
A mathematical technique for finding the maximum (or minimum) value for a linear function whose variables are subject to linear constraints.

		Required to Produce	Required to Produce
Resource	Total Available	1 Truck	1 Car
Labor	720 labor-hours	1 labor-hour	2 labor-hours
Machines	900 machine-hours	3 machine-hours	1 machine-hour
Steel	1,800 tons	5 tons	4 tons

Table 14A.1 Resources and Technology in a Hypothetical Economy

order to show how this technique works, we must first examine the factors in the economy that constrain the output choices that are feasible.

As we saw in Chapter 14, there are two types of constraints on the amount that can be produced by any economy: total quantities of various inputs are fixed, and certain technical rules (that is, production functions) must be followed in turning these inputs into outputs. For the purposes of our car-truck example, we assume that there are only three inputs: labor, machines, and steel. The quantities of these inputs that are assumed to be available are shown in the second column of Table 14A.1. No production plan can be implemented that uses more than 720 labor-hours, 900 machine-hours, or 1,800 tons of steel.

■ Production Functions for Cars and Trucks

Table 14A.1 also indicates the amount of each input required to produce one car or one truck. It takes one labor-hour, three machine-hours, and five tons of steel to build a truck; it takes two labor-hours, one machine-hour, and four tons of steel to build a car. The production techniques shown in Table 14A.1 are fixed proportions (see Chapter 8): no substitution between inputs is possible. This kind of technology is one characteristic of most linear programming problems.

■ Resource Constraints

We can now examine the constraints that the available amounts of inputs place on the combinations of cars and trucks that can be produced. With C representing the number of cars to be produced and T the number of trucks, the first line of Table 14A.1 shows that all possible choices of T and C must obey the inequality

$$1 \cdot T + 2 \cdot C \leq 720. \qquad [14A.2]$$

That is, the quantity of labor employed in truck production (one labor-hour to build one truck) plus the quantity employed in car production (two labor-hours per car) cannot exceed the 720 labor-hours available. Equation 14A.2 might be called the "labor-hours" constraint in production.

Similar constraints exist for machines and for steel. Again, these can be taken directly from Table 14A.1. The machine-hour constraint is

$$3 \cdot T + 1 \cdot C \leq 900 \qquad [14A.3]$$

and the steel constraint is

$$5 \cdot T + 4 \cdot C \leq 1,800. \qquad\qquad [14A.4]$$

These constraints record that no more machines or steel may be used in production than are available.

Given these three resource constraints, our problem is to find values of T and C that satisfy all constraints and to make the total value of output,

$$TV = 12,000 \cdot T + 15,000 \cdot C,$$

as large as possible. That, then, is our linear programming problem.

■ Construction of the Production Possibility Frontier

One very time-consuming solution to the problem would be to list all the combinations of C and T that satisfy the three constraints, calculate the total value obtained from each combination, and choose the one with the largest value. In practice, however, linear programming problems are usually solved by computer. We can show how such solutions are found by using a simple graphical approach. In Figure 14A.2 we have graphed the three resource constraints. Since any feasible combination of C and T must satisfy *all* three constraints, we are interested only in those points in the diagram that fall on or below all three lines. The heavy line in Figure 14A.2 indicates the outer perimeter of such feasible choices. Combinations of cars and trucks on or inside this curve can be produced. Those outside the perimeter cannot be produced because there is not enough of at least one of the resources to do so.

For example, should the central planner in the economy decide to produce only cars, the heavy line indicates that 360 could be produced. In producing only cars, the economy "runs out" of labor-hours first (there is enough steel to produce 450 cars and enough machine-hours to produce 900 cars). For trucks, on the other hand, the **binding constraint** is machine availability. There are only enough machine-hours to build 300 trucks. Other combinations of cars and trucks on or inside the heavy line in Figure 14A.2 similarly satisfy all the constraints. The curve is just the production possibility frontier for the simple economy we have described.

Binding constraint
The presence of one or more resources that effectively limits the amount that can be produced. If a particular input is not fully utilized, it does not pose a binding constraint in production.

Linear Programming Solution of the Problem

We can use the production possibility frontier derived in Figure 14A.2 to solve our maximum value problem in much the same way that the problem was solved in Figure 14A.1. Figure 14A.3 again shows the production possibility frontier together with several lines of equal revenue. From the figure, we can see that the value-maximizing point is output combination C*, T*, where

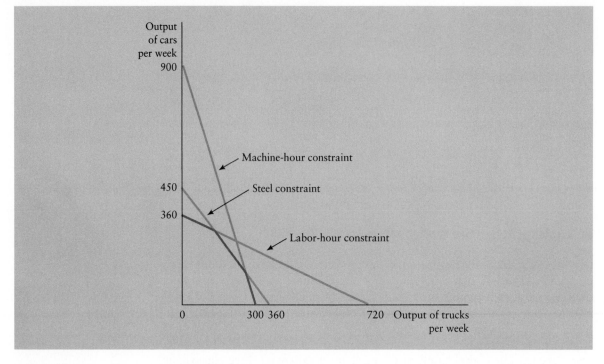

Figure 14A.2
Construction of the Production Possibility Frontier

The heavy line in this diagram is the production possibility frontier for cars and trucks implied by the input constraints. It is the perimeter of the set of output combinations that satisfies all the constraints.

the labor-hour constraint and the steel constraint intersect.[2] (Refer back to Figure 14A.2 to check that these are indeed the constraints that intersect at C^*, T^*.) Solving the two constraints for C^* and T^* gives

$$1T + 2C = 720 \text{ (labor-hour constraint)}$$

$$5T + 4C = 1{,}800 \text{ (steel constraint)} \qquad [14A.5]$$

or, from the labor-hour constraint,

$$T = 720 - 2C. \qquad [14A.6]$$

Therefore, by substitution into the steel constraint,

$$5(720) - 10C + 4C = 3{,}600 - 6C = 1{,}800. \qquad [14A.7]$$

[2]This point, in a sense, satisfies the rule that the RPT should equal the ratio P_T/P_C. The RPT along the labor-hour constraint is $-1/2$; along the steel constraint the RPT is $-5/4$. The vertex at C^*, T^* includes all slopes between $-1/2$ and $-5/4$. But the ratio $-P_T/P_C$ is given by $-4/5$, which lies between these two values. Hence, C^*, T^* is the revenue-maximizing point. In linear programming problems, the optimal solution will usually occur at corners, such as the one illustrated.

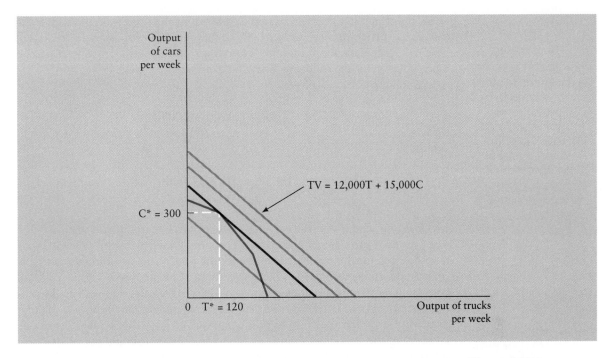

By superimposing several lines of equal revenue on the production possibility frontier, the point of maximum revenue can be found. This point occurs where the labor-hour and steel constraints intersect.

Figure 14A.3
Maximization of Revenue in the Linear Program

Hence, our optimal solution is

$$C^* = 300 \qquad T^* = 120. \qquad\qquad [14A.8]$$

That means that 120 trucks should be produced along with 300 cars. The revenue provided by these outputs is $5,940,000 (= $12,000 \cdot 120 + $15,000 \cdot 300). This is the maximum value possible given the resource constraints. At this production level not all the available machine-hours are being used. Production of 300 cars and 120 trucks requires only 660 machine hours, whereas 900 are available. The observation that at the optimal output level there are unused machines has important implications for the pricing of machines, as we will now demonstrate.

Duality and the Pricing of Inputs

So far we have said nothing about the price of inputs in this linear programming problem. The economy had certain amounts of inputs available, and the central planner set about the task of maximizing the value of the economy's output. A linear programming problem related to this *primal* maximization problem is the **dual linear programming problem** of finding the proper input prices associated with the optimal choice of car and pickup truck production. Formally, these dual input prices solve the following linear programming problem.

Minimize

$$M = 720P_L + 900\ P_K + 1,800P_S \qquad [14A.9]$$

subject to

$$P_L + 3P_K + 5P_S \geq 12,000$$
$$2P_L + P_K + 4P_S \geq 15,000 \qquad [14A.10]$$

where P_L, P_K, and P_S are the per-unit prices of labor, capital, and steel.

This dual problem can be given an economic interpretation. We are asked to find prices for the inputs that minimize the total value of all inputs available (that is, minimize total cost). These prices must not be too low (they can't all be zero). The two inequalities in Equation 14A.10 require that neither the production of cars nor trucks earns a pure economic profit. For example, the first inequality says that the costs of producing one pickup (that is, the cost of one labor-hour, three machine-hours, and five tons of steel) should not be less than the price of a truck ($12,000). Similarly, the input costs must be sufficiently high that their cost is not less than the price of a car ($15,000).

Without going into formal detail, it should be clear that the dual problem is related in some way to the original problem. All the constants that appeared in the primal problem also appear in the dual problem, but in different places. In particular, quantities of inputs that appeared in the original constraints now appear as coefficients in the dual objective function (Equation 14A.9) and vice versa. Also the constraints of the primal problem seem to have been "turned on their side" in the dual problem.

■ Solution to the Dual Problem

A graphic solution to the dual linear programming problem is not presented here because it would require a three-dimensional graph to show all three input prices. It must be taken on faith that the solution to the dual program turns out to be

$$P_L = \$4,500$$

$$P_K = \$0$$

$$P_S = \$1,500. \qquad [14A.11]$$

These are the prices of labor, machines, and steel that minimize Equation 14A.9 and obey the two constraints given by Equation 14A.10. You may wish to check if this is indeed true.

This solution has several important features:

- With these input prices, the inequalities in Equation 14A.10 are exactly satisfied. The cost of a pickup, for example, is $4,500 + 0 + 5 \cdot $1,500, which is precisely $12,000. A similar statement holds for cars. So, neither good is produced at a loss. Hence, both goods can be produced in the economy without needing a subsidy.

- The total value of all the inputs with these input prices is $5,940,000. It is no coincidence that this is identical to the maximum value for the total value of output that we found in the primal problem. Such a relationship holds between the primal and the dual solutions of all linear programs. Here this equality resembles the income-output identity in the *National Income and Product Accounts*. The total value of output is equal to the total value of inputs.

- The input that had some extra amount left over in the primal problem (machine-hours) is given a price of $0 in the dual problem. This result tells economists that adding machines in this economy would have no effect on the value of output. In formal terms, the **shadow price** of machinery in this example is 0 because machinery is not really scarce. On the other hand, since labor and steel are the binding constraints that prevent output from being increased, these inputs are given positive shadow prices. The values given in Equation 14A.11 for P_L and P_S indicate how much extra value would be provided by one more unit of these inputs. You may wish to show, for example, that an increase in labor-hours by one unit will cause the total output to increase by $4,500 if we allow the economy to produce fractional parts of cars and trucks.[3]

Further Observations on Duality

Our two linear programming problems demonstrate the relationship between the optimal choice of outputs and the correct choice of input prices. The optimal allocation of a fixed amount of inputs to the production of a variety of possible outputs always has associated with it a dual problem that involves the optimal pricing of those inputs available. The solution of one problem is equivalent to the solving of the other.[4] This relationship, which has an obvious similarity to Adam Smith's invisible hand image, has been widely used in practical problems as well.

The computation of input prices from a linear programming model can be very useful for economic planning in less-developed economies. Such shadow prices can provide information about how important certain inputs are, and occasionally such computed prices may differ greatly from the actual prices of

Shadow prices
Prices for resources in a dual linear programming problem. For resources that represent binding constraints on production, shadow prices will be positive. For resources that do not represent binding constraints, shadow prices are zero.

---

[3]The firm will produce five-sixths of an additional car in this situation but will cut truck production by two-thirds of a truck. Consequently, total revenue is changed by $5/_6 \cdot $15,000 − 2/_3 \cdot $12,000$, which is about $4,500.

[4]Linear programming problems may not always have solutions. If a linear programming problem and its associated dual have "feasible" solutions (solutions that satisfy the constraints of the problems), then they each have optimal solutions that have the properties listed above. For an elegant and concise discussion of the relationship between primal and dual linear programming problems with applications to a variety of allocational problems, see David Gale, *The Theory of Linear Economic Models* (New York: McGraw-Hill, 1960).

the inputs. For example, there are institutional reasons (labor unions, minimum wages, and so forth) why some groups of workers may have high wages even though labor is an overabundant resource in the particular country. On the other hand, linear programming models may suggest that the "real" value of labor is rather low, and planners should adopt production techniques that utilize labor to a greater extent than would seem economically warranted by looking only at market wage rates.

Corporations have used linear programming in a similar way to make more efficient management decisions. One such use arises when a firm wishes to decentralize its decision making. To do so, the firm often divides its operations among several profit centers, which are responsible for all production decisions within a specific area. One problem with which the management of such decentralized firms must contend is how to charge each profit center for the general company inputs (plant and equipment, administrative staff, advertising staff) it uses. Only by correctly choosing the bookkeeping prices of these inputs can the firm's management be sure that the decisions of the manager of each profit center will produce desirable overall results. Linear programming has been used extensively for calculating the prices of such intracompany resources.

These two examples merely hint at the huge number of applications that linear programming has had. Others include such widely different uses as the planning of natural gas pipelines and railway yards, investigating the optimal portfolio of stocks for a mutual fund to own, and studying the movement of seasonal labor forces in Africa. In many of these applications, a linear program's duality features are utilized.

Summary

This appendix describes the use of the mathematical tool of linear programming as a way to solve economic problems. In addition to illustrating the technique with a simple example, it also discusses the importance of the dual relationship between allocating resources efficiently and the correct pricing of these resources. The specific findings in the appendix are

- Linear programming can sometimes be used to find the maximum (or minimum) value for a linear function when the values of some of the variables in the function are subject to linear constraints.

- The optimal solution found by linear programming will have many of the characteristics of efficiency illustrated in Chapter 14. Specifically, the marginal rate of product transformation will be approximately equal to the relative prices of the goods being produced.

- Solving the dual to a linear programming problem can provide optimal prices for scarce resources. Resources that are not scarce will be assigned a price of zero in such solutions.

Thus far, our model of competitive price determination has assumed that economic actors have complete information. Both demanders and suppliers were assumed to know the prices of all available goods and to use those prices in making their decisions. As we pointed out in Chapter 7, however, such a complete degree of knowledge is unlikely to exist in the real world. Acquiring information about the prices and other characteristics of economic goods is a costly activity. We might, therefore, expect actual market information to be both imperfect and unevenly distributed.

In this chapter we will examine some of the consequences of such informational problems. We begin by examining some of the ways in which the existence of imperfect information might affect the ability of markets to establish equilibrium prices. We also discuss some of the ways in which nonequilibrium prices might occur. Finally, we ask whether equilibrium prices that are established in the presence of imperfect information will have the same efficiency properties as those in the simple models of the previous chapters.

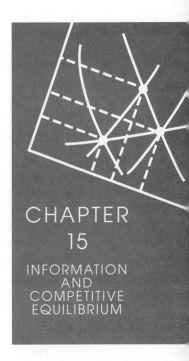

CHAPTER
15

INFORMATION AND COMPETITIVE EQUILIBRIUM

Establishing Competitive Equilibrium Prices

One of the most difficult problems faced by any competitive market is how an equilibrium price is discovered. What market signals do suppliers and demanders use to adjust their behavior toward equilibrium? Do they rely on temporary, nonequilibrium prices to make such decisions, or are other mechanisms available? We know from Chapter 12 that for most competitive markets an equilibrium price, P*, exists for which the quantity demanded is equal to the quantity supplied. Now we wish to examine how market price actually gets to P*. We begin with some theoretical answers proposed by economists, then turn to examine briefly some of the problems of information that arise in applying these theoretical suggestions to the real world.

■ The Impartial Auctioneer and Recontracting

To explain the movement of price to its equilibrium level, some economists have relied on the fictitious notion of an impartial auctioneer. The auctioneer is charged with calling out prices and recording the actions of buyers and sellers. Only when the auctioneer calls a price for which the quantity demanded is identical to that which is supplied will trading be permitted to take place. Presumably, the auctioneer will use information about the market supply and demand curves to guide the pricing decisions, but precise rules for this operation are seldom spelled out.

Although some markets do operate with actual auctioneers (the market for antiques is a good example), in general, no such agents are involved in price determination. Numerous attempts have, therefore, been made to give this fictional concept a behavioral interpretation. One such interpretation is the idea of *recontracting* in which buyers and sellers are assumed to enter into provisional contracts before the exchange of goods actually takes place. Each of these provisional contracts is voided if it is discovered that at the agreed-upon price, the market is not in equilibrium. Only when market-clearing prices for all markets are discovered will exchange take place. Recontracting is then a form of haggling over price, and price determination might be regarded as one aspect of contract theory.

■ Walrasian Price Adjustment

Excess demand

The extent to which quantity demanded exceeds quantity supplied at a particular price.

A second suggestion, which is similar to recontracting, was proposed by Leon Walras in the nineteenth century. In this scheme, equilibrium prices are a goal toward which the market struggles. Changes in price are motivated by information from the market about the degree of **excess demand** at any particular price.[1] It is assumed price will increase if there is positive excess demand, and decrease if excess demand is negative (that is, if supply exceeds demand).

---

[1]Leon Walras, *Elements of Pure Economics,* translated by William Jaffe (Homewood, Ill.: Irwin, 1954).

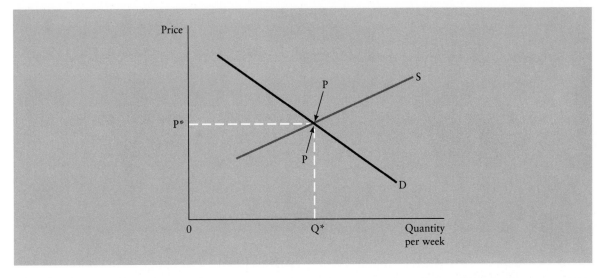

For prices above P*, supply exceeds demand. Such a price may set into motion a chain of events that causes price to fall. For prices less than P*, the quantity demanded exceeds that supplied. In reaction, price may rise.

Figure 15.1
Walrasian Price
Adjustment

Figure 15.1 shows the Walrasian process of adjustment schematically. For the supply and demand curves shown in the figure, P* is an equilibrium price. For prices less than P*, there will be an excess demand for this good. At such bargain prices, people will demand more than firms will be willing to supply. Crowds will descend on stores and buy all of this good off the shelves. Walras assumed that this behavior would be translated in the market into an increase in price and that this increase in price will serve to equilibrate supply and demand. In Figure 15.1 the upward-pointing arrow indicates the movement in price in response to excess demand. A similar argument follows for prices above P*. At such prices, the quantity supplied will exceed that which is demanded. Firms will be producing more than individuals demand, and the inventory of the good will begin to accumulate in the firms' warehouses. Eventually, this will lead to a fall in price that will again equilibrate supply and demand. The downward-pointing arrow in the figure indicates that result.

■ Marshallian Quantity Adjustment

The Walrasian adjustment process views price as the motivating force in the adjustment of markets to equilibrium. Individuals and firms respond to price changes by moving along their respective demand and supply curves until an equilibrium price-quantity combination is reached. A somewhat different picture of the adjustment process was suggested by Alfred Marshall in his classic

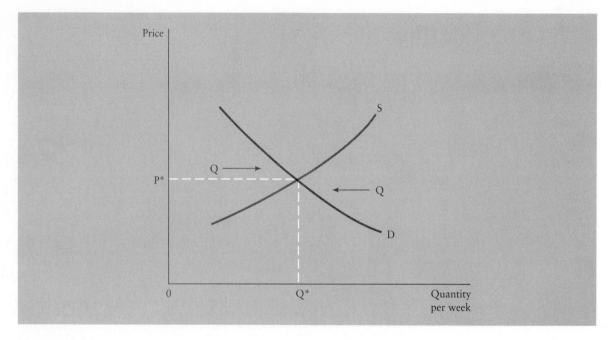

Figure 15.2

Marshallian Quantity
Adjustment

Under Marshallian adjustment, a difference between what demanders are willing to pay and what suppliers require sets up incentives for economic agents to alter output levels. If demand price exceeds supply price, Q will rise. If supply price exceeds demand price, Q will fall. The adjustment mechanism shown in the figure is stable, since Q converges to Q*.

Principles of Economics.[2] Marshall theorized that individuals and firms adjust quantity in response to imbalances in demand and supply, and that price changes follow from these changes in quantity. Movements in quantity toward equilibrium are motivated by discrepancies between the price individuals are willing to pay and the price firms wish to receive. When those two figures coincide, quantity adjustment ceases.

Quantity adjustment is illustrated in Figure 15.2. For quantities below equilibrium (Q*), what individuals are willing to pay exceeds what firms require to cover their marginal costs. Quantity produced and consumed therefore increases. For quantities above equilibrium, marginal costs exceed what demanders are willing to pay, which provides incentives for quantity reduction. As was the case for the price-adjustment mechanism, the Marshallian mechanism pictured in Figure 15.2 implies that the price-quantity equilibrium is a stable one. Starting from any initial position, forces come into play that move economic agents toward equilibrium. The precise mechanism by which the movement comes about, however, differs between the Walrasian and the Marshallian models.

[2]Alfred Marshall, *Principles of Economics*, 8th ed. (London: Macmillan, 1920), pp. 287–288.

■ Market Adjustments and Transactions Costs

Movement to an equilibrium price-quantity combination will usually involve changes in both price and quantity. The important questions concern the speed with which those variables are adjusted and how buyers and sellers perceive the need to make such adjustments. Although studying this issue in depth would take us beyond the scope of this book, the general approach to be followed is clear. Any theory of the adjustment process must focus on the costs to demanders and suppliers of changing their behavior. Those costs derive both from problems associated with gathering information about the true supply-demand configuration and from difficulties in adapting to this new information once it is acquired. We now turn to examine these costs.

In explaining why markets do not adjust immediately to bring about equilibrium, economists have tended to stress **transactions costs.** Bringing suppliers and demanders together is not as simple a process as the Marshallian diagram suggests. There may be significant costs involved. Such costs include not only the direct costs of finding a place in which to transact business but, more important, the costs to the participants of gaining information about the market. For demanders, all prices are not perfectly known. Rather, they must invest some time in search procedures that permit them to learn market prices.

Suppliers face similar costs in making transactions. The most important of these is the need to find out something about the demand for their product. Since production takes time, the absence of such information can lead to serious mistakes in the quantity a firm chooses to produce. Firms must also consider the random nature of demand over a short period. For example, no retailer knows exactly when he or she will sell shirts of particular sizes. One of the costs incurred in selling shirts is the cost of maintaining an inventory and making adjustments in that inventory.

As this brief discussion suggests, the competitive assumption of zero transactions costs is not likely to be fulfilled in the real world. Although supply and demand analysis provides information about equilibrium prices and about the direction of change in prices, various costs will prevent markets from adjusting promptly. Consequently, in the real world, we should observe examples not only of the systematic influence of supply and demand but also of *disequilibria* caused by transactions costs. In some cases, such as the simple laboratory experiments described in Application 15.1: Experimenting with Equilibrium, these disequilibrium results may be rather short-lived. In other cases, a market disequilibrium may be rather long-lasting, and there is a need to explain price determination in such situations.

Transactions costs
Costs involved in making market transactions and in gathering information with which to make those transactions.

Models of Disequilibrium Pricing

One difficulty with describing how markets establish equilibrium prices is that the competitive model pictures supply and demand decisions as being made simultaneously (remember again Marshall's scissors analogy). The model offers

APPLICATION 15.1

Experimenting with Equilibrium

Because real-world markets are constantly changing, some economists have tried to develop laboratory experiments to study the establishment of equilibrium prices in a simpler, controlled setting. These experiments usually involve students (because they can be hired at paltry wages) who are asked to assume the roles of various market participants and to conduct hypothetical transactions, usually over a computer network. One difficulty faced by the designers of such experiments is how to get students to behave like economic actors in the real world. Somehow they must be encouraged to maximize utility (for demanders) or profits (for suppliers) if their behavior is to resemble the ways economists believe actual market participants make decisions.

Experimental Design

One solution to this problem that has been adopted for experiments at several universities is to induce student subjects to follow their appropriate roles through monetary incentives. Table 1, for example, lists the marginal valuation for each of three demanders of a good and marginal costs for each of three suppliers. For each unit traded, demanders are told that they will be paid the difference between their marginal evaluation and the established price. Similarly, each supplier is told that he or she can pocket the difference between price and marginal cost. If, for example, Buyer 1 agrees to trade a first unit with Seller 2 for $4.25, the buyer will get to keep $.25 ($4.50 − $4.25), and the seller will get $2.25 ($4.25 − $2.00). This pair would not agree to make a second trade at this price (since Buyer 1 would lose on such a trade), but Seller 2 could still make a mutually beneficial trade with Buyers 2 or 3 at this price. Given these incentives, participating students sit at computer terminals and make any trades that can be arranged.

Experimental Results

Experiments similar to those illustrated in Table 1 have been replicated literally thousands of times. Usually buyers and sellers are able to focus in on an equilibrium

Table 1

Design for a Market Experiment

Number Bought or Sold	Market Value for Buyer Number			Marginal Cost for Seller Number		
	1	2	3	1	2	3
1	$4.50	$5.33	$5.00	$3.00	$2.00	$2.00
2	4.00	4.66	4.00	4.00	4.00	3.00
3	3.50	4.00	3.00	5.00	6.00	4.00
4	3.00	3.33	2.00	6.00	8.00	5.00

price (approximately $4.00 in the experiment illustrated in the table) at which all mutually beneficial transactions are exhausted. If a given set of players is allowed to repeat a game many times, they are able to get to equilibrium even more quickly.

Market experiments similar to those in Table 1 can be generalized in several ways.[1] More players can be added to the game, different formats for price determination can be used (in some experiments, for example, sellers can set "posted prices" for all buyers to see and change them only as the game proceeds), or the incentives facing a particular player can be varied. In most cases studied, the experimental participants still seem able to reach an equilibrium, but they may take a number of replays to do so. As in the real world that the experiments seek to mimic, the less information that is available to market participants, the more difficult it becomes to establish market equilibrium.

To Think About

1. In the experiment described in Table 1, no actual good is ever traded; participants only get the monetary value of the consumer or producer surplus that their trades generate. Do you think some actual goods would have to be traded to capture what really happens in market situations?
2. Given the experimental design in Table 1, how would you set up a computer network for the six players? How would buyers and sellers "find" each other? How would they set a price? How long would you give them to do all this?

[1]For a more detailed discussion, see V. Smith, "Experimental Methods in the Political Economy of Exchange," *Science* (October 1986): 167–173.

no guidance about how markets react when they are out of equilibrium. One way of developing a model in which transactions occur at nonequilibrium prices is to assume that either suppliers or demanders (or both) base their decisions on what they expect prices to be rather than on what market prices actually turn out to be. Under this approach, trading may occur at prices that are not what people expect. Only as market participants gain information and use this to modify their expected prices will prices move toward equilibrium.

◼ Cobweb Model

As a simple illustration of this approach, we first look at the **cobweb model** of price determination. In this model demanders base their decisions on actual market prices, but suppliers decide how much to produce based on last period's price (which they assume will continue into this period). This view of the market assumes the following sequence of events: Firms decide how much they will produce by referring to the previous period's price. They produce this output during the current period and sell it in the market for what demanders are willing to pay. Demanders then bid for this output (perhaps in auctions). In so doing they establish the current market price. This price enters into firms' production decisions for the next period. In this way suppliers exhibit a lagged response to the actions of demanders in determining price.

Figure 15.3 illustrates the working of the cobweb model. There P^* is an equilibrium price because the quantity demanded at this price is exactly equal

◼
Cobweb model
A model of price adjustment in which some trading takes place at nonequilibrium prices.

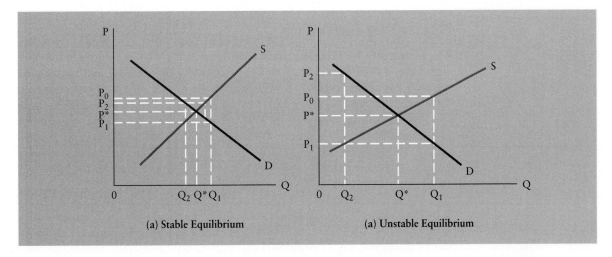

(a) Stable Equilibrium   (a) Unstable Equilibrium

The cobweb model of lagged response to price by firms provides a simple theory of market adjustment. Whether prices will approach an equilibrium level will depend on the relative slopes of the demand and supply curves. In the configuration shown in Panel a, convergence will take place, whereas in Panel b, it will not. A third possibility (not shown) would be for the supply and demand curves to have slopes such that the price perpetually oscillates about P^*.

Figure 15.3
Cobweb Model of Price Determination

to the quantity supplied. The price P^* can persist from one period to the next since firms, by referring to the previous period's price (which is also P^*), produce Q^*, which is what demanders are willing to buy at P^* in the current period.

We can see why this model is called the "cobweb" by analyzing the sequence of events that follows if price starts from a nonequilibrium position. Suppose that price starts at P_0 in Panel a in Figure 15.3. In period 1, firms will produce output level Q_1 by referring to P_0. For example, P_0 might represent the price of wheat from the 1993 grain harvest, and farmers use this information to decide the number of acres to be planted in 1994. Once Q_1 is produced, however, it must be sold in the market for whatever it will bring. Since Q_1 represents a relatively large output level, a low price must prevail in the market in period 1 (call this price P_1) to get demanders to buy this amount. In the grain harvest example, the price of wheat will fall substantially in 1994 from its 1993 level because of the overproduction in 1994.

In period 2, firms will base their output decisions on P_1. They will therefore produce a relatively low output level (Q_2). Demanders will bid for this output level and will drive the market price up to P_2. This price will then affect firms' output decision in period 3. As we can see in Panel a of Figure 15.3, this process will proceed until price converges to its equilibrium level at P^*. Over time, price therefore moves from P_0 to P^* because of the way in which supply and demand interact in the market. The price P^* is therefore a **stable equilibrium**, though nonequilibrium prices are observed for a number of periods.

Stable equilibrium

A situation in which market forces cause price to move to its equilibrium level.

■ Stability of Equilibrium

The interaction we have outlined does not necessarily lead to an equilibrium price. Panel b of Figure 15.3 shows a set of supply and demand curves for which the supply curve is somewhat flatter than that in the previous example. By starting at a price of P_0 in Panel b, an argument similar to the one we used for Panel a shows that price will oscillate in wider and wider movements away from P^*. You can follow the sequence of events by which market price moves from P_0 to P_1 to P_2. As Panel b in Figure 15.3 clearly shows, the price P^* is an **unstable equilibrium**. The workings of supply and demand will not suffice to move price to P^* with this particular configuration of supply and demand curves.[3] Since real-world prices probably do not oscillate as wildly as those in Panel b (though Application 15.2: Speculation and Bubbles shows some unusual cases where they have), we must conclude that either most real-world markets have a supply-demand pattern that resembles Panel a or that the real world is characterized by a more complex model than the cobweb model.

Unstable equilibrium

A situation in which market forces cause price to move away from its equilibrium level.

---

[3]Technically it can be shown that, for the linear demand curves used in this example, stability requires that the supply curve must be more steeply sloped (in absolute value) than the demand curve.

APPLICATION 15.2
Speculation and Bubbles

One of the most important illustrations of suppliers and demanders attempting to predict the direction of price movements is that of speculation. When some people believe there are good reasons for the price of a commodity to move in a particular direction, they may try to profit from such a movement. For example, if speculators believed that the price of a crop were going to move from P_1 to P_2 during the next period in Fig. 15.3, they might buy more of the crop this period hoping to make windfall profits on the price rise. Because speculators will find it profitable to acquire information about true supply-demand conditions in the market, they will maximize profits by taking actions that move the market toward equilibrium. Although speculation, in the long run, will help to stabilize equilibrium market prices, it is possible that in the short run it may lead to wild market gyrations.

Tulipomania

Following the spread of a tulip virus in Holland during the 1630s, a wide variety of new bulbs were developed.[1] Because there were no existing markets for these new bulbs, prices fluctuated widely. By 1634, speculating on price movements in bulbs had become a major preoccupation of the Dutch upper class and tulip trading had begun on the stock exchanges in Amsterdam and Rotterdam. Throughout 1635 and 1636, speculators pushed the price of rare bulbs ever higher with the hope of making profits on their purchases. At the height of the trading frenzy, some particularly prized bulbs sold for as much as the equivalent of $10,000. As might have been expected, however, "tulipomania" was short-lived. In 1637, the market price of bulbs fell sharply, and speculators moved rapidly to liquidate their stocks. Although the market for bulbs soon returned to relatively stable conditions, Dutch courts were clogged for many years with lawsuits that resulted from the debacle.

Bubbles

Extreme changes such as those experienced in seventeenth-century Holland have come to be called "bubbles." Other famous historical bubbles include John Law's financial schemes in eighteenth-century France and the rise and fall of prices for the shares of the South Sea Company in 1720. More recently, the concept of bubbles has been associated with rapid changes in stock market prices, most notable the 500 point decline in the Dow Jones average on October 19, 1987. The seemingly inexplicable magnitude of this decline convinced many observers (especially small investors) that prices of stocks were simply irrational. Economists (who tend to believe in the rational operations of markets) have been reluctant to accept this interpretation of price bubbles. Instead, they have tried to develop models of speculative trading in most markets in which information is imperfect and fundamentals change quickly. In this way, economists hope to demonstrate that large price fluctuations reflect the combined effects of rational traders rather than the herd instinct of an unruly crowd. Unfortunately the obstacles to developing models of rational bubbles have proved to be large, so there remains disagreement over how these traumatic episodes should be explained.[2]

To Think About

1. "Buy cheap, sell dear" is a basic principle that should yield speculators long-term profits. Use a simple supply and demand graph to show why this is so. Use the graph also to show why such speculation may help price to adjust to its equilibrium level.

2. To many people, speculators are undesirable, if not almost criminal. For a speculative good such as common stocks or foreign exchange, is it possible to differentiate between speculators and investors? Do they really have different motives?

---

[1]For a discussion of this episode together with some fascinating photographs see T. Berger, "Tulipomania Was No Dutch Treat to Gambling Burghers," *Smithsonian* (April 1977): 70–77. For a more detailed treatment see O. M. Garber, "Tulipomania," *Journal of Political Economy* (June 1989): 535–560. Garber believes that only common bulbs were subject to speculative price movements. He views the price moves for rare bulbs as being fairly typical of those in the flower industry.
[2]See J. E. Stiglitz, ed. "Symposium on Bubbles," *The Journal of Economic Perspectives* (Spring 1990): 13–101.

■ Rational Expectations

The cobweb model is an obvious oversimplification of reality. It would take a peculiar lack of sophistication on the part of buyers and sellers to accept a regularly oscillating price for long, and some kinds of adjustments based on people's expectations of prices are bound to be made. That is, the market participants may eventually figure out what the equilibrium price is and move to that point without further fluctuations.

A particularly intriguing hypothesis about the formation of price expectations was proposed by Muth in the early 1960s.[4] He suggested that one (and perhaps the only) method of forming expectations that is consistent with general optimizing behavior is to make such expectations on a "rational" basis by incorporating all available information about the market in question. Specifically, a supplier who knew the precise forms of the demand and supply curves in Figure 15.3 could calculate the equilibrium price, P*, as the expected price. If firms use this expected price, supply will be at its equilibrium level, and the market will be free of the fluctuations observed in the cobweb model. In the absence of any other information or transactions costs, equilibrium will be established instantly.

Rational expectations

Basing price expectations on complete information about the equilibrium price determined by the interaction of supply and demand in the market.

The information requirements for the **rational expectations** solution are quite severe. Not only must the supplier know the precise values of such magnitudes as the price elasticities of demand and supply, but it must also be assumed that no other unpredictable influences affect the supply or demand relationships. Models that relax both of these assumptions have been developed, principally in the field of macroeconomics. As might be expected, the results of the rational expectations approach are not so simple once more realistic assumptions are employed, but the approach has revolutionized economists' thinking about expectations and the attainment of market equilibrium. Application 15.3: Market Adjustment and the Business Cycle examines this approach.

Information and Economic Efficiency

Existence of imperfect information may not only affect the ability of markets to establish equilibrium prices, but may also call into question the correspondence between competitive prices and economic efficiency. Our proof of the efficiency of competitive prices in Chapter 14 assumed that these equilibrium prices were known to all economic actors. If some actors are not fully informed about prevailing prices or (what amounts to the same thing) if information about product quality is not freely available, Adam Smith's invisible

---

[4]John Muth, "Rational Expectations and the Theory of Price Movements," *Econometrica* (July 1961): 315–335.

hand may not be very effective. Incorrect decisions based on faulty information about price or quality can result in an inefficient allocation of resources.

A vast number of economic models seek to explore the consequences of imperfect information about prices. Here we will briefly review some of these models that are based on a competitive framework (that is, models with large numbers of buyers and sellers). In Chapter 17 we will return to the topic of information when we examine product differentiation in markets with relatively few producers.

■ Asymmetric Information and the "Lemons" Problem

A particularly intriguing problem involving imperfect information occurs when the parties to a transaction possess significantly different (**asymmetric**) amounts of **information**. Since this situation was first examined in detail for the case of used cars by George Akerlof, it is sometimes called the "lemons" problem.[5] Suppose used cars are of two types (good cars and lemons) and only the owner of a car knows for certain into which category that vehicle falls. Since buyers cannot differentiate between good cars and lemons, all used cars of a particular type will sell for the same price—somewhere between the true worth of the two types. The owner of a car will choose to keep his or her car if it is a good one (since a good car is worth more than the prevailing market price), but will sell the car if it is a lemon (since a lemon is worth less than the market price). Consequently, only lemons will be brought to the used-car market, and the quality of cars traded will be less than expected. Of course, this erosion in quality may be retarded by trustworthy used-car dealers, by development of car-buying expertise by the general public, or by sellers providing proof that their cars are trouble-free. But anyone who has ever shopped for a used-car knows the problem of potential lemons is a very real one.

> ■
> **Asymmetric information**
> A situation in which buyers and sellers have different amounts of information about a market transaction.

■ Adverse Selection

In formal terms, the lemons problem is another example of **adverse selection** in the marketplace (see also Chapter 7). Adverse selection in the used-car market is mirrored in many other markets for used durable goods. Indeed, in some cases (trading between individuals in precious gems, for example) the problem may be so severe as to foreclose practically all exchanges. As we saw earlier, the problem arises in insurance markets when buyers of health or life insurance know more about their own health than do sellers of such insurance. In this case, only high-risk individuals may choose to buy insurance since those who know they are low risk may find insurance too costly. In markets for inputs, adverse selection may be manifested if firms are less able to judge productivity than is the inputs' supplier. Especially productive workers may have

> ■
> **Adverse selection**
> When buyers and sellers have different information, market outcomes may exhibit adverse selection—the quality of goods or services traded will be biased toward market participants with better information.

---

[5]G. A. Akerlof, "The Market for 'Lemons': Quality Uncertainty and the Market Mechanism," *Quarterly Journal of Economics* (August 1970): 488–500.

APPLICATION 15.3
Market Adjustment and the Business Cycle

Explaining the business cycle is one of the main preoccupations of macroeconomists. Ever since the 1930s, the principal question has been whether the periodic declines in economic activity experienced by most market economies are best regarded as changing market equilibria or as short-term disruptions in which many markets are out of equilibrium. In his major writings during the Depression, J. M. Keynes tended to attribute the prevailing high unemployment rates to a failure of the labor market to reach equilibrium. More recent "Neo-Keynesian" economists have also incorporated disequilibrium outcomes in the market for goods into their models. Here we look briefly at both of these explanations for cyclical behavior.

An Equilibrium Model
Figure 1 illustrates a very simple model of how the labor market works. In this figure the wage rate[1] (w) influences both firms' willingness to hire workers (as reflected by the demand curve D) and individuals' willingness to work (as reflected by the supply curve S). Initially, the equilibrium wage in the labor market is w* with the quantity of labor hired being L*. There may be some unemployment in this equilibrium situation that arises out of the normal movement of workers from one job to another. But this unemployment should be regarded as part of the structure of any smoothly working labor market.

Suppose now that the demand for labor shifts to D'—perhaps a recession reduces the demand for the goods that workers produce. The equilibrium labor market model predicts that wages will fall to w' and that equilibrium will be reestablished at L'. Again, some normal level unemployment will exist at L', but the model in this simple form offers no reason for believing this would be any greater at L' than at L*.

Cyclical Unemployment
Explaining why unemployment varies over the business cycle, therefore, presents a major challenge to econo-

mists who believe in an equilibrium model of the labor market. During the 1930s, for example, the rate of unemployment in the United States exceeded 15 percent for six straight years. In both the 1975–1976 and 1982–1983 recessions, rates of 8 percent or more persisted for some time before they returned to a more usual 4 to 6 percent range. Such lengthy departures from the normal rate of unemployment are difficult to reconcile with a smoothly functioning equilibrium model.

Disequilibrium in the Labor Market
Although some economists have tried to develop elaborate equilibrium models to explain cyclical unemployment, a more common approach has been to assume that the market fails to adjust properly during recessions.[2] If, for example, the wage stays at w* when demand falls to D', there will be an excess supply of workers given by distance CE. These recession victims will remain unemployed until demand improves. Hence, wage rigidity represents a simple explanation for cyclical unemployment. But why should wages fail to change in response to the decline in the demand for labor? Firms could, after all, hire replacement workers at a wage of w'. Why should they continue to pay w*? Isn't this a violation of the assumption of profit maximization?

Attempting to answer these questions has posed a number of both theoretical and empirical challenges to economists. Most theories attempting to explain wage rigidities have focused on the kinds of implicit contracts (see Chapter 11) that firms have with their workers. Empirical examinations have tried to determine the actual extent of wage movements over the business cycle. Although all of this work has provided various pieces to the puzzle of how the labor market works, there is, as yet, no universally accepted explanation.

Disequilibrium in Other Markets
Recent Keynesian-type explanations of the business cycles have tended to focus on price rigidities in goods' markets. For this analysis a simple relabeling of the axes in Figure 1 will suffice—now regard the figure as representing the market for some product which has experienced a reduction in demand. Under our usual scenario, this

---

[1]Here the wage should be interpreted as a "real" wage—that is, a wage rate that is stated relative to the general cost of goods.
[2]For a more complete discussion, see R. E. Quandt and H. S. Rosen, *The Conflict between Equilibrium and Disequilibrium Theories: The Case of the U.S. Labor Market* (Kalamazoo: Upjohn Institute, 1988). One ex-

ample of how increasing unemployment might be explained as an equilibrium phenomenon argues that workers will take the decline in the wage as a sign to consume more leisure currently since the opportunity cost of doing so is temporarily low (see Chapter 20).

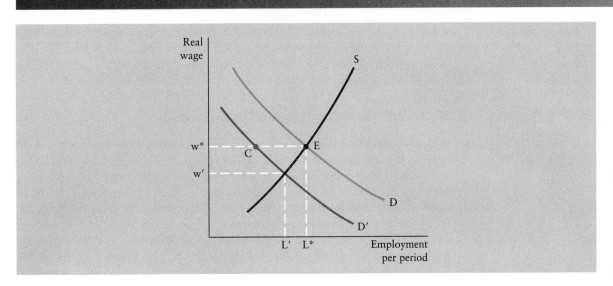

Initially the labor market is in equilibrium with a real wage of w*. If recession reduces the demand for labor to D', the real wage may not fall to w'. If it remains at w*, unemployment will increase by distance CE.

Figure 1
Operation of the Labor Market during Recession

decrease in demand would prompt a fall in market price and that would restore equilibrium. Suppose, however, that it were costly for firms to change the prices they charge. Costs associated with changing prices are sometimes termed "menu costs" to reflect the costs restaurants experience in printing new menus when prices change. Consideration of such factors as long-term contracts and the existence of complex pricing schemes, however, suggests that such costs may be more important than is implied by the triviality of the menu example.

The existence of menu costs may deter firms from lowering their prices immediately, especially if they are unsure whether the decline in market demand will be long-lasting. In this case, then, the effect of the decline of demand on output will be magnified. The decline in demand results in a greater sales loss (distance CE in Figure 1) than would have occurred if price had adjusted to its new equilibrium level. Such a decline in output may also cause firms to reduce employment. Thus,

higher unemployment will also be a feature of cyclical downturns in demand. Coupling the menu cost explanation with a variety of other observations about how real-world markets work (such as possibilities for imperfect competition or that prices are not fully known by all market participants) provides a new set of possible microeconomic foundations to the macroeconomic problem of explaining business cycles.[3]

To Think About

1. Why does it matter whether cyclical unemployment is an equilibrium or disequilibrium phenomenon? Would different policies to reduce unemployment be appropriate depending on its cause?

2. Can menu costs really explain market disequilibrium? In competitive markets, isn't price set by supply and demand, so won't firms have to change their menus no matter what it costs?

[3]For a summary, see L. Ball, N. G. Mankiw, and D. Romer, "The New Keynesian Economics and the Output Inflation Trade-off," *Brookings Papers on Economic Activity* (1988) #1: 1–82.

no way to illustrate their skills to would-be hirers and may turn down job offers based on employers' perceptions of the average skills of only "typical" workers. In all of these cases, therefore, informational asymmetries may cause competitively determined prices to depart from economic efficiency. Application 15.4: The Winner's Curse in Common Value Auctions looks at how such asymmetries may lead to possibly inefficient outcomes in auctions.

■ Acquisition and Provision of Information

In many situations, however, these conclusions drawn from the lemon model may be premature since they take no account of possible actions by market participants to improve information flows. The inefficiency inherent in the adverse selection outcomes provides a powerful incentive for economic actors to acquire information. It might, therefore, be expected that Smith's invisible hand would also be operating in the market for information. In the used-car case, for example, potential buyers might spend both time and money to appraise used cars they are considering. Sellers might also attempt to provide information by showing maintenance records or by offering limited warranties. That is, they will attempt to "signal" the quality of the car they wish to sell. Of course, information may not always be accurate. One might, for example, question a ten-year-old car with 45,000 miles on the odometer. Still, as Application 15.5: Looking for Lemons shows, for the case of pickup trucks, if not major league free agents, quality deterioration is not a foregone conclusion.

■ Information and Equilibrium

In general then, the lemons example suggests that information about product quality can be acquired and provided in many different ways and that such information may not always be perfectly accurate. To develop models of how competitive markets operate in such situations is very difficult, and there are no universally accepted results. To illustrate some of the problems in building such models, consider the comparatively simple question of how a market equilibrium should be defined. Suppose the quantity demanded of a product can be represented by

$$\text{Quantity demanded} = D(P, \alpha), \qquad [15.1]$$

where α is the information used by the demander in making his or her decisions. Similarly, supply can be represented by

$$\text{Quantity supplied} = S(P, \beta), \qquad [15.2]$$

where β represents the supplier's information. An equilibrium occurs where

$$D(P^*, \alpha) = S(P^*, \beta), \qquad [15.3]$$

where P^* is the equilibrium price for this good given the information α and β. However, as the used car example suggests, this information is chosen as part

APPLICATION 15.4

The Winner's Curse in Common Value Auctions

One of the most extensively examined instances of imperfect information is the behavior of participants in "common value" auctions. In such auctions a particular item is auctioned to a group of bidders, each of whom is uncertain as to its true value. When oil companies bid for a tract of land in the Gulf of Mexico or on the North Slope of Alaska, for example, they only have limited information about how much oil the tract will contain. Publishers are in a similar quandary when they make bids for the rights to publish a new novel—they really don't know how well it will sell. Similar informational problems affect the bidding for items as diverse as paintings of undetermined origin, baseball players in the free-agent draft, or guessing the number of beans in a jar. In all of these cases, the item being auctioned has a true value, which is the same for all potential auction winners. But the bidders are unsure about what this common value is; no one bidder knows what the other bidders believe the value to be.

The Winner's Curse

Faced with these uncertainties, each bidder will make some sort of estimate of what the good being sold is worth and bid accordingly. Because the person making the highest bid will win the item, it seems possible that this bid will be too high. The winner of the auction will be the bidder who has imagined the most inflated value for the item being sold. If we assume that the average bidder's assessment of the item is about right, the high bidder will have paid too much and is sure to be disappointed with the results. This result is sometimes called the "winner's curse."

Of course, a rational bidder will recognize the possibility of overbidding and will adjust his or her strategy accordingly. Even if every bidder at a particular auction follows such a prudent approach, however, deciding how much to bid can be a tricky business, especially for bidders who believe (possibly incorrectly) that the item is quite valuable. Each bidder must take account not only of his or her own valuation, but must also think about how many other bidders there are and what their valuations will be. Only by making such a complete assessment can a bidder with imperfect information guard against overbidding. Needless to say not all auction participants may be able to analyze such a difficult problem completely.

Evidence from Oil Lease Sales

The possibility of a winner's curse being associated with common value auctions was first recognized in connection with bidding for oil leases in the Gulf of Mexico. Several studies of such sales during the 1950s and 1960s tended to suggest that oil companies typically overbid for the leases they acquired. For example, winning bids often exceeded second place bids by a factor of 3 or more. Clearly the winning bids were based on very optimistic assessments. One 1987 study of over 1,200 leases concludes that firms systematically overbid by nearly 50 percent relative to what would have been (with perfect hindsight) an optimal bidding strategy.[1] They suggest that the winners in these lease sales should not be too pleased with their victories.

To Think About

1. Will the likelihood of a winner's curse be greater in an auction with many participants or one with few participants? How would you feel about winning over 3 or 4 bidders? How about winning over 100 bidders? How should you adapt your bidding strategy to reflect the number of bidders at an auction?

2. If oil companies typically overbid for leases, what can they do about it? Would it make sense for a firm to stay out of such auctions or to unilaterally reduce its bids? Might explicit or implicit collusion improve matters (though it might land the colluders in jail)?

---

[1] K. Hendricks, R. H. Porter, and B. Boudreau, "Information, Returns, and Bidding Behavior in OSL Auctions 1954–1969," *Journal of Industrial Economics* (June 1987): 517–542.

APPLICATION 15.5

Looking for Lemons

The lemons model suggests that asymmetric information will lead to a deterioration in the quality of goods traded in a market. In the used-car case, for example, the model predicts that used cars that are actually traded will be of a lower quality than those which are retained by their original owners. Given this clear prediction, economists have set out to examine a variety of markets to determine whether it is, in fact, borne out or whether various institutions have arisen that help to balance the information needs of buyers and sellers.

Pickup Trucks

Fairly good data exist on maintenance costs for pickup trucks, and these fail to show significant quality deterioration in the market. A 1982 study of pickup purchases during the 1970s found that approximately 60 percent of all such trucks were bought used.[1] After controlling for the mileage that the trucks had traveled, the author found no difference in the repair records for trucks purchased used versus those purchased new. Hence, although it seems likely that the used-truck market does exhibit asymmetric information, this does not appear to result in quality deterioration. Possibly sellers are able to "signal" a truck's true value to would-be buyers by providing repair records. Or possibly, buyers are able to gain some expertise in evaluating pickups by looking at several before they choose which to buy. Unfortunately, the available data do not permit a detailed examination of these various possibilities.

Free Agents in Baseball

After playing in major league baseball for five years, a player can elect to become a free agent. He is then able to accept contract offers from his own team or from any other team that may be interested. This market in "used" baseball players provides another illustration of asymmetric information since the player's present team will know a great deal more about his physical condition than will any other potential hirer. A team that knows one of its players is injured will let that player go into the free-agent market, and the team he moves to may be unpleasantly surprised by the player's inability to perform.

A 1984 study of player disabilities found that free agents spent almost twice as many days on the disabled list after they were signed than did players who had their contracts renewed by their teams.[2] These figures tend to suggest that quality deterioration occurs in this market—that many free agents are lemons. Of course, as in the market for pickup trucks, buyers may adapt their behavior to this situation. They may, for example, require physical examinations for players or simply reduce their bids for free agents. Because baseball owners do not want to be saddled with multimillion dollar contracts for "duds," they have a powerful incentive to mitigate the lemons problem.

To Think About

1. Under some versions of the lemons model, quality in a market deteriorates to such an extent that no trading occurs at all. Can you think of any examples of this? Why haven't institutions arisen in these markets to make trading possible by providing a better balance between the informational needs of buyers and sellers?

2. Should the lemons problem be considered an example of inefficiency? Are resources devoted to addressing the problem (for example, the time spent maintaining repair records for pickup trucks) "wasted"?

---

[1] E. W. Bond, "A Direct Test of the 'Lemons' Model: The Market for Used Pickup Trucks," *American Economic Review* (September 1982): 836–840.

[2] K. Lehn, "Information Asymmetries in Baseball's Free Agent Market," *Economic Inquiry* (January 1984): 37–44.

of demanders' and suppliers' overall decision processes. Furthermore, since the equilibrium price, P*, reflects this information, rational actors may draw additional information from this price itself. That is, actors may, to some extent, judge quality by price. A rational buyer of expensive cameras, for example, might reason that current prices reflect actual quality differences so he or she need not gain any more information before making a purchase. The fact that other buyers have read *Consumer Reports* can be relied on to ensure that quality differences are already reflected in the market prices. If everyone adopts this position, however, there will not be sufficient pressure on the demand side of the market to assure that such an assumption of efficient pricing is valid.

In these situations, then, the concept of market equilibrium is a complex one—it all depends on how people react to imperfect information. It is possible to develop models in which no such equilibrium exists or in which multiple equilibria exist.[6] Given the current state of information theory, it is not possible to state with any certainty which of these models can be considered to be of general validity.

■ Equilibrium and Pareto Efficiency

Because of these complexities in defining market equilibria in cases of imperfect information, it is not surprising that there are no fundamental results about the nature of efficient allocations in such situations. It is clear that equilibrium allocations with imperfect information will generally be inferior to allocations with perfect information (as the lemons model suggests). But that conclusion is not especially interesting. Information is imperfect and costly to acquire in all economic organizations. The relevant allocational question is which mechanisms produce efficient results from among all those that operate within a given environment with imperfect information. The cost and availability of information pose a series of constraints on any economic system, and efficiency must be defined subject to these constraints. Competitive markets incorporate powerful incentives both to generate and to reveal information. But their efficiency in a variety of contexts has not been clearly demonstrated.

Summary

In this chapter we have examined how perfectly competitive markets perform in situations of limited information. The general purpose of this examination was to explore the limits that should be placed on interpretations of the fundamental correspondence between competitive equilibria and economic efficiency. We showed that extending this correspondence to situations involving imperfect information raised many complex questions:

---

[6]For a discussion, see J. E. Stiglitz, "The Causes and Consequences of the Dependence of Quality on Price," *Journal of Economic Literature* (March 1987): 1–48.

- Information costs may determine how markets adjust to new equilibria and the time that such adjustments require. For example, whether Walrasian (price) or Marshallian (quantity) adjustment dominates will be importantly influenced by transactions and information costs.

- In some models of market adjustment, disequilibrium prices may occur. The path by which such prices approach equilibrium can be importantly affected by the information available and how expectations are based on that information.

- With asymmetric information, adverse selection may result in economic inefficient allocations, at least in models with no information acquisition possibilities.

- In general, economic actors will wish to acquire and to signal information about market transactions in which they participate. Equilibrium prices (if they exist) will incorporate prevailing information levels and may themselves be sources of information to market participants.

Review Questions

1. What balance of forces does an equilibrium price represent? Why would such forces not be balanced at a nonequilibrium price? How would economic actors know that supply and demand were not in balance?

2. Describe the Walrasian price adjustment mechanism. What types of information motivate price movements? With the usual configuration of supply and demand curves, would price always move toward its equilibrium value if it followed a Walrasian mechanism?

3. Whether markets adjust using the Walrasian or Marshallian mechanism depends mainly on costs. What are some of these costs? The stock market is usually believed to be a market characterized by price adjustment. Explain why this may be so. As Application 15.3 shows, the labor market may be characterized by quantity adjustment. Explain why this may be so and why "sticky wages" pose a problem for macroeconomic stability.

4. Why do "nonequilibrium" prices arise in the cobweb model? What information problems do these reflect? In what sense are the prices in the model really "nonequilibrium"?

5. "The only truly rational expectation about price is its equilibrium value." Do you agree? Doesn't this definition require actors developing such expectations to have too much information? What are some simpler, less costly (though perhaps less accurate) ways in which economic actors might form price expectations?

6. "If speculators follow the simple principle, 'buy cheap, sell dear,' they will both make money and help to equilibrate markets." Explain using a simple supply-demand graph.

7. If, as question 6 suggests, profitable speculation tends to stabilize markets, why are speculators often blamed for causing wild price gyrations? What kinds of price expectations might cause speculators to destabilize a market?

8. What kinds of information do demanders and suppliers need to make "informed" market transactions? Suppose you set out to hire someone to tutor you in microeconomics. Is the price of this transaction all you need to know, or should more go into your decision? Is the price all the tutor needs to know or might he or she care about other aspects of the transaction?

9. Explain why the "lemons problem" described in this chapter and the problem of adverse selection in insurance described in Chapter 7 are basically the same problem. Show that the definition provided fits both cases.

10. What does "judge quality by price" or "you get what you pay for" mean? Can you name some goods for which this approach to buying seems reasonable? What about the market for these goods suggests such a strategy may be reasonable? Suggest some situations where the strategy might backfire.

Problems

15.1 If the demand curve has a negative slope and the supply curve has a positive slope, the equilibrium price is stable under both Walrasian and Marshallian adjustment. Use a graphic analysis to show that for the case where both demand and supply curves have negative slopes, the equilibrium price will be stable under one method of adjustment, but unstable under the other.

15.2 Suppose that the demand for dog shampoos is given by

$$Q_D = 100 - 5P$$

and the supply by

$$Q_S = 20 + 3P$$

where Q_D and Q_S are the quantity of dog shampoos demanded and supplied each week, respectively.

a. What is the equilibrium price of dog shampoos in this market?
b. Explain why $P = 5$ and $P = 15$ are not equilibrium prices for dog shampoos. How would each of the participants in this market know these were not equilibrium prices?
c. Suppose producers of dog shampoos could lower their price by $1 if they didn't sell out in a week or raise it if they did. Explain the sequence of events by which the price would move from those in part b to its equilibrium value from part a.
d. Graph your results.

15.3 Sometimes economists use the notion of an excess demand function defined as $ED(P) = Q_D(P) - Q_S(P)$. That is, the excess demand for a good at any price is equal to the quantity demanded at that price minus the quantity supplied. Using this notion, show the following:

a. If we graph excess demand on the horizontal axis and price on the vertical axis, this function will usually have a negative slope.
b. An equilibrium price will be one for which $ED(P) = 0$.
c. The equilibrium price will be stable under the Walrasian criterion if the excess demand curve has a negative slope near that price.
d. An excess demand curve may have a negative slope under certain circumstances—what are these circumstances?
e. If the excess demand curve has a negative slope in the neighborhood of an equilibrium price, this price will be unstable under the Walrasian criterion.

15.4 Suppose that the market demand for a particular product is given by

$$Q_D = -2P + 13$$

and the industry supply curve by

$$Q_S = 2P^2 - 12P + 21.$$

What are the equilibrium prices for this market? Which of these prices is stable by the Walrasian criterion?

15.5 Suppose that the demand curve for corn at time t is given by

$$Q_t = 100 - 2P_t$$

and that supply in period t is given by

$$Q_t = 70 + E(P_t)$$

where $E(P_t)$ is what suppliers expect the price to be in period t.

a. If in equilibrium $E(P_t) = P_t$, what are the price and quantity of corn in this market?
b. Suppose that suppliers are myopic and use last period's price as their expectation of this year's price (that is, $E(P_t) = P_{t-1}$). If the initial market price of corn is $8, how long will it take for price to get within $.25 of the equilibrium price?
c. If farmers have "rational" expectations, how would they choose $E(P_t)$?

15.6 Under the assumptions of part b of problem 15.5, solve explicitly for P_t as a function of the initial price, P_0, and time. Graph this relationship and show that the oscillations about the equilibrium price are dampened. Suppose the supply function were instead given by

$$Q_t = 50 + 3P_{t-1}.$$

Would the equilibrium price now be stable?

15.7 The used-car supply in Metropolis consists of 10,000 cars. The values of these cars range from $5,000 to $15,000 with exactly one car being worth each dollar amount between these two figures. Used-car owners are always willing to sell their cars for what they are worth. Demanders of used cars in Metropolis have no way of telling the value of a particular car. Their demand depends on the average value of cars in the market ($\overline{P}$) and on the price of the cars themselves (P) according to the equation

$$Q = 1.5\,\overline{P} - P.$$

a. If demanders base their estimate of $\overline{P}$ on the entire used-car market, what will its value be and what will be the equilibrium price of used cars?
b. In the equilibrium described in part a, what will be the average value of used cars actually traded in the market?
c. If demanders revise their estimate of $\overline{P}$ on the basis of the average value of cars actually traded, what will be the new equilibrium price of used cars? What is the average value of cars traded now?
d. Is there a market equilibrium in this situation at which the actual value of $\overline{P}$ is consistent with supply-demand equilibrium at a positive price and quantity?

15.8 A market is "informationally efficient" if *all* available information is instantly and costlessly incorporated into the price of a good.

a. Explain why it is impossible to predict the arrival of new information in such a market.
b. Is it possible to earn private gains from information acquisition in this type of market? What is the optimal information acquisition strategy?
c. In view of your analysis in part b, under what circumstances do you think a market will be informationally efficient?

15.9 The "random walk" hypothesis of the pricing of share prices assumes that these prices move randomly in ways that are totally unpredictable.

a. Explain the relationship between the random walk hypothesis and the concept of informational efficiency defined in problem 15.8.
b. If share prices do follow a random walk, what do stock market advisers do and why are they paid so highly? Do the high salaries of such advisers tend to cast doubt on the random walk hypothesis?

"(The owner of a unique spring) could doubtless fix the price of a liter of water at 100 francs; but would soon see by the scant demand that this is not the way to make the most of his property."

Augustin Cournot

The Mathematical Principles of the Theory of Wealth, 1838.

One of the most important assumptions made throughout Part 4 was that both suppliers and demanders were price takers. All economic actors were assumed to exert no influence on prices, and, therefore, prices were treated as fixed in their decisions. In this part we will explore the consequences of dropping the price-taking assumption for suppliers of goods. We will use the general term *imperfect competition* to describe all such situations in which firms have some influence over the price of their products.

We begin our examination of imperfect competition in Chapter 16 with the case of a single supplier of a good. Such a firm is called a *monopoly.* This supplier faces the entire market demand curve for its product and can choose to operate at any point on that demand curve.

In Chapter 17 we move from the relatively simple case of monopoly to market structures involving a "few" firms. As we shall see, adding additional suppliers makes matters much more complicated. In such cases any one firm does not face the total market demand curve, but, rather, faces a demand curve for its own output that will have properties determined in part by its rivals' behavior. To develop a realistic model, therefore, some assumption must be made about how one firm believes its rivals will behave. The issue of intrafirm rivalry presented in Chapter 17 can also be approached formally as applications of the economic *theory of games.* In Chapter 18 we provide a brief introduction to some of the tools used in that field. We show how many strategic situations can be interpreted in game-theoretic terms.

PART
5

IMPERFECT
COMPETITION

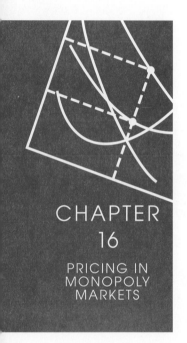

CHAPTER
16

PRICING IN
MONOPOLY
MARKETS

A producer of a good is described as a monopoly if it is the only producer of that good. This single firm faces the entire market demand curve for its output. Using its knowledge of this demand curve, the monopoly makes a decision on how much to produce. Unlike the perfectly competitive firm's output decision (which has no effect on market price), the monopoly output decision will completely determine the good's price. In this sense monopoly markets are the opposite, polar case from perfectly competitive ones. Of course, even though a monopoly has far more market power than a competitive firm, it is not all-powerful. It cannot sell all it wants at whatever price it chooses. The monopoly must still contend with the demand curve for its product and must recognize that it can sell more only by lowering its price.

Causes of Monopoly

The reason monopolies exist is that other firms find it unprofitable or impossible to enter the market. **Barriers to entry** are the source of all monopoly power. If other firms could enter the market, there would, by definition, no longer be a monopoly. There are two general types of barriers to entry: technical barriers and legal barriers.

Barriers to entry
Factors that prevent new firms from entering a market.

■ Technical Barriers to Entry

A primary technical barrier to entry is that the production of the good in question may exhibit decreasing average cost over a wide range of output levels. That is, relatively large-scale firms are more efficient than small ones. In this situation one firm may find it profitable to drive others out of the industry by price cutting. Similarly, once a monopoly has been established, entry by other firms will be difficult because any new firm must produce at relatively low levels of output and therefore at relatively high average costs. Because this barrier to entry arises naturally as a result of the technology of production, the monopoly created is sometimes called a **natural monopoly.**

The range of declining average costs for a natural monopoly need only be "large" relative to the market in question. Declining costs on some absolute scale are not necessary. For example, the manufacture of concrete does not exhibit declining average costs over a broad range of output when compared to the total U.S. market. In any particular small town, however, declining average costs may permit a concrete monopoly to be established. The high costs of transporting concrete tend to create local monopolies for this good.

Another technical basis of monopoly is special knowledge of a low-cost method of production. In this case the problem for the monopoly fearing entry by other firms is to keep this technique uniquely to itself. When matters of technology are involved, this may be extremely difficult, unless the technology can be protected by a patent (discussed below). Ownership of unique resources (such as mineral deposits or land locations) or the possession of unique managerial talents may also be a lasting basis for maintaining a monopoly.[1]

Natural monopoly
A firm that exhibits diminishing average cost over a broad range of output levels.

■ Legal Barriers to Entry

Many pure monopolies are created as a matter of law rather than as a matter of economic conditions. One important example of a government-granted monopoly position is the legal protection provided by a patent. Polaroid cameras and most prescription drugs are just two notable examples of goods that would-be competitors may be prevented from copying by patent law. Because the basic technology for these products was assigned by the government to

---

[1]"High costs" of entry into a market are sometimes mentioned as a basis for monopoly. Although there are probably cases in which this is correct, it is important to be careful in distinguishing these cases. If there were perfect capital markets, a firm would enter a market as long as the value of future profits exceeded the fixed costs of entry, since it could borrow these costs and repay the loan out of profits.

only one firm, a monopoly position was established. The rationale of the patent system, originally put forth by Thomas Jefferson, is that it makes innovation more profitable and therefore encourages technical advancement. Whether or not the benefits of such innovative behavior exceed the costs of creating monopolies is an open question.[2]

A second example of a legally created monopoly is the awarding of an exclusive franchise or license to serve a market. These are awarded in cases of public utility (gas and electric) services, communication services, the post office, some airline routes, some television and radio station markets, and a variety of other businesses. The argument usually put forward in favor of creating these monopolies is that having only one firm in the industry is more desirable than open competition.

In some instances it is argued that restrictions on entry into certain industries are needed to assure adequate quality standards (licensing of physicians, for example) or to prevent environmental harm (franchising businesses in the national parks). In many cases there are sound reasons for such entry restrictions, but in some cases, as Application 16.1: Entry Restriction by Licensing shows, the reasons are obscure. The restrictions act mainly to limit the competition faced by existing firms and seem to make little economic sense.

Profit Maximization

In order to maximize profits, a monopoly will choose to produce that output level for which marginal revenue is equal to marginal cost. Because the monopoly, in contrast to a perfectly competitive firm, faces a downward-sloping demand curve for its product, marginal revenue will be less than market price. To sell an additional unit, the monopoly must lower its price on all units to be sold in order to generate the extra demand necessary to absorb this marginal unit. In equating marginal revenue to marginal cost, the monopoly will produce an output level for which price exceeds marginal cost. This feature of monopoly pricing is the primary focus of our analysis of the distorting effect of a monopoly on resource allocation later in this chapter.

■ A Graphic Treatment

The profit-maximizing output level for a monopoly is given by Q^* in Figure 16.1.[3] For that output, marginal revenue is equal to marginal costs, and profits

---

[2]Some economists have argued that inventors should be rewarded directly by the government and that the invention should then be made available to all firms at no cost. Ideally the prize to inventors would provide the incentive that the patent system currently provides without creating the monopolies that arise under patents. In practice, however, it would be very difficult to decide how much a particular invention is "worth."

[3]In Figure 16.1, and in the other diagrammatic analyses in this chapter, no distinction is made between the behavior of a monopoly in the short run and in the long run. The analysis is the same in both cases, except that different sets of cost curves would be used depending on the possibilities for adjustment that are assumed to be feasible for the firm. Notice though that in the long run, a monopoly will not in general choose that level of capital output for which long-run average cost is a minimum. The only situation in which this would occur would be if MR and MC happened to intersect at the low point of the AC curve. For a multiplant monopoly, however, the firm may vary its number of plants so that production will take place at the minimum average cost of each of them.

APPLICATION 16.1

Entry Restriction by Licensing

State governments license many occupations and impose stiff legal penalties on people who run a business without a license. For some of these occupations, licensing seems warranted—no one wants to be treated by a quack doctor when he or she is seriously ill, for example. However, in some cases, licensing restrictions may go too far. In the state of California, it has been estimated that more than 25 percent of the work force is licensed by 52 different regulatory boards. Professionals such as embalmers, guide dog trainers, appliance repairers, and golf course designers are all licensed, though consumer gains in terms of quality or safety from such licensing seem to be minimal. Here we look in more detail at three specific cases of licensing.

Dry Cleaning

One rationale for requiring licensing is that existing firms find it in their interest to promote entry restrictions to preserve the market for themselves. A good illustration is provided by dry cleaners in California.[1] In order to enter the business, a would-be cleaner must pass examinations in a variety of specialties (fur cleaning, hat renovating, spot removal, and so forth). In order to even take the licensing exam, one must usually attend a dry cleaning school, and even then, pass rates tend to be very low. Those who try to skirt the process and do laundry on the side face stiff fines and even jail sentences for "practicing dry cleaning without a license." Whether Californians have cleaner clothes than the rest of us in the United States as a result of all of this is unclear, though several studies have found that profits in the industry are higher in California than in other states. Is it any wonder that existing dry cleaning firms are the staunchest defenders of regulation by the Board of Fabric Care?

Liquor Stores

Following Prohibition, states adopted a variety of restrictions on the ways in which liquor could be sold.

Currently, 16 states operate liquor store monopolies. In these states consumers must purchase liquor from a "state store," and usually they pay extra. In 34 other states, liquor stores are licensed and subject to restrictions on pricing and advertising. However, liquor licensing studies have failed to discern any clear benefits of such restrictions. They have, on the contrary, found that liquor prices are higher in states with stringent licensing and other regulations.[2] It is not surprising that existing license owners are among the most vocal opponents to the granting of additional licenses. (That "this town only needs one liquor store" is a sentiment frequently expressed.)

Taxicabs

Many cities limit the number of taxicabs allowed on their streets. Ostensibly, the purpose of such regulation is to control unscrupulous cab drivers who may overcharge uninformed passengers. This rationale is not wholly consistent with the evidence, however, that tends to show that taxi fares are higher in regulated markets. One recent study of Toronto, for example, found that costs may be about 25 percent higher than would prevail in an unregulated market.[3] Further evidence of the monopoly rents earned in regulated markets is provided by the price of taxi licenses, which run nearly $100,000 in Toronto. In New York City (where the number of taxi licenses has not changed since before World War II), the cost of a license may run twice this amount.

To Think About

1. Can you think of good reasons for regulating entry into the businesses described in this application? Is licensing needed to assure quality or other goals? How would you determine whether these goals are met?
2. Why do you think some states have chosen to license certain occupations, whereas others have not? What are the laws with regard to dry cleaners or liquor stores or taxis in your state? Who are the gainers and losers under the current arrangement relative to a competitive market?

---

[1]This example is based on David Kirp and Eileen Soffer, "Taking Californians to the Cleaners," *Regulation* (September/October 1985): 24–26. The puns in the article are highly recommended.
[2]For a discussion, see J. K. Smith, "An Analysis of State Regulations Governing Liquor Store Licensees," *Journal of Law and Economics* (October 1982): 301–319.
[3]D. W. Taylor, "The Economic Effects of the Direct Regulation of Taxicabs in Metropolitan Toronto," *Logistics and Transportation Review* (June 1989): 169–182.

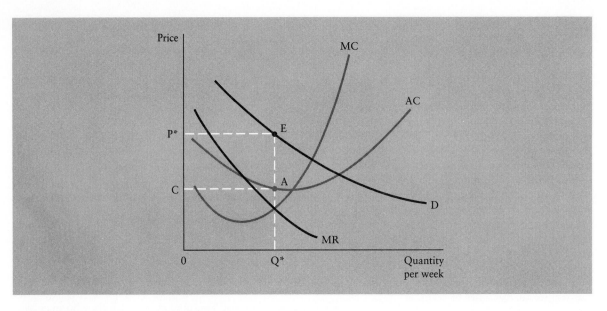

Figure 16.1
Profit Maximization and Price Determination in a Monopoly Market

A profit-maximizing monopolist produces that quantity for which marginal revenue is equal to marginal cost. In the diagram this quantity is given by Q^*, which will yield a price of P^* in the market. Monopoly profits can be read as the rectangle P^*EAC.

are maximized. If a firm produced slightly less than Q^*, profits would fall, since the revenue lost from this cutback (MR) would exceed the decline in production costs (MC). A decision to produce more than Q^* would also lower profits since the additional costs from increased production would exceed the extra revenues from selling the extra output. Consequently, profits are at a maximum at Q^*, and a profit-maximizing monopoly will choose this output level.

Given the monopoly's decision to produce Q^*, the demand curve D indicates that a market price of P^* will prevail. This is the price that demanders as a group are willing to pay for the output of the monopoly. In the market, an equilibrium price-quantity combination of P^*, Q^* will be observed.[4] This equilibrium will persist until something happens (such as a shift in demand or a change in costs) to cause the monopoly to alter its output decision.

■ Monopoly Supply Curve

In the theory of perfectly competitive markets we presented earlier, it was possible to speak of an industry supply curve. We constructed this curve by

---

[4]This combination will be on an elastic section of the demand curve. This will be true because MC is positive so for a profit maximum MR must also be positive. But, if marginal revenue is positive, demand must be elastic, as we showed in Chapter 10 (see especially Equation 10.8). One conclusion to be drawn is that industries that are found to operate along an inelastic portion of the demand curve for their product are not exercising strong monopoly power.

allowing the market demand curve to shift and observing the supply curve that was traced out by the series of equilibrium price-quantity combinations. This type of construction is not possible for monopoly markets. With a fixed market demand curve, the supply "curve" for a monopoly will be only one point—namely, the point corresponding to the quantity at which MR = MC (point E in Figure 16.1). If the demand curve should shift, the marginal revenue curve would shift along with it, and a new profit-maximizing output would be chosen. However, to connect the resulting series of equilibrium points would have little meaning and would not represent a supply curve. The set of points might have a very strange shape, depending on how the market demand curve's elasticity (and its associated MR curve) changed as the curve was shifted outward. In this sense the monopoly firm has no well-defined supply curve. Instead, each demand curve represents a unique profit-maximizing opportunity for a monopoly, and each has to be studied independently.

■ Monopoly Profits

Economic profits earned by the monopolist can be read directly from Figure 16.1. These are shown by the rectangle P*EAC and again represent the profit per unit (price minus average cost) times the number of units sold. These profits will be positive when, as in the figure, market price exceeds average total cost. Since no entry is possible into a monopoly market, these monopoly profits can exist even in the long run. For this reason some authors call the profits that a monopoly earns in the long run **monopoly rents**. These profits can be regarded as a return to the factor that forms the basis of the monopoly (such as a patent, a favorable location, or the only liquor license in town). Some other owner might be willing to pay that amount in rent for the right to operate the monopoly and obtain its profits. The huge prices paid for television stations or baseball franchises reflect the capitalized values of such rents.

■
Monopoly rents
The profits that a
monopoly earns in
the long run.

What's Wrong with Monopoly?

Firms that have a monopoly position in a market have been criticized for a variety of reasons. It has been argued that monopolies earn excess profits; give poor, unresponsive service; exploit their employees; stifle technical progress; and distort the allocation of resources. Although each of these complaints may have some truth to it, only two are discussed here: the profitability of monopoly and the effect of monopoly on resource allocation. Some of the other arguments are investigated in other sections of this chapter.

■ Profitability

Since perfectly competitive firms earn no pure profits in the long run, a firm with a monopoly in a market can earn higher profits than if the market were

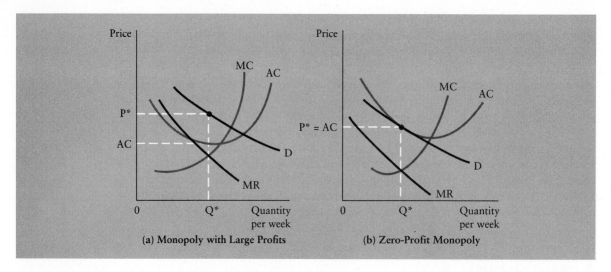

Figure 16.2
Monopoly Profits
Depend on the
Relationship between the Demand
and Average Cost
Curves

Both of the monopolies in this figure are equally "strong" in that they have similar divergences between market price and marginal cost. Because of the location of the demand and average cost curves, however, it turns out that the monopoly in Panel a earns high profits, whereas that in Panel b earns no profits. The size of profits is not a measure of the strength of a monopoly.

competitive. This does not imply, however, that monopolies necessarily earn huge profits. Two equally strong monopolies may differ greatly in their profitability. It is the ability of monopolies to raise price above *marginal* cost that reflects their monopoly power. Since profitability reflects the difference between price and *average* cost, profits are not necessarily a sign of monopoly power.

Figure 16.2 exhibits the cost and demand conditions for two firms with essentially the same degree of monopoly power (that is, the divergence between price and marginal cost is the same in both panels). The monopoly in Panel a earns a high level of profits, whereas the one in Panel b actually earns zero in profits since price equals average cost. Hence, excess profitability is not inevitable, even for a strong monopoly. Indeed, if monopoly rents accrue mainly to the inputs a monopoly uses (for example, rent on a favorably located piece of land), the monopoly itself may appear to make no profits.

More than the size of monopoly profits, people are likely to object to the distribution of these profits. If the profits go to relatively wealthy owners at the expense of less well-to-do consumers, there may be valid objections to monopoly profits no matter what their size. Profits from a monopoly may not necessarily always go to the wealthy, however. For example, consider the decision of Navajo blanket makers to form a monopoly to sell their products to tourists at the Grand Canyon. In this situation the monopoly profits make the income

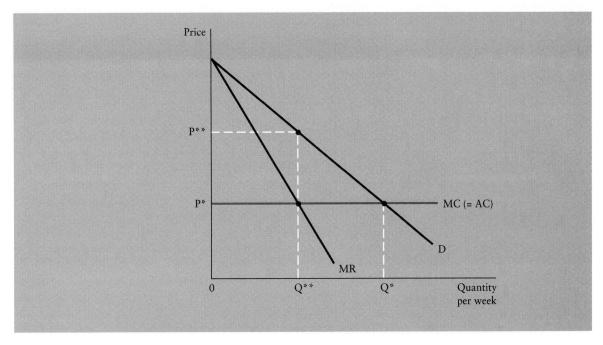

A perfectly competitive industry would produce output level Q* for which price equals marginal (and long-run average) cost. A monopoly, by recognizing the downward slope of the demand curve, would produce Q** where marginal revenue equals marginal cost. This output reduction is a measure of the allocational cost of monopolies. In some cases it may be possible to place a value on this loss in output.

Figure 16.3
Differential Effects of Perfect Competition and Monopoly in a Market

distribution more equal by transferring income from more wealthy tourists to low-income Navajos.

■ Distortion of Resource Allocation

Economists (who tend to worry about such matters) raise a second objection to monopolies: that their existence distorts the allocation of resources. Monopolies intentionally restrict their production in order to maximize profits. The discrepancy between price and marginal cost shows that at the monopoly's profit-maximizing output level consumers are willing to pay more for an extra unit of output than it costs to produce that output. From a social point of view, output is too low and some mutually beneficial transactions are being missed.

Figure 16.3 illustrates this observation by comparing the output that will be produced in a market characterized by perfect competition with the output that will be produced in the same market when it contains only one firm. The figure assumes that the monopoly produces under conditions of constant marginal cost[5] and that the competitive industry also exhibits constant costs with the same minimum long-run average cost as the monopolist—an assumption we question in the next section. In this situation a perfectly competitive industry would choose output level Q*, where long-run supply and demand intersect. At this point price is equal to average and marginal cost. A monopoly would choose output level Q**, for which marginal revenue is equal to marginal cost. The restriction in output (Q* – Q**) is then some measure of the allocation harm done by monopoly. Because of the way in which the market is organized, fewer resources are being devoted to the production of the good than the demand curve warrants. People would be willing to pay P** for additional output, which would only cost MC. However, the monopolist's market control and desire to maximize profits prevent the additional resources from being drawn into the industry to fill this demand.

As an admittedly inane example of this distortion, suppose a local hamburger joint has a monopoly in the production of chili dogs because its cook is the only one in town capable of concocting them. To maximize profits the owner of the monopoly restricts chili dog output to a point at which each dog sells for $2.00, but, at the margin, costs only $1.00 in terms of ingredients and the cook's time. Why is this inefficient? Because the well-being of both the cook and chili dog consumers could be improved by further trading. If the cook agreed to sell chili dogs at $1.50 to people who came around to the back door, overall welfare would be improved. Consumers would be better-off (since they would save $.50 per dog), and the cook would be better-off (by effectively getting a higher wage). Of course, the monopoly owner would prevent these illicit sales since they would undercut the profits being made. But the fact that such unexploited mutually beneficial trading opportunities exist is clear evidence that resources (here the cook's time) are not being used efficiently.

Measuring Monopolistic Distortions

Monopolies cause an artificial restriction in output together with an increase in price and thereby distort the allocation of resources. To put a dollar figure on this distortion, economists use the notion of consumer surplus that we introduced in Chapters 6 and 13.

Figure 16.4 repeats our previous illustration of the output restriction by a monopoly. When the market is competitively organized, Q* is produced at a price of P*. As we showed before, the total value to consumers of this output level is given by the area under the demand curve (that is, by area DEQ*0), for which they pay P*EQ*0. Total consumer surplus is given by the triangle DEP*.

---

[5]This assumption might be justified as reflecting the case of a multiplant monopoly that changes output by changing the number of plants it operates (see footnote 3).

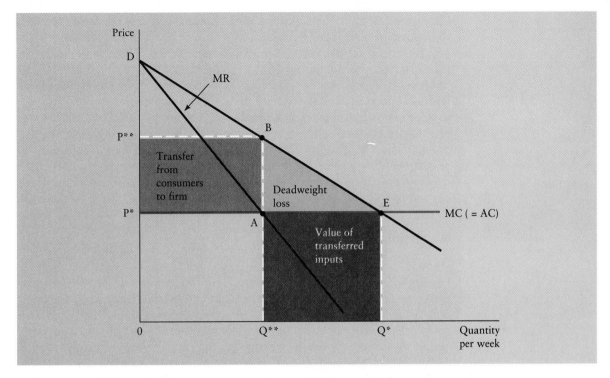

This figure repeats Figure 16.3 to study further the effects of monopolization. Consumer expenditures and productive inputs worth AEQ*Q** are reallocated into the production of other goods. Consumer surplus equal to P**BAP* is transferred into monopoly profits. There is a deadweight loss given by BEA.

Figure 16.4
Allocational and
Distributional Effects
of Monopoly

If this market is monopolized, only Q** is produced, and the price of this output is P**. The restriction in output and consequent price rise has had several effects. The total value of this good that consumers receive has been reduced in Figure 16.4 by the area BEQ*Q**. This reduction is not a total loss, however, since consumers previously had to pay AEQ*Q** for these goods, and they may now spend this money elsewhere. Since the monopoly produces less, it needs to hire fewer inputs. These released inputs will be used to produce those other goods that consumers buy. The loss of consumer surplus given by the area BEA is, however, an unambiguous reduction in welfare as a result of the monopoly. Some authors refer to triangle BEA as the deadweight loss from a monopoly. This loss is similar to the excess burden from a tax, which we illustrated in Chapter 13. It is the best single measure of the allocational harm caused by monopoly.

■ Distributional Effects

In addition to the allocational effect of monopolization of a market, there is a distributional effect, which can also be seen in Figure 16.4. At the monopoly's

output level of Q**, there exist monopoly profits given by the area P***BAP**.
In the case of perfect competition, this area was a part of the consumer's surplus triangle. If the market is a monopoly, that portion of a consumer's surplus is transferred into monopoly profits. The area P***BAP** in Figure 16.4 does not necessarily represent a loss of social welfare. It does measure the redistributional effects of a monopoly, and these may be undesirable. In order to make such an assessment, however, we would have to introduce an explicit concept of equity so that the welfare of the firm's owners and consumers could be compared. Concepts of equity are not necessary to demonstrate the nature of the allocational loss represented by area BEA. That is an unambiguous loss from the monopolization of the market. If the market were competitive, output would expand to Q*, and overall welfare would increase by the extent of this area.

■ Monopolists' Costs

Our analysis in Figures 16.3 and 16.4 assumed that monopolists and competitive firms have essentially the same costs of production. A deeper analysis suggests this may not in fact be the case. Monopoly profits, after all, provide a tantalizing target for firms, and they may spend real resources to achieve those profits. They may, for example, adopt extensive advertising campaigns or invest in ways to erect barriers to entry against other firms and hence obtain monopoly profits. Similarly, firms may seek special favors from the government in the form of tariff protection, restrictions on entry through licensing, or favorable treatment from a regulatory agency. Costs associated with these activities (such as lobbyists' salaries, legal fees, or advertising expenses) may make monopolists' costs exceed those in a competitive industry.

The possibility that costs may be different (and presumably higher) for a monopolist than for a firm in a competitive industry creates some complications for measuring monopolistic distortions to the allocation of resources. In this case, some potential monopoly profits will be dissipated into monopoly-creating costs, and it is possible that some of those costs (advertising, for example) may even shift the demand curve facing the producer. Such effects seriously complicate Figure 16.4, and we will not analyze them in detail here.[6] Application 16.2: Social Costs of Monopoly in the United States shows how the costs induced by monopoly-seeking activities may have a major impact on the estimated degree of the economic harm that monopolies do.

A Numerical Illustration of Deadweight Loss

As a numerical illustration of the types of calculations made by economists in studying the effects of monopoly, consider again the example of cassette tape sales

---

[6]For a relatively simple treatment, see R. A. Posner, "The Social Costs of Monopoly and Regulation," *Journal of Political Economy* (August 1975): 807–827.

APPLICATION 16.2
Social Costs of Monopoly in the United States

Arnold Harberger was one of the first economists to use the kind of analysis we have been discussing to estimate the allocational losses from monopolization of U.S. markets.[1] Harberger's method was rather simple. First, he assembled cost and profit data for 73 different industries. For each industry he estimated the percentage by which price exceeded average cost. This is equivalent to measuring the distance $P^{**} - P^*$ in Figure 16.3. For example, Harberger found that prices in the cement industry exceeded average (and, presumably, marginal) costs by 8.4 percent. Next, Harberger calculated the expansion in demand $(Q^* - Q^{**})$ that would occur by lowering prices to the competitive level. By assuming an elasticity of demand for cement of -1.0, the quantity of cement demanded would be increased by 8.4 percent if competitive prices prevailed. Using those two figures, he then calculated the area of the triangle BAE [$= 1/2 \times (P^{**} - P^*) (Q^* - Q^{**})$] as a measure of the welfare loss from monopoly (see Figure 16.4). For the case of cement, this loss amounted to $420,000 for the period under investigation (1924 to 1928). Making similar calculations for the other 72 industries in his sample, Harberger concluded that the total welfare loss from monopolies was about $150 million. This amounted to about 0.1 percent of gross national product during the period. Most recent studies arrive at similar estimates. Although monopoly losses may be relatively large in some industries, in comparison to the overall output of the economy, they are rather small.

Monopolist's Costs
Some economists believe these types of calculations substantially understate the social costs of monopoly because they do not account for possible differences in costs between monopolies and competitive firms. Taking account of such differences, it is claimed, may substantially reverse the notion that the allocational costs of monopoly are small. For example, a 1978 study by K. Cowling and D. C. Mueller estimated the portion of firms' costs that went toward creating monopoly profits.[2] From those estimates the authors calculated that monopolistic distortions may have represented as much as 13 percent of U.S. GNP in 1973. Estimates of such distortions were particularly large for automobile companies (they amounted to more than $1 billion for General Motors) and for household products companies (nearly $500 million each for Unilever and Procter & Gamble). However, the estimates are controversial because of the necessary arbitrariness in deciding which costs are really directed toward creating a monopoly position. For example, Cowling and Mueller included all advertising costs in that category, although they admit that some portion of these expenditures is probably unrelated to monopolistic goals. Despite this arbitrariness, the estimates illustrate the potential importance of the allocational effects of monopolies in situations where they may have significant effects on production costs.

To Think About
1. If the social cost of monopoly is so small (about 0.1 percent of GNP), why does the U.S. government spend so much on antimonopoly regulation through the Federal Trade Commission and the Department of Justice? Is the extent of such efforts misdirected, or does it seek goals other than just improving the allocation of resources (that is, preventing monopoly profits)?
2. The notion that monopolies may make expenditures in order to achieve monopoly profits has applications in other fields as well. Can you think of other ways in which firms may make rent seeking expenditures in order to obtain favorable market positions for themselves? (See Chapter 23 for a further discussion.)

[1]Arnold Harberger, "Monopoly and Resource Allocation," *American Economic Review* (May 1954): 77–87.

[2]K. Cowling and D. C. Mueller, "The Social Cost of Monopoly Power," *Economic Journal* (December 1978): 727–748.

Table 16.1
Effects of Monopolization on the Market for Cassette Tapes

	Demand Conditions				Consumer Surplus		
Price	Quantity (Tapes per Week)	Total Revenue	Marginal Revenue	Average and Marginal Cost	Under Perfect Competition	Under Monopoly	Monopoly Profits
$9	1	$9	$9	$3	$6	$3	$3
8	2	16	7	3	5	2	3
7	3	21	5	3	4	1	3
6	4	24	3	3	3	0	3
5	5	25	1	3	2	–	–
4	6	24	–1	3	1	–	–
3	7	21	–3	3	0	–	–
2	8	16	–5	3	–	–	–
1	9	9	–7	3	–	–	–
0	10	0	–9	3	–	–	–
				Totals	$21	$6	$12

▨ Competitive equilibrium: (P = MC).
▨ Monopoly equilibrium: (MR = MC).

introduced in Chapters 10 and 12. Table 16.1 repeats some of the information about this market originally presented in Table 10.1. Assume now that tapes have a marginal cost of $3 per tape. Under a situation of marginal cost pricing, tapes would also sell for $3 each, and as Table 16.1 shows, seven tapes per week would be bought. Consumer surplus can be computed as the amount people were willing to pay for each tape less what they actually pay ($3). For example, someone who was willing to pay $9 for the first tape sold paid only $3. He or she received a consumer surplus of $6. The sixth column of Table 16.1 makes a similar computation for each level of output from one to seven tapes. As the table shows, total consumer surplus is $21 per week when price is equal to marginal cost.

Suppose now that the tape market is monopolized by a single local merchant with a marginal cost of $3. This profit-maximizing firm will supply four tapes per week since at this level of output marginal revenue equals marginal cost. At this level of sales, price will be $6 per tape, profit per tape will be $3, and the firm will have total profits of $15. These profits represent a transfer of what was previously consumer surplus for the first four buyers of tapes. The seventh column of Table 16.1 computes consumer surplus figures for the monopolized situation. With a price of $6, for example, the buyer of the first tape now receives a consumer surplus of only $3 ($9 − $6)—the other $3 he or she enjoyed under marginal cost pricing has been transferred into $3 of profits for the monopoly. As Table 16.1 shows, total consumer surplus under the monopoly amounts to only $6 per week. When combined with the monopolist's profits of $12 per week, it is easy to see that there is now a deadweight loss of $3 per week ($21 − $18). Some part of what was previously consumer surplus has simply vanished with the monopolizing of the market.

Price Discrimination

So far in this chapter we have assumed that a monopoly sells all of its output at one price. The firm was assumed to be unwilling or unable to adopt different pricing strategies for different buyers of its product. There are two consequences of such a policy. First, as we illustrated in the previous section, the monopoly must forsake some transactions that would in fact be mutually beneficial if they could be conducted at a lower price. The total value of such trades is given by area BEA in Figure 16.5 (which repeats Figure 16.4). Second, although the monopoly does succeed in transferring a portion of consumer surplus into monopoly profits, it still leaves some consumer surplus to those individuals who value the output at a higher price than the monopoly charges (area DBP** in Figure 16.5). The existence of both of these areas of untapped opportunities suggests that a monopoly has the possibility of increasing its

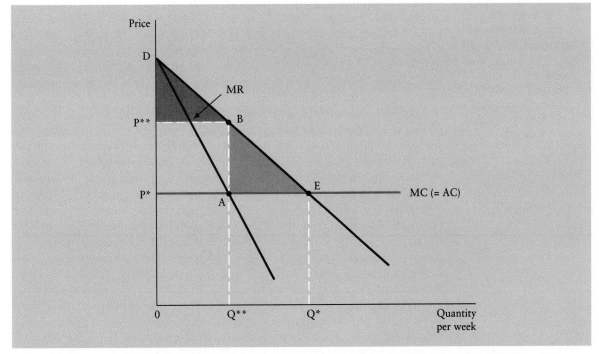

The monopolist's price-output choice (P** – Q**) provides targets for additional profits through successful price discrimination. It may obtain a portion of the consumer surplus given by area DBP** (shaded gray) through discriminatory entry fees, whereas it can create additional mutually beneficial transactions (area BEA, shaded in color) through quantity discounts.

Figure 16.5

Targets for Price Discrimination

profits even further by practicing **price discrimination**—that is, by selling its output at different prices to different buyers. In this section, we will examine some of these possibilities.

■ Perfect Price Discrimination

In theory, one way for a monopoly to practice price discrimination is to sell each unit of its output for the maximum amount that buyers are willing to pay for that particular unit. Under this scheme then, a monopoly faced with the situation described in Figure 16.5 would sell the first unit of its output at a price slightly below 0D, the second unit at a slightly lower price, and so forth. When the firm has the ability to sell one unit at a time in this way, there is no reason now to stop at output level Q^{**}. Because it can sell the next unit at a price only slightly below P^{**} (which still exceeds marginal and average cost by a considerable margin), it might as well do so. Indeed, the firm will continue to sell its output one unit at a time until it reaches output level Q^*. For output levels greater than Q^*, the price that buyers are willing to pay does not exceed average and marginal cost; hence, these sales would not be profitable.

The result of this **perfect price discrimination**[7] scheme will be the firm receiving total revenues of 0DEQ*, incurring total costs of 0P*EQ*, and, therefore, obtaining total monopoly profits given by area P*DE. In this case, all of the consumer surplus available in the market will have been transferred into monopoly profits. Consumers will have had all the extra utility they might have received by consuming this good wrung out of them by the monopolist's price discrimination scheme.

Perhaps somewhat paradoxically, this perfect price discrimination scheme results in an equilibrium that is economically efficient. Because trading proceeds to the point at which price is equal to marginal cost, there are no further unexploited trading opportunities available in this marketplace. Of course, this solution requires that the monopoly know a great deal about the buyers of its output in order to determine how much each is willing to pay. It also requires that no further trading occur in this good in order to prevent those who buy it at a low price from reselling to those who would have paid the most to the monopoly. The pricing scheme will not work for goods like toasters or concert tickets, which may easily be resold. But for some services, such as medical office visits or personalized financial or legal planning, providers may have the required monopoly power and may know their buyers well enough to permit some approximation to such a scheme. There may even be situations (such as providing physician services to small towns) where the greater profits available under perfect price discrimination are required in order for the service to be provided at all.

---

[7]Some authors refer to perfect price discrimination as "first degree price discrimination." In this (relatively unhelpful) terminology, quantity discounts and two-part tariffs where each individual faces the same pricing menu are referred to as "second degree price discrimination" and market separating strategies are referred to as "third degree price discrimination."

■ Quantity Discounts

One way to differentiate among buyers' willingness to pay is by offering quantity discounts. These have the advantage of retaining some sales at the monopolist's preferred price (P** in Figure 16.5), but earning additional profits for quantities greater than Q** sold at a lower price to consumers with lower marginal evaluations of the good. For example, the Pizza Hut restaurant chain offers customers a second pizza for below what it charges for the first one. Hungry consumers are tempted to make the additional purchase at a price that still yields profits for the restaurant. Similar quantity discounts occur with respect to supermarket coupons, video rental packages, and frequent-flyer programs.

As for other price discrimination schemes, an important problem for the monopolist utilizing quantity discounts is to prevent further transactions between customers who pay a low price and those who pay a high price. In the case of Pizza Hut and others, such resale is discouraged by custom; restaurant patrons seldom offer to buy a pizza for someone sitting at the next table (though a mutually beneficial transaction could probably be arranged). In the case of frequent-flyer coupons, however, resales can be a major problem for airlines, and they take many precautions (not always successfully) to prevent low-cost tickets from competing with their more profitable sales.

■ Two-Part Tariffs

Another way of increasing profits through price discrimination is to adopt a two-part pricing scheme under which consumers must pay an entry fee for the right to purchase the actual good being sold. The traditional example is popcorn pricing at movie theaters. The entry fee for the movie itself is the first part of this pricing scheme. Entry fees should be set in a way so as to extract as much of the available consumer surplus as possible from movie-goers. Presumably this should involve a variety of quantity discount schemes coupled with special charges for very popular films. Popcorn itself should be priced in a way that will maximize admissions; that is, it should be at marginal cost, since this will expand the pool of consumers paying entry fees.

Unfortunately, anyone who has purchased popcorn at inflated theater prices knows there must be more to the story than this. Theater owners price their comestibles well above marginal cost because they find it impossible to extract all available consumer surplus through their entry price schemes. They find it more profitable to raise popcorn prices above marginal cost, thereby losing movie attendance revenue extracted from some popcorn lovers with relatively little interest in movies; their hope is to make up for this by extracting additional consumer surplus from movie lovers who also buy popcorn.

Exploring a full analysis of optimal two-part pricing schemes is beyond our intentions here.[8] But the prevalence of combined sales arrangements such

---

[8] For a more complete discussion together with a good summary of the literature see L. Lecaz and A. Rodriguez, "Price Discrimination in Competitive Markets," *Journal of Political Economy* (October 1992): 954–965. As their title implies, these authors doubt that the monopoly model is adequate for explaining two-part pricing in what appear to be competitive markets (such as movie theaters).

as wine at restaurants, beer at baseball games, or fees for golf or tennis facilities at resort hotels suggests the topic is a fascinating one. Application 16.3: Pricing at the Magic Kingdom illustrates how the Disney empire has tried any number of schemes to draw consumer surplus from the demanders of its unique offerings.

■ Market Separation

A final way in which a monopoly may be able to practice price discrimination is to separate its potential customers into two or more categories and to charge different amounts in these markets. If buyers cannot shift their buying from one market to another in response to such differences, this practice may increase profits over what is obtainable under a single price policy.

Such a situation is shown graphically in Figure 16.6. The figure is drawn so that the market demand and marginal revenue curves in the two markets share the same vertical axis, which records the price charged for the good in each market. As before, the figure also assumes that marginal cost is constant over all levels of output. The profit-maximizing decision for the monopoly is to produce Q_1^* in the first market and Q_2^* in the second market; these output levels obey the MR = MC rule for each market. The prices in the two markets will then be P_1 and P_2, respectively. It is clear from the figure that the market

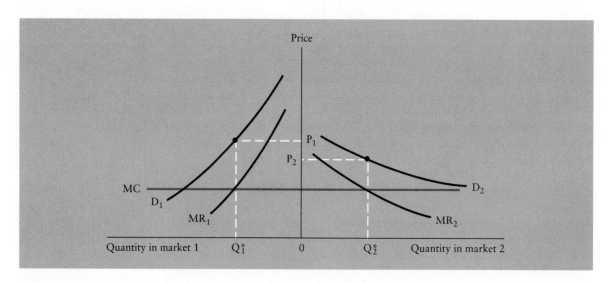

Figure 16.6
Separated Markets Raise the Possibility of Price Discrimination

If two markets are separate, a monopolist can maximize profits by selling its product at different prices in the two markets. The firm would choose that output for which MC = MR in each of the markets. The diagram shows that the market that has a less elastic demand curve will be charged the higher price by the price discriminator.

APPLICATION 16.3

Pricing at the Magic Kingdom

Disneyland and Disney World are unique entertainment attractions. Amusement park aficionados (including this author) agree there are few, if any, substitutes for Disney's products. Consequently, the company occupies a clear monopolistic position with regard to its pricing decisions. Given its position, it is not surprising that Disney adopts a bewildering array of pricing policies, all presumably with the purpose of converting available consumer surplus into profits.

The Disneyland Passport

Prior to the 1980s, Disney used a complicated multipart pricing schedule for its rides.[1] Under that schedule, Disneyland patrons had to purchase a "passport" containing a ticket for admission to the park together with coupons for admission to the rides themselves. (The contents of your author's old passport are summarized in Table 1 as are the prices of additional tickets for each type of ride.) Disney enjoyed a great deal of pricing flexibility with the passport arrangement. It could vary the basic price of a passport; it could vary the composition of tickets contained in a passport; it could redefine which rides required which tickets; and it could alter the prices of extra tickets. In short, the passport pricing method provided the firm with myriad opportunities to increase profits through price discrimination among different types of buyers. For example, the number of "E" ride tickets seemed to be carefully chosen to allow passport purchasers to ride most of the major attractions without permitting second rides, except at additional cost. The lesser attraction tickets in the passport spread patrons around the park. Notice that the price of extra tickets for "E" rides was quite high (certainly well above marginal cost). This pricing policy was consistent with the low price elasticity of "E" ride fanatics once they were already in the park and was also consistent with Disney's inability to extract full consumer surplus from these individuals paying their admissions prices.

Changes in Pricing Policy

Disney's passport pricing schedule posed problems for the parks. Most importantly, labor costs were substantially higher under such a system (since many ticket collectors

Table 1
Structure of a Typical Disneyland Passport

Item	Example	Number of Tickets in Passport	Price of Extra Ticket
Admission	—	1	$4.00
"A" ride	Shooting Gallery	2	.25
"B" ride	Dumbo, Train	3	.50
"C" ride	Peter Pan's Flight	3	.75
"D" ride	Autopia	2	1.00
"E" ride	Space Mountain	5	1.50

Source: Author's 1978 passport. *Note:* As discussed in this application, Disneyland now has a single price admission policy.

and salespersons were needed) than under the single price admission policy followed at other amusement parks (Great Adventure and Busch Gardens, for example). Consequently, in the early 1980s, Disney moved away from individual tickets for rides and toward a single entry fee with zero marginal prices for all rides. This single fee still provides the company with numerous opportunities for price discrimination, such as the ability to charge reduced prices for multiday tickets and to charge lower rates for local residents than for tourists. At Disney World (in Florida), the firm uses additional pricing strategies in the way it packages admission tickets to the Magic Kingdom, EPCOT, MGM World, and a number of minor attractions such as Discovery Island and its monorails. Probably only Disney financial executives fully understand all the pricing options available. The company still appears to be following the profit motive despite the different pricing schemes it employs.

To Think About

1. If you have been to Disneyland or Disney World, can you remember other examples of price discrimination? How is food priced? How about hotel accommodations? Can you explain why the company might adopt seasonal price differentials?
2. Why does Disney World still use a complex pricing scheme for entry into its major attractions? Why doesn't it adopt a single-entry price for all attractions?

[1]For an analytical treatment of these points see W. Y. Oi, "A Disneyland Dilemma: Two-Part Tariffs for a Mickey Mouse Monopoly," *Quarterly Journal of Economics* (February 1971): 77–96.

with the less elastic demand curve will have the higher price.[9] The price-discriminating monopolist will charge a higher price in that market in which quantity purchased is less responsive to price changes.

Whether a monopoly is successful in this type of price discrimination depends critically on its ability to keep the markets separated. In some cases, that separation may be geographic. For example, book publishers tend to charge higher prices in the United States than abroad because foreign markets are more competitive and subject to illegal copying. In this case, the oceans enforce market separation; few people would travel abroad simply to buy books. Such a discriminatory policy would not work if transportation costs were low, however. As chain stores that charge different prices in different parts of a town have discovered, people will flock to where the bargains are.

Price discrimination by time of sale may also be possible. For example, tickets to late night or afternoon showings of motion pictures are usually cheaper than for evening shows. Discriminating against those who wish to attend prime-time shows succeeds because the good being purchased cannot be resold later. A firm that tried to sell toasters at two different prices during the day might discover itself to be in competition with savvy customers who bought when the price was low and undercut the firm by selling to other customers during high price periods. If customers themselves can alter when they shop, a discriminatory policy may not work. A firm that offers lower post-Christmas prices may find its pre-Christmas business facing stiff competition from those sales. As always, arrival of competition (even from a monopoly's other activities) makes it impossible to pursue pure monopoly pricing practices.

Regulation of Monopolies

The regulation of natural monopolies is an important subject in applied economic analysis. The utility, communications, and transportation industries are highly regulated in most countries, and devising regulatory procedures that cause these industries to operate in a desirable way is an important practical problem. Here we look at a few aspects of the regulation of monopolies that relate to pricing policies.

■ Marginal Cost Pricing and the Natural Monopoly Dilemma

By analogy to the perfectly competitive case, many economists believe that it is important for the prices charged by regulated monopolies to accurately reflect marginal costs of production. In this way the deadweight loss from monopolies is minimized. The principal problem raised by an enforced policy of marginal cost pricing is that it may require natural monopolies to operate at a loss.

---

[9]*Proof:* Since $MR = P(1 + 1/e)$, $MR_1 = MR_2$ implies $P_1(1 + 1/e_1) = P_2(1 + 1/e_2)$. If $e_1 > e_2$ (if the demand in market 1 is less elastic), then P_1 must exceed P_2 for this equality to hold.

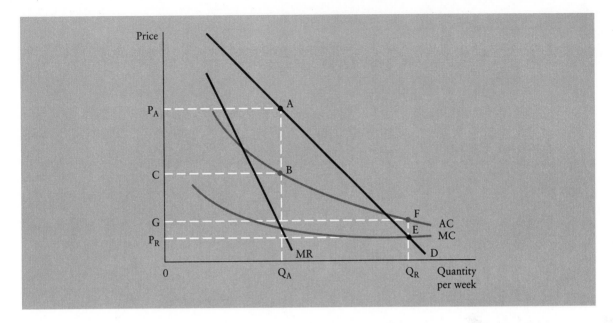

Because natural monopolies exhibit decreasing average cost, marginal costs fall below average cost. Enforcing a policy of marginal cost pricing will entail operating at a loss. A price of P_R, for example, will achieve the goal of marginal cost pricing but will necessitate an operating loss of $GFEP_R$.

Figure 16.7
Price Regulation for a Natural Monopoly

Natural monopolies, by definition, exhibit decreasing average costs over a broad range of output levels. The cost curves for such a firm might look like those shown in Figure 16.7. In the absence of regulation the monopoly would produce output level Q_A and receive a price of P_A for its product. Profits in this situation are given by the rectangle $P_A ABC$. A regulatory agency might set a price of P_R for this monopoly. At this price, Q_R is demanded, and the marginal cost of producing this output level is also P_R. Consequently, marginal cost pricing has been achieved. Unfortunately, because of the declining nature of the firm's cost curves, the price P_R (= marginal cost) falls below average costs. With this regulated price the monopoly must operate at a loss of $GFEP_R$. Since no firm can operate indefinitely at a loss, this poses a dilemma for the regulatory agency: either it must abandon its goal of marginal cost pricing, or the government must subsidize the monopoly forever.

■ Two-Tier Pricing Systems

One way out of the marginal cost pricing dilemma is a two-part pricing system. Under this system the monopoly is permitted to charge some users a high price while maintaining a low price for "marginal" users. In this way the demanders paying the high price in effect subsidize the losses of the low-price customers.

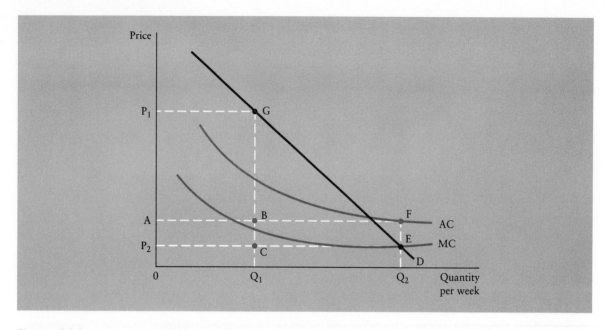

Figure 16.8
Two-Part Pricing
Schedule

By charging a high price (P_1) to some users and a low price (P_2) to others, it may be possible for a regulatory commission to (1) enforce marginal cost pricing and (2) create a situation where the profits from one class of user (P_1GBA) subsidize the losses of the other class (BFEC).

Such a pricing scheme is shown in Figure 16.8. Here the regulatory commission has decided that some users will pay a relatively high price, P_1. At this price, Q_1 is demanded. Other users (presumably those who would not buy the good at the P_1 price) are offered a lower price, P_2. This lower price generates additional demand of $Q_2 - Q_1$. Consequently, a total output of Q_2 is produced at an average cost of A. With this two-part pricing system, the profits on the sales to high-price demanders (given by the rectangle P_1GBA) balance the losses incurred on the low-priced sales (BFEC). Furthermore, for the "marginal user," the marginal cost pricing rule is being followed: it is the "intramarginal" user who subsidizes the firm so that it does not operate at a loss.

Although in practice it may not be so simple to establish pricing schemes that maintain marginal cost pricing and cover operating costs, many regulatory commissions do use multipart price schedules that intentionally discriminate against some users to the advantage of others. Application 16.4: The Breakup of AT&T illustrates how this was done for many years in the telephone industry and how this caused major problems in moving to a more competitive situation.

■ Rate of Return Regulation

Another approach to setting the price charged by a natural monopoly that is followed in many regulatory situations is to permit the monopoly to charge a

APPLICATION 16.4

The Breakup of AT&T

In 1974, the U.S. Department of Justice filed an antitrust suit against the American Telephone and Telegraph (AT&T) Company charging unlawful monopolization of the telephone equipment and long distance service markets. At the time, AT&T controlled virtually all of the telephone business in the United States and was regulated by a number of bodies at both the federal and state level. Filing an antitrust suit against a regulated natural monopoly was a highly unusual act, and legal wrangling over the suit lasted well into the 1980s. A settlement was finally realized in late 1982 and on January 1, 1984, AT&T formally divested itself of its seven local Bell Operating Companies (Ameritech, Atlantic Bell, Bell South, NYNEX, Pacific Telesis, Southwestern Bell, and U.S. West). AT&T itself retained its manufacturing operations (Western Electric Company) and its long distance operations. The goal of this huge restructuring was to improve the performance and competitiveness of the U.S. telephone industry, but these gains have proven very difficult to obtain.

Subsidization of Local Phone Service

Prior to the breakup, AT&T had been forced by regulators to provide local residential phone service at prices below average cost and to make up these losses by charging above average cost for long distance calls (see Figure 16.8). Over the years immediately prior to the breakup, the subsidies had grown larger as technical improvements (such as satellites) sharply reduced the costs of long distance service. But regulators chose to keep long distance rates high and local rates low. By the early 1980s, residential service was estimated to cost about $26 per month, but the typical charge was only $11 per month. Subsidies from long distance and other sources made up the $15 per month difference.[1] After the breakup, state regulators were faced with the politically unappealing prospect of implementing huge increases in residential telephone rates. Not surprisingly, local regulators instead opted for a continuation of subsidies from

AT&T (and, to a lesser extent, from other long distance companies such as MCI or Sprint) to the local operaters.

Performance of the Long Distance Market

Although the market for telephone equipment has become markedly more competitive since 1984 (mainly through the entry of Japanese producers), the long distance market has not. Long distance rates for AT&T have continued to be regulated at the federal level and other long distance carriers have found it difficult to gain much of the market despite their cost competitiveness. Both of these results, at least in part, are dictated by the continuing cross-subsidy to local service. Regulation of telephone rates is needed to assure adequate profits are generated to provide the subsidy and, because local companies get a larger subsidy from AT&T than from other long distance providers, local regulators have been reluctant to proceed to full-scale access for these providers.

Performance of Local Operating Companies

Because of a desire to ensure that operating subsidies are used to keep local rates low, regulators (and the federal judge overseeing the AT&T breakup) have been reluctant to provide much leeway for these companies to branch out into other fields. Most importantly, they have been forbidden to enter the long distance market and to enter the business of manufacturing telephone equipment for general sale. They have also been prevented from entering a variety of computer and data-transmission markets. What could have been strong competition among the seven operating companies has, therefore, generally failed to materialize except in relatively small markets such as those for cellular phones.

To Think About

1. Why should local phone service be subsidized? Are there socially desirable benefits from making sure phone service is available to practically everyone? If so, who should pay the subsidy?
2. Does the argument that local operating companies should be barred from many businesses because they might use their subsidies to gain an unfair advantage make sense? Would a local phone company find it in its interest to do this?

---

[1]P. W. MacAvoy and K. Robinson, "Losing by Judicial Policy Making: The First Year of the AT&T Divestiture," *Yale Journal on Regulation* (January 1985): 225–262.

price above average cost that will earn a "fair" rate of return on investment. Much analytical effort is then spent on defining the "fair" rate and on developing how it might be measured. From an economic point of view some of the most interesting questions about this procedure concern how the regulatory activity affects the firm's decisions. If, for example, the allowed rate of return exceeds what the firm might earn under competitive circumstances, the firm will have an incentive to use relatively more capital input than needed to truly minimize costs. If regulators typically delay in making rate decisions, firms may be given incentives to minimize costs that would not otherwise exist since they cannot immediately recover their costs through higher rates. Although it is possible to develop a formal analysis of all of these possibilities, we do not do so here.[10]

Benefits of Monopoly

Our analysis in this chapter makes two arguments against monopoly. The first concludes that the allocational effects of monopoly are harmful: too few resources are devoted to the production of a good for which the supply is monopolized. The second argument is somewhat more ambiguous but is probably more important from a policy perspective: monopolies have undesirable distributional effects. Monopolies may make long-run profits, and these profits may accrue to relatively rich owners at the expense of relatively poor consumers. This consideration of the distributional fairness of monopolies reinforces the allocational argument and provides the basis for the notion that monopolies are an unambiguous evil.

This simple conclusion is questioned by some economists. For example, J. A. Schumpeter stressed the beneficial role that monopoly profits can play in the process of economic development.[11] This section briefly reviews some of the possible beneficial aspects of monopoly that have been suggested.

■ Monopoly Profits and Economic Growth

Authors discussing the possible benefits of monopoly tend to take a dynamic view of the economic process. They emphasize innovation and the ability of particular types of firms to achieve technical advances. In this context, the profits that monopolistic firms earn play an important role. Profits provide the funds to invest in research and development. Whereas perfectly competitive firms must be content with a normal return on invested capital, monopolies have the surplus funds to undertake the risky process of research. More important, perhaps, the possibility of attaining a monopoly position, or the

---

[10]For a detailed treatment, see E. E. Bailey, *Economic Theory of Regulatory Constraint* (Lexington, Mass.: D. C. Heath, 1973).

[11]J. A. Schumpeter, *Capitalism, Socialism, and Democracy,* 3d ed. (New York: Harper & Row, 1950), especially Chapter 8.

APPLICATION 16.5
The IBM Case

On the final day of the Johnson administration, an antitrust case was filed by the U.S. Justice Department against International Business Machines Corporation (IBM). During the ensuing 13 years, the case developed all the elements of a television soap opera. Successive Justice Department officials had considerable difficulty in making a coherent case, legal careers were made and destroyed at the prestigious firm of Cravath, Swaine and Moore (IBM's attorneys), economists made tidy consultants' fees, and IBM even sought to have the judge in the case disqualified for being biased. In all, the case generated 66 million pages of documentation and probably cost taxpayers and IBM hundreds of millions of dollars. Despite the vast expenditures, the IBM case was ultimately dropped by the federal government on January 8, 1982, on the argument it was "flimsy" and "without merit." This farcical saga illustrates several economic elements of modern antitrust litigation.

Defining the Computer Market
In its original complaint, the Justice Department accused IBM of monopolizing the "general purpose computer" market in which, it was asserted, IBM had about a 70 percent share. In its defense, IBM continually sought to expand this market definition (to include all information-processing and retrieval systems, for example) and to show it was really a rather small fish in a big pond (which included, for example, American Telephone and Telegraph Company). At the time the case was dropped, the litigants had still not reached any agreement on the very basic question of what market IBM monopolized.

IBM's Conduct
Similar ambiguities surrounded the legal arguments of whether IBM had attempted to monopolize the computer market. Three of the government's specific charges against IBM's conduct illustrate the dispute. First, the government alleged that IBM introduced "fighting machines" (particularly model 360-70) whose timing was targeted specifically to undermine competitors' efforts to develop new products. Second, it was argued that

IBM's practice of selling its maintenance and programming services together with its machines made it difficult for competitors to gain a foothold in the market. Finally, IBM's use of discounts for educational institutions was deemed anticompetitive because they resulted in a generation of students trained only on IBM equipment.

IBM's Defense
IBM, in its defense, attacked each of these charges by asserting that they simply reflected aggressive competition and good corporate citizenship. Introduction of new machines, according to IBM, was just normal business practice in the fast-moving computer industry. Similarly, IBM argued, it bundled its services and equipment together simply to serve customers better. Other companies, after all, were free to adopt the same practice. Finally, educational discounts, according to IBM, were the natural response of a company seeking to promote general social well-being.

The decision to drop the IBM case probably reflected the sensible judgment that the case had reached a stage where the costs of further litigation outweighed any potential gains from a government victory. In the 13 years since the case was filed, the computer industry had changed greatly, with hundreds of new firms being founded and IBM's share of the market falling sharply. Problems experienced by IBM in the early 1990s in coping with the fast changing world of computer technology provides further evidence that whatever monopoly power the firm may have had was short-lived.

To Think About
1. What market was it that IBM may have monopolized in the 1960s? If you were a government attorney, how would you define the relevant market? What if you were an attorney for IBM?
2. In the Alcoa case, Judge Learned Hand ruled that because Alcoa controlled nearly two-thirds of the primary aluminum production capacity in the United States, it was a monopoly. Doesn't the definition of monopoly require 100 percent control of the market?

desire to maintain such a position, provides an important incentive to the monopoly to keep one step ahead of potential competitors. Innovations in new products and cost-saving production techniques may be integrally related to the possibility of monopolization. Without a monopoly position, the full benefits of innovation could not be obtained by the innovating firm.

■ Monopoly and Cost Saving

Schumpeter stresses that the monopolization of a market may make it less costly for a firm to plan its activities. Being the only source of supply for a product eliminates many of the contingencies that a firm in a competitive market must face. For example, a monopoly may not have to spend as much on selling expenses (such as advertising, brand identification, or visiting retailers) as would be the case in a more competitive industry. Similarly, a monopoly may know more about the specific demand curve for its product and may more readily adapt to changing demand conditions.

Of course, whether any of these purported benefits of monopolies outweigh their allocational and distributional disadvantages is an open question. Generally, economists have not been sufficiently convinced about the benefits of monopoly to favor deliberate creation of monopoly power through licensing or other barriers to entry. Instead they tend to regard such barriers as anticompetitive and probably unwise. Whether large firms should be subject to legal scrutiny for monopoly-like practices, however, raises more difficult questions, as Application 16.5: The IBM Case illustrates.

Summary

A market in which there is a single seller is called a "monopoly." In a monopoly situation the firm faces the entire market demand curve. Contrary to the case of perfect competition, the monopoly's output decision will completely determine market price. The major conclusions of our investigation of pricing in monopoly markets are

- The profit-maximizing monopoly will choose an output level for which marginal revenue is equal to marginal cost. Since the firm faces a downward-sloping demand curve, market price will exceed both marginal revenue and marginal cost.

- The divergence between price and marginal cost is a sign that the monopoly causes resources to be allocated inefficiently. Buyers are willing to pay more for one more unit of output than it costs the firm to produce it, but the monopoly prevents this beneficial transaction from occurring.

- Because of barriers to entry, a monopoly may earn positive long-run economic profits. These profits may have undesirable distributional effects.

- A monopoly may be able to increase profits further by practicing price discrimination. Adoption of such schemes depends on the specific nature of the market the monopoly serves.

- Governments may choose to regulate the prices charged by monopolies. In the case of a natural monopoly (for which average costs decline over a broad range of output), this poses a dilemma. The regulatory agency can opt for marginal cost pricing (in which case the monopoly will operate at a loss) or for average cost pricing (in which case an inefficient quantity will be produced).

Review Questions

1. In everyday discussions people tend to talk about monopolies "setting high prices," but in this chapter we have talked about the monopoly's profit-maximizing level of output. Are these two approaches saying the same thing? What do both assume about the demand curve facing a monopoly? What kind of rule would a monopoly follow if it wished to choose a profit-maximizing price? Why not charge the highest price possible?

2. Why are barriers to entry crucial to the success of a monopoly firm? Explain why all monopoly profits will show up as returns to the factor or factors that provide the barrier to entry.

3. "At a monopoly's profit-maximizing output, price will exceed marginal cost simply because price exceeds marginal revenue for a downward-sloping demand curve." Explain why this is so and indicate what factors will affect the size of the price-marginal cost gap.

4. The following conversation was overheard during a microeconomics cram session:

   Student A: "In order to maximize profits, a monopoly should obviously produce where the gap between price and *average* cost is the greatest."
   Student B: "No, that will only maximize profit per unit. To maximize total profits, the firm should produce where the gap between price and *marginal* cost is the greatest since that will maximize monopoly power and hence profits."
   Can you make any sense out of this drivel? Do these students still have a lot of studying to do?

5. "Increases in input costs will be passed on to consumers directly by a monopoly, but that would not happen in a competitive market. Hence, monopolies are a major cause of inflation." Do you agree?

6. Figure 16.4 illustrates the "deadweight loss" from the monopolization of a market. What is this a loss of? In the chili dog–cook example, what is the world missing out on?

7. Why must resale be prevented if a monopoly is to be able to practice price discrimination successfully? What factors can provide such prevention? Why don't markets obey the "law of one price" under price discrimination?

8. Explain the pricing policy followed by Disney, United Airlines, or any other firm that follows a complex pricing policy. How does this policy take advantage of its demand situation? How can the firm ensure that resale is prevented?

9. What is a "natural monopoly"? Why does electric power distribution or local telephone service have the characteristics of a natural monopoly? Why might this be less true for electric power generation or long distance telephone service?

10. Suppose the government wished to regulate the price of the monopoly firms illustrated in Figures 16.1 and 16.3. Would this price regulation pose the same dilemma posed by the natural monopoly in Figure 16.7? Suppose a monopoly owned many plants, each operating at the low point of its long-run average cost curve. Which of these figures would best reflect that situation? Would price regulation or some form of antitrust breakup promise better industry performance in this case?

Problems

16.1 A monopolist can produce at constant average and marginal costs of $AC = MC = 5$. The firm faces a market demand curve given by $Q = 53 - P$. The monopolist's marginal revenue curve is given by $MR = 53 - 2Q$.

a. Calculate the profit-maximizing price–quantity combination for the monopolist. Also calculate the monopolist's profits and consumer surplus.
b. What output level would be produced by this industry under perfect competition (where price = marginal cost)?
c. Calculate the consumer surplus obtained by consumers in part b. Show that this exceeds the sum of the monopolist's profits and consumer surplus received in part a. What is the value of the "deadweight loss" from monopolization?

16.2 A monopolist faces a market demand curve given by

$$Q = 70 - P.$$

The monopolist's marginal revenue curve is given by

$$MR = 70 - 2Q.$$

a. If the monopolist can produce at constant average and marginal costs of $AC = MC = 6$, what output level will the monopolist choose in order to maximize profits? What is the price at this output level? What are the monopolist's profits?

b. Assume instead that the monopolist has a cost structure where total costs are described by

$$TC = .25Q^2 - 5Q + 300$$

and marginal cost is given by

$$MC = .5Q - 5.$$

With the monopolist facing the same market demand and marginal revenue, what price–quantity combination will be chosen now to maximize profits? What will profits be?

c. Assume now that a third cost structure explains the monopolist's position with total costs given by

$$TC = .333Q^3 - 26Q^2 + 695Q - 5,800$$

and marginal costs given by

$$MC = Q^2 - 52Q + 695.$$

Again, calculate the monopolist's price–quantity combination that maximizes profits. What will profits be? (Hint: Set MC = MR as usual and use the quadratic formula or simple factoring to solve the equation for Q.)

d. Graph the market demand cruve, the MR curve, and the three marginal cost curves from parts a, b, and c. Notice that the monopolist's profit-making ability is constrained by (1) the market demand curve it faces (along with its associated MR curve) and (2) the cost structure underlying production.

16.3 A single firm monopolizes the entire market for Nixon masks and can produce at constant average and marginal costs of

$$AC = MC = 10.$$

Originally, the firm faces a market demand curve given by

$$Q = 60 - P$$

and a marginal revenue curve given by

$$MR = 60 - 2Q.$$

a. Calculate the profit-maximizing price–quantity combination for the firm. What are the firm's profits?

b. Now assume that the market demand curve shifts outward (becoming steeper) and is given by

$$Q = 45 - .5P$$

with the marginal revenue curve given by

$$MR = 90 - 4Q.$$

What is the firm's profit-maximizing price–quantity combination now? What are the firm's profits?

c. Instead of the assumptions of part b, assume that the market demand curve shifts outward (becoming flatter) and is given by

$$Q = 100 - 2P$$

with the marginal revenue curve given by

$$MR = 50 - Q.$$

What is the firm's profit-maximizing price–quantity combination now? What are the firm's profits?

d. Graph the three different situations of parts a, b, and c. Using your results, explain why there is no supply curve for this mask monopoly.

*16.4 Suppose that the market for hula hoops is monopolized by a single firm.

a. Draw the initial equilibrium for such a market.
b. Suppose now that the demand for hula hoops shifts outward slightly. Show that, in general (contrary to the competitive case), it will not be possible to predict the effect of this shift in demand on the market price of hula hoops.
c. Consider three possible ways in which the price elasticity of demand might change as the demand curve shifts—it might increase, it might decrease, or it might stay the same. Consider also that marginal costs for the monopolist might be rising, falling, or constant in the range where $MR = MC$. Consequently there are nine different combinations of types of demand shifts and marginal cost slope configurations. Analyze each of these to determine for which it is possible to make a definite prediction about the effect of the shift in demand on the price of hula hoops.

*16.5 Suppose a company has a monopoly on a game called Monopoly and faces a demand curve given by

$$Q_T = 100 - P$$

and a marginal revenue curve given by

$$MR = 100 - 2Q_T$$

where Q_T equals the combined total number of games produced per hour in the company's two factories ($Q_T = q_1 + q_2$). If factory 1 has a marginal cost curve given by

$$MC_1 = q_1 - 5$$

and factory 2 has a marginal cost curve given by

$$MC_2 = .5q_2 - 5,$$

how much total output will the company choose to produce and how will it distribute this production between its two factories in order to maximize profits?

---

*Denotes a problem that is rather difficult.

*16.6 Suppose a textbook monopoly can produce any level of output it wishes at a constant marginal (and average) cost of $5 per unit. Assume that the monopoly sells its books in two different markets that are separated by some distance. The demand curve in the first market is given by

$$Q_1 = 55 - P_1$$

and the curve in the second market is given by

$$Q_2 = 70 - 2P_2.$$

a. If the monopolist can maintain the separation between the two markets, what level of output should be produced in each market and what price will prevail in each market? What are total profits in this situation?
b. How would your answer change if it only cost demanders $5 to mail books between the two markets? What would be the monopolist's new profit level in this situation? How would your answer change if mailing costs were 0? (Hint: Show that for a downward-sloping linear demand curve, profits are maximized when output is set at $Q^*/2$, where Q^* is the output level that would be demanded when $P = MC$. Use this result to solve the problem.)

16.7 Suppose a perfectly competitive industry can produce Roman candles at a constant marginal cost of $10 per unit. Once the industry is monopolized, marginal costs rise to $12 per unit because $2 per unit must be paid to lobbyists to ensure that only this firm receives a Roman candle license. Suppose the market demand for Roman candles is given by

$$Q_D = 1,000 - 50P$$

and the marginal revenue curve by

$$MR = 20 - Q/25.$$

a. Calculate the perfectly competitive and monopoly outputs and prices.
b. Calculate the total loss of consumer surplus from monopolization of Roman candle production.
c. Graph your results.

16.8 Consider the following possible schemes for taxing a monopoly:

i. A proportional tax on profits
ii. A specific tax on each unit produced
iii. A proportional tax on the gap between price and marginal cost

a. Explain how each of these taxes would affect the monopolist's profit-maximizing output choice. Would the tax increase or decrease the deadweight loss from monopoly?
b. Graph your results for these three cases.

---

*Denotes a problem that is rather difficult.

16.9   Suppose a monopoly produces its output in a large number of identical plants, each characterized by a U-shaped long-run average cost curve. How should the firm decide how much to produce and how many plants to utilize? Will each plant be operated at the low point of its average cost curve? Does this imply that production is efficient in this situation? Explain.

16.10   Suppose a monopoly can choose the quality of its output in addition to the quantity of output. How will the monopolist's quality choice compare to that made by a competitive firm? How might this choice be affected by whether the good is durable (that is, lasts several periods) or not?

This chapter discusses the theory of pricing in markets that fall between the polar extremes of perfect competition and monopoly. Although no single model can be used to explain all possible forms of such imperfect competition, we look at a few of the basic elements that are common to many of the models in current use. To that end we focus on three specific topics: (1) pricing of homogeneous goods in markets in which there are relatively few firms; (2) product differentiation in these markets; and (3) how entry and exit possibilities affect long-run outcomes in imperfectly competitive markets. A related topic, strategy in the competition between firms, is taken up in Chapter 18.

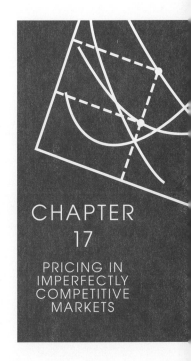

CHAPTER
17

PRICING IN
IMPERFECTLY
COMPETITIVE
MARKETS

Pricing of Homogeneous Goods

This section looks at the theory of pricing in markets in which relatively few firms produce a single homogeneous good. As before, we assume that the market is perfectly competitive on the demand side; that is, there are assumed to be many demanders, each of whom is a price taker. We also assume that there are no transactions or informational costs, so that the good in question obeys the law of one price and we may speak unambiguously of *the* price of the good. Later in this chapter we relax this assumption to consider cases where firms sell products that differ slightly from each other and may therefore have different prices. In this section we also assume that there is a fixed, small number of identical firms. Later in this chapter we allow the number of firms to vary through entry and exit in response to profitability.

■ Quasi-Competitive Model

The possible outcomes for prices when there are few firms are uncertain; they depend on how the firms react to competitors' activities. At one extreme is what we might call a **quasi-competitive model.** In this case each firm acts as a price taker. For example, a new gas station operator would be a price taker if he or she assumed that opening the station would not affect the local price of gasoline either directly (because opening the station doesn't change the local supply very much) or indirectly (because nearby stations will not change their prices in the face of the new competition). The price taker assumption may not always be valid, especially in volatile, cutthroat markets such as gasoline sales, but this (perhaps naive) assumption is a useful place to start.

If a firm acts as a price taker, it will, as before, produce where price equals long-run marginal cost. The market solution in this case will resemble a competitive one even though relatively few firms may be involved. Figure 17.1 shows a particularly simple market solution of this type. The figure assumes that marginal cost (and average cost) is constant for all output levels. Consequently, market price (P_C) must equal this marginal cost. Under this quasi-competitive solution Q_C will be produced and market equilibrium will occur at point C. This equilibrium represents the highest quantity and lowest price that can prevail in the long term with the demand curve D. A price lower than P_C would not cover firms' average cost, so it would not be sustainable in the long run.

■ Cartel Model

The assumption of price-taking behavior may be particularly inappropriate in concentrated industries in which each firm's decisions have an effect on price. An alternative assumption might be that firms as a group recognize that they

---

■
Quasi-competitive model

A model of oligopoly pricing in which each firm acts as a price taker.

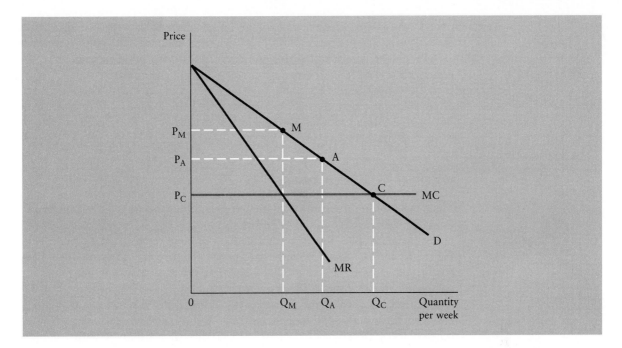

Market equilibrium under imperfect competition can occur at many points on the demand curve. In this figure (which assumes that marginal costs are constant over all output ranges), the quasi-competitive equilibrium occurs at point C and the cartel equilibrium at point M. Many solutions (such as A) may occur between points M and C, depending on the specific assumption made about firms' strategic interrelationships.

Figure 17.1
Pricing under
Imperfect
Competition

can affect price and coordinate their decisions to achieve monopoly profits. This case can be described by a **cartel model** in which the cartel acts as a multiplant monopoly and produces in each of its "plants" (that is, in each firm in the cartel) where marginal revenue equals marginal cost. Assuming, as before, that these marginal costs are equal and constant for all firms, the output choice is indicated by point M in Figure 17.1. Because this coordinated plan requires a specific output level for each firm, the plan also dictates how monopoly profits earned by the cartel are to be shared by its members. In the aggregate, these profits will be as large as possible, given the market demand curve and the industry's cost structure.

Maintaining this cartel solution poses three problems for the firms involved. First, cartel formations may be illegal. In the United States, for example, Section I of the Sherman Act of 1890 outlaws "conspiracies in restraint of trade," so would-be cartel members may expect a visit from the FBI. Similar laws exist in many other countries. A second problem with the cartel solution is that it requires that a considerable amount of information be available to the directors of the cartel—specifically, they must know the market demand function and each firm's marginal cost function. This information may be costly to

Cartel model

A model of oligopoly pricing in which firms coordinate their decisions to act as a multiplant monopoly.

obtain, and some cartel members may be reluctant to provide it. Finally, and most important, the cartel solution may be fundamentally unstable. Since each cartel member will produce an output level for which price exceeds marginal cost, each will have an incentive to expand output to increase its own profits. If the directors of the oligopoly are not able to police such "chiseling," the cartel solution may collapse. As Application 17.1: Diamonds Are Forever illustrates, even the famous DeBeers cartel occasionally finds itself unable to control its market.

■ Other Pricing Possibilities

The quasi-competitive and cartel models of pricing tend to determine the outer limits between which actual prices in an imperfectly competitive market will be set (for example, one such intermediate price is represented by point A in Figure 17.1). This band of outcomes may be very wide, so economists have tried to develop models to predict where market equilibrium will actually occur within these limits.[1] Developing these models is very difficult. For example, imagine developing a systematic description of how people play poker complete with betting strategies, bluffing, and each player guessing what the other players are doing. No model can predict such behavior with complete accuracy. The outcomes depend on the skills of the players, the way the cards are running, and even on seemingly irrelevant factors like the time of night or the temperature of the room. Exactly the same types of problems arise in creating a model of pricing in markets with relatively few firms. In this case the outcome depends entirely on how the firms play the game. In Chapter 18 we take up such strategic questions. Here we look at two very simple models that have been widely used.

The Cournot Model

One of the first people to use mathematics in economics was the nineteenth-century French economist Augustin Cournot.[2] Among other advances, Cournot devised what we now know as the concept of marginal revenue and used this both to discuss profit maximization by a monopoly and to develop a model in which two firms compete for the same market. Since a formal development of the **Cournot model** can become quite mathematical, a simple numerical example may suffice.

Cournot model

A model of duopoly in which each firm assumes the other firm's output will not change if it changes its own output level.

---

[1]For example, if the elasticity of demand is -2, Equation 10.8 shows that $P = 2 \cdot MR$. Under a quasi-competitive solution $P = MC$; under the cartel solution, price is twice that level ($P = 2MC$). A model that can predict prices only within a 100 percent range is not very useful.

[2]Augustin Cournot, *Researches into Mathematical Principles of the Theory of Wealth*, translated by N. T. Bacon (New York: Macmillan, 1897).

APPLICATION 17.1

Diamonds Are Forever

Although diamonds have been bought and sold throughout most of recorded history, it was not until the latter part of the nineteenth century that the diamond market became fully developed on a worldwide scale. The discovery of rich diamond fields in South Africa in the 1870s vastly expanded the world's diamond supply, which led eventually to the major gem and industrial markets that exist today. At first, diamond mining in South Africa was a very competitive enterprise—practically any prospector with a shovel could enter the market. Throughout the early 1880s, however, the richest diamond mines around Kimberly were unified under the ownership of Cecil Rhodes. By 1888, Rhodes incorporated his holdings into DeBeers Consolidated Mines, which, at that time, controlled about 90 percent of the world's total supply of diamonds. To this day, DeBeers continues to dominate the world diamond trade.

Operation of the DeBeers Cartel

Since the 1880s, diamonds have been found in many other places such as Namibia, Australia, and Siberia. DeBeers did not make most of these discoveries, nor does the firm actually own the resulting mines. Instead, the mine owners (often governments) have found it profitable to sell their output only to DeBeers, which then markets diamonds to final consumers through its central selling organization (CSO) in London. By carefully regulating the flow of diamonds into the market, the CSO manages to maintain high prices and assure significant profits for itself and its fellow cartel members. It is DeBeers' ability to add to its large diamond inventory if market conditions weaken that enables it to avoid the periodic swings in prices that the random nature of diamond finds might cause. By some estimates, high-quality gem diamonds sold by DeBeers are priced at a multiple of as much as one thousand times actual marginal production cost.

Threats to the Cartel

Because of this gap between price and marginal cost, any new diamond discovery is a potential threat to the DeBeers cartel. Historically, DeBeers has used its marketing strength to control any would-be chiselers. For example, when industrial diamonds from the former Soviet Union and Zaire started to enter the market in the early 1980s, DeBeers quickly flooded the market from its own inventory, thereby driving down prices and quickly convincing these newcomers of the wisdom of joining the cartel. Similarly, two very large diamond finds in Australia in the mid-1980s hardly disturbed the market at all; the owners found it more profitable to market through the CSO rather than fight it.

Recently, political instability in various parts of the world has come to pose one more threat to DeBeers' dominance. A long-running civil war in Angola combined with a major diamond discovery there led to a stampede of miners, many of whom sold their findings through illegal channels. Unrest in the former Soviet Union has also made it easier for diamond smugglers to get past the authorities (who prefer to deal with DeBeers). Whether the cartel will be able to reassert its influence on pricing in the world diamond market or will fall victim to the chiseling that has ultimately undermined practically all cartels remains an open question.[1]

To Think About

1. How does the fact that diamonds are durable affect the ability of DeBeers to control diamond prices? Could a cartel of producers of a perishable commodity (say, tomatoes or fish) be equally successful? How does CSO's ownership of a large inventory of diamonds help it enforce its pricing decisions?
2. Why would the owner of a large source of diamonds voluntarily choose to join the DeBeers cartel? How does such an owner's decisions depend on his or her expectations about how the cartel will treat new entrants into the market?

[1]See, for example, "Diamonds Aren't Forever," *Time* (October 12, 1992): 73.

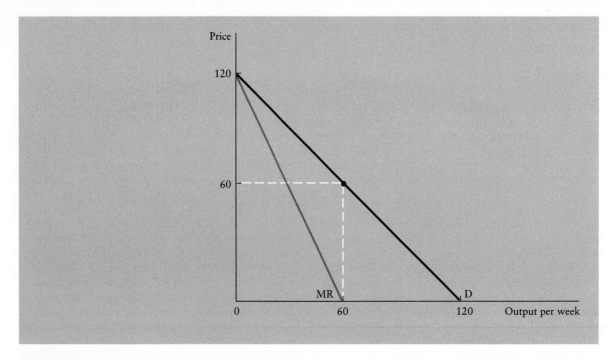

Figure 17.2
Spring Monopolist's
Output Choice

Given the market demand curve Q = 120 – P, a zero-cost monopolist would produce that output (60) for which marginal revenue is equal to 0. At this output, a price of $60 would prevail and profits would be $3,600. Notice that MR = 0 at an output level = $\frac{1}{2}Q_0$ (where Q_0 is the quantity demanded at P = 0). This result holds for any linear demand curve.

■ Market Conditions

Cournot began his study by looking at a very simple situation in which a single owner of a costless but healthful spring has to decide how to price its water. Early on he recognized that the owner must contend with a downward sloping demand for spring water—adoption of too high a price might be as unprofitable as adoption of too low a price (note the quotation from Cournot at the beginning of Part Five). Suppose, for example, the demand for spring water in terms of thousands of gallons per week (Q) depends on water price (P) according to the equation

$$Q = 120 - P. \qquad [17.1]$$

This demand curve is shown in Figure 17.2. Because water itself is costless to this firm, profits (and revenues) are maximized by proceeding to the point where marginal revenue equals zero. That is, the owner of the spring monopoly should produce Q = 60. At this output level P will be $60 and revenues will be $3,600 (= $60 × 60). For the future development of a duopoly model, it is important to note how the profit-maximizing output level is chosen. In this particular case, Q is chosen to be one-half of that quantity that would be demanded at a price of zero (that is, half of 120).[3] Using this conclusion we now turn to an examination of how two independent firms might respond to this market situation.

■ Duopoly Model

Cournot then allowed for a second spring to be discovered. In devising his model of this situation, the author assumed that each of the two firms in the market took the other firm's activities into account in only a very limited way. In particular, Cournot theorized that firm A, say, chooses its output level (q_A) on the assumption that the output of firm B (q_B) is fixed and will not be adjusted in response to firm A's actions. Total market output is then given by

$$Q = q_A + q_B = 120 - P. \qquad [17.2]$$

Assuming that q_B is fixed, the demand curve facing firm A is given by

$$q_A = (120 - q_B) - P. \qquad [17.3]$$

This simply says that some portion of market demand is assumed to be taken by firm B and firm A makes its choice from what is left. Using the rule discussed in footnote 3, it is obvious that firm A's profit-maximizing output level would be given by

$$q_A = \frac{120 - q_B}{2}. \qquad [17.4]$$

That is, firm A produces half the output demanded at a price of zero after allowing for firm B's production. Consequently, the output level actually chosen by firm A will depend on the level of output that firm B is assumed to produce. For example, if firm B chooses to produce 60, firm A would choose 30[= (120 − 60) ÷ 2]. Equation 17.4 is called the **reaction function** for firm A because it demonstrates how this firm reacts to firm B's actions. This reaction function is shown graphically in Figure 17.3.

Firm B might perform a similar analysis and arrive at a reaction function that expresses q_B as a function of q_A of the form

$$q_B = \frac{120 - q_A}{2}. \qquad [17.5]$$

This reaction function is also shown in Figure 17.3.

■

Reaction function

In the Cournot model a function or graph that shows how much one firm will produce given what the other firm produces.

---

[3]This result follows since, for a linear demand curve, the marginal revenue curve is twice as steep as the demand curve. Since both curves have the same P-intercept, the MR curve always bisects the horizontal distance between the price axis and the demand curve.

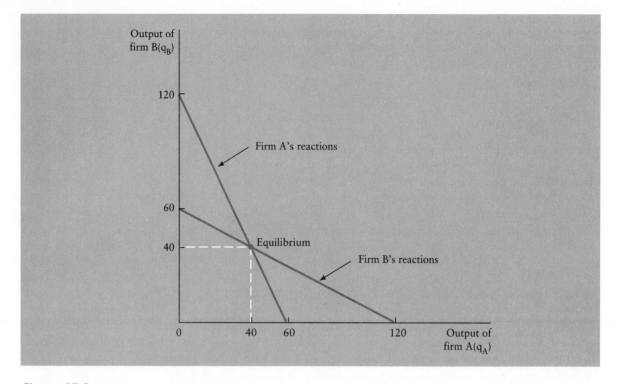

Figure 17.3
Cournot Reaction Functions in a Duopoly Market

The reaction function for firm A shows how that firm will react on the assumption that firm B's output choice is not affected by the level of q_A produced. The function for firm B shows a similar reaction for firm B. Only at the point of intersection of the two curves ($q_A = 40$, $q_B = 40$) will both of the firms' assumptions be realized. This point of intersection is called the Cournot equilibrium point.

Cournot Equilibrium

So far we know how firm A reacts to firm B's decisions and how firm B reacts to firm A's decisions. These decisions are consistent with each other only at the point where the two lines intersect. At all other points the two firms' output choices are inconsistent because each firm expects the other to be producing at some output level other than what it actually is. The point of interaction is the only **Cournot equilibrium** that can prevail in this two-firm market. It is easy to show that this point of intersection is given by

$$q_A = 40$$

$$q_B = 40. \qquad [17.6]$$

At the Cournot equilibrium both firms will produce 40, total output will be 80, and the market price will be \$40 (= 120 − 80). This Cournot equilibrium solution is stable because each firm has adjusted its output to the actual output

Cournot equilibrium

A solution to the Cournot model in which each firm makes the correct assumption about what the other firm will produce.

level being produced by the other firm. Total industry revenues and profits in this case ($3,200 − $1,600 for each firm) are lower than under the monopoly case ($3,600). This is a result of the failure of the firms in the duopoly situation to coordinate their actions perfectly. Only if the firms collude will they be able to achieve the full monopoly profits possible from the market demand curve for spring water. Otherwise, the uncertainties in the market lead to a greater level of production than in the cartel case, though price still remains well above the competitive solution (which here would require P = MC = 0).

■ Generalizations

It is relatively easy to generalize the Cournot equilibrium concept to cases involving more complex cost assumptions or to situations with three or more firms. Often such models provide a good starting point for examining outcomes that lie between the cartel and competitive equilibria.[4] However, the basic weakness of all such models is in the assumption that each firm takes no account of how its actions affect those of its rival. It would take a particularly obtuse owner of spring B, say, not to recognize that its decisions were affecting what the owner of spring A does. As we will see in Chapter 18, making more realistic assumptions about firms' strategies can involve a number of complications.

Price Leadership Model

A second model of pricing in markets with few sellers is called the **price leadership model**. It tends to accord with many real-world situations. In some markets one firm or group of firms is looked upon as the leader in pricing, and all firms adjust their prices to what this leader does. Two possible examples of price leadership are the computer industry in the 1970s and 1980s (where IBM used to play the role of a leader) and the commercial banking industry (where the prime rate tends to be determined by the major New York City banks).

A formal model of pricing in a market dominated by a leading firm is presented in Figure 17.4. The industry is assumed to be composed of a single price-setting leader and a **competitive fringe** of firms who take the leader's price as given in their decisions. The demand curve D represents the total demand curve for the industry's product, and the supply curve SC represents the supply decisions of all the firms in the competitive fringe. Using these two curves, the demand curve (D′) facing the industry leader is derived as follows. For a price of P_1 or above, the leader will sell nothing since the competitive fringe would be willing to supply all that is demanded. For prices below P_2 the leader has the market to itself since the fringe is not willing to supply anything. Between P_2 and P_1 the curve D′ is constructed by subtracting what the fringe

Price leadership model
A model in which one dominant firm takes reactions of all other firms into account in its output and pricing decisions.

Competitive fringe
A group of firms that act as price takers in a market dominated by a price leader.

---

[4]For a discussion see Walter Nicholson, *Microeconomic Theory*, 5th ed. (Fort Worth, Texas: The Dryden Press, 1992): 593–600.

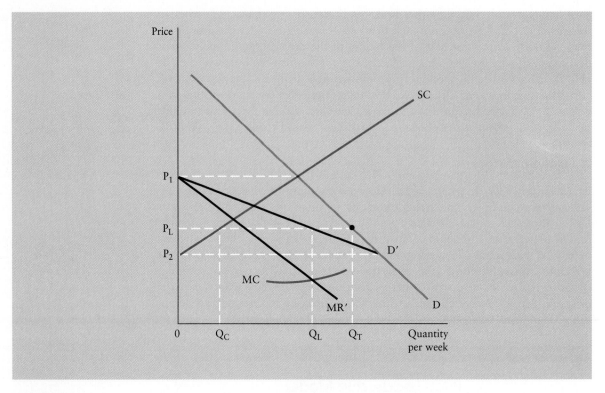

Figure 17.4
Formal Model of
Price Leadership
Behavior

The curve D′ shows the demand curve facing the price leader—it is derived by subtracting what is produced by the competitive fringe of firms (SC) from market demand (D). Given D′, the firm's profit-maximizing output level is Q_L, and a price of P_L will prevail in the market.

will supply from total market demand. That is, the leader gets that portion of demand not taken by the fringe firms.

Given the demand curve D′, the leader can construct its marginal revenue curve (MR′) and then refer to its own marginal cost curve (MC) to determine the profit-maximizing output level, Q_L. Market price will then be P_L. Given that price, the competitive fringe will produce Q_C and total industry output will be Q_T ($= Q_C + Q_L$).

This model does not answer such important questions as how the price leader in an industry is chosen, or what happens when a member of the fringe decides to challenge the leader for its position (and profits). The model does show how elements of both the perfectly competitive and the monopoly theories of price determination can be woven together to produce a model of pricing under imperfectly competitive conditions. Such a model may explain industry behavior in some important situations, as Application 17.2: OPEC Pricing Strategy illustrates.

APPLICATION 17.2
OPEC Pricing Strategy

The Organization of Petroleum Exporting Countries (OPEC) was formed in the early 1960s. Altogether, OPEC members represent about half of total world oil production and perhaps 60 to 70 percent of total crude oil reserves. During its first 10 years, OPEC had relatively little influence on world oil prices. But during the 1973 Arab-Israeli war and its associated oil embargo, that situation changed dramatically. In slightly more than one year, oil prices rose nearly fourfold—from about $2.50 to about $12 per barrel. After this initial price spurt, oil prices continued to rise (especially in reaction to supply disruptions, such as the Iranian revolution), although at a much slower rate. By 1982, crude oil sold for about $34 per barrel—a *fourteen*fold increase over the span of a decade. Since 1982 nominal prices have fallen to about one-half this level.

Modeling OPEC Behavior
Economists have developed two types of models to explain OPEC pricing. Both of these attempt to take account of the structure of OPEC membership, particularly the role played by Saudi Arabia and the nearby Persian Gulf states of Kuwait, Qatar, Bahrain, and the United Arab Emirates. These producers constitute more than one-third of total OPEC production and considerably more of its total crude oil reserves. The countries are relatively lightly populated compared to some other OPEC members, such as Indonesia, Nigeria, or Venezuela. They also seem to have substantial excess oil production capability. It is these features that make them crucial to the pricing story.

A Cartel Model
One approach to OPEC pricing treats the organization as a cartel. Under this model, Saudi Arabia is able to hold the cartel together by restricting its own output by the amount necessary to achieve the profit-maximizing level. Saudi Arabia's unique geological position (it has more than 500 billion barrels of crude oil) and its small population make it possible for this cartel to persist much longer than most cartels, since there is no need to enforce major output restrictions on other producers. In exchange for Saudi cooperation, other OPEC members must to some extent bend to that country's wishes. In particular, most observers agree that the Saudis exercise a moderating price influence within OPEC. Their large oil reserves make them more concerned than most other oil producers about possible long-run alternatives (such as nuclear or solar power) to oil-based energy being developed in response to oil's high price.

A Price Leadership Model
Another view of the world oil market assumes a much greater degree of competitiveness than the cartel model. In this view, Saudi Arabia is treated as a price leader with other OPEC nations (and, indeed, all other oil producers) constituting a competitive fringe. Members of the competitive fringe, as shown in Figure 17.4, act as price takers. If this model is correct, the elaborate, regular meetings of the OPEC oil ministers are simply a gaudy ritual with no particular significance for the actual pricing of oil. And Saudi Arabia's much-heralded position as a moderate in oil pricing simply derives from its position as a price leader with low marginal costs of production.

On the whole, the evidence seems to be most consistent with the price leadership model of OPEC behavior. Even during the late 1970s, prices seem to have been below those a cartelized monopoly would charge.[1] The sharp declines in 1984 and 1985 probably reflected a major shift in supply by the fringe producers as a result of significant oil discoveries, especially in non-OPEC countries.

To Think About
1. The sharp increase in oil prices between 1973 and 1982 is still a bit of a mystery to economists. Can such a large increase be fully explained with either the cartel or the price leadership model? In the absence of any very large increase in demand, wouldn't both models predict rather modest price rises in response to slowly growing demand?
2. Why is the level of a nation's petroleum reserves relevant to their desired sales patterns? How do future oil prices enter into each nation's calculations?

---

[1] By most estimates, the demand for oil is price inelastic at current price levels. Since an inelastic demand implies a negative marginal revenue, current prices are inconsistent with monopoly profit maximization.

Product Differentiation

Up to this point we have assumed the good being produced in an imperfectly competitive market is homogeneous. Demanders were assumed to be indifferent about which firm's output they bought, and the law of one price was assumed to hold in the market. These assumptions may not hold in many real-world markets. Firms often devote considerable resources to make their products different from those of their competitors through such devices as quality and style variations, warranties and guarantees, special service features, and product advertising. These activities require firms to employ additional resources, and firms will choose to do so if profits are thereby increased. Product variation also results in a relaxation of the law of one price, since now the market will consist of goods that vary from firm to firm and consumers may have preferences about which supplier to patronize.

■ Market Definition

That possibility introduces a certain fuzziness into what we mean by the "market for a good," since now there are many closely related, but not identical, products. For example, if toothpaste brands vary somewhat from supplier to supplier, should we consider all these products to be in the same market or should we differentiate among fluoridated products, gels, striped toothpaste, smokers' toothpaste, and so forth? Although this question is of great practical importance in industry studies, we do not pursue it here. Instead, we will assume that the market is composed of a few firms, each producing a slightly different product, but that these products can usefully be considered a single **product group.** That is, each firm produces a product that is highly substitutable for that of its rivals. Although this definition has its own ambiguities (arguments about the definition of a product group often dominate antitrust lawsuits, for example), it should suffice for our purposes.

Product group

Set of differentiated products that are highly substitutable for one another.

■ Firms' Choices

Let us assume that there are a few firms competing within a particular product group. Each firm can choose the amount to spend on differentiating its product from those of its competitors. Again, the profit-maximization model provides some insight about how firms will do this; they will incur additional costs associated with differentiation up to the point at which the additional revenue brought in by such activities equals each activity's marginal cost. With this view, producing differentiated products involves the same types of decisions that firms use in selecting any input.

■ Market Equilibrium

Although this description of firms' choices seems straightforward, the choices are actually quite complex. Since the demand curve facing any one firm depends on the prices and product differentiation activities of its competitors, that demand curve may shift frequently, and its position at any particular time may only be partly understood. The firm must make some assumptions in order to make decisions. And, whatever one firm decides to do may affect its competitors' actions.

Developing models of markets with differentiated products poses more complex strategic issues than does devising models for the homogeneous good case. Not surprisingly, there are few definite theoretical results about the nature of the market equilibrium that results from the differentiated oligopoly situation. Two very general conclusions might be mentioned, however. First, because of the differentiated nature of goods in the product group, price-taking behavior is unlikely. Each firm will believe that its activities have some effect on the price of its product. Price will exceed marginal revenue and marginal cost, and there may be some allocational inefficiency. Second, because of the uncertain demand facing each firm, information costs may be quite high. Firms may opt for strategies that economize on such costs. For example, they may adopt relatively simple "rules of thumb" in their decisions, such as adopting markup pricing (see Chapter 10) or aiming for a particular share of the market.

As a result of these types of behavior, market equilibria may be somewhat more stable over time than might at first be suggested by the complexities and uncertainties of the problem. Both prices and product types may converge around some median values, so that the homogeneous oligopoly models become appropriate. For example, product attributes may come to approximate those desired by the "typical" consumer, since any firm that departs very far from producing such a good may find itself outflanked by competitors. The tendency of television networks to produce the same types of shows and of political candidates to gravitate to the middle of the road in their positions are probably the most familiar instances of such behavior, but other occurrences come readily to mind. In Application 17.3: Brand Proliferation in Breakfast Cereals, we look at some of the issues of product differentiation that arise in one such market.

Advertising

Producers of differentiated products may seek to expand the demand for this output even further by advertising. To the extent that advertising shifts the demand curve facing the firm outward, it will offer the firm more favorable price–quantity combinations. Profit-maximizing firms will devote additional dollars to advertising activities so long as the extra profits brought in exceed the costs of these activities.

Economists have tended to focus on two aspects of advertising: (1) the effects of advertising on market structure; and (2) the informational content of advertising messages. With respect to the first issue, it seems clear that advertising may either decrease or increase the degree of competition in a marketplace depending on the particular circumstances. If advertising expenditures

APPLICATION 17.3
Brand Proliferation in Breakfast Cereals

Production of ready-to-eat breakfast cereals in the United States is highly concentrated. The top four firms in the industry (Kellogg's, General Mills, General Foods, and Quaker) supply about 85 percent of total industry output. According to most estimates, the industry is highly profitable with significantly higher rates of return on firms' investments than the average manufacturing companies enjoy. Despite these high profits, entry by new firms into the industry has been virtually nonexistent. Although many large food companies could conceivably enter the industry, they have chosen not to do so. Economies of scale in cereal production do not seem to explain this reluctance. In fact, it appears that efficient size operations can be attained at a fairly small fraction of total industry output of about 2 to 3 percent. There must be some other explanation for the absence of entry.

The FTC Charge
In 1972, the U.S. Federal Trade Commission issued a complaint against the four largest cereal producers charging that through proliferating brands and intensive advertising the firms had erected substantial entry barriers, thereby insuring monopoly-type returns to themselves. The brand proliferation argument ran as follows: By creating a huge number of cereal brands (about 80 in 1972) the largest firms had substantially covered all the attributes (sweetness, crunchiness, grain composition, and so forth) that mattered to consumers. There was no room in the market for potential entrants to differentiate their products successfully. Crucial to this argument were the related issues of intensive advertising and brand identification preventing potential entrants from duplicating the characteristics of an existing cereal at a lower price. That is, it was claimed that consumers would generally be unwilling to purchase a less expensive version of Cheerios, for example.[1]

Even More Product Differentiation
Although this explanation of entry barriers is intriguing, it is not airtight. The notion that there is no room for

new cereal brands implicitly assumes a limit to firms' ingenuity that may not, in fact, exist. For example, the introduction of natural cereals in the 1970s seems to have filled a market niche that had been overlooked by the major companies. Similarly, the belief that look-alike, cheap imitations of major brands will not sell seems to be contradicted by the growing number of house brand cereals offered by supermarkets in the 1980s. New cereals that cater to health concerns (such as those made from oat bran) have also had a period of rapid growth in sales. Cereal companies have, therefore, shown no slackening in their ability to develop new brands, though the gains in consumer welfare from such activities may be open to question.

Demise of the Legal Case
In its complaint, the FTC tried to show that cereal firms had engaged in implicit collusion to proliferate brands with the intent of foreclosing entry. The distinction between such collusion and simple head-to-head competition between major firms proved to be difficult to make. To a large extent the case against the cereal makers remained unproven and the case was dropped in early 1982. The reasons for brand proliferation in breakfast cereals and whether this has any undesirable economic effects therefore remains unclear.

To Think About
1. Do large cereal producers have advantages that permit them to develop new brands at relatively low cost? Why aren't such techniques available to other firms? Can you think of other products where brand proliferation is an important strategy for the firms involved (for example, how about cigarette firms)?
2. Can you think of other ways that producers of differentiated products attempt to prevent the entry of rival producers? How would you explain their decisions to make such expenditures? What would determine their success? Are these strategies subject to other, more favorable interpretations?

---

[1]For a detailed development of this theory see Richard Schmalensee, "Entry Deterrence in the Ready-to-Eat Breakfast Cereal Industry," *The Bell Journal of Economics* (Autumn 1978): 305–327.

exhibit significant economies of scale and if such expenditures tend to promote strong brand allegiances, advertising may help large firms gain additional control of a marketplace. For example, major television advertising campaigns for successive types of Crest toothpaste undoubtedly helped the Proctor and Gamble Corporation hold onto a commanding position in this market. On the other hand, advertising may also ease the entry of new firms into a market, thereby having a positive effect on competition. The highly successful advertising campaigns for Volkswagen beetles in the early 1960s and similar campaigns for Japanese automobiles in the 1970s undoubtedly played a major role in opening up the U.S. auto market to foreign competition. Overall, then, the effects of advertising on market structure must be judged on a case-by-case basis.

Advertising may provide a variety of information to consumers about product characteristics and prices. Presumably, if this information is accurate, it will be valuable to consumers, permitting them to achieve higher levels of utility than would otherwise be possible. As for many topics in the economics of information, the issue of whether resources are efficiently allocated to advertising raises a number of difficult conceptual issues. Advertising messages are not directly bought and sold; rather, consumers indirectly "buy" advertising when they purchase an advertised product. But even consumers who don't buy an advertised product may find advertising information valuable, if only to convince them not to buy. In this respect, advertising messages have some of the characteristics of public goods (see Chapters 14 and 23). These kinds of goods usually pose problems in resource allocation. To pursue all of these issues here would take us too far afield, but Application 17.4: Cigarette Advertising illustrates some of the complexities that arise in attempting to regulate advertising in the real world.

Entry by New Firms

The possibility of new firms entering an industry plays an important part in the development of the theory of perfectly competitive price determination. This possibility assures that any long-run profits will be eliminated by new entrants and that firms will produce at the low points of their long-run average cost curves. With relatively few firms, the first of these forces continues to operate. To the extent that entry is possible, long-run profits are constrained. If entry is completely costless, long-run economic profits will be zero (as in the competitive case).

■ Zero-Profit Equilibrium

Whether or not firms in an imperfectly competitive industry with free entry will be directed to the low point of their average cost curves depends on the nature of the demand curve facing them. If firms are price takers, the analysis given for the competitive case carries over directly. Since $P = MR = MC$ for

APPLICATION 17.4
Cigarette Advertising

Prior to 1970, cigarettes were one of the most highly advertised products. Cigarette advertising constituted about 15 percent of all television advertising and a significantly higher fraction of advertising in magazines. Because of this dominance, expenditures on cigarette advertising have been extensively studied. The general conclusion of these studies was that advertising of cigarette brands had a major impact on the choice of brand (a favorite example is the hugely successful "Marlboro Man" advertising campaigns of the 1960s), but that such advertising had relatively little effect on the overall level of smoking.

The Advertising Ban

In the late 1960s, cigarette advertising became an extremely controversial subject. As a result of the 1964 Surgeon General's Report linking smoking to lung cancer, Congress passed the Cigarette Labeling and Advertising Act. That act required that all cigarette packs carry a warning label about the possible health hazards of smoking, and that the warning be prominently displayed in advertisements. In response to requests from the American Cancer Society and others, the Federal Communications Commission also decided that the "fairness doctrine" required free television air time be granted for antismoking commercials to combat advertising by cigarette companies. By 1970 antismoking commercials totaled about one-third of cigarette advertising time. In that year, however, Congress, impatient with the continued high level of cigarette sales despite their known health hazards, passed the Public Health Cigarette Smoking Act banning cigarette advertising from radio and television. Banning television advertising of cigarettes had the unintended side effect of sharply reducing antismoking commercials, since the fairness doctrine no longer applied.

Effects of the Ban

In a 1972 paper, J. L. Hamilton tried to sort out the effects of these changes in the advertising environment on total cigarette sales.[1] He found that cigarette advertising increased average annual cigarette consumption by about 95 cigarettes per year (about 3 percent of average annual consumption). The health scare resulting from the Surgeon General's Report, on the other hand, was estimated to have reduced average sales by 253 cigarettes per year. Even more dramatic results were estimated by Hamilton for the antismoking commercials, which reduced average sales by an average of over 530 cigarettes per year. It appears that scenes of smoke-filled lungs and the appeal of actor William Talman, who was dying of lung cancer, left a more vivid impression on viewers than did the Marlboro Man. The failure of cigarette sales to decline very rapidly over the decades since the Surgeon General's Report may also be the result of the reduced level of antismoking commercials or possibly of the continuing advertising of cigarettes in other media.

To Think About

1. Did the advertising ban really hurt cigarette sales? Might it actually have helped such sales? Might the ban have helped cigarette companies? How hard do you think they fought the ban?

2. The cigarette example raises the question of how, if at all, the government should regulate advertising. Currently, various rules require that advertisements be "truthful" with respect to claims being made for a product or against a competitor's product. Do these rules seem necessary? Can't consumers decide for themselves whether advertising claims make sense? What should the government do if it finds that some advertising claims have been untruthful?

[1]J. L. Hamilton, "The Demand for Cigarettes: Advertising the Health Scare, and the Cigarette Advertising Ban," *Review of Economics and Statistics* (November 1972): 401–411.

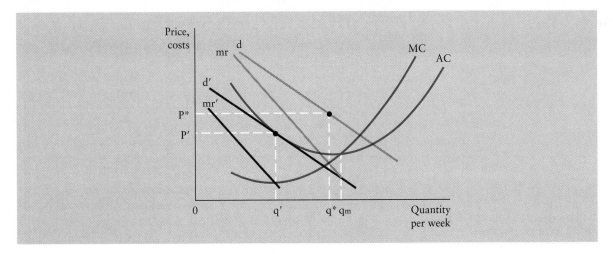

Initially the demand curve facing the firm is d. Marginal revenue is given by mr, and q^* is the profit-maximizing output level. If entry is costless, new firms attracted by the possibility for profits may shift the firm's demand curve inward to d', where profits are zero. At output level q', average costs are not a minimum, and the firm exhibits excess capacity given by $q_m - q'$.

Figure 17.5
Entry Reduces Profitability in Oligopoly

profit maximization and since P = AC if entry is to result in zero profits, production will take place where MC = AC (that is, at minimum average cost).

If firms have some control over the price they receive (perhaps because each produces a slightly differentiated product), each firm will face a downward-sloping demand curve, and the competitive analysis may not hold. Entry still may reduce profits to zero, but now production at minimum average cost is not assured. This situation (which is sometimes termed **monopolistic competition** because it has features of both perfect competition and monopoly) is illustrated in Figure 17.5. Initially, the demand curve facing the typical firm is given by d and economic profits are being earned. New firms will be attracted by these profits, and their entry will shift d inward (because now a larger number of firms are contending with a given market demand curve). Indeed, entry can reduce profits to zero by shifting the demand curve to d'. The level of output that maximizes profits with this demand curve, q', is not, however, the same as that level at which average costs are minimized, q_m. Rather, the firm will produce less than that "efficient" output level and will exhibit "excess capacity," given by $q_m - q'$. Some economists have hypothesized that this outcome characterizes industries such as service stations, convenience stores, and fast-food franchisers, where product differentiation is prevalent but entry is relatively costless.[5]

■
Monopolistic competition

Market in which each firm faces a negatively sloped demand curve and there are no barriers to entry.

---

[5]This analysis was originally developed by E. H. Chamberlain, *The Theory of Monopolistic Competition* (Cambridge, Mass.: Harvard University Press, 1950).

■ Contestable Markets and Market Equilibrium

The conclusion that a zero-profit equilibrium with price above marginal cost (such as that pictured in Figure 17.5) is sustainable in the long run has been challenged recently by several economists.[6] They argue that the model neglects the effects of potential entry on market equilibrium by focusing only on the behavior of actual entrants. This argument introduces the distinction first made by Harold Demetz between competition *in* the market and competition *for* the market by showing that the latter concept provides a more appropriate perspective for analyzing the free entry assumption.[7] Within this broader perspective, the "invisible hand" of competition becomes even more constraining on firms' behavior, and perfectly competitive-type results are more likely to emerge.

■

Contestable market

Market in which entry and exit are costless.

The expanded examination of entry begins by defining a **contestable market** as one in which no potential competitor can enter by cutting price and still make profits (since if profit opportunities existed, potential entrants would take advantage of them). A perfectly contestable market drops the perfectly competitive assumption of price-taking behavior but expands a bit upon the concept of free entry by permitting potential entrants to operate in a hit-and-run manner, snatching up whatever marginal profit opportunities are available. Such an assumption, as we will point out, is not necessarily accurate in many market situations, but it does provide a different starting place for a simplified theory of pricing.

The equilibrium illustrated in Figure 17.5 is unsustainable in a contestable market, provided that two or more firms are already in the market. In such a case a potential hit-and-run entrant could turn a quick profit by taking all the first firm's sales by selling q′ at a price slightly below P′ and making up for the loss this would entail by selling a further increment in output to another firm's customers at a price in excess of average cost. That is, because the equilibrium in Figure 17.5 has a market price that exceeds marginal costs, it permits a would-be entrant to take away one zero-profit firm's market and encroach a bit on other firms' markets where, at the margin, profits are attainable. The only type of market equilibrium that would be impervious to such hit-and-run tactics would be one in which firms earn zero profits and price at marginal costs. As we saw in Chapter 12, this requires that firms produce at the low points of their long-run average cost curves where $P = MC = AC$. Hence, even in the absence of price-taking behavior in markets with relatively few firms, contestability provides an "invisible hand" that guides market equilibrium to a perfectly competitive type of result.

■ Determination of Industry Structure

This analysis can be taken one step further by showing how industry structure is determined. If, as in Chapter 12, we let q^* represent that output level for

---

[6]See W. J. Baumol, "Contestable Markets: An Uprising in the Theory of Industry Structure," *American Economic Review* (March 1982): 1–19, and W. J. Baumol, J. C. Panzar, and R. D. Willig, *Contestable Markets and the Theory of Industry Structure* (San Diego, Calif.: Harcourt Brace Jovanovich, 1982).

[7]Harold Demetz, "Why Regulate Utilities?" *Journal of Law and Economics* (April 1968): 55–65.

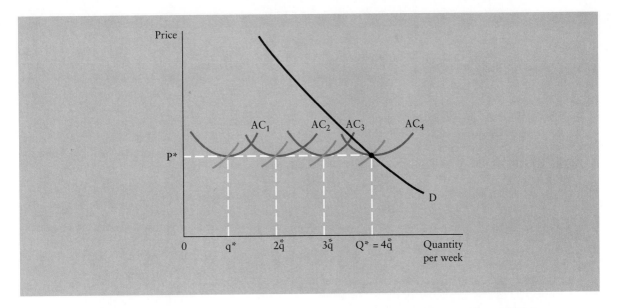

In a contestable market, equilibrium requires that P = MC = AC. The number of firms is determined by market demand (Q*) and by the output level that minimizes average cost (q*).

Figure 17.6
Contestability and
Industry Structure

which average costs are minimized and Q* represent the total market for the commodity when price equals marginal (and average) cost, then the number of firms in the industry, n, is given by

$$n = \frac{Q^*}{q^*}. \qquad [17.7]$$

Contrary to the perfectly competitive case, this number of firms may be relatively small. In Figure 17.6, for example, exactly four firms fulfill the market demand for Q*. The contestability assumption will ensure competitive behavior, even though these firms may recognize strategic relationships among themselves. The ability of potential entrants to seize any possible opportunities for profit sharply constrains the types of behavior that are possible and thereby provides a well-defined equilibrium market structure. One of the most important industries that seems to have contestable characteristics is the airline industry, and in Application 17.5: Airline Deregulation, Revisited, we look at one aspect of its recent history.

■ Barriers to Entry

All of the analysis presented so far in this section has assumed free entry and exit. When various barriers prevent such flexibility, these results must be modified. Possible barriers to entry include many of those already discussed in

APPLICATION 17.5

Airline Deregulation, Revisited

In Application 10.2 we showed how the passage of the Airline Deregulation Act of 1978 caused major changes in the way airlines operate. Here we look at the market repercussions of these activities. Especially interesting is whether experiences under deregulation have tended to confirm the predictions of the model of contestable markets.

Airlines Contestability

In many respects the airline industry represents a perfect illustration of contestability. Because the industry's principal capital assets (planes) are mobile, they can in principle be quickly moved into any market that promises excess profitability. The possibility of such "hit-and-run" entry by potential competitors should keep prices at competitive levels even in markets with relatively few actual competitors.

The predictions of the contestable model are not, however, ironclad for the case of airlines. A portion of airlines' capital is invested in terminal facilities and is, therefore, committed to a specific market. Similarly, many flyers tend to prefer to patronize a specific airline (perhaps they belong to their Frequent Flyer Club), so they may not be willing to respond very quickly to differences in price. Finally, some airports (Chicago's O'Hare, Washington, D.C.'s National, and New York's LaGuardia) are operating very close to capacity and have restricted new entrants.

Effects of Deregulation

Most studies of airline deregulation have found that fares declined dramatically after 1978. For example, S. Morrison and C. Winston looked at over 800 city-pairs for flights and calculated that by 1983 travelers and airlines had yearly gains of about $8.6 billion from the passage of the Deregulation Act.[1] They note that such estimated gains would be even larger if potential benefits to aircraft manufacturers and to travelers on buses and trains (from lower fares on these modes) were also taken into account. Still, the authors find that, even

after deregulation, the airline industry has some elements of imperfectly competitive behavior. Further annual welfare gains of about $2.5 billion might be obtainable if airline markets more closely approximated the perfectly contestable ideal. Some of these gains might be obtainable by adopting better ways of rationing landing slots at major airports or by making airline computer reservation systems more competitive, since existing systems may aid in price collusion.

Trends in Airline Competition

One result of airline deregulation was a remarkable shakeup in the structure of the industry. At first, many new firms entered the industry, but often these were quickly consolidated into the larger carriers. In other cases, some major airlines (such as Eastern or Pan American) fell on hard times and were broken up among existing airlines. Adding to this increasing concentration in the air travel market were significant changes in the ways airlines organize their flight networks. By developing hub-and-spoke designs, airlines have been able to economize on total distance traveled and to encourage passengers to make their trips on a single carrier. One undesirable side effect of this reorganization is an increasing dominance of one or two airlines in particular hub cities. For example, Delta Airlines provides most of the traffic at the Atlanta airport; and the Dallas–Fort Worth Airport is dominated by American and United. Since several studies have found that concentration of the traffic at a single airport is correlated with higher fares, there is some concern that such changes in the airline market may eventually reverse some of the gains from deregulation.[2]

To Think About

1. Who were the principal gainers from air fare deregulation? Were there any losers?
2. How might hub-and-spoke operations undercut the predictions of the contestable markets model in air travel markets? What would determine the limits on how much price might rise above marginal cost?

---

[1] S. Morrison and C. Winston, *Economic Effects of Airline Deregulation* (Washington, D.C.: The Brookings Institution, 1986).

[2] For a discussion, see S. Borenstein, "The Evolution of U.S. Airline Competition," *Journal of Economic Perspectives* (Spring 1992): 45–74.

connection with monopoly in Chapter 16. They also include those arising specifically out of some features of imperfectly competitive markets. Product differentiation, for example, may raise entry barriers by promoting strong brand loyalty. Or producers may so proliferate their brands that no room remains for would-be entrants to do anything different. In Application 17.3 we showed how this has been alleged to be true in the ready-to-eat breakfast cereal industry. The possibility of strategic pricing decisions may also deter entry if existing firms use them to convince firms wishing to enter that it would be unprofitable to do so. Firms may, for a time, adopt lower, entry-deterring prices in order to accomplish this goal, with the intent of raising prices once potential entrants disappear (assuming they do). A somewhat different version of this theory assumes that large firms may be able to buy up small ones by practicing "predatory pricing." Prices are reduced until the small firms can be bought at a low price, then the large firm can reestablish its high prices. In Chapter 18 we will look more closely at the logic behind these various possibilities.

Finally, the completely flexible type of hit-and-run entry behavior assumed in the theory of contestable markets may be subject to two other types of barriers in the real world. First, some types of capital investments made by firms may not be reversible. A firm cannot build an automobile assembly plant for a week's use and then dismantle it at no loss. In this case there are exit costs that will make recurrent raids on the industry unprofitable. Of course, in other cases, such as the trucking or airline industry, capital may be easily rented for short periods, and exit here poses few costs. So competitive-type results might occur in these industries. Second, the contestable market model requires that quantity demanded respond quickly to price differentials. If, instead, demanders switch slowly to a new product, potential entrants cannot establish themselves in a market rapidly. Hence, their ability to enforce marginal cost pricing in existing firms in the market will be constrained.[8] The importance of all such entry restrictions for market behavior is ultimately an empirical question.

Summary

Many real-world markets resemble neither of the polar cases of perfect competition or monopoly. Rather, such markets are characterized by relatively few firms that have some effect on market price—they are not price takers—but no single firm exercises complete market control. In these circumstances there is no generally accepted model of market behavior. Aspects of both competitive and monopoly theory must be used, together with particular institutional details of the market in question, in order to develop a realistic picture of how

---

[8]For some additional criticism of this type, see Michael Spence, "Contestable Markets and the Theory of Industrial Structure," *Journal of Economic Literature* (September 1983): 981–990.

price and output decisions are made. Several specific issues that must be addressed in developing such a model are the following:

- The number of firms and the importance of feedback effects in firms' decision-making processes.

- The potential benefits from cartelization of a market and the legal and resource costs associated with maintaining such a position.

- The importance of nonprice methods of competition, such as product differentiation and advertising.

- Entry conditions in the market and the constraints that potential entry places on attaining monopoly profits.

- The uncertainty faced by individual firms and the strategies they may adopt to cope with it (see Chapter 18).

Review Questions

1. One way of differentiating among various market structures is by the nature of the demand curve that faces the individual firm. What kind of demand curve faces a firm in a perfectly competitive industry? What demand curve faces a monopolist? In what way is the demand curve facing a firm in an imperfectly competitive industry a mixture of these two extremes?

2. Why is the cartel solution to the oligopoly pricing problem unstable? If one firm in a cartel believes it can increase profits by chiseling on price, what is it implicitly assuming about the pricing behavior of other cartel members?

3. What does the Cournot model assume about the way a firm treats its rival's output decision? Is this assumption consistent with profit maximization by the rival?

4. What does a price leader assume about the behavior of its rivals? If two firms tried to be the price leader, why would both be thwarted? Why would you generally expect the largest firm in an industry to be the price leader?

5. Explain how product differentiation and advertising can be treated as inputs in the firm's decisions. How do these inputs differ from other types of inputs in the way they affect profitability? How would the firm's profit-maximizing decisions about these inputs differ from its decisions about capital or labor input?

6. In Figure 17.5 the demand curve facing a firm in a monopolistically competitive industry is shown as being tangent to its average cost curve at q'. Explain why this is a long-run equilibrium position for this firm. That is, why does marginal revenue equal marginal cost and why are long-run profits zero?

7. Why does the model of a contestable market require that there be no costs of entry or exit? What kinds of costs might a firm incur exiting an industry? Why might such "sunk" costs inhibit entry in the first place?

8. Can firms themselves through their behavior deter entry into a market? What kinds of strategic actions might deter entry? Do firms already "in" a market have advantages over would-be entrants in choosing such strategies?

9. Concentration ratios are one of the most frequently used measures of market structure. These show the fraction of an industry's output produced by, say, the four largest firms. Under what conditions would such ratios be fairly good indicators of the kind of pricing behavior that occurs in an industry? When might such measures be particularly inappropriate?

10. Why does the application of U.S. (and most other) antitrust laws require definition of a relevant market? Why will this definitional process usually be somewhat difficult and subject to dispute? How might the concept of the cross-price elasticity of demand help to clarify matters?

Problems

17.1 Suppose there are two firms selling ice cream cones in a small town. The prices charged by the firms are given by P_1 and P_2. Because the firms sell different types of cones, their goods are only partial substitutes for one another. The demand facing firm 1 is given by

$$q_1 = 10 - P_1 + \tfrac{1}{2}P_2$$

and that facing firm 2 is

$$q_2 = 10 - P_2 + \tfrac{1}{2}P_1.$$

Both firms have a constant marginal cost of $2 per cone.

a. Suppose each firm sets a price equal to marginal cost. How many cones will each sell and what will each firm's profits be?
b. Suppose firm 1 believes firm 2 will have a price of $2 per cone. How much should this firm charge to maximize profits? (Hint: Price should be halfway between P = MC and the price for which $q_1 = 0$.) What will this firm's profits be if $P_2 = 2$?
c. Suppose firm 2 also follows the strategy described in part b. What price will it charge and what will its profits be if $P_1 = 2$?
d. Are the decisions in parts b and c consistent with each other? How might the firms choose their prices in a consistent way?
e. Suppose the two firms merged. What pricing policy would maximize their total joint profits? (Hint: Assume they should each charge the same price.)

17.2 A carrot monopolist can product at constant average (and marginal) costs of $AC = MC = 5$. The firm faces a weekly market demand curve for carrots given by

$$Q = 53 - P.$$

a. Calculate the profit-maximizing price–quantity combination for this monopolist. Also calculate the monopolist's profits. (Hint: Use footnote 3 of this chapter.)

b. Suppose that a second firm enters the carrot market. Let q_A be the output of firm A and q_B the output of firm B. Market demand now is given by

$$q_A + q_B = 53 - P.$$

On the assumption that firm B has the same costs as firm A, calculate the profits of firms A and B as functions of q_A and q_B.

c. Suppose (as in the Cournot model) that each of these two firms chooses its level of output so as to maximize profits on the assumption that the other's output is fixed. Calculate each firm's reaction function (which expresses desired output of one firm as a function of the other's output).

d. On the assumption in part c, what is the only level for q_A and q_B with which both firms will be satisfied (what q_A, q_B combination satisfies both reaction curves)?

e. With q_A and q_B at the equilibrium level specified in part d, what will be the market price of carrots, the profits for each firm, and the total profits earned?

17.3 Some critics contend that U.S. automobile companies pursue a strategy of planned obsolescence: that is, they produce cars that are intended to become obsolete in a few years. Would that strategy make sense in a monopoly market? How might the production of obsolescence depend on the characteristics of market demand? How would oligopolistic competition affect the profitability of the strategy?

17.4 Suppose advertising expenditures are able to increase a firm's sales. How should a firm decide on the profit-maximizing level of advertising? What marginal rule should it use?

17.5 Under monopolistic competition, each firm sells a product that is slightly different from its competitors. Suppose two firms in this industry merged. Would they continue to produce two different goods? Or should they focus on a single product? Develop an intuitive argument to suggest what the profit-maximizing solution might be.

17.6 In the 1945 Alcoa case, Judge Learned Hand was faced with deciding whether Alcoa had a monopoly in aluminum production. A crucial issue concerned the distribution between "primary" aluminum production (P) and "secondary" (recycled) production (S). Three different market share measures were used to evaluate Alcoa's position:

$$I = P_A/P$$

$$II = P_A/(P + S)$$

$$III = (P_A - F)/(P + S)$$

where P_A = Alcoa's primary production (Alcoa was not significantly engaged in recycling) and F = the amount of Alcoa's primary production that it used for its own fabricated products.

a. Which of these definitions seems to provide the best approximation for the market for aluminum production?
b. How would you answer part a if you were an Alcoa attorney? How would you answer if you were a government attorney?
c. The figures showed the following results for each of the three market share measures:

$$I = .90$$

$$II = .64$$

$$III = .33.$$

If you were Judge Hand, how would you rule on the charge that Alcoa had a monopoly? How did the Judge actually rule?

17.7 In the Clorox case, Procter & Gamble was alleged to be a potential entrant into the liquid bleach market and was therefore prevented from buying Clorox. Can you devise a way to use firms' cost curves and the demand curves facing the firms to differentiate among actual entrants? Potential entrants? Nonentrants? Use your analysis to suggest what the court should have looked for in this antitrust case.

*17.8 Suppose that the total market demand for crude oil is given by

$$Q_D = -2,000P + 70,000$$

where Q is the quantity of oil in thousands of barrels per year and P is the dollar price per barrel. Suppose also that there are 1,000 identical small producers of crude oil, each with marginal costs given by

$$MC = q + 5$$

where q is the output of the typical firm.

a. Assuming that each small oil producer acts as a price taker, calculate the typical firm's supply curve ($q = \ldots$), the market supply curve ($Q_S = \ldots$), and the market equilibrium price and quantity (where $Q_D = Q_S$).
b. Suppose a practically infinite supply of crude oil is discovered in New Jersey by a would-be price leader and that this oil can be produced at a constant average and marginal cost of $AC = MC = \$15$ per barrel. Assume also that the supply behavior of the competitive fringe described in part a is not changed by this discovery. Calculate the demand curve facing the price leader.
c. Assuming that the price leader's marginal revenue curve is given by

$$MR = -Q/1,500 + 25,$$

how much should the price leader produce in order to maximize profits? What price and quantity will now prevail in the market?

---

*Denotes a problem that is rather difficult.

    d. Graph your result indicating the market demand curve, the supply curve for the competitive fringe, and the price leader's demand, MR, and MC curves.

    e. Does consumer surplus increase as a result of the New Jersey oil discovery? How does consumer surplus after the discovery compare to what would exist if the New Jersey oil were supplied competitively?

17.9 Suppose a firm is considering investing in research that would lead to a cost-saving innovation. Assuming the firm can retain this innovation solely for its own use, will the additional profits from the lower (marginal) costs be greater if the firm is a competitive price taker or if the firm is a monopolist? Develop a careful graphical argument. More generally, develop a verbal analysis to suggest how market structure may affect the adoption of cost-saving innovations.

17.10 Suppose a firm facing a downward-sloping demand curve for its product can shift that demand curve outward by undertaking an advertising campaign that involves a certain additional level of fixed costs (that is, the level of advertising does not depend on the amount produced).

    a. Show that if the firm is a monopoly this advertising campaign will definitely increase the amount the monopoly chooses to produce.

    b. Show that if this firm is initially in equilibrium in an industry characterized by monopolistic competition, the advertising campaign will also cause it to increase output. Will this firm operate closer to minimum average cost than was previously the case?

In Chapter 17 we examined some of the problems that arise in modeling markets in which there are only a few firms. Perhaps the most difficult of these problems concerns questions of strategy. That is, with few firms each firm must, to some extent, be concerned with what its rivals will do. Under perfect competition such strategic thinking is unnecessary because the prevailing market price conveys all the market information that is relevant to the firm. With relatively few firms the situation may be more complicated, since price-taking behavior is less likely.

One of the primary tools that economists use to study strategic choices is *game theory*. This subject was originally developed during the 1920s and grew rapidly during World War II in response to the need to develop formal ways of thinking about military strategy.[1] In this chapter, we will provide a brief introduction to game theory with a primary focus on its use in explaining pricing and entry behavior in imperfectly competitive markets.

---

[1]Much of the pioneering work in game theory was done by the mathematician John von Neumann. The main reference is J. von Neumann and O. Morgenstern, *The Theory of Games and Economic Behavior* (Princeton, N.J.: Princeton University Press, 1944).

CHAPTER
18
STRATEGY AND GAME THEORY

Basic Concepts

Game theory models seek to portray complex strategic situations in a highly simplified setting. Much like the previous models in this book, game theory models abstract from most of the personal and institutional details of a problem in order to arrive at a representation of the situation that is mathematically tractable. The greatest strength of this type of modeling is that it enables us to get to the heart of the problem.

Any situation in which individuals must make strategic choices and in which the final outcome will depend on what each person chooses to do can be viewed as a *game*. All games have three basic elements: (1) players; (2) strategies; and (3) payoffs. Some games may be *cooperative*, in which players can make binding agreements, or *noncooperative*, where such agreements are not possible. Here we will be concerned primarily with noncooperative games. Again, the following basic elements are always included in such games.

■ Players

Each decision maker in a game is called a player. The players may be individuals (as in poker games), firms (as in imperfectly competitive markets), or entire nations (as in military conflicts). All players are characterized as having the ability to choose among a set of possible actions. Usually the number of players is fixed throughout the "play" of a game and games are often characterized by the number of players (that is, two-player, three-player, or n-player games). In this chapter, we will primarily study two-player games and will denote these players (usually firms) by A and B. An important assumption usually made in game theory (as in most of economics) is that the specific identity of players is irrelevant. There are no "good guys" or "bad guys" in a game, and players are not assumed to have any special abilities or shortcomings. Each player is simply assumed to choose the course of action that yields the most favorable outcome.

■ Strategies

Each course of action open to a player in a game is called a strategy. Depending on the game being examined, a strategy may be a very simple action (taking another card in blackjack) or a very complex one (building a laser-based antimissile defense, for example), but each strategy is assumed to be a well-defined, specific course of action. Usually the number of strategies available to each player will be few in number; many aspects of game theory can be illustrated for situations in which each player has only two strategies available.[2] In

---

[2]Players may also adopt "mixed" strategies by choosing to play their pure strategies randomly (say, by flipping a coin). We will analyze this possibility only briefly in footnotes.

noncooperative games, players cannot reach binding agreements with each other about what strategies they will play; each player is uncertain about what the other will do.

■ Payoffs

The final returns to the players of a game at its conclusion are called payoffs. Payoffs are usually measured in levels of utility obtained by the players, although frequently monetary payoffs (say, profits for firms) are used instead. In general, it is assumed that players can rank the payoffs of a game from most preferred to least preferred and will seek the highest ranked payoff attainable. Payoffs incorporate all aspects associated with outcomes of a game; these include both explicit monetary payoffs and the implicit feelings of the players about the outcomes, such as whether they are embarrassed or whether they gain self-esteem. Naturally, players prefer payoffs that offer more utility to those that offer less. In some games the payoffs are simply transfers among the players—what one player wins, the other loses. Most of the games we look at are not of this zero-sum type, however. Instead, some outcomes offer higher total payoffs than do others.

Equilibrium Concepts

In our examination of the theory of markets, we developed the concept of equilibrium in which both suppliers and demanders were content with the market outcome. Given the equilibrium price and quantity, no market participant has an incentive to change his or her behavior. The question therefore arises whether there are similar equilibrium concepts in game theory models. Are there strategic choices that, once made, provide no incentives for the players to alter their behavior further? Do these equilibria then offer believable explanations of market outcomes?

Although there are several ways to formalize equilibrium concepts in games, the most frequently used approach is similar to that originally proposed in the nineteenth century by Cournot (see Chapter 17) and generalized in the early 1950s by J. Nash. Under this procedure a pair of strategies, say (a*, b*), is defined to be a **Nash equilibrium** if a* represents player A's best move when B plays b* and b* represents B's best move when A plays a*. Even if one of the players reveals the (equilibrium) strategy he or she will use, the other player cannot benefit from knowing this. For nonequilibrium strategies, as we shall see, this is not the case. If one player knows what the other's strategy will be, he or she can often benefit from that knowledge and, in the process, take actions which reduce the payoff received by the player who has revealed his or her strategy.

Not every game has a Nash equilibrium. And, in some cases, a game may have many different Nash equilibria, some of which are more plausible than others. Some Nash equilibria may not be especially desirable to the players in

■

Nash equilibrium

A pair of strategies (a*, b*) in a two-player game such that a* is an optimal strategy for A against b* and b* is an optimal strategy for B against a*.

a game. And, in some cases, other equilibrium concepts may be more reasonable than those proposed by Nash. Hence, there is a rather complex relationship between game theory equilibria and more traditional market equilibrium concepts. Still, the concept provides an initial working definition of equilibrium with which to start our study of game theory.

An Illustrative Advertising Game

As a way of illustrating the game theoretic approach to strategic modeling, we will examine a simple example in which two firms (A and B) must decide how much to spend on advertising. Each firm may adopt either a high (H) budget or a low (L) budget, and we wish to examine possible equilibrium choices in this situation. It should be stressed at the outset that this game is not especially realistic—it is intended for pedagogic purposes only.

■ The Game in Extensive Form

Figure 18.1 illustrates the specific details of the advertising game. In this game "tree," the action proceeds from left to right, and each "node" represents a de-

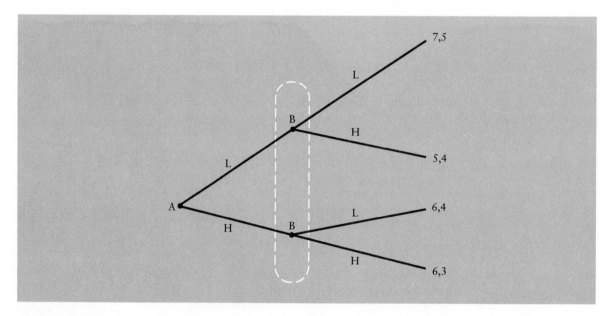

Figure 18.1
The Advertising
Game in Extensive
Form

In this game A chooses a low (L) or a high (H) advertising budget, then B makes a similar choice. The oval surrounding B's nodes indicates that they share the same (lack of) information—B does not know what strategy A has chosen. Payoffs (with A's first) are listed at the right.

cision point for the firm indicated there. The first move in this game belongs to firm A: it must choose its level of advertising expenditures, H or L. Because Firm B's decisions occur to the right of A's, the tree indicates that firm B makes its decision after firm A. At this stage, two versions of the game are possible depending on whether B is assumed to know what choice A has made. First we will look at the case where B does not have this information. The larger oval surrounding B's two decision nodes indicates that both nodes share the same (lack of) information. Firm B must choose H or L without knowing what A has done. Later we will examine the case where B does have this information.

The numbers at the end of each tree branch indicate payoffs, here measured in thousands or millions of dollars of profits. Each pair of payoffs lists A's profits first. For example, the payoffs in Figure 18.1 show that if firm A chooses H and firm B chooses L, profits will be 6 for A and 4 for B. Other payoffs are interpreted similarly.

■ The Game in Normal Form

Although the game tree in Figure 18.1 offers a useful visual presentation of the complete structure of a game, sometimes it is more convenient to describe games in tabular (or "normal") form. Table 18.1 provides such a presentation for the advertising game. In the table, firm A's strategies (H or L) are shown at the left, and B's strategies are shown across the top. Payoffs (again with firm A's coming first) corresponding to the various strategic choices are shown in the body of the table. The reader should check that Figure 18.1 and Table 18.1 convey the same information about this game.

■ Dominant Strategies and Nash Equilibria

Table 18.1 makes clear that adoption of a low advertising budget is a **dominant strategy** for firm B. No matter what A does, the L strategy provides greater profits to firm B than does the H strategy. Of course, since the structure of the game is assumed to be known to both players, firm A will recognize that B has such a dominant strategy and will opt for the strategy that does the best against it; that is, firm A will also choose L. Considerations of strategy dominance, therefore, suggest that the A:L, B:L strategy choice will be made and that the resulting payoffs will be 7 (to A) and 5 (to B).

■
Dominant strategy
A strategy which is optimal regardless of the strategy adopted by an opponent.

			B's Strategies		Table 18.1 The Advertising Game in Normal Form
			L	H	
A's Strategies	L		7, 5	5, 4	
	H		6, 4	6, 3	

Table 18.2
Two Simple Games

(a) Rock, Scissors, Paper—No Nash Equilibria

		B's Strategies					
		Rock		Scissors		Paper	
A's Strategies	Rock	0	0	1	−1	−1	1
	Scissors	−1	1	0	0	1	−1
	Paper	1	−1	−1	1	0	0

(b) Battle of the Sexes–Two Nash Equilibria

		B's Strategies			
		Mountain		Seaside	
A's Strategies	Mountain	2	1	0	0
	Seaside	0	0	1	2

The A:L, B:L strategy choice also obeys the Nash criterion for equilibrium. If A knows that B will play L, its best choice is L. Similarly, if B knows A will play L, its best choice is also L (indeed, since L is a dominant strategy for B, this is its best choice no matter what A does). The A:L, B:L choice, therefore, meets the symmetry required by the Nash criterion.

To see why the other strategy pairs in Table 18.1 do not meet the Nash criteria, let us consider them one at a time. If the players announce A:H, B:L, this provides A with a chance to better its position—if firm A knows B will opt for L, it can make greater profits by choosing L. The choice A:H, B:L is therefore not a Nash equilibrium. Neither of the two outcomes in which B chooses H meets the Nash criterion because, as we have already pointed out, no matter what A does, B can improve its profits by choosing L instead. Since L strictly dominates H for firm B, no outcome in which B plays H can be a Nash equilibrium.

■ Nature of Nash Equilibria

Although the advertising game illustrated in Figure 18.1 contains a single Nash equilibrium, that is not a general property of all two-person games.[3] Table 18.2 illustrates two familiar games that reflect differing possibilities for Nash equilibria. In part (a) of the table, the children's finger game "Rock, Scissors, Paper" is depicted. The zero payoffs along the diagonal show that if players adopt the same strategy, no payments are made. In other cases, the payoffs indicate a $1 payment from loser to winner under the usual hierarchy (Rock breaks Scissors, Scissors cut Paper, Paper covers Rock). As anyone who has played this game knows, there is no equilibrium. Any strategy pair is unstable

---

[3]Nash equilibria can be shown always to exist in certain types of games. For example, in zero-sum games, a Nash equilibrium always exists in mixed strategies (strategies that consist of various pure strategies played with certain probabilities).

because it offers at least one of the players an incentive to adopt another strategy. For example, (A: Scissors, B: Scissors) provides an incentive for either A or B to choose Rock. Similarly (A: Paper, B: Rock) obviously encourages B to choose Scissors. The irregular cycling behavior exhibited in the play of this game clearly indicates the absence of a Nash equilibrium.

In the "Battle of the Sexes" game, a husband (A) and wife (B) are planning a vacation. A prefers mountain locations, B prefers the seaside. Both players prefer a vacation spent together to one spent apart. The payoffs in part (b) of Table 18.2 reflect these preferences. Here both of the joint vacations represent Nash equilibria. With (A: Mountain, B: Mountain) neither player can gain by taking advantage of knowing the other's strategy. Similar comments apply to (A: Seaside, B: Seaside). Hence this is a game with two Nash equilibria. Application 18.1: Nash Equilibrium Tariff Policy applies this concept to real-world strategic interactions.

The Prisoner's Dilemma

The *Prisoner's Dilemma* game was first discussed by A. W. Tucker in the 1940s. The title stems from the following game situation. Two people are arrested for a crime. The district attorney has little evidence in the case and is anxious to extract a confession. She separates the suspects and tells each, "If you confess and your companion doesn't, I can promise you a reduced (six-month) sentence, whereas on the basis of your confession, your companion will get 10 years. If you both confess, you will each get a three-year sentence." Each suspect also knows that if neither of them confesses, the lack of evidence will cause them to be tried for a lesser crime for which they will receive two-year sentences. The normal form payoff matrix for this situation is illustrated in Table 18.3. The "confess" strategy dominates for both A and B. Hence these strategies constitute a Nash equilibrium and the district attorney's ploy looks successful. However, an agreement by both not to confess would reduce prison terms from three years to two years. This "rational" solution is not stable, and each prisoner has an incentive to squeal on his or her colleague. This, then, is the dilemma—outcomes that appear to be optimal from the prisoners' points of view are not stable, and cheating will usually prevail.

		B	
		Confess	Not Confess
A	Confess	A: 3 years B: 3 years	A: 6 months B: 10 years
	Not Confess	A: 10 years B: 6 months	A: 2 years B: 2 years

Table 18.3
The Prisoner's Dilemma

APPLICATION 18.1

Nash Equilibrium Tariff Policy

To many economists, free trade among nations seems a feasible route to welfare maximization. As we showed in Application 1.6, national surveys report that approximately 90 percent of economists polled tend to support free trade. Still, many economists recognize that there are situations where a country may find it desirable to adopt trade barriers, especially if other countries already do so. In such instances, choices among trade policies can resemble game theoretic situations—each country must take other country's reactions into account when choosing its own optimal policy.

Optimal Tariff Policy

For example, it is well known that implementation of a tariff (that is, a tax on imports) may, in some cases, improve a country's welfare. Adoption of such a policy can allow a country to behave as a monopolist in its trading relationships with the rest of the world, enabling it to effect domestic welfare gains. The difficulty in choosing such an "optimal" tariff policy is, of course, that other countries may retaliate with tariffs of their own. The gains promised from a tariff can quickly evaporate if other nations respond forcefully. One possible outcome from this strategic situation is that the nations involved may reach a Nash equilibrium set of tariff choices. In other words, each country makes its best choice, given what the other countries have chosen to do. Hence, the situation is stable and repeated tariff wars are avoided. Whether this equilibrium outcome is also better than free trade, however, is open to question.

A Canada–U.S. Example

Devising models of the trading relationships among all of the countries in the world is a formidable undertaking. Economists sometimes try to simplify matters by looking only at bilateral relationships between two countries, taking the rest of the world's trading decisions as a given. This is the approach followed by Markusen and Wigle in an examination of Canadian-U.S. tariff policy.[1] The authors asked how various tariff policies

that might be adopted by these countries would affect their overall welfare. Not surprisingly, they found that relative to current tariff rates (an average of 4.6 percent in the U.S. and 13.2 percent in Canada), both countries would gain by adopting free-trade policies. However, they also found the solution may be unstable in that an ironclad decision by one of the trading partners to adopt free trade offers the other a chance to choose an optimal tariff. For example, a Canadian commitment to free trade might offer the United States a chance to gain by taxing imports of Canadian natural gas.

To study the consequences of various tariff policies, the authors compute payoff matrices for Canada and the United States. They show that for Canada tariff reductions from current levels represent a dominant strategy. No matter what the United States does, Canada gains by reducing its tariff rate. For the United States there is no dominant strategy—its optimal tariff depends on what Canada does. Still, the authors show that there is a Nash equilibrium where the United States adopts fairly large increases in its current tariff rates. At this equilibrium the tariff pattern is reversed from what it actually is—equilibrium Canadian rates are only about one third of equilibrium U.S. rates. Such a result is consistent with the notion that the United States, because of its size in world markets, might gain from higher tariffs (assuming, probably contrary to fact, that other countries do not retaliate), but that smaller Canada would gain by moving closer to free trade.

To Think About

1. Payoffs in the tariff "game" analyzed here are measured as total changes in economic welfare. Why might these not provide a very good indication of what tariff policies would actually be adopted by the countries?

2. In further analyses the authors also show that Canada's gains from cutting tariffs are more likely if Canadian industry experiences increasing returns to scale. Can you provide an intuitive explanation for this result?

---

[1] J. R. Markusen and R. W. Wigle, "Nash Equilibrium Tariff Rates for the United States and Canada," *Journal of Political Economy* (April 1989): 368–386.

		B's Strategies		Table 18.4
		L	H	An Advertising
A's Strategies	L	7, 7	3, 10	Game with a Desirable Outcome
	H	10, 3	5, 5	that Is Unstable

		B's Strategies		Table 18.5
		L	H	A Threat Game in
A's Strategies	L	20, 5	15, 10	Advertising
	H	10, –50	5, –25	

Applications

Prisoner's Dilemma–type problems may arise in many real-world market situations. Table 18.4 contains an illustration of the dilemma in the advertising context. Here the twin L strategies are most profitable, but this choice is unstable. In this game, advertising might be regarded as "defensive" in the sense that a mutual agreement to reduce expenditures would be profitable to both parties. Such an agreement in the situation of Table 18.4 would be unstable. Either firm could increase its profits even further by cheating on the agreement. Similar situations arise in the tendency for airlines to give "bonus mileage" (there would be larger profits if all firms stopped offering free trips, but such a solution is unstable) and in the instability of farmers' cartels' agreements to restrict output (it is just too tempting for an individual farmer to try to sell more milk). As these examples show, the difficulty of enforcing agreements can be very detrimental to the profits of an industry.

Cooperation and Repetition

Communication between participants can be an important part of a game. In the Prisoner's Dilemma, for example, the inability to reach a cooperative agreement not to confess leads to a second-best outcome. If the parties could agree to cooperate, they might do better. As an example of how communications can affect the outcome of a game, consider the payoff matrix shown in Table 18.5. In this version of the advertising game, the adoption of strategy H by firm A has disastrous consequences for firm B, causing a loss of –50 when B plays L and –25 when H is chosen. Without any communication A would choose L (this dominates H) and B would choose H (which dominates L). Firm A would therefore end up with +15 and B with +10. However, by recognizing the potency of strategy H, A may be able to improve its situation. It can threaten to play H unless B plays L. If this threat is credible (a topic we take up later), A can increase its profits from 15 to 20.

If games are to be played many times, communication may be fostered. In the Prisoner's Dilemma game, for example, it seems doubtful that the district attorney's ploy would work if it were used repeatedly. In this case, prisoners might hear about the method and act accordingly in their interrogations. In other contexts, firms that are continually exasperated by their inability to obtain favorable market outcomes may come to perceive the kind of cooperative behavior that is necessary. In antitrust theory, for example, some markets are believed to be characterized by "tacit collusion" among the participants. Firms act as a cartel even though they never meet to plot a common strategy. We will explore the formal aspects of this problem later. Finally, repetition of the threat game (Table 18.5) offers player A the opportunity to take reprisals on B for failing to choose L. Imposing severe losses on B for "improper" behavior may be far more persuasive than simply making abstract threats.

Many-Period Games

These observations suggest that repeated games, perhaps with some types of communication or cooperation, may involve complex scenarios that better reflect real-world markets than do the simple single-period models we have studied so far. In order to illustrate the formal aspects of such games in a simple setting, we return to a reformulated version of the advertising game presented at the beginning of this chapter. Figure 18.2 repeats that game, but now we

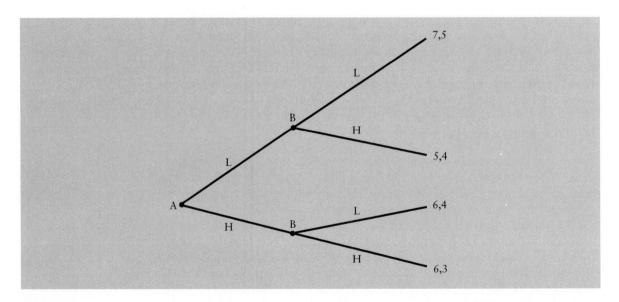

Figure 18.2
The Advertising Game in Sequential Form

In this form of the advertising game, firm B knows firm A's advertising choice. Strategies for B must be phrased taking this information into account. (See Table 18.6.)

		B's Strategies			
		L,L	L,H	H,L	H,H
A's Strategies	L	7, 5	7, 5	5, 4	5, 4
	H	6, 4	6, 3	6, 4	6, 3

Table 18.6
Contingent
Strategies in the
Advertising Game

assume that firm B knows which advertising spending level A has chosen. In graphical terms, the oval around B's nodes has been eliminated in Figure 18.2 to indicate this additional information. B's strategic choices now must be phrased in a way that takes the added information it has into account. In Table 18.6, we indicate such an extended delineation of strategies. In all, there are four such strategies covering the possible informational contingencies. Each strategy is stated as a pair of actions indicating what B will do depending on its information. The strategy (L,L) indicates that B chooses L if A chooses its first strategy and L also if A chooses its second strategy. Similarly (H,L) indicates that B chooses H if A chooses its first strategy and B chooses L if A chooses its second strategy. Although this table conveys little more than did the previous illustration of the advertising game (Table 18.1), explicit consideration of contingent strategy choices does enable us to explore equilibrium notions for dynamic games.

■ Credible Threats

There are three Nash equilibria in this game: (1) A:L, B:(L,L); (2) A:L, B:(L,H); and (3) A:H, B:(H,L). Each of these strategy pairs meets the criterion of being optimal for each player given the strategy of the other. Pairs (2) and (3) are implausible, however, because they incorporate a noncredible threat that firm B would not carry out if it were in a position to do so. Consider, for example, the pair A:L, B:(L,H). Under this choice B promises to play H if A plays H (its second strategy). A glance at Figure 18.2 shows that this threat is not credible. If B were presented with the fact of A having chosen H, it will make profits of 3 if it chooses H, but 4 if it chooses L. The threat implicit in the (L,H) strategy is therefore not credible. Even though B's strategy (L,H) is one component of a Nash equilibrium, firm A should be able to infer the noncredibility of the threat implicit in it and thereby eliminate it as a possible choice B might make.

By eliminating strategies that involve noncredible threats, A can conclude that B would never play (L,H) or (H,L).[4] Proceeding in this way, the advertising game is reduced to the payoff matrix originally shown in Table 18.1 and, as we discussed previously, in that case always playing L (that is, choosing (L,L)) is a dominant strategy for B. Firm A can recognize this and will opt for

---

[4]The process of eliminating strategies involving noncredible threats is termed "backward induction." This method of solving games by "folding back the tree" was developed by H. Kuhn. See "Extensive Games and the Problem of Information," in H. Kuhn and A. Tucker, eds., *Contributions to the Theory of Games* (Princeton, N.J.: Princeton University Press, 1953): 193–216.

■
Perfect equilibrium

A Nash equilibrium in which the strategy choices of each player do not involve noncredible threats. That is, no strategy in such an equilibrium requires a player to carry out an action that would not be in its interest at the time.

strategy L. The Nash equilibrium A:L, B:(L,L) has therefore been shown to be the only one of the three in Table 18.6 that does not involve noncredible threats. Such an equilibrium is termed a **perfect equilibrium.** By using the concepts of strategic dominance, Nash equilibrium, and perfect equilibrium, we are now in a position to examine a few game theoretic models of firm behavior.

Models of Pricing Behavior

We begin our discussion of the economic applications of game theory by illustrating some of the insights that this approach can provide to the analysis of pricing. As in Chapter 17, most of the interesting results can be shown for the duopoly case. Later in the chapter we briefly discuss some complications involved in extending game theory models to markets that include many firms.

■ The Bertrand Equilibrium

Suppose there are two firms (A and B) each producing a homogeneous good at constant marginal cost, c. The demand for the good is such that all sales go to the firm with the lowest price and that sales are split evenly if $P_A = P_B$. The available pricing strategies here consist of choosing any price greater than or equal to c—no firm would choose to operate at a loss in the long run by choosing a price less than c.

In this case, the only Nash equilibrium is $P_A = P_B = c$. That is, the Nash equilibrium is the competitive solution with marginal cost pricing even though there are only two firms. To see why, suppose firm A chooses a price greater than c. The profit-maximizing response for firm B is to choose a price slightly less than P_A and corner the entire market. But B's price, if it exceeds c, still cannot be a Nash equilibrium since it provides A with further incentives for price cutting. Only by choosing $P_A = P_B = c$ will the two firms in this market achieve a Nash equilibrium in which they share the market equally. This pricing strategy is sometimes referred to as a "Bertrand equilibrium" after the French economist who discovered it.[5]

■ Two-Stage Price Games

The simplicity and definiteness of the Bertrand result depend crucially on the assumptions underlying the model. If firms do not have equal costs (see problem 18.4) or if the goods produced by the two firms are not perfect substitutes, the competitive result no longer holds. Other duopoly models that depart from the Bertrand result treat price competition as only the final stage of a two-stage game in which the first stage involves various types of entry or investment considerations for the firms. In Chapter 17 we examined Cournot's example of a

---

[5]J. Bertrand, "Théorie Mathematique de la Richess Sociale," *Journal de Savants* (1883): 499–508.

natural spring duopoly in which each spring owner chose how much water to supply. In the present context we might assume that each firm in a duopoly must choose a certain capacity output level for which marginal costs are constant up to that level and infinite thereafter. It seems clear that a two-stage game in which firms choose capacity first (and then price) is formally identical to the Cournot analysis. The quantities chosen in the Cournot equilibrium represent a Nash equilibrium because each firm correctly perceives what the other's output will be. Once these capacity decisions are made, the only price that can prevail is that for which total quantity demanded equals the combined capacities of the two firms.

To see why Bertrand-type price competition will result in such a solution, suppose Cournot capacities are given by $\bar{q}_A$ and $\bar{q}_B$ and that $\bar{P}$ is the price that would prevail when production is at capacity for both firms. A situation in which

$$P_A = P_B < \bar{P} \qquad [18.1]$$

is not a Nash equilibrium. With this price, total quantity demanded exceeds total capacity, so firm A could increase its profits by raising price slightly and still selling $\bar{q}_A$. Similarly,

$$P_A = P_B > \bar{P} \qquad [18.2]$$

is not a Nash equilibrium because now total sales fall short of capacity. At least one firm (say, firm A) is selling less than its capacity. By cutting price slightly, firm A can increase its profits by taking all possible sales up to $\bar{q}_A$. Of course, B will respond to a loss of sales by dropping its price as well. Hence the only Nash equilibrium which can prevail is the Cournot result.[6]

$$P_A = P_B = \bar{P}. \qquad [18.3]$$

In general, this price will fall short of the monopoly price but will exceed marginal cost. Results of this two-stage game are therefore indistinguishable from those arising from the Cournot model of the previous chapter.

The contrast between the Bertrand and Cournot games is striking. The former predicts competitive outcomes in a duopoly situation whereas the latter predicts monopoly-like inefficiencies in which price exceeds marginal cost. This suggests that actual behavior in duopoly markets may exhibit a wide variety of outcomes depending on the precise way in which competition occurs. The principal lesson of the two-stage Cournot game is that, even with Bertrand price competition, decisions made prior to this final (price-setting) stage of a game can have an important impact on market behavior. This lesson will be reflected again in some of the game theory models of entry we describe later in this chapter. Application 18.2: Price Leadership in Steel shows how the jockeying for price advantages portrayed in these models seems to characterize one major market.

---

[6]For completeness, it should also be noted that no situation in which $P_A \neq P_B$ can be an equilibrium since the low-price firm has an incentive to raise price and the high-price firm wishes to cut price.

APPLICATION 18.2
Price Leadership in Steel

The Prisoner's Dilemma, Bertrand, and Cournot models suggest that pricing decisions in an industry can, at times, become quite chaotic. In some concentrated industries, price leadership positions tend to be established over many years, and disruptions are relatively rare. When unexpected factors cause leadership changes, however, past patterns can quickly unravel, and competitive-type results can spring up. This was the case in the U.S. steel industry throughout the 1960s and beyond.

U.S. Steel as the Price Leader
In 1901, Andrew Carnegie brought together 12 steel and related companies to form the United States Steel Corporation, the first billion-dollar company. For the next fifty years, U.S. Steel occupied the undisputed role of leader in determining the price of steel products. At times, price coordination in the industry resulted from explicit collusion (U.S. Steel chairman Elbert Gary was famous for holding regular "dinners" at which the general "industry situation" was discussed). More often, however, other firms in the industry demurred in allowing the largest firm to act as the price setter.

The Politics of Price Leadership
Public concern about inflation in the early 1960s brought this practice under increased scrutiny. U.S. Steel was harshly criticized by President Kennedy in 1962 after announcing a price increase and was forced to retract it due to the public outcry that followed. With its price leader politically paralyzed, the steel industry floundered in search of a new pricing policy. Discounts from list prices became widespread, and several leading firms took turns being knocked down as the price leader.[1] One consequence of this turmoil was a sharp decline in the profitability of the industry as a whole. By the early 1970s, rates of return in the steel industry had dropped far below those of other manufacturing industries.

Enlisting the Government's Help
Steel imports grew throughout the 1960s, reaching about 18 percent of total production by the end of the decade. This undoubtedly contributed to the loss of cartel-like price discipline in steel, but the industry's political position was so weakened by its earlier confrontations with the Kennedy Administration that it was unable to press for price protection. The situation began to change in the 1970s, especially with the closing of three major steel plants by Youngstown and Bethlehem Steel in 1977. Fearing for the overall health of the U.S. industry, the Carter Administration developed a schedule of "reference prices" for steel below which various trade restrictions would be implemented. In the 1980s, a similar pricing scheme was adopted by European steel producers. Although these actions did not explicitly reestablish price leadership within the steel industry, they did increase coordination of pricing decisions. Major U.S. producers were able to return to positions of price leaders. The threat of Japanese imports allowed them to enlist government support in what they could not effectively do for themselves.

To Think About
1. How might the situation described in this application be framed as a problem in game theory? Who are the players, what are their strategies, is there a Nash equilibrium?
2. How can the announcement by the government of steel (minimum) "trigger" prices for steel imports aid in establishing domestic pricing discipline? How do these prices constrain what domestic leaders can do? Do you think that the industry leaders try to influence what trigger prices the government chooses?

---

[1]For a description of one particularly dramatic confrontation between U.S. Steel and Bethlehem Steel in 1968, see F. M. Scherer, *Industrial* *Market Structure and Economic Performance,* 2nd ed. (Chicago: Rand McNally, 1980): 178–179.

■ Tacit Collusion

Our analysis of the Prisoner's Dilemma concluded that if the game were played several times the participants might devise ways to adopt more cooperative strategic choices. A similar issue might be raised about the Bertrand game. Would repetition of this game offer some mechanism for the players to attain supra-competitive profits by pursuing a monopoly pricing policy? One possibility, discussed in Chapter 17, would be for the players to establish a cartel and explicitly set price or output targets. As we demonstrated, such explicit agreements can be difficult to enforce. Here we adopt a noncooperative approach to the collusion question by exploring models of "tacit" collusion. That is, we use game theory concepts to see whether there exist equilibrium strategies that, though not explicitly coordinated, would allow firms to achieve monopoly profits.

Finite Time Horizon. Our initial result from the Bertrand model poses a significant stumbling block to achieving tacit collusion. Since the single-period Nash equilibrium in this model results in $P_A = P_B = c$, we need to ask whether this situation would change if the game were repeated during many periods. With any small number of repetitions, it seems clear that the Bertrand result remains unchanged. Any strategy in which firm A, say, chooses $P_A > c$ during the final period offers firm B the possibility of earning profits by setting $P_A > P_B > c$. The threat of charging $P_A > c$ in the last period is therefore not credible. Because a similar argument applies to any period prior to the last one too, we can conclude that the only perfect equilibrium is one in which firms charge the competitive price in every period. The strict assumptions of the Bertrand model make tacit collusion impossible over any finite period.

Infinite Time Horizon. If firms are viewed as having an infinite time horizon, however, matters change significantly. In this case there is no "final" period so there may exist collusive strategies that are not undermined by the logic of the Bertrand result. One such possibility is for firms to adopt "trigger" strategies in which each firm (again, say firm A) sets $P_A = P_M$ (where P_M is the cartel price) in every period for which firm B adopts a similar price, but chooses $P_A = c$ if firm B has cheated in the previous period.

To determine whether these trigger strategies constitute a perfect equilibrium, we must discern whether they constitute a Nash equilibrium in every period. Suppose the firms have colluded for a time and firm A thinks about cheating in this period. Knowing that firm B will choose $P_B = P_M$ it can set its price slightly below P_M and, in this period, obtain the entire market for itself. It will thereby earn (almost) the entire monopoly profits (π_M) in this period. But, by doing this, firm A will lose its share of profits ($\pi_M/2$) forever after because its treachery will trigger firm B's retaliatory strategy. Since the present value (see Chapter 21) of these lost profits is given by

$$\pi_M/2 \cdot \frac{1}{r} \qquad \qquad [18.4]$$

(where r is the per period interest rate), cheating will be unprofitable if

$$\pi_M < \pi_M/2 \cdot \frac{1}{r} \, . \qquad [18.5]$$

This condition holds for values of r less than $\frac{1}{2}$. We can therefore conclude that the trigger strategies constitute a perfect equilibrium for sufficiently low interest rates. The collusion implicit in these strategies is totally noncooperative. The firms never actually have to meet in seedy hotel rooms to adopt strategies that yield monopoly profits.

■ Generalizations and Limitations

The contrast between the competitive results of the Bertrand model and the monopoly results of the tacit collusion model suggests that the viability of collusion in game theory models is very sensitive to the particular assumptions made. Two assumptions in our simple model of tacit collusion are especially important: (1) that firm B can easily detect whether firm A has cheated; and (2) that firm B responds to cheating by adopting a harsh response that not only punishes firm A, but also condemns itself to zero profits forever. In more general models of tacit collusion, these assumptions can be relaxed, for example, by allowing for the possibility that it may be difficult for firm B to recognize cheating by A. Some models examine alternative types of punishment B might inflict on A—for example, B could cut price in some other market in which A also sells. Other categories of models explore the consequences of introducing differentiated products into models of tacit collusion or of incorporating reasons why the demand for a firm's product may not respond instantly to price changes by its rival. As might be imagined, results of such modeling efforts are quite varied.[7] In all such models, the notions of Nash and perfect equilibria continue to play an important role in identifying whether tacit collusion can arise from strategic choices that appear to be viable. Real-world markets often exhibit aspects of both tacit and explicit collusion as Application 18.3: The Great Electrical Equipment Conspiracy shows.

Entry, Exit, and Strategy

Our treatment of entry and exit in previous chapters left little room for strategic thinking. A potential entrant was concerned only with the relationship between prevailing market price and its own (average or marginal) costs. We assumed that making that comparison involved no special problems. Similarly, we assumed firms will promptly leave a market they find to be unprofitable.

---

[7]See J. Tirole, *The Theory of Industrial Organization* (Cambridge, Mass.: MIT Press, 1988), Chapter 6.

APPLICATION 18.3
The Great Electrical Equipment Conspiracy

Even though an industry may be reasonably profitable, the lure of monopoly profits provides the industry a considerable incentive to create cartels. The lure is especially strong when there are relatively few firms in an industry and when it is fairly easy for the members of the cartel to police what the other members are doing. This was the case with the electrical equipment industry in the early 1950s when it developed an elaborate price-rigging scheme. However, the scheme came under both increasing internal friction and external legal scrutiny. By the 1960s, the scheme had failed, and executives of several major companies had been imprisoned.[1]

The Markets for Generators and Switchgear

Electric turbine generators and high-voltage switchgear are sold to electric utility companies. Often they are customized to unique specifications, and, consequently, they can cost many millions of dollars, constituting a lucrative business. Following World War II, the 1950s saw a period of rapid growth in electricity use and the building of new generation facilities. At that time, the electrical equipment industry tended to be dominated by only a few firms: General Electric, Westinghouse, Allis Chalmers, I.T.E. Corporation, and Federal Pacific. Although the growth expected in the industry created good prospects for most of these firms, the possibility for cartelization seemed to promise even greater profits.

Bid Rigging Schemes

The principal problem faced by the electrical equipment firms seeking to create a cartel was that most sales took place through sealed bidding. To avoid competition, they therefore had to devise a method for coordinating the bids each firm would make. Through a complex strategy that involved dividing up the United States into bidding regions and using the lunar calendar to decide whose turn it was to "win" a bid in a region, the firms were able to overcome the secrecy usually involved in submitting sealed bids. The practice worked quite well until the end of the decade, probably increasing total

profits of electrical equipment manufacturers by as much as $50 to 100 million over the period.

Demise of the Conspiracy

Toward the end of the 1950s, the electrical equipment conspiracy came under increasing internal friction as its leaders (General Electric and Westinghouse) were asked to give a greater share of the business to other firms. New entries into the industry by importers and low-cost domestic producers also caused some problems for the cartel. The final blow to the conspiracy came with a series of widely publicized hearings under Senator Kefauver in 1959 and the federal indictment of 52 executives of the leading generator, switchgear, and transformer companies. Although the government recommended jail sentences for thirty of these defendants, only seven actually served time in jail. Still, the notoriety of the case and the personal disruption it caused to those involved probably had a chilling effect on the future establishment of other cartels of this type.

To Think About

1. Why did the electrical equipment manufacturers opt for a clearly illegal bid rigging scheme rather than settling for some other form of tacit collusion? What about the nature of transactions in this business made the explicit price-fixing solution a desirable one?

2. Prosecution of the electrical equipment conspirators was one of the few cases of a successful "cops and robbers" approach to antitrust law. It involved wire tapping, government informers, and so forth. Without such evidence, how could the government prosecute a tacit collusion case?

[1]For a popularized and somewhat sensationalized version of this episode, see J. G. Fuller, *The Gentlemen Conspirators* (New York: Grove Press, 1962).

Upon closer inspection, however, the entry and exit issue can become considerably more complex. The fundamental problem is that a firm wishing to enter or leave a market must make some conjecture about how its action will affect market price in subsequent periods. Making such conjectures obviously requires the firm to consider what its rivals will do. What appears to be a relatively straightforward decision comparing price and average cost may therefore involve a number of possible strategic ploys, especially when a firm's information about its rivals is imperfect.

■ Sunk Costs and Commitment

Many game theoretic models of the entry process stress the importance of a firm's *commitment* to a specific market. If the nature of production requires that firms make specific capital investments in order to operate in a market and if these cannot easily be shifted to other uses, any firm that makes such an investment has committed itself to being a market participant. As we saw in Chapter 9, expenditures on such investments are called *sunk costs*. Sunk costs might include expenditures on such items as unique types of equipment (for example, a newsprint-making machine) or on job-specific training for workers (developing the skills to use the newsprint machine). Sunk costs have many characteristics of fixed costs in that these costs are incurred even if no output is produced. Rather than being incurred periodically as are many fixed costs (heating the factory), these costs are incurred only once in connection with the entry process. When the firm makes such an investment, it has committed itself to the market, which may have important consequences for its strategic behavior.

■ First-Mover Advantages

Although at first glance it might seem that incurring sunk costs by making the commitment to serve a market puts a firm at a disadvantage, in most models that is not the case. Rather, one firm can often stake out a claim to a market by making a commitment to serve it and in the process limit the kinds of actions its rivals find profitable. Many game theory models, therefore, stress the advantage of moving first.

As a simple numerical example, consider again Cournot's example of two springs. In our discussion in Chapter 17, we assumed each firm chose its output capacity simultaneously and this resulted in a price of $40 with a total output of 80 (thousand gallons). Suppose now, instead, that firm A has the option of moving first. Since this firm can safely assume that firm B will maximize profits given what it has done, firm A can take account of this insight in its decision. Specifically, since firm A knows that firm B reacts by

$$q_B = \frac{120 - q_A}{2},$$

[18.6]

it can use this to compute the net demand for its own spring's water:

$$q_A = 120 - q_B - P = 120 - (120 - q_A)/2 - P = 60 + \frac{q_A}{2} - P. \qquad [18.7]$$

Solving for q_A gives

$$q_A = 120 - 2P. \qquad [18.8]$$

Hence marginal revenue equals zero (and total revenues are maximized) when firm A chooses a capacity of $q_A = 60$ (that is, half of 120—the quantity demanded when $P = 0$). With firm A taking advantage of its first-mover position, firm B chooses to produce

$$q_B = \frac{120 - q_A}{2} = \frac{(120 - 60)}{2} = 30. \qquad [18.9]$$

With total output of 90, spring water sells for $30 and firm A's total revenues are $1,800—an improvement over the $1,600 collected in the Cournot equilibrium. Firm B's revenues have correspondingly been reduced to $900—a sign of the disadvantage faced by a late mover.[8]

■ Entry Deterrence

In some cases, first-mover advantages may be large enough to deter all entry by rivals. Intuitively, it seems plausible that the first mover could opt for a very large capacity and thereby discourage all other firms from entering the market. The economic rationality of such a decision is not clear-cut, however. In the Cournot model, for example, the only sure way for one spring owner to deter all entry is to satisfy the total market demand at the firm's marginal and average cost; that is, firm A would have to offer $q_A = 120$ at a price of zero if it is to have a fully successful entry deterrence strategy. Obviously such a choice results in zero profits for the firm and would not represent profit maximization. Instead, it would be better for firm A to accept some entry.

    With economies of scale in production, the possibility for profitable entry deterrence is increased. If the firm that is to move first can adopt a large enough scale of operation, it may be able to limit the scale of the potential entrant. The potential entrant will therefore experience such high average costs that there would be no way for it to earn a profit.

■ A Numerical Example

The simplest way to incorporate economies of scale into the Cournot model is to assume each spring owner must pay a fixed cost of operations. If that fixed

---

[8]Sometimes this solution is referred to as a "Stackelberg equilibrium" after the German economist who first discovered the advantage of moving first in the Cournot case.

cost is given by \$784 (a carefully chosen number!), firm B would still find it attractive to enter if firm A moves first and opts to produce $q_A = 60$. In this case, firm B would earn profits of \$116 (= \$900 − \$784) per period. However, if the first mover opts for $q_A = 64$, this would force firm B to choose $q_B = 28$ [= (120 − 64) ÷ 2]. At this combined output of 92, price would be \$28 and firm B would break even (profits = TR − TC = 28 · 28 − 784 = 0) and choose not to enter. Firm A would now have the market to itself, obtain a price of \$56 (= 120 − 64), and earn profits of \$2,800 (= 56 · 64 − 784). Economies of scale, combined with the ability to move first, provide firm A with a very profitable entry-deterring strategy. Of course, in the real world, the advantages of entering a market first may not be so clear-cut as Application 18.4: First-Mover Advantages illustrates.

■ Limit Pricing

So far our discussion of strategic considerations in entry decisions has focused on issues of sunk costs and output commitments. Prices were assumed to be determined through auction or Bertrand processes only after such commitments were made. A somewhat different approach to the entry deterrence question has concerned the possibility of an incumbent monopoly accomplishing this goal through its pricing policy alone. That is, are there situations where a monopoly might purposely choose a low ("limit") price policy with the goal of deterring entry into its market?

In most simple cases, the limit pricing strategy does not seem to yield maximum profits nor to be sustainable over time. If an incumbent monopoly opts for a price of $P_L < P_M$ (where P_M is the profit-maximizing price), it is obviously hurting its current-period profits. But this limit price will deter entry in the future only if P_L falls short of the average cost of any potential entrant. If the monopoly and its potential entrant have the same costs (and if capacity choices do not play the role they did in the previous example), the only limit price that is sustainable in the presence of potential entry is $P_L = AC$, adoption of which would obviously defeat the purpose of being a monopoly since profits would be zero. Hence, the basic monopoly model offers little room for limit price behavior—either there are barriers to entry that allow the monopoly to sustain P_M, or there are no such barriers in which case competitive pricing prevails.

■ Incomplete Information

Believable models of limit pricing behavior must therefore depart from traditional assumptions. The most important set of such models are those involving incomplete information. If an incumbent monopoly knows more about a particular market situation than does a potential entrant, it may be able to take advantage of its superior knowledge to deter entry. As an example, consider

APPLICATION 18.4
First-Mover Advantages

The first-mover advantages that arise in game theory are illustrated in a number of actual markets. Here we look at two types of advantages: (1) advantages that stem from economies of scale in production; and (2) advantages that arise in connection with the introduction of pioneering brands.

Economies of Scale

If there are economies of scale in production, the first firm into a market may "overbuild" its initial plant in the interest of achieving low costs in the future as demand for the product expands. In this way, future entry will be deterred. One of the first instances of this behavior studied by economists concerned the expansion of the Aluminum Company of America (Alcoa) immediately after World War II. In an important antitrust suit against the company, it was claimed that Alcoa, in an effort to foreclose entry by others, built far larger plants than was justified by current demand. Ultimately, however, the rapid growth in post-war aluminum demand together with the sale of government aluminum plants to Alcoa's competitors meant that this strategy did little to deter entry.

A similar case occurred during the 1970s in connection with the production of titanium dioxide.[1] DuPont was the largest producer of this product (which is the primary coloring agent in white paint), but the firm worried about potential expansions by its principal competitors. In an attempt to forestall new investment, DuPont decided to embark on a major expansion in its capacity to produce titanium dioxide. Several studies of this episode have concluded that DuPont's strategy was largely successful in deterring investment by others. In fact, the move brought a 1978 Federal Trade Commission antitrust complaint against the company. But the Commission ultimately could not prove that DuPont had intended to monopolize the titanium dioxide market.

Pioneering Brands

Introducing the first brand of a new product to its market seems to give it considerable advantages over its later arriving rivals. Such advantages have been obtained by a number of prescriptive drugs, by consumer products like laundry detergents (Tide), fluoride toothpaste (Crest), and deodorant soap (Dial), and by convenience items like disposable razors and lighters (Bic). Although traditional arguments about economies of scale in the production of these brands or in the advertising related to their introduction may explain some of these first-mover advantages, a more important reason may arise from the information problems faced by consumers.[2] Invention of a new product poses difficulty for consumers because they don't know whether it will do what it is supposed to do. Someone who buys the product thereby exposes herself to risk. If the product does work as advertised, a consumer may then decide to stick with it as other "me-too" brands are developed. Being first, therefore, has the advantage of prompting consumers to obtain initial information; they then see little gain from repeating the process. Only if there is a substantial price advantage will they depart from a pioneering brand that seems to do the job.

To Think About

1. Are economies of scale crucial to implementation of a successful strategy of entry-deterring plant expansion? Would such expansion be a profitable strategy under conditions of constant returns to scale?
2. Why is the existence of imperfect information crucial to the first-mover advantage of pioneering brands? Would pioneering brands enjoy any advantage in a world of homogeneous products and perfect information?

---

[1]See E. A. Hall, "An Analysis of Preemptive Behavior in the Titanium Dioxide Industry," *International Journal of Industrial Organization* (September 1990): 469–484.

[2]For additional details, see R. Schmalensee, "Product Differentiation Advantages of Pioneering Brands," *American Economic Review* (June 1982): 349–365.

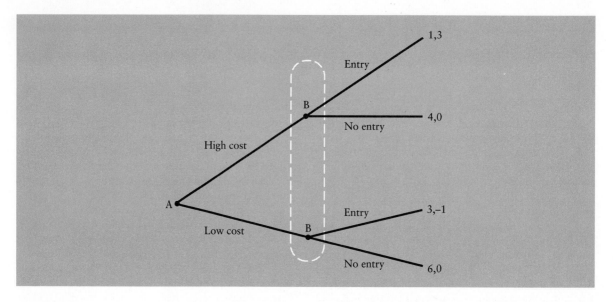

Figure 18.3
An Entry Game

Firm A has either a "high" or a "low" cost structure that cannot be observed by B. If B assigns a subjective probability (ρ) to the possibility that A is high cost, it will enter providing $\rho > \frac{1}{4}$. Firm A may try to influence B's probability estimate.

the game tree illustrated in Figure 18.3. Here firm A, the incumbent monopolist, may have either "high" or "low" production costs as a result of its past decisions. Firm A does not actually choose its costs currently but, because these costs are not known to B, we must allow for the two possibilities. Clearly the profitability of B's entry into the market depends on A's costs—with high costs B's entry is profitable ($p_B = 3$) whereas if A has low costs, entry is unprofitable ($p_B = -1$). What is B to do? One possibility would be for B to use whatever information it has to develop a subjective probability estimate of A's true cost structure. That is, B must assign probability estimates for whether firm A is "low cost" or "high cost." If B assumes there is a probability r that A has high cost and $(1 - \rho)$ that it has low cost, entry will yield a positive expected profit (see Chapter 7) provided

$$E(p_B) = \rho(3) + (1 - \rho)(-1) > 0 \qquad [18.10]$$

which holds for

$$\rho > 1/4. \qquad [18.11]$$

The particularly intriguing aspects of this game concern whether A can influence B's probability assessment. Clearly, regardless of its true costs, firm A is better-off if B adopts the no-entry strategy, and one way to assure that is for A to make B believe that it is likely it has low costs. As an extreme case, if A can convince B that it is definitely a low-cost producer ($r = 0$), B will be deterred from entry even if the true cost situation is otherwise. For example, if A chooses a low-price policy when it serves the market as a monopoly, this may signal to B that A's costs are low and thereby deter entry. Such strategy might be profitable for A even though it would require it to sacrifice some profits. This provides a possible rationale for low-limit pricing as an entry deterrence strategy.

■ Predatory Pricing

Tools used to study limit pricing can also shed light on the possibility for "predatory" pricing. Ever since the formation of the Standard Oil monopoly in the late nineteenth century, part of the mythology of American business is that John D. Rockefeller was able to drive his competitors out of business by charging ruinously low (predatory) prices. Although both the economic logic and the empirical facts behind this version of the Standard Oil story have generally been discounted (see Application 18.5: The Standard Oil Legend), the possibility of encouraging exit through predation continues to provide interesting opportunities for theoretical modeling.

The structure of many models of predatory behavior is similar to that used in limit pricing models; that is, the models stress asymmetric information. An incumbent firm wishes to encourage its rival to exit the market so it takes actions intended to affect the rival's view of the future profitability of market participation. The incumbent may, for example, adopt a low-price policy in an attempt to signal to its rival that its costs are low—even if they are not. Or the incumbent may adopt extensive advertising or product differentiation activities with the intention of convincing its rival that it has economies of scale. Once the rival is convinced that the incumbent firm possesses such advantages, it may recalculate the expected profitability of its production decisions and decide to exit the market. Of course, as in the limit pricing models, such successful predatory strategies are not a foregone conclusion. Their viability depends crucially on the nature of information in the market. Only if the monopoly can take advantage of its better information can predatory behavior succeed.

n-Player Game Theory

All of the game theory examples we have developed so far in this chapter involve only two players. Although this limitation is useful for illustrating some of the strategic issues that arise in the play of a game (or the operation of a duopoly market), it also tends to obscure some important questions. The most important additional element added to game theory when the study moves beyond two players is the possibility for the formation of subsets of players who agree on coordinated strategies. Although the possibility for forming such *coalitions* exists in two-player games (the two firms in a duopoly could form a cartel), the number of possible coalitions expands rapidly as games with larger

APPLICATION 18.5

The Standard Oil Legend

The Standard Oil case of 1911 was one of the landmarks of U.S. antitrust law. In that case, John D. Rockefeller's Standard Oil Company was found to have "attempted to monopolize" the production, refining, and distribution of petroleum in the United States, violating the Sherman Act. As a result of this finding, the company was split into several independent companies, many of which still exist today (Exxon, Amoco, Chevron, Mobile, and so forth). One of the ways that Standard Oil was found to have established its monopoly was through the use of "predatory pricing." It was claimed that the company would cut prices dramatically to drive rivals out of a particular market and then raise prices back to monopoly levels after the rivals had left the market or had sold out to Standard Oil. This view of how Standard Oil operated is one of the more durable ones on nineteenth-century business practices.

Theory of Predatory Pricing

Unfortunately, the notion that Standard Oil practiced such predatory pricing policies in order to discourage entry and discourage exit by its rivals makes little sense in terms of economic theory. As we have seen, if a would-be monopolist wishes to impose such costs on its rivals, it must sell its output below average cost, perhaps below marginal cost. It must also be willing to absorb the extra sales that such lowered prices would bring. The predator must, therefore, operate with relatively large losses for some time in the hope that the smaller losses this may cause rivals will eventually prompt them to give up. This strategy is inferior to the strategy of simply buying smaller rivals in the marketplace. Even if such mergers were illegal, it is unclear that the predator has longer staying power than its rivals in sticking to a low-price policy—especially since rivals know that price must eventually return to providing a normal profit.

Actual Evidence on Standard Oil

These thoughts prompted J. S. McGee to re-examine the historical record of what Standard Oil actually did. In a famous 1958 article, McGee concludes that Standard Oil neither tried to use predatory policies, nor did its actual price policies have the effect of driving rivals from the oil business.[1] In all, McGee looks at over 100 refineries that were bought by Standard Oil between 1871 and 1900. He finds no evidence that predatory behavior by Standard Oil caused these firms to sell out. Indeed, in many cases Standard paid quite good prices for these refineries, which themselves were reasonably profitable. McGee also looks in detail at the effect that Standard Oil's retailing activities had on the network of jobbers and small retailers who had grown up around the oil and kerosene business in the late nineteenth century. It seems clear that Standard's retailing methods were superior to those used previously (and were quickly adopted by other firms). The use of local price cutting does not seem to have been practiced by the company, however. Hence, although Standard Oil did eventually obtain an oil refining monopoly, which probably required some attention by policy makers, it did not appear to attain this position through predatory behavior.

To Think About

1. If the facts do not support the notion of predatory pricing by Standard Oil, why do you think the company is so widely believed to have practiced it? What kinds of market-wide trends were influencing oil pricing during the late nineteenth century? Might these have been mistaken for predatory behavior?

2. Another claim in the Standard Oil case is that Rockefeller obtained preferential rates from railroads to transport oil. Why might railroads have granted such rates to Rockefeller? Would they have an interest in refusing such rates to other similar shippers?

[1] J. S. McGee, "Predatory Price Cutting: The Standard Oil Case," *Journal of Law and Economics* (October 1958): 137–169.

numbers of players are considered. In some games, simply listing the number of potential coalitions and the payoffs they might receive can be a major task.

As in the formation of cartels in oligopolistic markets, the likelihood of forming successful coalitions in *n*-player games is importantly influenced by organizational costs. These costs involve both information costs associated with determining coalition strategies and enforcement costs associated with ensuring that a coalition's chosen strategy is actually followed by its members. If there are incentives for members to cheat on established coalition strategies, then monitoring and enforcement costs may be high. In some cases, such costs may be so high as to make the establishment of coalitions prohibitively costly. For these games, then, all *n*-players operate independently, and many of the insights from two-person game theory continue to hold.

Summary

In this chapter we have briefly examined the economic theory of games with particular reference to the use of that theory to explain strategic behavior in duopoly markets. Some of the conclusions of this examination include the following:

- Concepts such as players, strategies, and payoffs are common to all games.

- Many games also possess a number of types of equilibrium solutions. With a Nash equilibrium each player's strategic choice is optimal given its rival's choice. In multi-period games only Nash equilibria that involve credible threats are viable.

- The Prisoner's Dilemma represents a particularly instructive two-person game. In this game the most preferred outcome is unstable, though in repeated games the players may adopt various enforcement strategies.

- Game theoretic models of duopoly pricing start from the Bertrand result that the only Nash equilibrium in a simple game is competitive (marginal cost) pricing. Consideration of possible output commitment and first-mover strategies may result in noncompetitive results, however. Tacit collusion at the monopoly price is sustainable in infinite-period games under certain circumstances.

- Much of the game theoretic modeling of entry and exit stresses the importance of the informational environment. In situations of asymmetric information, incumbent firms may be able to capitalize on superior information by adopting strategies that result in entry deterrence.

Review Questions

1. In game theory the identity of players is usually assumed to be irrelevant—relabeling players has no effect on the analysis of the game. Describe the ways in which this assumption is similar to assumptions made about economic actors in competitive markets. Are there important ways in which they differ?

2. Express the notion of a Nash equilibrium as a maximization problem. What does each player maximize? What are the constraints in the problem? What is consistent about these constraints at the Nash equilibrium?

3. Is the Cournot equilibrium described in Chapter 17 also a Nash equilibrium? How might your answer depend on the way in which we define the potential players' strategies in this game?

4. Which of the following activities might be represented as a zero-sum game? Which are clearly not zero-sum?

   a. Flipping a coin for $1;
   b. Playing Blackjack;
   c. Choosing which candy bar to buy from a vendor;
   d. Reducing taxes through various "creative accounting" methods and seeking to avoid detection by the IRS;
   e. Deciding when to rob a particular house knowing that the residents may adopt various counter-theft strategies.

5. Why is the Prisoner's Dilemma a "dilemma" for the players involved? How might they solve this dilemma through pre-game discussions? If the game were repeated many times, can you also think of ways in which the dilemma might be resolved?

6. What does the Bertrand equilibrium assume about the nature of demand? Are the producers assumed to produce identical goods? How do consumers decide which producer to buy from? What are the consequences of changing these assumptions?

7. Why can the Cournot model from Chapter 17 be regarded as a choice of firms' "capacities"? What is "capacity" and how is this concept related to firms' cost functions?

8. What is a credible threat? Why are such threats more likely to play an important role in multi-period games than in single-period games?

9. "Tacit collusion only can exist in games of infinite duration." Explain why this is so and discuss its relevance to real-world markets.

10. What conditions are required for a firm to practice successful entry deterrence? How does imperfect information play a role in the most believable formulations of the strategy?

Problems

18.1 The table below reports the payoff matrix for an advertising game. Explain why the strategy pair "A:high, B:low" is a Nash equilibrium in this game and all the other strategy pairs are not.

		B's Strategies	
		High	**Low**
A's Strategies	**High**	A:5 B:2	A:3 B:3
	Low	A:4 B:3	A:2 B:4

18.2 Players A and B are engaged in a coin-matching game. Each shows a coin as either heads or tails. If the coins match, B pays A $1. If they differ, A pays B $1.

  a. Write down the payoff matrix for this game, and show that it does not contain a Nash equilibrium.
  b. How might the players choose their strategies in this case?

18.3 Smith and Jones are playing a number-matching game. Each chooses either 1, 2, or 3. If the numbers match, Jones pays Smith $3. If they differ, Smith pays Jones $1.

  a. Describe the payoff matrix for this game, and show that it does not possess a Nash equilibrium strategy pair.
  b. Show that with mixed strategies this game does have a Nash equilibrium if each player plays each number with probability $1/3$. What is the value of this game?

18.4 Suppose firms A and B each operate under conditions of constant average and marginal cost, but that $MC_A = 10$, $MC_B = 8$. The demand for the firms' output is given by

$$Q_D = 500 - 20P.$$

  a. If the firms practice Bertand competition, what will be the market price under a Nash equilibrium?
  b. What will the profits be for each firm?
  c. Will this equilibrium be Pareto efficient?

18.5 The entire world's supply of kryptonite is controlled by 20 people with each having a large supply of this potent material. The annual world demand for kryptonite is given by

$$Q = 10,000 - 1,000P$$

where P is the price per gram.

a. If all owners could conspire to rig the price of kryptonite, what price would they set and how much of their supply would they sell?
b. Why is the price computed in part a an unstable equilibrium?
c. Does a price for kryptonite exist that would be a stable equilibrium in the sense that no firm could gain by altering its output from that required to maintain this market price?

18.6 The game of "chicken" is played by two macho teens who speed toward each other on a single lane road. The first to veer off is branded the chicken whereas the one who doesn't turn gains peer group esteem. Of course, if neither veers, both die in the resulting crash. Payoffs to the chicken game are provided in the following table.

		B's Strategies	
		Chicken	Not Chicken
A's Strategies	Chicken	2, 2	1, 3
	Not Chicken	3, 1	0, 0

a. Does this game have a Nash equilibrium?
b. Is a threat by either not to chicken-out a credible one?
c. Would the ability of one player to firmly commit to a no chicken strategy (by, for example, throwing away the steering wheel) be desirable for that player?

18.7 Two firms (A and B) are considering bringing out competing brands of a healthy cigarette. Payoffs to the companies are as follows (A's profits are given first):

		Firm B	
		Produce	Don't Produce
Firm A	Produce	3, 3	5, 4
	Don't Produce	4, 5	2, 2

a. Does this game have a Nash equilibrium?
b. Does this game present any first-mover advantages for either firm A or firm B?
c. Would firm B find it in its interest to bribe firm A enough to stay out of the market?

18.8 The Wave Energy Technology (WET) company has a monopoly on the production of vibratory waterbeds. Demand for these beds is relatively inelastic—at a price of $1,000 per bed, 25,000 will be sold whereas at a price of $600, 30,000 will be sold. The only costs associated with waterbed production are the initial costs of building a plant. WET has already invested in a plant capable of producing up to 25,000 beds and this sunk cost is irrelevant to its pricing decisions.

    a. Suppose a would-be entrant to this industry could always be assured of half the market but would have to invest $10 million in a plant. Construct the payoff matrix for WET's strategies (P = 1,000 or P = 600) against the entrant's strategies (enter, don't enter). Does this game have a Nash equilibrium?

    b. Suppose WET could invest $5 million in enlarging its existing plant to produce 40,000 beds. Would this strategy be a profitable way to deter entry by its rival?

18.9 An individual is thinking of going on a picnic but fears it might rain. Utilities possible in this situation are reflected in the following table:

	Rain	No Rain
Picnic	0	20
No Picnic	5	10

    a. Suppose this individual adopts the pessimistic attitude that "whatever can go wrong will go wrong," which strategy should she choose? (Technically this is called a maximin strategy because it is the maximum utility from all the worst outcomes.)

    b. Suppose instead this individual assigns a probability to the possibility of rain and maximizes expected utility. What is the maximum probability of rain for which she will still opt to go on the picnic?

18.10 Smith and Jones are stranded on a desert island with fixed initial endowments of clams and bread. Instead of seeking mutually beneficial trades directly, they opt for a bidding strategy in which they use their initial clam endowments to bid for bread. The bread is deposited in a safe place, and each person states how many clams he or she will offer for it. When the bids are revealed, the available bread is then split in proportion to each bid, and the net difference in clams bid is paid from one trader to the other. If, for example, Smith bids one clam and Jones bids two clams, Smith gets $1/3$ of the bread and Jones gets $2/3$. On net, one clam is transferred from Jones to Smith.

    a. Sketch an Edgeworth box diagram that shows the initial endowments of Smith and Jones.

    b. On your Edgeworth box, show how a final allocation is determined given a particular set of bids by Smith and Jones.

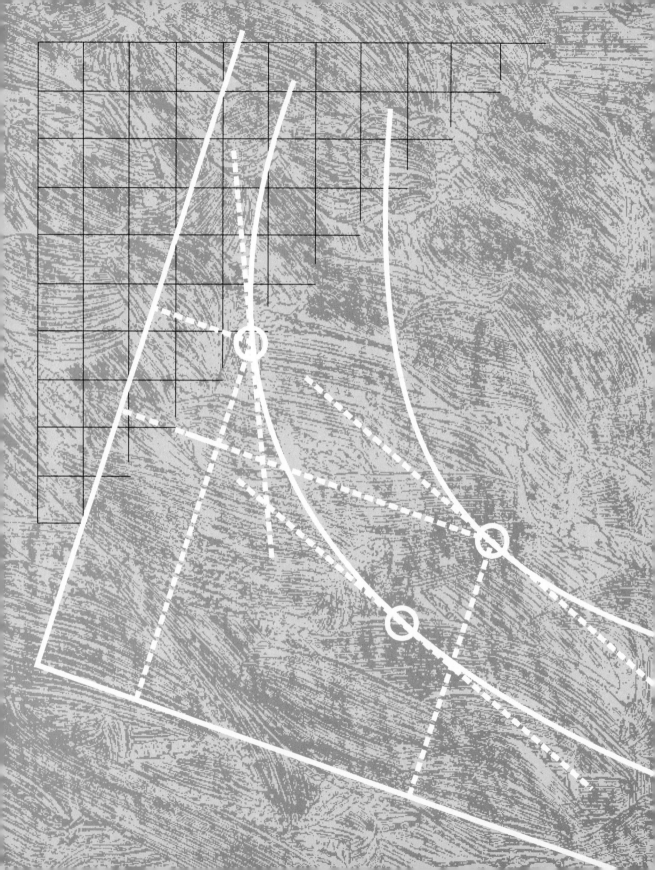

"The produce of the earth . . . is divided among . . . the proprietor of land, the owner of the stock of capital necessary for its cultivation, and the laborers by whose industry it is calculated. To determine the laws which regulate this distribution is the principal problem of Political Economy."

David Ricardo

Principles of Political Economy and Taxation, 1817

Part Six illustrates that factors of production also have prices. Labor services are purchased for a wage rate per hour, machines have rental rates, and rent must usually be paid for the use of land. In this part we investigate how those prices are determined.

Chapter 19 discusses the demand for factors of production, which differs in several ways from the demand concepts we have been using so far. Most important, here firms are doing the hiring, and their demand for any factor of production is a *derived demand.* It depends indirectly on the demand for the good that the firm produces. Much of the discussion in Chapter 19 assumes that firms hire inputs in perfectly competitive markets. That is, firms are assumed to be price takers— their actions have no effect on the wage rate they must pay for labor or the rental rate they must pay for capital. In the final sections of the chapter, however, we explore the situation of a monopsony (single buyer) and show how the market power possessed by the monopsony can lead to the same general kinds of distortions in the allocation of resources that we described earlier for the case of monopoly.

In Chapter 20 we discuss three particular aspects of the labor supply. First we analyze the simple labor supply decisions of one person and then construct a market supply of labor curve. Next we briefly discuss occupational choice and the concept of compensating wage differentials. Finally, we show how unions can be incorporated into the general theory of how wages are determined.

In Chapter 21 we look at the market for capital. The central purpose of the chapter is to emphasize the connection between capital and the allocation of resources over time. The appendix to Chapter 21 presents some mathematical results about interest rates that are widely used in the study of capital and investment.

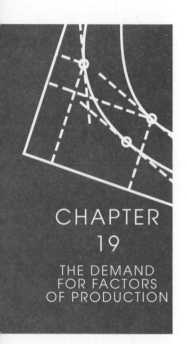

CHAPTER
19

THE DEMAND
FOR FACTORS
OF PRODUCTION

As is true for any market price, the prices of factors of production are determined by the combined influence of demand and supply. In this case, however, the identities of the market participants are reversed from the situation we have been concerned with so far. Now firms appear on the demand side of the market, hiring resources that they can use in their production activities. Any theory of resource demand must therefore start from a model of firms' behavior. In this chapter, we will examine several such models. In the process, we will say relatively little about the supply side of the market. We implicitly assume that there are a large number of individuals who supply productive inputs (that is, labor, capital, and natural resources) and that these individuals act as price takers. We will also assume for the most part that individuals as a group will supply more of an input to the market as its price rises. Any attempt to describe in detail the economics of these supply decisions will be postponed to Chapters 20 and 21, however.

Marginal Productivity Theory of Factor Demand

In Chapter 13 we looked briefly at Ricardo's theory of economic rent. This theory was an important start to the development of marginal economics. Ricardo's notion that price is determined by output demand and by the costs of the marginal producer in many ways represents the seed from which modern microeconomics grew. One application of his approach was the development of the "marginal productivity" theory of the demand for factors of production. This section investigates that theory in detail.

■ Profit-Maximizing Behavior and the Hiring of Inputs

The basic concept of the marginal productivity theory of factor demand has already been stated in Chapter 10 when we discussed profit maximization. There we showed that one implication of the profit-maximization hypothesis is that the firm will make marginal input choices. More precisely, we showed that a profit-maximizing firm will hire additional units of any input up to the point at which the additional revenue from hiring one more unit of the input is exactly equal to the cost of hiring that unit. If we use ME_K and ME_L to denote the marginal expense associated with hiring one more unit of capital and labor, respectively, and let MR_K and MR_L be the extra revenue that hiring these units of capital and labor allows the firm to bring in, then profit maximization requires that

$$ME_K = MR_K;$$

$$ME_L = MR_L. \qquad [19.1]$$

Our analysis in the remainder of this chapter applies this marginal concept in various situations.

■ Price-Taking Behavior

If the firm is a price taker in the capital and labor markets, it is easy to simplify the marginal expense idea. In this case, the firm can always hire an extra hour of capital input at the prevailing rental rate (v) and an extra hour of labor at the wage rate (w). Therefore, Equation 19.1 reduces to

$$v = ME_K = MR_K;$$

$$w = ME_L = MR_L. \qquad [19.2]$$

These equations simply say that a profit-maximizing firm that is a price taker for the inputs it buys should hire these inputs up to the point at which their unit cost is equal to the revenue generated by the last one hired. If the firm's hiring decisions affect input prices it will have to take that into account. We will look at such a situation later in this chapter.

■ Marginal Revenue Product

To analyze the additional revenue yielded by hiring one more unit of an input is a two-step process. First we must ask how much output the additional input can produce. As we discussed in Chapter 8, this magnitude is given by the input's marginal physical productivity. For example, if a firm hires one more worker for an hour to make shoes, the worker's marginal physical productivity (MP_L) is simply the number of additional pairs of shoes per hour that the firm can make.

Once the additional output has been produced, it must be sold. Assessing the value of that sale is the second step in analyzing the revenue yielded by hiring one more unit of an input. We have looked at this issue quite extensively in previous chapters—the extra revenue obtained from selling an additional unit of output is, by definition, marginal revenue (MR). So, if an extra worker can produce two pairs of shoes per hour and the firm can take in $4 per pair from selling these shoes, then hiring the worker for an hour has increased the firm's revenues by $8. This is the figure the firm will compare to the worker's hourly wage to decide whether he or she should be hired. So now our profit-maximizing rules become

$$v = ME_K = MR_K = MP_K \cdot MR;$$

$$w = ME_L = MR_L = MP_L \cdot MR. \qquad [19.3]$$

Marginal revenue product

The extra revenue obtained from selling the output produced by hiring an extra worker or machine.

The terms on the right side of Equation 19.3 are called the **marginal revenue product** of capital and labor, respectively. They show how much extra revenue is brought in by hiring one more unit of the input. These are precisely what we need to study the demand for inputs and how the demand might change if wages or rental rates change.

■ A Special Case—Marginal Value Product

The profit-maximizing rules for input choices can be made even clearer if we assume that the firm we are examining sells its output in a competitive market. In that case, the firm will also be a price taker in the goods market, so the marginal revenue it takes in from selling one more unit of output is the market price (P) at which the output sells. Using the result that, for a price taker in the goods market, marginal revenue is equal to price, Equation 19.3 becomes

$$v = MP_K \cdot P;$$

$$w = MP_L \cdot P \qquad [19.4]$$

as the conditions for a profit maximum.[1] We call the terms on the right-hand side of Equation 19.4 the **marginal value product** (MVP) of capital and labor, respectively, since they do indeed put a value on these inputs' marginal physical productivities. Our final condition for maximum profits in this simple situation is

$$v = MVP_K;$$

$$w = MVP_L. \qquad [19.5]$$

To see why these are required for profit maximization, consider again our shoe worker example. Suppose the worker can make two pairs of shoes per hour and that shoes sell for $4. The worker's marginal value product is $8 per hour. If the hourly wage is less than this (say, $5 per hour), the firm can increase profits by $3 by employing the worker for one more hour; profits were not at a maximum so the extra labor should be hired. Similarly, if the wage is $10 per hour, profits would rise by $2 if one less hour of labor were used. Only if the wage and labor's marginal value product are equal will profits truly be as large as possible. Application 19.1: Jet Fuel and Hybrid Seeds looks at profit-maximizing choices for these vital inputs. Of course, as Application 19.2: Input Demand by Nonprofit Firms shows, if a firm has no interest in profits, it will not necessarily follow these rules, though they still may offer some useful insights.

■ A Graphical Demonstration

Figure 19.1 shows the profit-maximizing choice of, say, labor input graphically. The horizontal axis in the figure records the hours of labor hired, and the vertical axis shows the MVP for each of these levels.[2] We can construct an MVP curve for labor directly from the marginal physical product of labor curve (MP_L) introduced in Chapter 8 by multiplying MP_L by the market price of the firm's output. The resulting MVP_L curve is shown in Figure 19.1. The downward slope of that curve reflects the assumption of a diminishing marginal physical productivity: the more labor hired, the lower will be labor's marginal physical productivity and the lower also will be its marginal value product.

The profit-maximizing amount of labor to hire can be found by recording the hourly wage rate (w^*) that firms must pay on the vertical axis. At that wage, profit maximization requires hiring L^* workers. Only for this level of

Marginal value product

A special case of marginal revenue product in which the firm is a price taker for its output.

---

[1]Equation 19.4 implies cost minimization for this firm. Dividing the two equations gives

$$MP_L/MP_K = w/v,$$

but in Chapter 8 we showed that RTS (of L for K) = MP_L/MP_K. A firm that pursues a marginal productivity approach to input demand will equate

$$RTS \text{ (of L for K)} = w/v,$$

and this is what is required for (long-run) cost minimization.

[2]Although here we analyze only the case of labor input, an analysis of the demand for capital input would proceed in exactly the same way. Throughout our discussion we assume the firm is a price taker in the output market so that the marginal value product is the correct demand concept.

APPLICATION 19.1
Jet Fuel and Hybrid Seeds

Although much of our discussion of factor demand has focused on general capital and labor resources, in many cases the theory is illustrated most clearly by looking at more narrowly defined inputs. Here we look at two of these.

Jet Fuel

The price of aviation jet fuel has fluctuated widely over the past twenty years. Between 1972 and 1980 prices increased more than sevenfold, and fuel costs rose from 13 percent to nearly 30 percent of total airline costs. From 1980 to 1990, on the other hand, jet fuel prices fell nearly 40 percent, and their relationship to total costs returned to near the 1972 level. Airlines' reactions to these changes were relatively modest over the short-run. With existing fleets of aircraft, little could be done to fly them along more fuel-efficient flight paths. Over the long run, however, entirely new fleets of fuel-efficient planes could be brought into service, and that appears to be what happened during the late 1970s and early 1980s. Between 1972 and 1986 passenger miles per gallon of fuel approximately doubled, rising from 14 to 28 miles per gallon. Declining fuel prices throughout the 1980s significantly reduced the incentive to continue these efficiency improvements, and average miles per gallon actually fell a bit toward the end of the decade. Introductions of new fuel-efficient aircraft were also curtailed as the need to economize declined. Airlines' fuel demands were clearly being influenced by a series of very careful profitability calculations.[1]

Hybrid Seeds

The use of hybrid seeds to grow corn began during the 1930s, and in ensuing decades, the use of this newly invented input spread throughout the world. In one of the first studies of the proliferation of such a technical innovation, Z. Griliches examined U.S. farmers' decisions to adopt hybrid seeds.[2] He showed how adoption decisions were motivated mainly by profitability calculations. In states where conditions resulted in large increases in corn yields from hybrids (such as Iowa), adoptions came rapidly. For states where growing conditions were not favorable to hybrids (such as Alabama), adoptions proceeded much more slowly. Farmers' decisions to adopt hybrids also seemed to be based primarily on the productivity of the innovations. More recent studies of adoptions of hybrids reach a similar conclusion. In nations where hybrid seeds are profitable (such as India), they are widely adopted by farmers, and have resulted in a vast increase in agricultural output (the Green Revolution). Elsewhere (in West Africa, for example), hybrid seeds do not appear to be profitable innovations and are little used.

To Think About

1. Would different airlines react in the same way to rising (or falling) prices for jet fuel? What factors would determine these reactions? How would airlines' competitive positions be affected by their ability to restrain the effects of fuel price increases or cuts?

2. The Griliches' article on hybrid corn was part of a larger debate on the "rationality" of U.S. farmers. Do farmers really maximize profits? Are their decisions dictated by marginal productivity considerations? What other explanation might account for Griliches' findings on the adoption of hybrid seeds?

---

[1]Numbers in this application are from the U.S. Statistical Abstract, 1991. For a discussion of the interaction between fuel costs and the demand for air travel, see D. Gately, "Taking Off: The U.S. Demand for Air Travel and Jet Fuel," *Energy Journal* (October 1988): 63–91.

[2]Z. Griliches, "Hybrid Corn: An Exploration in the Economics of Technical Change," *Econometrica* (October 1957): 501–522.

APPLICATION 19.2

Input Demand by Nonprofit Firms

Our discussion of input demand so far has assumed that firms seek maximum profits. If firms do not behave in this way, they may not make the kinds of marginal input choices we have described. Studies of nonprofit firms, for example, suggest that these firms' input choices may depart in systematic ways from those dictated by profit maximization and that such departures can have important implications for the relative efficiency with which various inputs are used. Here we look at two examples: cultural institutions and hospitals.

Cultural Institutions

Practically all symphonic, theater, opera, and ballet companies operate on a nonprofit basis. Often these firms rely on outside sources of funding (such as gifts or government aid) to cover perennial deficits between costs and revenues. Given this arrangement, it is not surprising that these firms may not employ the various inputs they use (artists, support personnel, and capital) in the same way that profit-maximizing firms would. For example, one study by J. Gapinski of 154 performing arts companies found that these firms typically over-employed artists and under-employed support personnel throughout the 1960s and 1970s.[1] Although profit maximization suggests that an input's marginal value product should equal its price, Gapinsky found that an artist's marginal value product was only about 60 percent of his or her wage in theater and ballet and was less than 40 percent of his or her wage in opera or in an orchestra. For support personnel such as janitors, ushers, and administrators, on the other hand, the author found that most arts companies operated in a range of increasing marginal productivities—implying that more support personnel should be hired by a profit maximizer.

Why should cultural institutions depart in these ways from profit maximization in their input choices? One explanation may be that contributors to the arts have strong preferences favoring the employment of artists. If governments want to subsidize not only the arts but the artists too, or if private donors enjoy post-performance gatherings, administrators will probably respond to these preferences. They may then find it necessary to skimp on support personnel to save on costs.

Hospitals

Most hospitals in the United States also operate on a nonprofit basis. They consequently have characteristics that resemble cultural institutions in that their input choices may be different from those that a profit-maximizing firm might make. Indeed, several studies have found that nonprofit hospitals tend to use more highly-skilled labor (physicians, registered nurses) and less low-skilled labor than do proprietary (for profit) hospitals.[2]

Nonprofit hospitals also tend to make more extensive use of high-technology surgical and diagnostic equipment than might be warranted by the costs and productivities involved. A possible explanation is that hospital decisions are often made by physicians and other administrators who have preferences favoring use of such inputs. That is, nonprofit hospitals may employ rather elaborate technology such as CAT scanners or intensive-care facilities that offer training or other opportunities for their physicians. Profit-making hospitals, on the other hand, may make do with lower-cost facilities.

To Think About

1. Does it make sense to talk about an opera, ballet, or orchestra substituting one input for another? After all, it takes a certain size cast to produce *Aida* or *Fidelio* and a full orchestra and chorus to perform Beethoven's *Ninth Symphony*. How could firms economize on artists and use more ancillary personnel?
2. If profit-making hospitals use less elaborate technology than do nonprofit hospitals, do they necessarily provide lower-quality care?

---

[1]J. H. Gapinski, "The Production of Culture," *Review of Economics and Statistics* (November 1980): 578–586.

[2]See J. P. Newhouse, "Toward a Theory of Non-Profit Institutions: An Economic Model of a Hospital," *American Economic Review* (March 1970): 64–74.

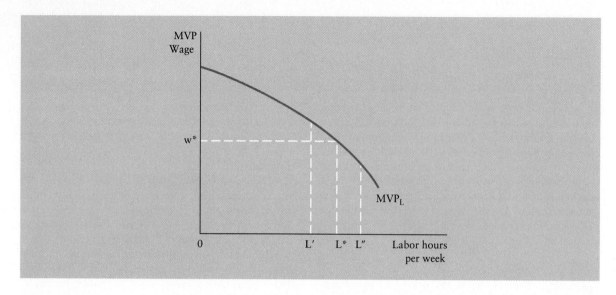

**Figure 19.1
Profit-Maximizing
Input Choice**

The marginal value product curve for labor (MVP_L) is constructed by multiplying labor's marginal physical productivity times the market price of the firm's output. The curve is downward sloping because of the assumption that labor exhibits a diminishing marginal physical productivity. At a wage of w^*, profit maximization requires that L^* units of labor input be hired.

labor input does $w^* = MVP_L$. For levels of labor input less than L^* (say, L') labor's MVP will exceed the market wage, and it would be profitable to hire more workers. Quantities of labor input greater than L^* (say, L''), on the other hand, have an MVP that falls short of w^*, and profits would be increased by cutting back on employment. Only at L^* is the cost of hiring an extra worker exactly equal to the revenue that hiring the worker provides to the firm: only at L^* is the firm maximizing profits.

If the market wage were to change, we would expect the profit-maximizing quantity of labor input to change also. We examine that possibility in the next section. In our investigation we continue to assume that the firm is a price taker for both the inputs it buys and the output it sells. The analysis would be only slightly changed if we studied a case of imperfect competition in the goods market. In this case marginal revenue (MR) would be less than market price (P), but it would be a simple matter to take that into account.

Responses to Changes in Input Prices

Suppose the price of labor (w) were to fall. It seems reasonable that firms might demand more labor in response to such a change. In this section we provide a detailed analysis of why the model of a profit-maximizing firm supports this conclusion.

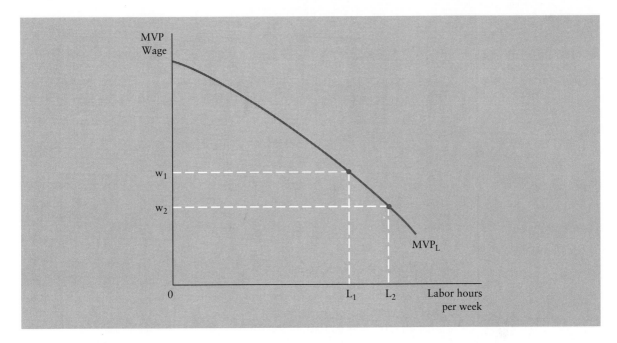

At a wage rate w_1, profit maximization requires that L_1 labor input be hired. If the wage rate falls to w_2, more labor (L_2) will be hired because of the assumed negative slope of the MVP_L curve.

Figure 19.2
Change in Labor Input When Wage Falls: Single-Input Case

■ Single-Input Case

As a simple first case, let us assume that a firm uses only labor to produce its output. The firm's marginal value product curve is shown in Figure 19.2. At a wage of w_1 the firm's profit-maximizing choice of labor input is given by L_1. The firm will persist in hiring L_1 units of labor as long as the conditions it faces do not change.

If the wage rate were to fall to w_2, more labor (L_2) would be demanded. At such a lower wage, more labor can be hired because the firm can "afford" to have a lower marginal physical productivity from the labor it employs. If it continued to hire only L_1, the firm would not be maximizing profits since, at the margin, labor would now be capable of producing more in additional revenue than hiring additional labor would cost. For the single-input case, the assumption of a diminishing marginal productivity of labor ensures that a fall in the price of labor will cause more labor to be hired.[3] The marginal value product curve shows this response.

---

[3]Since the marginal productivity of labor is positive, hiring more labor also implies that output will increase when w declines.

Table 19.1	Labor Input per Hour	Hamburgers Produced per Hour	Marginal Product (Hamburger)	Marginal Value Product ($1.00 per Hamburger)
Hamburger Heaven's Profit-Maximizing Hiring Decision	1	20.0	20.0	$20.00
	2	28.3	8.3	8.30
	3	34.6	6.3	6.30
	4	40.0	5.4	5.40
	5	44.7	4.7	4.70
	6	49.0	4.3	4.30
	7	52.9	3.9	3.90
	8	56.6	3.7	3.70
	9	60.0	3.4	3.40
	10	63.2	3.2	3.20

■ A Numerical Example

As a numerical example of these input choices, let's look again at the hiring decision for Hamburger Heaven first discussed in Chapter 9. Table 19.1 repeats the productivity information for the case in which Hamburger Heaven uses four grills (K = 4). As the table shows, the marginal productivity of labor declines as more workers are assigned to use grills each hour—the first worker hired turns out 20 (heavenly) hamburgers per hour, whereas the tenth hired produces only 3.2 hamburgers per hour. To calculate these workers' marginal value products, we simply multiply these physical productivity figures by the price of hamburgers, $1.00. These results appear in the final column of Table 19.1. With a market wage of $5.00 per hour, Hamburger Heaven should hire four workers. The marginal value product of each of these workers exceeds $5.00, so the firm earns some incremental profit on each of them. The fifth worker's MVP is only $4.70, however, so it does not make sense to add that worker.

The number of workers hired in this example is precisely the number required to minimize average cost with four grills in operation (see Chapter 9). Profit maximization and cost minimization yield the same result. If the price of hamburgers had been higher than $1.00, however, the MVP figures in the final column of Table 19.1 would have been higher, and the firm might have hired more workers (how many would be hired if hamburgers sold for $1.25?). A rise in the price of hamburgers would provide an incentive for Hamburger Heaven to produce more burgers and, in the short run, to do so by adding more workers to use its fixed number of grills.

At a wage other than $5.00 per hour, Hamburger Heaven would hire a different number of workers. At $6.00 per hour, for example, only three workers would be hired. With wages of $4.00 per hour, on the other hand, six workers would be employed. The MVP calculation provides complete information about Hamburger Heaven's short-run hiring decisions. Of course, a change in the wages of burger-flippers might also cause the firm to reconsider how many grills it uses—a subject that we now investigate.

■ Two-Input Case

For the case where the firm can vary two (or more) inputs the story is considerably more complex. The assumption of a diminishing marginal physical product of labor can be misleading here. If w falls, there will be a change not only in labor input but also in capital input as a new cost-minimizing combination of inputs is chosen (see our analysis in Chapter 9). When capital input changes, the entire MP_L function shifts (workers now have a different amount of capital to work with), and our earlier analysis of how wages affect hiring cannot be made. The remainder of this section presents a series of observations that establish that even with many inputs, a fall in w will lead to an increase in the quantity of labor demanded.

■ Substitution Effect

In some ways analyzing the two-input case is similar to our analysis of the individual's response to a change in the price of a good in Chapter 4. When w falls, we can decompose the total effect on the quantity of L hired into two components: a substitution effect and an output effect.

To study the **substitution effect,** we hold q constant at q_1. With a fall in w there will be a tendency to substitute labor for capital in the production of q_1. This effect is illustrated in Panel a in Figure 19.3. Since the condition for minimizing the cost of producing q_1 requires that RTS = w/v, a fall in w will necessitate a movement from input combination A to combination B. Because the isoquants have been assumed to exhibit a diminishing RTS, it is clear from

■
Substitution effect

In the theory of production, the substitution of one input for another while holding output constant in response to a change in the input's price.

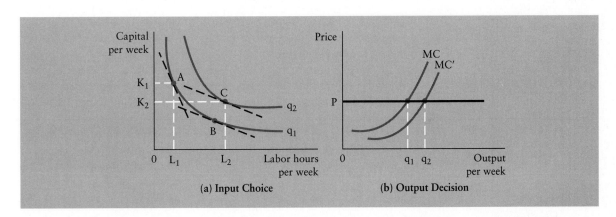

(a) Input Choice   (b) Output Decision

When the price of labor falls, the substitution effect causes more labor to be purchased even if output is held constant. This is shown as a movement from point A to point B in Panel a. The change in w will also shift the firm's expansion path and its marginal cost curve. A normal situation might be for the MC curve to shift downward in response to a decrease in w, as shown in Panel b. With this new curve (MC') a higher level of output (q_2) will be chosen. The hiring of labor will increase (to L_2) from this output effect.

Figure 19.3
Substitution and Output Effects of a Decrease in the Price of Labor

the diagram that this substitution effect must cause labor input to rise in response to the fall in w. The firm now decides to produce q_1 in a more labor-intensive way.

▪ Output Effect

▪
Output effect

The effect of an input price change on the amount of the input that the firm hires that results from a change in the firm's output level.

It is, however, not completely correct to hold q output constant when w falls. When the firm changes its level of production—the **output effect**—the analogy to a person's utility-maximization problem breaks down. The reason for this is that consumers have budget constraints, but firms do not. Firms produce as much as profit maximization requires; their need for inputs is derived from these production decisions. In order to investigate what happens to the quantity of output produced, we must therefore investigate the firm's profit-maximizing output decision. A fall in w, because it changes relative factor costs, will shift the firm's expansion path. Consequently, all the firm's cost curves will be shifted, and probably some output level other than q_1 will be chosen.

Panel b in Figure 19.3 illustrates the most common case. As a result of the fall in w, the marginal cost curve for the firm has shifted downward to MC'. The profit-maximizing level of output rises from q_1 to q_2.[4] The profit-maximizing condition (P = MC) is now satisfied at a higher level of output. Returning to Panel a, this increase in output will cause even more labor input to be demanded. The combined result of both the substitution and the output effects is to move the input choice to point C on the firm's isoquant for output level q_2. Both effects work to increase L in response to a decrease in w.[5]

▪ Summary of a Firm's Demand for Labor

We can summarize our findings about a firm's response to a fall in w by concluding that a profit-maximizing firm will increase its hiring of labor for two reasons. First, the firm will substitute the now cheaper labor for other inputs that are now relatively more expensive. This is the substitution effect. Second, the wage decline will reduce the firm's marginal costs, thereby causing it to increase output and to increase the hiring of all inputs including labor. This is the output effect.

This conclusion holds for any input, and it can be reversed to show that an increase in the price of an input will cause the firm to hire less of that input. We have shown that the firm's demand curve for an input will be unambiguously downward sloping: the lower its price, the more of the input will be demanded.[6]

---

[4]Price (P) has been assumed to be constant. If all firms in an industry were confronted with a decline in w, all would change their output levels; the industry supply curve would shift outward, and consequently P would fall. As long as the market demand curve for the firm's output is negatively sloped, however, the analysis in this chapter would not be seriously affected by this observation since the lower P will lead to more output being demanded.

[5]No definite statement can be made about how the quantity of capital (or any other input) changes in response to a decline in w. The substitution and output effects work in opposite directions (as can be seen in Figure 19.3), and the precise outcome depends on the relative sizes of these effects.

[6]Actually, a proof of this assertion is not as simple as is implied here. The complicating factor arises when the input in question is "inferior," and it is no longer true that the marginal cost curve shifts downward when the price

Responsiveness of Input Demand to Price Changes

The notions of substitution and output effects help to explain how responsive to price changes the demand for a factor might be. Suppose the wage rate rose. We already know that less labor will be demanded. Now we wish to investigate whether this decrease in quantity demanded will be large or small.

■ Ease of Substitution

First, consider the substitution effect. The decrease in the hiring of labor from a rise in w will depend on how easy it is for firms to substitute other factors of production for labor. Some firms may find it relatively simple to substitute machines for workers, and for these firms the quantity of labor demanded will decrease substantially. Other firms may produce with a fixed proportions technology. For them substitution will be impossible. The size of the substitution effect may also depend on the length of time allowed for adjustment. In the short run, a firm may have a stock of machinery that requires a fixed complement of workers. Consequently, the short-run substitution possibilities are slight. Over the long run, however, this firm may be able to adapt its machinery to use less labor per machine; the possibilities of substitution may now be substantial. For example, a rise in the wages of coal miners will have little short-run substitution effect since existing coal-mining equipment requires a certain number of workers to operate it. In the long run, however, there is clear evidence that mining can be made more capital intensive by designing more complex machinery. In the long run, capital has been substituted for labor on a large scale.

■ Costs and the Output Effect

An increase in the wage rate will also raise firms' costs. In a competitive market this will cause the price of the good being produced to rise, and people will reduce their purchases of that good. Consequently, firms will lower their levels of production; because less output is being produced, the output effect will cause less labor to be demanded. In this way the output effect reinforces the substitution effect. The size of this output effect will depend on (1) how large the increase in marginal costs brought about by the wage rate increase is, and (2) how much quantity demanded will be reduced by a rising price. The size of the first of these components depends on how "important" labor is in total production costs, whereas the size of the second depends on how price-elastic the demand for the product is.

---

of such a factor declines. Nevertheless, it can be shown that, as long as the good that is being produced has a downward-sloping demand curve, the firm's demand for the factor will also be negatively sloped.

In industries for which labor costs are a major portion of total costs and for which demand is very elastic, output effects will be large. For example, an increase in wages for restaurant workers is likely to induce a large negative output effect in the demand for such workers, since labor costs are a significant portion of restaurant operating costs and the demand for meals eaten out is relatively price-elastic. An increase in wages will cause a big price rise, and this will cause people to reduce sharply the number of meals they eat out. On the other hand, output effects in the demand for pharmaceutical workers are probably small. Direct labor costs are a small fraction of drug production costs, and the demand for drugs is price-inelastic. Wage increases will have only a small effect on costs, and any increases in price that do result will not cause demand for drugs to be reduced significantly.

Overall, then, the effect of a wage change will be determined by the size of the substitution and income effects it causes. In Application 19.3: The Minimum Wage, we look at how these insights can help to explain the possible effects of increases in the minimum wage.

Monopsony

In many situations, the firm is not a price taker for the inputs it buys. It may be necessary for the firm to offer a wage above that currently prevailing to attract more employees, or the firm may be able to get a better price on some equipment by restricting its purchases. To explore these situations, it is most convenient to examine the polar case of **monopsony** (a single buyer) in a factor market.

■ Marginal Expense

If there is only one buyer of an input, that firm faces the entire market supply curve for the input. In order to increase its hiring of labor, say, by one or more units, the firm must move to a higher point on this supply curve. This will involve paying not only a higher wage to the last worker hired but also additional wages to those workers already employed. The marginal cost of hiring the extra unit of labor therefore exceeds its wage rate, and the price-taking assumption we made earlier no longer holds. Instead, for a monopsonist facing an upward-sloping supply curve for an input, the **marginal expense** will exceed the market price of the input. For labor input, for example, the marginal expense (ME_L) of hiring one more worker exceeds the market wage (w).

Notice the similarity between the concept of the marginal expense of an input and the marginal revenue for a monopolist. Both concepts are intended to be used when firms possess market power and their choices have an effect

■ Monopsony

A firm that is the only hirer in a particular input market.

■ Marginal expense

The cost of hiring one more unit of an input. Will exceed the price of the input if the firm faces an upward-sloping supply curve for the input.

APPLICATION 19.3
The Minimum Wage

The Fair Labor Standards Act of 1938 established a national minimum wage of $.25 per hour. Since that time, the minimum wage has been raised several times in response to general inflation and changing social values. In the early 1990s, the minimum wage will rise to $4.55.

A Graphic Analysis

Figure 1 illustrates the possible effects of a minimum wage. Panel a shows the supply and demand curves for labor. Given these curves, an equilibrium wage rate, w_1, is established in the market. At this wage, a typical firm hires l_1 (shown on the firm's isoquant map in Panel b). Suppose now that a minimum wage of ($w_2 > w_1$) is imposed by law. This new wage will cause the firm to reduce its demand for labor from l_1 to l_2. At the same time, more labor (L_3) will be supplied at w_2 than was supplied at the lower wage rate. The imposition of the minimum wage will result in an excess of the supply of labor over the demand for labor of $L_3 - L_2$. This excess supply is what we mean by "unemployment."

Minimum Wages and Teenage Unemployment

There is some empirical evidence that changes in the minimum wage law have had serious effects in increasing teenage unemployment. Teenagers are the labor-market participants most likely to be affected by minimum wage laws, because their skills usually represent the lower end of the spectrum. An increase in minimum wages may cause employers to substitute capital and skilled labor for what has become more expensive, unskilled teenage labor. It may also have large negative output effects, because the products produced by teenage employees (services, for example) usually have a fairly high price elasticity. In recent years, teenage unemployment has increased rapidly. Particularly hard hit have been teenage minority group members, for whom unemployment rates often exceed 30 percent. Although there are several factors that may account for such statistics (unstable employment opportunities, discrimination in employment, long periods of searching for jobs),

Figure 1
Effects of a Minimum Wage in a Perfectly Competitive Labor Market

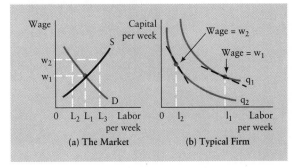

(a) The Market **(b) Typical Firm**

The imposition of a minimum wage (w_2) causes the firm to reduce labor usage to l_2 because it will both substitute capital (and other inputs) for labor and cut back output.

many economists assign an important role to statutory changes in the minimum wage. For example, one major study in the 1970s found that each 1 percent increase in the minimum wage resulted in a reduction of 0.3 percent in teenagers' share of total employment.[1]

Minimum Wages and Poverty

Of course, those who keep their jobs when minimum wages increase do earn more. The notion that minimum wages may help the poor is probably the most important reason for the policy's political popularity. It is important, however, to be careful about equating minimum wage workers with "the poor" because many people who work in minimum wage jobs live in nonpoor families. Indeed, one study reports that only about 11 percent of the gains from raising the minimum wage go to poor families.[2]

To Think About

1. Does a minimum wage increase or decrease total wages received by workers affected by it? How does your answer depend on the elasticity of demand for labor?
2. How does a minimum wage affect the demand for workers who are paid wages above the minimum wage?

[1]Finis Welch, "Minimum Wage Legislation in the United States," *Economic Inquiry* (September 1974): 285–318.

[2]R. V. Burkhauser and T. A. Finegan, "The Minimum Wage and the Poor: The End of a Relationship," *Journal of Policy Analysis and Management* (Winter 1989): 54–71.

on prices. In such situations firms are no longer price takers. Instead, firms will recognize that their actions affect prices and will use this information in making decisions.

■ A Numerical Illustration

This distinction is easiest to see with a numerical example. Suppose (as is probably the case) that the Yellowstone Park Company is the only hirer of bear wardens. Suppose also that the number of people willing to take this job (L) is a simple positive function of the hourly wage (w) given by

$$L = \tfrac{1}{2} w. \qquad [19.6]$$

This relationship between the wage and the number of people who offer their services as bear wardens is shown in the first two columns of Table 19.2. Total labor costs (w · L) are shown in the third column, and the marginal expense of hiring each warden is shown in the fourth column. The extra expense associated with adding another warden always exceeds the wage rate paid to that person. The reason is clear. Not only does a newly hired warden receive the higher wage, but all previously hired wardens also get a higher wage. A monopsonist will take these extra expenses into account in its hiring decisions.

A graph can be used to help to clarify this relationship. Figure 19.4 shows the supply curve (S) for bear wardens. If Yellowstone wishes to hire three wardens, it must pay $6 per hour, and total outlays will be $18 per hour. This situation is reflected by point A on the supply curve. If the firm tries to hire a fourth warden, it must offer $8 per hour to everyone—it must move to point B on the supply curve. Total outlays are now $32 per hour, so the marginal expense of hiring the fourth worker is $14 per hour. By comparing the sizes of the total outlay rectangles, we can see why the marginal expense is higher than the wage paid to the fourth worker. That worker's hourly wage is shown by the gray rectangle—it is $8 per hour. The other three workers, who were previously earning $6 per hour, now earn $8. This extra outlay is shown in color. Total labor expenses for four wardens exceed those for three by the area of both the color and gray rectangles. In this case, marginal expense exceeds the wage since the Yellowstone Company is the sole hirer of people in this unusual occupation.

Table 19.2 Labor Costs of Hiring Bear Wardens in Yellowstone Park	Hourly Wage	Workers Supplied per Hour	Total Labor Cost per Hour	Marginal Expense
	$2	1	$2	$2
	4	2	8	6
	6	3	18	10
	8	4	32	14
	10	5	50	18
	12	6	72	22
	14	7	98	26

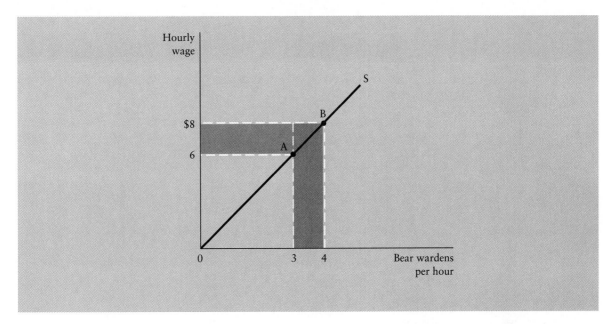

Figure 19.4
Marginal Expense of
Hiring Bear Wardens

Since Yellowstone Park is (probably) the only hirer of bear wardens, it must raise the hourly wage offered from $6 to $8 if it wishes to hire a fourth warden. The marginal expense of hiring that warden is $14—his or her wage ($8, shown in gray) plus the extra $2 per hour that must be paid to the other three wardens (shown in color).

Monopsonist's Input Choice

As for any profit-maximizing firm, a monopsonist will hire any input up to the point at which the additional revenue and additional cost of hiring one more unit are equal. For the case of labor this requires

$$ME_L = MVP_L. \qquad\qquad [19.7]$$

In the special case of a price taker that faces an infinitely elastic labor supply ($ME_L = w$), Equations 19.5 and 19.7 are identical. However, if the firm faces a positively sloped labor supply curve, Equation 19.7 dictates a different level of input choice, as we now show.

A Graphical Demonstration

The monopsonist's choice of labor input is illustrated in Figure 19.5. The firm's demand curve for labor (D) is drawn initially on the assumption that the firm is a price taker. This curve is negatively sloped, as we have shown it must be. The ME_L curve associated with the labor supply curve (S) is constructed in much the same way that the marginal revenue curve associated with a demand curve can be constructed. Because S is positively sloped, the ME_L curve always

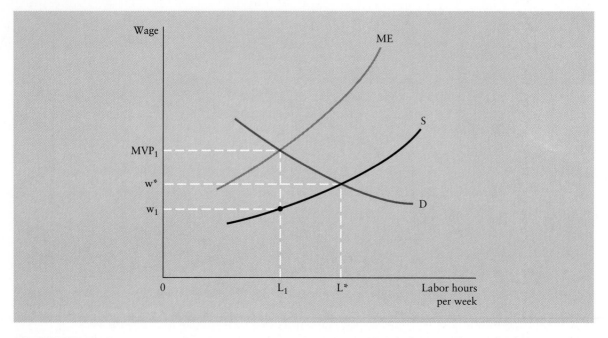

**Figure 19.5
Pricing in a Monop-
sonistic Labor Market**

If a firm faces a positively sloped supply curve for labor (S), it will base its decisions on the marginal expense of labor curve (ME_L). Because S is positively sloped, ME_L lies above S. The curve S can be thought of as an average cost of labor curve, and the ME_L curve is marginal to S. At L_1 the equilibrium condition $ME_L = MVP_L$ holds, and this quantity will be hired at a market wage rate w_1.

lies above S. The profit-maximizing level of labor input for the monopsonist is given by L_1. At this level of input use, marginal expense is equal to marginal value product. At L_1 the wage rate in the market is given by w_1. The quantity of labor demanded falls short of that which would be hired in a perfectly competitive market (L^*). The firm has restricted input demand to take advantage of its monopsonistic position in the labor market.

The formal similarities between this analysis and the monopoly analysis we presented in Chapter 16 should be clear. In particular, the actual "demand curve" for a monopsonist consists of a single point. In Figure 19.5 this point is given by L_1, w_1. The monopsonist has chosen this point as the most desirable of all those points on the supply curve S. A different point will not be chosen unless some external change (such as a shift in the demand for the firm's output or a change in technology) affects labor's marginal value product.

■ **Monopsonistic Exploitation**

In addition to restricting its input demand, the monopsonist pays an input less than its marginal value product. This result is also illustrated in Figure 19.5. At the monopsonist's preferred choice of labor input (L_1), a wage of

w_1 prevails in the market. For this level of input demand, the firm is willing to pay an amount equal to MVP_1: this is the amount of extra revenue that hiring another worker would provide to the firm. At L_1 the monopsonist pays workers less than they are "worth" to the firm. In the absence of effective competition, the monopsonist can persist in this behavior. Some authors refer to this gap between an input's MVP and its market price as monopsonistic exploitation. It should be clear from Figure 19.5 that the extent of this exploitation will be greater the more inelastic the supply of labor is to the monopsonist. The less responsive to low wages the supply of labor is, the more the monopsonist can take advantage of this situation.

Causes of Monopsony

To practice monopsonistic exploitation a firm must possess considerable power in the market for a particular input. If the market is reasonably competitive, monopsonistic exploitation cannot occur because other firms will recognize the profit potential reflected in the gap between MVPs and input costs. They will therefore bid for these inputs, driving their prices up to equality with marginal value products. Under such conditions the supply of labor to any one firm will be nearly infinitely elastic (because of the alternative employment possibilities available), and monopsonistic behavior will be impossible. Our analysis suggests monopsonistic outcomes will be observed in real-world situations in which, for some reason, effective competition for inputs is lacking. We now examine three such causes: geography, specialized employment, and monopsonistic cartels.

■ Geography

Some firms may occupy a monopsonistic position by being the only source of employment in a small town. Because moving costs for workers are high, alternative employment opportunities for local workers are unattractive, and the firm may be able to exert a strong effect on wages paid. This possibility may, in part, explain the low wage rates that prevailed in the southern United States prior to World War II. Many small southern towns had isolated labor markets that were dominated by one or two firms. The term *company town* originated in this situation and carried a connotation of exploitation that may have been appropriate. A number of factors tend to undermine such monopsonistic positions. Workers may be willing to relocate in response to wage rate differences. The entry of new firms may improve workers' alternative earnings possibilities. Finally, opposing forces, such as unionization, may also have an effect on monopsonistic practices.

■ Specialized Employment

It may sometimes be the case that only one firm hires a particularly specialized type of input. If the alternative earnings prospects for that input are unattractive, its supply to the firm will be inelastic, presenting the firm with the opportunity for monopsonistic behavior. For example, marine engineers with many years of experience in designing nuclear submarines must work for the one or two companies that produce such vessels. Because other jobs would not make use of these workers' specialized training, alternative employment is not particularly attractive. Similarly, experienced telephone circuit designers may find they have to work for the local phone company if they wish to capitalize on their skills without having to move. As a nonlabor example, the McDonald's Corporation for many years bought more than 50 percent of all frozen french fried potatoes produced in the United States; the corporation probably occupied a monopsonistic position in that market.

■ Monopsonistic Cartels

These examples suggest that monopsonistic hiring of specialized inputs is often associated with a monopoly position in the sale of an output (nuclear submarines, local telephone service, or french fries). A particularly prevalent example of this relationship is in hiring by the federal government. Since the government occupies a monopoly position in the production of a number of goods requiring specialized inputs (space travel, armed forces, and national political offices, to name a few), it would be expected to be in a position to exercise monopsony power. In other cases a group of firms may combine to form a cartel in their hiring decisions (and, perhaps, in their output decisions too). Application 19.4: Monopsony in the Market for Baseball Players illustrates this relationship between a firm's monopoly position and monopsonistic hiring in major league baseball, a situation in which it is possible to obtain direct measures of workers' marginal value.

Discrimination in Hiring

If a monopsony can segregate the supply of a factor into two or more distinct markets, it may be able to increase profits. For example, a monopsony may be able to discriminate in hiring between men and women. Because the firm can readily identify which market a prospective employee belongs to, it will find it profitable to pay different wages in the two markets.

■ A Graphical Analysis

Such a situation is shown in Figure 19.6. The figure assumes that men and women are equally productive and that the firm has a constant marginal

APPLICATION 19.4

Monopsony in the Market for Baseball Players

Occasionally, powerful cartels of hirers can achieve a successful monopsony. An important example was provided by major league baseball teams during the period prior to 1970 in which the reserve clause was in effect. That clause combined with player drafts effectively bound each player to a single team and prevented interteam competition for salaries. Even though there were 18 major league clubs (or firms), their hiring was effectively cartelized—creating the potential for monopsonistic exploitation.

Empirical Estimates

Numerical estimates of the degree of exploitation in major league baseball were constructed by G. W. Scully in a 1974 article.[1] Because baseball players' salaries are more or less a matter of public record, the principal problem Scully faced in measuring the effect of monopsony was to estimate the players' marginal value products. He adopted a two-step procedure. First, he examined the correlation between a team's winning percentage and its attendance figures. He concluded that winning did indeed produce additional revenues. Next, he analyzed which aspects of individual player performance were most closely related to a team's overall performance. Two significant variables were identified: For hitters, the "slugging average" seemed most important, whereas for pitchers, the ratio of strikeouts to walks proved most relevant. A few of the estimates are presented in Table 1. These data show that most players' MVPs exceed their salaries by a substantial margin.

Erosion of the Cartel

It was only a matter of time before players came to recognize the cartelizing effect of the reserve clause and took organized action against it. A players' strike in 1972 (coupled with legal action in a suit brought by St. Louis Cardinal outfielder Curt Flood) eventually led to the adoption of a free-agent provision in players' contracts as a partial replacement of the reserve clause. Recent spectacular contract settlements for some star players are indicative of the bidding competition that has continued since the breakdown of the cartel. Although the leagues

Table 1
Monopsonistic Exploitation in Major League Baseball, 1969

Hitters		
Slugging Average	**Hitters' Net MVP[a]**	**Estimated Salary**
255	$-39,100	$9,700
305	103,600	14,100
350	137,800	32,700
375	156,800	39,000
427	296,500	42,200
490	350,400	60,500
525	383,700	68,000

Pitchers		
Ratio of Strikeouts to Walks	**Pitchers' Net MVP[a]**	**Estimated Salary**
1.50	$-20,800	$9,000
2.00	132,000	16,500
2.30	169,200	36,900
2.79	349,600	47,200
3.09	405,300	66,800
3.54	479,700	86,300

[a]Estimated gross MVP less training and related costs. For poor players the net figure is negative.

Source: G. W. Scully, "Pay and Performance in Major League Baseball," *American Economic Review* (December 1974): 928.

have tried several actions to re-establish their cartel position (such as player drafts and limiting league expansion), they have been unable to return to the powerful position they occupied prior to 1970.

To Think About

1. If players could be freely traded among teams, could monopolistic exploitation arise?
2. How might mergers between two rival leagues (for example, the American and National Football Leagues or the American and National Basketball Associations) affect players' salaries?

[1]G. W. Scully, "Pay and Performance in Major League Baseball," *American Economic Review* (December 1974): 915–930. For more detail on the current status of the players' labor market, see Scully's *The Business of Major League Baseball* (Chicago: The University of Chicago Press, 1989).

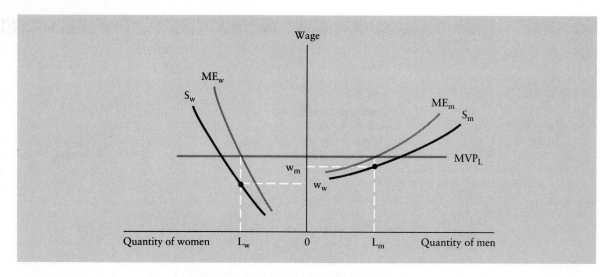

**Figure 19.6
Discrimination in
Hiring by a
Monopsonist**

By segregating the labor market, say, between men and women, a monopsonist will minimize labor costs by choosing those quantities of labor such that the marginal revenue product of labor is equal to the marginal expense in each market. In this diagram, the wages of women (w_w) will be below the wages of men (w_m), even though the marginal value product for both types of labor is identical.

value product of labor no matter how much labor is hired. This curve is shown by the horizontal MVP_L curve. The supply curves for men and women are shown in the figure as sharing the same vertical axis. Given these supply curves the firm will choose that quantity of labor in each market for which the marginal expense (ME) is equal to labor's marginal revenue product. Consequently, the firm will hire L_m from the men's market and L_w from the women's. The wage rate in the two markets will be w_m and w_w, respectively. The way we have drawn Figure 19.6, men's wages will exceed women's. This happens because women's labor supply is relatively inelastic.

■ Limits to Discrimination

A similar analysis can be developed for any situation in which a monopsony can segregate the market for its inputs into two separate parts. In order to do so, it must be able to identify workers as belonging to particular markets so that its segmentation strategy will work. It must know how much of each kind of worker it is hiring. For this reason, wage discrimination among geographically distinct labor markets or among individuals with readily identifiable personal characteristics (sex, race, age) would be expected to be the types of discrimination most often encountered. Application 19.5: Sex Discrimination shows that some U.S. data are consistent with this model. But, because it is

APPLICATION 19.5

Sex Discrimination

Table 1 shows median earnings in different occupations for men and women for the year 1989. Overall women's earnings averaged about 68 percent of those of men. Although some part of the differences may be explained by objective characteristics (for example, age, education, or job experience), a number of statistical studies have found that the gap in earnings continues to persist even after these factors are controlled. Such findings are in general accord with the monopsony model of labor-market discrimination.

Can the Monopsony Model Explain Wage Differences?

It is hard to believe that monopsony can be an important explanation for the wage differences that are observed in the U.S. labor market. Very few (if any) firms in the United States are the only employer in the labor market from which they draw. If we are to apply the simple monopsony model, it must be assumed that all the firms in a particular labor market are able to collude perfectly in their discriminatory hiring decisions. Because economists generally believe that such collusion is very difficult to achieve (again there are incentives to cheat on any collusive agreement that is reached), they have instead turned their attention to examining how discrimination might arise in a competitive labor market.

Wage Discrimination in Competitive Markets

An initial observation about discrimination in a competitive market is that it is costly to the discriminator. For example, a firm that decides not to hire female workers is increasing its labor costs over what they would be if it hired workers solely on the basis of their skills. Nevertheless, discrimination persists, and this fact indicates that firms, workers, and consumers may be willing to pay these costs. The importance of this observation is to demonstrate that discrimination is costly not only to those being discriminated against, but also to those doing the discriminating. The total income of both groups would be higher in the absence of discrimination.[1]

Table 1

Median Earnings for Full-Time, Year-Round Workers by Sex and Occupation, 1989

Occupation	Median Earnings		Ratio Women: Men
	Men	Women	
Manager	$40,103	$24,589	.61
Technical	31,371	21,768	.69
Service	18,903	11,669	.63
Precision Production	26,499	17,457	.66
Operators and Inspectors	22,343	14,463	.65

Source: Statistical Abstract of the United States, 1991 (Washington, D.C.: U.S. Department of Commerce, 1991), Table 680.

Antidiscrimination Policy

Following from this analysis is the question of what should be done about the discriminatory preferences of employers. In part, they may be based on ignorance. Employers, for example, may discriminate against black or female workers because they incorrectly believe that these workers have lower productivity levels. Providing more information to employers may alter these perceptions. More significantly, governmental equal opportunity and affirmative action programs may lead firms to make hiring decisions they would not freely make; as a result, they may gain more accurate information about true productivities.

To Think About

1. What factors other than wage discrimination might explain the figures in Table 1? Should factors such as education, job skills, or work experience be controlled for in looking at male-female wage differences, or might these too reflect discrimination?
2. How would you explain the economic rationale for affirmative action programs that establish hiring guidelines for minorities and women? Under what conditions might such programs have an effect on the male-female wage differential? When might such policies fail?

---

[1]One of the first economists to study discrimination in detail was Gary S. Becker. In his book, *The Economics of Discrimination* (Chicago: University of Chicago Press, 1957), he develops a simple model that shows that discrimination harms both the majority and minority groups. This finding is in contrast to other views that discrimination in some way benefits the discriminator.

doubtful that many firms have the kind of monopsony hiring power that such discrimination requires, these data raise more questions about discrimination than they answer.

Summary

In this chapter we examined firms' demands for the inputs they buy. The most fundamental observation was that this demand is necessarily derived from the demand for the output being produced. Firms don't hire workers just to have them around to keep the chief executive company. Rather, a firm's hiring decisions are one aspect of its desire to maximize profits. In analyzing the demand for factors, this connection between factor and goods markets must be kept clearly in mind. Several specific conclusions emerged from our examination of this relationship:

- Firms will hire any input up to the point at which the marginal expense of hiring one more unit is equal to the marginal revenue yielded by selling what that input produces.

- If the firm is a price taker in both the market for its inputs and the market for its output, profit maximization requires that it employ that level of inputs for which the market price of the input (for example, the wage) is equal to the marginal value product of that input (for example, $P \cdot MP_L$).

- If the price of an input rises, the firm will hire less of it for two reasons. First, the higher price will cause the firm to substitute other inputs for the one whose price has risen. Second, the higher price will raise the firm's costs and reduce the amount it is able to sell. This output effect will also cause fewer units of the input to be hired.

- If a firm is the sole hirer of an input (a monopsony), its hiring decisions will affect market prices of inputs. The marginal expense associated with hiring an additional unit of an input will exceed that input's price. Firms will take this into account in their hiring decisions—they will restrict hiring below what it would be under competitive conditions.

- If a firm has a monopsony in two markets, it may increase profits further by practicing input price discrimination.

Review Questions

1. In the supply-demand model of factor pricing, who are the demanders? What type of assumptions would you use to explain their behavior? In this model, who

are the suppliers? What types of assumptions would you use to explain their behavior?

2. If the pricing of a particular factor of production can be explained by a simple supply-demand model, what labels should be put on the axes? What types of influences might cause the demand curve or the supply curve to shift?

3. In Chapter 13 we described the notions of consumer and producer surplus as they relate to a competitive equilibrium. How should similar areas be interpreted in a supply-demand graph of the competitive equilibrium in a factor market?

4. Profit maximization implies that firms will make input choices in a marginal way. Explain why the following marginal rules found in this chapter are specific applications of this general idea:

    a. $MR_L = ME_L$.
    b. $MP_L \cdot MR = ME_L = w$.
    c. $MVP_L = ME_L = w$.
    d. $MVP_L = w$.
    e. $MVP_L = ME_L > w$.

    If firms follow these various rules, will they also be producing a profit-maximizing level of output? That is, will they produce when $MR = MC$? Will they also be minimizing costs if they use these rules?

5. Explain why if a price-taking firm has only one variable input the MVP curve is also its demand curve for that input, but if the firm has two or more variable inputs, its demand curve for one of them reflects a whole family of MVP curves.

6. A fall in the price of an input induces a profit-maximizing firm to experience both substitution and output effects that cause it to hire more of that input. Explain how the profit-maximizing assumption is used in explaining the direction of each of these effects. Did you have to use the assumption that the input is not inferior in your analysis? Do you think a similar statement can be made about inferior inputs?

7. Suppose the price of an input used by firms with fixed proportions production functions were to fall. Why would such a change not cause any substitution effects for these firms' input demand? Would there, however, be output effects? What would determine the size of these effects?

8. Why does the relationship between the firm's marginal expense of hiring an input and the market price of that input depend on the shape of the input supply curve facing the firm? For a price-taking firm, what kind of supply curve faces the firm and what is the relationship between these concepts? What is different about a monopsony? Illustrate the similarity between these ideas and the notion of the output demand curve that faces a firm.

9. How would you measure the strength of a monopsonist in an input market? Would a monopsony necessarily be very profitable? What would you need to add to Figure 19.5 in order to show a monopsonist's profit graphically?

10. To practice input price discrimination, a monopsony must have market power in two separated markets. Why would an inability to separate markets make such discrimination impossible?

Problems

19.1 Suppose the demand for labor is given by

$$L = -50w + 450$$

and the supply is given by

$$L = 100w$$

where L represents the number of people employed and w is the real wage rate per hour.

a. What will be the equilibrium levels for w and L in this market?
b. Suppose the government wishes to raise the equilibrium wage to $4 per hour by offering a subsidy to employers for each person hired. How much will this subsidy have to be? What will the new equilibrium level of employment be? How much total subsidy will be paid?
c. Suppose instead the government declared a minimum wage of $4 per hour. How much labor would be demanded at this price? How much unemployment would there be?
d. Graph your results.

19.2 Assume that the market for rental cars for business purposes is perfectly competitive with the demand for this capital input given by

$$K = 1,500 - 25v$$

and the supply given by

$$K = 75v - 500$$

where K represents the number of cars rented by firms and v is the rental rate per day.

a. What will be the equilibrium levels for v and K in this market?
b. Suppose that following an oil embargo gas prices rise dramatically so that now business firms must take account of gas prices in their car rental decisions. Their demand for rental cars is now given by

$$K = 1,700 - 25v - 300g$$

where g is the per gallon price of gasoline. What will be the equilibrium levels for v and K if g = $2? If g = $3?

   c. Graph your results.

   d. Since the oil embargo brought about decreased demand for rental cars, what might be the implication for other capital input markets as a result? For example, employees may still need transportation, so how might the demand for mass transit be affected? Since businesspeople also rent cars to attend meetings, what might happen in the market for telephone equipment as employees drive less and use the telephone more? Can you think of any other factor input markets that might be affected?

19.3 A landowner has three farms (A, B, and C) of differing fertility. The levels of output for the three farms with one, two, and three laborers employed are as follows:

	Level of Output		
Number of Laborers	Farm A	Farm B	Farm C
1	10	8	5
2	17	11	7
3	21	13	8

For example, if one laborer were hired for each farm, the total output would be $10 + 8 + 5 = 23$. This would represent a poor allocation of labor, since if the farm C laborer were assigned to farm A the total output would be $17 + 8 = 25$.

   a. If market conditions caused the landowner to hire five laborers, what would be the most productive allocation of that labor? How much would be produced? What is the marginal product of the last worker?

   b. If we assume that farm output is sold in a perfectly competitive market with one unit of output priced at $1, and we assume that labor market equilibrium occurs when five workers are hired, what wage is paid? How much profit does the landowner receive?

19.4 Assume that the quantity of envelopes licked per hour by Sticky Gums, Inc. is $q = 10,000 \sqrt{L}$ where L is the number of laborers hired per hour by the firm. Assume further that the envelope-licking business is perfectly competitive with a market price of $.01 per envelope. The marginal product of a worker is given by

$$MP_L = 5,000/\sqrt{L}.$$

   a. How much labor would be hired at a competitive wage of $10? $5? $2? Use your results to sketch a demand curve for labor.

   b. Assume that Sticky Gums hires its labor at an hourly wage of $10. What quantity of envelopes will be licked when the price of a licked envelope is $.10? $.05? $.02? Use your results to sketch a supply curve for licked envelopes.

*19.5 Suppose there are a fixed number of 1,000 identical firms in the perfectly competitive concrete pipe industry. Each firm produces the same fraction of total market output and each firm's production function for pipe is given by

$$q = \sqrt{KL}$$

and for this production function

$$RTS \ (L \text{ for } K) = K/L.$$

Suppose also that the market demand for concrete pipe is given by

$$Q = 400,000 - 100,000P$$

where Q is total concrete pipe.

a. If $w = v = \$1$, in what ratio will the typical firm use K and L? What will be the long-run average and marginal cost of pipe?
b. In the long-run equilibrium what will be the market equilibrium price and quantity for concrete pipe? How much will each firm produce? How much labor will be hired by each firm and in the market as a whole?
c. Suppose the market wage, w, rose to $2 while v remained constant at $1. How will this change the capital-labor ratio for the typical firm, and how will it affect its marginal costs?
d. Under the conditions of part c, what will the long-run market equilibrium be? How much labor will now be hired by the concrete pipe industry?
e. How much of the change in total labor demand from part b to part d represents the substitution effect resulting from the change in wage and how much represents the output effect?

19.6 Suppose that the supply curve for the labor to a firm is given by

$$L = 100w$$

and the marginal expense of labor curve is given by

$$ME_L = L/50$$

where w is the market wage. Suppose also that the firm's demand for labor (marginal revenue product) curve is given by

$$L = 1,000 - 100MRP_L.$$

a. If the firm acts as a monopsonist, how many workers will it hire in order to maximize profits? What wage will it pay? How will this wage compare to the MRP_L at this employment level?
b. Assume now that the firm must hire its workers in a perfectly competitive labor market, but it still acts as a monopoly when selling its output. How many workers will the firm hire now? What wage will it pay?
c. Graph your results.

---

*Denotes a problem that is rather difficult.

19.7 Carl the clothier owns a large garment factory on an isolated island. Carl's factory is the only source of employment for most of the islanders, and thus Carl
acts as a monopsonist. The supply curve for garment workers is given by

$$L = 80w$$

and the marginal expense of labor curve is given by

$$ME_L = L/40$$

where L is the number of workers hired and w is their hourly wage. Assume
also that Carl's labor demand (marginal value product) curve is given by

$$L = 400 - 40MVP_L.$$

a. How many workers will Carl hire in order to maximize his profits and what
wage will he pay?
b. Assume now that the government implements a minimum wage law covering all garment workers. How many workers will Carl now hire and how
much unemployment will there be if the minimum wage is set at $3 per
hour? $3.33 per hour? $4.00 per hour?
c. Graph your results.
d. How does the imposition of a minimum wage under monopsony differ in
results from a minimum wage imposed under perfect competition (assuming the minimum wage is above the market determined wage)?

19.8 Under what conditions would you expect the imposition of a minimum wage to:

a. Have no effect on wages or on the number of workers employed?
b. Increase wages and leave the number of workers unaffected?
c. Increase wages and decrease the number of workers?
d. Increase both wages and the number of workers?

*19.9 The Ajax Coal Company is the only employer in its area. It can hire any num-
ber of female workers or male workers it wishes. The supply curve for women
is given by

$$L_f = 100w_f$$

$$ME_f = L_f/50$$

and for men by

$$L_m = 9w_m^2$$

$$ME_m = \tfrac{1}{2}\sqrt{L_m}$$

---

*Denotes a problem that is rather difficult.

where w_f and w_m are, respectively, the hourly wage rate paid to female and male workers. Assume that Ajax sells its coal in a perfectly competitive market at $5 per ton and that each worker hired (both men and women) can mine two tons per hour. If the firm wishes to maximize profits, how many female and male workers should be hired and what will the wage rates for these two groups be? How much will Ajax earn in profits per hour on its mining machinery? How will that result compare to one in which Ajax was constrained (say, by market forces) to pay all workers the same wage based on the value of their marginal products?

19.10 Assume employers have no "taste for discrimination" against blacks but that the white employees do. A white employee considers the "psychic wage" to be a combination of the money wage and the percentage of blacks in the firm. That is, a white worker demands higher wages in order to work with blacks. Both blacks and whites offer their services in a perfectly competitive market and are equally productive. The wages for whites and blacks are given by

$$w_1 = \text{MVP}(1 + \text{percentage of blacks in firm})$$

and

$$w_2 = \text{MVP},$$

respectively. How might you expect a cost-minimizing firm to adjust the racial mix of its employees?

I n this chapter we examine some aspects of factor pricing that are particularly related to the labor market. Because we have already discussed the demand for labor (or any other factor of production), here we are concerned primarily with the supply of labor. The theory of labor supply provides another useful application of the model of individual choice developed in Part 2. With this model it is possible to explain many of the important trends in the U.S. labor market. This chapter also examines labor unions. The tools used to study union behavior and bargaining can be applied to other situations in which both buyers and sellers exercise some market power.

CHAPTER
20

PRICING OF
LABOR

Allocation of Time

Part 2 analyzed how an individual will choose to allocate a fixed amount of income among a variety of available goods. People must make similar choices in deciding how they will spend their time. The number of hours in a day (or in a year) is absolutely fixed, and time must be used as it passes by. Given this fixed amount of time, any person must decide how many hours to work; how many hours to spend consuming a wide variety of goods, ranging from cars and television sets to operas; how many hours to devote to self-maintenance; and how many hours to sleep. Table 20.1 shows that there is considerable variation in time use between men and women and among various countries around the world. By studying the division of time people choose to make among their activities, economists are able to understand labor supply decisions. Viewing work as only one of a number of choices open to people in the way they spend their time enables us to understand why these decisions may be adjusted in response to changing opportunities.

■ A Simple Model of Time Use

Leisure

Time spent in any activity other than market work.

We first assume that there are only two uses to which any person may devote his or her time: either engaging in market work at a wage rate of w per hour or not working. We refer to nonwork time as **leisure,** but to economists this word does not mean idleness. Time that is not spent in market work can be used to work in the home, for self-improvement, or for consumption (it takes time to use a television set or a bowling ball).[1] All of these activities contribute to a person's well-being, and time will be allocated to them in a utility-maximizing way.

More specifically, assume that utility depends on consumption of market goods (C) and on the amount of leisure time (H) used. Figure 20.1 presents an indifference curve map for this utility function. The diagram has the familiar shape introduced in Chapter 3, and it shows those combinations of C and H that yield an individual various levels of utility.

To discuss utility maximization we must first describe the budget constraint that faces this person. If the period we are studying is one day, the individual will work (24 − H) hours. That is, he or she will work all of the hours not devoted to leisure. For this work she or he will earn w per hour and will use this to buy consumption goods.

---

[1]For a more theoretical treatment of the allocation of time, see G. S. Becker, "A Theory of the Allocation of Time," *The Economic Journal* (September 1965): 493–517. The author treats the household as both a provider of labor services and a producer of utility, which is made by combining time with goods. The household is seen to be bound by a time constraint and must allocate available time among a number of activities. The implications drawn by Becker are far-reaching and affect most of the traditional theory of individual behavior.

	Men			Women			Table 20.1
	U.S.	Japan	Soviet Union	U.S.	Japan	Soviet Union	Time Allocation (Percentage of Time during Typical Week)
Market work	28.3%	33.6%	35.1%	15.4%	15.3%	25.4%	
Housework	8.2	2.1	7.1	18.2	18.5	16.1	
Personal care and sleep	40.6	43.1	40.4	42.6	42.9	41.6	
Leisure and other	22.9	21.2	17.4	23.8	23.3	16.9	

Source: Adapted from F. T. Juster and F. P. Stafford, "The Allocation of Time: Empirical Findings, Behavioral Models and Problems of Measurement," *Journal of Economic Literature* (June 1991), Table 1.

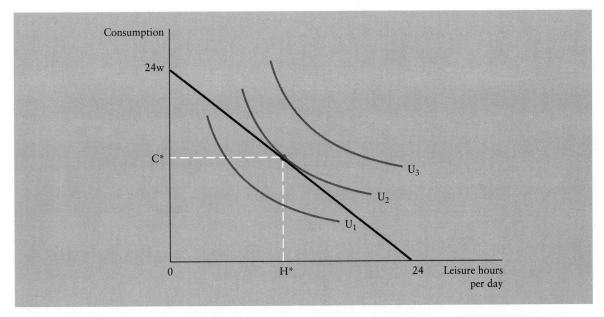

Given his or her budget constraint, this person will maximize utility by choosing H* hours of leisure and consumption of C*. At this point, the rate at which he or she is willing to trade H for C (the MRS) is equal to the rate at which he or she is able to trade these in the market (the real hourly wage—w).

Figure 20.1
Utility-Maximizing Choice of Hours of Leisure and Work

■ The Opportunity Cost of Leisure

Each extra hour of leisure this person takes reduces his or her income (and consumption) by w dollars. The hourly wage therefore reflects the opportunity cost of leisure. People have to "pay" this cost for each hour they do not work. The wage rate used to make these calculations should be a real wage in that it should reflect the prevailing price level for consumer goods. A nominal wage of $1 per hour provides the same purchasing power when the typical item costs $.25 as does a wage of $100 per hour when that item sells for $25. In either case, the person must work 15 minutes to buy the item. Alternately, in both cases, the opportunity cost of taking one more hour of leisure is to do without four consumption items. In Application 20.1: The Opportunity Cost of Time, we look at some cases of competing uses of time and illustrate how the opportunity cost notion can explain the choices people make.

■ Utility Maximization

To show the utility-maximizing choices of consumption and leisure, we must first graph the relevant budget constraint. This is done in Figure 20.1. If this person doesn't work at all, he or she can enjoy 24 hours of leisure. This is shown as the horizontal intercept of the budget constraint. If, on the other hand, this person works 24 hours per day, he or she will be able to buy $24 \cdot w$ in consumption goods. This establishes the vertical intercept in the figure. The slope of the budget constraint is $-w$. This reflects opportunity costs—each added hour of leisure must be "purchased" by doing without w worth of consumption items. For example, if $w = \$10$, this person will earn $240 if he or she works 24 hours per day. Each hour not worked has an opportunity cost of $10.

Given this budget constraint, this person will maximize utility by choosing to take H* hours of leisure and to work the remaining time. With the income earned from this work, he or she will be able to buy C* units of consumption goods. At the utility-maximizing point, the slope of the budget ($-w$) is equal to the slope of indifference curve U_2. In other words, the person's real wage is equal to the marginal rate of substitution of leisure hours for consumption.

If this were not true, utility would not be as large as possible. For example, suppose a person's MRS were equal to 5, indicating a willingness to give up five units of consumption to get an additional hour of leisure. Suppose also that the real wage is $10. By working one more hour, he or she is able to earn enough to buy ten units (that is, $10 worth) of consumption. This is clearly an inefficient situation. By working one hour more, this person can buy ten extra units of consumption. But he or she required only five units of consumption to be as well-off as before. By working the extra hour, this person earns five ($= 10 - 5$) more units of consumption than required. Consequently he or she could not have been maximizing utility in the first place. A similar proof can be constructed for any case in which the MRS differs from the market wage, which proves that the two trade-off rates must be equal for a true utility maximum.

■ Flexibility of Work

Before we examine how these choices might be affected by a change in the real wage rate, it is important to ask whether this theory of choice has any relevance to the real-world decisions people must make. While we all are relatively free to determine what we will do in our spare time, we may not have complete freedom of choice in selecting our own hours of work. Most jobs require that

APPLICATION 20.1
The Opportunity Cost of Time

Choices that people must make among competing uses of time can often be clarified by recognizing the opportunity costs involved.

Transportation Choices

In choosing among alternative ways of getting to work, people will take both time and dollar costs into account. Most studies have found that commuters are quite sensitive to time costs, especially those associated with walking to a bus or train station or with waiting for the bus or train to come.[1] By examining people's willingness to pay to avoid such waits, the studies generally conclude that people value travel time at about one-half of their market wage. For example, studies conducted in connection with the Bay Area Rapid Transit System (BART) in San Francisco concluded that fares involved in using the system were less than one-fourth of the total costs people faced. Far more important were the time costs involved in getting to suburban BART stations, waiting for trains, and walking from downtown BART stations to the final destination. Given the size of these costs, it is not surprising that most commuters in the Bay Area continue to use private cars for their trips.

The Economics of Childbearing

People's decisions to have children are affected by a number of social, religious, and economic factors. Economists have tended to focus primarily on the costs associated with having children and how those costs vary among individuals. One of the most important costs is the forgone wages of parents who choose to care for their children rather than to pursue market employment. Indeed, by some estimates, this cost is far in excess of all other costs of childbearing combined. This calculation has led some economists to speculate that higher real wages earned by women in the United States since World War II are the principal reason for the decline in the birthrate during the same period. Similarly, the lower birthrates in North America and Western Eu-

rope as compared to the less-developed world might be attributed to wage-rate differences (and hence cost of children differences) between these regions.[2]

Job Search Theory

When seeking new jobs, people are often faced with considerable uncertainty about available openings. Consequently, they must invest some time (and possibly other resources, such as telephone calls or advertising) in finding a suitable job match. To the extent that people must reduce work time to accommodate their job search plans, the hourly cost of a search can be approximated by the market wage. The higher an individual's market wage, the more likely he or she would be to adopt search techniques that economize on time (such as using an employment agency). If, on the other hand, search time is subsidized (say, by unemployment insurance benefits), search time may be prolonged in the hope of finding a better job. By one estimate, a 10 percent increase in weekly unemployment benefits is associated with about one-half week of additional unemployment.[3]

To Think About

1. Why do empirical studies of commuting patterns find that people value their time at about one-half the market wage? Doesn't our theory suggest that the value should be the full wage rate?
2. The evidence about people's job search activities is that receipt of unemployment insurance benefits causes them to be more choosy about the jobs they take. Isn't that a good thing?

---

[1]See, for example, T. A. Domencich and Daniel McFadden, *Urban Travel Demand* (Amsterdam: North Holland Press, 1975).
[2]For a seminal contribution to the economics of fertility, see G. S. Becker, "An Economic Analysis of Fertility," in *Demographic and Economic Change in Developed Countries* (Princeton, N.J.: Princeton University

Press, 1960).
[3]For a summary of some studies of this effect see Daniel Hamermesch, *Jobless Pay and the Economy* (Baltimore: Johns Hopkins University Press, 1976).

you work about 35 to 40 hours a week, and this figure is not very flexible in response to people's preferences. Nevertheless, the freedom of choice in hours of work that we have been assuming may be justified in several ways. First, the model might apply to a very long period, perhaps a lifetime. Over such a period you have considerable flexibility in the number of hours to be worked since you may choose to work 35 hours during some weeks (or years) and zero hours during others. By moving in and out of the labor market at different stages in their lifetimes, people can adjust their hours of work rather precisely.

A second and similar justification for our model is to regard it as applying to the average person. At any one point in time, some individuals will work 35 hours and others will not work. Consequently, average hours of work will depend on how many people fall into each category. If nearly everyone works, the average person will work about 35 hours, whereas if 60 percent of all people work 35 hours and 40 percent do not work, the average person will be working 21 hours.

A final way to justify the assumption of time flexibility is to note that people do have considerable freedom in choosing the jobs they take. By choosing among the comforts and discomforts of particular jobs, people can be thought of as making a marginal choice, even though actual hours of work are fixed by the employer. For example, someone taking a low-paying job as a surfing instructor can be regarded as choosing an occupation with a significant leisure component, and he or she is thereby adjusting the hours of actual work. We examine some additional questions about occupational choice later in this chapter.

Income and Substitution Effects of a Change in the Real Wage Rate

■

Substitution effect of a change in w

Movement along an indifference curve in response to a change in the real wage. A rise in w causes an individual to work more.

■

Income effect of a change in w

Movement to a higher indifference curve in response to a rise in the real wage rate. If leisure is a normal good, a rise in w causes an individual to work less.

A change in the real wage rate can be analyzed the same way we studied a price change in Chapter 4. When w rises, the price of leisure becomes higher—people must give up more in lost wages for each hour of leisure consumed. The **substitution effect** of an increase in w on the hours of leisure will therefore be to reduce them. As leisure becomes more expensive, there is reason to consume less of it. However, the **income effect** of a rise in the wage will tend to increase leisure. Since leisure is a normal good, the higher income resulting from a higher w will increase the demand for it. Hence income and substitution effects work in the opposite direction. It is impossible to predict whether an increase in w will increase or decrease the demand for leisure time. Because leisure and work are mutually exclusive ways to use time, this shows that it is impossible to predict what will happen to the number of hours worked. When the wage rises, the substitution effect tends to increase hours worked. The income effect, because it increases the demand for leisure time, tends to decrease the number of hours worked. Which of these two effects is the stronger is an important empirical question whose answer depends on people's preferences for consumption and leisure.

■ A Graphical Analysis

Figure 20.2 illustrates two possible reactions to an increase in w. In both graphs the initial wage rate is w_0, and the optimal choices of consumption and leisure are given by C_0 and H_0. When the wage rate increases to w_1, the utility-maximizing combination moves to C_1, H_1. This movement can be divided into two effects. The substitution effect is represented by the movement along the indifference curve U_0 from C_0, H_0 to S. This effect works to reduce the number of hours of leisure in both parts of Figure 20.2. People substitute consumption for leisure since the relative price of leisure has increased.

The movement from S to C_1, H_1 represents the income effect of a higher real wage. Since it is assumed that leisure time is a normal good, increases in income will cause more leisure to be demanded. Consequently, the income and substitution effects induced by the increase in w work in opposite directions. In Panel a in Figure 20.2 the demand for leisure is reduced by the rise in w; that is, the substitution effect outweighs the income effect. On the other hand, in Panel b the income effect is stronger, and the demand for leisure increases in response to an increase in w. This person actually chooses to work fewer hours when w increases. In our analysis of demand we would have considered this result unusual—when the price of leisure rises, this person demands more of it. For the case of normal consumption goods, income and substitution effects work in the same direction, and both cause quantity to decline when price increases. In the case of leisure, however, income and substitution effects work in opposite directions. An increase in w makes a person better-off because he or she is a *supplier* of labor. In the case of a consumption good, an individual is made worse-off by a rise in price because he or she is a *consumer* of that good. Consequently, it is not possible to predict how a person will respond to a wage increase—he or she may work greater or fewer hours depending on his or her preferences.

■ Individual Supply Curve for Labor

In Figure 20.3 we have drawn an individual's supply of labor curve by calculating the number of hours he or she is willing to work at every possible real wage rate. In Panel a the individual's supply curve is drawn with an upward slope: at higher real wage rates this person chooses to work longer hours. The substitution effect of a higher wage outweighs its income effect. This need not always be the case, however, as Panel b shows. There the supply curve is **backward bending**—once real wages exceed a certain level, even higher wage rates induce this person to work fewer hours. Such a curve is entirely consistent with the theory of labor supply we have developed. At relatively high wage rates, an increase in the wage may cause people to choose to work fewer hours, since the income effect may be stronger than the substitution effect. In this situation a person uses his or her higher real wage rate to "buy" more leisure. High-priced lawyers taking Wednesday afternoons off to play golf is a rational response to their situations, though it does result in the loss of some potential legal fees.

■
Backward-bending labor supply curve
Labor supply curve in which higher real wages cause less labor to be supplied because the income effect outweighs the substitution effect.

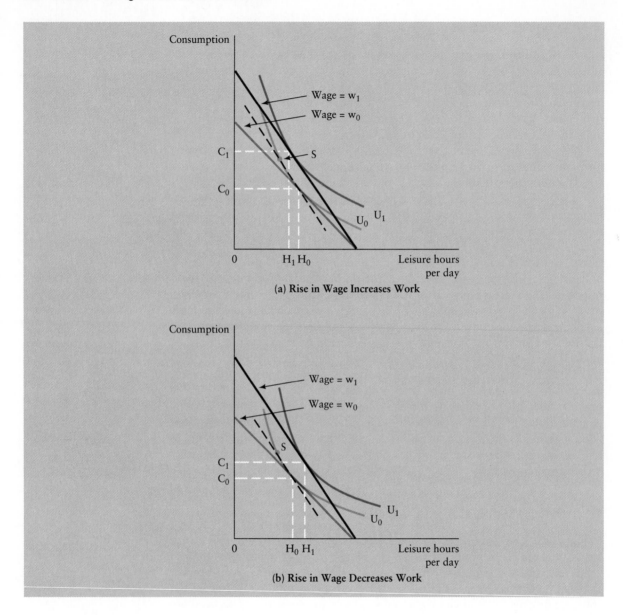

(a) Rise in Wage Increases Work

(b) Rise in Wage Decreases Work

Figure 20.2

Income and
Substitution Effects
of a Change in the
Real Wage Rate

Since the individual is a supplier of labor, the income and substitution effects of an increase in the real wage rate work in opposite directions in their effect on the hours of leisure demanded (or on hours of work). In Panel a the substitution effect (movement to point S) outweighs the income effect, and a higher wage causes hours of leisure to decline to H_1. Hours of work, therefore, increase. In Panel b the income effect is stronger than the substitution effect, and H increases to H_1. Hours of work in this case fall.

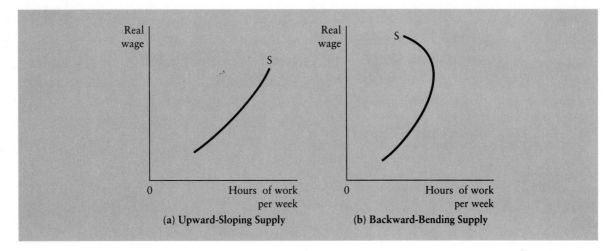

In Panel a, a higher real wage induces the individual to supply more labor. The substitution effect of the higher wage outweighs the income effect. In Panel b, on the other hand, the supply curve for labor is backward bending. For relatively high wage rates, the income effect of a higher wage outweighs the substitution effect and causes the individual to demand more leisure.

Figure 20.3
Two Shapes for an Individual's Supply Curve for Labor

Do people's labor supply curves more nearly resemble that shown in Panel a or Panel b in Figure 20.3? Although there is substantial evidence that short-run labor supply curves have a positive slope (consider, for example, the positive effect on hours of work that offering premium overtime wages has), it appears that over the long run labor supply curves at times may have been backward bending. In 1890 the average workweek in the United States in the manufacturing industry was about 60 hours. Real wages in 1890 were about $3.40 per hour (in terms of 1989 prices). By 1929 the workweek in manufacturing had dropped to 40 hours, in spite of the fact that real wages had risen to about $5.85 per hour. American workers chose to take a large part of their increasing incomes in the form of leisure, and this is consistent with the notion of a backward-bending supply curve. Since 1929, real wages in manufacturing have continued to rise (to about $10 per hour in 1989), but the workweek has not fallen much below 40 hours per week (though in other industries it has fallen to about 35 hours). It appears that in recent years the substitution effect of higher wages has almost exactly balanced the income effect—at least for manufacturing workers. Of course, these numbers only represent average wages for the whole economy. Across occupations and industries relative wages change over time, and this has the effect of causing people to change the kinds of jobs they take. Application 20.2: The Volunteer Army and the Draft shows that the supply curve of labor to any one occupation (here the military) is undoubtedly upward sloping and possibly quite elastic.

APPLICATION 20.2

The Volunteer Army and the Draft

The question of the elasticity of the supply of labor played an important role in the mid-1960s debate over the costs of establishing an all-volunteer army in the United States. If the supply of labor to the military were elastic, volunteers could be attracted with relatively small increases in existing pay schedules. An inelastic supply, on the other hand, would require sharp increases in defense costs as a result of the elimination of military conscription.

Labor Supply and the Costs of the Draft

To study this issue, in 1967 W. Y. Oi calculated a supply curve for military personnel.[1] His basic results are presented in Table 1. There is clear evidence that increases in military pay encouraged enlistments. For example, Oi showed that an increase in the first-term pay of enlistees from the then-present level of $2,500 to a level more nearly approximating civilian wages (about $3,600 for unskilled 18-year-olds in 1965) would have increased enlistments by 40 percent. Notice, however, that the supply curve tended to become more inelastic as potential wages were raised still further. Raising wages from $4,700 to $5,900 would attract only 13 percent more enlistments. This may indicate that people's willingness to enlist voluntarily in the military varies widely across the population and those with preferences against serving can be attracted only at very high wages. It also suggests that the military draft may involve very high implicit costs for some draftees who would be willing to pay quite a lot to avoid service.

The Volunteer Force

Following cessation of hostilities in Vietnam in the early 1970s, the U.S. military moved rapidly toward the establishment of an all-volunteer force. Experiences since that time have been quite consistent with what had been predicted by Oi and others; that is, enlistments proved to be rather responsive to military pay. One study of the

Table 1

Supply Curve of Voluntary Enlistments in the Armed Forces in 1965

Annual First-Term Pay	Enlistments
$2,500	260,000
3,600	365,000
4,700	415,000
5,900	470,000

Source: W. Y. Oi, "The Economic Cost of the Draft," *American Economic Review* (May 1967): 39–62.

years 1967 to 1979, for example, found that the supply elasticities for enlistments in the Army and Navy exceed 1 and are especially high for later years in which the threat of a draft had largely disappeared.[2] Interestingly, these authors also found that supply elasticities to the Marines and Air Force were much lower than for the other armed services. For the case of the Marine Corps, they attributed this finding to the special nature of that branch of the armed forces: It appears that a segment of the population wants to join almost regardless of wages. The Air Force is also a special case because of the specialized training it provides. The allure of high-wage civilian jobs following service in the Air Force appears to outweigh the effects of current wages on enlistments.

To Think About

1. The "costs" of hiring soldiers usually mean the wages they are paid. With a military draft, is that a correct way to account for costs? How would you measure the costs of military service to a draftee?

2. Some people say that a draft is the only fair way to raise an army since only with a draft would the burden of military service be "equally shared." Do you agree? Ideally, how would the costs of military service be shared under a draft relative to the costs under a volunteer force?

---

[1] W. Y. Oi, "The Economic Cost of the Draft," *American Economic Review* (May 1967): 39–62. Oi's calculations have been simplified in this example, and they do not correspond exactly to those in the original article.

[2] See Colin Ash, Bernard Udis, and R. F. McNowan, "Enlistments in the All-Volunteer Force: A Military Personnel Supply Model and Its Forecasts," *American Economic Review* (March 1983): 145–155.

Market Supply Curve for Labor

We can construct a market supply of labor curve from individual supply curves by "adding" them up. At each possible wage rate, we add together the quantity of labor offered by each person in order to arrive at a market total. One particularly interesting aspect of this procedure is that as the wage rate rises, more people may be induced to enter the labor force. That is, rising wages may induce some people who were not previously employed to take jobs. Figure 20.4 illustrates this possibility for a simple case of two individuals. For a real wage below w_1, neither person chooses to work in the market. Consequently, the market supply curve of labor (Panel c) shows that no labor is supplied at real wages below w_1. A wage in excess of w_1 causes person 1 to enter the labor market. However, as long as wages fall short of w_2, person 2 will not work. Only at a wage rate above w_2 will both people choose to take a job. As Panel c in Figure 20.4 shows, the possibility of the entry of these new workers makes the market supply of labor somewhat more responsive to wage rate increases than would be the case if we assumed that the number of workers was fixed. Changing wage rates may not only induce current workers to alter their hours of work, but perhaps more important, they may change the composition of the work force. As Application 20.3: Changing Labor Force Participation for Married Women and Older Males shows, such effects have been especially pronounced for these two groups in the United States over the past 25 years.

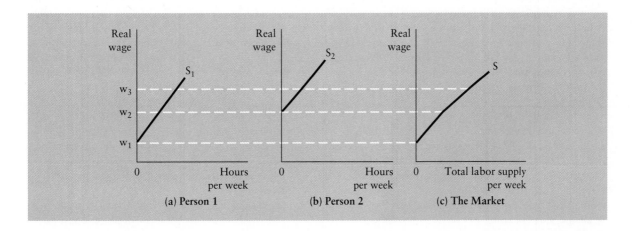

(a) Person 1   **(b) Person 2**   **(c) The Market**

As the real wage rises, the supply of labor may increase for two reasons. First, higher real wages may cause each person to work more hours. Second, higher wages may induce more people (for example, person 2) to enter the labor market.

Figure 20.4
Construction of the Market Supply Curve for Labor

APPLICATION 20.3

Changing Labor Force Participation for Married Women and Older Males

Probably the two most significant trends in labor market behavior in the United States during the past three decades has been (1) the increasing tendency for married women to hold paying jobs, and (2) the decline in employment of older men. Both of these trends are illustrated in Table 1.

Expanding Female Labor Force Participation

For women in the prime age category 25 to 34, the increase in labor force participation has been spectacular. The fraction of married women aged 25 to 34 who are in the work force more than doubled between 1960 and 1989. Many reasons have been proposed to explain this major social phenomenon. Economists have tended to focus on expanding job opportunities and real wages for women as a principal explanation. Because married women have good alternative uses for their time (such as working in the home versus working in the market), substitution effects from higher real wages would be expected to be large; hence, labor supply will increase in response to higher wages. Sociologists, on the other hand, tend to attribute the increasing work by married women to political and cultural factors. That is, they attribute the change to a shift in the supply curve rather than a move along it in response to higher wages. Whatever the cause, these labor force statistics show greater responsiveness in labor supply behavior of a large segment of the population than was believed likely in earlier times.

The Case of Older Men

Interestingly, the labor force trend for older married men has been precisely opposite to that for younger married women. As Table 1 shows, between 1960 and 1989 the labor force participation rate for married men over 65 fell to less than half its initial level. The pattern is all the more puzzling given the improvement in the health of older men that had occurred over this period.

Table 1

Labor Force Participation Rates, 1960–1989

Year	Married Females Age 25–34	Married Males Age 65 and Over
1960	28.8%	36.6%
1970	38.8	29.9
1975	48.4	23.3
1980	58.8	20.5
1985	65.8	16.8
1989	69.0	17.8

Source: Statistical Abstract of the United States, 1991 (Washington D.C.: U.S. Government Printing Office, 1991), Table 641.

Such improvements should have resulted in more rather than less work activity by this group.

Although it is possible that the figures simply reflect a backward bending supply of labor in response to higher wages, most economists have instead focused on issues of retirement as being the primary cause. Most importantly, the rapid growth in Social Security coverage of the elderly coupled with rising real benefit amounts may have encouraged increasingly large numbers of workers to retire in recent years. Other provisions of the program (such as reduction in benefits that results when the elderly do take jobs) have had a similar effect of discouraging work. Policymakers have been especially concerned about these trends (most importantly because they threaten the financial integrity of Social Security) and have taken some steps to try to reverse them.[1]

To Think About

1. How does income taxation affect the labor supply decisions of married women? Would special tax treatment of the earnings of married couples increase or decrease labor supply by married women?
2. Would the availability of Social Security benefits at retirement cause people to work more or less during their prime working years?

---

[1] For a more complete discussion of these issues in the theory of labor supply see R. G. Ehrenberg and R. G. Smith, *Modern Labor Economics,* 4th ed. (Glenview, Ill.: Scott, Foresman, 1991), Chapters 6 and 7.

Occupational Choice and Compensating Wage Differentials

So far this chapter has primarily treated the labor market as a single market. All labor was assumed to be of the same quality and all jobs were assumed to be equally attractive so we could speak of the wage as being set by supply and demand in one market. In reality, of course, wages differ greatly among individuals and among jobs.

There are three reasons for these differentials. First, workers have different levels of skills. These differences in skills may cause some workers to be more productive than others; in a competitive market for labor, those with greater skills will earn higher wages. Second, some workers may receive wages that are essentially monopoly rents. If workers can successfully limit access to certain jobs, they may succeed in improving their own wages. Finally, wage rates may differ among jobs because some jobs are more pleasant than others. More enjoyable jobs will attract a large supply of applicants, and this may cause the wage rates to be lower than in less desirable ones. In this section we restrict our attention to this third reason for wage differentials.

The notion that differing characteristics of jobs may lead to differential wages has long been noted by economists. In *The Wealth of Nations*, for example, Adam Smith observed that

> . . . the whole of the advantages and disadvantages of the different employments of labour . . . must, in the same neighbourhood, be either equal or continually tending to equality. If in the same neighbourhood there is any employment either more or less advantageous than the rest, so many people would crowd into it in the one case, and so many would desert it in the other, that its advantages would soon return to the level of other employments. . . .

> [But] pecuniary wages . . . are everywhere in Europe extremely different according to the different employments of labour . . . this difference arises partly from certain circumstances in the employments themselves, which, either really, or at least in the imaginations of men, make up for a small pecuniary gain in some and counter-balance a great one in others. . . .[2]

Smith then stresses the difference between the "whole advantages and disadvantages" of a particular job and the wages paid for the job. Even with perfect freedom of access to jobs and no skill differentials, wage rate differences can persist because of differences in the attractiveness of certain jobs. The market operates to equate the total attractiveness of jobs, not just the pecuniary rewards of these jobs. To capture such effects economists use the term **compensating wage differentials** to describe differences in wages that arise solely because of differing characteristics of jobs. The wage rate differences "compensate" for the differing job characteristics.

Compensating wage differentials

Differences in wages caused by differing job characteristics.

[2]Adam Smith, *The Wealth of Nations*, Cannan ed. (New York: Modern Library, 1937), Chapter 10, p. 1.

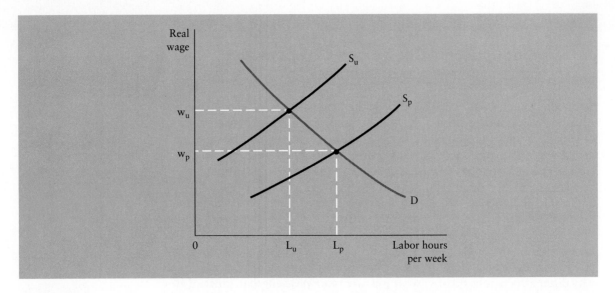

Figure 20.5
Compensating
Wage Differentials

The demand curve for labor is assumed to be the same for both a "pleasant" job and an "unpleasant" one. However, the supply curves (S_p and S_u, respectively) differ for the two types of jobs. This causes wages to differ between the jobs. The higher wage rate for the unpleasant job (w_u) is said to "compensate" for the nature of the job.

■ A Graphical Demonstration

Figure 20.5 illustrates a simple example of the way in which compensating differentials might arise. It assumes that there are two jobs: one "pleasant," the other "unpleasant." The demand curves of firms for workers to fill those jobs are assumed to be the same for both jobs. There are no differences in the skills of workers that might lead to differing marginal value products. The demand curve for both jobs is represented by the curve D.

Because the jobs differ in their attractiveness, however, the supply of labor to them will differ. The curve S_u represents the supply curve to the unpleasant job, and the equilibrium wage is given by w_u. At this wage firms in the unpleasant industry will demand L_u hours of labor input, and this is what individuals are willing to supply. Similarly, the curve S_p represents the supply curve of workers to the pleasant job. This curve lies to the right of the S_u curve because of the differences in the jobs. At any given wage individuals are willing to supply more labor to the pleasant job. Through the interaction of supply and demand, an equilibrium wage rate of w_p will be established for the pleasant job. This wage will be below w_u, and the difference between w_u and w_p is the wage differential that compensates for the unpleasantness of the first job.

The equilibrium shown in Figure 20.5 is stable: there is no incentive for a worker to transfer from one job to the other. As Smith predicted, the "net advantages" of the two jobs have been equalized. Measuring these differentials is not only interesting in itself, but the information may be useful for a variety of other purposes, as Application 20.4: Compensating Wage Differentials shows.

APPLICATION 20.4

Compensating Wage Differentials

Tables 1 and 2 provide some very tentative estimates of compensation wage differentials. Table 1 shows that jobs that have high mortality rates also have higher annual wages (other things being the same). In 1967 individuals chose among jobs as if they were putting an implicit value of about $176,000 on their own lives.[1] In other words, employees seem willing to accept an increase in the annual probability of dying on a job of one-tenth of 1 percent in exchange for $176 extra in annual salary. Although that conclusion is controversial and may, for a variety of reasons, be too low (for instance, it disregards the costs that a person's death may impose on his or her family), there are many situations in which assigning some estimated value for a life is essential. Workplace health and safety legislation, for example, must reach some compromise between the benefits of safer methods of production and the costs of such safety.

Table 1

Compensating Wage Differentials for Differential Death Rates, by Occupations, 1967

Occupation	Additional Annual Deaths per 100,000	Estimated Increment to Annual Salary
Bartenders	179	$315
Boilermakers	230	405
Fire fighters	44	77
Lumberjacks	256	451
Mine operatives	176	310
Police and detectives	78	137
Taxicab drivers	182	320
Teamsters	114	201

Source: R. Thaler and S. Rosen, "The Value of Saving a Life: Evidence from the Labor Market," in *Household Production and Consumption,* N.E. Terleckyj, ed. (New York: National Bureau of Economic Research, 1975), pp. 265–298. Data computed from Tables 1 and 3.

Table 2

Compensating Wage Differentials for Unpleasant Working Conditions, 1967

	Addition to Wage Provided by Job Attribute			
	White Males	Black Males	White Females	Black Females
Repetitive jobs	10.3%	7.7%	22.3%	25.6%
Jobs in a poor work environment	6.8	−7.7	3.3	19.5

Source: R. E. B. Lucas, "Hedonic Wage Equations and Psychic Wages in the Returns to Schooling," *American Economic Review* (September 1977): Table 1, p. 554.

Valuing Working Conditions

Because it is very difficult to define "working conditions" of jobs in objective and quantifiable ways, measuring compensating differentials for "unpleasant" jobs is even more difficult than measuring differentials associated with risks of loss of life. The results of R. E. B. Lucas's attempt at measurement are reported in Table 2. These results show that, on the whole, people do seem to receive somewhat higher wages for jobs that are repetitive in nature or that require working in an unpleasant environment (that is, one characterized by heat, cold, noise, or some other unpleasant feature).

To Think About

1. Why bother to put a value on life at all? Isn't all life essentially beyond valuation?
2. How can the idea of compensating wage differentials be reconciled with the everyday observation that some very unpleasant jobs (such as those of trash collectors or day laborers) are not paid very well whereas executives in fancy, comfortable offices may be paid a great deal?

[1]For an up-to-date summary of studies of the value of a life, see A. Fisher, L. G. Chestnut, and D. M. Violette, "The Value of Reducing Risks from Death," *Journal of Policy Analysis and Management* (Winter 1989): 88–100.

Labor Unions

Workers may at times find it useful to join a labor union in order to pursue goals that can more effectively be achieved through group action. Sometimes joining a union is completely voluntary. In many cases, however, compulsory membership (the closed shop) is required in order to maintain an effective union and prevent other workers from getting a free ride without paying union dues. This section examines the goals that an effective union might pursue, and how this pursuit will affect the wage rate.

■ Unions' Goals and the Monopoly Supply Decision

As in our discussion of the theory of the firm, we start our analysis of union behavior by describing the goals a union might seek. A first assumption we might make is that the goals of a union represent what its members want. This assumption avoids the problem of modeling the personal aspirations of union leaders, which may be in conflict with rank-and-file goals. Union leaders are therefore assumed to be conduits for expressing the desires of the membership.

Strong unions can be treated in the same way as monopoly firms. The union faces a demand curve for labor; because it is the sole source of supply, it can choose the point on this curve at which it will operate. The point that is actually chosen by the union will obviously depend on the particular goals it has decided to pursue. Three possible choices are illustrated in Figure 20.6. The union may, for example, choose to offer that quantity of labor that maximizes the total wage bill $(w \cdot L)$. If this is the case, it will offer that quantity for which the marginal revenue from labor demand is equal to zero. This quantity is given by L_1 in Figure 20.6, and the wage rate associated with this quantity is w_1. The point E_1 is therefore this union's preferred wage-quantity combination. Notice that at wage rate w_1 there may be an excess supply of labor, and the union must somehow allocate those jobs that are available among the workers who want them. It may, for example, adopt a seniority or apprenticeship scheme that preserves high-wage jobs for its most senior workers.

Another possible goal that the union may pursue would be to choose to supply the quantity of labor that maximizes the total economic rent obtained by its members. In this way the union would be acting in a way similar to a monopoly firm by maximizing the "profits" (that is, wages in excess of opportunity costs) of its members. To do so would require the union to choose that quantity of labor for which the additional total wages obtained by having one more employed union member (the marginal revenue) are equal to the extra cost of luring that member into the market. The union should therefore choose that quantity, L_2, at which the marginal revenue curve crosses the supply curve. The wage rate associated with this quantity is w_2, and the desired wage-

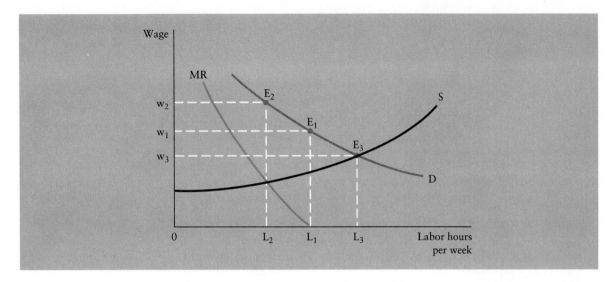

A union that has a monopoly in the supply of labor may choose any point on the demand curve for labor that it prefers. Three such points are shown in the figure. At point E_1 total labor payments (w · L) are maximized; at E_2 the economic rent that workers receive is maximized; and at E_3 the total amount of labor hired is maximized.

Figure 20.6
Three Possible Points on the Labor Demand Curve that a Monopoly Union Might Choose

quantity combination is labeled E_2 in the diagram. Again, under this combination, some workers who desire to work at the prevailing wage are left unemployed. Perhaps the union may "tax" (by charging dues) the large economic rent earned by those who do work in order to transfer income in the form of layoff benefits to those who don't.

A third possibility would be for the union to aim for maximum employment of its members. This would involve choosing the point w_3, L_3, which is precisely the point that would result if the market were organized in a perfectly competitive way. No employment greater than L_3 could be achieved, since the quantity of labor that union members supply would be reduced for wages less than w_3.

■ Other Union Goals: Job Security and Fringe Benefits

Although the union goals illustrated in Figure 20.6 are those that are easiest to diagram, that list is by no means exhaustive. Two other important goals that unions may seek, for example, are job security and a variety of nonwage fringe benefits. Job security is particularly important in industries such as durable goods manufacturing or construction in which there are major cyclical influences on product demand and on the demand for labor. Unions may seek to reduce the risks of such fluctuations for their members by establishing

APPLICATION 20.5
The Effects of Unions

Collective bargaining may have an effect on many aspects of labor contracts. Figure 20.6 illustrates how unions might affect wages and employment, but our discussion suggests that they may also have effects on job security and other fringe benefits. In this application, we look at some of the empirical evidence regarding these effects.

Union Wage Effects
There is clear evidence that unions raise wages for their members. Studies of a wide variety of industries suggest that the union wage premium is on the order of 10 to 20 percent and rose significantly during the 1970s and 1980s.[1] Union effects seem larger in those industries in which the demand for labor is less elastic, perhaps because in these cases unions face a more attractive wage-employment trade-off. Economists have been especially interested in union wage effects in the public sector—a sector with presumably a low elasticity of demand for workers. However, most studies have failed to find these expected large union wage effects. They do suggest that public sector unions may succeed in obtaining more attractive fringe benefit packages, possibly because these may be less visible than wages to voters who must ultimately support the resulting labor contracts.[2]

The Decline of Unionization
Between 1965 and 1985 the fraction of the U.S. workforce covered by collective-bargaining agreements fell dramatically from approximately 30 percent to less than 16 percent. In part, this trend reflected a restructuring of total output in the economy away from sectors that are highly unionized (manufacturing) toward those with much lower rates of unionization (services). More active employer opposition to unions coupled with a less favorable legislative climate may also have contributed to the decline. Unions themselves may also have helped their demise through their wage and fringe

benefits policies. Rising union wage premia may have contributed to rapid growth of nonunionized employment in construction and several service sectors.[3]

Unions and Productivity
Although some economists take a benign view of the decline of unionism as reflecting the normal workings of the labor market, others view the decline with alarm. To these economists, unions provide a valuable "voice" in the industrial-relations system that may promote productivity advances by improving communications within firms. Empirical evidence does tend to confirm that output per worker is higher in unionized firms than in nonunionized firms in some industries. Of course, such effects might be expected given the ability of unions to raise wages—*ceteris paribus,* higher wages will always be associated with higher marginal productivities for profit-maximizing firms. Whether unions have actually fostered technical improvements is open to question.

To Think About
1. How do unions choose among the various wage-employment options offered by the labor demand curve? Whose preferences enter into considerations? Whose preferences are disregarded?
2. Some studies of labor demand focus on "unit labor costs"—that is, the cost of production per unit of output. How might the effects of unions on wages and productivity affect unit labor costs? How does this concept affect the competitiveness of unionized versus nonunionized firms?

[1]See B. T. Hirsh and J. T. Addison, *The Economic Analysis of Unions: New Approaches and Evidence* (Boston: Allen & Unwin, 1988).
[2]R. B. Freeman, "Unionism Comes to the Public Sector," *Journal of Economic Literature* (March 1986): 41–86.
[3]All of these issues are discussed in the symposium, "Unions in Decline: Causes and Consequences," *American Economic Review* (May 1986): 92–108.

contractual rights to jobs. In that way the variability in workers' wage incomes will be reduced, and (as we showed in Chapter 7) this reduction raises workers' utility.

Fringe benefits such as pensions, vacations, insurance coverage, and generally better working conditions are also of considerable value to workers. Because such benefits are frequently of low public visibility in negotiating sessions and are often nontaxable to workers, they have come to constitute an increasingly important part of firms' total labor costs.

Such additional union goals can be taken into account in two ways. First, the price of labor should be generalized to include indirect forms of compensation in addition to the usual hourly wage rate. Obviously, firms and workers bargain over the total package of compensation, not just one part of it. Related to this is a second observation: Unions may be willing to forgo wage rate increases to obtain other types of benefits. Although diagramming such other goals may be difficult, these goals do play a major role in many labor negotiations. Application 20.5: The Effects of Unions looks at some of the evidence about the effects that unions have on labor market outcomes.

Summary

In this chapter we have examined several questions about the supply of labor. Our primary conclusions are

- The market wage rate represents the opportunity cost of leisure for individuals. It shows how nonwork time can be traded for income (and consumption) in the marketplace.

- A utility-maximizing individual will choose to work that number of hours for which the MRS of leisure for consumption is equal to the market wage. That is, the individual will equate the rate at which he or she is willing to trade leisure for consumption to the market opportunity cost of that leisure.

- A change in the wage rate has both substitution and income effects on people's choices. The effects work in opposite directions. A higher real wage, for example, will have a substitution effect that encourages people to work more, but an income effect that encourages them to work less.

- If jobs differ in their attractiveness, this will show up in the supply of labor for those jobs. Differentials in wage rates will arise that compensate people for differing job characteristics.

- If workers join together to form a union, they may exert some monopoly power in the labor market. The supply decisions made by the monopoly union will depend on the goals it chooses to pursue. It is likely that unions can raise market wages for those who get jobs.

Review Questions

1. Economists tend to approach the study of labor supply in a relatively backward way by looking at the demand for "leisure." What do economists mean by "leisure"? Why does an individual's demand for leisure also constitute a supply of labor? If leisure is viewed as a consumption good, what is its price?

2. Use the concept of the opportunity cost of time to discuss the following:

   a. Who might be expected to pay the higher fares to fly the faster Concorde to Europe.
   b. Who would be likely to stand in long lines and even camp out overnight to purchase tickets to a sporting event.
   c. For whom greens fees are a larger fraction of the total cost of a golf game—a prospering physician or an unemployed laborer.
   d. How the degree of traffic congestion affects who drives to work and who takes mass transit.

3. In Chapter 4 we showed that, for a normal good, income and substitution effects tend to work in the same direction causing price rises to result in a decline in quantity demanded. Can a similar argument be made for the relationship between the price and quantity of leisure consumed? What is different about these two situations?

4. Use the time allocation model to discuss the effects on an individual's hours of work of

   a. The receipt of a substantial amount of outside income.
   b. The imposition of a tax on wages.
   c. An increase in the general price level with no concomitant increase in wages.
   d. National legislation establishing a maximum workweek of 35 hours.

5. Why might a person choose not to work? How would Figure 20.2 look in this case? What changes in such a person's budget constraint might lure him or her into the labor market?

6. The illustration of compensating wage differentials in Figure 20.5 shows two supply curves together with a single demand curve. Why is only the demand curve shown even though the figure shows the wages for two occupations? What does the use of the single demand curve implicitly assume about the workers who might take either job? Why is that an appropriate assumption for measuring compensation differentials?

7. Explain how information on compensating wage differentials might be used to find the value that workers implicitly place on their lives. What would such an

estimate assume about workers' knowledge of the risks of various jobs? Can you think of reasons why such labor market information might understate the true value of a life?

8. Why do workers join a union? What do they expect to gain? What do they have to give up? Why is a union more effective than a single worker in bargaining with employers?

9. If a union can be analyzed as a monopoly supplier of labor, why is that analysis so much more complicated than our analysis of the monopoly supplier of a good? Why is the profit-maximization assumption not applicable to a union?

10. Suppose a monopoly union represented all of the employees of a firm that was a monopsony hirer of these workers. Why might the goals of these two market participants be in conflict? How might such a conflict be resolved? (See also problem 20.10.)

Problems

20.1 Suppose there are 8,000 hours in a year (actually there are 8,760) and that an individual has a potential market wage of $5 per hour.

   a. What is the individual's full potential income if he or she could work 8,000 hours? If he or she chooses to devote 75 percent of this income to leisure, how many hours will be worked?

   b. Suppose a rich uncle dies and leaves the individual an annual income of $4,000 per year. If he or she continues to devote 75 percent of full income to leisure, how many hours will be worked?

   c. How would your answer to part b change if the market wage were $10 per hour instead of $5 per hour?

   d. Graph the individual's supply of labor curve implied by parts b and c.

20.2 Mrs. Smith has a guaranteed income of $10 per day from an inheritance. Her preferences require her always to spend half her potential income on leisure (H) and consumption (C).

   a. What is Mrs. Smith's budget constraint in this situation?

   b. How many hours will Mrs. Smith devote to work and to leisure in order to maximize her utility given that her market wage is $1.25? $2.50? $5.00? $10.00?

   c. Graph the four different budget constraints and sketch in Mrs. Smith's utility-maximizing choices. (Hint: when graphing budget constraints, remember that when H = 24, C = 10, not 0.)

   d. Graph Mrs. Smith's supply of labor curve.

20.3 Mr. Peabody has a utility function of $U = \sqrt{C \cdot H}$ and is maximizing his utility at U = 20 when he works 14 hours a day. Would he be willing to give up an hour of his leisure to drive Mrs. Atterboy to the wrestling match if she offered him $5?

20.4 John Q. Public always devotes two-thirds of his potential income to leisure. Mr. Public's real wage is $10 per hour.

    a. In the absence of any income taxation, how will Mr. Public allocate his time each day?

    b. Suppose the government institutes a proportional income tax with a tax rate of one-fourth. How will this affect Mr. Public's time allocation? How much in taxes will be collected?

    c. Suppose instead that the government instituted a lump sum of $20 per day. Now how will Mr. Public allocate his time? Explain why this result differs from your result in part b.

20.5 An individual's time horizon consists of two "days." During the first day her wage will be $5 per hour and this wage will rise to $10 per hour for the second day. This person always wishes to allocate two-thirds of her full income to leisure time.

    a. What is this person's full income?

    b. If this person is indifferent about which day she takes her leisure hours, how will she allocate her work hours over these two days so as to maximize these hours?

    c. Suppose this person feels she must have at least 16 hours of leisure each day. How would this change her time allocation?

    d. How would a rise in the second day's wage to $20 per hour affect the time allocations described in part b? Explain why such a rise would have no effect on the allocation described in part c.

    e. How would a rise in the first day's wage to $8 per hour affect the time allocation described in part b (assuming the second day's wage is $10 per hour)?

20.6 Returning to problem 20.1, suppose the rich uncle described in part b does not die, but decides to move in with the relative in question. The uncle agrees to give this person 40 percent of his earnings as rent. Obviously, if the uncle earns $10,000 per year, parts b and c to problem 20.1 will have the same answer as before. How would the answers change if the uncle earned $5,000 per year? or, how about $20,000 per year? Explain how this individual's labor market behavior is related to that of her uncle.

20.7 Suppose a union has a fixed supply of labor to sell. If the union desires to maximize the total wage bill, what wage rate will it demand? How would your answer change if unemployed workers were paid unemployment insurance at the rate u per worker and the union now desired to maximize the sum of the wage bill and the total amount of unemployment compensation?

*20.8 An individual receives utility from daily income (Y), given by

$$U(Y) = 100Y - \tfrac{1}{2}Y^2.$$

---

*Denotes a problem that is rather difficult.

The only source of income is earnings. Hence $Y = wL$, where w is the hourly wage and L is hours worked per day. The individual knows of a job that pays $5 per hour for a certain 8-hour day. What wage must be offered for a construction job where hours of work are random with a mean of 8 hours and a variance of 36 hours to get the individual to accept this more "risky" job? Hint: This problem makes use of the statistical identity

$$E(X^2) = \text{Var } X + E(X)^2,$$

where E means "expected value."

* 20.9   A welfare program for low-income people offers a family a basic grant of $6,000 per year. This grant is reduced by $.75 for each $1 of other income the family has.

   a. How much in welfare benefits does the family receive if it has no other income? If the head of the family earns $2,000 per year? How about $4,000 per year?

   b. At what level of earnings does the welfare grant become zero?

   c. Assume that the head of this family can earn $4 per hour and that the family has no other income. What is the annual budget constraint for this family if it does not participate in the welfare program? That is, how are consumption (C) and hours of leisure (H) related?

   d. What is the budget constraint if the family opts to participate in the welfare program? (Remember, the welfare grant can only be positive.)

   e. Graph your results from parts c and d.

   f. Suppose the government changes the rules of the welfare program to permit families to keep 50 percent of what they earn. How would this change your answer to parts d and e above?

   g. Using your results from part f, can you predict whether the head of this family will work more or less under the new rules described in part f?

* 20.10 Suppose the supply curve for labor to a firm has the form

$$L = 100w$$

where w is the market wage. Suppose that the marginal expense of hiring workers is

$$ME_L = L/50.$$

Suppose also that the firm's demand (marginal value product) curve has the form

$$L = -50MVP_L + 450.$$

   a. If the firm is a monopsonist, how many workers will it hire in order to maximize profits? What wage will it pay?

---

*Denotes a problem that is rather difficult.

b. If the supply of labor is monopolized, how many workers should be provided to the firm in order to maximize the total wage bill (wL)? What will the wage rate be?

c. If the market has both a monopsony on the demand side and a monopoly on the supply side, what can you say about the "equilibrium" outcome? How will this compare to the competitive solution?

The study of capital as a factor of production is extremely important in economics. For example, economists have traditionally assigned an important role to capital accumulation as a source of economic growth. One of the major reasons for income increasing over time is the increasing amount of productive equipment workers have at their disposal. Similarly, Keynesian economic theory assigns an important role to investment as one component of aggregate demand. For this reason, capital theory is central to modern macroeconomics. The purpose of Chapter 21 is to provide a simple analysis of capital pricing that is relevant to these and many other issues.

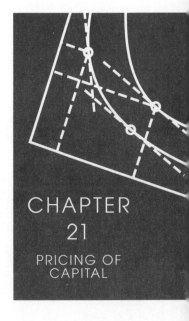

CHAPTER
21
PRICING OF CAPITAL

Definition of Capital

■
Capital stock

The total amount of machines, buildings, and all other produced, nonlabor resources in an economy.

When we speak of the **capital stock** of an economy, we mean the total amount of machines, buildings, and other nonlabor resources that are in existence at some point in time. These assets represent some portion of an economy's past output that was not consumed when it was produced. This past output was instead invested to be used for production in the future. All societies, from the most primitive to the most advanced, engage in this sort of capital accumulation. A bushman's taking time off from hunting to make arrows, people in a modern society using part of their incomes to buy houses, or governments taxing citizens in order to purchase dams and post office buildings are all pursuing the same sort of activity—some portion of the economy's current output is being invested for use in producing additional goods in future periods. Present sacrifice for future gain is the essential aspect of all capital accumulation.

Rate of Return

The process of capital accumulation is pictured schematically in Figure 21.1. In both panels of the figure, society is initially consuming level C_0 and has been doing so for some time. At time 1 a decision is made to withhold some current output (amount s) rather than consuming it. Starting in time 2 this investment

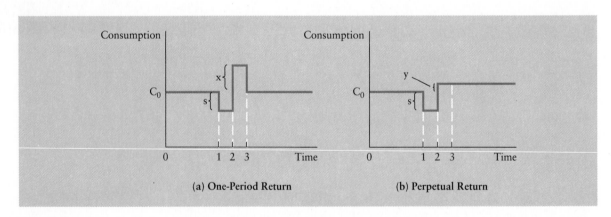

Figure 21.1
Two Views of Capital Accumulation

In Panel a, society withdraws some current consumption (s) in order to gorge itself (with x extra consumption) in the next period. The one-period rate of return would be measured by $x/s - 1$. The society in Panel b takes a more long-term view and uses s to increase its consumption perpetually by y. The perpetual rate of return would be given by y/s.

is put to use producing additional consumption goods. An important concept connected with this process is the **rate of return** earned on this investment. In Panel a, all of the investment is used to produce additional output only in time 2. Consumption is increased by amount x in time 2 and then returns to its prior level, C_0. Society has saved for one period in order to have an orgy of consumption in the next one. A measure of the one-period rate of return from this activity would be

$$r_1 = \frac{x}{s} - 1. \qquad [21.1]$$

If $x > s$ (if more consumption comes out of this process than went into it), we would say that the one-period rate of return to capital accumulation is positive. For example, if investing 100 units of current output permitted society to consume an extra 110 units next year, the one-period rate of return would be .10 (= 110/100 − 1) or 10 percent.

In Panel b of Figure 21.1 society is assumed to take a more long-term view in its consumption activities. Again, an amount s is invested at time 1. Now, however, this investment is used to raise the consumption level for all periods in the future. If the permanent level of consumption is raised to $C_0 + y$, we define the perpetual rate of return to be

$$r_\infty = \frac{y}{s}. \qquad [21.2]$$

If capital accumulation succeeds in raising C_0 permanently, r will be positive. For example, suppose society invested 100 units of output in time 1 to be devoted to capital accumulation. If this capital would permit output to be raised by 10 units for every period in the future (starting at time 2), the perpetual rate of return would be 10 percent.

When economists speak of the rate of return on capital, they have in mind something between these two extremes. They define the rate of return in an economy to be the terms at which current output that is invested can be turned into goods consumed at some future date. The next section shows how market forces operate to determine this rate.

Determination of the Rate of Return

In a market economy the actual rate of return on capital will depend on the technical possibilities of investing present goods to make future goods, and on the preferences of people for present versus future goods. An equilibrium rate of return will reflect both the return to capital accumulation that is technically feasible and the return that individuals are willing to accept.

Rate of return

The increase in future output made possible by investing one unit of current output in capital accumulation.

■ A Supply-Demand Analysis

Determination of this equilibrium rate of return can be illustrated by considering the supply and demand for what we might call **future goods.** Such goods are "purchased" today by setting aside some capital investment. When the output from that capital is consumed, it is called a future good. Simple examples of future goods include those yielded by growing grapes for wine or trees for lumber. Once an investment in these goods has been made, they increase in value over time—wine and timber offer a rate of return. Although purchasing machinery in the U.S. economy is much more complicated than planting trees, the activities are similar in that they represent investing present goods for use in producing goods to be consumed in the future. It is the market equilibrium that arises in this process that we wish to study.

A simple market for future goods is pictured in Figure 21.2. The horizontal axis shows the quantity of future goods traded (F). This is the quantity of actual consumption that will occur in the future. On the vertical axis we have recorded the relative price of these future goods (P_F). This price records the number of current goods (for example, pounds of seedlings) that must be sacrificed to get one future good (for example, one pound of lumber). The demand curve for future goods is drawn sloping downward on the assumption that the lower their price, the greater the quantity people will demand. In other

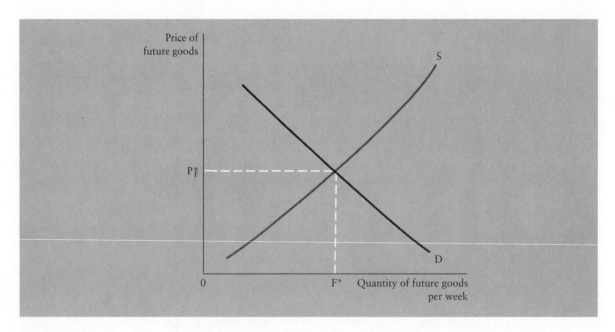

Figure 21.2
The Market for
Future Goods

The terms at which present goods trade for future goods (P_F) through capital accumulation is set by demand and supply conditions. It is likely that P_F^* will be less than one. We define the rate of return (r) by the formula $(1/1 + r) = P_F^*$. Since $P_F^* < 1$, r will be positive.

words, the smaller the required sacrifice of present goods, the greater will be people's demand for goods in the future. The supply curve for future goods slopes upward because of the assumption that the process of investing capital for the production of future goods may run into diminishing returns. As the amount of future goods produced increases, the marginal cost (in terms of the present investment required) of producing them rises. Expanding the production from a wood lot of a fixed size requires progressively more in the way of initial investment of workers' time, soil improvements, and care in spacing seedlings.

■ Equilibrium Price of Future Goods

Equilibrium in the market shown in Figure 21.2 is at P_F^*, F^*. At that point the supply and demand for future goods are in balance, and the required amount of current goods will be invested in order to produce F^* in the future.[1]

There are a number of reasons to expect that P_F^* will be less than one: that is, it will cost less than the sacrifice of one current good to "buy" one good in the future. On the demand side it might be argued that people require some reward for waiting. Everyday slogans ("a bird in the hand is worth two in the bush," "live for today") and more substantial realities such as the uncertainty of the future and the finiteness of life suggest that people are generally impatient in their consumption decisions. Capital accumulation such as that shown in Figure 21.1 will take place only if the current sacrifice is in some way worthwhile.

There are also supply reasons for believing P_F^* will be less than one. All of these involve the idea that capital accumulation is "productive": investing one good currently will ultimately yield more than one good in the future. Tree farmers, vineyard operators, and cheesemakers "abstain" from selling their wares currently in the belief that time will make them more valuable in the future.[2] Similarly, building steel mills or power stations may ultimately yield more in the future value of output than was used to produce these capital goods. Application 21.1: The Rate of Return to Storing Wine illustrates a particularly rewarding example of this productivity from investing.

■ The Equilibrium Rate of Return

We can show the relationship of the rate of return (r) to what we have called the price of future goods by the formula

$$P_F^* = \frac{1}{1+r}. \qquad [21.3]$$

---

[1]This is a much simplified form of an analysis originally presented by Irving Fisher in *The Rate of Interest* (New York: Macmillan, 1907).

[2]For a discussion of these examples in the context of "Austrian" capital theory, see Marc Blaug, *Economic Theory in Retrospect*, 4th ed. (Cambridge, U.K.: Cambridge University Press, 1985), Chapter 12.

APPLICATION 21.1

The Rate of Return to Storing Wine

Laying down rare wine to age is a simple example of capital accumulation—present consumption of wine is forgone in the hope of obtaining more enjoyable consumption in the future. Although there are no objective standards to measure how much a wine's taste improves each year, prices for bottles of wine of various ages provide a good estimate of the returns obtained by oenophiles. In a 1981 study, Elizabeth Jaeger examined results for the Hueblein Wine Auction for red bordeaux and California cabernet sauvignon over the period 1969 to 1977.[1] Overall, she calculated that wines being auctioned yielded average annual rates of return of over 20 percent, a figure well in excess of returns available on financial investments (such as Treasury bills) during the period. At least for these particular years, it appears that aging of wine offered a substantial incentive to delay consumption.

Is Wine a Good Investment?

One question immediately suggested by these results is why returns to storing wine are so high. Jaeger suggests the principal explanation is that storing wine is a risky enterprise. Besides the problem of protecting wine against breakage and temperature changes, there is major uncertainty as to whether a particular vintage will age properly. The chemistry involved in the changing properties of wine over time is very delicate. Undetectable differences among rare wines when they are first bottled may lead to major discrepancies in their quality as they age. Discovering that a particular red vintage is aging poorly can lead to sharp price drops, reflecting the wine's lowered quality. Jaeger finds some evidence to support this explanation for wine's high rates of return by comparing older and younger vintages. She calculates a much higher rate of return on the younger vintages since these are subject to great risks and potential disappointments. For these older vintages, rates of return were not significantly higher than those obtainable on relatively safe financial investments.

Wine Auctions and Price Information

Using auction records (as Jaeger does) to judge the rate of return to owning wines (or paintings, stamps, coins) poses additional problems. Many wines come to auction only occasionally, so price records are not as complete as those for, say, stock prices. Wines also may not obey the law of one price, selling at different prices in transactions only minutes apart in the same auction. Wine prices also may be significantly affected by experts' announced opinions even though these may not accurately reflect reality. Vintages touted by experts may offer lower appreciation potential than those vintages not mentioned. Such information effects incorporate important random elements into observed prices. Hence, although wine prices from auctions do provide some indication of relative value, limited samples of these data must be used with care in judging investment returns.[2]

To Think About

1. When is the right time to sell wine that is rising in value? Should a winery hold onto its product until it has ceased to appreciate further? Or should the product be sold while it is still rising in value? What is the opportunity cost of keeping wine in the barrel?
2. Why do people hold wine (or other collectibles such as paintings or coins) as an investment? What returns do they expect? Wouldn't the returns to financial investments generally be superior since these pay a definite monetary return?

---

[1]Elizabeth Jaeger, "To Save or Savor: The Rate of Return to Storing Wine," *Journal of Political Economy* (June 1981): 584–592.

[2]See G. Ashenfelter, "How Auctions Work for Wine and Fine Art," *Journal of Economic Perspectives* (Summer 1989): 23–36.

Since we believe that P_F^* will be less than one, r will be positive. For example, if $P_F^* = .9$, r will equal approximately .1, and we would say that the rate of return to capital accumulation is 10 percent.[3] By investing one unit of current output, the consumption of future goods can be increased by 1.1. The rate of return and P_F are equivalent ways of measuring the terms on which present goods can be turned into future goods.[4]

In the remainder of this chapter we assume that the equilibrium real rate of return, r, has been established by the process shown in Figure 21.1. That rate provides a measure of the benefits of capital accumulation to all people who are considering it. We will show how they take account of r in all of the decisions they make that concern the allocation of resources over time.

Rental Rate on Machines and the Theory of Investment

Any firm will rent machines in accordance with the principles of profit maximization derived in Chapter 19. Specifically, a profit-maximizing firm will hire that number of machines for which the marginal value product (MVP) from hiring one more is equal to the machine's market rental rate (v). This section first investigates the determinants of machines' market rental rates by assuming that firms rent all the equipment they use. Later, we examine the particular problems raised because most firms own the machines they use rather than renting them from others.

■ Determinants of Market Rental Rates

Consider a firm in the business of leasing machines to other firms. Hertz and Avis lease automobiles, banks lease computers and aircraft to other operators, and Taylor Rental rents everything from punch bowls to chain saws. Suppose that such a rental firm owns a machine that has a current market value of P. If it sold the machine outright, the firm could get P for it. How much will the firm charge its clients for the use of the machine?

The firm owning this machine faces two kinds of costs: physical depreciation on the machine and the opportunity cost of having its funds tied up in the machine rather than in an investment earning the prevailing rate of return. If

---

[3]More precisely, if $P_F^* = .9$, r will be .11111 . . . since

$$.9 = \frac{1}{1 + .1111 \ldots} .$$

[4]It is important to make a distinction between the rate of return (r) and interest rates (i) observed in real-world markets (say, on savings accounts or on bonds). Since we live in a world of inflation, market interest rates will reflect both the rate of return on capital accumulation and the expected change in prices (since lenders will want to be compensated for the fact that they will be repaid in devalued dollars). If the expected proportional change in the price level is given by P_e, i and r are related by

$$i = r + P_e.$$

For example, if r = .05 (5 percent) and P_e = .04 (4 percent), the market interest rate will be i = .09 (9 percent).

depreciation costs per period (say, each year) are a constant percentage (d) of the machine's market value (P) and if the market rate of return on other investments is given by r, then the total costs to the machine owner for one year are given by

$$dP + rP = P(r + d). \qquad [21.4]$$

If we assume that the machine rental market is perfectly competitive, the workings of the market will ensure that the rental rate per year for the machine (v) is exactly equal to these long-run costs of the machine owner. Hence we have the basic result that

$$v = P(r + d). \qquad [21.5]$$

The annual rental rate is the sum of opportunity and depreciation costs that the rental company incurs. For example, suppose that the rate of return on alternative investments is 5 percent per year (that is, .05) and that the physical depreciation rate is 4 percent per year (.04). Suppose also that the current market price of a particular machine is $100. In this simple example, the machine would have a rental rate of $9 [$100 × (.05 + .04)] per year. The opportunity cost of the funds invested in the machine is $5, and the remaining $4 reflects the costs of physical deterioration over the year.

■ A Nondepreciating Machine

In the case of a machine that does not depreciate (d = 0), Equation 21.5 can be written in a simpler way:

$$\frac{v}{P} = r. \qquad [21.6]$$

This says that in equilibrium an infinitely long-lived (nondepreciating) machine is equivalent to a perpetual bond and must yield the prevailing rate of return. The rental rate as a percentage of the machine's price must be equal to r. If v/P exceeds r, everyone would rush out to buy machines, since they yield more than the prevailing rate of return on other investments. For example, if v = $10 per year and a machine sells for $100, a firm in the machine rental business will earn 10 percent on the funds it invests in machines. If alternative investments yield only 8 percent, the rental business is a very profitable one and new firms would enter it. Alternatively, if v/P is below r, no one would be in the business of leasing out machines, since more could be made on alternative investments. Hertz would do better putting its funds in a bank (at a 3 percent real rate of return) rather than investing in cars if each $20,000 car rented for only $400 per year (2 percent) net of depreciation.

■ Ownership of Equipment

To this point we have assumed that firms rent all of the machines they use. Although such rental does take place in the real world, more commonly firms own the machines they use. A firm will buy a machine and use its services, in combination with the labor the firm hires, to produce output. Ownership of machines makes the analysis of the demand for capital slightly more complicated than analyzing the demand for labor. By recognizing the important distinction between a stock and a flow, we can show that these two demands are quite similar.

A firm uses capital services to produce output. These services are a flow magnitude. It is the number of machine-hours that is relevant to the productive process (just as it is labor-hours), not the number of machines per se. Frequently, the assumption is made that the flow of capital services is proportional to the stock of machines (100 machines can, if fully employed for one hour, deliver 100 machine-hours of service). In this case, these two different concepts can be used synonymously. If during a period a firm desires a certain number of machine-hours, this is usually taken to mean that the firm needs a certain number of machines to provide them. The firm's demand for capital services is also a demand for capital ownership.

A profit-maximizing firm in perfect competition will choose its level of inputs so that the marginal value product from an extra unit of any input is equal to its cost. This result also holds for the demand for machine-hours. The cost of capital services is given by the rental rate (v) in Equation 21.5. This cost is borne by the firm whether it rents the machine in the open market or owns the machine itself. In the former case, machine rental is an explicit cost; in the latter case, it is an implicit cost since the firm could lease its equipment to another user if it chose to do so. In either case the opportunity cost of machine use is given by the market rental rate v. The fact of ownership is, to a first approximation, irrelevant to the determination of cost, and we can treat all firms as if they rent capital equipment. Firms that own machines can be viewed as renting those machines from themselves. In the process, they incur an opportunity cost of v.

■ Theory of Investment

If a firm finds that it desires more capital services than can be provided by its currently existing stock of machinery, it has two choices. First, it may hire the additional machines that are needed in the rental market. This would be formally identical to its decision to hire additional labor. Second, the firm can buy new machinery to meet its needs. We call this purchase of new equipment by the firm (net) **investment**.

Investment demand is an important component of aggregate demand in macroeconomic theory. Usually it is assumed that investment demand (that is, the demand for machines) is inversely related to the rate of return on alternative investments. It is easy now to demonstrate the links in this argument. A fall in the prevailing rate of return, r, will, *ceteris paribus*, decrease the rental rate on capital (Equation 21.5). Because forgone investment returns represent an implicit cost for the owner of a machine, a fall in r in effect reduces the cost of capital inputs. This fall in v implies that capital has become a relatively less expensive input and, as we showed in Chapter 19, this will prompt firms to

Investment

The purchase of new capital.

increase their capital use. Firms may then either rent additional machines from others or buy new equipment for their own use.

It is this latter effect (the buying of new equipment) that is termed investment. The relationship between changes in r and investment demand is therefore just one aspect of the theory of firms' demand for inputs. Because the rate of return is an important determinant of the rental rate on capital, a fall in r has an effect on investment by causing the quantity of capital demanded by firms to increase. If the firm's current stock of machinery cannot deliver the desired number of machine-hours, investment in new machinery will take place.

Tax Policy and Investment

Taxes represent a third type of cost that can also influence decisions on capital use. In the United States and many other countries, the corporate profits tax is not only an important source of government revenue, it is also a major policy tool that has been used to influence investment decisions.[5]

■ A Graphical Demonstration

When taxes are imposed on capital equipment, Equation 21.5 must be modified to take them into account. Now there are three costs that a machine owner must pay: interest, physical depreciation, and taxes. Consequently, the rental rate on a machine will now be

$$v = P(r + d) + T, \qquad [21.7]$$

where T represents the taxes on a machine that must be paid by the owner each period. A higher T implies a higher rental cost, and a lower T implies a lower cost. Figure 21.3 shows the effect that a reduction in T (and v) will have on the firm's desired level of capital inputs. Initially, the rental rate on capital is given by v_1; the firm produces q_1 by using K_1 units of capital input per period.

Now suppose T declines. Using Equation 21.7, this will cause a machine's rental rate to fall to v_2. As was the case for labor, this fall in the rental rate will create both substitution and output effects, which cause more capital to be hired. In Panel a in Figure 21.3 the substitution effect causes the optimal input combination to move to point B on the q_1 isoquant. The fall in v also causes the firm's marginal cost curve to shift downward to MC′. Output is increased to q_2; at this output level, the firm now wishes to hire K_2 units of capital input. Since the firm may not have a sufficient stock of capital equipment on hand to

---

[5]Although this tax is termed a profits tax, as we showed in Chapter 10, it is not a tax on economic profits, but rather on both economic profits and on the net output (marginal value product) of machines. It is this taxation of machines' net returns that affects investment decisions. A tax only on economic profits would have no such effect since it would not affect profit-maximizing or cost-minimizing input choices.

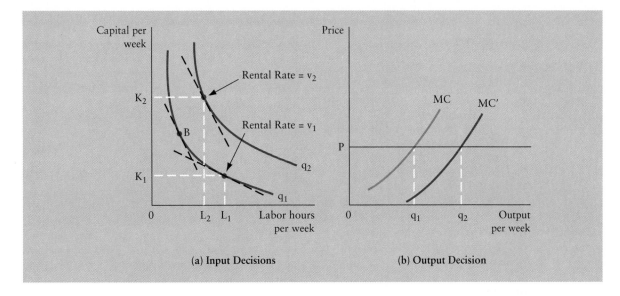

(a) Input Decisions

(b) Output Decision

If tax policies change the rental rate on capital, this will change the demand for capital services. For example, a reduction in taxes will cause the rental rate to fall from v_1 to v_2. This will create both substitution (from K_1, L_1 to B) and output (from B to K_2, L_2) effects, which cause the quantity of capital services demanded to increase (from K_1 to K_2). This increased demand for services may prompt firms to buy new machines.

Figure 21.3
Effects of a Reduction in Taxes on the Demand for Capital Services

provide this level of services, it may have to buy additional equipment. In other words, it may engage in investment. This is the sequence of events by which changes in government tax policy are related to the generation of investment incentives. In Application 21.2: Effects of Tax Policies on Investment, we examine the success of some specific tax measures that were intended to spur investment in this way.

Present Discounted Value and Investment

The theory of firms' demand for capital is often presented in a form different from the one we have used. This alternative form is termed the **present discounted value** theory of investment demand. Rather than treating the renting of machines similarly to the hiring of labor and centering attention on the rental rate (as we have done), this other approach looks directly at the firm's decision to purchase a machine. The theory concerns the demand for machines rather than the demand for the services of machines. This distinction between the two approaches is, however, not very important. Here we will show that this alternative approach predicts the same behavior as does the rental rate approach we have been using.

■
Present discounted value

The present value of funds payable in the future after taking account of the opportunity cost of interest forgone.

APPLICATION 21.2
Effects of Tax Policies on Investment

Federal tax policies have been widely used to influence the overall level of investment over the past 40 years. While the general thrust of these policies has been to seek to increase investment by lowering taxes, changes in the overall tax rate on profits have not been the primary way this has been accomplished. Rather, complex changes have been made in accounting procedures, and special credits have been allowed for investment. Although it would be inappropriate to describe these changes in detail, a brief sketch of the three most important policies will indicate how investment incentives have been provided.

Accelerated Depreciation

In 1954, federal tax policy was changed to allow firms to write off the costs of their investments in plant and equipment more rapidly than previously. That policy allowed firms to postpone the taxes owed on the income generated by newly purchased machinery. In essence, firms received an interest-free loan of their tax liability from the government. By one estimate this relatively subtle change in accounting principles reduced the rental rate on capital by as much as 20 percent.[1] Depreciation policies have been changed many times since 1954.

Useful Lifetime Guidelines

Another provision for accelerated depreciation was instituted in 1962. Under this provision what was defined as the "useful lifetimes" of various types of equipment for tax purposes were shortened. For example, the statutory minimum useful life of a car was reduced from four to three years. This made it possible for firms to gain further benefits from accelerated depreciation, and effective rental rates on capital were reduced another 2 or 3 percent.

Investment Tax Credit

An additional tax change in 1962 was the institution of an investment tax credit for machinery and equipment

purchases. Under that policy, 7 percent of the amount firms invested could be taken as a credit against taxes due. That policy reduced effective rental rates by 7 percent—essentially the U.S. Treasury paid for 7 percent of all machinery and equipment purchases. Similar credits have been instituted on a temporary basis several times during the past thirty years.

Effects of the Tax Policies in the Early 1960s

Table 1 shows the estimated effect of each of these tax policies on firms' total gross investment in equipment in 1963. As our theoretical discussion suggested, the reduction in rental rates had a substantial effect on the demand for capital equipment, increasing total purchases by about 20 percent over what they would have been under older, less generous tax laws. Clearly, tax policy provides a powerful lever with which the federal government can affect investment, and through investment, the overall pace of economic activity. The relatively high levels of employment experienced during the mid-1960s in the United States may have been in part the result of such policies.

Tax Policies of the Early Reagan Administration

In the first year of the Reagan administration, a similar set of investment-oriented tax policies was enacted as part of the Economic Recovery Tax Act of 1981 (ERTA). Changes introduced under this act included a new form of accelerated depreciation (Accelerated Cost Recovery System—ACRS) and an increased investment tax credit. Adoption of the ACRS was a particularly important innovation. It eliminated the prior concept of "useful lifetime guidelines" for determining depreciation allowances and substituted a simplified scheme in which any asset fell into one of four classes with tax lives of 3, 5, 10, or 15 years. For most capital assets these lives were considerably shorter than had been the case previously. Adoption of the ACRS also brought much greater uniformity into the tax treatment of various industries' investments. For example, under prior laws, depreciation periods for producers' equipment ranged from over 14 years for ships and boats to over 12 years for turbines to 5 years for trucks and tractors.

---

[1] R. E. Hall and D. W. Jorgenson, "Tax Policy and Investment Behavior," *American Economic Review* 57 (June 1967): 391–414. All numbers for the 1960s in this example are also taken from this source.

Similarly, depreciation periods for buildings ranged from 17 to more than 40 years. Under the ACRS, depreciation periods were set at a uniform 5 years for most equipment and 10 or 15 years for buildings. It was hoped that such changes would result in a more uniform tax treatment of investment decisions across industries.

Raising Taxes on Investment

The overall effect of the ERTA changes was to reduce taxes substantially (reducing effective rental rates) on firms' capital investments. Indeed, some analysts even suggested that the tax rates under ERTA on many types of equipment were negative; that is, the government was effectively subsidizing this type of investment.[2] Possibilities for this subsidy having a major effect on firms' investment behavior were rather limited, however. The tax law was again changed in 1982 (under the pompously titled Tax Equity and Fiscal Responsibility Act), and the prior subsidy was largely eliminated. Indeed, this latter law raised the tax rates on some types of investment to above their pre-1981 levels. The overall effect of the Reagan changes on actual investment incentives was therefore unclear. Actual investment performance during the 1980s was similarly erratic.

Tax Policies of the Clinton Administration

Initial priorities of the Clinton administration included both the need to increase employment in the short run and to encourage long-run economic growth. To pursue these goals, the administration proposed the reinstitution of investment tax credits. Unlike similar credits in the Kennedy and Ford administrations, these credits were narrowly focused on smaller firms and on firms making new investment commitments. Developing regulations that achieve this precise targeting is no easy task since firms have an incentive to make their investments qualify for the credit. For example, similar credits for "equipment" investments in the 1960s led to major increases in "office partition systems" instead of renovations which were not eligible for the credit. The effectiveness of investment targeting in improving the overall investment performance of the U.S. economy remains to be seen.

Table 1

Change in Gross Investment in Equipment as a Result of Federal Tax Policy, 1963 (Billions of 1954 Dollars)

	Manufacturing Equipment	Non-manufacturing Equipment
Total gross investment	$8.461	$17.982
Change due to:		
Accelerated depreciation	0.549	1.141
Useful lifetime guidelines	0.315	0.656
Investment tax credit	0.867	1.808
Total effect of federal tax policy	1.731	3.605
Tax effect as a percentage of total gross investment	20.5%	20.0%

Source: R. E. Hall and D. W. Jorgenson, "Tax Policy and Investment Behavior," *American Economic Review* 57 (June 1967): 391–414, Tables 3, 4, and 5.

To Think About

1. Why does the government adopt policies to encourage investment? Won't private markets make enough investment without government subsidies? What goals is the government trying to achieve with such tax policies? Should tax policy favor investments in some industries and discourage it in others?

2. Depreciation policies are usually based on the actual purchase price of a machine. Is this definition of depreciation consistent with economists' notions of production costs? What are the actual costs involved in using a machine? Are these necessarily related to the machine's price of possibly many years ago? How does the failure to use accurate cost measures for firms' depreciation affect their investment decisions?

---

[2]See Donald Fullerton and Y. K. Henderson, "Long Run Effects of the Accelerated Recovery System," *National Bureau of Economic Research Working Paper,* No. 828 (revised, February 1983).

■ Present Discounted Value

In order to describe the present discounted value criterion for investment, we must first discuss the procedure that should be used to add up sums of money that are to be received in different time periods. Since the purchaser of a machine will collect net income (or, more properly, the marginal value product) from the machine over several periods into the future, we need to know how to add up these amounts. Although some formal aspects of this question are presented in the appendix to this chapter, it is possible here to provide an intuitive explanation of the logic that economists employ.

One dollar today is worth more than a dollar that will not be received until a later date. If a dollar is available today, it can be invested and earn a return given by the prevailing rate, r. Conversely, if a dollar is not received until next year, some return must be forgone. The current dollar is more valuable. Specifically, a dollar today will grow to $1 + r$ dollars next year. We might therefore define the present value of $1 to be paid next year as $1/(1 + r)$. This is the amount that, if invested today at an annual interest rate r, will yield $1 in one year. If you invest $.95 today at 5 percent, you will have $1 next year. The present value of $1 to be received one year from now is $.95.

■ Present Value for Many Periods

It is easy to generalize the idea of present value to any number of periods. If $1 is invested for two years, for example, it will grow to $1 \cdot (1 + r) \cdot (1 + r) = \$1 \cdot (1 + r)^2$. The present value of $1 payable in two years would be $1/(1 + r)^2$. This is the amount that would have to be invested today in order to obtain $1 in two years. These results can be summarized by

$$\text{Present value of \$1 payable in one year} = \frac{\$1}{(1+r)};$$

$$\text{Present value of \$1 payable in two years} = \frac{\$1}{(1+r)^2};$$

$$\text{Present value of \$1 payable in three years} = \frac{\$1}{(1+r)^3};$$

$$\text{Present value of \$1 payable in n years} = \frac{\$1}{(1+r)^n}. \qquad [21.8]$$

In order to illustrate the implications of the present value concept, Table 21.1 shows the present value of $1 payable in 1, 2, 3, 10, and 20 years in the future for five possible rates of return. For example, if r is 4 percent, the present value of $1 payable in one year is $.962. If about $.96 is invested today at 4 percent, it will grow to $1 by the end of one year. If the rate of return is 7 percent, an investment of only $.26 will grow to $1 in 20 years. In general, the present value of a dollar to be paid at some date in the future declines as the rate of return increases. The higher r is, the more heavily future payments are discounted since the

Rate of Return (r)	1 Year	2 Years	3 Years	10 Years	20 Years
3%	$.970	$.943	$.915	$.744	$.544
4	.962	.925	.899	.676	.456
5	.952	.907	.864	.614	.377
6	.943	.890	.840	.558	.312
7	.935	.873	.816	.508	.258

Table 21.1
Present Value of $1
Payable at Various
Dates

opportunity costs of lost investment returns are greater. Similarly, for any particular rate of return, dollars payable in the distant future are worth less than those payable in the near term. Again, such distant payments are discounted more heavily because of the greater opportunity costs involved. Published tables and calculators are available for calculating present values, and these can be most helpful for economic analyses that involve sums of money payable over time.

■ Present Discounted Value Approach to Investment Decisions

When a firm buys a machine, it is in effect buying a stream of net revenues in future periods. In order to decide whether to purchase the machine, the firm must assign some value to this stream. Since the revenues will accrue to the firm in many future periods, the logic of the preceding argument suggests that the firm should compute the present discounted value of this stream. Only by doing so will the firm have taken adequate account of the opportunity costs associated with alternative assets it might have bought.

Consider a firm in the process of deciding whether to buy a particular machine. The machine is expected to last n years and will give its owner a stream of monetary returns (that is, marginal value products) in each of the n years. Let the return in year i be represented by R_i. If r is the rate of return on alternative investments, and if this rate is expected to prevail for the next n years, the present discounted value (PDV) of the machine to its owner is given by

$$PDV = \frac{R_1}{1+r} + \frac{R_2}{(1+r)^2} + \ldots + \frac{R_n}{(1+r)^n}. \qquad [21.9]$$

This represents the total value of the stream of payments that is provided by the machine, once adequate account is taken of the fact that these payments occur in different years. If the PDV of this stream of payments exceeds the price (P) of the machine, the firm should make the purchase. Even when opportunity costs are taken into account, the machine promises to return more than it will cost to buy, and firms would rush out to buy machines. On the other hand, if P exceeds the machine's PDV, the firm would be better-off investing its funds in some alternative that promises a rate of return of r. When account is taken of forgone returns, the machine does not pay for itself. No profit-maximizing firm would buy such a machine.

In a competitive market the only equilibrium that can persist is one where the price of a machine is exactly equal to the present discounted value of the net revenues it provides. Only in this situation will there be neither an excess demand for machines nor an excess supply of machines. Hence, market equilibrium requires that

$$P = PDV = \frac{R_1}{1+r} + \frac{R_2}{(1+r)^2} + \ldots + \frac{R_n}{(1+r)^n}. \qquad [21.10]$$

■ Present Discounted Value and the Rental Rate

For simplicity, assume now that machines do not depreciate and that the marginal value product is the same in every year. This uniform return will then also equal the rental rate for machines (v), since that is what another firm would be willing to pay for the machine's use during each period. With these simplifying assumptions we may write the present discounted value from machine ownership as

$$PDV = \frac{v}{1+r} + \frac{v}{(1+r)^2} + \ldots + \frac{v}{(1+r)^n} + \ldots, \qquad [21.11]$$

where the dots (...) indicate that payments go on forever. But since in equilibrium P = PDV, the appendix to this chapter shows how we can solve Equation 21.11 as

$$P = \frac{v}{r} \qquad [21.12]$$

or

$$r = \frac{v}{P}, \qquad [21.13]$$

which is the same as Equation 21.6 (v/P = r). For this case the present discounted value criterion gives results identical to those outlined earlier using the rental rate approach. In equilibrium a machine must promise owners the prevailing rate of return.

We have again demonstrated the algebraic relationship between a machine's current price, the rental rate on the machine, and the market rate of return. In particular, an increase in r will decrease the machine's PDV, and firms will be less willing to buy machines for the same reasons that we discussed before—opportunity costs are too high. This result is quite general. The present discounted value approach to investment and the rental rate approach are alternative ways of phrasing the same idea. However, as Application 21.3: The Economist and the Car Dealer illustrates, PDV calculations can be useful in a wide variety of other contexts. Many of these are encountered every day.

APPLICATION 21.3

The Economist and the Car Dealer

In 1985 an economist well known to this author ventured into an automobile showroom to buy a new car. He quickly settled on a no-frills family car with a final price tag of $10,000 (in round numbers). Before reaching final agreement with the salesman, the nervous economist was introduced to the manager of the firm who was supposed to close the deal.

A Common Sales Pitch

The manager's pitch was a smooth one. "You look like a sensible and frugal buyer," he said. "Do I have a deal for you! We have just signed a great financing package with a local bank to make car loans. I can let you have this car now and all you have to do is pay $3,100 per year for the next four years. You will pay back $12,400—$10,000 for the car and $2,400 in finance charges. If you instead pay for the car with $10,000 in cash you'll lose, say, 7 percent each year by taking your money out of the bank. This amounts to $2,800 over four years. By financing with us you save $400."

The Economist Smells a Rat

This final appeal to opportunity cost sounded good to the economist, but he smelled a rat. How could the car dealer (or dealer's bank) offer more favorable financing than the economist made on his account at that same bank? Something was wrong. As the startled car dealer looked on, the economist pulled out his calculator to evaluate the present value of the repayment scheme being proposed. He used 7 percent as his opportunity cost since that was what he was then earning from the bank:

$$\text{PDV of auto loan} = \frac{\$3,100}{(1.07)} + \frac{\$3,100}{(1.07)^2} + \frac{\$3,100}{(1.07)^3}$$
$$+ \frac{\$3,100}{(1.07)^4} = \$10,500.$$

So this loan was actually more costly than paying for the car with cash even after accounting for opportunity

costs. To cinch the analysis the economist pressed the dealer to reveal the true interest rate in his offer (which by law he was required to do). After some foolishness about how such figures "distort the real picture," he announced the true cost as 9.2 percent—considerably more than the economist made in his paltry savings account. The "deal" being offered was no deal at all. After a bit more verbal sparring, the economist was handed back to the salesman (who seemed embarrassed by the whole episode) and proceeded to buy the car with cash. He has not taken the car back to this dealer for service since then, however.

An Explanation

The trick in the car dealer's offer is obvious. He was not offering to lend the purchase price of the car for four years. Instead, the scheme he proposed (similar to all consumer credit purchase schemes) required repayment of some of the loan's principal each year. Effectively, the economist would have been borrowing much less than the full $10,000 for the entire period. The car dealer's opportunity cost calculations were misleading, and the economist was (at least on this occasion) saved from a costly mistake by a simple application of the present value concept.

To Think About

1. Suppose the car dealer had allowed his entire $12,400 charge to be paid at the end of four years. Then, would his argument be correct? How much would the economist save by taking such a deal?

2. How would you compute the "true" interest charge on the car dealer's offer? Does this figure actually "distort the true picture"? In general, do laws requiring disclosure of true interest charges seem desirable? What is the economic rationale for such laws?

Human Capital

One important application of the theory of capital concerns the investment people can make in themselves. They can do this in a variety of ways. Individuals can acquire a formal education, they may accept apprenticeships and learn skills on the job, they can spend considerable efforts in looking for better jobs, or they can purchase various kinds of medical services that maintain them in good health. All of those activities can be looked upon as "investments" since both time and resources are sacrificed currently in the hope that this will somehow pay off in the future.

By acquiring skills or buying good health, people are adding to their stock of **human capital** in much the same way that the purchase of machines by firms adds to the firm's stock of physical capital. There is evidence that most additions to human capital are quite productive—they help people to increase their earnings in future years. In fact, it has been found that individuals make many investments in themselves that yield returns substantially in excess of the prevailing rate of return on other investments.[6] In this section we discuss how such calculations are made and look at some of the ways in which human capital differs from physical capital.

Human capital

Capital in the form of learned abilities acquired through training, education, or experience.

■ Calculating the Yield on an Investment

Conceptually, it is an easy matter to compute the **yield** that an individual receives from an investment in human capital (or on any other kind of capital investment, for that matter). Suppose that the cost of an investment that someone is intending to make is given by C. Suppose also that the investment is expected to raise this person's earnings in each year in the future and that these additions to earnings are given by $I_1, I_2, \ldots, I_n$. We wish to know what discount rate, i, will discount these earnings increments to make them exactly equal to C. Mathematically, we know C and I, and we wish to find that value of i that solves the equation

Yield

The discounting rate at which the present discounted value of the returns from an investment are exactly equal to the investment's current cost.

$$C = \frac{I_1}{1+i} + \frac{I_2}{(1+i)^2} + \ldots + \frac{I_n}{(1+i)^n}.$$ [21.14]

The value of i that solves Equation 21.14 would be called yield (or, sometimes, rate of return) on this particular investment (see the appendix to this chapter for a discussion of this calculation). Application 21.4: Yields on Investments in Schooling and On-the-Job Training illustrates some results that are typically obtained from this kind of calculation in the study of the returns on schooling or on-the-job training. These studies tend to confirm that human capital investment is very important and often yields surprisingly high returns.

---

[6]For a thorough analysis of the educational aspects of human capital formation, see G. S. Becker, *Human Capital*, National Bureau of Economic Research (New York: Columbia University Press, 1964).

APPLICATION 21.4

Yields on Investments in Schooling and On-the-Job Training

The two most important human capital investments people make are in formal schooling and in on-the-job training. Costs of investment in schooling are of two types. First are explicit costs such as tuitions and fees, transportation costs, and other incidental expenses. A second, and probably larger, component of schooling costs is the implicit opportunity costs of forgone earnings while in school. Because people could hold jobs instead of attending school, potential earnings on those jobs must be considered a cost of formal education. A similar opportunity cost argument suggests that if people forsake some earnings in order to learn skills that will be useful to them in the future, these forgone earnings represent a cost of accumulating job skills.

Costs of Human Capital Investments

A 1970 study by Thomas Johnson attempted to estimate the dollar costs of these two types of human capital investments.[1] A few of the author's results for males in 1959 are presented in Table 1. As would be expected, the costs of formal schooling rise rapidly for individuals with higher educational levels. Workers with less than a high school education have invested relatively little in formal schooling (less than $4,000—composed primarily of forgone earnings). More than three-quarters of these workers' total human capital investments are in on-the-job training. For more highly-educated people, formal schooling costs may be quite high. Those with education beyond the college level have a total investment that may average over $40,000 (in 1959 dollars). Again, the principal component of this cost is the earnings that college graduates forgo when they attend graduate school.

Yields on these Investments

The investments in human capital shown in Table 1 seem to pay off in increasing total lifetime incomes. For example, on average, individuals with a college education earned nearly $100,000 more over their lifetimes than did those with only a high school education. The final

Table 1

Investments in Human Capital and the Yield of Those Investments for White Males in the Northern United States, 1959

Years of Education Completed	Total Investment in Human Capital	Total Lifetime Income	Yield on Investment in Human Capital
9–11	$19,076	$220,025	24.6%
12	24,112	245,433	21.5
13–15	28,463	278,323	17.5
16	46,016	341,856	15.5
17+	63,771	380,626	13.5

Source: Thomas Johnson, "Returns from Investment in Human Capital," *American Economic Review* (September 1970): 546–560, Table 3.

column of Table 1 presents the percentage yields on total human capital investments. These yields were calculated using a formula similar to Equation 21.14. All of the yields are positive, indicating that formal schooling and on-the-job training do indeed pay off in increased earnings. The yields diminish for higher levels of formal education, however, suggesting that some kind of diminishing return to human capital investments may exist. As for any other economic activity, it appears to be possible to push investments in human capital too far. Indeed, more recent data tend to indicate that the returns to college education have been rather erratic, falling during the 1970s and rising during the 1980s, primarily in response to college attendance patterns.[2]

To Think About

1. If education offers a high return, why should it be subsidized by the government? Doesn't the high return give people an adequate incentive to purchase their own education?
2. If workers obtain higher wages as a result of on-the-job training, who pays for that training? Do firms have an incentive to provide the training or do workers in effect pay for it by accepting low wages when they are new on the job?

[1]Thomas Johnson, "Returns from Investment in Human Capital," *American Economic Review* (September 1970): 546–560.
[2]For a summary and comparison among various countries in the return to education, see G. Psacharapoulos, "Returns to Education: A Further

International Update and Implications," *Journal of Human Resources* (Fall 1985): 584–604.

■ Special Features of Human Capital

Although the analogy between human and physical capital provides many insights into the nature of people's decisions about gaining skills and education, it should not be pushed too far. Human capital has a number of special properties that make it unique among the assets an individual can buy. Contrary to other assets, human capital cannot (in the absence of slavery) be sold. The owner of human capital is inextricably tied to his or her past investments. Although a person may "rent" out this investment to employers for a wage, he or she may not sell it in the way a firm might sell a machine it no longer needed. Human capital also depreciates in a rather unusual way. It is totally lost upon the death of its owner. This makes the investment rather risky. Finally, the acquisition of human capital may take substantial time. Whereas a firm seeking to buy a drill press may only have to spend five minutes to make a phone call, people who wish to improve their skills must usually invest considerable time, perhaps years, in doing so. The irreversibility of time makes this process of human capital investment all the more risky. It is not surprising, therefore, that these investments frequently offer high returns.

Pricing of Exhaustible Natural Resources

As a final application of capital theory, we consider how markets will price finite natural resources over time. Much concern has been expressed about the possible exhaustion of some finite resources. In the mid-1970s, for example, considerable attention was focused on the adequacy of known petroleum reserves. More recently, concern has been expressed about the supply of a wide variety of exhaustible resources ranging from stocks of various fish and wildlife species to the amount of farmland. Our principal focus here is on the implications for the pricing of such resources that stem from the fact that these resources can be used up. In Chapter 22 we look at some other questions about the allocation of both exhaustible and renewable natural resources.

■ Scarcity Costs

Scarcity costs

The opportunity costs of forgone future production that cannot be made because of current production that uses exhaustible resources.

What makes the production of exhaustible resources different from the production of any other economic good is that current production from a finite resource stock reduces the amount of the resource available for the future. This might be contrasted to the usual case of production in which firms' activities during one year have no effect on their production activities the next year. Producers of an exhaustible resource must therefore take an additional cost into account in their current production decisions: the opportunity cost of forgone sales in the future. Economists define the **scarcity costs** associated with current production of an exhaustible resource as the value of forgone future sales that cannot be made because of this current production. Recognition of such costs does not imply that profit-maximizing firms will produce no output and con-

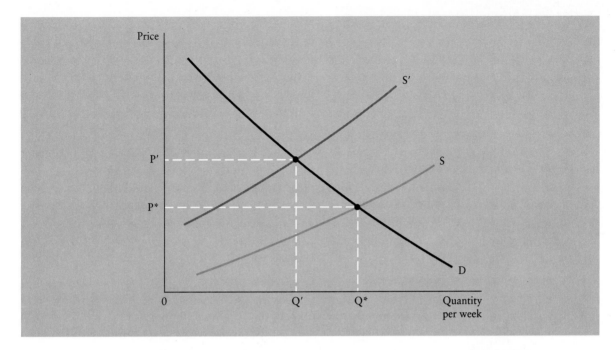

Firms that produce exhaustible resources will take into account both current marginal production costs and the opportunity costs of forgone future production. The market supply curve for such firms (S′) will be above their marginal cost curves to the extent of those scarcity costs.

Figure 21.4
Scarcity Costs
Associated with
Exhaustible
Resources

stantly hoard their resources for some future time. But they will be careful to incorporate the full opportunity costs of current sales in their decisions.

The implications of scarcity costs for pricing are illustrated in Figure 21.4. In the absence of those costs, the industry supply curve for the resource would be given by S, and that curve would, as usual, reflect the marginal costs of actually producing (that is, drilling, mining, or refining) the resource. Scarcity costs (related to the finiteness of the ultimately available resource supply) shift firms' marginal cost curves upward. The new market supply curve is S′. The gap between S′ and S reflects the opportunity costs associated with forgone future sales. Current output is reduced (from Q* to Q′) when firms recognize the finiteness of the resource supply. This reduction reflects firms' preference for withholding some of the resource from current supply in order to be able to sell it in the future.

■ Scarcity Costs and Resource Prices

The actual value of scarcity costs depends on firms' perceptions about what resource prices will be in the future. Knowledge of those prices is required if owners are to be able to calculate correctly the opportunity costs associated with current sales from their resource stocks. As a simple example, suppose a firm that owns a copper mine knows that copper will sell for $1 per pound in 20 years. Since the amount of copper in the mine is fixed, selling a pound today will mean forgoing this $1 sale in 20 years. If we assume that the real interest rate is 3 percent, Table 21.1 shows that the present value of this opportunity cost is $.54. Assuming the mine owner is indifferent about selling the copper in 20 years or today, the current market price should also be $.54 per pound. That is the only price that reflects an equilibrium between present and future sales. Any lower current price would encourage the mine owner to leave the copper in the ground since it will be worth more later even taking account of forgone interest in the meantime. A current price above $.54 would, on the other hand, cause the owner to sell as much copper as possible today and not wait for 20 years.

Our calculation of scarcity costs proceeds by comparing the price of copper to its actual production costs. If the marginal cost of producing a pound of copper is $.30, then scarcity costs would be $.24 per pound—the amount by which the current equilibrium price exceeds marginal production cost. In this case, the fact that price exceeds marginal cost is not a sign of inefficiency. Instead, it shows that all costs are fully reflected in the price.

■ The Time Pattern of Resource Prices

An important implication of this discussion is that in the absence of any changes in production costs or in expectations about future prices, the market price of copper would be expected to increase over time at the rate of return on alternative investments. If r is 3 percent, for example, real copper prices would be expected to rise at 3 percent a year.[7] Only by following that path would prices always equal the present value of $1 in year 20.

This result can be shown intuitively from another perspective. Any firm will evaluate its resource holdings in the same way as it evaluates any other investment. Investments in resources should yield the same return (r) as those alternatives. Only if the real prices of finite resources increase at the rate r will they provide such a return to their owners. If resource prices were rising slower than this rate, natural resources would be an inferior investment, and owners should put their funds elsewhere. A rate of price rise above r per year is also unsustainable in the long run because investors would bid up the current price of resources to reflect their investment desirability. This bidding up of prices would continue until the possibility for further increases in excess of the prevailing rate was eliminated. This principle of the pricing of scarce finite resources can be used to study a variety of economic issues, as Application 21.5: Are Any Resources Scarce? illustrates.

---

[7]Since r is a "real" rate of return (that is, corrected for inflation), the prediction here is that the price of the resource relative to the price of all other goods should rise at the rate r. This result was first rigorously shown by Harold Hotelling in "The Economics of Exhaustible Resources," *Journal of Political Economy* (April 1931): 137–175.

APPLICATION 21.5
Are Any Resources Scarce?

The question, Are any resources scarce?, is, of course, rhetorical. After all, the earth is a finite size so (barring mining in space) the total quantity of natural resources is ultimately fixed. Any production today necessarily reduces the amount that can be produced tomorrow. By this test, all natural resources are scarce. The economic consequences of this scarcity, however, are another issue.

Resource Price Trends

During the past century, the primary trend for natural resource prices has been downward in real terms. As Table 1 shows, annual rates of decline between 1 and 2 percent characterize the price histories for such diverse resources as petroleum, coal, and aluminum. Similarly, farmland prices seem to have declined in real terms, though at a slower rate than natural resources. It is, however, difficult to infer actual scarcity values from these figures since declining relative costs of extraction and development may have masked rising scarcity costs. Since 1970, the decline in real resource prices appears to have slowed (but not stopped, as Application 1.5 illustrated) and this may indeed indicate an increasing relevance of scarcity costs. Nevertheless, the prospect of rising real resource prices driven by scarcity is not yet a forgone conclusion.

Implications of Scarcity

Even if real prices of natural resources were to follow a rising path indicating their scarcity, the economic consequences of such a trend are far from clear. The ultimate effect on overall output would depend on such factors as the ability of firms to substitute inputs that have stable prices for those that were rising in price; the tendency of rising resource prices to induce various types of resource-saving technical innovations; and the willingness of consumers to reduce their consumption of resource-intensive goods. Modeling all of these various reactions is a formidable undertaking. One fairly careful

Table 1
Real Prices for Natural Resources (1989 = 100)

Resource	1870	1910	1950	1970	1989
Petroleum	700	250	150	80	100
Coal	550	350	200	110	100
Copper	1,000	500	250	160	100
Iron Ore	1,000	750	200	120	100
Aluminum	–	800	180	110	100
Farmland	200	375	80	105	100

Source: Adapted from W. P. Nordhaus, "Lethal Model 2: Limits to Growth Revisited," *Brookings Papers on Economic Activity*, no. 2 (1992): 24–26.

estimate suggests that resource scarcity might reduce real economic growth rates by about 0.3 percent by the year 2050 with more than half of the decline being attributed to the increasing scarcity of energy resources.[1] Whether this relatively modest effect will prove accurate is, of course, anyone's guess.

To Think About

1. How should changing costs of resource extraction be factored into an explanation of market prices? In what way might such changes mask changing scarcity values? What is the maximum effect that changing relative extraction costs might be expected to have?

2. Why do economists and environmentalists have such different views on resource scarcity? Don't environmentalists understand how the price system works to mitigate the effects of scarcity? Or is it economists who mistakenly disregard the sharp discontinuities and irreversibilities that environmentalists fear?

[1]W. D. Nordhaus, "Lethal Model 2: Limits to Growth Revisited," *Brookings Papers on Economic Activity* No. 2 (1992): 1–43.

Summary

The fundamental concept introduced in this chapter is the rate of return (or real interest rate), which shows the terms at which present goods can be exchanged for future goods. It is this "price" that ties together economic decisions made in different time periods. The rate of return is a primary influence on the allocation of resources over time. We show these effects in several contexts:

- The rate of return, because it represents an important opportunity cost incurred by firms that own machines, directly affects firms' input choices. A higher rate of return raises the rental costs of capital and thereby discourages investment.

- The rate of return, or real interest rate, is also important for calculating the present value of payments to be made in different time periods. Such payments can only be compared once the opportunity costs of interest forgone are taken into account.

- Human capital represents a particular type of investment that people may make in themselves. Rates of return on such investments may be rather high, possibly because of the risky features of these investments.

- Exhaustible resources pose important allocational problems because using some quantity of them in one year precludes the use of those resources in later years. The logic of interest rate computations suggests that the relative price of finite resources should increase over time at a rate equal to the real rate of interest.

Review Questions

1. What is capital? How does an economy "accumulate" capital? Could an economy ever experience a decline in its stock of capital? How is the abstract view of capital accumulation pictured in Figure 21.1 related to the actual process of firms increasing the capital stock by purchasing new machines? Can you explain these ideas using a production possibility frontier for present and future goods?

2. Suppose that the economy produced only one, all-purpose good called jelly. How would capital accumulation occur in such an economy? How would you measure the rate of return as described in Figure 21.1? Would the jelly rate of return (that is, the ratio of final jelly output to jelly investment) be a real or a nominal rate of return?

3. A simple formula for the rental rate on a piece of capital equipment is $v = P(r + d)$. Explain why the price (P) used here is the current price of the machine. Why

wouldn't it be correct to use the machine's original purchase price? How might the analysis be expanded to allow for the possibility that the machine's price might change over time?

4. Explain the sequence of events through which a change in the interest rate affects a firm's demand for capital input. Why is this sequence essentially the same regardless of whether the firm owns its capital or rents it from someone else?

5. Why does a tax on capital affect a firm's profit-maximization input choice but a tax on pure economic profits does not? How might the U.S. corporate profits tax (see Application 10.1) be changed so that it more closely resembles a tax on pure corporate profits?

6. In our discussion of present discounted value we usually only examined the value of "one dollar" payable at various times. How is the case of any number of dollars a trivial generalization of this? More importantly, explain why the PDV of any given number of dollars is lower the higher the interest rate is or the longer the time until the dollars are to be paid.

7. Suppose the general level of prices was increasing and that capital rental rates were rising in line with all other prices. Can a firm use these nominal rental rates in making a PDV calculation for an intended investment? If so, should the firm use a nominal or a real interest rate to make its calculation? Alternatively, if the firm decides to adjust future rental rates for inflation, which interest rate should it use?

8. Why does the analysis of Chapter 20 suggest that the opportunity cost of time may be a major cost of human capital accumulation? Give some examples of this opportunity cost. For example, what fraction of the total cost of your education would you estimate is represented by such costs?

9. Why are scarcity costs relevant for the pricing of finite natural resources but not for the production of standard manufactured goods? Doesn't the sale of, say, one more automobile reduce the stock of potentially available new cars in exactly the same way that the sale of a barrel of oil reduces the stock of oil? What is the economic difference?

10. In our numerical example of copper pricing we had to make some assumption about the price of copper in 20 years in order to be able to calculate current scarcity costs. Why was such an assumption necessary? Should the price in 20 years be the nominal price of copper then or should it be adjusted to the current price level to control for inflation?

Problems

21.1 Mr. Moneybags is thinking of buying a bond issued by the ABC Corporation. Mr. Moneybags' economist friend tells him that a fair price for the bond is the bond's present discounted value. The face value of the bond is $10,000, which will be given to Mr. Moneybags at the end of five years. In addition, the bond promises to pay five "coupons" of $1,000 at the end of each year. Assuming the market interest rate (i) is 12 percent annually, what is a fair price for the bond? What if i = 8 percent instead? What is the relationship between bond prices and interest rates?

21.2　The president of the Acme Landfill Company has estimated that the purchase of 10 more deluxe dump trucks can bring in added revenues of $100,000 a year for the life of the trucks. The trucks have a life span of seven years and cost $50,000 each. If the company can earn a 10 percent rate of return on investments in alternative ventures, should it go ahead and purchase the trucks? What if the company found that it could only earn a 9 percent return on its alternative investments? Should it go ahead with the purchase?

21.3　A high pressure life insurance salesman was heard to make the following argument: "At your age a $100,000 whole life policy is a much better buy than a similar term policy. Under a whole life policy you'll have to pay $2,000 per year for the first four years, but nothing more for the rest of your life. A term policy will cost you $400 per year, essentially forever. If you live 35 years, you'll pay only $8,000 for the whole life policy, but $14,000 for the term policy. Surely the whole life is a better deal."

Assuming the salesman's life expectancy assumption is correct, how would you evaluate this argument? Specifically, calculate the present discounted value of the premium costs of the two policies assuming that the interest rate is 10 percent.

21.4　Suppose J. P. Miser obtains utility from present and future consumption (C_1 and C_2) and that she has a certain amount of dollars (Y) to allocate between these goods.

a.　If the interest rate is r, what will the budget constraint in this problem be?
b.　Using the budget constraint from part a, show graphically how Y will be allocated between C_1 and C_2 to maximize utility. What will the tangency condition for a utility maximum be in this situation?
c.　Suppose r were to increase. What will happen to the utility-maximizing choices for C_1 and C_2?

* 21.5　Assume that an individual expects to work for 40 years, then retire with a life expectancy of an additional 20 years. Suppose also that the individual's earnings rise at a rate of 3 percent per year and that the interest rate is also 3 percent (the overall price level is constant in this problem). What (constant) fraction of income must the individual save in each working year to be able to finance a level of retirement income equal to 60 percent of earnings in the year just prior to retirement?

21.6　The No-Flite Golfball Company manufactures cut-proof golfballs and is thinking of investing in a new name. Its media personnel have come up with two suggestions: "Astro-Flite" and "Jack Nickless." It is cheaper to switch to Astro-Flite since the second name will involve legal fees for dealing with a well-known golfer who is likely to get upset by the whole thing. The second name,

---

*Denotes a problem that is rather difficult.

however, is expected to bring in more business than the first. If the costs and payoffs are as given below, and the firm expects to go out of business in five years, is it worth it to make a name switch, and if so, to which name?

	Cost	Yearly Return	Interest Rate
Astro-Flite	$3,800	$1,000	10%
Jack Nickless	5,000	1,400	10

Would your answer change if the interest rate were 15 percent?

21.7 Some foresters suggest that timber plots be managed so as to achieve "maximum sustainable yield." Would an economist agree that a single tree should be grown to maturity before it is cut down and sold as lumber (since trees begin to grow more slowly as they get older)? How would an economist manage a whole forest of trees? How might the problem be complicated by a forest of trees of widely different ages (and growth rates)?

*21.8 Suppose Scotch increases in value as it ages. In particular, the value of Scotch at any time t is given by $V = 100t - 6t^2$ and the proportional growth rate in that value is $(100 - 12t)/V$. Graph this Scotch function. At what value of t is V as large as possible? Is that when the Scotch should be bottled? If the interest rate is 5 percent, when should the Scotch be bottled?

*21.9 Suppose an individual has a fixed amount of money to allocate between consumption this period (C_1) and consumption next period (C_2). Assume also that this person's utility is simply the sum of the utility he or she receives from consumption in each period

$$\text{Utility} = U(C_1) + U(C_2).$$

a. If the interest rate is zero between the two periods, explain why utility maximization requires this individual to choose $C_1 = C_2$.
b. If the interest rate is positive, explain why utility maximization requires this person to choose $C_2 > C_1$.
c. If this person discounts future utility at a ratio of d so that

$$\text{Utility} = U(C_1) + \frac{U(C_2)}{1+d},$$

explain why utility maximization requires $C_1 > C_2$ if d exceeds the interest rate and $C_1 < C_2$ if d is smaller than the interest rate.
d. What do you conclude about the relationship between interest rates and individuals' time preference?

*Denotes a problem that is rather difficult.

21.10 An individual who has a planning horizon of two periods expects to earn an income of Y_1 in period 1 and Y_2 in period 2. These incomes are to be used to purchase consumption in the two periods (C_1 and C_2).

a. Show this individual's "initial endowment" (Y_1 and Y_2) and his or her indifference curve map. If there is no borrowing or lending, what will determine utility?

b. Show that if the individual can borrow and lend at an interest rate of 0, he or she can raise the level of utility obtainable from Y_1 and Y_2.

c. Would a positive interest rate raise or lower utility relative to the situation described in part b? How would your answer depend on this person's initial utility-maximizing choices?

d. If this individual faced a higher interest rate for borrowing than for lending, how might this affect his or her utility-maximizing choices?

People encounter compound interest concepts almost every day. Calculating returns on bank accounts, deciding on the true cost of an automobile loan, and buying a home with a mortgage all involve the use of interest rate computations. This appendix shows how some of those computations are made. The methods introduced are useful not only in economics classes, but in many personal economic decisions too.

Interest

Interest is payment for the time value of money. A borrower gets to use funds for his or her own purposes for a time and in return pays the lender some compensation. Interest rates are usually stated as some percentage of the amount borrowed (the principal). For example, an annual interest rate of 5 percent would require someone who borrowed $100 to pay $5 per year in interest.

Throughout this appendix we assume that the market has established an annual interest rate, i, and that this interest rate will persist from one year to the next. It is a relatively simple matter to deal with interest rates that change from one period to another, but we do not consider them here. We are also not particularly interested in whether i is a "nominal" interest rate (such as a rate quoted by a bank) or a "real" interest rate that has been adjusted for any inflation that may occur over time.[1] The mathematics of compound interest is the same for both nominal and real interest rates.

Compound Interest

If you hold funds in a bank for more than one period, you will receive **compound interest**—that is, you will receive interest not only on your original principal but also on the interest that you earned in prior periods and left in the bank. Compounding is relatively complicated and results in rather dramatic growth over long periods.

■ Interest for One Year

If you invest $1 at the interest rate of i, at the end of one year you will have

$$\$1 + \$1 \cdot i = \$1 \cdot (1 + i). \qquad [21A.1]$$

For example, if i is 5 percent, at the end of one year, you will have

$$\$1 + \$1 \cdot (.05) = \$1 \cdot (1.05) = \$1.05. \qquad [21A.2]$$

■
Interest
Payment for the current use of funds.

■
Compound interest
Interest paid on prior interest earned.

---

[1]Nominal and real interest rates can be related by the formula i = r + P_e, where i is the nominal interest rate per year, r is the real interest rate, and P_e is the expected annual rate of inflation. Often the real interest rate, r, is assumed to equal the rate of return on capital accumulation, a concept we discussed in detail in Chapter 21.

■ Interest for Two Years

If at the end of the first year you leave your money in the bank, you will now earn interest on both the original $1 and on your first year's interest. At the end of two years you will therefore have

$$\$1 \cdot (1 + i) + \$1 \cdot (1 + i) \cdot i = \$1 \cdot (1 + i)(1 + i)$$
$$= \$1 \cdot (1 + i)^2. \qquad [21A.3]$$

To understand Equation 21A.3 it is helpful to expand the term $(1 + i)^2$. Remember from algebra that

$$(1 + i)^2 = 1 + 2i + i^2. \qquad [21A.4]$$

At the end of two years, $1 will grow to

$$\$1 \cdot (1 + i)^2 = \$1 \cdot (1 + 2i + i^2)$$
$$= \$1 + \$1 \cdot (2i) + \$1 \cdot i^2. \qquad [21A.5]$$

At the end of two years you will have the sum of three amounts:

1. Your original $1.
2. Two years' interest on your original $1, that is, $1 \cdot 2i$.
3. Interest on your first year's interest, that is, $[(\$1 \cdot i) \cdot i] = \$1 \cdot i^2$.

   If, again, the interest rate is 5 percent, at the end of two years you will have

$$\$1 \cdot (1.05)^2 = \$1 \cdot (1.1025) = \$1.1025. \qquad [21A.6]$$

This represents the sum of your original $1, two years' interest on the $1 (that is, $.10), and interest on the first year's interest (5 percent of $.05, which is $.0025). The fact that you will have more than $1.10 is a reflection of compounding. As we look at longer and longer periods of time, the effects of this compounding become much more pronounced.

■ Interest for Three Years

If you now leave these funds, which after two years amount to $1 \cdot (1 + i)^2$, in the bank for another year, at the end of this third year you will have

$$\$1 \cdot (1 + i)^2 + \$1 \cdot (1 + i)^2 \cdot i = \$1 \cdot (1 + i)^2(1 + i)$$
$$= \$1 \cdot (1 + i)^3. \qquad [21A.7]$$

For an interest rate of 5 percent, this amounts to

$$\$1 \cdot (1 + .05)^3 = \$1 \cdot 1.157625 = \$1.157625. \qquad [21A.8]$$

The fact that you get more than simply your original $1 and three years' simple interest ($.15) again reflects the effects of compounding.[2]

■ A General Formula

By now the pattern should be clear. If you leave your $1 in the bank for any number of years, n, you will have, at the end of that period,

---

[2]As an exercise, you may wish to expand $(1 + i)^3$ and see whether you can explain the meaning of each of the four terms in the expression.

	Interest Rate				Table 21A.1 Effects of Compound Interest for Various Interest Rates and Time Periods with an Initial Investment of $1
Years	1 Percent	3 Percent	5 Percent	10 Percent	
1	$1.01	$1.03	$1.05	$1.10	
2	1.0201	1.0609	1.1025	1.2100	
3	1.0303	1.0927	1.1576	1.3310	
5	1.051	1.159	1.2763	1.6105	
10	1.1046	1.344	1.6289	2.5937	
25	1.282	2.094	3.3863	10.8347	
50	1.645	4.384	11.4674	117.3909	
100	2.705	19.219	131.5013	13,780.6123	

$$\text{Value of \$1 compounded for n years} = \$1 \cdot (1 + i)^n. \qquad [21A.9]$$

With a 5 percent interest rate and a period of 10 years, you would have

$$\$1 \cdot (1.05)^{10} = \$1 \cdot 1.62889 \ldots = \$1.62889. \qquad [21A.10]$$

Without compounding you would have had $1.50—your original $1 plus 10 years' interest at $.05 per year. The extra $.12889 comes about through compounding.

To illustrate the effects of compounding further, Table 21A.1 shows the value of $1 compounded for various time periods and interest rates.[3] Notice how compounding becomes very important for long periods. For instance, Table 21A.1 shows that, at a 5 percent interest rate, $1 grows to be $131.50 over 100 years. This represents the original $1, simple interest of $5 ($.05 per year for 100 years), and a massive $125.50 in interest earned on prior interest. At higher interest rates the effect of compounding is even more pronounced since there is even more prior interest on which to earn interest. At a 1 percent interest rate, only about 26 percent of the funds accumulated over 100 years represent the effects of compounding. At a 10 percent interest rate more than 99.9 percent of the huge amount accumulated represents the effects of compounding.

■ Compounding with Any Dollar Amount

The use of $1 in all of the computations we have made so far was for convenience only. Any other amount of money grows in exactly the same way. Investing $1,000 is just the same as investing a thousand one-dollar bills—at an interest rate of 5 percent this amount would grow to $1,050 at the end of 1 year [$1,000 · (1.05)]; it would grow to $1,629 at the end of 10 years [$1,000 · (1.629)]; and to $131,501 at the end of 100 years [$1,000 · 131.501].

[3]Because these computations are burdensome, they are often made using either a calculator or interest rate tables. Calculators capable of doing fairly sophisticated interest calculations can be purchased for about $10.

Algebraically, D dollars invested for n years at an interest rate of i will grow to

$$\text{Value of \$D invested for n years} = \$D \cdot (1+i)^n. \qquad [21A.11]$$

Application 21A.1: Compound Interest Gone Berserk illustrates some particularly extreme examples of using this formula.

Present Discounted Value

Because interest is paid on invested dollars, a dollar you get today is more valuable than one you won't receive until next year. You could put a dollar you receive today in a bank and have more than a dollar in one year. If you wait a year for the dollar, you will do without this interest that you could have earned.

Economists use the concept of present discounted value (sometimes called *present value*) to reflect this opportunity cost notion. The present discounted value of the dollar you will not get for one year is simply the amount you would have to put in a bank now to have $1 at the end of one year. If the interest rate is 5 percent, for example, the present value of $1 to be obtained in one year is about $.95—if you invest $.95 today, you will have $1 in one year, so $.95 accurately reflects the present value of $1 in one year.

■ An Algebraic Definition

More formally, if the interest rate is i, the present discounted value of $1 in one year is $\$1/(1+i)$ since

$$\frac{\$1}{1+i} \cdot (1+i) = \$1. \qquad [21A.12]$$

If i = 5 percent, the present discounted value (PDV) of $1 in one year is

$$\text{PDV} = \frac{\$1}{1.05} = \$.9524 \qquad [21A.13]$$

and

$$\$.9524 \cdot 1.05 = \$1. \qquad [21A.14]$$

A similar computation would result for any other interest rate. For example, the PDV of $1 payable in one year is $.971 if the interest rate is 3 percent, but $.909 when the interest rate is 10 percent. With a higher interest rate, the PDV is lower because the opportunity costs involved in waiting to get the dollar are greater.

Waiting two years to get paid involves even greater opportunity costs than waiting one year since now you forgo two years' interest. At an interest rate of

APPLICATION 21A.1
Compound Interest Gone Berserk

The effects of compounding can be gigantic if a sufficiently long period is used. Consider the author's three favorite examples.

Manhattan Island

Legend has it that in 1623 Dutch settlers purchased Manhattan Island from the native Americans living there for trinkets worth about $24. Suppose these native Americans had invested this $24 at 5 percent interest for the 370 years between 1623 and 1993. Using Equation 21A.11, in 1990 they would have

$$\$24 \cdot (1.05)^{370} = \$24 \cdot (69,189,574)$$
$$= \$1,660,549,773.$$

Over 370 years, their $24 would have grown to more than $1.6 billion. With a higher interest rate (say 10 percent) the figure would be much larger—probably exceeding by far the entire actual value of Manhattan Island today.

Horse Manure

In the 1840s the horse population of Philadelphia was growing at nearly 10 percent per year. Projecting this growth into the future, the city fathers began to worry about excessive crowding and potential pollution of the streets from manure. So they passed restrictions on the number of horses allowed in the city. It's a good thing! If the 1840 horse population of 50,000 had continued to grow at 10 percent per year into the 1990s, there would have been quite a few:

$$\text{Number of horses} = 50,000 \cdot (1 + i)^{150}$$
$$= 50,000 \cdot (1.10)^{150}$$
$$= 80,886,000,000.$$

With these 81 billion horses the manure problem would have been severe—amounting to perhaps 500 feet per year over the entire city. The City of Brotherly Love (the

author's hometown) was spared this fate through timely governmental action.

Rabbits

Rabbits were first introduced into Australia in the early 1860s. There they found a country free of predators and a country highly conducive to rabbit multiplication. By some estimates, the rabbit population grew at 100 percent per year during the 1860–1880 period. Assuming there were only two rabbits to start, by 1880 there would have been

$$\text{Number of rabbits} = 2(1+i)^{20}$$
$$= 2(1+1)^{20} = 2(2)^{20}$$
$$= 2,097,152$$

Continuing this growth for the next one hundred years would have resulted in more than 10^{36} rabbits in Australia by 1980—or over a trillion rabbits per square foot.

To Think About

1. The tongue-in-cheek nature of these examples suggests there is probably something wrong with such simplistic applications of compound interest. For each of the examples explain carefully why the calculations are pure nonsense.

2. As the rabbit problem shows, with high interest rates, compounding can produce spectacular results even for relatively short time periods. In the late 1970s, for example, it was possible to invest in bonds that yielded 15 percent per year. How much would you have to invest now at 15 percent to have $1 million in, say, 45 years when you retire? Do you think this calculation is "reasonable"? What does it overlook?

5 percent, $.907 will grow to be $1 in two years—that is, $1 = $.907 \cdot (1.05)^2$. Consequently, the present value of $1 payable in two years is only $.907. More generally, for any interest rate, i, the present value of $1 payable in two years is

$$\text{PDV of \$1 payable in two years} = \$1/(1 + i)^2 \qquad [21A.15]$$

and for the case of a 5 percent interest rate

$$\begin{aligned}\text{PDV of \$1 payable in two years} &= \$1/(1.05)^2 \\ &= \$1/1.1025 \\ &= \$.907. \qquad [21A.16]\end{aligned}$$

■ General PDV Formulas

The pattern again should be obvious. With an interest rate of i, the present value of $1 payable after any number of years, n, is simply

$$\text{PDV of \$1 payable in n years} = \$1/(1 + i)^n. \qquad [21A.17]$$

Calculating present values is the reverse of computing compound interest. In the compound interest case (Equation 21A.9) the calculation requires multiplying by the interest factor $(1 + i)^n$ whereas in the present discounted value case (Equation 21A.17) the calculation proceeds by dividing by that factor. Similarly, the present value of any number of dollars ($D) payable in n years is given by

$$\text{PDV of \$D payable in n years} = \$D/(1 + i)^n. \qquad [21A.18]$$

Again, by comparing Equations 21A.11 and 21A.18 you can see the different ways that the interest factor $(1 + i)^n$ enters into the calculations.

In Table 21A.2 the author has again put his calculator to work to compute the present discounted value of $1 payable at various times and for various inter-

Table 21A.2 Present Discounted Value of $1 for Various Time Periods and Interest Rates	Year until Payment Is Received	Interest Rate			
		1 Percent	3 Percent	5 Percent	10 Percent
	1	$.99010	$.97087	$.95238	$.90909
	2	.98030	.94260	.90703	.82645
	3	.97059	.91516	.86386	.75131
	5	.95147	.86281	.78351	.62093
	10	.90531	.74405	.61391	.38555
	25	.78003	.47755	.29531	.09230
	50	.60790	.22810	.08720	.00852
	100	.36969	.05203	.00760	.00007

Note: These amounts are the reciprocals of those in Table 21A.1.

est rates. The entries in this table are the reciprocals of the entries in Table 21A.1 since compounding and taking present values are different ways of looking at the same process. In Table 21A.2 the PDV of $1 payable in some particular year is smaller, the higher the interest rate. Similarly, for a given interest rate, the PDV of $1 is smaller the longer it is until the $1 will be paid. With a 10 percent interest rate, for example, a dollar that will not be paid for 50 years is worth less than one cent ($.00852) today. Application 21A.2: Zero-Coupon Bonds shows how such PDV calculations apply to a rapidly growing type of financial asset.

Discounting Payment Streams

Dollars payable at different points of time have different present values. One must be careful in calculating the true worth of streams of payments that occur at various times into the future—simply adding them up is not appropriate. Consider a situation that has irritated the author for some time. Many state lotteries promise grand prizes of $1 million (or, sometimes, much more) that they pay to the winners over 25 years. But $40,000 per year for 25 years is not "worth" $1 million. Indeed, at a 10 percent interest rate the present value of such a stream is only $363,200—much less than half the amount falsely advertised by the state. This section describes how such a calculation can be made. There is really nothing new to learn about discounting streams of payments— performing the calculations always involves making careful use of the general discounting formula from Equation 21A.18. However, repeated use of that formula may be very time consuming (if a stream of income is paid, say, at one hundred different times in the future), and our main purpose here is to present a few shortcuts.

■ An Algebraic Presentation

Consider a stream of payments that promises $1 per year starting next year and continuing for three years. By applying Equation 21A.18 it is easy to see that the present value of this stream is

$$\text{PDV} = \frac{\$1}{1+i} + \frac{\$1}{(1+i)^2} + \frac{\$1}{(1+i)^3}. \qquad [21A.19]$$

If the interest rate is 5 percent, this value would be

$$\frac{\$1}{1.05} + \frac{\$1}{(1.05)^2} + \frac{\$1}{(1.05)^3} = \$.9523 + \$.9070 + \$.8639$$

$$= \$2.7232. \qquad [21A.20]$$

Consequently, just as for the lottery, $1 a year for three years is not worth $3, but quite a bit less because of the need to take forgone interest into account in making present value calculations.

APPLICATION 21A.2
Zero-Coupon Bonds

Federal Treasury bonds sometimes include coupons that promise the owner of the bond a certain semiannual interest payment. For example, a thirty-year $1 million bond issued in 1990 with a 10 percent interest rate would include 60 semiannual coupons that represent the government's promise to pay $50,000 (that is, half of 10 percent of $1 million) on January 1 and July 1 of each year. The image of a Scrooge-like "coupon clipper" collecting regular interest payments in this way is a popular figure for financial cartoonists.

The Invention of Zero-Coupon Bonds

Unfortunately, this form of bond is not particularly convenient for investors. Bonds (and their attached coupons) may be lost, cashing the coupon necessitates a trip to the bank, and there is no easy way to reinvest interest payments to obtain the benefits of compounding. As a remedy for some of these problems, in the late 1970s some financial firms began to introduce *zero-coupon bonds* based on the Treasury obligations. These worked as follows: A brokerage firm would buy a bond (say, the $1 million bond described above). Then it would "strip" the coupons from the bond and sell these as separate investments. For example, it would sell a coupon representing a $50,000 interest payment on January 1, 2013 to an investor who wished to invest his or her funds until then.

Use of the PDV Formula

How much would such a stripped coupon be worth? The present discounted value formula gives the answer. If the interest rate is 10 percent, the present value of $50,000 payable in 2013 (20 years from January 1, 1993) is

$$\frac{\$50,000}{(1+i)^{20}} = \frac{\$50,000}{(1.10)^{20}} = \frac{\$50,000}{6.728} = \$7,432.$$

So the coupon would sell for $7,432 and would grow to about seven times this amount by 2013 when it was redeemed. Such a financial investment offers considerable advantages to an investor who does not want to be bothered with semiannual coupons, and zero-coupon bonds have proven to be quite popular. Prices for Treasury strips are now quoted daily in all financial newspapers.

A Specific Example

For example, *The Wall Street Journal* on June 24, 1993, reported that a Treasury strip worth $1,000 in August 2013 has a current value of $213.90. An investor thinking of retiring on that date could invest $214 today and be assured of $1,000 in twenty years, earning an interest rate of about 7.27 percent.

To Think About

1. Does an investor who buys a zero-coupon bond have to leave his or her funds in that investment until the payment is due? Would someone who sells before this due date lose all interest earned? Are zero-coupon investments more risky than ordinary bonds?

2. Do the financial institutions offering zero-coupon bonds have to use Treasury coupons for their promises of future payments? Couldn't they just make the promises themselves and sell them in the market? What advantages are offered by using Treasury bond coupons as the basis for zero-coupon investments?

If the promised stream of payments extends for longer than three years, additional terms should be added to Equation 21A.19. The present value of $1 per year for five years is

$$PDV = \frac{\$1}{1+i} + \frac{\$1}{(1+i)^2} + \frac{\$1}{(1+i)^3} + \frac{\$1}{(1+i)^4} + \frac{\$1}{(1+i)^5}, \qquad [21A.21]$$

which amounts to about $4.33 at a 5 percent interest rate. Again, $1 per year for five years is not worth $5.

The PDV equation can be generalized to any number of years (n) by just adding the correct number of terms:

$$PDV = \frac{\$1}{1+i} + \frac{\$1}{(1+i)^2} + \ldots + \frac{\$1}{(1+i)^n}. \qquad [21A.22]$$

Table 21A.3 uses this formula to compute the value of $1 per year for various numbers of years and interest rates. Several features of the numbers in this table are important to keep in mind when discussing present values. As noted previously, none of the streams is worth in present value terms the actual number of dollars paid. The figures are always less than the number of years for which $1 will be paid. Even for low interest rates the difference is substantial. With a 3 percent interest rate, $1 per year for 100 years is worth only $31 in present value. At higher interest rates, the effect of discounting is even more pronounced. A dollar each year for 100 years is worth less than $10 in present value terms with an interest rate of 10 percent.

■ Perpetual Payments

The value of a stream of payments that goes on "forever" at $1 per year is reported as the final entry in each column of Table 21A.3. To understand how this is calculated, we can pose the question in a slightly different way. How much ($X) would you have to invest at an interest rate of i to yield $1 a year forever? That is, we wish to find $X that satisfies the equation

$$\$1 = i \cdot \$X. \qquad [21A.23]$$

Years of Payment	Interest Rate				Table 21A.3 Present Value of $1 per Year for Various Time Periods and Interest Rates
	1 Percent	3 Percent	5 Percent	10 Percent	
1	$.99	$.97	$.95	$.91	
2	1.97	1.91	1.86	1.74	
3	2.94	2.83	2.72	2.49	
5	4.85	4.58	4.33	3.79	
10	9.47	8.53	7.72	6.14	
25	22.02	17.41	14.09	9.08	
50	39.20	25.73	18.26	9.91	
100	63.02	31.60	19.85	9.99	
Forever	100.00	33.33	20.00	10.00	

But this just means that

$$\$X = \$1/i, \qquad\qquad [21A.24]$$

which is the way the entries in the table were computed. For example, the present value of $1 per year forever with an interest rate of 5 percent is $20 (= $1/.05). With an interest rate of 10 percent the figure would be $10 (= $1/.10). Such a permanent payment stream is called a **perpetuity.** Although these are technically illegal in the United States (although many people set up "permanent" endowments for cemetery plots, scholarships, and prize funds) other countries do permit such limitless contracts to be written. In the United Kingdom, for example, perpetuities originally written in the 1600s are still bought and sold. Equation 21A.24 shows that even though such perpetuities in effect promise an infinite number of dollars (since the payments never cease), in present value terms they have quite modest values. Indeed, for relatively high interest rates, there isn't much difference between getting $1 a year for 25 or 50 years and getting it forever. At an interest rate of 10 percent, for example, the present value of a perpetuity (which promises an infinite number of dollars) is only $.92 greater than a promise of a dollar a year for only 25 years. The infinite number of dollars to be received after year 25 are only worth $.92 today![4]

■ **Perpetuity**

A promise of a certain number of dollars each year, forever.

■ Varying Payment Streams

The present value of payment stream that consists of the same number of dollars each year can be calculated by multiplying the value of $1 per year by that amount. In the lottery illustration with which we began this section, for example, we calculated the present value of $40,000 per year for 25 years. This is 40,000 times the entry for $1 per year for 25 years at 10 percent from Table 21A.3 (40,000 · $9.08 = $363,200). The present value of any other constant stream of dollar payments can be calculated in a similar fashion.

When payments vary from year to year, the computation can become more cumbersome. Each payment must be discounted separately using the formula given in Equation 21A.18. We can show this computation in its most

---

[4]Using the formula for perpetuities provides a simple way of computing streams that run for only a limited number of years. Suppose we wished to evaluate a stream of $1 per year for 25 years at a 10 percent interest rate. If we used Equation 21A.22, we would need to evaluate 25 terms. Instead, we could note that a 25-year stream is an infinite stream less all payments for year 26 and beyond. The present value of a perpetual stream is

$$\frac{\$1}{i} = \frac{\$1}{.10} = \$10$$

whereas the present value of a perpetual stream that starts in year 25 is

$$\frac{\$10}{(1+i)^{25}} = \frac{\$10}{(1+.10)^{25}} = \frac{\$10}{10.83} = \$.92.$$

The value of a 25-year stream is

$$\$10 - \$.92 = \$9.08,$$

which is the figure given in Table 21A.3.

More generally, a stream of $1 per year for n years at the interest rate i has a present value of

$$PDV = \frac{\$1}{i} - \frac{\$1/i}{(1+i)^n}.$$

general form by letting D_i represent the amount to be paid in any year i. Then the present value of this stream would be

$$PDV = \frac{D_1}{1+i} + \frac{D_2}{(1+i)^2} + \frac{D_3}{(1+i)^3} + \ldots + \frac{D_n}{(1+i)^n}. \qquad [21A.25]$$

Here each D could be either positive or negative depending on whether funds are to be received or paid out. In some cases the computations may be rather complicated (as Application 21A.3: Mortgage Market Innovations illustrates) so it may be a good idea to get a calculator that does the drudgery for you.

Frequency of Compounding

So far we have talked only about interest payments that are compounded once a year. That is, interest is paid at the end of each year and does not itself start to earn interest until the next year begins. In the past that was how banks worked. Every January 1 depositors were expected to bring in their bank books so that the past year's interest could be added to them. People who withdrew money from the bank prior to January 1 often lost all the interest they had earned so far in the year.

Since the 1960s, however, banks and all other financial institutions have started to use more frequent, usually daily, compounding. This has provided some extra interest to investors, because more frequent compounding means that prior interest earned will begin itself to earn interest more quickly. In this section we use the tools we have developed so far to explore this issue.

■ Semiannual Compounding

As before, assume the annual interest rate is given by i (or in some of our examples 5 percent). But now suppose the bank agrees to pay interest two times a year—on January 1 and on July 1. If you deposit $1 on January 1, by July 1 it will have grown to be $1 \cdot (1 + i/2)$ since you will have earned half a year's interest. With an interest rate of 5 percent, you will have $1.025 on July 1. For the second half of the year you will earn interest on $1.025, not just on $1. At the end of the year you will have $1.025 \cdot 1.025 = \$1.05063$, which is slightly larger than the $1.05 you would have with annual compounding. More generally, with an interest rate of i, semiannual compounding would yield

$$\$1(i + 1/2)(1 + i/2) = \$1(1 + i/2)^2 \qquad [21A.26]$$

at the end of one year. That this is superior to annual compounding can be shown with simple algebra:

$$\$1 \cdot (1 + i/2)^2 = \$1(1 + i + i^2/4)$$
$$= \$1 \cdot (1 + i) + \$1 \cdot i^2/4, \qquad [21A.27]$$

APPLICATION 21A.3
Mortgage Market Innovations

High interest rates that prevailed during the late 1970s made it very difficult for young people to afford to buy a house using an ordinary mortgage. With an ordinary mortgage, the borrower agrees to pay a fixed amount each month for the duration of the mortgage (usually 30 years). For example, with an interest rate of 10 percent a would-be buyer of a $100,000 home would have to pay $10,600 in annual mortgage payments ($883 per month) because the present value of $10,600 per year for 30 years is precisely the $100,000 needed to buy the house. Since such high mortgage payments may not be affordable by many young people—especially in the early years of trying to establish a family when their incomes are fairly low—they may seek alternative payment schedules that more closely meet their economic circumstances. It is important to understand the nature of the problem young people face. They are not "too poor" to afford a $100,000 house in any absolute sense. But, they are at an early stage in their careers when their earnings are low and are expected to grow. They also can reasonably expect the values of their homes to increase, if only they can get into the market in the first place.

In response to these needs, banks have tried to devise mortgages with payment streams that more closely meet people's life patterns. There are, of course, an infinite number of possible payment streams that have a present value of $100,000 so there is plenty of room for innovations. Here we illustrate two of them.

Balloon Payments

With a balloon payment mortgage, some interest charges are pushed to the end of the mortgage in order to reduce monthly costs early in the mortgage. For example, a borrower can reduce his or her annual payments to about $8,800 ($733 per month) by agreeing to make a single balloon payment of $300,000 at the end of 30 years (presumably when the house will have appreciated substantially).

Graduated Payments

With this scheme, mortgage payments will increase over time to reflect the borrower's increased earnings. For example, the borrower might agree to pay $7,000 per year for the first ten years, $15,000 for the next ten years, and $23,000 for the final ten years and still get $100,000 currently to buy the house. Numerous other schemes were devised during the early 1980s to further cushion the initial shock of mortgage payments.

Recent Trends

Mortgage interest rates fell during the early 1990s, and this reduced the attractiveness of unusual mortgage payment schemes. Banks were reluctant to lend at very low fixed rates for long periods, however, so "adjustable rate" mortgages became an important alternative. With such mortgages, effective interest rates are adjusted every three years to reflect current market conditions. In this way, banks can better match their returns from mortgages to what they must pay for funds.

To Think About

1. Doesn't paying $300,000 at the end of 30 years seem like a huge amount to save only $2,000 per year in mortgage payments? Explain why the balloon payment has to be so large to obtain a sizeable reduction in payments.

2. Why don't people always opt for graduated payment schemes (assuming their incomes will grow)? Why might people want to spend a higher fraction of their income on housing when they are young than when they are old? Does the desire for fixed payments come more from the preferences of lenders or those of borrowers?

Years on Deposit	Frequency			
	Annual	Semiannual	Monthly	Daily
1	$1.0500	$1.0506	$1.0512	$1.0513
2	1.1025	1.1038	1.1049	1.1052
3	1.1576	1.1596	1.1615	1.1618
5	1.2763	1.2801	1.2834	1.2840
10	1.6289	1.6386	1.6471	1.6487
25	3.3863	3.4371	3.4816	3.4900
50	11.4674	11.8137	12.1218	12.1803
100	131.5013	139.5639	146.9380	148.3607

Table 21A.4
Value of $1 at a 5 Percent Annual Interest Rate Compounded with Different Frequencies and Terms

which is clearly greater than $1 \cdot (1 + i)$. The final term in Equation 21A.27 reflects the interest earned in the first half of the year $1 \cdot (i/2)$ times the interest rate in the second half of the year $(i/2)$. This is the bonus earned by semiannual compounding.

■ A General Treatment

We could extend this algebraic discussion to more frequent compounding—quarterly, monthly, or daily—but little new information would be added. More frequent compounding would continue to increase the effective yield that the 5 percent annual interest rate actually provides. Table 21A.4 shows how the frequency of compounding has this effect over time periods of various durations. The gains of using monthly rather than annual compounding are relatively large, especially over long periods of time when small differences in effective yields can make a big difference. Gains in going from monthly to daily compounding are fairly small, however. The extra yield from compounding even more frequently (every second?) are even smaller.[5] Most banks currently utilize daily compounding both because they have been forced to do so by competitive pressures and because they find it fairly easy to adapt computer programs to make such payments.

Calculating Yields

The compound interest formulas we have introduced so far can be easily reversed to solve for the interest return promised on an investment if the payments

---

[5]An approximation to daily compounding is provided by the instantaneous compounding formula

$$\text{Value of \$1 in year } n = e^{in},$$

where i is the annual interest rate and e is the base of natural logarithms ($= 2.71828\ldots$). For an explanation, see Walter Nicholson, *Microeconomic Theory: Basic Principles and Extensions,* 5th ed. (Fort Worth, Texas: The Dryden Press, 1992), pp. 734–735.

and the investment's present value are known. As a very simple example, suppose someone promises to give you \$105 in one year if you give them \$100 today. Obviously, the interest rate promised here (what is more formally called the yield) is 5 percent. By comparing this yield to the yield on other investment options available, you can decide whether to give your \$100 to this person.

In general, if an investment promises to pay D dollars n years from now and will charge you P dollars for this promise, we can use Equation 21A.18 to write

$$P = D/(1 + i)^n, \qquad \text{[21A.28]}$$

but now we wish to solve this equation for the yield, i. To find the yield on a promise of, say, \$1,000 in 10 years that costs \$400 today, we would write

$$\$400 = \$1,000/(1 + i)^{10} \qquad \text{[21A.29]}$$

and manipulate this expression to solve for i:

$$(1 + i)^{10} = \$1,000/\$400 = 2.5$$

or

$$1 + i = (2.5)^{1/10}. \qquad \text{[21A.30]}$$

At this stage you will need either a calculator or a set of yield tables since raising numbers to strange exponential powers is not easy to do by hand. Performing such a calculation gives

$$1 + i = (2.5)^{1/10} = 1.096 \qquad \text{[21A.31]}$$

or

$$i = .096. \qquad \text{[21A.32]}$$

So this investment has a yield of 9.6 percent.

■ More Complex Cases

In more complex cases investments will often promise different payments in various future periods, and the rights to these payments can be purchased for some present cost. For example, when a firm buys a machine, it is really purchasing the right to the stream of future profits that the machine generates. Calculating the yield (or what is sometimes called the *internal rate of return*) on such an investment again requires use of the present value formulas introduced earlier. Suppose that an automobile repair shop is thinking of buying an electronic engine tester that costs \$10,000. The shop will earn \$2,000 each year on this tester and will be able to sell it for \$5,000 in five years when a new model becomes available. What is the yield from buying the tester? Using the present value formula from Equation 21A.25 gives

$$\$10,000 = \frac{\$2,000}{1+i} + \frac{\$2,000}{(1+i)^2} + \frac{\$2,000}{(1+i)^3} + \frac{\$2,000}{(1+i)^4}$$

$$+ \frac{\$2,000}{(1+i)^5} + \frac{\$5,000}{(1+i)^5} \qquad\qquad \text{[21A.33]}$$

—that is, the present cost of the tester ($10,000) should be equated to the present value of $2,000 per year for five years plus the present value of the price the machine will bring when it is sold.

Solving Equation 21A.33 by hand for the yield, i, is no simple task, but it can easily be done by modern calculators. The author's calculator provides a solution of i = 12.15 percent as the yield on this testing machine. The repair shop can compare this yield to that available on other equipment it might buy or to the return banks are offering to decide whether to purchase the tester. Making such yield calculations therefore offers a convenient way of comparing the returns available from alternative investments that may provide very different payment streams.

Summary

This appendix surveys the mathematical calculations that surround compound interest concepts. Dollars payable at different points in time are not equally valuable (since those payable in the distant future require the sacrifice of some potential interest), and it is important to be careful in making comparisons among alternative payment schedules. Discussing this issue we show:

- In making compound interest calculations, it is necessary to take account of interest that is paid on prior interest earned. The interest factor $(1+i)^n$—where n is the number of years over which interest is compounded—reflects this compounding.

- Dollars payable in the future are worth less than dollars payable currently. To compare dollars that are payable at different dates requires using present discounted value computations to allow for the opportunity costs associated with forgone interest.

- Evaluating payment streams requires that each individual payment be discounted by the appropriate interest factor. It is incorrect simply to add together dollars payable at different times.

- More frequent compounding leads to higher effective returns since prior interest paid begins to earn interest more quickly. There is an upper limit to the increased yield provided, however.

- The present discounted value formula can also be used to calculate yields on investments. The availability of such yields provides a convenient way to compare alternative investments for which the actual payment streams may be quite different.

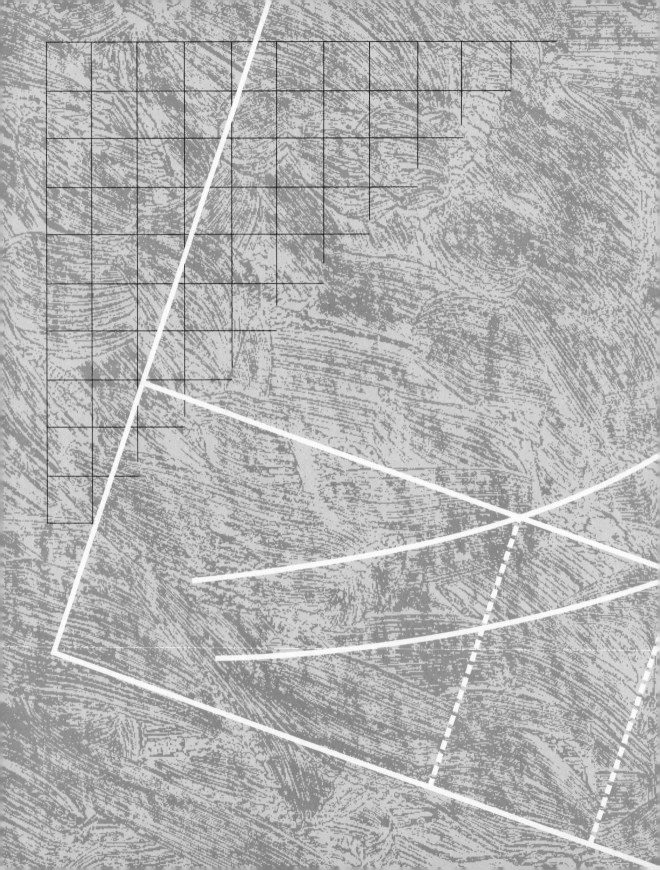

"In devising and choosing among social arrangements, we should have regard for the total effect."

Ronald Coase

"The Problem of Social Cost," 1960

Part 7 explores the limits of the market. Prior sections of this book have focused at length on the ways in which markets allocate resources. Although the equilibria described were not always efficient, they were arrived at through some type of interaction of the forces of supply and demand. In this final part, we will move away somewhat from our examination of market forces and explore some situations where nonmarket influences may be quite important. We will show that, for some allocational questions, markets will perform relatively poorly and other economic institutions (most importantly, the government) may play decisive, though not necessarily better, allocational roles.

Chapter 22 addresses problems raised by goods that have externality or spillover effects. For these goods simple market transactions may not accurately reflect all of the economic consequences of consumption and production—some misallocations of resources may occur.

Chapter 23, the final chapter in this book, focuses on goods that benefit a large number of individuals who cannot be prevented from receiving such benefits. These goods are called "public goods." Besides examining in detail the attributes of such goods, we also investigate some of the problems involved in achieving an efficient level of output for them.

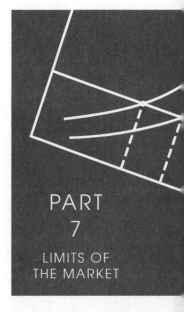

PART
7

LIMITS OF
THE MARKET

CHAPTER
22

EXTERNALITIES
AND PROPERTY
RIGHTS

Externalities are effects of the actions of one economic actor on other actors that are not adequately reflected in the market. A manufacturing plant that pollutes the air causing serious health problems for people nearby is creating such an externality. Our goal in this chapter is to analyze why markets may fail to allocate resources efficiently in this situation. We also show various ways in which the problems posed by externalities can be controlled. More generally, our study of externalities provides insights into the nature and problems of private property; the issue of property rights and how they influence the allocation of resources is an underlying theme of this chapter.

Defining Externalities

Before launching into a detailed analysis, we should be precise in defining exactly what an externality is, since there has been substantial confusion over this point in economics. An **externality** is an effect of one economic actor's activities on another actor's well-being that is not taken into account by the normal operations of the price system. This definition stresses the direct, non-market effect of one actor on another such as soot falling out of the air or toxic chemicals appearing in drinking water. The definition does not include effects that take place through the market. If I buy an item that is on sale before you do, I may keep you from getting it and thereby affect your well-being. That is not an externality in our sense because the effect took place in a market setting.[1] Its occurrence does not affect the ability of markets to allocate resources efficiently. Before examining why true externalities may distort the allocation of resources, our definition may be made more concrete by giving a few examples.

Externality

The effect of one party's economic activities on another party that is not taken into account by the price system.

Examples of Externalities

Externalities can occur between any two economic actors. Here we first illustrate negative (harmful) and positive (beneficial) externalities between firms. We then examine externalities between people and firms and conclude by considering a few externalities between people.

Externalities between Firms

Consider two firms—one producing eyeglasses, another producing charcoal (this is an actual example from nineteenth-century English law). The production of charcoal is said to have an external effect on the production of eyeglasses if the output of eyeglasses depends not only on the amount of inputs chosen by the eyeglass firm but also on the level at which the production of charcoal is carried on. Suppose these two firms are located near each other, and the eyeglass firm is downwind from the charcoal firm. In this case, the output of eyeglasses may depend not only on the level of inputs the eyeglass firm uses itself but also on the amount of charcoal in the air, which affects its precision grinding wheels. The level of pollutants, in turn, is determined by the output of the charcoal firm. Increases in charcoal output would cause fewer high-quality eyeglasses to be produced even though the eyeglass firm has no control over this negative effect.[2]

---

[1]Sometimes such effects are called "pecuniary" externalities to distinguish them from the "technological" externalities we will be discussing.

[2]We will find it necessary to redefine the assumption of "no control" considerably as the analysis of this chapter proceeds.

The relationship between two firms may also be beneficial. Most examples of positive externalities are rather bucolic in nature. Perhaps the most famous, proposed by James Meade, involves two firms, one producing honey by raising bees and the other producing apples.[3] Because the bees feed on apple blossoms, an increase in apple production will improve productivity in the honey industry. The beneficial effects of having well-fed bees is a positive externality to the beekeeper. Similarly, bees pollinate apple crops and the beekeeper provides an external benefit to the orchard owner. Later in this chapter we examine this situation in greater detail since, surprisingly enough, the beekeeper–apple grower relationship has played an important role in economic research on the significance of externalities.

■ Externalities between Firms and People

Firms' productive activities may impact directly on individuals' well-being. A firm that produces air pollution imposes costs on people living near the firm in the form of ill health and increased dust and grime. Similar effects arise from firms' pollution of water (for example, mining firms that dump their waste into Lake Superior, reducing the lake's recreational value to people who wish to fish there), misuse of land (strip mining that is an eyesore and may interfere with water supplies), and production of noise (airports that are located near major cities). In all of these cases, at least on first inspection, it seems that firms will not take any of these external costs into consideration when making decisions on how much to produce.

Of course, people may also have external effects on firms. Drivers' auto pollution harms the productivity of citrus growers, cleaning up litter and graffiti is a major expense for shopping centers, and the noise of Saturday night rock concerts on college campuses probably affects motel rentals. In each of these cases, as for the cases of externalities produced by firms, there may be no simple way for the affected parties to force the people who generate the externalities to take the full costs of their actions into account.

■ Externalities between People

Finally, the activity of one person may affect the well-being of someone else. Playing a radio too loud, smoking cigars, or driving during peak hours are all consumption activities that may negatively affect the utility of others. Planting an attractive garden or shoveling the snow off one's sidewalk may, on the other hand, provide beneficial externalities. Often, however, these activities will not be reflected in market transactions among the people involved.

■ Reciprocal Nature of Externalities

Although these examples of externalities picture one actor as the cause of the problem and some other actor as the helpless victim (or beneficiary), that is

---

[3]James Meade, "External Economies and Diseconomies in a Competitive Situation," *Economic Journal* (March 1952): 54–67.

not in fact the case. By definition, externalities require (at least) two parties and in a sense each should be regarded as the "cause." If the producer of eyeglasses had not located its factory near the charcoal furnace, it would not have suffered any negative effects on its grinding wheels; if individuals didn't live below airport flight paths, noise would only be a minor problem; and if you were out of earshot, it wouldn't matter that someone else had the radio's volume turned up. Recognizing these reciprocal relationships is not intended to exonerate polluters, only to clarify the nature of the problem. In all of these cases two economic actors are seeking to use the same resource, and (as we illustrate in Application 22.1: Reciprocal Effects of Externalities, Past and Present) there are no unambiguous economic principles for deciding whose claim is stronger. Rather, as we shall see, in studying externalities it is important to understand their reciprocal nature and how this affects the allocation of resources. In this way we can explore how various ways of coping with externalities may affect the behavior of all of the parties involved.

Externalities, Markets, and Allocational Efficiency

It has traditionally been argued that the presence of externalities such as those we have just described can cause a market to operate inefficiently. We discussed the reasons for this briefly in Chapter 14, and will repeat these reasons here using the example of eyeglass and charcoal producers. Production of eyeglasses is assumed to produce no externalities, but is assumed to be negatively affected by the level of charcoal output. We now show that resources may be allocated inefficiently in this situation. Remember that for an allocation of resources to be efficient it is required that price be equal to social marginal cost in each market (see Chapter 14 for a discussion of this point). If the market for eyeglasses is perfectly competitive (as we assume both markets to be), their price will indeed be equal to this good's private marginal cost. Since there are no externalities in eyeglass production, there is no need to make a distinction between private and social marginal cost in this case.

For charcoal production, the story is more complex. The producer of charcoal will still produce that output for which price is equal to private marginal cost. This is a direct result of the profit-maximization assumption. However, because of the negative effect that production of charcoal has on eyeglass production, it will not be true that private and social marginal costs of charcoal production are equal. Rather, the true **social cost** of charcoal production is equal to the private cost *plus* the cost that charcoal production imposes on eyeglass firms in terms of reduced or inferior output. The charcoal-producing firm does not recognize this effect and produces where price is equal to private marginal cost (which in this case is lower than social marginal cost). Since now the social marginal cost of charcoal production exceeds charcoal's price, this is a clear sign that too much charcoal is being produced. Society would be made better-off by reallocating resources away from charcoal production and toward

Social costs

Costs of production that include both input costs and costs of the externalities that production may cause.

APPLICATION 22.1
Reciprocal Effects of Externalities, Past and Present

Sometimes the reciprocal effects of externalities are made explicit in the law. Legal doctrine is constantly evolving as such interrelationships become more apparent. This is illustrated by two important concerns occurring nearly one hundred years apart.

Steam Engines and Crops

As railroads spread throughout the English countryside in the latter part of the nineteenth century, they began to have a variety of effects on the environment. Cultivation moved toward rail lines since they promised reduced transportation costs for crops. At the same time, however, the steam engines of the day tended to spew sparks and cinders over the landscape, thereby posing the threat of fire. As these types of interactions along rail lines became more frequent, a body of common law developed to sort out legal liability in various instances.

A. C. Pigou was one of the first economists to explore the train–crops relationship in detail. In his view, the operators of steam engines were at fault and should be made liable for any damage done. R. M. Coase attacked this conclusion in his famous article on social cost[1] by pointing out that as early as 1860 railroads had been granted exemption from such liability, possibly because Parliament recognized the reciprocal nature of the externality and found it preferable to encourage the growth of railroads. One side effect of such a stance was to discourage cultivation along rail right-of-ways and thereby minimize the number of accidental fires. By not getting embroiled in a fruitless pursuit of who was "at fault" in this situation, Parliament may have improved the allocation of resources.

Anti-Smoking Laws

A modern day equivalent of the railroad sparks question is the debate over cigarette smoke. Again, the situation is a reciprocal one—both smokers and nonsmokers wish to use the air around them. Although it may be difficult for nonsmokers to admit, their demand for fresh air has no more intrinsic worth than does the smoker's demand for the right to enjoy his or her habit unencumbered.

Despite this symmetry, government at all levels has been adopting increasingly more stringent rules about smoking. In many localities, smoking is banned in public places, federal law bans smoking on all flights shorter than two hours, and laws are starting to appear that guarantee a "smoke-free" workplace. Through all of this, smokers have been relatively docile in yielding their rights. Perhaps the anti-smoking laws represent a relatively efficient way of defining matters since those who can most easily change their behavior are being asked to do so (it is, for example, easier for a smoker not to smoke on a plane flight than it is for a nonsmoker to exit the plane). In establishing such laws, the government is not necessarily adopting a position about whose rights are more "worthy" (although there are public health reasons for discouraging smoking for smokers and nonsmokers alike). Rather, the government can be viewed as deciding how the air can be used best from an overall allocational perspective.

To Think About

1. Isn't the idea of reciprocal externalities fairly far-fetched in some situations? How can the victims of toxic waste disposal (such as those at Love Canal) in a chemical dumpsite, for example, be assigned blame for what is happening to them? Doesn't the Coase view of matters seem to disregard common-sense notions of cause and effect?

2. Should colleges and universities impose a no-smoking ban in classrooms and dormitories? How are objections to smoking handled without such a ban? Would matters be improved through administrative action? Does Coase-type bargaining occur on college campuses?

---

[1]For a complete discussion, see R. M. Coase, "The Problem of Social Cost," *Journal of Law and Economics* (October 1960): 1–44.

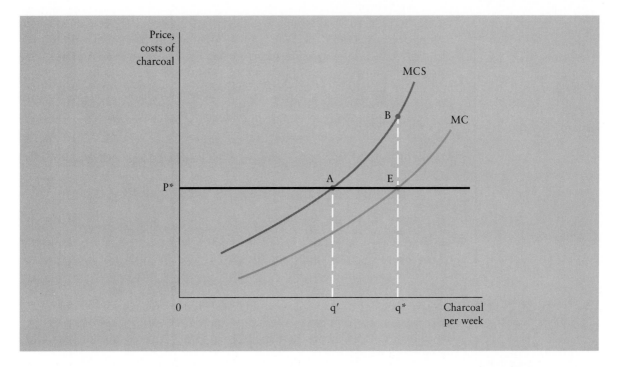

Because production of charcoal imposes external costs on eyeglass makers, social marginal costs (MCS) exceed private marginal costs (MC). In a competitive market the firm would produce q* at a price of P*. At Q*, however, MCS > P* and resource allocation could be improved by reducing output to q'.

Figure 22.1
An Externality in Charcoal Production Causes an Inefficient Allocation of Resources

the production of other goods (including eyeglasses). Because of the externality in charcoal production, prices no longer carry the correct information about marginal costs that is necessary to achieve efficiency.

■ A Graphic Demonstration

Figure 22.1 illustrates the possible misallocation of resources that results from the externality in charcoal production. Assuming that the charcoal producer is a price taker, the demand curve for its output is simply a horizontal line at the prevailing market price (say, P*). Profits are maximized at q* where price is equal to the private marginal cost of producing charcoal (MC). Because of the externality that charcoal production imposes on eyeglass makers, however, the social marginal cost of this production (MCS) exceeds MC as shown in Figure 22.1. The vertical gap between the MCS and the MC curves is a measure of the harm that producing an extra unit of charcoal imposes on eyeglass makers. At q*, the social marginal cost of producing charcoal exceeds the price people are willing to pay for this output (P*). Resources are misallocated, and production should be reduced to q′ where social marginal cost and price are equal. In making this reduction, the reduction in total social costs (area ABq*q′) exceeds the reduction in total spending on charcoal (given by area AEq*q′). This comparison shows that the allocation of resources is improved by a reduction in charcoal output since costs are reduced to a greater extent than are consumers' expenditures on charcoal. Consumers can reallocate their spending toward something else that involves lower social costs than charcoal does.

Traditional Solutions to the Externality Problem

To study possible solutions to the problems that externalities pose for the allocation of resources, we will first assume that production techniques are fixed.[4] Under this assumption, prescriptions such as "force charcoal producers to use alternative production techniques that yield less soot" are outside the frame of analysis. Later in this chapter we will look at such other ways of coping with externalities, but to do so here would obscure the issue of how the charcoal producer can be prompted to reduce output. Even in this limited case, there are still three approaches that may bring about reduced output—taxation, merger, and bargaining.

■ Taxation

By imposing a suitable excise tax on the firm generating an externality, the government can cause the output of this firm to be reduced—thereby shifting resources into other uses. This classic remedy to the externality problem was first lucidly put forward in the 1920s by A. C. Pigou.[5] Although it has been somewhat modified, it remains one of the "standard" answers given by economists. The central problem for regulators becomes one of obtaining sufficient empirical information so that the correct tax structure can be enacted.

The taxation solution is illustrated in Figure 22.2. Again, MC and MCS represent the private and social marginal costs of charcoal production, and the market price of charcoal is given by P*. An excise tax of amount t (see Chapter 13) would reduce the net price received by the firm to P* − t, and at that price the firm would choose to produce q′. The tax causes the firm to reduce its output to the socially optimal amount. At q′ the firm incurs private marginal costs of P* − t and imposes external costs on eyeglass makers of t per unit. The per-unit tax is therefore exactly equal to the extra costs that charcoal produc-

---

[4]It is also assumed that the detrimental effects of the production of charcoal do not affect anyone else in the economy other than eyeglass producers. Similarly, our discussion of externalities takes place within a partial equilibrium framework in which the rest of the economy is assumed to be perfectly competitive.

[5]A. C. Pigou, *The Economics of Welfare*, 4th ed. (London: Macmillan, 1946). Pigou also stressed the desirability of providing subsidies to firms that produce beneficial externalities. More recent literature has stressed that such taxes and subsidies must be based directly on the costs (or benefits) of the externalities (rather than on the total costs of the goods themselves) if efficiency is to be achieved. Later in this chapter we show this result.

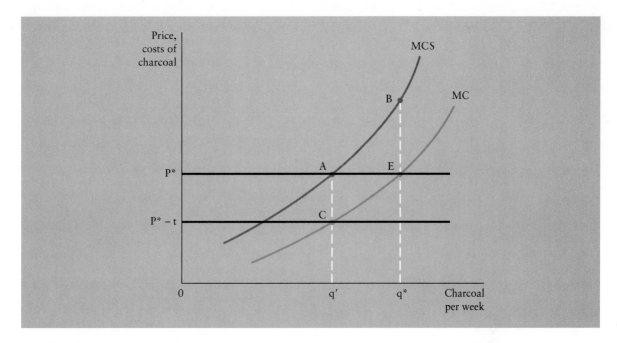

An excise tax of amount t would reduce the net price of charcoal to P* − t. At that price the firm would choose to produce the socially optimal level of charcoal output (q').

Figure 22.2
Taxation Solution to the Externality Problem

ers impose on eyeglass producers.[6] Application 22.2: Acid Rain shows how such a **Pigovian tax** might work in practice as a partial solution to the problem of electric power plant emissions.

■ **Merger and Internalization**

A second traditional cure for the allocation problems caused by externalities between two firms would be for these firms to merge. If there were a single firm producing both charcoal and eyeglasses, this firm would recognize the detrimental effect that charcoal production has on its glass-grinding equipment. In effect, the combined firm would now pay the full social marginal costs of charcoal production because it now incurs these costs directly. In other words, the firm's manager would now take the marginal cost curve for charcoal production to be MCS and would produce q', where price equals this marginal cost. This is exactly what is required for efficiency. Economists would say that the externality in production has been **internalized** as a result of the merger.

■ **Pigovian tax**

A tax or subsidy on an externality that brings about an equality of private and social marginal costs.

■ **Internalization of an externality**

Incorporation of the social marginal costs of an externality into an economic actor's decisions (as through taxation or merger).

---

[6]If the charcoal firm here represents an entire industry, then the tax would, as in Chapter 13, raise the market price of charcoal. If the industry exhibited constant costs, in the long run price would rise by the exact amount of the tax and demand would be reduced to the socially optimal level by that price rise. In this case the tax would be fully paid by charcoal consumers in the long run. If charcoal production exhibited increasing costs, some portion of the Pigovian tax would be paid by suppliers of inputs to the charcoal industry.

APPLICATION 22.2
Acid Rain

Electric power plants that burn coal emit a variety of unhealthy by-products, most importantly sulfur which combines with oxygen to produce sulfuric acid. Existing environmental regulations require such power plants to achieve certain emission standards, mainly by "scrubbing" the coal fumes in their exhaust stacks. Since that process is very costly, a number of economists and other observers have suggested that taxing sulfur emissions might obtain the same results at much lower resource costs.

A Pigovian Tax Proposal

For example, an early proposal by Wisconsin Senator William Proxmire would have taxed sulfur emissions at an initial rate of 5 cents per pound, with the rate rising to 20 cents over a period of years. A. Schlottman and L. Abrams attempted to estimate the effects of this tax on coal production and sulfur emissions in the United States.[1] Overall, the authors estimated that a 5 cent per pound tax would reduce annual sulfur emissions by about 1 million tons (a 12 percent reduction), with the 20-cent tax leading to nearly a 5 million ton reduction (a greater than 40 percent reduction). These reductions came partly from a reduced level of coal use and partly from a shift in coal supplies from regions with high-sulfur-content coal (parts of Appalachia and the Midwest) to regions with low-sulfur-content coal (the West). These changes would have imposed additional costs on utilities, but these costs may be rather small compared to alternative ways of dealing with sulfur.

The Acid Rain Debate

During the 1980s the debate over power plant emissions came to focus more explicitly on the problem of "acid rain." Evidence of increasing levels of acidity in lakes in the Northeast United States and Canada suggested (though by no means proved) that sulfur emissions from midwestern power plants were having greater effects than had previously been believed. Environmentalists were quick to adopt the image of "acid" falling from the sky to argue for much stricter controls on electric power generation.

Unfortunately, the debate over what to do about acid rain quickly became mired in both scientific and political controversy. On the scientific level, there is relatively little long-term data with which to test the acid rain hypothesis. Comparisons among various areas of the country also pose problems since it is very difficult to identify two areas that are similar in every respect except this exposure to power plant emissions. One major government assessment concludes that "about half" of all the lakes in sensitive areas might acidify if subjected to enough pollutants, but that conclusion is at best only a guess.[2]

Because the benefits and costs of policies to reduce sulfur emissions would be unevenly distributed among regions of the country, the politics of acid rain are even more complex than the scientific issues. The basic problem is that power plants in the midwestern states of Illinois, Indiana, Michigan, and Ohio are the major source of sulfur dioxide emissions, but the northeastern states would be the major beneficiaries of a program to reduce those emissions. Most proposed plans for dealing with acid rain take no account of such differences, but instead stress the adoption of national emission standards or national taxes on coal. Because such approaches do not focus on areas where emissions pose the greatest danger, they may not be economically efficient.[3]

To Think About

1. Would an excise tax on coal have the same effect as a tax on sulfur emissions? How would the two taxes affect utilities' choices of inputs?
2. Suppose the sole goal of an anti-acid rain policy were to reduce the danger to rivers and lakes in the northeastern United States. Would a uniform tax on all emissions achieve that goal at minimal cost?

---

[1]A. Schlottman and L. Abrams, "Sulfur Emission Taxes and Coal Resources," *Review of Economics and Statistics* (February 1977): 50–55.
[2]U.S. Congress, Office of Technology Assessment, *Acid Rain and Transported Air Pollutants: Implications for Public Policy* (Washington,

D.C.: U.S. Government Printing Office, 1984).
[3]See R. W. Crandall, *Controlling Industrial Pollution: The Economics and Politics of Clean Air* (Washington, D.C.: The Brookings Institution, 1983).

Bargaining

One important question we might still ask about this analysis is if the charcoal producer's actions impose a cost on the eyeglass maker, why doesn't the eyeglass maker "bribe" the charcoal firm to cut back on its output? Presumably the gain of a cutback to the eyeglass firm (the reduction in eyeglass costs is given by area ABEC in Figure 22.2) would exceed the loss of profits to charcoal makers (area AEC in the figure), and some bargaining arrangement might be worked out that would monetarily benefit both parties. Both firms would be irrational not to recognize such a possibility, and it would seem that the benefits of internalization could be obtained without actually going through a merger. After all, people do bargain with their neighbors about loud music or maintaining the yard. Such bargaining between economic actors might therefore be a third way to attain efficiency. Because this possibility suggests that the externality problem may, in some cases, "cure itself," we will examine it in a bit more detail.

Property Rights, Bargaining, and the Coase Theorem

To explore the bargaining issue further, we need to introduce the concept of property rights to show how these rights might be traded voluntarily between the two firms. Simply put, **property rights** are the legal specification of who owns a good and of the types of trades that the current owner is allowed to make. Some goods may be defined as **common property** that is owned by society at large and may be used by anyone; others may be defined as **private property** that is owned by specific people. Private property may either be *exchangeable* or *nonexchangeable,* depending on whether the good in question may or may not be traded to someone else. In this book we have been primarily concerned with exchangeable private property, and we will consider these types of property rights here.[7]

■ Costless Bargaining and Competitive Markets

For the purposes of the charcoal–eyeglass externality, it is interesting to consider the nature of the property right that might be attached to the air shared by the charcoal and eyeglass firms. Suppose property rights were defined so as to give sole rights to use of the air to one of the firms, but that the firms were free to bargain over exactly how the air might be used. At first, you might think that if rights to the air were given to the charcoal producer, pollution would result, whereas if rights were given to the eyeglass firm, the air would remain pure and grinding machines would work properly. This might not be

■
Property rights
The legal specification of who owns a good and the trades the owner is allowed to make with it.

■
Common property
Property that may be used by anyone without cost.

■
Private property
Property that is owned by specific people who may prevent others from using it.

---

[7] Two important examples of privately owned goods that are not exchangeable are a person's human capital (this could be sold only in a society that permitted slavery) and a person's vote (a private good that is provided by the state).

the case since your snap conclusion disregards the bargains that might be reached by the two parties. Indeed, some economists have argued that if *bargaining is costless,* the two parties left on their own will arrive at the efficient output (q′), and this result will be true regardless of who "owns" the rights to use the air.

■ Ownership by the Polluting Firm

Suppose the charcoal firm owns the right to use the air as it wishes. It must then add the costs (if any) related to this ownership into its total costs. What are the costs associated with air ownership? Again the opportunity cost notion provides the answer. For the charcoal firm, the costs of using the air as a dumping place for its dust are what someone else is willing to pay for this resource in its best alternative use. In our example, only the eyeglass maker has some alternative uses for the air (to keep it clean), and the amount that this firm would be willing to pay for clean air is precisely equal to the external damage done by charcoal pollution. If the charcoal firm calculates its costs correctly, its marginal cost curve (including the implicit cost of air use rights) becomes MCS in Figure 22.2. The firm will therefore produce q′ and sell the remaining air use rights to the eyeglass maker for a fee of some amount between AEC (the lost profits from producing q′ rather than q* tons of charcoal) and ABEC (the maximum amount the eyeglass maker would pay to avoid having charcoal output increased from q′ to q*).

■ Ownership by the Injured Firm

A similar result would occur if eyeglass makers owned the rights to use the air as they pleased. In this case the charcoal producer would be willing to pay up to its total profits for the right to pollute the air (assuming, as we have all along, that there is no less damaging way to make charcoal). The eyeglass maker will accept these payments as long as they exceed the costs imposed on it by the charcoal firm's pollution. The ultimate result of bargaining will be for the charcoal firm to offer a payment for the right to "use" the air to dispose of the amount of soot and ash associated with output level q′. The eyeglass maker will not sell the rights to undertake any further pollution into "its" air because what the charcoal firm would be willing to pay (P − MC) falls short of the cost of this additional pollution (MCS − MC). Again, as when the charcoal firm had the property rights for air usage, an efficient allocation can be reached by relying on voluntary bargaining between the two firms. In both situations some production of charcoal takes place, and there will therefore be some air pollution. Having no charcoal output (and no pollution) would be inefficient in the same sense that producing q* is inefficient—scarce resources would not be efficiently allocated. In this case there is some "optimal level" of air pollution that may be achieved through bargains between the firms involved.

■ The Coase Theorem

We have shown that the two firms left on their own can arrive at the efficient output level (q'). Assuming that bargaining is costless, both parties will recognize the advantages of striking a deal. Each will be led by the "invisible hand" to the same output level that would be achieved through an ideal merger. That solution will be reached no matter how the property rights associated with air use are assigned. The pollution-producing firm has exactly the same incentives to choose an efficient output level as does the injured firm. The ability of the two firms to bargain freely causes the true social costs of the externality to be recognized by each in its decisions. This result is sometimes referred to as the **Coase theorem** after the economist Ronald Coase, who first proposed it in this form.[8]

■ Distributional Effects

There are distributional effects that do depend on who is assigned the property rights to use the air. If the charcoal firm is given the air rights, it will get the fee paid by the eyeglass maker, which will make the charcoal producer at least as well off as it was producing q*. If the eyeglass firm gets the rights, it will receive a fee for air use that at least covers the damage the air pollution does. Because, according to the Coase result, the final allocation of resources will be unaffected by the way in which property rights are assigned,[9] any assessment of the desirability of the various possibilities might be made on equity grounds. For example, if the owners of the charcoal firm were very wealthy and those who make eyeglasses were poor, we might argue that ownership of the air use rights should be given to eyeglass makers on the basis of distributional equity. If the situation were reversed, one could argue for giving the charcoal firm the rights. The price system may often be capable of solving problems in the allocation of resources caused by externalities, but, as always, it will not necessarily achieve equitable solutions. Such issues of equity in the assignment of property rights arise in every allocational decision, not only in the study of externalities, however.

■ The Role of Bargaining Costs

The result of the Coase theorem depends crucially on the assumption of zero bargaining costs. If the costs (real or psychological) of striking bargains were high, the workings of this voluntary exchange system might not be capable of achieving an efficient result. In the next section we examine an important type of externality for which bargaining costs are indeed quite high—environmental externalities. We show that for such externalities it is unlikely that the competitive market will attain an efficient outcome and then proceed to look

■
Coase theorem
If bargaining is costless, the social cost of an externality will be taken into account by the parties, and the allocation of resources will be the same no matter how property rights are assigned.

---

[8]See Ronald Coase, "The Problem of Social Cost," *Journal of Law and Economics* (October 1960): 1–44.

[9]Assuming that the wealth effects of how property rights are assigned do not affect demand and cost relationships in the charcoal market.

at other remedies. Still, as Application 22.3: Bargains in the Orchard—Bees and Apples shows, the price system often has a surprising power to handle certain types of externalities.

Bargaining Costs, Environmental Externalities, and Environmental Regulation

It is commonly believed that markets seem to have failed to cope with many externalities related to the environment. Firms and individuals routinely pollute the air and water through their disposal activities; noise levels in urban areas are often so high as to be harmful to residents' health; and the array of signs and posters along most major highways creates what some people regard as "visual pollution." In view of the Coase theorem, a natural first question to ask about these externalities is why they have not been internalized through bargaining. It would seem that those who are harmed by the externalities could bargain with those who create them and thereby improve the allocation of resources.

The principal reason that Coase-type agreements do not occur in these cases is that *high bargaining costs* are often associated with most environmental externalities. It is frequently difficult to organize people harmed by these externalities into an effective bargaining unit and to calculate the monetary value of the losses each has suffered.[10] Similarly, most legal systems have been set up primarily to adjudicate disputes between two specific plaintiffs rather than to represent the rights of large, diffuse groups such as those who may be affected by environmental damage. These factors make bargaining costs extremely high in many cases. It is possible that these costs exceed the possible efficiency gains that can be obtained by successful bargaining.

■ Bargaining Costs and Allocation

In cases characterized by high transactions or bargaining costs, the assignment of ownership rights can have significant allocational effects. If, as is normally the case, disposal of refuse into air and water is treated as use of common property, this in effect assigns use rights to each firm. The firm may use the air and water around it in any way it chooses, and high bargaining costs will prevent it from internalizing any external costs into its decisions. For this reason, pollution-producing activities may be operated at a higher level than would be optimal unless specific types of control mechanisms (such as Pigou-type taxes) are employed.

---

[10]Many of the problems that arise in the provision of public goods are important impediments to group environmental action. Once pollution is abated, it is abated for everyone. The benefits are nonexclusive. Consequently, it may be to the advantage of each person to adopt the position of a free rider. See Chapter 23 for a further discussion of this free rider issue.

APPLICATION 22.3

Bargains in the Orchard—Bees and Apples

Earlier in this chapter we described James Meade's example of the beneficial externalities between beekeepers and apple growers—bees pollinate apples, and apples provide nectar for honey. However, since the costs of bargaining between these two producers are probably low, the Coase theorem suggests that there may be incentives to internalize these externalities through private contracts, thereby reversing Meade's conclusion.

Bee Contracting in Washington

Cheung's fascinating investigation of beekeeping in Washington state shows that contract bargaining is very well developed.[1] Terms of contracts between beekeepers and farmers typically take into account both the benefits that various crops provide to beekeepers (in the form of honey) and the benefits that farmers get from having bees pollinate their crops. For crops such as clover and alfalfa, which have high honey yields, beekeepers usually pay rent to farmers for the right to have their bees graze off the farmers' crops. On the other hand, apple and cherry growers must "rent" bees to provide pollination because the honey yield from those crops is low. Although Meade's classic example has a certain bucolic appeal, the economic facts seem to offer limited support to his theorizing.

Lessons from the Bees

This episode clearly illustrates the importance of the interplay between theory and empirical evidence in developing economic models. To an economic theorist, Meade's example was compelling—generations of students (including your author) were taught it as "gospel." But, despite the theory, beekeepers and orchard owners continued to develop their elaborate set of contracts. Indeed, a quick look in the Yellow Pages in many cities confirms the importance of these contracts—by all appearances bee rental is a thriving business. Indeed, some "migratory beekeepers" regularly drive their hives around the United States on large flatbed trucks, following whatever crop needs pollinating. Free contracting combined with the interstate highway system seems to have solved Meade's problem in even the most far flung areas.[2] Other examples of hypothetical market imperfections that have been undermined by real-world evidence include a purported absence of markets for recyclable material (these markets, in fact, are flourishing for some items), the presumed undesirable properties of markets for human blood or human organs (which seem to operate rather well where they are permitted), and (as we shall see in the next chapter) the presumption that public-type goods (such as lighthouses or roads) must be provided by the government. In all of these cases the benefits from voluntary transactions that are predicted by the Coase theorem keep occurring despite the most dire predictions based on incomplete theories.

To Think About

1. Not every beekeeper enters into contracts with growers for nectar. Instead, many allow their bees to forage (and pollinate) anywhere the bees choose to go. What sort of factors would determine whether there were formal contracts between beekeepers and growers?

2. Can you think of other examples of beneficial externalities in which some kind of payment is made by the beneficiary? For example, how do apartment and condominium complexes pay for landscaping services? Or, how do mall owners pay for indoors plants, fountains, and parking lot maintenance?

---

[1]S. N. S. Cheung, "The Fable of the Bees: An Economic Investigation," *Journal of Law and Economics* (April 1973): 11–33.

[2] "America's Beekeepers: Hives for Hire," *National Geographic* (May 1993): 73–93.

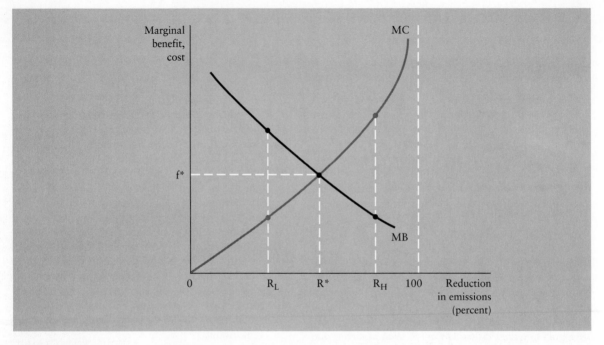

Figure 22.3
Optional Pollution
Abatement

The MB and MC curves show the marginal benefits and marginal costs, respectively, of pollution abatement. R* represents an optimal allocation of resources to this purpose. Such an outcome may be attained through the imposition of an effluent fee of f*, through the sale of marketable pollution permits, or through direct controls.

■ Modeling Environmental Regulation

In order to examine a few of the issues that arise in designing environmental controls, we shall adopt a very simple model of this regulatory process.[11] The horizontal axis in Figure 22.3 shows percentage reductions in environmental pollution from some source below what would occur in the absence of any regulation. The curve MB in the figure shows the additional social benefits obtained by reducing such pollution by one more unit. These benefits consist of possibly improved health, the availability of additional recreational or aesthetic benefits, and improved production opportunities for other firms. The curve is intended to reflect all of the potentially valuable outcomes that antipollution efforts might have. As for most economic activities, this provision of benefits is assumed to exhibit diminishing returns—the curve MB slopes downward to reflect the fact that the marginal benefits from additional reductions in pollution decline as stricter controls are implemented. The health gains from removing the final .001 percent of pollutants are therefore assumed to be

[11]For a more complete discussion, see W. J. Baumol and W. E. Oates, *The Theory of Environmental Policy*, 2d ed. (Cambridge, U.K.: Cambridge University Press, 1988).

rather small, perhaps because the natural environment can easily handle some amount of pollutants on its own.

The curve MC in Figure 22.3 represents the marginal costs incurred in reducing environmental emissions. These costs include both forgone profits from a lower output and actual costs associated with using anti-pollution equipment. The positive slope of this curve reflects our usual assumptions of increasing marginal costs. Controlling the first 50 or 60 percent of pollutants is assumed to be a relatively low-cost activity, but controlling the last few percentage points is assumed to be rather costly. As reductions in emissions approach 100 percent, marginal costs associated with further reductions rise very rapidly.

■ Optimal Regulation

Given this configuration, it is clear that R^* is the optimal level of pollution reduction. For reductions less than R^* (say, R_L), the marginal benefits associated with further tightening of environmental controls exceed the marginal cost of achieving lower pollution levels, so emissions should be reduced further. Reductions in excess of R^* are also inefficient, however—environmental control can be pushed too far. At R_H the marginal cost of emissions control exceeds the marginal benefits obtained so less strict regulation may be desirable. To noneconomists the notion that there is an optimal level of pollution (that R^* is less than 100 percent) may sound strange, but this result simply reflects the general principles of resource allocation we have been studying throughout this book. As Application 22.4: Regulatory Zealotry shows, excessive environmental control can be as costly to society as inadequate control.

■ Fees, Permits, and Direct Controls

There are three general ways that emissions reductions of R^* might be attained through environmental policy.[12] First, the government may adopt a Pigovian-type "effluent fee" of f^* for each percent that pollution is not reduced. Faced with such a charge, the polluting firm will choose the optimal emissions reduction level, R^*. For reductions less than R^*, the fee exceeds the marginal cost of pollution abatement so a profit-maximizing firm will opt for abatement. Reductions in emissions of more than R^* would be unprofitable, however, so the firm will opt to pay the fee on $100 - R^*$ percent. One important feature of the fee approach is that the firm itself is free to choose what combination of output reduction and adoption of pollution control technology achieves R^* at minimal cost.

A similar allocational result would be attained if governmental regulators issued permits that permitted firms to "produce" $100 - R^*$ percent of their

---

[12]In our discussion we will assume that government regulators face no adverse incentives of their own—they only seek to achieve R^*. Some of the discussion in Chapter 23 may suggest the possible shortcomings of this assumption, since regulators themselves may face a variety of adverse incentives.

APPLICATION 22.4

Regulatory Zealotry

Environmental and consumer safety groups have become very effective at lobbying for their causes. Frequently the goals of these groups are laudable and their actions promote the adoption of desirable public policies. At times, however, regulatory proposals would impose costs that seem far in excess of the social benefits provided.

Phosphates

In the late 1970s, responding to pressure from environmental groups, several localities banned the sale of laundry detergents containing phosphates, and some states also followed suit. Because these bans were easy to impose and seemed to represent only trivial inconvenience for consumers (there are other types of detergents available), they did not involve the extensive debate that many other environmental regulations have. Still, our analysis in this chapter suggests that such dramatic measures seldom produce efficient results. For example, a 1984 study of phosphate bans in Wisconsin and North Carolina estimated that these imposed costs of about $50 to $70 per household per year in the form of extra laundry additives needed, increased fabric wear, and decreased wash quality.[1] Gains in terms of improved water quality were generally not detectable. Even if there were gains for water quality, the author shows that these could be obtained more cheaply (for about one-fourth to one-third the cost) by adoption of waste water treatment methods than by banning phosphate detergents.

Toxins, Carcinogens, and the Delaney Amendments

Similar inefficiencies may arise from regulatory attempts to control toxins and carcinogens. For example, several clauses of the Food, Drug, and Cosmetic Act (the "Delaney Amendments") require the banning of any substance that has been found to cause cancer in laboratory animals. The use of massive dosages in animal experiments combined with the ability to detect minute dosages in human food has led to situations where practically any food can be banned based on the scientific evidence. Indeed, many natural foods would have to be banned on the basis of such evidence too. Dissatisfaction with the absolutism of the Delaney Amendments (especially in a series of cases involving the artificial sweetener, saccharine, and a number of artificial food colors) has led the U.S. Food and Drug Administration to experiment with a somewhat more flexible balancing of risks and benefits. Often, however, outcomes that do not accord with the letter of the Delaney Amendments are challenged in courts, making it difficult to achieve any careful weighing of benefits and costs.[2]

Debate over possible amendments to the Clean Air Act in 1990 raised similar issues about the regulation of emissions of toxic chemicals from industrial plants. One bill (which did not pass) would have required the closing of any plant that presented a risk of greater than one additional death per million lifetimes to nearby residents. Since risks were again to be judged by animal tests using massive doses, this amendment might have meant the shutdown of much of U.S. industrial capacity. Dissatisfaction with such dire possibilities prompted Congress to set up a commission to study alternative, more flexible ways of assessing risks.

To Think About

1. What other regulatory strategies (instead of an outright ban) might be used to address the problem of toxic chemicals? How would a Pigovian tax operate in this case? Would it be preferable to a ban?

2. If the toxicity of a particular chemical is uncertain, how should its use be regulated? How should the dangers from both over- and under-regulation be taken into account?

---

[1] The report is summarized in W. Kip Viscusi, "Phosphates and the Environmental Free Lunch," *Regulation* (September/December 1984): 53–55.

[2] For a discussion, see R. M. Cooper, "Stretching Delaney Till It Breaks," *Regulation* (November/December 1985): 11–17.

unregulated emissions levels. Figure 22.3 implies that if such permits were freely tradable, they would sell for a price of f*. In this case, a competitive market for pollution permits ensures that the optimal level of emissions reductions will be attained at minimal social cost.

A third regulatory strategy would be simply to implement reductions of R* through direct controls. In this case, which tends to be the one most often followed in the United States, firms would be told the level of emissions they would be allowed. Such a direct approach can, in principle, duplicate the allocational solutions provided by Pigovian taxation and marketable permits. If, as is often the case, direct control is also accompanied by specification of the precise mechanism by which R* is to be achieved (for example, through the installation of a special kind of pollution control equipment) the cost-minimization incentives incorporated in the other two approaches may be lost.

■ Uncertainty in Environmental Regulation

Of course, the approach to environmental regulation illustrated in Figure 22.3 is extremely simplistic. For many actual environmental problems (such as the "greenhouse effect," which is discussed in Application 22.5), both the benefits and costs associated with various abatement strategies may be very poorly understood. Simply calculating the optimal level of pollution abatement may be subject to considerable uncertainty. In such cases, the three control mechanisms discussed in the previous section may no longer be equivalent—some approaches may be more likely to achieve an efficient outcome than others. Actual outcomes will depend on the incentives the various control strategies offer and on the degree to which property rights are fully defined and whether some limited Coase-type bargaining is able to occur.

The Evolution of Property Rights—Economics and the Law

Legal definitions of property rights change over time. Some goods that were at one time commonly owned (most land, for example) have in more recent times become primarily private property. Similarly, some goods that were at one time private (such as roads, bridges, lighthouses, and fire companies) have increasingly become publicly owned. Traditionally, such changes have been regarded as having a legal or political origin. Although economic analysis could illustrate the implications of various property rights assignments, it was believed to have little to say about how assignments were in fact made.

More recently, several economists have argued that the way societies choose to define property rights is strongly motivated by economic considerations. In particular, it has been suggested that private property rights come into existence when it becomes efficient for those affected by externalities to internalize them through transactions in private property; that is, when the benefits of coping with the externalities exceed the costs of enforcing private

APPLICATION 22.5

The Greenhouse Effect and What to Do about It

In recent years considerable concern has been voiced that the continued burning of fossil fuels combined with declining forestation throughout the world will lead to a buildup of carbon dioxide in the atmosphere. This buildup will, it is feared, result in a gradual warming of the earth, prompting vast climatic changes. This possibility has come to be known as the "greenhouse effect."

Scientific Evidence
Most evidence suggests that the earth has been gradually warming over the past 100 years. A best guess puts the increase in mean temperature at about 0.5°C from 1880 to 1980. During the same period concentrations of carbon dioxide and other gases from combustions in the atmosphere have also increased—primarily as a result of increasing industrialization. One estimate puts the increase at about 20 percent over the past 100 years.[1] There is considerable uncertainty about whether these two facts are connected. Attempts at modeling carbon dioxide buildup in the atmosphere have encountered numerous theoretical difficulties and the actual data continue to pose unanswered puzzles (for instance, there appears to have been little buildup during the period 1945 to 1970—a period of rapid economic growth throughout the world).

The Policy Dilemma
The uncertainties in the scientific basis for the greenhouse effect pose a major dilemma for policymakers. This dilemma is illustrated in Figure 1. The marginal costs associated with combating the greenhouse effect (say, by imposing major restrictions on electricity production and automobile use) are shown by the MC curve. The increasingly steep slope of this curve illustrates the sharply increasing costs associated with heroic efforts to combat the effect. The curve MB in Figure 1 reflects the best scientific estimate of the benefits from restricting carbon dioxide emissions. Uncertainty about these benefits is reflected by the curves MB′ and MB″—the benefits may be either greater or smaller than those based on the best guess. Notice that although emissions reductions of R*

Figure 1
Optimal Abatement and Scientific Uncertainty

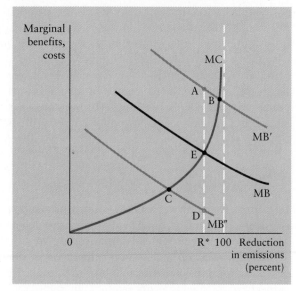

Losses from a policy of R* are given by area ABE if benefits prove to be larger than expected, but they are given by area EDC if benefits prove to be smaller than expected.

are optimal if the best scientific estimates prove correct, the possible losses from such a policy are not symmetric. If the true benefits are given by MB′, losses given by area ABE will be encountered because of under-regulation. On the other hand, if true benefits are given by MB″, much greater losses, given by area EDC, will be encountered from over-regulation. The effect of sharply increasing marginal costs combined with scientific uncertainty is to suggest caution in the adoption of heroic control efforts.[2]

To Think About
1. The notion that the greenhouse effect should be approached cautiously seems directly contrary to the dramatic approach advocated by many environmentalists. Under what conditions would a more aggressive policy approach be favored?
2. Can you think of historical environmental externalities for which scientific evidence about their effects was highly uncertain? Are these situations accurately reflected by Figure 1?

[1]G. J. MacDonald, "Scientific Evidence for the Greenhouse Effect," *Journal of Policy Analysis and Management* (Spring 1988): 425–444.
[2]For a further discussion of the economic issues involved in the green-house effect, see W. D. Nordhaus, "A Sketch of the Economics of the Greenhouse Effect," *American Economic Review* (May 1991): 146–150.

property rights.[13] In broad terms, the hypothesis is that legal institutions (notably the way in which property rights are defined) evolve over time toward economically efficient arrangements. For example, during the California gold rush or the stampede to Kimberly, South Africa to find diamonds, most claims were initially available for the taking. Mining land was quickly divided into private plots in response to the rapid rise in its value. Other cases of rapidly changing definitions of property rights that have been examined include instances from product liability law, land zoning law, and even criminal law.[14] As a more extensive illustration of the issues, we look briefly at how economic incentives may encourage the conversion of common property to private property.

■ The Common Property Problem

Resources are termed *common property* if they can be used by anyone without a direct charge. As our discussion of air and water pollution showed, this is frequently the case for the natural environment—enforcement of private property rights is simply too costly. Other examples of common property include the radio and television spectrum (although rights to particular wavelengths have been created by the government), fishing and mining in the oceans or Antarctica, and the use of outer space for satellites or other purposes. As a specific example we examine the case of ocean fishing, but similar issues arise in all cases of common ownership.

■ Ocean Fisheries and Common Property

Ocean fisheries are, in most cases, common property. Anyone wishing to catch fish need only rent or buy a boat and proceed to a desirable location. Because most fishing grounds are treated as common property, there may be a tendency for the areas to be overfished from a long-run viewpoint. Each fisher will adopt a policy of increasing his or her catch up to the point at which the marginal cost of catching additional fish is equal to the price of fish. Although such a policy may lead to short-run profit maximization, it also runs the risk of so depleting the stock of fish that the future catch may be endangered. Because the fisheries are "owned" in common, individual fishermen will not take these additional costs of resource depletion into account.

This argument is illustrated in Figure 22.4. Suppose that the price of fish is given by P^* and the marginal cost curve for the current year's output is given by MC. Under common ownership, each fishing firm will produce output level q_c since this output level maximizes current profits. If the fishery were solely owned by one firm, that firm would consider both the present and future operating costs of its actions. Since increasing the current year's catch tends to reduce the catch (and the profits) in future years, the firm will regard its marginal cost curve as being MCS. This curve reflects both current operating costs and

---

[13]See Harold Demsetz, "Toward a Theory of Property Rights," *American Economic Review, Papers and Proceedings* (May 1967): 347–359.

[14]R. A. Posner, *Economic Analysis of Law*, 2d ed. (Boston: Little, Brown and Company, 1977).

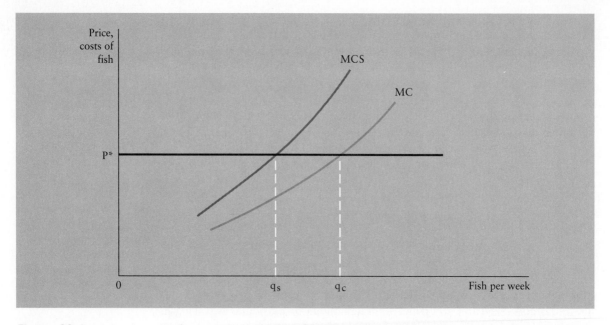

Figure 22.4
Differential Effects
of Common and
Sole Ownership
of a Fishery

Under common ownership, fishermen will recognize only current operating costs as reflected by MC and will produce output level q_c. If the fishery is owned by a single firm, this firm would produce at a point (q_s) where price is equal to a comprehensive measure of marginal costs (MCS). The efficiency gains associated with such private ownership may encourage the evolution of legal specifications of property rights.

the future costs of reduced harvests. The sole owner would choose to produce output level q_s since this provides maximum profits when full costs are taken into account.

■ Private Property and Internalization

This analysis shows that when resources are commonly owned they may be overused. Under common ownership, each fishing firm imposes an external cost on others by not recognizing the effect its fishing has on future harvests. A firm that could enforce sole ownership of the fishery would internalize this externality and would operate the fishery on a sustained yield basis. Moves in recent years by several countries such as the United States, Canada, and Chile to define 200-mile "economic zones" beyond the traditional 12-mile territorial limit can be viewed as a partial application of this principle. By expanding their limits, these countries are attempting to create a property right to surrounding fisheries and thereby to internalize the negative externalities of overfishing. In cases where property rights are more easily enforced (on land, along the shore, or in rivers and lakes), this process has gone even further, leading to potentially large efficiency gains. Application 22.6: Applying Economics to Oysters and Elephants illustrates some of these gains.

APPLICATION 22.6

Applying Economics to Oysters and Elephants

Any wildlife species that has economic value can be threatened by the destructive incentives inherent in a common property system. Moving to a private property regime (perhaps surprisingly) can sometimes lead to greater wildlife populations because of the incentives for value maximization that such a system provides.

Oysters

Some direct evidence of this possibility was provided in a 1975 study of oyster production in various states by R. J. Agnello and L. P. Donnelley.[1] The authors noted that states differ widely in the proportion of privately-owned oyster grounds. In Virginia, for example, about 74 percent of oysters produced are from privately owned grounds, whereas in neighboring Maryland the figure is less than 17 percent. The authors found there was clear evidence that oyster producers were more productive in states with a high level of private property. In Virginia, for example, the average physical productivity of oyster fishermen was nearly 60 percent higher than in Maryland. More generally, the authors found that a 10 percent increase in the proportion of oyster grounds that were privately owned led to an increase of 338 pounds in the annual oyster catch of each producer. They attribute this result to the greater efficiency with which private oyster beds can be managed to achieve high, sustained levels of oyster growth.

Elephants

Similar results are suggested by the experiences of several African nations in attempting to preserve their elephant herds. Because elephants are primarily treated as common property, their numbers have been seriously depleted by ivory hunters. International pressure on ivory sales and a ban on hunting in some countries seem to have had little effect on this trend since the rising prices engendered by these actions raised the return to ivory poachers. During the 1980s the population of African elephants declined by more than 50 percent by some estimates with an especially severe decline in countries such as Kenya, which seem to have been most aggressive in enforcing the ban on hunting.

Several southern African countries such as Botswana and Namibia have taken a different approach to the preservation of elephants. These countries have granted local villages the rights to sell hunting permits for elephants with the number of permits allowed depending on herd size. Essentially, elephants have been converted to the private property of the villages. The result has been a rapid expansion in herd sizes (more than doubling in Botswana, for example) as local villages have undertaken long-run strategies to maximize their permit revenues.

To Think About

1. Many New England towns used to have "commons." This was land owned by the town that anyone could use—primarily as a place for livestock to graze. What would you expect might happen to such common land?
2. Doesn't Botswana's solution to the elephant problem seem rather crass? Wouldn't a solution in which everyone agreed to nurture elephants be preferable to one in which shooting is turned into a commercial enterprise?

---

[1] R. J. Agnello and L. P. Donnelley, "Property Rights and Efficiency in the Oyster Industry," *Journal of Law and Economics* (October 1975): 521–533.

Summary

We began this chapter with a demonstration of the misallocation of resources that may be created by an externality. That misallocation occurs because of a divergence between private and social marginal costs that leads economic actors, acting in their own self-interest, to make choices that may not be efficient. Using this concept we showed that:

- The traditional method for correcting the allocational harm of an externality, first proposed by A. C. Pigou, is to impose an optimal tax on the firm creating the externality.

- When bargaining costs are low and property rights are fully specified, no governmental intervention may be required to cope with an externality. Private negotiations between the parties may result in an efficient allocation regardless of how the property rights are assigned (the Coase theorem).

- Some externalities, such as those associated with environmental pollution, involve high bargaining costs. In this case, governmental regulation may be required to achieve an efficient allocation (although regulation does not guarantee such a result).

- Environmental regulation can proceed through the use of fees, pollution permits, or direct control. In the simplest case, these can have identical outcomes. In actuality, however, the incentives incorporated under each may yield quite different results.

- In some cases, legal specification of private property rights will evolve as a way of solving various allocational problems. Common property may become private as a way of controlling overuse externalities.

Review Questions

1. If one firm raises the costs of another firm by bidding against it for its inputs, that is not an externality by our definition. But, if a firm raises the costs of another firm by polluting the environment, that is an externality. Explain the distinction between these two situations. Why does the second lead to an inefficient allocation of resources but the first does not?

2. Explain why externalities usually arise from two parties trying to use the same resource. Why does this demonstrate that externalities are reciprocal in nature? Why is it important to recognize this reciprocal nature in designing policies to address externalities?

3. Our general definition of economic efficiency focuses on mutually beneficial transactions. Explain why the presence of externalities may result in some mutually beneficial transactions being forgone. Illustrate these using Figure 22.1.

4. The taxation and merger solutions to the externality problem both succeed by transforming a social cost into an explicit cost. For each solution explain why this is so and how recognition of social costs prompts firms to behave efficiently.

5. The proof of the Coase theorem requires that firms recognize both the explicit and implicit costs of their decisions. Explain a situation where a firm's failure to curtail pollution may cause it to incur implicit costs. Why is the assumption of zero bargaining costs crucial if the firm is to take account of these costs?

6. Why are bargaining costs in two-person externalities likely to be low? Why are these costs likely to be quite high when many economic actors are involved? Provide examples of each type of situation.

7. Explain why the level of emissions control R^* in Figure 22.3 is economically efficient. Why would the levels of abatement given by R_L and R_H result in inefficiency? What kinds of inefficient trades would be occurring at these levels of abatement?

8. Figure 22.3 shows that an emissions fee can be chosen that attains the same level of pollution reduction as does direct control. Explain why firms would make the same choices under either control method. Would this equivalence necessarily hold if government regulators did not know the true marginal costs of emissions control?

9. If the conditions of the Coase theorem hold, the allocation of resources will be the same no matter which party is assigned the property rights. Why, if bargaining is costly, does it matter how property rights are defined? Provide an example of how the definition of property rights might affect the allocation of resources in such a situation. Consider, for example, how the definition of property rights might affect the allocation of resources when a firm produces air pollution.

10. Suppose certain legal contracts were defined in an inefficient manner. Why would this generate pressures to change the law? What forces might prevent such changes?

Problems

22.1 A firm in a perfectly competitive industry has patented a new process for making widgets. The new process lowers the firm's average costs, meaning this firm alone (although still a price taker) can earn real economic profits in the long run.

   a. If the market price is $20 per widget and the firm's marginal cost curve is given by $MC = .4q$ where q is the daily widget production for the firm, how many widgets will the firm produce?

   b. Suppose a government study has found that the firm's new process is polluting the air and estimates the social marginal cost of widget production by this firm to be MCS = .5q. If the market price is still $20, what is the socially optimal level of production for the firm? What should the amount of a government-imposed excise tax be in order to bring about this optimal level of production?

c. Graph your results.

22.2 On the island of Pago-Pago there are two lakes and 20 fishers. Each fisher gets to fish on either lake and gets to keep the average catch on that lake. On Lake X the total number of fish caught is given by

$$F^X = 10L_X - \tfrac{1}{2}L_X^2,$$

where L_X is the number of fishers on the lake. The amount an additional fisher will catch is $MP_X = 10 - L_X$.
For Lake Y the relationship is

$$F^Y = 5L_Y.$$

a. Under this organization of society, what will the total number of fish caught be?
b. The chief of Pago-Pago, having once read an economics book, believes that she can raise the total number of fish caught by restricting the number of fishers allowed on Lake X. What is the correct number of fishers on Lake X to allow in order to maximize the total catch of fish? What is the number of fish caught in this situation?
c. Being basically opposed to coercion, the chief decides to require a fishing license for Lake X. If the licensing procedure is to bring about the optimal allocation of labor, what should the cost of a license be (in terms of fish)?
d. Does this problem prove that a "competitive" allocation of resources may not be optimal?

* 22.3 Suppose that the oil industry in Utopia is perfectly competitive and that all firms draw oil from a single (and practically inexhaustible) pool. Each competitor believes that he or she can sell all the oil he or she can produce at a stable world price of $10 per barrel, and that the cost of operating a well for one year is $1,000.

Total output per year (Q) of the oil field is a function of the number of wells (N) operating in the field. In particular,

$$Q = 500N - N^2,$$

and the amount of oil produced by each well (q) is given by

$$q = \frac{Q}{N} = 500 - N.$$

The output from the Nth well is given by

$$MP_N = 500 - 2N.$$

---

*Denotes a problem that is rather difficult.

a. Describe the equilibrium output and the equilibrium number of wells in this perfectly competitive case. Is there a divergence between private and social marginal cost in the industry?

b. Suppose that the government nationalizes the oil field. How many oil wells should it operate? What will total output be? What will the output per well be?

c. As an alternative to nationalization, the Utopian government is considering an annual license fee per well to discourage overdrilling. How large should this license fee be to prompt the industry to drill the optimal number of wells?

*22.4 Three types of contracts are used to specify how tenants of a plot of agricultural land may pay rent to the landlord. Rent may be paid (1) in money (or a fixed amount of agricultural produce); (2) as a fixed proportionate share of the crop; or (3) in "labor dues," by working on other plots owned by the landlord. How might these alternative contract specifications affect tenants' production decisions? What sorts of transaction costs might occur in the enforcement of each type of contract? What economic factors might affect the type of contract specified in different places or during various historical periods?

22.5 There is currently considerable legal controversy concerning product safety. Two extreme positions might be termed *caveat emptor* (let the buyer beware) and *caveat vendor* (let the seller beware). Under the former scheme, producers would have no responsibility for the safety of their products: buyers would absorb all losses. Under the latter scheme this liability assignment would be reversed; firms would be completely responsible under law for losses incurred from unsafe products. Using simple supply and demand analysis, discuss how the assignment of such liability might affect the allocation of resources. Would safer products be produced if firms were strictly liable under law?

22.6 Inventors are not usually able to capture all the profits arising from their inventions. Inventions tend to become public property that can be freely used without paying royalties to the inventor. Develop a supply-demand diagram that demonstrates how this externality may cause too few inventions to be produced. How might the adoption of patent laws mitigate this problem by granting property rights to inventions? What inefficiencies might be created by patents?

22.7 Develop an example of interpersonal externalities similar to the one that illustrates interfirm externalities in Chapter 22. Show how the assumption of zero bargaining costs permits exchanges between the two persons to bring about an optimal allocation of resources even in the presence of this type of externality.

22.8 Suppose a monopoly produces a harmful externality. Use the concept of consumer surplus to analyze whether an optimal tax on the polluter would necessarily be a welfare improvement.

22.9 As an illustration of the apple–bee externality, suppose that a beekeeper is located next to a 20-acre apple orchard. Each hive of bees is capable of pollinating ¼ acre of apple trees, thereby raising the value of apple output by $25.

---

*Denotes a problem that is rather difficult.

a. Suppose the market value of the honey from one hive is \$50 and that the beekeeper's marginal costs are given by

$$MC = 30 + .5Q$$

where Q is the number of hives employed. In the absence of any bargaining, how many hives will the beekeeper have and what portion of the apple orchard will be pollinated?

b. What is the maximum amount per hive the orchard owner would pay as a subsidy to the beekeeper to prompt him or her to install extra hives? Will the owner have to pay this much to prompt the beekeeper to use enough hives to pollinate the entire orchard?

22.10 A government study has concluded that the marginal benefits from controlling cow-induced methane production are given by

$$MB = 100 - R$$

where R represents the percentage reduction from unregulated levels. The marginal cost to farmers of methane reduction (through better cow feed) is given by

$$MC = 20 + R.$$

a. What is the socially optimal level of methane reduction?
b. If the government were to adopt a methane fee that farmers must pay for each percent of methane they do not reduce, how should this fee be set to achieve the optimal level of R?
c. Suppose there are two farmers in this market with differing costs of methane reduction. The first has marginal costs given by

$$MC_1 = 20 + \tfrac{2}{3}R_1$$

whereas the second has marginal costs given by

$$MC_2 = 20 + 2R_2.$$

Total methane reduction is the average from these two farms. If the government mandates that each farm reduce methane by the optimal amount calculated in part a, what will the overall reduction be and what will this reduction cost (assuming there are no fixed costs to reducing methane)?
d. Suppose, instead, that the government adopts the methane fee described in part b. What will be the total reduction in methane and what will this reduction cost?
e. Explain why parts c and d yield different results.

In Chapter 14 we showed that some goods are not necessarily suited to production through private markets since they have zero marginal costs of serving another person and benefit everyone. Such goods tend to be produced by the government and are paid for through compulsory taxation. Our goal in this chapter is to study some of the issues that arise in this process. We begin by defining public goods and examining the problems that such goods pose for the allocation of resources. We then show why these goods will often be produced by governments and show that, at least in theory, such actions could result in an efficient allocation of resources. In the final sections of the chapter, we examine the ways governments actually work and raise some doubts about whether they will ultimately choose efficient solutions.

CHAPTER
23
PUBLIC GOODS
AND
PUBLIC CHOICE

Public Goods

What does a government do? Economists might define governmental activities with one general statement: A government produces public goods. The term *public goods* in this definition could refer to all those effects a government has on the members of society. These effects include all the tangible goods and services provided by the government (for example, national defense, postal services, education, and so forth) and are also intended to include the various intangible benefits (or costs) of citizenship, such as providing justice or building national character. In a sense, governments are not very different from other organizations (such as labor unions, professional associations, fraternities and sororities, or the American Legion) that provide benefits to, and impose obligations on, their members. The distinguishing characteristic of government is its ability to produce public goods on a very large scale and to finance these goods with compulsory taxes.

■ Attributes of Public Goods

The above discussion of public goods is circular—governments are defined as producers of public goods, and public goods are defined as the stuff government produces. Many economists (starting with Paul Samuelson) have tried to attach a more specific, technical definition to the term *public good*.[1] The purpose of such a definition is to differentiate those goods that are public by nature from those that are suitable for private markets.[2] The most common definitions of public goods stress two attributes that seem to characterize many of the goods governments produce: nonexclusivity and nonrivalry.

■ Nonexclusivity

One property that distinguishes public goods is whether people may be excluded from the benefits the goods provide. For most private goods, exclusion is indeed possible. I can easily be excluded from consuming a hamburger if I don't pay for it. In some cases, exclusion is either very costly or impossible. National defense is the standard example. Once an army or navy is set up, everyone in a country benefits from its protection whether they pay for it or not. Similar comments apply on a local level to such goods as mosquito control or inoculation programs against disease. In these cases, once the programs are implemented, all of the residents of a community benefit from them and no one can be excluded from those benefits, regardless of whether he or she pays for them. These **nonexclusive goods** can be contrasted with exclusive private consumption goods (such as automobiles or motion pictures) for which exclu-

Nonexclusive goods
Goods that provide benefits that no one can be excluded from enjoying.

---

[1]See Paul A. Samuelson, "The Pure Theory of Public Expenditure," *Review of Economics and Statistics* (November 1954): 387–389.

[2]Usually the implication is that governments should not produce private goods since the competitive market will do a better job of this.

sion is a simple matter. Those who do not pay for such private goods do not receive the services these goods promise.

Nonrivalry

A second property that characterizes many public goods is nonrivalry. **Nonrival goods** are goods for which benefits can be provided to additional users at zero marginal social cost. For most goods, consumption of additional amounts involves some marginal costs of production. Consumption of one more hot dog, for example, requires that various resources be devoted to its production. For some goods, however, this is not the case. Consider one more automobile crossing a highway bridge during an off-peak period. Since the bridge is already there anyway, one more vehicle crossing it requires no additional resources and does not reduce consumption of anything else. One more viewer tuning into a television channel involves no additional cost even though this action would result in additional consumption taking place. Consumption by additional users of such a good is nonrival in that this additional consumption involves zero marginal social costs of production; such consumption does not reduce other people's ability to consume.

Categories of Public Goods

The concepts of nonexclusivity and nonrivalry are in some ways related. Many goods that are nonexclusive are also nonrival. National defense and mosquito control are two examples of goods for which exclusion is not possible and for which additional consumption takes place at zero marginal cost. Many other instances might be suggested.

These concepts are not identical. Some goods may possess one property, but not the other. It is, as shown in Chapter 22, impossible (or at least very costly) to exclude some fishing boats from ocean fisheries, yet one more boat imposes social costs in the form of a reduced catch for all concerned. Similarly, use of a bridge during off-peak hours may be nonrival, but it is possible to exclude potential users by erecting toll booths. Table 23.1 presents a cross-classification of goods by their possibilities for exclusion and their rivalry. Several examples of goods that fit into each of the categories are provided. Many of the examples in boxes other than the upper left corner in the table (exclusive, rival private goods) are often produced by the government. Nonrival goods are sometimes privately produced—there are private bridges, swimming pools, and highways that consumers must pay to use even though this use involves zero marginal cost. Nonpayers can be excluded from consuming these goods, so a private firm may be able to cover its costs.[3] Still, even in this case the resulting allocation of resources will be inefficient because price will exceed marginal cost.

For simplicity we will define **public goods** as having both of the properties listed in Table 23.1. That is, such goods provide nonexclusive benefits and can

Nonrival goods
Goods that additional consumers may use at zero marginal costs.

Public goods
Goods that provide nonexclusive benefits to everyone in a group and that can be provided to one more user at zero marginal cost.

---

[3]Nonrival goods that permit imposition of an exclusion mechanism are sometimes referred to as *club goods* since provision of such goods might be organized along the lines of private clubs. Such clubs might then charge a "membership" fee and permit unlimited use by members. The optimal size of a club is determined by the economies of scale present in the production process for the club good. For an analysis, see R. Cornes and T. Sandler, *The Theory of Externalities, Public Goods, and Club Goods* (Cambridge, England: Cambridge University Press, 1986).

Table 23.1 Types of Public and Private Goods		Exclusive		
		Yes		No
Rival	Yes	Hot dogs, automobiles, houses		Fishing grounds, public grazing land, clean air
	No	Bridges, swimming pools, scrambled satellite television signals		National defense, mosquito control, justice

be provided to one more user at zero marginal cost. Public goods are both nonexclusive and nonrival.

Public Goods and Market Failure

Our definition of public goods suggests why private markets may not produce them in adequate amounts. For exclusive private goods, the purchaser of that good can appropriate the entire benefits of the good. If Smith eats a pork chop, for example, that means the chop yields no benefits to Jones. The resources used to produce the pork chop can be seen as contributing only to Smith's welfare, and he or she is willing to pay whatever this is worth.

For a public good, this will not be the case. In buying a public good, any one person will not be able to appropriate all the benefits the good offers. Since others cannot be excluded from benefiting from the good and since others can use the good at no cost, society's potential benefits from the public good will exceed the benefits that accrue to any single buyer. However, the purchaser will not take the potential benefits of this purchase to others into account in his or her expenditure decisions. Consequently, private markets will tend to underallocate resources to public goods.

■ A Graphical Demonstration

Problems raised by the nature of public goods can be demonstrated with partial equilibrium analysis by examining the demand curve associated with such goods. In the case of a private good, we found the market demand curve (see Chapter 5) by summing people's demands horizontally. At any price, the quantities demanded by each person are summed up to calculate the total quantity demanded in the market. The market demand curve shows the marginal evaluation that people place on an additional unit of output. For a public good (which is provided in about the same quantity to everyone) we must add individual demand curves vertically. To find out how society values some level of public good production, we must ask how each person values this level of output and then add up these valuations.

This idea is represented in Figure 23.1 for a situation with two people. The total demand curve for the public good is the vertical sum of each person's

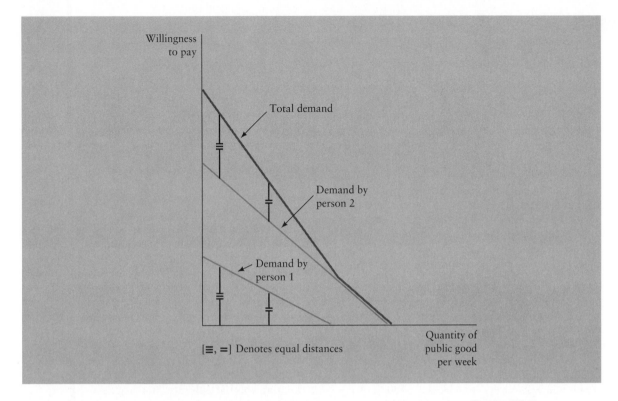

Willingness to pay

Total demand

Demand by person 2

Demand by person 1

[≡, =] Denotes equal distances

Quantity of public good per week

Since a public good is nonexclusive, the price that people are willing to pay for one more unit (their marginal valuations) is equal to the sum of what each individual would pay. Here person 1's willingness to pay is added vertically to person 2's to get the total demand for the public good.

Figure 23.1
Derivation of the Demand for a Public Good

demand curve. Each point on the curve represents what person 1 and person 2 together are willing to pay for the particular level of public good production. Producing one more unit of the public good would benefit both people; so, to evaluate this benefit, we must sum each person's evaluation of the good. This is shown in Figure 23.1 by adding what person 1 is willing to pay to what person 2 is willing to pay. In private markets, on the other hand, the production of one more unit benefits only the person who ultimately consumes it.[4] Because each person's demand curve in Figure 23.1 is below the total demand for the public good, no buyer is willing to pay what the good is worth to society as a whole. Therefore, although Application 23.1: Are Lighthouses Public Goods?

---

[4]If MC_P and MC_G represent the marginal costs of a public and a private good, respectively, then (somewhat loosely) the conditions for optimality in the production of a private good are given by

$$MC_G = MV_G^1 = MV_G^2 = \ldots = MV_G^n$$

and for the public good by

$$MC_P = MV_P^1 + MV_P^2 + \ldots + MV_P^n,$$

where MV_G and MV_P are the marginal valuations (that is, the amount each individual is willing to pay for one more unit) of the two goods. For a more extensive discussion, see Paul A. Samuelson, "The Pure Theory of Public Expenditure," *Review of Economics and Statistics* (November 1954): 387–389.

APPLICATION 23.1

Are Lighthouses Public Goods?

Lighthouses have played an important role in the development of the theory of public goods. Our categories in Table 22.1 suggest that lighthouses have both properties that tend to be associated with public goods: (1) the light provided is a nonexclusive good, offering guidance to everyone who sees it; and (2) the light is nonrival since an additional ship can make use of it at zero marginal cost. It is not surprising that lighthouses are often used as textbook examples of public goods.

Private Lighthouses

Just because lighthouses have the characteristics of public goods does not mean that they must be owned and operated by the government. Private ownership is still possible, provided the owners have some way to collect tolls from those who use the lighthouse in order to pay for its operations. In a fascinating history of lighthouses in England, Ronald Coase shows that during the seventeenth and eighteenth centuries most were indeed privately owned.[1] Owners were then provided by the king with the legal right to collect "light dues" from shipowners who stopped at British ports. Apparently, the business of operating lighthouses was a thriving one during this period, and many enterprising entrepreneurs entered the market in response to profit opportunities.

The Government Takeover

In 1836 the British Parliament granted an exclusive franchise to operate all lighthouses to Trinity House, a quasi-governmental body. The era of private ownership came to an end. Reasons for Parliament's decision are somewhat unclear. Some members argued that monopoly provision of lighthouse services through the government would be more efficient (though, as for many cases of multiplant monopolies, the source of such efficiencies is not obvious since each productive unit remains small). Others adopted a more political stance, arguing that lighthouses simply should be government-owned as a source of national pride (or, indeed, of

political patronage). Regardless of which of these arguments was finally persuasive, the debate showed that in some cases whether the government decides to produce a particular good may be less a matter of the good's technical properties than of prevailing political institutions and attitudes.

Modern Lighthouses

The airport and air traffic control system represent the modern equivalent of the nineteenth century lighthouse-port network. Throughout the world, these systems tend to be government controlled, although private control was common in the early history of aviation. As we saw in Application 9.4, governments have been slow to move toward more efficient pricing policies for these facilities, particularly with regard to charging correctly for congestion costs. Some economists have suggested that privatization of airports and some local traffic control operations would provide better performance by limiting political influences in the system's operations.[2] So far, however, governments have shown little interest in relinquishing control.

To Think About

1. Lighthouses may not necessarily provide nonexclusive benefits—conceivably a lighthouse keeper could turn off the light for ships that haven't paid their dues. With modern communications equipment, especially radar for ship or aircraft sightings, this is even more feasible today than in eighteenth-century England. Would adoption of a system of communications that resulted in lighthouses' output becoming an exclusive good improve the efficiency of resource allocation?
2. In the case of lighthouses and other public goods that might be "privatized," is it necessary for the government to set prices for these goods? How would prices be determined if they were not set by the government?

[1]Ronald Coase, "The Lighthouse in Economics," *Journal of Law and Economics* (October 1974): 357–376.

[2]For a discussion see S. Borenstein, "The Evolution of U.S. Airline Competition," *Journal of Economic Perspectives* (Summer 1992): 45–73.

offers a warning about jumping to conclusions, in many cases private markets seem to undervalue the benefits of public goods and underallocate resources to them.

Voluntary Solutions for Public Goods

Since public goods cannot be traded efficiently in competitive markets, a number of economists have examined how such goods might be provided by the government and financed through taxation. One approach investigates whether an efficient allocation of resources to public goods might come about voluntarily; that is, people would agree to be taxed in exchange for the benefits that the public good provides. Perhaps the earliest statement of how such an equilibrium might arise was provided by the Swedish economist Erik Lindahl in 1919.[5] Lindahl's argument can be illustrated graphically for a society with only two individuals (again the ever-popular Smith and Jones). In Figure 23.2 the curve labeled SS shows Smith's demand for a particular public good. Rather than using the price of the public good on the vertical axis, we instead assume that the share of the public good's cost that Smith must pay varies from 0 percent to 100 percent. The negative slope of SS indicates that at a higher tax "price" for the public good, Smith will demand a smaller quantity of it.

Jones's demand for the public good is derived in much the same way. Now, however, we record the proportion paid by Jones on the right-hand vertical axis on Figure 23.2 and reverse the scale so that moving up the axis results in a lower tax price paid. Given this convention, Jones's demand for the public good (JJ) has a positive slope.

■ The Lindahl Equilibrium

The two demand curves in Figure 23.2 intersect at C, with an output level of OE for the public good. At this output level Smith is willing to pay, say, 60 percent of the good's cost whereas Jones pays 40 percent. That point C is an equilibrium is suggested by the following argument. For output levels less than OE, the two people combined are willing to pay more than 100 percent of the public good's cost. They will vote to increase its level of production (but see the warnings about this statement in the next section). For output levels greater than OE, the people are not willing to pay the total cost of the public good being produced and may vote for reductions in the amount being provided. Only for output level OE is there a **Lindahl equilibrium** where the tax shares precisely pay for the level of public good production undertaken by the government.

Not only does this allocation of tax responsibilities result in an equilibrium in people's demands for public goods, but it is also possible to show that

■

Lindahl equilibrium
Balance between people's demand for public goods and the tax shares that each must pay for them.

---

[5]Excerpts from Lindahl's writings are reprinted in translation in R. A. Musgrave and A. T. Peacock, eds., *Classics in the Theory of Public Finance* (London: Macmillan, 1958).

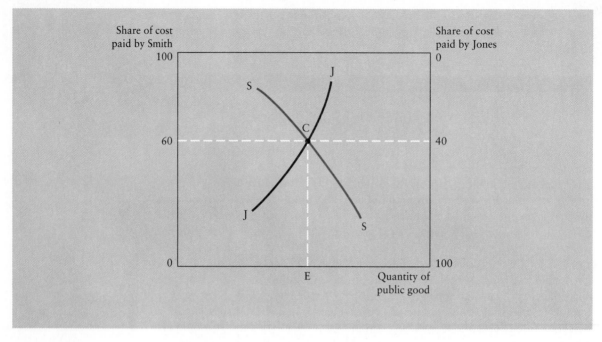

Figure 23.2
Lindahl Equilibrium in the Demand for a Public Good

The curve SS shows that Smith's demand for a public good increases as the tax share that Smith must pay falls. Jones's demand curve for the public good (JJ) is constructed in a similar way. The point C represents a Lindahl equilibrium at which OE of the public good is supplied with Smith paying 60 percent of the cost. Any other quantity of the public good is not an equilibrium since either too much or too little funding would be available.

this equilibrium is efficient.[6] The tax shares introduced in Lindahl's solution to the public goods problem play the role of "pseudo" prices that mimic the functioning of a competitive price system in achieving efficiency. Unfortunately, for reasons we now examine, this solution is at best only a conceptual one.

Discovering the Demand for Public Goods: The Free Rider Problem

Deriving the Lindahl solution requires knowledge of the optimal tax share for each person. A major problem arises in how such data might be collected. Although, through their voting patterns, people may provide some information about their preferences for public goods (a topic we take up later in this chapter), that information is usually too sketchy to permit Lindahl's tax shares to

[6]For a derivation, see Walter Nicholson, *Microeconomic Theory: Basic Principles and Extensions,* 5th ed. (Fort Worth: The Dryden Press, 1992), pp. 764–765.

be computed. As an alternative, a government might ask people how much they are willing to pay for particular packages of public goods, but the results of this poll might be extremely inaccurate. In answering the question, people may feel that they should understate their true preferences for fear they will ultimately have to pay what the good is worth to them in the form of taxes. From each person's point of view, the proper strategy is to understate true preferences in the hope that others will bear the burden of paying taxes. Since no one can be excluded from enjoying the benefits of a public good, the best position to occupy is that of a **free rider.** Each person, by acting in his or her own self-interest, may ensure that society underestimates the demand for public goods and underallocates resources to their production.

The free rider problem arises in all organizations that provide collective goods to their members. For example, as we saw in Chapter 20, labor unions generally are able to obtain better wages and working conditions in unionized plants. Workers in such plants have an incentive to enjoy the benefits of unionization while at the same time refusing to join the union. They thereby avoid the payment of dues. In order to combat such free rider problems, unions quite often insist on a "closed," or "union," shop. Similar problems arise in collecting blood on a voluntary basis. Since people know that they will get all the blood they need if they have to be hospitalized, the tendency is to be a free rider and refrain from donating. Even in your own home, you may understate your interest in a clean room in the hope someone else will clean it.

■ **Free rider**

A consumer of a nonexclusive good who does not pay for it in the hope that other consumers will.

■ Compulsory Taxation

As these examples illustrate, the free rider problem can be solved only by some sort of compulsion. This compulsion may arise out of a sense of group solidarity or civic pride (people do give blood in America, and far more do in England), or it may require legal or quasi-legal force (as in the union case). For governments, the necessity to tax people to force them to pay for public services is inescapable, and some voting schemes have been proposed that gather the sort of information required for a Lindahl equilibrium. None of these offers a particularly effective solution to the free rider problem, however. As Application 23.2: Searching for Free Riders illustrates, this type of behavior is relatively common, and a variety of social mechanisms are used to control it.

■ Local Public Goods

Some economists have suggested that the public goods problem may be more tractable on a local than on a national level.[7] Because individuals are relatively free to move from one locality to another, they may indicate their preferences for local public goods by choosing to live in communities that offer them utility-maximizing public-goods taxation packages. "Voting with one's feet" provides a mechanism for revealing public goods demand in much the same way that "dollar voting" reveals private goods demand. People who want high-quality

---

[7]See C. M. Tiebout, "A Pure Theory of Local Expenditures," *Journal of Political Economy* (October 1956): 416–424.

APPLICATION 23.2
Searching for Free Riders

The notion that people will behave as free riders when making decisions about public goods seems intuitively reasonable. It draws directly on the model of rational decision making that we develop in Part 2. Finding actual examples of free rider behavior in the real world is difficult, however. Of course, everyone has experiences of people shirking group responsibilities (the author's children tend to disappear when it's time to do yardwork). A major problem arises in deciding whether this represents free riding or simply indicates that the good being provided is of little value to a person (perhaps the children don't care what the yard looks like). Since preferences are difficult, if not impossible, to measure, the search for free riders has turned in other directions.

A Free Rider Experiment

Some researchers have tried to demonstrate free rider behavior in experiments. The subjects (usually college students) are given some money that they may either keep or contribute to some public good (often a pot of money) that they will share equally. For example, five students might each be given $10 and told that they can keep the $10 or put some of it into a common fund that will be doubled and split evenly. If every student contributes $10, each will receive $20 in return. Each person has an incentive to cheat on this deal, however. If one student doesn't contribute and the four others do, the one who doesn't contribute will get to keep the original $10 and will receive $16 more ($40 contributed and then doubled, then split five ways) for a total of $26. Each person has an incentive to be a free rider. What is individually rational is collectively irrational if everyone is a free rider, since everyone then ends up with only $10.

Results of such simple experiments indicate that free ridership exists and may become more significant as an experiment is repeated.[1] Sometimes as many as half or more of the students involved take the free rider position. In many cases, cooperative behavior tends also to appear. Especially if the students can talk together, they may choose cooperative solutions that outwit the game and the professor who is conducting it. There will, however, often be some students who will cheat on such cooperative strategies to their own advantage.

Free Riders in Religious Organizations

A second way to investigate the free rider problem is to study methods that various organizations use to control it. For example, religions that expect major commitments from their members need to ensure that only those willing to make such investments will join. They may therefore utilize dietary, dress, or behavioral prohibitions that screen out those who would be free riders. Only individuals with a true commitment are willing to incur the costs that dietary or dress restrictions impose. One study of religious choices found that those who join denominations with such stringent entry requirements are significantly more likely to then participate in the religion's formal activities (attending services, raising money, or proselytizing) than do individuals who make less significant commitments to their religion.[2]

To Think About

1. How do you solve the free rider problems that arise in your own living arrangements? Who (if anyone) cleans the room, buys essential provisions, or plans the parties? By what methods do you control free riding?
2. Charities also face a free rider problem in getting people to contribute. What are some of the methods used by charities such as United Way, the Red Cross, or the local public television station to coerce would-be free riders into contributing?

---

[1]For a summary of some of these experiments, see T. S. McCaleb and R. E. Wagner, "The Experimental Search for Free Riders," *Public Choice* (September 1985): 479–490.

[2]L. R. Iannaccone, "Sacrifice and Stigma: Reducing Free-Riding in Cults, Communes, and Other Collectives," *Journal of Political Economy* (April 1992): 271–291.

schools or a high level of police protection can "pay" for them by choosing to live in highly taxed communities. Those who prefer not to receive such benefits can choose to live elsewhere. Similar arguments apply to other types of organizations that offer packages of public goods for their members—people can choose which package of goods they prefer by choosing which clubs to join. Whether such actions can completely reveal the demand for public goods (even on a local level) remains an unsettled question, however. We now examine the most common ways in which people express their demands for public goods—through the political process.

Direct Voting and Resource Allocation

Voting is used to decide on allocational questions in many institutions. In some instances, people vote directly on policy questions. That is the case in New England town meetings and many statewide referenda (such as those discussed later in Application 23.5) and for many of the public policies adopted in Switzerland. Direct voting also characterizes the social decision procedure used for many smaller groups and clubs such as farmers' cooperatives, university faculties, or the local Rotary Club. In other cases, societies have found it more convenient to utilize a representative form of government in which people directly vote only for political representatives, who are then charged with making decisions on policy questions.

To study how public choices are made, we begin with an analysis of direct voting. Direct voting is important not only because such a procedure may apply to some cases but also because elected representatives often engage in direct voting (such as in the U.S. Congress), and the theory we illustrate applies to those instances also. Later in the chapter we take up special problems of representative government.

■ Majority Rule

Because so many elections are conducted on a majority rule basis, we often tend to regard that procedure as a natural and, perhaps, optimal one for making social choices. But a quick examination suggests that there is nothing particularly sacred about a rule requiring that a policy obtain 50 percent of the vote to be adopted. In the U.S. Constitution, for example, two-thirds of the states must adopt an amendment before it becomes law. And 60 percent of the U.S. Senate must vote to limit debate on controversial issues. Indeed, in some institutions (Quaker meetings, for example), unanimity may be required for social decisions. Our discussion of the Lindahl equilibrium concept suggests that there does indeed exist a distribution of tax shares that would obtain unanimous support in voting for public goods. But arriving at such unanimous agreements poses difficult information problems and may be subject to strategic ploys and free rider behavior by the voters involved. To examine in detail the forces that lead societies to move away from unanimity and to choose some other determining fraction would take us too far afield here. We instead assume throughout our discussion

Table 23.2	Voter	Order of Preferences		
Preferences That Produce the Paradox of Voting	Smith	A	B	C
	Jones	B	C	A
	Fudd	C	A	B

A=Low-spending policy.
B=Medium-spending policy.
C=High-spending policy.

of voting that decisions are made by majority rule. You may be able to think of some situations that might call for a decisive proportion of other than 50 percent.

■ The Paradox of Voting

In the 1780s the French social theorist M. de Condorcet observed an important peculiarity of majority rule voting systems—they may not arrive at an equilibrium but instead may cycle among alternative options. Condorcet's paradox is illustrated for a simple case in Table 23.2. Suppose there are three voters (Smith, Jones, and Fudd) choosing among three policy options. These policy options represent three levels of spending on a particular public good (A = low, B = medium, and C = high). Preferences of Smith, Jones, and Fudd among the three policy options are indicated by the order listed in the table. For example, Smith prefers option A to option B and option B to option C, but Jones prefers option B to option C, and option C to option A. The preferences described in Table 23.2 give rise to Condorcet's paradox.

Consider a vote between options A and B. Option A would win, since it is favored by Smith and Fudd and opposed only by Jones. In a vote between options A and C, option C would win, again by two votes to one. But in a vote of option C versus option B, the previously defeated option B would win, and consequently social choices would cycle. In subsequent elections, any choice that was initially decided upon could later be defeated by an alternative, and no decision would ever be reached. In this situation, the option finally chosen will depend on such seemingly unimportant issues as when the balloting stops or how items are ordered on an agenda rather than being derived in some rational way from the preferences of voters.

■ Single-Peaked Preferences and the Median Voter Theorem

Condorcet's voting paradox arises because of the degree of irreconcilability in the preferences of voters. We might ask whether restrictions on the types of preferences allowed might yield situations where equilibrium voting outcomes are more likely. A fundamental result about this probability was discovered by Duncan Black in 1948.[8] Black showed that equilibrium voting outcomes can

---

[8]Duncan Black, "On the Rationale of Group Decision Making," *Journal of Political Economy* (February 1948): 23–24.

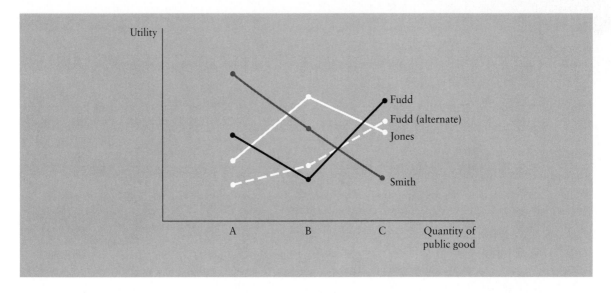

This figure illustrates the preferences in Table 23.2. Smith's and Jones's preferences are single-peaked, but Fudd's have two peaks, and these yield the voting paradox. If Fudd's instead had been single-peaked (the dashed lines), option B would be chosen as the preferred choice of the median voter (Jones).

Figure 23.3
Single-Peaked
Preferences and
the Median Voter
Theorem

always occur in cases where the issue being voted upon is one-dimensional (such as how much to spend on public goods) and where voters' preferences are "single-peaked."

To understand what *single-peaked* means, consider again Condorcet's paradox. In Figure 23.3 we illustrate the preferences that gave rise to the paradox by assigning hypothetical utility levels to options A, B, and C that are consistent with the preferences recorded in Table 23.2. For Smith and Jones, preferences are single-peaked—as levels of public goods' expenditures rise, there is only one local utility-maximizing choice (A for Smith, B for Jones). Fudd's preferences, on the other hand, have two local peaks (A and C). It is these preferences that produced the cyclical voting pattern. If, instead, Fudd had preferences represented by the dashed line in Figure 23.3 (where C is now the only local peak), there would be no paradox. In that case, option B would be chosen since that option would defeat both A and C by votes of two to one. Here B is the preferred choice of the *median voter* (Jones) whose preferences are "between" the preferences of Smith and the opposing preferences of Fudd.

Black's result is quite general and applies to any number of voters. If choices are one-dimensional and preferences are single-peaked, majority rule will result in selection of that project that is most favored by the **median voter**. Therefore, that voter's preference will determine what social choices are made. Application 23.3: Voting for School Budgets shows that in some cases this theory can explain observed decisions on public spending fairly well.

Median voter

A voter whose preferences for a public good represent the middle point of all voters' preferences for the good.

APPLICATION 23.3
Voting for School Budgets

Decisions about spending for public schools provide examples of public choice theory in which the median voter theorem may be applicable. Voters have rather definite preferences about the proper level for such spending and, on the whole, those preferences are probably single-peaked. For this reason, voting patterns in elections related to school financing questions have been more intensively studied by economists than any other public issue.

Voting on Long Island

For example, Robert Inman examined voting patterns in 58 Long Island (New York) school districts that determine their annual funding for schools through a budget referendum.[1] He found that levels of per-pupil spending in these towns were heavily influenced by the income of the median voter and by the share of taxes this voter would be expected to bear. Although higher income voters can expect to pay higher taxes (principally because they own more expensive houses upon which school property taxes are levied), the author still found that high median-income districts will choose to spend more on education than low-income districts; that is, a high income elasticity of demand for education tends to dominate voters' decisions.

Influence of Small Groups

Although Inman's results suggested that the median voters (in his case, moderate-income, middle-aged homeowners with children) tend to dominate the voting patterns, he also found that some smaller segments of the population may affect the voting results. Most important of these groups are older voters whose children have already passed through the public schools. These voters tend to favor smaller school budgets and have had the effect of reducing public school spending somewhat. Other groups, such as renters and Catholic parents (who may not send their children to public schools), also tend to have some influence in Inman's results. In

most cases, however, preferences of the median voter prove to be decisive in setting school budgets.

School Budgets in Massachusetts

Strict budgeting limits imposed in the early 1980s in Massachusetts (see Application 23.5) eventually had the effect of requiring that many local budgets be subject to an "override process" in which citizens could vote directly on whether to raise taxes. Overall, citizens tended to be more likely to favor overrides intended for schools than those intended for other purposes. Still, studies of override votes exhibited many of the results found in Inman's study of Long Island voting—characteristics of the median voter proved to be good predictors of how votes on overrides would go. In this case, political variables related to the override process itself also seemed to have a significant influence on the outcome, since local voters tended to be skeptical of overrides in certain situations.[2]

To Think About

1. In many localities, school budgets are determined by elected school boards, not by direct referenda. How do you think such indirect budget-setting procedures would affect the results of the median voter theorem? What pressures might bring about systematic departures of actual spending from what might be chosen by the median voter?

2. Are there ways in which median voter groups could encourage other groups to vote with them on school budget issues? How, for example, might median voters blunt the low spending preferences of older voters, renters, or people who send their children to private schools?

[1] Robert Inman, "Testing Political Economy's 'As If' Proposition: Is the Median Income Voter Really Decisive?" *Public Choice* (1978): 45–65.
[2] See K. L. Bradbury, "Can Government Give Citizens What They Want?" Referendum Outcomes in Massachusetts," *New England Economic Review* (May/June 1991): 3–22.

	Utility Gain or Loss			Table 23.3
Voter	Project A	Project B	Project C	

Voter	Project A	Project B	Project C
1	−5	2	2
2	−5	6	6
3	3	2	10
4	3	−5	−5
5	3	−7	−7

Table 23.3
Intensity of
Preferences and
Logrolling

Unfortunately, the median voter theorem may be of only limited general importance, since many issues of public choice, unlike voting for school budgets, are not one-dimensional. Consider, for example, choosing among alternative environmental policies. These may involve varying levels of spending, choices of locations for polluting firms, and types of pollution permitted. In such a case, people's preferences are likely to be both varied and quite complex. In describing how people vote on these issues, the single-peaked notion loses much of its intuitive appeal, and there are no simple median voter theorems.

■ Intensity of Preferences, Logrolling, and Efficient Resource Allocation

So far, we have discussed voting schemes in which voters can choose which of two options they prefer but have no opportunity to express the intensity of their feelings. In these situations majority rule can result in adoption of policies that are only mildly favored by the majority but are despised by a minority. To prevent that, minority voters may adopt logrolling (or vote-trading) techniques.

Table 23.3 provides an example of logrolling. In it the preferences about three projects (in terms of utility gains or losses) for five voters are recorded. If all the projects are voted on individually, all will pass—always by a vote of three to two. That these outcomes may not be desirable can be seen by summing the utility levels (assuming that can be done) for each project; by this criterion, only project C is "worthwhile." Both A and B yield a net negative utility level to society as a whole. These examples clearly show why majority rule may not result in an efficient allocation of revenues.

Perhaps the inefficient projects in Table 23.3 might be stopped through logrolling. Suppose voters 1 and 5 agree to "trade" votes; that is, voter 1 agrees to oppose project B, providing voter 5 will oppose project A. Such a trade makes both people better-off than they would be should both projects be adopted. With the trading of votes, both projects fail by three to two votes.[9]

Unlike voluntary trading in competitive markets, however, vote trading does not promise Pareto optimality. Not all projects that are beneficial will be

[9]This trade imposes a negative externality on voters 2 and 3 (who are worse-off without both projects than with both) and a positive externality on voter 4.

accepted, and not all of those that are harmful will be turned down. Consider a two-way choice between projects A and C. In that case, voters 1 and 5 can still profitably trade votes, ensuring that both project A (undesirable) and project C (desirable) are defeated.

As this example suggests, there is no very close connection between the concept of free trading in votes and attaining efficient resource allocations. There are no general efficiency theorems about vote trading and resource allocation. Nevertheless, the prevalence of "back-scratching" and "pork barrel" politics in legislative bodies is a prevalent phenomenon that clearly does affect which public goods are produced.

Analysis of Representative Government

In a representative government, voters vote for candidates, not policies. Successful candidates represent their constituencies in making policy choices. Here we examine a few of the issues that have been raised about this kind of indirect representation of individual preferences.

As in the theory of the firm, we start our analysis by examining the motives of government leaders. It might, for instance, be proposed that government leaders act for the "social good." At least two realities argue against assuming such benevolent motivations. First, the notion of "social good" is extremely ill-defined. It is simply not true that everyone in society has the same view of the way things should be. Second, the assumption of selfless political leadership is in marked contrast to the self-interest assumption that underlies both the theory of the individual and the theory of the firm we developed earlier. There seems no very persuasive reason why people should change their basic motivations upon elevation to political office.

■ The Majority Principle

One theory of political motivation has been put forward by Anthony Downs. In *An Economic Theory of Democracy*, he hypothesizes that

> parties in democratic politics are analogous to entrepreneurs in a profit-seeking economy. So as to attain their private ends, they formulate whatever policies they believe will gain the most votes, just as entrepreneurs produce whatever products will gain the most profits. . . .[10]

In other words, parties act to maximize votes. In order to pursue this goal, parties must contend with uncertainty in many respects. A party is uncertain how any particular policy choice will affect political support. This is true not only because it may be hard to find out who benefits from government action, but also because policies must be adopted before the policies of the party (or

---

[10]Anthony Downs, *An Economic Theory of Democracy* (New York: Harper & Row, 1957), p. 295.

parties) out of power are known. This strategic advantage of those out of power is significantly modified, however, by the control that the party in power has over the public's access to information.

Perhaps the most interesting general conclusion that Downs draws from his model is that the party in power will generally adopt a *majority principle* in its policy decisions. It will pursue only those policies for which more votes are gained than are lost, and it will pursue such policies up to the point at which the marginal gain in votes from those benefiting from the policy equals the marginal loss in votes from those being hurt by the policy. The analogy between vote maximization and profit maximization is quite close.

■ Pluralism

Downs's view of the nature of the political process can be contrasted with another, more commonly held view. This alternative conception examines the *pluralistic* nature of democratic government. Social decisions are assumed to be made by the interaction of many powerful special interest groups. Presumably these groups wield some influence over political leaders by virtue of campaign contributions, friendship, superior knowledge of special issues, or perhaps by direct measures of corruption. Whatever the avenues of control, it is assumed that interest groups are the primary molders of the legal system.

Two assessments of pluralism have been put forward. The first optimistically predicts that the interaction of numerous pressure groups will, in some sense, produce a socially desirable outcome. Laws that are ultimately passed represent an equilibrium among numerous groups. Because no one group has significant power (at least not on all issues), the resulting equilibrium will generally be representative of the society as a whole.

■ Interest Groups and Rent-Seeking Behavior

This beneficial assessment of pluralism has been questioned by many authors. One of the most interesting objections was put forward by Mansur Olson.[11] He pointed out that there is a systematic bias in a pluralistic society that causes only certain kinds of interest groups to exercise political power. In particular, Olson argues that only groups that represent narrow special interests will arise; groups representing the broad "public" interest will be weak or nonexistent. The reason for this tendency, Olson explains, lies in the nature of the public good a special interest group provides to its members. In a close-knit group, each member can recognize the benefits of group action, and there may be strong sanctions against being a free rider. Groups such as the National Rifle Association or the United Automobile Workers may be quite effective in pursuing their goals through government action. In some cases the gains will be largely psychological—for example, members of the Sierra Club enjoy knowing that national parks will be protected and enlarged. In other cases the gains will be monetary. In the early 1980s, as we have seen, some U.S. automobile

---

[11]See Mansur Olson, *Logic and Collective Action* (Cambridge, Mass.: Harvard University Press, 1965), especially Chapters 5 and 6.

companies pressed for and won "voluntary" export restraints with the Japanese, presumably with the goal of increasing their profits. Similarly, specialized groups of agricultural producers may find it in their economic interest to enlist the government's help in restricting supply, as shown in Application 23.4. Economists call these activities examples of **rent-seeking behavior.** Special interest groups who feel they may have success in obtaining profits by seeking government favors will probably do so. Such behavior is simply another application of the profit-maximization hypothesis.

For representing broad questions of public interest, Olson sees a problem. In such cases the direct gains to the people who participate in the political process may be small even though social gains from the policies they advocate may be large. People will have a tendency to refrain from such political activities—they will be susceptible to the free rider problem. Consider, for example, the benefits of free trade. Economists have expounded on these benefits at least since Ricardo's time, but any single person would probably gain little direct benefit from petitioning the government for free trade. Although the total social benefits of a free trade policy may be quite large, the gains are spread so broadly over the population that no one person (unless he or she happens to be a Toyota dealer) would be interested in spending the time and effort necessary for a successful lobbying effort. According to Olson, broad issues of public interest will be underrepresented and special interests will be overrepresented in the political process.

■ **Rent-seeking behavior**

Firms or individuals influencing government policy to increase their own welfare.

■ Reelection Constraint

By combining these theories of government action, we can construct a more realistic third alternative. It is undoubtedly true that interest groups exercise considerable influence over legislation, and Olson is probably right when he theorizes that the public interest will be underrepresented. Lobby groups probably do give utility (and money!) to political leaders, and these leaders may sometimes follow the dictates of the lobbyists. But a legislator does not have an unconstrained utility-maximization problem. Rather, he or she must operate subject to the *constraint of reelection*. The legislator must pay some attention to the vote-maximization majority principal, although this attention will by no means be absolute.

■ Bureaucracies

Although government policies in a representative democracy are enacted by elected officials, they are usually implemented by and operated through bureaucratic agencies. Because those agencies typically possess monopoly power in the production of the services with which they are charged, it is possible that they exercise an independent influence on the direction of policy. For example, Niskanen hypothesizes that government agencies seek to maximize their budgets (perhaps because high budgets yield utility to bureaucrats).[12] A major

---

[12]W. A. Niskanen, *Bureaucracy and Representative Government* (Chicago: Aldine, 1971).

APPLICATION 23.4

Rent Seeking through Agricultural Marketing Orders

The agricultural marketing order program operated by the U.S. Department of Agriculture provides a clear example of how the rent-seeking activities of narrow special interest groups can affect legislation. Under the program, the government imposes supply restrictions on 47 relatively minor agricultural commodities, including almonds, cranberries, navel oranges, lemons, spearmint oil, raisins, and, to take an extremely odd case, kiwi fruit. These supply restrictions take a variety of forms including limiting what planters may grow, prorationing orders on how much may be sold during any given week, and restricting the kinds of technology that can be used for production in the industry. The reasons given for such constraints on supply vary. Most often, these are claimed to be needed in order to "assure stable prices" or to "guarantee" that the produce supplied is of sufficient quality.

Economic Effects of the Orders

Most economists who have examined these programs carefully, however, conclude that their primary result is to increase both overall costs to consumers and growers' profits. Even seemingly minor restrictions can be quite effective in this regard. For example, it is estimated that restrictions on the number of lemons that may be harvested cost consumers about $45 million per year and that the overall impact of the program for lemons is probably much higher because of the limits placed on new production techniques such as "shrink-wrap" packaging. For navel oranges, costs as high as $72 million per year arise from the use of quality grading systems that restrict the supply of fresh oranges sold and require that many navel oranges be crushed for concentrate—a use for which they are ill-suited.[1]

Why the Special Interests Often Succeed

Of course, none of these costs contributes a very large part of the typical person's spending for food. In total, it is doubtful that the programs add a few tenths of 1 percent to such costs. Kiwi fruits and cranberries are simply not important enough in people's budgets for them to get very excited about the restrictions. For the growers involved, however, the supply restrictions may be extremely important. It is not surprising, therefore, that grower organizations tend to dominate congressional lobbying about the market order program.

Sometimes Consumers Win

Sometimes lobbying activities fail, however. In December, 1992 the Bush administration finally succeeded in killing production quotas for navel oranges and lemons that had been in effect since the 1930s despite intensive efforts by the Sunkist citrus cooperative to save them. Widespread publicity about the effects of the quotas (including television pictures of rotting oranges) may have generated sufficient public outcry to overcome these efforts—at least, for a time. Of course, agricultural marketing order restrictions (and antitrust exemption for growers' cooperatives) remain in effect for many other food items since voter outrage does not seem to have spread to such minor commodities as almonds or nectarines.

To Think About

1. A purported benefit of the market order program is to stabilize prices for the goods involved. How might the program have this effect? Would a stabilized, high price be preferable to fluctuating prices for consumers?

2. Why are market order programs accepted by Congress? After all, cranberries or almonds are only grown in a few congressional districts. Why don't the vast majority of members (who have no growers in their districts) vote to stop the programs since at least some of their constituents would be made better-off by such a move, if only slightly?

---

[1]See, for example, T. M. Lenard and M. P. Mazur, "Harvest of Waste: The Marketing Order Program," *Regulation* (May/June 1985): 19–26.

APPLICATION 23.5

Economics and the Tax Revolt

In recent years a number of states have passed tax limitation statutes, and a constitutional amendment has been proposed to serve the same purpose at the federal level. In this example we summarize some of the empirical research that has tried to explain the nature of this "tax revolt." The tax limitation idea largely originated in California with the passage of "Proposition 13" in 1977. This ballot initiative required that property in California be taxed at a maximum rate of 1 percent of the 1975 fair market value and imposed sharp limits on tax increases in future years. It resulted in a decline in local property tax revenues of nearly 60 percent between fiscal 1978 and fiscal 1979.

Theories of the Revolt

Two hypotheses have been proposed to explain why voters demanded such a drastic change in policy. The first views Proposition 13 as a demand for changing the sources of local tax revenues without reducing local expenditures significantly. Under this view citizens were largely content with the existing levels of local services but wanted state tax sources (primarily income and sales taxes) to take over a larger share of the burden. A second hypothesis views Proposition 13 as a statement by voters that local government had grown too large and that voters wished to see a cutback in both taxes and expenditures.

Results from Proposition 13

In a 1979 paper, Attiyeh and Engle examined voting patterns on Proposition 13 in an attempt to differentiate between these hypotheses.[1] They found such patterns tended to contradict the notion that voters simply wished to change the sources of local government financing. For example, communities in which property tax levies had been rising most dramatically did not appear to favor Proposition 13 disproportionately. On the other hand, the authors found clear evidence that voters wished a reduction in both tax rates and expenditures, although their results suggested that a somewhat less dramatic reduction might have received even more voter

support. In all then, Attiyeh and Engle's results imply that local government in California had expanded beyond the bounds that voters believed to be optimal. The success of Proposition 13 clearly showed, however, that there were limits to that expansion.

Tax Limitation in Massachusetts and Michigan

Evidence from studies of other tax limitation initiatives tends to be somewhat contradictory as to voters' motivation. For example, Ladd and Wilson used personal survey data to examine voter patterns in Massachusetts in connection with the 1980 passage of "Proposition 2½"—a proposal very similar to Proposition 13.[2] Consistent with the California study they also found evidence to contradict the notion that voters simply wanted to shift the source of local revenues (say, from the property tax to the income tax). But voters feared the loss of "vital" services and did not seem to want large cutbacks. Instead they preferred "greater efficiency" in government but seemed to be quite vague as to what actual policies that might require. Similar conclusions have been obtained by studying voters' opinions in connection with a 1978 vote in Michigan on the "Headler Amendment" to limit state taxes. Hence, whether tax limitation proposals represent a rather confused quest for a nonexistent "free lunch" or whether voters have in mind some more systematic alteration in existing tax expenditure patterns is difficult to determine given the data currently available.

To Think About

1. Since World War II the fraction of GDP devoted to government has risen in virtually every Western country. How do you explain this rise? Would a law that limited government spending to a set fraction of GDP be a good idea?

2. Many American politicians favor a balanced-budget amendment to the U.S. Constitution. Does the analysis of this chapter provide any reasons for thinking this amendment is a good idea? What kinds of economic arguments might you use to support the amendment? What arguments might be used to oppose?

---

[1]Richard Attiyeh and Robert F. Engle, "Testing Some Propositions about Proposition 13," *National Tax Journal* (June 1979): 131–146.

[2]H. Ladd and J. B. Wilson, "Why Voters Support Tax Limitations—Proposition 2½." *National Tax Journal* (June 1982): 127–148.

implication of that hypothesis is that in the interchange between elected officials and bureaucracies, decisions will be reached that tend to overallocate resources to the public sector (relative to what would be preferred by the median voter).

Several authors have attempted to estimate such allocational effects empirically.[13] They generally conclude that the data are consistent with the budget-maximization hypothesis. However, this empirical work is, of necessity, quite simple. More sophisticated modeling awaits the development of better data sources and more precise analytic models of the bureaucratic process. Application 23.5: Economics and the Tax Revolt illustrates some of the problems in analyzing how voters feel about whether actual levels of resources allocated to the government are too high.

Summary

In this chapter we examine the economic theory of public goods and of the public choices involved in providing such goods. Studying such subjects is a fairly recent activity for economists, and the theory described here is far from complete. Still, applying economic logic to what are basically political issues leads to a number of important conclusions:

- Pure public goods have the property of nonexclusivity and nonrivalry—once the good is produced, no one can be excluded from receiving the benefits it provides, but additional people may benefit from the good at zero cost.

- These properties pose a problem for private markets since people will not freely choose to purchase such goods in economically efficient amounts. Resources may be underallocated to public goods.

- In theory, compulsory taxation can be used to provide public goods in efficient quantities by charging taxpayers what the goods are worth to each of them. However, measuring this demand may be very difficult because each person has an incentive to act as a free rider by understating his or her preferences.

- Direct voting may produce paradoxical results. However, in some cases, majority rule will result in the adoption of policies favored by the median voter.

- Analysis of representative government is made complicated by the need to consider the actual motives of elected political leaders. In some cases, leaders will make choices in ways that maximize political appeal (that is, maximize votes). Narrow special interests and bureaucracies may often result in other choices being made, however.

---

[13]See, for example, T. E. Borcherding, *Budgets and Bureaucrats: The Sources of Government Growth* (Durham, N.C.: Duke University Press, 1975).

Review Questions

1. For each of the following goods, explain whether it possesses the nonexclusive property, the nonrival property, or both. If the good does not have the characteristics of a public good but is, nevertheless, produced by the government, can you explain why?

   a. Television receivers
   b. Over-the-air television transmissions
   c. Cable TV transmissions
   d. Elementary education
   e. College education
   f. Electric power
   g. Delivery of first-class mail
   h. Low-income housing

2. Explain why private production of nonexclusive or nonrival goods may be inefficient. Is the nature of the inefficiency the same for both types of goods? What principles of economic efficiency are violated in each case?

3. The Lindahl solution to the public goods problem promises economic efficiency on a voluntary basis. Why would each person voluntarily agree to the tax assessments determined under the Lindahl solution? What choice is he or she being asked to make?

4. What information would a government need if it wished to institute a Lindahl scheme for public goods provision? Why is it unlikely to be able to obtain that information accurately?

5. Why is the "paradox of voting" a paradox? What, if anything, is undesirable about a voting scheme that cycles?

6. The median voter theorem predicts that majority rule voting will result in selecting that level of expenditure that is favored by the median voter. To what types of public questions might this theorem be applicable? For what cases would it probably not apply? What role does the "single-peaked" assumption play in the theorem?

7. "Under perfect competition voting with dollars achieves economic efficiency, but democratic voting (one person—one vote) offers no such promise." Do you agree? Why does the specification of one vote per person interfere with the ability to achieve economic efficiency?

8. Why would elected representatives vote in a way not favored by the median voter? What types of information problems arise in representatives judging voters' preferences? What problems arise in voters assessing representatives' performance?

9. Why would individuals or firms engage in rent-seeking behavior? How much will they spend on such behavior? What are the externalities associated with rent seeking?

10. Why might bureaucracies have special information about certain public goods? In what ways might such access to information affect the process of providing such goods?

Problems

23.1 Suppose there are only two people in society. The demand curve for person A for mosquito control is given by

$$q_A = 100 - P.$$

For person B the demand curve for mosquito control is given by

$$q_B = 200 - P.$$

a. Suppose mosquito control is a nonexclusive good—that is, once it is produced everyone benefits from it. What would be the optimal level of this activity if it could be produced at a constant marginal cost of $50 per unit?

b. If mosquito control were left to the private market, how much might be produced? Does your answer depend on what each person assumes the other will do?

c. If the government were to produce the optimal amount of mosquito control, how much will this cost? How should the tax bill for this amount be allocated between the individuals if they are to share it in proportion to benefits received from mosquito control?

23.2 Suppose there are three people in society who vote on whether the government should undertake specific projects. Let the net benefits of a particular project be $150, $140, and $50 for persons A, B, and C, respectively.

a. If the project costs $300 and these costs are to be shared equally, would a majority vote to undertake the project? What would be the net benefits to each person under such a scheme? Would total net benefits be positive?

b. Suppose the project cost $375 and again costs were to be shared equally. Now would a majority vote for the project and total net benefits be positive?

c. Suppose (presumably contrary to fact) votes can be bought and sold in a free market. Describe what kinds of results you might expect in parts a and b.

23.3 Suppose that education provides both private benefits and nonexclusive public benefits to individuals. Any particular level of educational output provides equal amounts of these types of benefits. How should resources be allocated in order to attain efficient production of this semipublic good? How might production of the good be financed?

23.4 Suppose that there are N individuals in an economy with three goods. Two of the goods are pure nonexclusive public goods, whereas the third is an ordinary private good.

a. What conditions must hold for resources to be allocated efficiently between either of the public goods and the private good?

b. What conditions must hold for resources to be allocated efficiently between the two public goods?

23.5 In an economy characterized by a hierarchy of government units (for example, federal, state, and local government), what criteria might be used to determine which public goods are produced by which level of government? How would economies of scale in production affect your answer?

*23.6 Suppose that both spending and taxation decisions about public goods are decided by a voting process that faithfully reflects the preferences of the median voter. How will the allocation of resources adopted under such a system compare to an efficient allocation of resources under which tax shares are computed by a Lindahl scheme?

23.7 The demand for gummy bears is given by

$$Q = 200 - 100P$$

and these confections can be produced at a constant marginal cost of $.50.

a. How much will Sweettooth, Inc. be willing to pay in bribes to obtain a monopoly concession from the government for gummy bear production?
b. Do the bribes represent a welfare cost from rent seeking?
c. What is the welfare cost of this rent-seeking activity?

23.8 How does the free rider problem arise in the decision of eligible voters to vote? How might voter participation decisions affect median voter results?

23.9 Suppose the government wished to choose among several job training projects on the basis of which provided the largest gain to economic output. Which of the following effects should it include in its cost-benefit analysis? Explain the logic of your choice.

a. Increased earnings by trained workers
b. Reduced unemployment among trained workers
c. Increased tax collections from trained workers
d. Reduced welfare benefits to trained workers
e. Reduced auto thefts by trained workers
f. Wages paid to job training instructors

23.10 Local authorities go to considerable trouble to assess houses for purposes of taxation (see Application 2.1).

a. Explain why a scheme that allowed each person to state his or her own assessment would run afoul of the free rider problem.
b. Would the free rider problem be mitigated by requiring each person to be willing to sell his or her house at the value submitted for assessment?
c. Would the proposal suggested in part b actually identify the "fair market value" of houses?

---

*Denotes a problem that is rather difficult.

This section contains brief solutions to the odd-numbered problems in this book. These should be helpful both for students trying to solve specific problems and as a general review for many of the concepts presented.

Chapter 1

1.1   a.

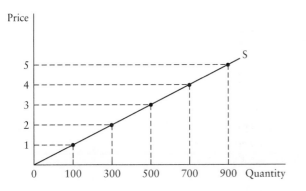

b. The points seem to be on a straight line. Use
   $\Delta P/\Delta Q$ for slope = 1/200.
   If $P = a + bQ = a + 1/200\ Q$
   at $P = 2, Q = 300, 2 = a + 1.5$, or $a = 0.5$.
   Hence, the equation is $P = 0.5 + 1/200\ Q$,
   or $Q = 200P - 100$.
c. Using $Q = 200P - 100$
   If $P = 0$, $Q = -100$.
   If $P = 6$, $Q = 1100$.

1.3   a. Supply: $Q = 200P - 100$
      Demand: $Q = -100P + 800$
      Supply = Demand: $200P - 100 = -100P + 800$
      $300P = 900$ or $P = 3$
      When $P = 3, Q = 500$.

b. At $P = 2$, Demand = 600, and Supply = 300.
   At $P = 4$, Demand = 400, and Supply = 700.

c.

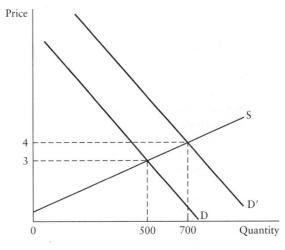

d. Demand is now $Q = -100P + 1100$.
e. Supply = Demand: $200P - 100 = -100P + 1100$
   $300P = 1200$.
   $P = 4, Q = 700$.

1.5   If P and Q rise or fall together, this must reflect a demand shift along a stationary supply curve. If P rises and Q falls (or vice versa), this reflects a shift of supply along a stationary demand curve.

1.7   a.

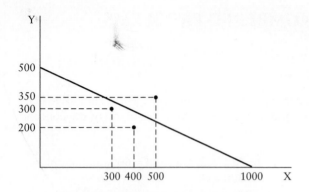

b. Both these points lie below the frontier.
c. This point lies beyond the frontier.
d. Opportunity cost of 1Y is 2X independent of production levels.

1.9   a. $x^2 + 4y^2 = 100$.
If $x = y$, then $5x^2 = 100$, and $x = \sqrt{20}$
and $y = \sqrt{20}$.

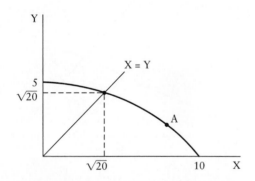

b. Can consume where any combination y
$= -x + a$ that is tangent to the PPF.
The slope of PPF $= -x/4y$.
If the slope $= -1$ $x = 4y$
$20y^2 = 100$ $y = \sqrt{5}$ $x = 4\sqrt{5}$
(given by point A in graph).
c. Can trade from A by
$y = -x + a$, $\sqrt{5} = -4\sqrt{5} + a$
$a = 5\sqrt{5}$
If $x = y$ $2x = 5\sqrt{5}$
$x = y = 2.5\sqrt{5}$

d. The cost of forgone trade is $2.5\sqrt{5} -$
$\sqrt{20} = .5\sqrt{5}$ units of both x and y.

Chapter 2

2.1   a. If $x = 0$, then $y = 15$.
b. $y = 0$, $0 = 15 + 3x$
$-3x = 15$
$x = -5$.
c. $x = 3$, $y = 15 + 3(3) = 15 + 9 = 24$.
$x = 4$, $y = 15 + 3(4) = 15 + 12 = 27$.
If x increases by 1, y increases by 3.
d., e., f. (graph)

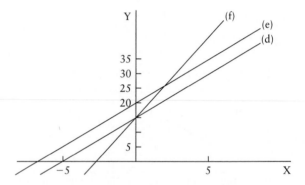

e. (graph)
  i. If $x = 0$, then $y = 20$.
  ii. $y = 0$, $0 = 20 + 3x$
  $-3x = 20$
  $x = -20/3 = -6\ 2/3$.
  iii. $x = 3$, $y = 20 + 3(3) = 20 + 9$
  $= 29$.
  $x = 4$, $y = 30 + 3(4) = 20 + 12$
  $= 32$.
If x increases by 1, y increases by 3.
f. (graph)
  i. If $x = 0$, $y = 15$.
  ii. $y = 0$, $0 = 15 + 5x$
  $-5x = 15$
  $x = -3$.
  iii. $x = 3$, $y = 15 + 5(3) = 15 + 15$
  $= 30$.
  $x = 4$, $y = 15 + 5(4) = 15 + 20$
  $= 35$.
If x increases by 1, y increases by 5.

2.3

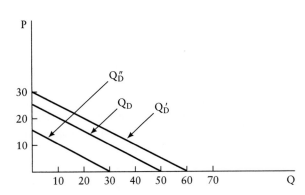

The algebraic solution proceeds as follows:

a. $Q_D = 40 - 2P + .001 I$, $I = 10,000$, so $Q_D = 50 - 2P$.

If $P = 0$, then $Q_D = 50$.
If $P = 10$, then $Q_D = 50 - 2(10) = 30$.
If Q_D equals 0, then $0 = 50 - 2P$.
$$2P = 50$$
$$P = 25.$$

b. $I = 20,000$ changes Q_D to $Q_{D'} = 60 - 2P$.
If $P = 0$, then $Q_D = 60$.
If $P = 10$, then $Q_D = 40$.
If Q_D equals 0, then $0 = 60 - 2P$
$$2P = 60$$
$$P = 30.$$

c. $Q_D = 40 - 2P + .001 I$, $P = P_p + 10$.
Substituting:
$$Q_{D''} = 40 - 2(P_p + 10) + .001 I$$
$$= 40 - 2P_p - 20 + .001 I$$
$$= 20 - 2P_p + .001 I.$$
If $I = 10,000$, then $Q_{D''} = 30 - 2P_p$.
If $P_p = 10$, then $Q_D = 10$.
If $P_p = 0$, then $Q_D = 30$.
If Q_D equals 0, then $0 = 30 - 2P_p$
$$2P_p = 30$$
$$P_p = 15.$$

2.5

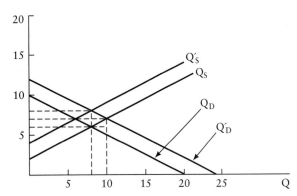

The algebraic solution proceeds as follows:

a. $Q_D = -2P + 20$.
$Q_S = 2P - 4$.
Set $Q_D = Q_S$: $-2P + 20 = 2P - 4$
$$24 = 4P$$
$$P = 6.$$
Substituting for P gives: $Q_D = Q_S = 8$.

b. Now $Q_{D'} = -2P + 24$.
Set $Q_D = Q_S$: $-2P + 24 = 2P - 4$
$$28 = 4P$$
$$P = 7.$$
Substituting gives: $Q_{D'} = Q_S = 10$.

c. $P = 8$, $Q = 8$ (see graph)

2.7 a. $T = .01 I^2$.
$I = 10$, $T = .01(10)^2 = 1$.
Taxes = $1,000.
$I = 30$, $T = .01(30)^2 = 9$.
Taxes = $9,000.
$I = 50$, $T = .01(50)^2 = 25$.
Taxes = $25,000.
$I = 100$, $T = 100$.

b.

	Average Rate	Marginal Rate
$I = 10,000$	10%	20%
$I = 30,000$	30%	60%
$I = 50,000$	50%	100%

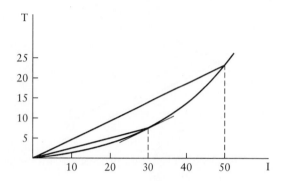

2.9

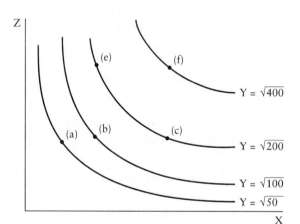

a. $2X + Z = 20$, $Z = -2X + 20$,
   $-Z/X = -2$, $Z = 2X$, $X = 5$, $Z = 10$.
b. $X + Z = 20$, $Z = -X + 20$, $-Z/X = -1$,
   $Z = X = 10$.
c. $X + 2Z = 40$, $Z = -1/2X + 20$,
   $-Z/X = -1/2$, $X = 20$, $Z = 10$.
d. $X + 5Z = 100$, $Z = -1/5X + 20$,
   $-Z/X = -1/5$, $X = 50$, $Z = 10$.
e. $2X + Z = 40$, $Z = -2X + 40$,
   $-Z/X = -2$, $X = 10$, $Z = 20$.
f. $X + Z = 40$, $Z = -X + 40$,
   $-Z/X = -1$, $Z = 20 = X$.

Chapter 3

3.1 a. $\dfrac{\$8.00}{\$.40/\text{apple}} =$ 20 apples can be bought.

   b. $\dfrac{\$8.00}{\$.10/\text{orange}} =$ 80 oranges can be bought.

   c. 10 apples cost:
       10 apples × $.40/apple = $4.00, so there is $8.00 – $4.00 = $4.00 left to spend on oranges which means
       $\dfrac{\$4.00}{\$.10/\text{an orange}} =$ 40 oranges can be bought.

   d. One less apple frees $.40 to be spent on oranges, so $\dfrac{\$.40}{\$.10/\text{orange}} = 4$ more oranges can be bought.

   e. $8.00 = $.40 × number of apples + $.10 × number of oranges = $.40A + .10 \cdot O$.

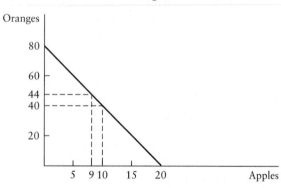

3.3 To graph the indifference curves, use U^2 instead of U. U = 10 means $U^2 = 100 = D \cdot C$. Hence, indifference curves are rectangular hyperbolas.

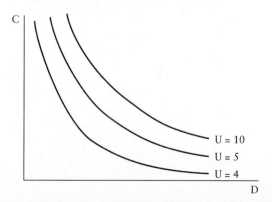

3.5

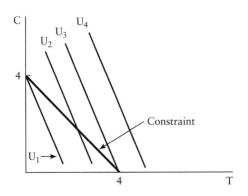

Indifference curves are straight lines: The slope of these lines is − 4/3. Therefore, MRS = 4/3 —this person is willing to give up 4/3 units of C to get one more T. She would buy where her budget constraint intersects her indifference curve (maximizing U), which is at T = 4, C = 0. If she had more income, she would not buy more coffee (she would maximize utility by buying more tea). If the price of coffee fell to $2, she would buy all coffee maximizing her utility at U = 3C + 4T = 3(6) + 4(0) = 18.

3.7

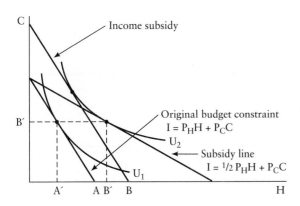

Income subsidy is cheaper since AB < A′B′.

3.9   Such a policy would be more likely to reduce utility of low-income people. High-income people would probably buy the required housing quality anyway.

Chapter 4

4.1

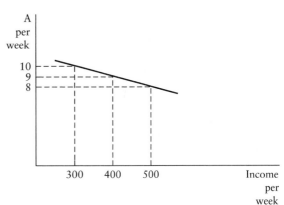

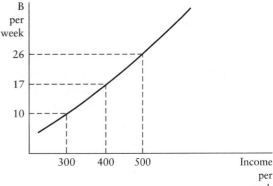

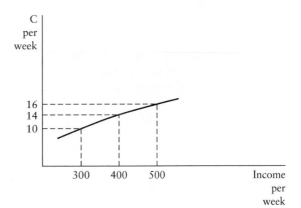

Note: A is inferior
B is a luxury
C is a necessity

4.3   In the figure, Mr. Wright is required to buy $50 worth of clothing. Given this constraint, he can only attain utility level U_0. With an unconstrained choice, U_1 can be attained.

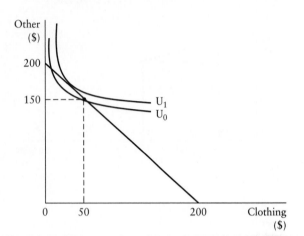

d.

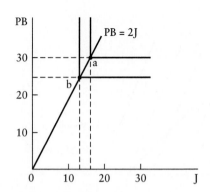

e. Since David uses only PB + J to make sandwiches (in fixed proportions), and because bread is free, it is just as though he buys sandwiches where $P_{sandwich} = 2P_{PB} + P_J$.

4.5   If the price of potatoes rises, the quantity purchased will also rise. Hence the amount available to spend on automobiles falls. Since the price of automobiles is unchanged, the quantity bought must fall.

4.7   a. PB = 2J and .05PB + .1J = 3
             5PB + 10J = 300
             PB + 2J = 60
        ∴ 4J = 60   J = 15,   PB = 30
     b. P_J = \$.15   PB = 2J   .05PB + .15J = 3
        5PB + 15J = 300   25J = 300
        J = 12, PB = 24
     c. To continue buying J = 15, PB = 30, David would need to buy 3 more ounces of jelly and 6 more ounces of peanut butter.
        Increase by: 3(.15) + 6(.05) = \$.75.

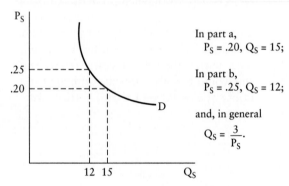

In part a,
   P_S = .20, Q_S = 15;

In part b,
   P_S = .25, Q_S = 12;

and, in general

   $Q_S = \dfrac{3}{P_S}$.

f. There is no substitution effect due to the fixed proportion. A change in price results in only an income effect.

4.9

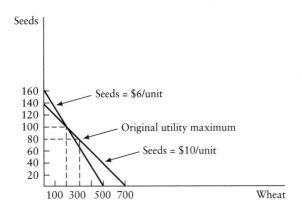

Seeds = $6/unit

Original utility maximum

Seeds = $10/unit

a. Started with 200 wheat, 100 sunflower seeds. Since he sells 20 units of sunflower seeds, he can buy 100 more units of wheat (will consume 300 in all).

b. If he continues to sell 20 units of sunflower seeds, he will only be able to get an additional $120/$2 = 60 units of wheat, so he'd be worse off. It is clear from the graph that the new constraint is northeast (Sam can be better off) of the old one only where Sam consumes more sunflower seeds than he produces, so he must sell wheat and buy sunflower seeds with the new prices.

c. In this case, the income effect is not the usual one since the lower sunflower seed price does not imply a higher real income, as in the usual case, since Sam's income is a function of the price of sunflower seeds.
(Graphically, the lower price causes a rotation around the point 200 wheat, 100 sunflower seeds rather than around the wheat intercept.)

Chapter 5

5.1 $Q = 500 - 50P$.
a. If $P = 2, Q = 400$.
   $P = 3, Q = 350$.
   $P = 4, Q = 300$.
   $P = 0, Q = 500$.

b.

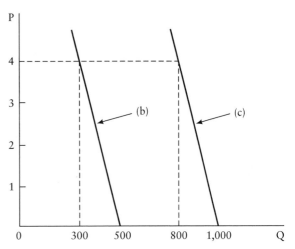

c. $Q = 1000 - 50P$.
If $P = 2, Q = 900$.
   $P = 3, Q = 850$.
   $P = 4, Q = 800$.
   $P = 0, Q = 1000$.
(See previous graph.)

5.3   a. Demand Function (Q)

	(i)	(ii)	(iii)
$P = 1$	100	100	100
$P = 1.1$	90.9	95.3	86.7

b. Demand Function (i) has e = -1.
Demand Function (ii) has e = -0.5.
Demand Function (iii) has e = -1.5.
Note: Values are not exact because of the relatively large price change. Elasticities would more closely predict changes in Q for smaller changes.
Demand Function (Q)

	(i)	(ii)	(iii)
$P = 4$	25	50	12.5
$P = 4.4$	22.7	47.7	10.8

These are constant elasticity demand functions.

5.5   a.

	Tom	Dick	Harry	Total
$P = 50$	0	0	0	0
$= 35$	30	20	0	50
$= 25$	50	60	25	135
$= 10$	80	120	100	300
$= 0$	100	160	150	410

b. "Total" column in part a.

c.

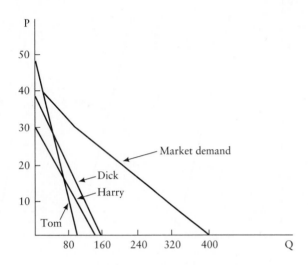

d. Above graph.

5.7 a. If price of X rises by 1 percent, quantity will fall by 2 percent since $e_{x,P_x} = -2$. Therefore X will be 980.

b. If the price of Y rises by 1 percent, quantity of X will rise by 0.5 percent since $e_{x,P_y} = 0.5$. Therefore, X will be 1005.

c. If income rises by 1 percent, quantity of X demanded will increase by 0.8 percent since $e_{x,I} = 0.8$. Therefore, quantity of X demanded will increase to 1008.

5.9 A numerical example will be sufficient here. Since ham and cheese are used in a fixed relationship, there is really only one good—ham and cheese sandwiches. Since this is the only good, the price elasticity of demand for it must be –1—that is, P · Q is constant.

a. If $P_H = P_C$, then ham constitutes 1/2 the price of a sandwich. If P_H rises by, say, 10 percent, cost of a sandwich rises by 5 percent so quantity purchased falls by 5 percent. Elasticity is, therefore, 5%/10% = –1/2.

b. For similar reasons, using the same numerical example, cross price elasticity is –1/2.

c. If $P_H = 2P_C$, ham now constitutes 2/3 the cost of a sandwich. If P_H rises by 10 percent, the cost of a sandwich rises by 6.6 percent and quantity must fall by 6.6 percent. Elasticity is 6.6%/10% = –2/3. Similar logic shows that cross price elasticity is –1/3.

Chapter 6

6.1 a. Pizza = 40 Chianti = 20 Cost = $100
b. Pizza = 50 Chianti = 25 Cost = $100
c. –f.

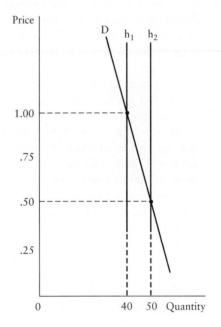

The compensated curves, h_1 and h_2, are vertical because there are no substitution effects in Irene's demand for pizza. Curves intersect at actual price–quantity choices.

6.3

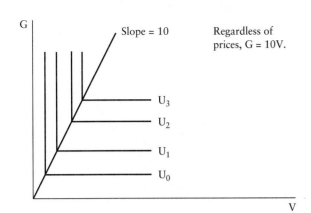

Slope = 10

Regardless of prices, $G = 10V$.

Base year index :

$$\frac{I_2}{I_1} = \frac{P_{G1}G_2 + P_{V1}V_2}{P_{G1}G_1 + P_{V1}V_1} = \frac{P_{G1}G_2 + P_{V1}(10G_2)}{P_{G1}G_1 + P_{V1}(10G_1)}$$

$$= \frac{G_2(P_{G1} + 10P_{V1})}{G_1(P_{G1} + 10P_{V1})} = \frac{G_2}{G_1}.$$

Current year index:

$$\frac{I_2}{I_1} = \frac{P_{G2}G_2 + P_{V2}V_2}{P_{G2}G_1 + P_{V2}V_1} = \frac{P_{G2}G_2 + P_{V2}(10G_2)}{P_{G2}G_1 + P_{V2}(10G_1)}$$

$$= \frac{G_2(P_{G2} + 10P_{V2})}{G_1(P_{G2} + 10P_{V2})} = \frac{G_2}{G_1}.$$

6.5 a. $U_{1992} = \sqrt{40 \cdot 40} = 40$

$U_{1993} = \sqrt{20 \cdot 80} = 40$

b. $I^{92} = P_X^{92} \cdot X^{92} + P_Y^{92}Y^{92}$

$= \$1 \cdot 40 + \$1 \cdot 40 = \$80$

$I^{93} = P_X^{92} \cdot X^{93} + P_Y^{92}Y^{93}$

$= \$1 \cdot 20 + \$1 \cdot 80 = \$100$

$\dfrac{I^{93}}{I^{92}} = \dfrac{5}{4} > 1$, so real income in 92 prices is higher in 1993.

c. $I^{92} = P_X^{93} X^{92} + P_Y^{93} Y^{92}$

$= \$4 \cdot 40 + \$1 \cdot 40 = \$200$

$I^{93} = P_X^{93} X^{93} + P_Y^{93} Y^{93}$

$= \$4 \cdot 20 + \$1 \cdot 80 = \$160$

$\dfrac{I^{93}}{I^{92}} = \dfrac{4}{5} < 1$, so real income in 93 prices is lower in 1993.

d. Results of calculations depend on which prices are used. It may be necessary to use some combination of the two indices to get a true picture.

6.7

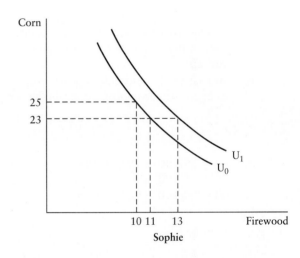

Sophie

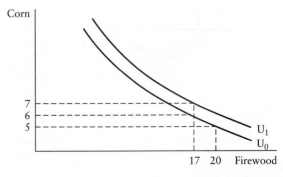

Jack

6.9 a.

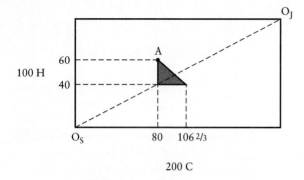

Mutually beneficial trades fall in the shaded triangular region.

b. Since Smith requires fixed proportions, anything else gives him an extra amount of one of the goods that could be given away with no loss of utility.

c. Contract curve is entire diagonal of box in part a; only shaded portion is attainable.

Chapter 7

7.1 a. $E(1) = .50(100) + .50(-100) = 0.$
       $E(2) = .75(100) + .25(-300) = 0.$
       $E(3) = .90(100) + .10(-900) = 0.$

     b.

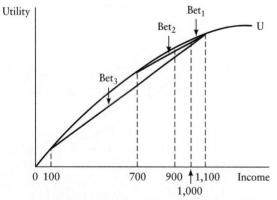

Assume, for simplicity, current income is $1,000.

c. Bet 1 will be preferred since it has smaller variability.

7.3

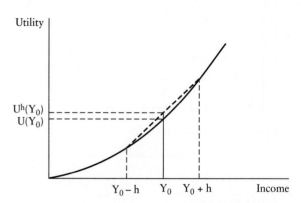

Since $U^h > U$, the individual will gamble, even on unfair bets. This would be limited by the individual's resources; he or she could eventually run out of money by taking unfair bets.

7.5 P must be large enough so that expected utility with bet is greater than or equal to that without bet:

$$P \ln(1,100,000) + (1 - P) \ln(900,000)$$
$$\geq \ln(1,000,000)$$

$13.9108P + 13.7102(1 - P) \geq 13.8155$
$.2006P \geq .1053$
$P \geq .525.$

7.7

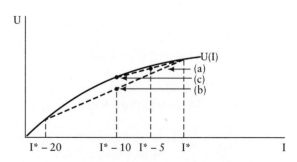

Note $U_c > U_b$. Hence, increasing fine is more effective.

7.9   a.   Let state 1 represent keeping the watch, state 2 losing the watch. Initial point A has $C_1 > C_2$.

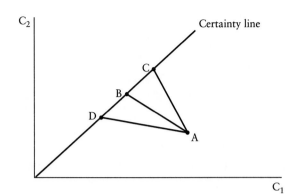

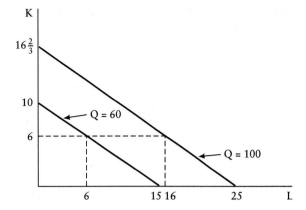

b.   Could spend time and resources on preventing watch loss. It would depend on whether move from A raises utility.

c.   Watch loss insurance could permit move to B, raising utility.

d.   AC might represent brown-eyed purchases, AD represents blue-eyed purchases.

e.   Blue-eyed people would try to buy insurance intended for brown-eyed people.

Chapter 8

8.1   a. $K = 6$, $Q = 6K + 4L = 6(6) + 4L$
$$= 36 + 4L.$$
If $Q = 60$, $4L = 60 - 36 = 24$, $L = 6$.
If $Q = 100$, $4L = 100 - 36 = 64$, $L = 16$.

b. $K = 8$, $Q = 6K + 4L = 6(8) + 4L$
$$= 48 + 4L.$$
If $Q = 60$, $4L = 60 - 48 = 12$, $L = 3$.
If $Q = 100$, $4L = 100 - 48 = 52$, $L = 13$.

c.   RTS = 2/3: If L increases by 1 unit, can keep Q constant by decreasing K by 2/3 units.

8.3   a.

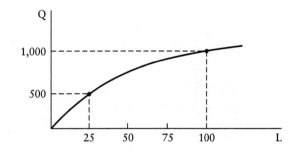

b. $AP_L = \dfrac{Q}{L} = \dfrac{100}{\sqrt{L}}$

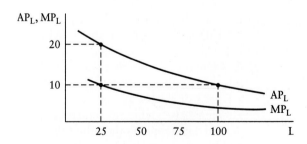

c.   Graph above. Since the AP_L is everywhere decreasing, then each additional worker must be contributing less than the average of the existing workers, bringing the average down. Therefore, the marginal productivity must be lower than the average. Here $MP_L = 1/2\ AP_L$.

8.5 $Q = KL - .8K^2 - .2L^2$
Average productivity
$$\frac{Q}{L} = K - .8\frac{K^2}{L} - .2L = 10 - \frac{80}{L} - .2L$$

a. Average productivity reaches maximum at $L = 20$, $Q = 40$.
b. $MP_L = 0$ at $L = 25$.

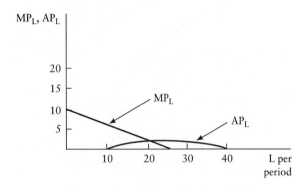

$MP_L = 10 - .4L$
c. $K = 20$. $Q = 20L - 320 - .2L^2$
$$Q/L = 20 - \frac{320}{L} - .2L$$

Average productivity reaches maximum at $L = 40$, $Q = 472$. $MP_L = 0$ at $L = 50$.

8.7   a. In 8.4 $a = b = 1/2$.
b. If we use 2K, 2L have $Q = (2K)^a(2L)^b = 2^{a+b}K^aL^b$ and if $a + b = 1$, this is twice K^aL^b.
c. d. From b it follows that output will less than double or more than double if $a + b < 1$ or $a + b > 1$.
e. Function can exhibit any returns to scale desired depending on the values of a and b.

8.9   a. $Q = 100\sqrt{KL} = 1,000$
so $\sqrt{KL} = 10$, or, $K \cdot L = 100$.

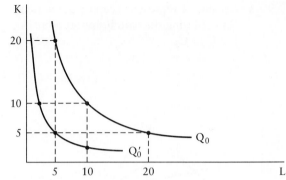

b. If $K = 10$, $L = 10$
$AP_L = Q/L = 1000/10 = 100$ boxes per hour per worker.
c. If $Q = 200\sqrt{KL} = 1000$
$\sqrt{KL} = 5$, or, $KL = 25$
Isoquant shifts to Q_0'.
Now, if $K = 10$ $L = 2.5$
$AP_L = Q/L = 1000/2.5 = 400$ boxes per hour per worker.

Chapter 9

9.1   a.

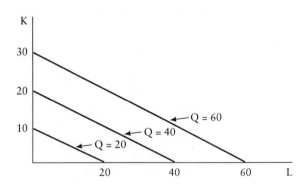

$RTS = 1/2$ since if L is increased by one, K can be reduced by 1/2 while holding Q constant.

b. Since RTS = 1/2 < w/v = 1, the manufacturer will use only K. For Q = 20, K = 10; Q = 40, K = 20; Q = 60, K = 30. The manufacturer's expansion path is simply the K axis.

c. If v = $3, RTS = 1/2 > w/v = 1/3, the manufacturer will use only L. For Q = 20, L = 20; Q = 40, L = 40; Q = 60, L = 60. Now the manufacturer's expansion path is the L axis.

9.3 a. This is a cubic cost curve. It resembles Figure 9.4d.

b. AC = TC/Q = $Q^2 - 40Q + 430$
This is a parabola. It reaches a minimum at the axis of symmetry:
Q = −(− 40)/2 = 20
At Q = 20   AC = 400 − 800 + 430
= 30.

c. At Q = 20   MC = 3(400) − 1600
+ 430 = 30.

d.

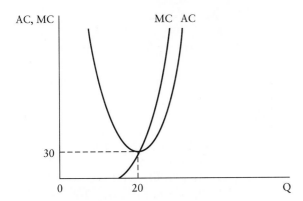

9.5 a. $Q = 2\sqrt{K \cdot L}.$ K = 100,
$Q = 2\sqrt{100 \cdot L}.$ $Q = 20\sqrt{L}.$
$\sqrt{L} = \dfrac{Q}{20}.$ $L = \dfrac{Q^2}{400}.$
$STC = vK + wL = 1(100) + 4\dfrac{(Q^2)}{400}$
$= 100 + \dfrac{Q^2}{100}.$
$SAC = \dfrac{STC}{Q} = \dfrac{100}{Q} + \dfrac{Q}{100}.$

b. $SMC = \dfrac{Q}{50}.$
If Q = 25,
$STC = 100 + \dfrac{(25)^2}{100} = 106.25.$
$SAC = \dfrac{100}{25} + \dfrac{25}{100} = 4.25.$
$SMC = \dfrac{25}{50} = .50.$
If Q = 50,
$STC = 100 + \dfrac{(50)^2}{100} = 125.$
$SAC = \dfrac{100}{50} + \dfrac{50}{100} = 2.50.$
$SMC = \dfrac{50}{50} = 1.$
If Q = 100,
$STC = 100 + \dfrac{(100)^2}{100} = 200.$
$SAC = \dfrac{100}{100} + \dfrac{100}{100} = 2.$
$SMC = \dfrac{100}{50} = 2.$
If Q = 200,
$STC = 100 + \dfrac{(200^2)}{100} = 500.$
$SAC = \dfrac{100}{200} + \dfrac{200}{100} = 2.50.$
$SMC = \dfrac{200}{50} = 4.$

c.

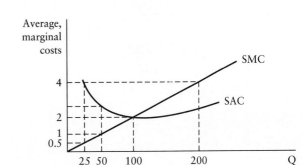

d. As long as the marginal cost of producing one more unit is below the average cost curve, average costs will be falling. Similarly, if the marginal cost of producing one more unit is higher than the average cost, then average costs will be rising. Therefore, the SMC curve must intersect the SAC curve at its lowest point.

9.7 To minimize, costs should equate the marginal productivities of labor in each plant. If labor were more productive in one plant than another, costs could be lowered by moving workers.

a. $MP_{L1} = MP_{L2}$. $5/2\sqrt{L_1} = 5/\sqrt{L_2}$.

$2\sqrt{L_1} = \sqrt{L_2}$. $L_2 = 4L_1$.

$Q_1 = 5\sqrt{L_1};\ Q_2 = 10\sqrt{L_2} = 10\sqrt{4L_1}$

$\qquad\qquad = 20\sqrt{L_1}$

Hence $Q_2 = 4Q_1$.

b. $4Q_1 = Q_2$ so, $Q_1 = 1/5Q$. $Q_2 = 4/5Q$ where Q is total output.

STC (Plant 1) $= 25 + wL_1 = 25 + \dfrac{Q_1^2}{25}$

STC (Plant 2) $= 100 + wL_2$

$\qquad\qquad = 100 + \dfrac{Q_2^2}{100}$

STC = STC (Plant 1) + STC (Plant 2)

$\qquad = 25 + \dfrac{Q_1^2}{25} + 100 + \dfrac{Q_2^2}{100}$

$\qquad = 125 + \dfrac{(1/5Q)^2}{25} + \dfrac{(4/5Q)^2}{100}$

$\qquad = 125 + \dfrac{1/25Q^2}{25} + \dfrac{16/25Q^2}{100}$

$\qquad = 125 + \dfrac{20/25Q^2}{100}$

$\qquad = 125 + \dfrac{Q^2}{125}$.

$MC = \dfrac{2Q}{125}$. $AC = \dfrac{125}{Q} + \dfrac{Q}{125}$.

$MC(100) = \dfrac{200}{125} = \$1.60$.

$MC(125) = \$2.00$. $MC(200) = \$3.20$.

c. In the long run, because of constant returns to scale, can change K so doesn't really matter where production occurs. Could split evenly or produce all output in one plant.
$TC = K + L = 2Q$. $AC = 2 = MC$.

d. If there were decreasing returns to scale, then should let each firm have equal share of production. AC and MC, not constant anymore, are increasing functions of Q so do not want either plant to be too large.

9.9 a. Now K = L so Q = 20L.
$\qquad TC = vK + wL = 5K + 5L = 10L$
$\qquad$ so $TC = 0.5Q$
$\qquad\qquad AC = TC/Q = 0.50$
$\qquad\qquad MC = \Delta TC/\Delta Q = 0.50$.
These costs are half what they were before.

b. All costs will fall at the rate r per year.

Chapter 10

10.1 a. Set P = MC. $20 = .2q + 10$.
$\qquad 10 = .2q.\ q = 50$.

b. Maximum Profits = TR − TC = $(50 \cdot 20)$ $- [.1(50)^2 + 10(50) + 50] = 1000 - 800 =$ 200.

c.

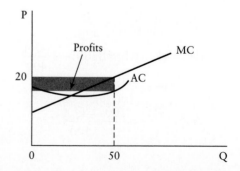

10.3 If P is constant, then $TR = P \cdot q$ is simply a straight line through the origin. Profits will be maximized where the slope of the TR curve (which is the price) is equal to the slope of the TC curve (that is to marginal cost).

10.5 Here the demand curve has a constant elasticity of -2. Hence,

$$MR = P\left(1 + \frac{1}{e}\right) = \frac{1}{2}P$$

but $P^2 = \dfrac{256}{q}$, so $P = \dfrac{16}{\sqrt{q}}$ so $MR = \dfrac{8}{\sqrt{q}}$.

For profit maximization, $MR = MC$,

$$\frac{8}{\sqrt{q}} = .001q,$$

$$8000 = q^{3/2}$$

Hence, $q = 400$. $P = \dfrac{16}{20} = .80$.

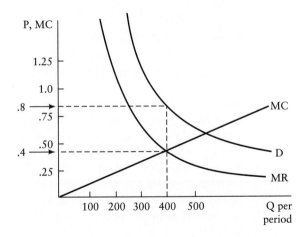

10.7 a. $TR = P \cdot q = \dfrac{(100 - q) \cdot q}{2}$

$$= 50q - \frac{1}{2}q^2.$$

$MR = 50 - q$.

Noncalculus proofs can be done graphically or with a table.

b. Max. π: $MR = MC$.
MR = 50 - q.
MR = MC: 50 - q = 10. q = 40,
P = 30, $\pi = P \cdot q - 10q$
= 1200 - 400 = 800.

c. Max. Revenue: $MR = 0$. 50 - q = 0.
q = 50, P = 25,
$\pi = P \cdot q - 10q$
= 1250 - 500 = 750.

d. Constraint $\pi = 768$. $50q - q^2/2 - 10q = 768$. Use quadratic formula or factor: q = (32,48), but trying to max revenue so choose q = 48, P = 26.

e.

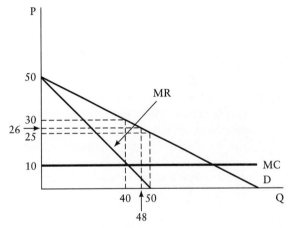

10.9 a. John's supply function is q = 5P - 50.
If P = 15, q = 25.
If P = 25, q = 75.

b. When P = 15, $\pi = 15 \cdot 25 - 362.5 = 375 - 362.5 = 12.5$.
When P = 25, $\pi = 25 \cdot 75 - 1362.5 = 1,875 - 1,362.5 = 512.5$.
Average $\pi = (512.5 + 12.5) \div 2 = 262.5$.

c. If P = 20, q = 50, $\pi = 1000 - 800 = 200$.
The father's deal makes John worse-off.

d.

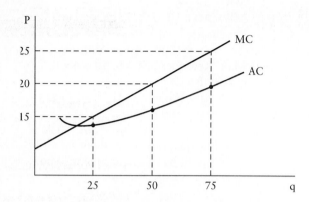

Since high profits are associated with high P,q combination, it's more profitable to let price fluctuate.

Chapter 11

11.1 For temporary price changes, hiring and severance costs might be regarded as marginal costs since they arise in connection with short-term changes in input use. For permanent price changes, however, these are more like fixed costs since they do not affect hourly wage rates.

11.3 a. $STC = vK + wL$
$$= 10 \cdot 100 + wL$$
$$= 1,000 + 5L,$$

but $q = 10\sqrt{L}$ so $L = \dfrac{q^2}{100}$.

Hence, $STC = 1,000 + q^2/20$.

b. Use $P = MC$.
$20 = .1q$, so $q = 200$.
$L = q^2/100$, so $L = 400$.

c. If $P = 15$, $P = MC$ implies $15 = .1q$ or $q = 150$, $L = 225$.

d. Cost will be 175 to reduce L from 400 to 225. With $q = 150$, Profits $= TR - TC$
$= 15(150) - (1,000 + .05q^2) = 2,250 - (1,000 + 1,125) = 125$.
After paying severance cost of 175 the firm will incur a loss of 50.

e. If the firm continues to hire 400 workers it will have no severance costs and profits of
$TR - TC = 15(200)$
$$- 1,000 + .05(200^2)$$
$$= 3,000 - (1,000 + 2,000)$$
$$= 0,$$
which is better than in part d. An output level of 180 ($L = 324$) would yield an overall profit for the firm.

11.5

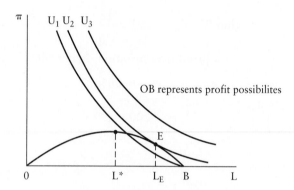

OB represents profit possibilites

a. Draw π, L indifference curves – optimum point of E. If optimum is to be at L^*, slope of indifference curve must be 0 there, i.e.:
$MRS = MU_L/MU_H = 0$ ∴ $MU_L = 0$.

b. Draw indifference curve through point B,0. Call this U_1. This shows levels of π, L indifferent to $L = B$, $\pi = 0$.

c. π' (Marshallian profits) equals distance between curve 0B and U_1. If that is to be maximized at E, slope of U_1 at L_E must equal slope of 0B at E = slope U_2 at E. QED.

11.7 a. Again we use $P = MC$.
$30 = .02q$, so $q = 1,500$.
Profits $= TR - TC$
$$= 30(1500) - (.01q^2 + 10,000)$$
$$= 45,000 - (22,500 + 10,000)$$
$$= 12,500.$$

b. Now costs $= .75 \cdot STC$
$$= .0075q^2 + 7,500.$$
$$SMC = .75(.02q) = .015q.$$
$P = MC$ implies $30 = .015q$ or $q = 2,000$.
In this case
Profits $= TR - TC$
$$= 30(2,000)$$
$$- (.0075q^2 + 7,500)$$
$$= 60,000 - (30,000 + 7,500)$$
$$= 22,500.$$

c. Ted would pay up to $22,500 - 12,500 = 10,000$ per week for the company.

11.9 a. Produce each output where $P = MC$.
For Q
$$.2Q = 10 \quad Q = 50$$
For C
$$.4C = 4 \quad C = 10$$
$TR = 10Q + 4C = 540$.
$TC = .1Q^2 + .2C^2 - 125 = 250 + 20 - 125 = 145$.
$\pi = TR - TC = 540 - 145 = 395$.

b. If $Q = C$, $TR = 14Q$.
$TC = .3Q^2 - 125$
$TR = TC$: $14Q = .3Q^2 - 125$.
$.3Q^2 - 14Q - 125 = 0$.
Quadratic formula yields $Q = C = 54.3$.

Chapter 12

12.1 a. Set supply equal to demand to find equilibrium price:
$Q_S = 1,000 = Q_D = 1,600 - 600P$.
$$1,000 = 1,600 - 600P.$$
$$600 = 600P$$
$$P = 1/lb.$$

b. $Q_S = 400 = 1,600 - 600P$.
$$600P = 1,200.$$
$$P = 2/lb.$$

c. $Q_S = 1,000 = 2,200 - 600P$.
$$1,200 = 600P.$$
$$P = 2/lb.$$
$Q_S = 400 = 2,200 - 600P$.
$$600P = 1800.$$
$$P = 3/lb.$$

d.

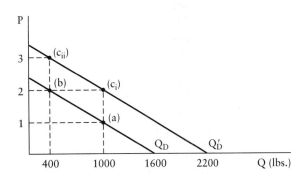

12.3 a. Supply $= 100,000$. In equilibrium,
$100,000 = Q_S = Q_D = 160,000 - 10,000P$ or $P = 6$.

b. For any one firm, quantity supplied by other firms is fixed at 99,900. Demand curve is
$Q_{D'} = 160,000 - 10,000P - 99,900$
$$= 60,100 - 10,000P.$$
If quantity supplied is 0, $Q_{S'} = 0 = Q_{D'}$
$= 60,100 - 10,000P$, or $P = 6.01$.
If quantity supplied is 200, $Q_{S'} = 200 = Q_{D'} = 60,100 - 10,000P$, or
$P = 5.99$.
Elasticity = Slope of demand × P/Q for market.
$$e_{Q,P} = -10,000 \cdot \frac{6}{100,000} = -.6.$$

For a single firm, demand is much more elastic:
$$e_{Q,P} = -10,000 \cdot \frac{6}{100} = -600.$$

A change in quantity supplied does not affect price very much.

12.5 a. Short Run: $MR = P$ so $P = MC$.
$P = q^2 + 20q + 100$.
$P = (q + 10)^2$.
$\sqrt{P} = q + 10$.
$q = \sqrt{P} - 10$.

b. $P = 121$. $q = \sqrt{121} - 10 = 1$.
$P = 169$. $q = \sqrt{169} - 10 = 3$.
$P = 256$. $q = \sqrt{256} - 10 = 6$.

c. $\pi = TR - TC$. $P = 121$.
$$\pi = 1 \cdot (121) - [.33(1)^3 + 10(1)^2$$
$$+ 100(1) + 48].$$
$$= 121 - 158.33 = -37.33.$$
$P = 169$.
$$\pi = 3(169) - [.33(3)^3 + 10(3)^2$$
$$+ 100(3) + 48].$$
$$= 507 - 447 = 60.$$
$P = 256$.
$$\pi = 6(256) - [.33(6)^3 + 10(6)^2$$
$$+ 100(6) + 48].$$
$$= 1536 - 1080 = 456.$$

12.7 $C = q^2 + wq = q^2 + .002Qq$
a. If $w = 10$, $C = q^2 + 10q$.
$MC = 2q + 10 = P$. Hence, $q = P/2 - 5$.

Industry Supply: $Q = \sum_{1}^{1,000} q$
$$= 500P - 5,000.$$
At $P = 20$, $Q = 5,000$; at $P = 21$,
$Q = 5,500$.

b. Here $MC = 2q + .002Q$. Set $= P$.
$q = P/2 - .001Q$.

Total $Q = \sum_{i}^{1,000} q = 500P - Q$.

Therefore, $Q = 250P$.
$P = 20$, $Q = 5,000$.
$P = 21$, $Q = 5,250$.
Supply is more steeply sloped in this case of interactions—increasing production bids up the wages of diamond cutters.

12.9 a. In long-run equilibrium, $AC = P$ and $MC = P$, so $AC = MC$.
$$.01q - 1 + \frac{100}{q} = .02q - 1.$$

$$\frac{100}{q} = .01q.$$

$$\frac{10,000}{q} = q, \text{ so, } q^2 = 10,000.$$

$q = 100$ gallons.

$$AC = .01(100) - 1 + \frac{100}{100}$$
$$= 1 - 1 + 1 = 1.$$
$MC = .02(100) - 1 = 2 - 1 = 1$.

b. In the long run, $P = MC$ $P = \$1$.
$Q_D = 2,500,000 - 500,000(1) =$
$2,000,000$ gallons. The market supplies $200,000$ gallons so

$$\frac{2,000,000 \text{ gallons}}{100 \text{ gallons/station}} = \frac{20,000 \text{ gas}}{\text{stations}}.$$

c. In the long run, $P = \$1$ still since the AC curve has not changed.
$Q_D = 2,000,000 - 1,000,000(1) =$
$1,000,000$ gallons

$$\frac{1,000,000 \text{ gallons}}{100 \text{ gallons/station}} = \frac{10,000 \text{ gas}}{\text{stations}}.$$

Chapter 13

13.1 a. With $Q = 400$, demand curve yields $400 = 1000 - 5P$, or $P = 120$.
For supply, $400 = 4P - 80$, or $P = 120$.
Hence, P is an equilibrium price. Total spending on broccoli is $400 \cdot 120 = 48,000$.
On the demand curve when $Q = 0$, $P = 200$. Hence, area of the consumer surplus triangle is $.5(200 - 120)(400) = 16,000$.
On the supply curve, $P = 20$ when $Q = 0$. Producer surplus is then $.5(120 - 20)(400) = 20,000$.

b. With $Q = 300$, the total loss of surplus would be given by the area of the triangle between the demand and supply curves which is
$.5(140 - 95)(100) = 2,250$.

c. With $P = 140$, consumer surplus is
$.5(200 - 140)(300) = 9,000$.
Producer surplus is
$.5(95 - 20)(300) + 45(300) = 24,750$.
Consumers lose 7,000, producers gain 4,750, net loss is 2,250.
With $P = 95$, consumer surplus is
$.5(200 - 140)(300) + 45(300) = 22,500$.
Producer surplus is
$.5(95 - 20)(300) = 11,250$.
Consumers gain 6,500, producers lose 8,750, again net loss is 2,250.

d. With Q = 450, demand price would be 110, supply price is 132.50. Total loss of surplus is
.5(132.5 − 110)(5) = 562.50.
Net loss is shared depending on where price falls between 110 and 132.5.

e.

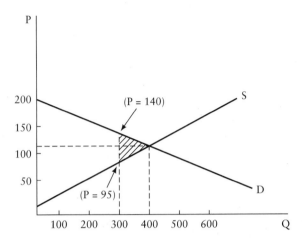

13.3 a.

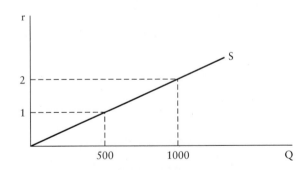

b. Since P = AC = 10 + r = 10 + .002Q, substitute this into demand:
Q = 1,050 − 50P = 1,050 − 500 − .1Q
or
1.1Q = 550, Q = 500.
Since each firm produces 5 tapes, there will be 100 firms. Royalty is r = .002(500) = 1 so P = 11.

c. With Q = 1,600 − 50P, same substitution gives
Q = 1,600 − 500 − .1Q
or
1.1Q = 1,100, Q = 1000.
So now there are 200 firms.
r = .002(1000) = 2 so P = 12.

d.

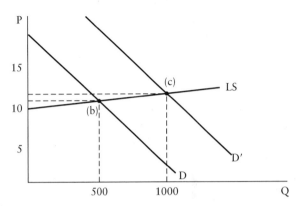

Producer surplus when P = 11 is .5(11 − 10) · 500 = 250. When P = 12, it is .5(12 − 10) · 1000 = 1000.

e. Royalties when Q = 500 are 500. Increment when Q rises to 1,000 is (2 − 1)(500) + .5(2 − 1)(1000 − 500) = 500 + 250 = 750 which is precisely the increase in consumer surplus in part d.

13.5 a. With a tax of 45, the price paid by demanders will exceed the price received by suppliers by 45. Setting demand equal to supply yields
Q = 1,000 − 5(P + 45) = 4P − 80
so 9P = 855, P = 95, Q = 4P − 80 = 300.
Consumers pay 95 + 45 = 140.

b. Tax collections = 45(300) = 13,500.
Consumers pay (140 − 120)(300) = 6,000.
Producers pay (120 − 95)(300) = 7,500.

c. Excess burden is
.5(140 − 95)(100) = 2,250.
Compare to problem 13.1 and graph in part e.

13.7 **a.** From 13.2, supply curve is $Q = 100P - 1,000$ and initial equilibrium is $P = 14$, $Q = 400$. Producer surplus is 800 composed of profits of 300 and fixed costs of 500. With a tax of 3, supply is $Q = 100P - 1,000$, demand is $Q = 1,100 - 50(P + 3)$. Setting demand = supply yields $950 - 50P = 100P - 1,000$ $P = 13$, $P + 3 = 16$, $Q = 300$.

b. Total tax collections are 900; consumers pay 600, firms pay 300.

c. Producer surplus is now $.5(13 - 10)$ $(300) = 450$—a loss of 350. Short-run profits are $(P - AC) \cdot 300$. $STC = 39.5$, $SAC = 39.5/3$. $\pi = (13 - 39.5/3) \cdot 300 = -50$. Since profits before were 300, this is a loss of 350—which is the same as the loss of total producer surplus from 800 to 450. Fixed costs remain at 500 since there are a fixed number of firms.

13.9 **a.** Set supply equal to demand. $150P = 5,000 - 100P$; $P = 20$, $Q = 3,000$.

b. P will fall to 10. $Q_D = 4,000$, $Q_S = 1,500$. 2,500 radios will be imported.

c. Price would now rise to 15. $Q_D = 3,500$, $Q_S = 2,250$. Imports are now 1,250. Tariff revenue is $5(1,250) = 6,250$. With free trade, consumer surplus is $.5(50 - 10)(4,000) = 80,000$. Domestic producer surplus is $.5(10)(1,500) = 7,500$. With the tariff, consumer surplus is $.5(50 - 15)(3,500) = 61,250$, a loss of 18,750. Producer surplus is now $.5(15)(2,250) = 16,875$, a gain of 9,375.

Deadweight loss is $18,750 - 6,250 - 9,375 = 3,125$, as can be found by measuring triangles.

d.

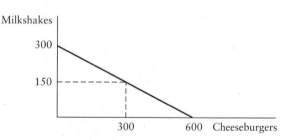

Chapter 14

14.1 **a.** Production possibility frontier:

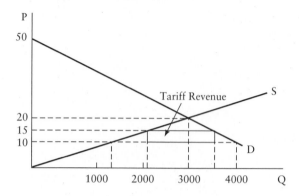

b. $M = 1/2C$. $C + 2M = 600$. $C + 2(1/2C) = 600$. $2C = 600$. $C = 300$. $M = 150$.

c. $-$slope = RPT = 1/2. Under efficient economy, $RPT = MRS = \dfrac{P_C}{P_M}$ so $\dfrac{P_C}{P_M} = \dfrac{1}{2}$.

14.3 a. Production possibility frontier:

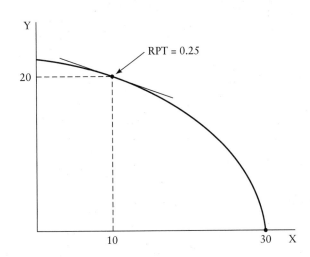

b. If $Y = 2X$, $X^2 + 2(2X)^2 = 900$.
    $9X^2 = 900$; $X = 10$, $Y = 20$.

c. If $X = 9$ on the production possibility frontier,

$$Y = \sqrt{\frac{819}{2}} = 20.24.$$

If $X = 11$ on the frontier,

$$Y = \sqrt{\frac{779}{2}} = 19.74.$$

Hence, RPT is about $\dfrac{20.24 - 19.74}{2} = .25$.

14.5 $H = 16$, $L_F + L_C = 8$ so $F^2 + C^2 = 8$.
    $U = 4F^{1/4}C^{1/4}$.
    $C = F$ since the goods enter utility symmetrically.
    $C = F = 2$, $H = 16$, $U = 4\sqrt{2} = 5.66$.

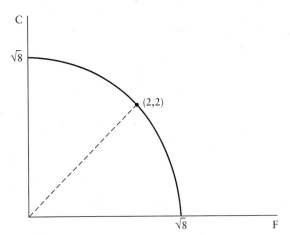

14.7 a. $X_A^2 = L_X$, $Y_A^2 = L_Y$, $X_A^2 + Y_A^2 = L_X + L_Y = 100$. Same for region B $\therefore$ $4X_B^2 + 4Y_B^2 = 100$.

b. RPT's should be equal.

c. $RPT_A = X_A / Y_A$.
    $RPT_B = X_B / Y_B$.
    But $X_A^2 + Y_A^2 = 4(X_B^2 + Y_B^2)$.
    Some algebra shows that
    $X_A = 2X_B$; also $Y_A = 2Y_B$.
    $X_T = X_A + X_B = 3X_B$. $X_T^2 = 9X_B^2$.
    $Y_T = Y_A + Y_B = 3Y_B$. $Y_T^2 = 9Y_B^2$.
    $X_T^2 + Y_T^2 = 9(X_B^2 + Y_B^2) = 9/4 \times 100$
        $= 225$.
    If $X_T = 12$ $X_T^2 = 144$
    $Y_T = \sqrt{225 - 144} = 9$.
    Note : If labor could move, would set marginal physical products equal.
    In this case, can show that
    $X_T^2 + Y_T^2 = 250$
    If $X_T = 12$ $Y_T = \sqrt{250 - 144}$
                 $= 10.3$.

Note improvement over c.

14.9 a. D
   b. E
   c. $E(U) = .6(L) + .4(H)$.
      $EU_A = 50$, $EU_B = 52$, $EU_C = 48.6$, $EU_D = 51.5$, $EU_E = 50$, . . . Choose B.
   d. Max $E(U) - |U_1 - U_2|$
      Values: A: $50 - 0 = 50$.
              B: $55 - 30 = 25$.
              C: $49.5 - 9 = 40.5$
              D: $51.75 - 2.5 = 49.25$.
              E: $57 - 54 = 3$.
      Choose A.
   e. It shows that a variety of different social choices might be made depending on the criteria being used.

Chapter 15

15.1

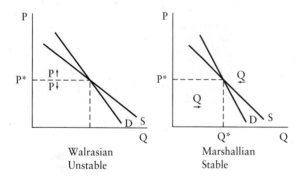

Walrasian
Unstable

Marshallian
Stable

15.3

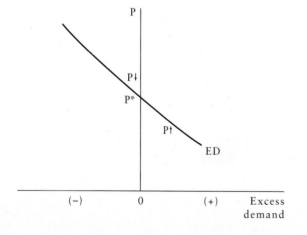

a. ED is negatively sloped since usually D is negatively sloped, S is positively sloped.
b. ED = 0 when D = S.
c. ED > 0; P rises; ED < 0; P falls—see graph.
d. ED could be positively sloped if S were negatively sloped and the absolute value of its slope exceeded that of the demand curve.
e. Process described in (c) would be reversed.

15.5 a. $Q_t = 100 - 2P_t$ $Q_t = 70 + E(P_t)$
      In equilibrium, $E(P_t) = P_t$
      $100 - 2P_t = 70 + P_t$, $3P_t = 30$
      $P^* = \$10$, $Q^* = 80$.
   b. If suppliers use last year's price to predict this year's price yields:
      $E(P_t) = P_{t-1}$, thus $Q_t = 70 + P_{t-1}$,
      $Q_t = 100 - 2P_t$. Equating Q^D and Q^S gives $70 + P_{t-1} = 100 - 2P_t$ or
      $$P_t = -\frac{1}{2}P_{t-1} + 15.$$
      If initial $P_0 = \$8$, then next period's price will be
      $$P_1 = -\frac{1}{2}(8) + 15 = \$11$$
      $$P_2 = -\frac{1}{2}(11) + 15 = \$9.5$$
      $$P_3 = -\frac{1}{2}(9.5) + 15 = \$10.25$$
      Therefore, it will take three periods for the price to get within \$.25 of equilibrium price of \$10.
   c. The farmers would notice the oscillating price and make some more "rational" prediction. Perhaps, $E(P_t) = P^* = 10$.

15.7 a. $\overline{P} = 10{,}000$ so demand is
      $Q_D = 15{,}000 - P$.
      Supply assumption implies
      $Q_S = P - 5{,}000$.
      $Q_D = Q_S$ implies $P^* = 10{,}000$.
   b. With $P^* = 10{,}000$ $\overline{P}$ of cars traded is 7,500.
   c. Now $Q_D = 11{,}250 - P$
      $Q_D = Q_S$ implies $P^* = 8{,}125$
      $\overline{P} = 6{,}562$.

d. As these cases suggest, there is no equilibrium price at which $\overline{P} = P^*$.

15.9 a. Assuming new information arrives in unpredictable random ways, the two theories are equivalent.

b. They can't outguess the market, but they may provide diversification or "prudence" for those who demand it.

Chapter 16

16.1 a. $P = 53 - Q$.

For maximum profits, set MR = MC:
MR $= 53 - 2Q =$ MC $= 5$.
Q $= 24$, P $= 29$.
$\pi =$ TR $-$ TC $= 24 \cdot 29 - 24 \cdot 5 = 696 - 120 = 576$.

Consumer surplus $= \dfrac{1}{2}(53 - 29)$.
$24 = 288$.

b. MC $=$ P $= 5$, P $= 5$, Q $= 48$.

c. Consumer surplus $= \dfrac{1}{2}(48)^2 = 1152$.

$1152 >$ Profits $+$ consumer surplus $= 576 + 288 = 864$
Deadweight loss $= 1152 - 864 = 288$
Also $\frac{1}{2}\Delta Q \cdot \Delta P = \frac{1}{2}(24)(24)$.

16.3 a. AC $=$ MC $= 10$, Q $= 60 -$ P, MR $= 60 - 2Q$. For profit max., MC $=$ MR. $10 = 60 - 2Q$, $2Q = 50$, Q $= 25$, P $= 35$.
$\pi =$ TR $-$ TC $= (25)(35) - (25)(10) = 625$.

b. AC $=$ MC $= 10$, Q $= 45 - .5P$.
MR $= 90 - 4Q$. For profit max., MC $=$ MR, $10 = 90 - 4Q$, $80 = 4Q$, Q $= 20$, P $= 50$.
$\pi = (20)(50) - (20)(10) = 800$.

c. AC $=$ MC $= 10$, Q $= 100 - 2P$, MR $= 50 - Q$. For profit max., MC $=$ MR, $10 = 50 - Q$, Q $= 40$, P $= 30$.
$\pi = (40)(30) - (40)(10) = 800$.

d.

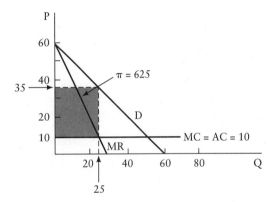

Part a

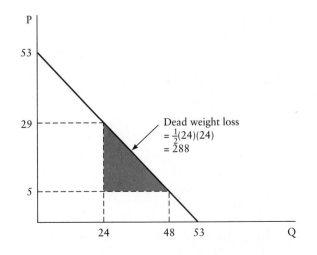

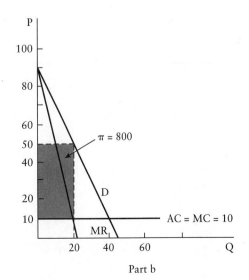

Part b

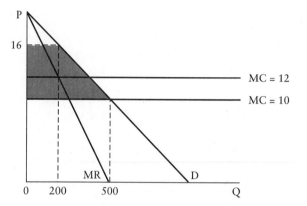

Part c

The supply curve for a monopoly is the single point on the demand curve that corresponds to profit maximization. Any attempt to connect equilibrium points (price-quantity points) on the market demand curves has little meaning and brings about a strange shape. One reason for this is that as the demand curve shifts, its elasticity (and its MR curve) often changes, bringing about widely varying price and quantity changes.

16.5 A multiplant monopolist will still produce where MR = MC and will equalize MC among factories.
  $MR = 100 - 2(q_1 + q_2)$ and $MC_1 = MC_2$.
  $q_1 - 5 = .5q_2 - 5$. $q_1 = .5q_2$.
  $MR = 100 - 2(.5q_2 + q_2)$.
  $MR = MC_2$. $100 - 2(1.5q_2) = .5q_2 - 5$.
  $3.5q_2 = 105$.
  $q_2 = 30$ and $q_1 = 15$, so $Q_T = 45$.

16.7 $Q_D = 1000 - 50P$ $MR = 20 - Q/25$
  $MC = 10$ under PC
  $MC = 12$ under monopoly

  a. *Perfect competition:*
    $P = MC = 10$.
    $Q_D = 1000 - 50(10) = 500 = Q_S$.
    Monopoly:
    $MC = MR$
    $12 = 20 - Q/25$
    $300 = 500 - Q$
    $Q = 200$ $200 = 1000 - 50P$
    $50P = 800$ $P = 16$

b. Loss of consumer surplus due to monopolization can easily be obtained from the graph (shaded portion). Area of shaded portion = $(16 - 10)(200) + \frac{1}{2}(16 - 10)(500 - 200) = 1200 + 900 = 2100$. This area is much larger than loss of consumer surplus if monopolist's $MC = 10$.

c.

16.9 As in Problem 16.5, the monopolist will equate marginal costs in each plant. It will choose the number of plants to minimize the total cost of producing its profit-maximizing output level. Assuming optimal plant size is small relative to this desired output level it will operate each at minimum average cost. This is still inefficient because $P > MC$, and there is a loss of consumer surplus because too little is being produced.

Chapter 17

17.1 a. $q_1 = 9$ $q_2 = 9$
    Profits of each = 0.
  b. $q_1 = 11 - P_1$. Set $P = \frac{1}{2}(11 + 2) = 6.5$.
    Now $q_1 = 4.5$
    $\pi = 4.5(6.5 - 2) = 20.25$.
  c. Same as (b) $P_2 = 6.5$ $q_2 = 4.5$.
  d. (b) and (c) are inconsistent. Need to use Cournot reaction functions to determine equilibrium.

e. $q_1 = 10 - \frac{1}{2}P$
   $q_2 = 10 - \frac{1}{2}P$
   Set $P = \frac{1}{2}(20 + 2) = 11$
   $q_1 = q_2 = 4.5$
   Profits of each $= 4.5(11 - 2) = 40.5$

17.3 Most literature suggests that "planned obsolescence" is a profitable strategy for a monopoly, but not so under perfect competition since entrants would produce more durable commodities. The difficult part of the theory of durability is how to treat the market for used goods and the degree of substitutability between new and used goods in the demand curve facing the monopoly.

17.5 Might still produce different goods depending on nature of demand and cost conditions.

17.7 Might compare low point of AC curve to what price would be if firm producing that output were to enter.

17.9

Fellner gives the following analysis:
$MR_C = P_C$ is demand facing competitive firm.

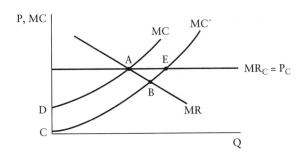

MR is the marginal revenue curve for the monopolist.
Innovation shifts MC to MC′.
Potential profits for competitive firms are CDAE.
For monopoly CDAB.

Hence innovation is more profitable for the competitive firm. It is more likely to adopt the innovation.

Chapter 18

18.1 Against A:high, B's best strategy is low. Against B:low, A's strategy is high. Any other strategy choices give one player an incentive to switch.

18.3 a. The payoff matrix is (payoffs are recorded from Smith's perspective)

		Jones		
		1	2	3
	1	+3	−1	−1
Smith	2	−1	+3	−1
	3	−1	−1	+3

There is no Nash equilibrium in this game.

b. Expected payoff for Smith is $+\frac{1}{3}$, for Jones it is $-\frac{1}{3}$. This is a Nash equilibrium assuming each strategy choice is purely random since neither player can achieve more than these expected values by playing another strategy.

18.5 a. If owners act as a cartel, they will maximize total revenue. This will require a price of $5 = (10 + 0)/2$. At $P = 5$, $Q = 5,000$, each firm sells $q = 250$ with revenues of 1,250.

b. $P = 5$ is unstable since if one firm produces 251, $Q = 5,001$ and $P = 4.999$. Revenues $= 1,254.7$ so chiseling increases revenues for that firm.

c. With a suitably low price, there will be no incentive to cheat. With $P = .30$, for example, $Q = 9,700$ and $q = 485$. Revenues $= 145.50$.
   If $q = 486$, $P = .299$. Revenues $= 145.31$ so there is no incentive to cheat.
   With fewer cartel members, this stable price is higher. With 2 firms, for example, if $P = 3$, $Q = 7,000$ and

q = 3,500. Revenues = 10,500.
If q = 3,501, P = 2.999. Revenues = 10,499.50 so there is no incentive to chisel.

18.7 a. This game has two Nash equilibria—(1) A = Produce; B = Don't produce and (2) A = Don't produce; B = Produce.

b. If A moves first, it can dictate that Nash equilibrium (1) is chosen. Similarly, if B goes first, it can assure that Nash equilibrium (2) is chosen.

c. Firm B could offer a bribe of 1 to firm A not to enter (if it is A's move first). But this would yield identical profits to those obtained when A moves first anyway.

18.9 a. With a maximin strategy, this person will choose "no picnic" since this assures a utility of at least 5.

b. If p is the probability of rain, expected utilities are
Picnic = $p(0) + (1 - p)(20) = 20 - 20p$.
No picnic = $p(5) + (1 - p)(10) = 10 - 5p$.
Setting these equal yields $p = 2/3$ as the maximum p for which the picnic might be chosen.

Chapter 19

19.1 Demand: L = −50w + 450.
Supply: L = 100w.

a. Set S = D. 100w = −50w + 450. w = 3, L = 300.

b. Demand is now: L = −50(w − s) + 450. where s = subsidy
w = $4. L_s = 400 = −50 (4 − s) + 450.
s = 3.
Total subsidy is 400 × 3 = $1,200.

c. w = $4. D = 250. S = 400. U = 150.

d.

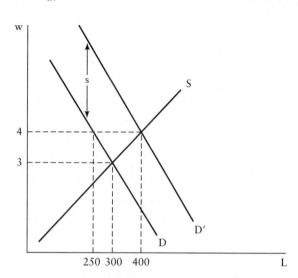

19.3 a. Five laborers: Put them where MP_L is greatest. First laborer goes to A, second goes to B, third goes to A, fourth goes to C, fifth goes to A. Output = 21 + 8 + 5 = 34.
MP of last worker is 4.

b. $P \cdot MP_L = \$1.00 \times 4 = \$4.00 = w$.
Five laborers, wL = $20.
$\pi = TR - TC = PQ - wL$
$= \$34 - \$20 = \$14$.

19.5 a. w = v = $1, so K and L will be used in a one-to-one ratio.
$TC = w \cdot L + v \cdot K = L + K = 2L$,
so $AC = \dfrac{2L}{q} = \dfrac{2L}{\sqrt{KL}} = \dfrac{2L}{\sqrt{LL}} = 2$ and
$MC = 2$.

b. P = 2, so Q = 400,000 − 100,000(2) = 200,000 pipe.
$q = \dfrac{200,000 \text{ pipe}}{1,000 \text{ firms}} = 200$ pipe/firm.
$q = 200 = \sqrt{L \cdot K} = L$, so 200 workers are hired per firm, 200,000 by the industry.

c. $w = \$2$, $v = \$1$, so $K/L = 2$
$TC = wL + vK$
$\quad = 2L + K = 4L = 2\sqrt{2}q.$
so $AC = MC = 2\sqrt{2}.$

d. $P = 2\sqrt{2}.$ $Q = 400{,}000 -$
$100{,}000(2\sqrt{2}) = 117{,}157.$
$L = \dfrac{117{,}157}{\sqrt{2}} = 83{,}000$ workers hired
by the industry.

e. If $Q = 200{,}000$ at the new wage,
$L = \dfrac{200{,}000}{\sqrt{2}} = 141{,}000$ workers

would have been hired by the industry. So if Q were unchanged, 59,000 fewer workers would have been hired = substitution effect. The remaining 58,000 fewer workers are the result of the lower output; that is, the output effect.

19.7 Supply : $L = 80w.$ $ME_L = \dfrac{L}{40}.$
Demand: $L = 400 - 40MVP_L$

a. For monopsonist $ME_L = MVP_L$
$L = 400 - 40MVP_L.$
$40MVP_L = 400 - L.$
$MVP_L = 10 - \dfrac{L}{40} \cdot$ Using the profit maximizing condition,

$\dfrac{L}{40} = 10 - \dfrac{L}{40}.$
$\dfrac{2L}{40} = 10.$ $L = 200.$
Get w from supply curve :
$w = \dfrac{L}{80} = \dfrac{200}{80} = \$2.50.$

b. For Carl, the marginal expense of labor now equals the minimum wage and in equilibrium the marginal expense of labor will equal the marginal revenue product of labor.
$w_m = ME_L = MVP_L$
$w_m = \$3.00.$

Carl's Demand	Supply
$L = 400 - 40MVP_L$	$L = 80w$
$L = 400 - 40(3)$	$L = 80(3)$
$L = 280.$	$L = 240.$

Demand > supply. Carl will hire 240 workers, with no unemployment. To study effects of minimum, try $3.33 and $4.00
$w_m = \$3.33$
$L = 400 - 40(3.33)$ $L = 80(3.33)$
$\quad = 267.$ $\quad = 267.$
Demand = supply, Carl will hire 267 workers, with no unemployment.
$w_m = \$4.00$
$L = 400 - 40(4.00)$ $L = 80(4.00)$
$\quad = 240.$ $\quad = 320.$
Supply > demand, Carl will hire 240 workers, unemployment = 80.

c.

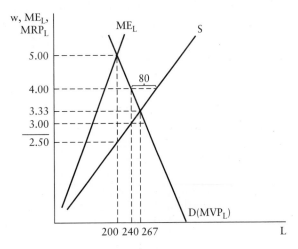

d. Under perfect competition, a minimum wage means higher wages but fewer workers employed. Under monopsony, a minimum wage may result in higher wages and more workers employed as shown by cases studied in part b.

19.9 Here marginal value product is $10 per hour:

$$ME_{Lm} = \frac{\sqrt{L_m}}{2} = 10, \text{ so } L_m = 400,$$

$$w_m = \frac{20}{3} = 6.67.$$

$$ME_{Lf} = \frac{L_f}{50} = 10, \text{ so } L_f = 500, \ w_f = 5.$$

$L_T = 900.$

Profits on machinery $= 9,000 - 5(500) - 6.67(400) = 3,833$. If Ajax must pay the same wage $w = MVP_L = 10$, $L = 1,000 + 900 = 1,900$.

Profits $= 19,000 - 1900 \cdot w = 19,000 - 19,000 = 0$.

Chapter 20

20.1 a. 8,000 hrs/year × $5/hr = $40,000/year. 3/4 × $40,000/yr = $30,000/yr at leisure.

$$\frac{\$30,000}{5} = 6,000 \text{ hours of leisure.}$$

Work = 2,000 hours.

b. 3/4 × $44,000/yr = $33,000/yr at leisure.

$$\frac{\$33,000}{5} = 6,600 \text{ hours of leisure.}$$

Work = 1,400 hours.

c. Now full income = $84,000. 3/4 × $84,000 = $63,000. Leisure = 6,300 hours. Work = 1,700 hours. Hence, higher wage leads to more labor supply. Note that in part a, labor supply is perfectly inelastic at 2,000 hours.

d.

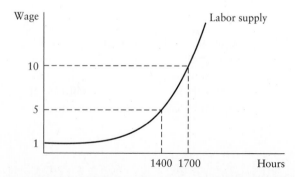

20.3 $U = 20$ $\sqrt{C \cdot H} = 20 = \sqrt{10C}$

$10C = 400$

$C = 40.$

If he gives up 1 hour of leisure $H = 9$, but 5 more dollars, $C = 45$.

$\sqrt{45 \cdot 9} = 20.13 > 20$, ∴ yes, he will be willing to drive.

20.5 a. Ignoring discounting, full income is $5(24) + 10(24) = 360$.

b. Wants to take $2/3(360) = 240$ in leisure time. This can be done with maximal leisure by taking all of day one off and half of day two off. This leaves 120 earned in day two for consumption. Leisure amounts to 36 hours.

c. She would take 16 hours of leisure in each day. This would still leave 120 for consumption, but only 32 hours of leisure in total.

d. With a wage of 20, full income increases to 600. Taking 16 hours of leisure in each day leaves 200 for consumption.

e. Now full income is 432. She wants to spend 288 on leisure and will maximize leisure hours by taking all of day one in leisure and 9.6 hours of day two. This leaves 144 earned in day two with 14.4 hours of work. A rise in the day one wage raises labor supply in day two.

20.7 This can be most easily solved using a graph.

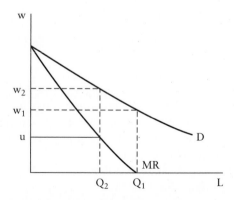

To maximize wage bill, set wage at w_1. Here marginal revenue is 0. With unemployment compensation at u, set wage at w_2. Beyond Q_2 additional revenue brought in by offering one more worker on the market falls short of what that worker could get from unemployment insurance.

20.9 a. Grant = 6,000 − .75(I)
 If I = 0   Grant = 6,000.
 I = 2,000   Grant = 4,500.
 I = 4,000   Grant = 3,000.
 b. Grant = 0 when 6,000 − .75I = 0.
  I = 6,000/.75 = 8,000.
 c. Assume there are 8,000 hours in the year.
  Full income = 4 · 8,000 = 32,000 = C + 4H.
 d. Full income = 32,000 + grant
  $$= 32,000 + 6,000 − .75 \cdot 4(8,000 − H)$$
  $$= 38,000 − 24,000 + 3H$$
  $$= C + 4H$$
  or 14,000 = C + H.

 e.

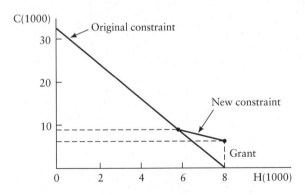

 f. New budget constraint is
  22,000 = C + 2H.
 g. Income and substitution effects of change work in opposite directions (see graph).

Chapter 21

21.1 If i = 12%,

$$\text{price} = \text{PDV} = \frac{1,000}{(1+.12)} + \frac{1,000}{(1+.12)^2}$$
$$+ \frac{1,000}{(1+.12)^3} + \frac{1,000}{(1+.12)^4}$$
$$+ \frac{1,000}{(1+.12)^5} + \frac{10,000}{(1+.12)^5}$$

PDV = $9,279.
If i = 8%,

$$\text{price} = \text{PDV} = \frac{1,000}{(1+.08)} + \frac{1,000}{(1+.08)^2}$$
$$+ \frac{1,000}{(1+.08)^3} + \frac{1,000}{(1+.08)^4}$$
$$+ \frac{1,000}{(1+.08)^5} + \frac{10,000}{(1+.08)^5}$$

PDV = $10,799.
When interest rates go down, bond prices go up. It is an inverse relationship.

21.3 Assuming premiums paid at end of year, $\text{PDV}_{\text{whole life}} = \$6,340$. $\text{PDV}_{\text{term}} = \$3,858$. The salesman is wrong, the term policy represents a better value to this consumer.

21.5 Let Y_t = Income in year t = $Y_0(1.03)^t$
 S_t = Savings in year t = $sY_t = sY_0(1.03)^t$.
 Accumulated savings

$$= \sum_{t=0}^{40} S_t (1.03)^{40-t}$$

$$= \sum_{t=0}^{40} sY_0 (1.03)^t (1.03)^{40-t}$$

$$= 40sY_0 (1.03)^{40}$$

PDV of dissavings:

$$\text{PDV} = \sum_{t=0}^{20} .6Y_0 (1.03)^{40} \cdot (1.03)^{t-20}$$

Equate the two streams to solve for s:

$$s = \frac{PDV}{40Y_0(1.03)^{40}}$$

$$= \frac{6Y_0(1.03)^{40}(15.9)}{40Y_0(1.03)^{40}}$$

$$= \frac{.6(15.9)}{40} = .24,$$

which is much higher than the average savings rate in the United States (about 5%).

21.7 Each tree should be cut down when the rate of interest (opportunity cost) is equal to the tree's rate of growth. Maximum sustainable yield proceeds to point where growth becomes zero. It neglects the opportunity cost of interest.

21.9 a. For utility maximization, set MRS = 1 + r.

If r = 0 $MRS = \dfrac{u'(c_1)}{u'(c_2)} = 1.$

So, since u is the same function, $c_1 = c_2$.

b. If r > 0, then $u'(c_1) > u'(c_2)$ which implies $c_1 < c_2$ for diminishing marginal utility.

c. Now $MRS = \dfrac{u'(c_1)}{u'(c_2)} \cdot (1+d).$

For utility maximization,

$$\frac{u'(c_1)}{u'(c_2)} = \frac{1+r}{1+d}$$

If d > r, $u'(c_1) < u'(c_2)$ therefore $c_1 > c_2$
If d < r, $u'(c_1) > u'(c_2)$ therefore $c_1 < c_2$.

d. Discounting future consumption raises c_1, but will have $c_1 > c_2$ only when d > r.

Chapter 22

22.1 a. MC = .4q. P = $20. Set P = MC.
20 = .4q. q = 50.

b. SMC = .5q. Set P = SMC. 20 = .5q.
q = 40.
At optimal production level of q = 40, the marginal cost of production is MC = .4q = .4(40) = 16, so the excise tax t = 20 − 16 = $4.

c.

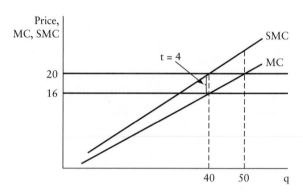

22.3 AC = MC = 1000/well.
a. Produce where revenue/well = 1,000 = 10q = 5,000 − 10N. N = 400. There is an externality here because drilling another well reduces output in *all* wells.
b. Produce where MVP = MC of well.
Total value = 5,000N − 10N².
MVP = 5,000 − 20N = 1,000.
N = 200.
c. Let Tax = X. Want revenue/well − X = 1,000 when N = 200. At N = 200, average revenue/well = 3,000. Charge X = 2,000.

22.5 Under *caveat emptor*, buyers would assume all losses. The demand curve under such a situation might be given by D. Firms (that assume no liability) might have a horizontal long-run supply curve of S. A change in liability assignment would shift both supply and demand curves. Under *caveat vendor*, losses (of amount L) would now be incurred by firms, thereby shifting the long-run supply curve to S′.

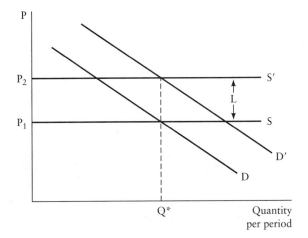

Individuals now no longer have to pay these losses and their demand curve will shift upward by L to D′. In this example then, market price rises from P_1 to P_2 (although the real cost of owning the good has not changed) and the level of production stays constant at Q*. Only if there were major information costs associated with either the *caveat emptor* or *caveat vendor* positions might the two give different allocations. It is possible also that L may be a function of liability assignment (the moral hazard problem) and this would also cause the equilibria to differ.

22.7 One example of this type of externality would be an individual who refused to trim a hedge that bordered a neighbor's property. The neighbor might, if he or she valued a trimmed hedge, offer to trim it (at least one side of it) thereby internalizing the externality. In general, one might expect that such agreements are common since bargaining costs are low when only two individuals are involved.

22.9 a. For profit maximization, set P = MC, 50 = 30 + .5Q. Hence Q = 40. Bees will pollinate 10 acres.

b. Orchard owner would pay up to $25. A $20 subsidy would result in 70 = 30 + .5Q or Q = 80—enough to pollinate the entire 20 acres.

Chapter 23

23.1 a. Marginal valuation for a = P = 100 − q_a; for b, marginal valuation = P = 200 − q_b. Because of the public good nature of mosquito control these should be added "vertically."

Marginal value = 300 − 2q (since q_a = q_b).
Set this equal to MC of 50, gives q = 125.

b. Free rider problem could result in having no production.

c. Total cost = 50 × 125 = $6,250. Area under demand curve for a = $4,688; for b = $17,188. May want to share costs in proportion to these values.

23.3 Resources should be allocated so that the sum of people's marginal valuations of education's public benefits plus the private benefit for the marginal buyer equals the marginal cost of producing one more unit. It might be financed through a combination of compulsory taxes and user fees. For example, elementary and secondary education might be publicly financed (if it provided all public goods), whereas university education might be funded privately if its benefits were private.

23.5 If different localities have different tastes for a certain public good, then it should be produced by local governments. But if the good can be supplied uniformly over the whole state (example, state police), then it should be produced by the state. Diseconomies of scale may make it more efficient to produce countrywide or statewide services on a statewide or local basis.

23.7 a. Since $P = 2 - .01Q$, $MR = 2 - .02Q$. Profit maximum where $MC = .5 = MR = 2 - .02Q$, $Q = 75$, $P = 1.25$, $\pi = (1.25 - .5)(75) = 56.25$
   Firm will be willing to pay up to this amount as a bribe.
   b. The bribe is only a transfer from monopoly profits to the government official. This is not a welfare cost.
   c. Welfare cost is the loss of consumer surplus from the monopoly itself. The value of this loss is $.5(1.25 - .5)(75) = 28.125$.

23.9 Here want to differentiate between social benefits, opportunity costs, and transfers.
   a. A benefit (increased output).
   b. A benefit (increased output, but some reduced value of leisure).
   c. A transfer (neither benefit nor cost).
   d. Reduction in a transfer.
   e. Usually treated as a transfer, but may not want to give thieves standing. Then this is a true benefit.
   f. An opportunity cost since instructors could be doing something else.

Glossary

A

Accounting cost The concept that goods or services cost what was paid for them. (p. 227)

Adverse selection When buyers and sellers have different information, market outcomes may exhibit adverse selection—the quality of goods or services traded will be biased toward market participants with better information. (p. 181, 425)

Agent The role of making economic decisions for another party, e.g., the manager of a firm being hired to act for the owner. (p. 297)

Asymmetric information A situation in which buyers and sellers have different amounts of information about a market transaction. (p. 425)

Average cost Total cost divided by output: a common measure of cost per unit. (p. 235)

Average productivity The ratio of total output produced to the quantity of a particular input employed. (p. 202)

B

Backward-bending labor supply curve Labor supply curve in which higher real wages cause less labor to be supplied because the income effect outweighs the substitution effect. (p. 561)

Barriers to entry Factors that prevent new firms from entering a market. (p. 439)

Binding constraint The presence of one or more resources that effectively limits the amount that can be produced. If a particular input is not fully utilized, it does not pose a binding constraint in production. (p. 409)

Budget constraint The limit that income places on the combinations of goods and services that an individual can buy. (p. 74)

C

Capital stock The total amount of machines, buildings, and all other produced, nonlabor resources in an economy. (p. 580)

Cartel model A model of oligopoly pricing in which firms coordinate their decisions to act as a multiplant monopoly. (p. 471)

***Ceteris paribus* assumption** In economic analysis, holding all other factors constant so that only the factor being studied is allowed to change. (p. 59)

Coase theorem If bargaining is costless, the social cost of an externality will be taken into account by the parties, and the allocation of resources will be the same no matter how property rights are assigned. (p. 635)

Cobweb model A model of price adjustment in which some trading takes place at nonequilibrium prices. (p. 421)

Common property Property that may be used by anyone without cost. (p. 633)

Compensated demand curve A demand curve drawn on the assumption that other prices and utility are held constant. Income effects of price changes are compensated for along the curve, and it reflects only substitution effects. (p. 150)

Compensating wage differentials Differences in wages caused by differing job characteristics. (p. 567)

Competitive fringe A group of firms that act as price takers in a market dominated by a price leader. (p. 477)

Complements Two goods such that when the price of one increases, the quantity demanded of the other falls. (p. 109)

Complete preferences The assumption that an individual is able to state which of any two options is preferred. (p. 62)

Composite good Combining expenditures on several different goods whose relative prices do not change into a single good for convenience in analysis. (p. 85)

Compound interest Interest paid on prior interest earned. (p. 607)

Constant cost industry An industry in which the entry or exit of firms has no effect on the cost curves of the firms in the industry. (p. 327)

Consumer Price Index (CPI) The current value of the market basket of goods and services purchased by a typical household compared to a base year value of the same market basket. (p. 155)

Consumer surplus The extra value individuals recieve from consuming a good over what they pay for it. What people would be willing to pay for the right to consume a good at its current price. (p. 153, 343)

Contestable market Market in which entry and exit are costless. (p. 486)

Contour lines Lines in two dimensions that show the sets of values of the independent variables that yield the same value for the dependent variable. (p. 41)

Contract curve The set of all efficient allocations of the existing goods in an exchange situation. Points off that curve are necessarily inefficient, since individuals can be made unambiguously better-off by moving to the curve. (p. 166)

Cournot equilibrium A solution to the Cournot model in which each firm makes the correct assumption about what the other firm will produce. (p. 476)

Cournot model A model of duopoly in which each firm assumes the other firm's output will not change if it changes its own output level. (p. 472)

Cross-price elasticity of demand The percentage change in the quantity demanded of a good in response to a 1 percent change in the price of another good. (p. 137)

D

Deadweight loss Losses of consumer and producer surplus that are not transferred to other parties. (p. 357)

Decreasing cost industry An industry in which the entry of firms decreases the costs of the firms in the industry. (p. 333)

Demand function A representation of how quantity demanded depends on prices, income, and preferences. (p. 92)

Dependent variable In algebra, a variable whose value is determined by another variable or set of variables. (p. 31)

Direct approach A method of verifying economic models that examines the validity of the assumptions on which the model is based. (p. 18)

Diversification The spreading of risk among several options rather than choosing only one. (p. 183)

Dominant strategy A strategy which is optimal regardless of the strategy adopted by an opponent. (p. 499)

Dual linear programming problem A minimization problem related to a primal linear programming maximization problem; often involves computation of appropriate resource prices. (p. 412)

E

Economic cost The cost concept that goods or services cost the amount required to keep them in their present use: the amount that they would be worth in their next best alternative use. (p. 227)

Economic profits The difference between a firm's total revenues and its total economic costs. (p. 230)

Economically efficient allocation of resources A technically efficient allocation of resources in which the output combination also reflects people's preferences. (p. 382)

Economics The study of the allocation of scarce resources among alternative end uses. (p. 3)

Edgeworth box diagram A graphic device for illustrating all of the possible allocations of two goods (or two inputs) that are in fixed supply. (p. 375)

Efficient wage A wage above the market wage paid to encourage a worker to remain with a firm. (p. 296)

Elasticity The measure of the percentage change in one variable brought about by a 1 percent change in some other variable. (p. 126)

Equilibrium price The price at which the quantity demanded by buyers of a good is equal to the quantity of the good supplied by sellers. (p. 10, 313)

Equity The fairness of the distribution of goods or utility. (p. 392)

Excess demand The extent to which quantity demanded exceeds quantity supplied at a particular price. (p. 416)

Expansion path The locus of cost-minimizing input combinations a firm will choose to produce at vari-

ous levels of output (when the prices of inputs are held constant). (p. 233)

Expected value The average outcome from an uncertain gamble. (p. 173)

External price effects Effects that changes in the level of production of an industry have on the prices of inputs to that industry. (p. 317)

Externality The effect of one party's economic activities on another party that is not taken into account by the price system. (p. 387, 625)

F

Fair games Games that cost their expected value. (p. 173)

Fair insurance Insurance for which the premium is equal to the expected value of the loss. (p. 178)

Firm Any organization that turns inputs into outputs. (p. 197)

Fixed costs Costs associated with inputs that are fixed in the short run. (p. 242)

Fixed-proportions production function A production function in which the inputs must be used in a fixed ratio to one another. (p. 212)

Free rider A consumer of a nonexclusive good who does not pay for it in the hope that other consumers will. (p. 659)

Functional notation A way of denoting the fact that the value taken on by one variable (Y) depends on the value taken on by some other variable (X) or set of variables. (p. 31)

Future goods Goods that are purchased today by investing some present output as capital whose output is then consumed in the future. (p. 582)

G

General equilibrium model An economic model of a complete system of markets. (p. 15)

Giffen's paradox A situation in which the increase in a good's price leads people to consume more of the good. (p. 104)

H

Homogeneous demand function Quantity demanded does not change

when prices and income increase in the same proportion. (p. 93)

Human capital Capital in the form of learned abilities acquired through training, education, or experience. (p. 596)

I

Imperfect competition A market situation in which buyers or sellers have some influence on the prices of goods or services. (p. 387)

Income effect (in demand theory) The part of the change in quantity demanded that is caused by a change in real income. (p. 98)

Income effect of a change in w Movement to a higher indifference curve in response to a rise in the real wage rate. If leisure is a normal good, a rise in w causes an individual to work less. (p. 560)

Income elasticity of demand The percentage change in the quantity demanded of a good in response to a 1 percent change in income. (p. 136)

Increase or decrease in demand The change in demand for a good caused by changes in the price of another good, income, or preferences. Graphically represented by a shift of the entire demand curve. (p. 116)

Increase or decrease in quantity demanded The increase or decrease in quantity demanded caused by a change in the good's price. Graphically represented by the movement along a demand curve. (p. 116)

Increasing cost industry An industry in which the entry of firms increases the costs of the firms in the industry. (p. 331)

Independent variable In an algebraic equation, a variable that is unaffected by the action of another variable and may be assigned any value. (p. 31)

Index number An average of many different trends into one number. (p. 153)

Indifference curve All the combinations of goods or services that provide the same level of utility. (p. 64)

Indifference curve map A contour map that shows the utility an individual obtains from all possible consumption options. (p. 68)

Indirect approach A method of verifying economic models that asks if the model can accurately predict real-world events. (p. 18)

Individual demand curve A graphic representation of the relationship between the price of a good and the quantity of it demanded by a person, holding all other factors constant. (p. 111)

Inferior good A good that is bought in smaller quantities as income increases. (p. 94)

Initial endowments The initial holdings of goods from which trading begins. (p. 393)

Intercept The value of Y when X equals zero. (p. 33)

Interest Payment for the current use of funds. (p. 607)

Internalization of an externality Incorporation of the social marginal costs of an externality into an economic actor's decisions (as through taxation or merger). (p. 631)

Investment The purchase of new capital. (p. 587)

Isoquant A curve that shows the various combinations of inputs that will produce the same amount of output. (p. 203)

Isoquant map A contour map of a firm's production function. (p. 203)

J

Job-specific skills Skills learned on a job that enable a worker to do that specific job better. (p. 293)

L

Law of diminishing returns Hypothesis that the cost associated with producing one more unit of a good rises as more of that good is produced. (p. 8)

Leisure Time spent in any activity other than market work. (p. 556)

Lindahl equilibrium Balance between people's demand for public goods and the tax shares that each must pay for them. (p. 657)

Linear function An equation that is represented by a straight-line graph. (p. 33)

Linear programming A mathematical technique for finding the maximum (or minimum) value for a linear function whose variables are subject to linear constraints. (p. 407)

Long run The period of time in which a firm may consider all of its inputs to be variable in making its decisions. (p. 238)

Long-run elasticity of supply The percentage change in quantity supplied in the long run in response to a 1 percent change in price. (p. 333)

M

Marginal cost The additional cost of producing one more unit of output. (p. 235)

Marginal expense The cost of hiring one more unit of an input. Will exceed the price of the input if the firm faces an upward-sloping supply curve for the input. (p. 538)

Marginal physical productivity The additional output that can be produced by one more unit of a particular input while holding all other inputs constant. (p. 198)

Marginal rate of substitution (MRS) The rate at which an individual is willing to reduce consumption on one good when he or she gets one more unit of another good while remaining equally well-off. The negative of the slope of an indifference curve. (p. 65)

Marginal rate of technical substitution (RTS) This shows the amount by which one input can be reduced while holding output constant when one more unit of another input is added. The negative of the slope of an isoquant. (p. 205)

Marginal revenue The extra revenue a firm receives when it sells one more unit of output. (p. 266)

Marginal revenue curve A curve showing the relation between the quantity a firm sells and the revenue yielded by the last unit sold. Derived from the demand curve. (p. 271)

Marginal revenue product The extra revenue obtained from selling the output produced by hiring an extra worker or machine. (p. 528)

Marginal value product A special case of marginal revenue product in which the firm is a price taker for its output. (p. 529)

Market demand The total quantity of a good or service demanded by all potential buyers. (p. 122)

Market demand curve The relationship between the total quantity demanded of a good or service and its price, holding all other factors constant. (p. 122)

Market period A short period of time during which quantity supplied is fixed. (p. 313)

Markup pricing Determining the selling price of a good by adding a percentage to the average cost of producing it. (p. 277)

Median voter A voter whose preferences for a public good represent the middle point of all voters' preferences for the good. (p. 663)

Microeconomics The study of the economic choices individuals and firms make and how those choices create markets. (p. 3)

Models Simple theoretical descriptions that capture the essentials of how the economy works. (p. 5)

Monopolistic competition Market in which each firm faces a negatively sloped demand curve and there are no barriers to entry. (p. 485)

Monopoly rents The profits that a monopoly earns in the long run. (p. 443)

Monopsony A firm that is the only hirer in a particular input market. (p. 538)

Moral hazard The effect that having insurance has on the behavior of the insured. (p. 181)

N

Nash equilibrium A pair of strategies (a*, b*) in a two-player game such that a* is an optimal strategy for A against b* and b* is an optimal strategy for B against a*. (p. 497)

Natural monopoly A firm that exhibits diminishing average cost over a broad range of output levels. (p. 439)

Nonexclusive goods Goods that provide benefits that no one can be excluded from enjoying. (p. 652)

Nonrival goods Goods that additional consumers may use at zero marginal costs. (p. 653)

Normal good A good that is bought in greater quantities as income increases. (p. 93)

Normative analysis Theories that make judgments about how the economy's resources should be used. (p. 19)

O

Opportunity cost The cost of a good or service as measured by the alternative uses that are forgone by producing the good or service. (p. 16, 227)

Output effect The effect of an input price change on the amount of the input that the firm hires that results from a change in the firm's output level. (p. 536)

P

Pareto efficient allocation An allocation of available resources in which no mutually beneficial trading opportunities are unexploited. That is, an allocation in which no one person can be made better-off without someone else being made worse-off. (p. 166)

Partial equilibrium model An economic model of a single market. (p. 13)

Perfect equilibrium A Nash equilibrium in which the strategy choices of each player do not involve noncredible threats. That is, no strategy in such an equilibrium requires a player to carry out an action that would not be in its interest at the time. (p. 506)

Perfect price discrimination Selling each unit of output for the highest price obtainable. Extracts all of the consumer surplus available in a given market. (p. 452)

Perfectly competitive price system An economic model in which individuals maximize utility, firms maximize profits, there is perfect information about prices, and every economic actor is a price taker. (p. 370)

Perpetuity A promise of a certain number of dollars each year, forever. (p. 616)

Pigovian tax A tax or subsidy on an externality that brings about an equality of private and social marginal costs. (p. 631)

Positive economic analysis Theories that explain how resources actually are used in an economy. (p. 19)

Present discounted value The present value of funds payable in the future after taking account of the opportunity cost of interest forgone. (p. 589)

Price discrimination Selling identical units of output at different prices. (p. 452)

Price elasticity of demand The percentage change in the quantity demanded of a good in response to a 1 percent change in its price. (p. 126)

Price leadership model A model in which one dominant firm takes reactions of all other firms into account in its output and pricing decisions. (p. 477)

Price taker A firm or individual whose decisions regarding buying or selling have no effect on the prevailing market price of a good or service. (p. 267)

Private property Property that is owned by specific people who may prevent others from using it. (p. 633)

Probability The relative frequency with which an event occurs. (p. 173)

Producer surplus The extra value producers get for a good in excess of the opportunity costs they incur by producing it. What all producers would pay for the right to sell a good at its current market price. (p. 343)

Product group Set of differentiated products that are highly substitutable for one another. (p. 480)

Production function The mathematical relationship between inputs and outputs. (p. 197)

Production possibility frontier A graph showing all possible combinations of goods that can be produced with a fixed amount of resources. (p. 15)

Property rights The legal specification of who owns a good and the trades the owner is allowed to make with it. (p. 633)

Public goods Goods that provide nonexclusive benefits to everyone in a group and that can be provided to one more user at zero marginal cost. (p. 391, 653)

Q

Quadratic function An equation that includes terms in X^2 and (possibly) X. (p. 36)

Quasi-competitive model A model of oligopoly pricing in which each firm acts as a price taker. (p. 470)

R

Rate of product transformation The slope of the production possibility frontier that shows the opportunity costs involved in producing more of one good and less of some other good. (p. 379)

Rate of return The increase in future output made possible by investing one unit of current output in capital accumulation. (p. 581)

Rational expectations Basing price expectations on complete information about the equilibrium price determined by the interaction of supply and demand in the market. (p. 424)

Reaction function In the Cournot model a function or graph that shows how much one firm will produce given what the other firms produces. (p. 475)

Rental rate (v) The cost of hiring one machine for one hour. (p. 228)

Rent-seeking behavior Firms or individuals influencing government policy to increase their own welfare. (p. 668)

Returns to scale The rate at which output increases in response to proportional increases in all inputs. (p. 207)

Revenue maximization A goal for firms in which they work to maximize their total revenue rather than profits. (p. 275)

Ricardian rent Long run profits earned by owners of low cost firms. May be capitalized into the price of these firms' inputs. (p. 346)

Risk aversion The tendency of people to refuse to accept fair games. (p. 175)

S

Scarcity costs The opportunity costs of forgone future production that cannot be made because of current production that uses exhaustible resources. (p. 598)

Shadow prices Prices for resources in a dual linear programming problem. For resources that represent binding constraints on production, shadow prices will be positive. For resources that do not represent binding constraints, shadow prices are zero. (p. 413)

Short run The period of time in which a firm must consider some inputs absolutely fixed in making its decisions. (p. 238)

Short-run elasticity of supply The percentage change in quantity supplied in the short run in response to a 1 percent change in price. (p. 320)

Short-run supply curve The relationship between market price and quantity supplied of a good in the short run. (p. 316)

Short-run supply curve for a price-taking firm The positively-sloped section of a firm's SMC curve above the point of minimum SAVC. Shows the supply decisions of a price-taking firm. (p. 281)

Shutdown price The price below which the firm will choose to produce no output in the short run. Equal to minimum average variable cost. (p. 283)

Simultaneous equations A set of equations with more than one variable that must be solved together for a particular solution. (p. 45)

Slope The direction of a line on a graph. Shows the change in Y that results from a unit change in X. (p. 34)

Social costs Costs of production that include both input costs and costs of the externalities that production may cause. (p. 627)

Stable equilibrium A situation in which market forces cause price to move to its equilibrium level. (p. 422)

Substitutes Two goods such that if the price of one increases, the quantity demanded of the other rises. (p. 109)

Substitution effect (in demand theory) The part of the change in quantity demanded that is caused by substitution of one good for another. A movement along an indifference curve. (p. 96)

Subsitution effect (in production theory) The substitution of one input for another while holding output constant in response to a change in the input's price. (p. 535)

Substitution effect of a change in w Movement along an indifference curve in response to a change in the real wage. A rise in w causes an individual to work more. (p. 560)

Sunk cost Expenditure that once made cannot be recovered. (p. 228)

Supply-demand model A model describing how a good's price is determined by the behavior of the individuals who buy the good and the firms that sell it. (p. 5)

Supply response The change in quantity of output in response to a change in demand conditions. (p. 313)

Survivorship principle The idea that in competitive markets only profit-maximizing firms are likely to survive. (p. 274)

T

Tax incidence theory The study of the final burden of a tax after considering all market reactions to it. (p. 353)

Tariff A tax on an imported good. May be equivalent to a quota or a nonquantitative restriction on trade. (p. 361)

Technical progress A shift in the production function that allows a given output level to be produced using less inputs. (p. 215)

Technically efficient allocation of resources An allocation of the available resources such that producing more of one good requires producing less of some other good. (p. 373)

Theory of choice The interaction of preferences and income that causes people to make the choices they do. (p. 59)

Transactions costs Costs involved in making market transactions and in gathering information with which to make those transactions. (p. 419)

Transivity of preferences The property that if A is preferred to B, and B is preferred to C, then A must be preferred to C. (p. 63)

U

Unstable equilibrium A situation in which market forces cause price to move away from its equilibrium level. (p. 422)

Utility The pleasure, satisfaction, or need fulfillment that people get from their economic activity. (p. 59)

V

Variable costs Costs associated with inputs that can be varied in the short run. (p. 242)

Variables The basic elements of algebra, usually called X, Y, and so on, that may be given any numerical value in an equation. (p. 31)

W

Wage rate (w) The cost of hiring one worker for one hour. (p. 227)

Y

Yield The discounting rate at which the present discounted value of the returns from an investment are exactly equal to the investment's current cost. (p. 596)

Name Index

Subject Index